THE ROUTLEDGE COMPANION
AND POPULAR CULT

"Overall, this is an impressive collection of essays that encapsulates many of the important points of interface between religion and popular culture. It will become an important marker in the development of the field and its introduction at this point is timely."

Steve Knowles, *University of Chester, UK*

"Lyden and Mazur offer a fascinating collection of essays from a wide range of contributors exploring religion and popular culture. This is a terrific resource for the classroom and scholars will be impressed with their contribution to the field."

Gina Messina-Dysert, *Claremont Graduate University, USA*

Religion and popular culture is a fast-growing field that spans a variety of disciplines. This volume offers the first real survey of the field to date and provides a guide for the work of future scholars. It explores:

- key issues of definition and of methodology
- religious encounters with popular culture across media, material culture and space, ranging from videogames and social networks to cooking and kitsch, architecture and national monuments
- representations of religious traditions in the media and popular culture, including important non-Western spheres such as Bollywood.

This *Companion* will serve as an enjoyable and informative resource for students and a stimulus to future scholarly work.

John C. Lyden is the Liberal Arts Core Director and Professor of Liberal Arts at Grand View University, USA. He is editor of *The Routledge Companion to Religion and Film* (Routledge 2009).

Eric Michael Mazur is Gloria and David Furman Professor of Judaic Studies and Professor of Religious Studies at Virginia Wesleyan College, USA. He is co-editor of *God in the Details: American Religion in Popular Culture* with Kate McCarthy (Routledge, 2nd edition 2010).

ROUTLEDGE RELIGION COMPANIONS

Available:

THE ROUTLEDGE COMPANION TO RELIGION AND POPULAR CULTURE

Edited by
John C. Lyden and Eric Michael Mazur

LONDON AND NEW YORK

First published in paperback 2019

First published 2015
by Routledge
2 Park Square, Milton Park, Abingdon, Oxon OX14 4RN

and by Routledge
711 Third Avenue, New York, NY 10017

Routledge is an imprint of the Taylor & Francis Group, an informa business

British Library Cataloguing-in-Publication Data
A catalogue record for this book is available from the British Library

Library of Congress Cataloging-in-Publication Data
The Routledge companion to religion and popular culture / edited by John C. Lyden
and Eric Michael Mazur.
pages cm. – (Routledge religion companions)
Includes bibliographical references and index.
ISBN 978-0-415-63866-1 (hardback) – ISBN 978-1-315-72447-8 (ebk) 1. Popular
culture–Religious aspects. 2. Religion and culture. I. Lyden, John, 1959– editor.
II. Mazur, Eric Michael, editor.
BL65.C8R65 2015
201'.7–dc23
2014036433

ISBN: 978-0-415-63866-1 (hbk)
ISBN: 978-1-138-32273-8 (pbk)
ISBN: 978-1-315-72447-8 (ebk)

Typeset in Monotype Goudy
by Taylor & Francis Books

Printed and bound in Great Britain by
TJ International Ltd, Padstow, Cornwall

To my mother, Corinne Lyden, who has always encouraged and inspired me.

J.L.

To Claudia, *my* companion.

E.M.M.

CONTENTS

FIGURES

ACKNOWLEDGEMENTS

Our thanks go to all our contributors for their patience and cooperation as we worked on a volume of this size and scope. At Routledge—a familiar and welcome partner for both co-editors—Katherine Ong also had immense patience with us as she encouraged and assisted us with all the details of moving the volume toward completion. Leslie Riddle pitched the idea for the volume to us originally, and it would never have happened without her encouragement and vision at the outset. Eve Mayer saw the volume to its completion and made sure that it met the high standards of Routledge, and Helena Power provided expert assistance editing the copy to make sure it all made sense.

Eric would like to thank his wife, Claudia, for her suggestions, patience, and support, particularly as life has unfolded over the past two years; and John, who called one day "out of the blue" with an invitation to collaborate, and has proven to be a most supportive and patient person—a real mensch—as well as a generous and insightful scholar.

John would like to thank his wife Liz for her tremendous support for his scholarship and editorial work, as she assisted with his juggling of the many obligations of life and jobs. Grand View University helped with travel costs to conferences where key ideas for the volume were developed. John would also like to thank Eric for saying "yes," and for being an assiduous editor devoted to detail—and for knowing how to find excellent contributors, as well as how to properly assemble all the pieces.

CONTRIBUTORS

Nikki Bado (Iowa State University) is the author of *Coming to the Edge of the Circle: A Wiccan Initiation Ritual* (2005/2012), and co-author (with Rebecca Sachs Norris) of *Toying with God: The World of Religious Games and Dolls* (2010). She has written on the pedagogical nature of embodied ritual practice, the philosophy of Kūkai, and the Triple Goddess in Wicca, and has been a Visiting Research Fellow at the Nanzan Institute for Religion and Culture in Japan, doing fieldwork on ritual and pilgrimage. Bado is currently working on two books, *The Vagina Festival Comes First: Fertility Festivals in Modern Japan*, and *Returning the Body to Belief: Ritual and the Embodied Nature of the Divine*. She is co-editor (with Chas Clifton) of the "Equinox Studies in Contemporary and Historical Paganism" series, and serves on the editorial boards of the *Journal of Magic, Ritual, and Witchcraft* and *The Pomegranate: The International Journal of Pagan Studies*.

Heidi A. Campbell is Associate Professor of Communication and Affiliate Faculty in Religious Studies at Texas A&M University, USA, and she teaches in media studies, popular culture, and religion. Since 1997 she has studied the practice of religion online and the influence of new media on religious communities. Her work has appeared in numerous academic venues including the *Journal of the American Academy of Religion*, *Journal of Computer-Mediated Communication*, *Journal of Contemporary Religion*, *New Media and Society*, and *The Information Society*. She is the author of *Exploring Religious Community Online* (2005), *When Religion Meets New Media* (2010), and editor of *Digital Religion: Understanding Religious Practice in New Media Worlds* (2012).

Darryl Caterine (Le Moyne College) is a historian of religions and ethnographer whose research focuses on the intersections of religion and culture in the United States and parts of Latin America. His first book, *Conservative Catholicism and the Carmelites: Identity, Ethnicity and Tradition in the Modern Church* (2001), records the appropriation of Catholic symbolism by first- and second-generation Mexican and Cuban Americans to reconstitute ethnic identity in the United States. His recent book, *Haunted Ground: Journeys through a Paranormal America* (2011), analyzes our nation's fascination with paranormal phenomena through a series of thick descriptions of Spiritualist, ufological, and dowsing conventions. Caterine has published several articles on popular religion in the United States, including essays on civil religion, Nature religion, and the religion of the Boston Red Sox. In the wake of *Haunted Ground*, he is currently working on a number of articles focusing on metaphysical movements and American cultural religion.

Jennie Chapman is a Lecturer in American Literature, University of Hull, UK. Her research interests include Evangelical popular fiction, particularly the "Left Behind" series; popular apocalyptic discourse and culture; and the intersections of literature and religion in America. She is the author of *Plotting Apocalypse: Reading, Agency, and Identity in the Left Behind Series* (2013). Her current research project examines literary representations of life after death in US fiction since 1850.

Edward Dutton is Adjunct Professor of the Anthropology of Religion, Oulu University, Finland. He has taught at a number of universities, including Riga Stradins University (Latvia) and Aberdeen University (Scotland). Dutton is the author of *Culture Shock and Multiculturalism* (2012), *The Duttons of Stanthorne Hall: A Victorian Non-Conformist Family in Cheshire and their Male Line Ancestors* (2012), *The Finnuit: Finnish Culture and the Religion of Uniqueness* (2009), and *Meeting Jesus at University* (2008). He studied theology at Durham University and earned a PhD in religious studies at Aberdeen University. Also a journalist, Dutton's articles have appeared in such publications as *Chronicles in Higher Education*, *University Affairs*, *Times Higher Education*, and *Times Educational Supplement*. In his spare time he enjoys Indian cooking.

Paul Emerson Teusner earned a PhD from the School of Media and Communication at RMIT University in Melbourne, Australia. His research investigates the use of digital devices and social software by young people to construct social, gender, religious, and cultural identities, and how networked individualism is changing religion in the public sphere, shaping social identities, changing the aesthetic experience of and interaction with religious text, and shaping the spaces where young people experience "family," "work," and "friends." He has been quoted in the *Guardian* and has discussed his research on Australia's *ABC Radio National*.

Tona Hangen is Associate Professor of Nineteenth and Twentieth Century History, teaches social, cultural, and religious history at Worcester State University, and consults on historical pedagogy for Teaching American History grant partnerships with public school systems across Massachusetts. She is the author of *Redeeming the Dial: Radio, Religion and Popular Culture in America* (2002) and a contributing author to *Radio Reader: Essays in the Cultural History of Radio* (ed. M. Hilmes and J. Loviglio, 2001) as well as *Radio Cultures: The Sound Medium in American Life* (ed. M. Keith, 2008).

Mark Hulsether is Professor of Religious Studies and Director of the Interdisciplinary Program in American Studies, University of Tennessee, Knoxville. He has authored a wide range of articles on intersections between religion and public culture in the fields of US history, American studies, and religious studies. His most recent book is *Religion, Culture and Politics in the Twentieth Century United States* (2007).

Christine Hoff Kraemer (Cherry Hill Seminary) is Managing Editor of the Pagan Channel at Patheos.com, co-editor with A. David Lewis of *Graven Images: Religion in Comic Books and Graphic Novels* (2010), and author of *Eros and Touch from a Pagan Perspective* (Routledge, forthcoming). Her research interests include body and queer theology, contemporary Pagan studies, and religion and popular culture.

A. David Lewis is co-editor of *Graven Images: Religion in Comic Books and Graphic Novels* (2010), an editorial board member for the *International Journal of Comic Art*, and writer of the graphic novels *The Lone and Level Sands* (2005) and *Some New Kind of Slaughter* (2009). His research interests include eschatology, thanatology, Islam, and narratology in popular culture.

John C. Lyden is the Liberal Arts Core Director and Professor of Liberal Arts at Grand View University, USA. He is the author of *Film as Religion: Myths, Morals, and Rituals* (2003), and the editor of *Enduring Issues in Religion: Opposing Viewpoints* (1995) and *The Routledge Companion to Religion and Film* (2009). He is also the editor of the *Journal of Religion and Film*.

Clive Marsh is Director of Lifelong Learning, University of Leicester, UK, and the author of a number of works on theology and culture, including *Christianity in a Post-Atheist Age* (2002), *Cinema and Sentiment: Film's Challenge to Theology* (2004), *Christ in Focus: Radical Christocentrism in Christian Theology* (2005), *Christ in Practice: A Christology of Everyday Life* (2006), and *Theology Goes to the Movies: An Introduction to Critical Christian Thinking* (2007), as well as articles and co-edited books. His most recent work has been on popular music and includes, with Vaughan S. Roberts, *Personal Jesus: How Popular Music Shapes Our Souls* (2012). His next project seeks to bring together his three main areas of interest and expertise: theology, adult education, and popular culture.

Eric Michael Mazur is the Gloria and David Furman Professor of Judaic Studies and Professor of Religious Studies, Virginia Wesleyan College, USA. He is the author of *The Americanization of Religious Minorities* (1999), co-author of *Religion on Trial* (2004), co-editor of *God in the Details: American Religion in Popular Culture* (2000/2010), and editor of *Art and the Religious Impulse* (2002) and the *Encyclopedia of Religion and Film* (2011). He is also a former book review co-editor for the *Journal of American Culture* and the *Journal of Religion and Popular Culture*.

Jolyon P. Mitchell is Professor of Communications, Arts and Religion, University of Edinburgh, UK, Director of the Centre for Theology and Public Issues (CTPI), and Acting Director of the Institute for Advanced Studies in the Humanities (IASH). He is also the President of the UK's national association for Theology and Religious Studies. His recent books include *Promoting Peace, Inciting Violence: The Role of Religion and Media* (2012), *Religion and the News* (2012), and *Martyrdom: A Very Short Introduction* (2012). He is currently directing several research projects relating to *Peacebuilding through the Media Arts*. Prior to working in Edinburgh, he worked as a producer and journalist with BBC World Service.

Sheila J. Nayar (Greesboro College) is the author of *The Sacred and the Cinema: Reconfiguring the "Genuinely" Religious Film* (2012) and *Cinematically Speaking: The Orality-Literacy Paradigm for Visual Narrative* (2010), winner of the 2011 award for Outstanding Book in the Field of Media Ecology. Her essays have appeared in *Film Quarterly*, *Journal of the American Academy of Religion*, *PMLA*, and *Visual Anthropology*, among others. Currently she is working on a book, forthcoming with Bloomsbury, in which she examines the sacramental imagery in Dante's *Divine Comedy*.

Chad B. Newswander is Assistant Professor of Political Science, University of South Dakota, USA, and his research interests include constitutional governance, power and politics, administrative statesmanship, and domestic security.

Lynita K. Newswander is Adjunct Professor of Political Science, University of South Dakota, USA. She is co-author with Lee Trepanier of *LDS in the USA: Mormonism and the Making of American Culture* (2012). Dr. Newswander's research includes work on religion and politics, American political thought, and the effects of multidisciplinary approaches to teaching and learning.

Rebecca Sachs Norris is Professor of Religious and Theological studies, Merrimack College, USA. She is the co-author (with Nikki Bado) of *Toying with God: The World of Religious Games and Dolls* (2010), co-editor (with David Cave) of *Religion and the Body: Modern Science and the Construction of Religious Meaning* (2012), and author of works on neurobiology and emotion, pain, suffering, and religion, and "religiotainment." She is also the co-editor (with Richard Carp) of the Rowman and Littlefield series "Studies in Body and Religion." Prof. Norris is the co-founder of the "Anthropology of Religion" and the "Body and Religion" units of the American Academy of Religion, and has served in various leadership positions for the New England-Maritimes Region of the American Academy of Religion.

Rodger M. Payne is Chair of the Department of Religious Studies, University of North Carolina, USA. His publications include *The Self and the Sacred: Conversion and Autobiography in Early American Protestantism* (1998) and *Southern Crossroads: Perspectives on Religion and Culture* (co-edited with Walter H. Conser, Jr., 2008). He is currently completing a project titled "The Saint of the Sugar Fields: St. Amico, Italian Immigrant Labor, and Jim Crow in South Louisiana" that examines the way in which a popular devotion in honor of an obscure Italian saint contributed to racial discourse in the rural twentieth-century South. When not reading and writing about religion and culture in the American South, he hikes the storied mountains of western North Carolina and indulges his inner "lapsed Catholic" by listening to the music of Jimmy Buffett.

Leonard Norman Primiano is Professor and Chair of the Department of Religious Studies, Cabrini College, USA. He teaches courses on vernacular religion, American Catholicism, American religious movements, the history of Christianity, and religious folklife. He was awarded The Kennedy Center/Stephen Sondheim Inspirational Teacher Award in 2014. He is the co-producer and co-founder of "The Father Divine Project," a multimedia documentary and video podcast about The Peace Mission Movement. Recent research and publications include an examination of the theologies of food of Father and Mother Divine and a study of Roman Catholic ephemeral culture as exemplified by the "holy card."

Graham St John is currently Adjunct Research Fellow at the Griffith Centre for Cultural Studies, Griffith University, Queensland, Australia, and is a cultural anthropologist and researcher of electronic dance music cultures and festivals. He is the author of six books, including *Global Tribe: Spirituality, Technology and Psytrance* (2012), *Technomad: Global Raving Countercultures* (2009), and the edited collections *The Local Scenes and Global Culture of Psytrance* (2010), *Victor Turner and Contemporary Cultural Performance* (2008), and *Rave Culture and Religion* (2004). He is executive editor of the peer reviewed open-access journal *Dancecult: Journal of Electronic Dance Music Culture* (dj.dancecult.net), and his Web site is at www.edgecentral.net.

Jeffrey Scholes (University of Colorado, Colorado Springs) is the author of *Vocation and the Politics of Work: Popular Theology in a Consumer Culture* (2013) and *Religion and Sports in American Culture* (2013). He is currently working on a book on the political theology of charity.

Tricia Sheffield (independent scholar) is an ordained minister in the Reformed Church in America (RCA). She is the author of *The Religious Dimensions of Advertising* (2006), and she has also written on issues of gender and religion, including "Cover Girls: Toward a Theory of Female Divine Embodiment" (*Journal of Religion and Society*, 2002) and "Performing Jesus: A Queer Counternarrative of Embodied Transgression" (*Theology and Sexuality*, 2008).

James Mark Shields (Bucknell University) conducts research on modern Buddhist thought, Japanese philosophy, comparative ethics, and philosophy of religion. He has published articles and translations in *Asian Philosophy*, *The Eastern Buddhist*, *Japan Review*, the *Japanese Journal of Religious Studies*, *Journal of Religion and Society*, *Kultura i Politkya*, *Philosophy*, *Culture and Traditions*, and *Studies in Religion/Sciences religieuses*. He is the author of *Critical Buddhism: Engaging with Modern Japanese Buddhist Thought* (2011) and co-editor of *Teaching Buddhism in the West: From the Wheel to the Web* (2003). He is currently working on a book manuscript titled *Warp and Woof: Modernism and Progressivism in Japanese Buddhism, 1886–1936*.

Elijah Siegler teaches courses on religion and film and religion and popular culture, among many others, at College of Charleston, USA. He has published an introductory textbook on New Religious Movements (2006), and articles on the film director David Cronenberg, the TV producer Tom Fontana, cop shows, and American Daoism, as well as several articles on religious studies pedagogy. He is currently working on two book projects: *Dream Trippers: Global Daoism and the Predicament of Modern Culture*, and *The Coen Brothers' Religion: Mythology, Morality and the American Landscape*.

Sarah McFarland Taylor teaches in the areas of religious studies, American studies, and environmental policy and culture, Northwestern University, USA. She is the author of *Green Sisters: A Spiritual Ecology* (2007), which was awarded first prize by the Catholic Press Association for "Best Book on Gender Issues" and "Best Book on Social Concerns." Taylor has co-chaired American Academy of Religion program units on "Religion and Popular Culture" and "Religion and Ecology," and is currently a co-chair of the "Religion, Media, and Culture" unit. Her current book project is titled *Green Convergence: Religion and Environment in American Popular Culture*, in which she looks through the lens of American popular culture at the environment as a site of contested morality. She is also editing a special issue on "Environment, Religion, and Popular Culture" for the *Journal for the Study of Religion, Nature, and Culture*.

Lee Trepanier is Professor of Political Science, Saginaw Valley State University, USA. He is co-author with Lynita K. Newswander of *LDS in the USA: Mormonism and the Making of American Culture* (2012), and editor of several volumes, the latest being *Teaching in the Age of Ideology* (2012).

Jodie Ann Vann is working toward a PhD in the anthropology of religion, Arizona State University, USA. Her dissertation examines Contemporary Paganism through theories of gender, place, and the postmodern religious imagination. Her other current work examines physical elements of Pagan pilgrimage to the village of Glastonbury, England, and the role of imagination in both alternative religions and the fantasy and science fiction genres.

Rachel Wagner (Ithaca College) is the author of *Godwired: Religion, Ritual, and Virtual Reality* (2011) and has written chapters for a number of volumes on religion and media, including *Digital Religion: Understanding Religious Practice in New Media Worlds* (2013), *God in the Details* (2010), *Halos and Avatars* (2010), and others. She is co-chair of the Religion, Film, and Visual Culture Group of the American Academy of Religion, and is currently working on her second book, an examination of apocalyptic media culture in a globalizing world.

William Lafi Youmans (The George Washington University) is a scholar of global media and communication. He has contributed articles to the *Journal of Communication*, *Journal of Intercultural Communication Research* and *Arab Media & Society*, and is working on a book about Al Jazeera in the United States.

Benjamin E. Zeller is Assistant Professor of Religion, Lake Forest College, USA. He is author of *Prophets and Protons: New Religious Movements and Science in Late Twentieth-Century America* (2010), and co-editor of *Religion, Food, and Eating in North America* (2014) and *The Bloomsbury Companion to New Religious Movements* (2014). His research interests focus on new or alternative religious currents, including new religions, the religious engagement with science, and the quasi-religious relationship people have with food.

INTRODUCTION

John C. Lyden

The study of "Religion and Popular Culture" is not entirely new, but at this writing it still lacks maturity in that few works exist which reflect with much subtlety on its methods or with any suggestion at a comprehensive approach to its contents. Of course, it is notoriously difficult to define its subject matter (as Chapter 1 makes clear), but it still seems legitimate to try to define the areas that might be involved and the issues and questions posed by them for the study of religion and popular culture. This volume attempts such a task, and so comprises a general introduction to this nascent area of study.

While a volume of this sort can hardly pretend to cover *everything* related to religion and popular culture—given that the subject matter of both is constantly changing—we have attempted to include chapters on as many areas within popular culture as possible. The volume is organized into three main sections: first, methodological concerns; second, chapters on the forms that popular culture takes and their dimensions in relation to religion; and third, discussion of the representation of various religious communities within popular culture.

The methodological essays forming Chapters 1 and 2 in Part I, written by the editors, seek to set out some basic ground rules (or perhaps the lack thereof) for the study of religion and popular culture. John Lyden's chapter shows the slippery nature of the terms involved in this "field," in the difficulties involved in defining "religion," "culture," and "popular," as well as the slippages that exist in relation to these terms. He shows that we need not set down hard and fast definitions in order to study this intersection, and that perhaps the study is valuable precisely because it indicates the overlaps and complicated relations between these categories. Eric Michael Mazur's chapter discusses the question of why people study this subject and what that says about them as well as those who read their work, which constitutes an example of how the reflexivity of the scholar of religion and popular culture can add to our understanding of what we are studying as well as why; we all live within this subject, as people who exist in culture and who are implicated in various communities that create meaning out of combinations of religious and cultural materials.

These initial chapters lay the basis for what follows, as the authors of the subsequent chapters show the slippery lines between "religion" and "culture" in much of this study. It is difficult to define where one begins and the other ends, as one can look to ways that religious traditions are represented in popular culture, as well as the ways that popular culture has been influenced (sometimes unwittingly) by religion; one can look to obvious religious content in popular form, as well as popular culture itself mimicking the forms and practice of religion. The authors use a variety of methods as they approach their subjects, but they are generally informed by the notion of a "circuit of culture," as it has been understood by cultural studies methodology, which insists that we can only understand elements of popular culture (in relation to religion, or for that matter anything else) by examining the processes of production, what is produced, how it is distributed or marketed, and how it is received by a population. The latter shows that artifacts and practices only have meaning when appropriated, and that the various products of popular culture can be given diverse meanings depending on the interpretations and uses given to them by the populations that appropriate them. There is no single way in which a given aspect of popular culture can be interpreted religiously, and in this study we can see the multivalent nature of both culture and religion reflected fully in their intersection.

Part II, "Encounters with popular culture," contains three separate sections. "Mediated encounters" explores religious encounters through electronic transmission, such as while watching television (news or entertainment) or film, listening to music (on the radio or in other formats), while playing videogames or interactive net-based games, while engaging in Internet-based social networks, or through advertising. These are in some cases very recently developed media, and they have changed the way in which culture as well as religion is conveyed and understood; religious communities have used these media, but all of these media also convey ideas about religion often even when they do not intend to do so, and the practice of using these media also has "religion-like" elements to it. Section B ("Material encounters") explores religious encounters with material (physical) items: in print media (in written or graphic form), while cooking (or eating, or drinking), in fashion, and with games, toys, and "tchotchkes" (gewgaws, trinkets, kitsch). These sorts of material encounters indicate the physicality of experience within both religion and popular culture, and in their areas of overlap. Section C ("Locative encounters") explores religious encounters with popular culture in real space: while shopping, at social events, while engaging in (or attending) sporting events, and while visiting monuments of civic and patriotic significance.

The tremendous range of types of encounters indicates how broad the study of popular culture has become, but it also indicates that religion and religious ideas and practices have been implicated in all of these forms as well. By attending to this diversity, we can see very clearly that the days are gone when scholars of religion and popular culture simply looked for the interpolation of rather obvious religious symbols into (e.g.) movies or television shows. Rather, we can see that any number of aspects of popular culture can be understood in relation to religions in multiple ways, as they utilize and react to recognizable religious concepts as well as mimic religions more implicitly in their form, content, and ritualized practices.

Part III, "Religious traditions," explores the portrayal of certain religious traditions within popular culture, whether by "outsiders" or by members of those traditions ("insiders"). These traditions include Buddhism, Hinduism, Islam, Judaism, Contemporary Paganism, Mormonism, Protestant Christianity, and Roman Catholic Christianity. This list is not intended to be exhaustive, nor is it meant to indicate that these religious traditions are somehow more significant or important in the study of religion and popular culture. Rather, the list is illustrative of a range of traditions that have been portrayed more often in popular culture, especially in the West. These chapters are not restricted to Western portrayals of these traditions, but it remains true that global, commercial popular culture has been produced and distributed most aggressively by the West (especially the USA), which has therefore had more influence on global culture than the smaller popular culture industries outside the West. At the same time, non-Western products and commercial industries (such as "Bollywood" films) are included as well.

It is our hope that readers will find that this volume fills an important niche in the developing study of religion and popular culture. It is intended to be a conversation starter, and if it raises more questions than it answers, then it will have served the valuable purpose of contributing to the agenda for this study. The study of religion and popular culture will continue to be diverse in its subject, as both religions and popular culture continue to generate new forms and interact in new ways. The terms themselves will continue to inspire lively debates about definitions that have a bearing on how we understand religions or culture, and how we apply our concepts to them. In short, this field can only become more relevant to our understandings of ourselves and our cultures, as we all increasingly realize how embedded we are in the multiplicity of worldviews that have shaped our beliefs, our habits, and our histories.

Part I

APPROACHING THE DISCIPLINE OF RELIGION AND POPULAR CULTURE

1
DEFINITIONS
What is the subject matter of "religion and popular culture"?

John C. Lyden

If a companion volume on a subject exists, one might presume that the editors have a pretty good idea of what the subject matter of that field is, and how it is best defined. The defining characteristics of any academic discipline or subject matter will, of course, be open to constant discussion as those involved with it continually revise their understandings of both its methodology and what properly constitutes its object. But for many fields of study, there is at least enough of a history of its study, or a semblance of orthodoxy about how to approach its study, that some degree of consensus exists about the field's definition which can serve as a starting point for discussion. The subject matter of the study of religion, for example, has become a topic of considerable debate in recent years, but it has been around long enough that these debates can take place in the comfort of established departments in elite universities. The study of religion and popular culture, on the other hand, has not established a solid foothold in the halls of academia, perhaps because it is too recent in origin, or because it appears to lack the coherence and discernment required for inclusion.

In this chapter, it is not my aim to insist that such coherence is well established among those who study religion and popular culture, and only needs to be recognized; nor am I bold enough to propose a formula for such coherence on behalf of the nascent discipline. Rather, I would argue that the difficulties inherent in defining this field are not the result of its youth and indiscretions but are part and parcel of its subject matter. Furthermore, I would suggest that the difficulties inherent in defining the terms of this field of study are endemic to all study of religion and of culture, and that this sub-field therefore can offer a fine lesson to its more established parent disciplines that we should be wary of overconfidence in defining our subject matter. Although it is natural to wish for such careful definitions of our academic disciplines—especially when we are trying to justify adding a tenure-track position to our department—the fact is that all such definitions are quite artificial.

At the same time, as I will make clear below, this is not an argument that there is no subject matter for the field, as if academics invented it from their imaginations with no reference for the concepts in the world. There is something we call religion, and something we call popular culture, however contested and slippery the definitions of these terms remain. And not only can both of these be studied, but we can also study their interactions. At the same time, given the slippery nature of both religion and popular culture, that interaction is no easier to define than the terms, as they tend to mix together in ways that make it hard to see where one ends and the other begins. And yet again: this is due not to our lack of methodological sophistication in approaching them, but to the very nature of the things we label in these ways—as they combine and develop, raising questions about the very nature of religion and of culture which can have a bearing on how we may perceive both in the future.

To advance our understanding of the nature of the study of *religion and popular culture*, then, I propose to look at the problematic nature of each of the words in this italicized phrase, suggesting some of the difficulties inherent in defining them as well as the lessons that can be learned from this exercise. In the process, we can approach an understanding of the subject matter of the field of religion and popular culture—not by eliminating ambiguity, but by coming to realize that that very ambiguity in interpretation helps us to better understand the phenomena in question.

"Religion"

Although the study of religion or religious studies has existed in academia for some time, it has recently come under attack as an artificial concept that has been illegitimately imposed on reality, distorting the content it seeks to explicate. Jonathan Z. Smith has famously declared that, "Religion is solely the creation of the scholar's study" and therefore, "Religion has no existence apart from the academy" (Smith 1982: xi). More recently, this view has been further developed by scholars such as Russell McCutcheon (1999, 2001, 2003) and Timothy Fitzgerald (2000). Such scholars claim that the modern sense of the term "religion" as a separate aspect of culture, largely private and related to personal belief in a transcendent power, evolved as part of an attempt to justify the superiority of Christianity over other "religions." Western colonialist attitudes to other cultures either suggested that these cultures had no "religion" (and so needed to acquire Christianity) or that their inferior "religions" required replacement by Christianity in order to correspond more clearly to the "true" notion of religion. "Religion" then appears to be a descriptive term, but actually functions normatively to exalt one worldview over another.

Such ideological critique of the concept of religion is important as it reveals the biases present in the concept since the development of the modern academic study of religion. It is particularly relevant to definitions that clearly import a Christian or Western bias, such as those that define religion in relationship to a single transcendent reality or a quest for salvation; the definitions of Schleiermacher, Otto, Eliade, and Tillich all appear to fall into this category (Lyden 2003: 37–40). Even definitions that are less obviously Western, however, may still be said to be based on Western theological assumptions that may be concealed by the ways in which they are stated.

But the recognition that "religion" is a construct, even one that has included bias, does not necessitate the conclusion that there is no object to which the study of religion corresponds. Kevin Schilbrack has argued that something is no less "real" for being socially constructed; it exists only in the framework of human societies, and not as a natural kind (like lightning, or frogs), and so "[r]eligion does not exist apart from human ways of thinking, speaking, and acting" (Shilbrack 2010: 1118). But politics, sports, and economics similarly do not exist apart from humans, and yet no one would suggest that what they describe does not exist; even though they describe "socially dependent facts," it remains true that there are "realities" described by them, including elections, games, and business transactions.

Critics who would dispense with the term "religion," however, also wish to do so because they believe that the concept distorts what it seeks to describe, and is ideologically motivated. They would claim we are well rid of the academic concept of religion for these reasons. But it is not only Western academics who use the term "religion"—practitioners use the term to refer to their own activities, even though it may not have arisen from within their own traditions. For that matter, individual "religions" have often been first "named" by outsiders (including Christianity and Hinduism), but the terms have then been accepted by insiders as a description of themselves. It might well be said that Christianity and Hinduism did not exist until they were so named, but that does not take away from the fact that they are identified as social realities now by their own members. In the same way, cultures have come to exist: "Native American" identity is a creation of outsiders, but has become a term of self-identification for those to whom it applies. In fact, the term "Indian" which preceded it functioned in much the same way; both terms can be seen as equally foreign to the peoples so named, but both have been accepted in various periods by the populations thereby designated as terms which unify them historically, religiously, and culturally, across traditional tribal lines.

It is also true that the scholar may use the term "religion" to apply to activities that are not so named by a group, if the term serves as a helpful way of interpreting the phenomena in question. Schilbrack argues that if the scholar recognizes features that relate to a particular definition of religion, and has not *imposed* those features on the phenomena in question, the term can be legitimately used, as "the interpreter is claiming … that there is a cultural pattern or structure that exists independent of the label of it as a religion and … the label of 'religion' fits or illuminates that pattern" (2010: 1124). Of course, one may debate whether the label illuminates or distorts; but to conclude *a priori* that it can *only* do the latter, seems to be a conclusion that would ignore all information to the contrary. The concept of religion has evolved over time in a variety of ways, as scholars have sought to better understand the features that are often classified by this term. Terry Godlove points out that although "religion" is an abstract intellectual construct, it is one based on empirical data, and our definitions of it have evolved as we seek to generalize and classify information which might fall under that term. As such, we are continually re-defining the term itself as the result of our study of phenomena, which informs the way we define the general term (Godlove 2010: 1040–41).

Furthermore, even if the term "religion" evolved out of an ideological desire to subjugate other peoples, this does not justify the genetic fallacy that because the term *has* been so used, it always *will* be so used for ideological purposes. As noted below, the term "culture" has an equally ideological history (having been used to condemn other "cultures" as inferior to one's own) but those who argue for the abolition of the term "religion" do not seem ready to discard the term "culture" as well (Schilbrack 2010: 1130). Were we to stop using all words that have been used ideologically, we would be rendered mute in our descriptions of anything. A better alternative may be to continue seeking better understandings and definitions of the term which are informed by study of the phenomena we so classify, so that "religion" remains a useful category, although one in constant need of revision (just like "culture," "ritual," "myth," or indeed any other terms evolved within fields such as religious studies, history, or social science).

I have devoted this much space to the critique of "religion" as a concept because it stands at the center of much academic discourse in what some might call "the field formerly known as religious studies," and because this debate serves as a useful marker of some of the disputes about such labels that are apposite to the definition of our larger term, *religion and popular culture*. If "religion" does not exist, one can hardly speak about the larger term. But if it does, the disputes about its definition may also illuminate the slippery nature of all these terms, and the fact that one tends to blend into the other. This supports the contention of many scholars of religion and popular culture, including many of the authors of this volume, that we cannot neatly divide "religion" from "culture."

When one looks to the definitions of "religion" used by scholars of religion and popular culture, we find a variety, as one would expect—but there are family resemblances among them. David Chidester defines religion as "the activity of being human in relation to superhuman transcendence and sacred inclusion, which inevitably involves dehumanization and exclusion" (2005: viii). He also acknowledges that this is hardly the only definition one might use, and that he has adopted this one for heuristic purposes of illuminating certain features of how religions function; in particular, he is interested in ritual performance and exchange, sacred objects, and experiences of community in sacred time and place (ibid.: 30–51). Eric Michael Mazur and Kate McCarthy resist giving a set definition, instead identifying a "set of markers that are suggestive of religious meaning" including "the formation of communities of shared meanings and values, the presence of ritualized behaviors, the use of language of ultimacy and transcendence, the marking of special, set-aside 'sacred' times and spaces, and the manipulation of traditional religious symbols and narratives" (2011: 6). They suggest that the presence of one or more of these markers merits an analysis in terms we could call "religious." Bruce Forbes resists a definition of religion as well, as he is content to list some of the standard academic definitions along with their criticisms, but he also points to a range of phenomena that usually merit religious discussion such as devotional acts, ritual patterns, or "reflections on the struggles of life" (Forbes and Mahan 2005: 9).

I will also avoid giving a formal definition of "religion" here, noting only that the various aspects often associated with this term in both popular conversation and academic discourse make appearances throughout the chapters of this volume. The term is one that is under constant negotiation, and it may be sufficient to acknowledge that the debate about what is or is not religion is found here as well. In any case, the term has not disappeared, and it does appear to refer to a real set of human behaviors and activities.

"Culture"

The term "culture" first evolved in modern times out of the notion of the "cultured person" who has cultivated his or her capacities. This idea is often associated with Matthew Arnold, but also has roots in Francis Bacon's resuscitation of the idea from Cicero, and the German notion of *Bildung* as the cultivation of the national virtues, such as that developed by Johann Gottfried Herder (Tanner 1997: 3–5). In this way, it functioned as a way to view the culture of one's own group or nation as superior, and so in turn provided the ideological basis for colonialism and the "white man's burden" to educate and civilize the "savage" or *uncultured* peoples of the world. Obviously, this was itself a rationale for controlling and exploiting the natural resources and human beings of these locales. (In these ways, it is much like the notion of religion critiqued by McCutcheon and others.)

This notion of culture then gave way to a more evolutionary idea that suggested cultures are not entirely distinct as previously thought, but instead the primitive evolves into the more complex; still, there is judgment implied on the "primitive" culture which tends to be associated with contemporary non-Western cultures, particularly those at a preliterate or tribal level (Tanner 1997: 16–18). Finally, this cultural evolutionism, associated with Social Darwinism and the notion of the superiority of the allegedly more advanced culture, gives way to the critique of Ruth Benedict (1934) and others in the development of twentieth-century anthropology. These thinkers embraced cultural relativism, the notion that no culture should be viewed as inferior to any other, as the differences should be embraced as expressive of the diversity of humans and not evaluated by any single cultural perspective (as none can claim that superior position) nor by any transcultural standard (as this does not exist, in their view).

It is indeed commendable that the cultural relativists criticized Social Darwinism as an illegitimate effort to justify colonialist exploitation in the name of Western cultural superiority. At the same time, cultural relativism was not entirely logically consistent. If there are no universal values, then the value of universal tolerance which cultural relativism seeks to espouse is also simply a particular cultural value, with no relevance beyond the cultures that hold it. If a culture prefers genocide and slavery as its values, cultural relativists cannot say those values are wrong.

There are other problems with the modern anthropological notion of culture. It assumes a *holistic* notion of "culture" which implies that a society has a single culture composed of a shared set of meanings and values, held by all; this suggests homogeneity in a given population which may not exist. There may be multiple sets of values in different subsets of a population and so no single set of values. If I am to follow the cultural relativist view, I must somehow determine what the culture in a certain area is, so that I can suggest that those values are the correct ones for that group; but what if the group is diverse? If one half of the population wants to enslave the other half, which determines the correct or normative cultural value? Do the enslavers have as much right to their values as the enslaved have the right to resist? Or does the hegemonic culture determine the values of a society in practice, minority rights be damned? These problems also demonstrate the fallacies that follow when a descriptive definition is utilized normatively, to suggest what values "should" be accepted as determinative of a culture.

This notion of culture also generally assumes that cultures are unchanging over time; and yet, a society's values evolve, so that one cannot define precisely what the cultural values are. Again, for the cultural relativist, one would have to say that slavery was correct in the USA in 1850, but not in 1870. This view seems arbitrary, and does not pay attention to the conflicts over values that ensue and that comprise culture as it evolves; nor does it note how power structures often determine which values prevail.

Noticing the checkered past of the term "culture" and the continuing difficulties with its definition, one might be tempted to discard it altogether, just as some have regarded the term "religion" as worth dismissing. But as with the latter term, "culture" does refer to a set of practices, even though it is an abstraction created by scholars (and others) to refer to those activities. Those activities are not less "real" for being described by a construct that has been invented as a way of classifying those activities, and the term may still be useful for drawing some connections and generalizations about the activities of societies in which they develop shared attitudes, practices, and beliefs. We can develop a fluid and flexible notion of "culture," just as we can for "religion."

Kathryn Tanner has suggested a view of culture that does not assume unanimity of views or lack of tension within cultures; in today's world, we know that nations contain diverse groups that cannot be expected to share a single cultural identity such as the allegedly homogeneous cultures imagined by Johann Herder or Matthew Arnold. Cultures are not "sharply bounded, self-contained units" (Tanner 1997: 53) but instead are "internally fissured wholes" made up of diverse groups that battle over meanings. Cultures are in this sense "sites of resistance and contradiction" united not by a shared sense of the meaning of their cultural elements, but rather by a group of issues over which they argue. What unites them is not values that have been agreed upon, but a set of questions about a set of values that can be debated (Tanner 1997: 57). Consider the contemporary characterization of US culture as made up of "Red" and "Blue" states; these allegedly represent populations that argue about the relationship of the values of church and state, homosexuality, war, abortion, stem cell research, and other issues. American culture is composed, to some extent, of these tensions and debates.

We see, then, that "culture," much like "religion," is an abstract construct that has an ideologically tainted past, and yet the term has evolved to include greater diversity and a more accurate description of the phenomena it attempts to describe, as those who study cultures seek to develop better conceptual tools for understanding them. Neither "culture" nor "religion" is monolithic or easy to define, nor are they ideologically neutral, but this does not mean they cannot be used, or that they have no object that they describe. We can continue to utilize these terms, recognizing that they are fluid and continually revisable on the basis of more empirical study and closer reflection.

"Popular culture"

If there is no such thing as a homogeneous culture of shared values—if, instead, cultures are simply systems of conflict, tension, and contradictory approaches to certain values—then what would *popular* culture be? If we once again look at how the term evolved, we see an attempt to contrast "high culture" (which comes from an elitist view like that of Matthew Arnold, that the educated have superior cultural values) with the so-called "popular" culture; in this case, the latter is denigrated as inferior in taste and quality, expressing the less desirable values of the uneducated majority. The elitist basis of this definition has become more obvious over time, so that it is no longer automatically assumed that the values of the educated or privileged are to be preferred in all cases (Lynch 2005: 7). Furthermore, the lines between the two are slippery; e.g., jazz might have begun as a popular art form, but it soon became so sophisticated that the majority of the population lost interest in it, and now it is primarily played and studied more in academic settings than in nightclubs. This also shows how new forms of elite culture evolve which may not come from the privileged class in all cases; avant-garde art often styles itself as a leftist critique of both the uncritical preferences of the majority and the traditional values of elite culture, associated with the rich and powerful. But again, where does one draw the line? There is considerable overlap between all of these categories (Lynch 2005: 6–11).

Popular culture may also be viewed as a mass product of industrialization, made in assembly-line style by a capitalist economy (or a totalitarian government) as part of a modern effort to control the people through ideology maintenance. The Frankfurt School of Adorno and Horkheimer had this view, and their spirits are still very much with us, although this view has also received a great deal of criticism (e.g., Hollows and Jancovich 1995). Its assumption that the people have no taste at all, and simply accept whatever the powers put before them, betrays the fact that people can create what they wish out of their culture (to some extent) as they shape its meaning in the process of reception. Popular culture creates an opportunity for resistance against the dominant culture, as the Birmingham School of Cultural Studies has made clear through the work of scholars like Stuart Hall and Tony Jefferson (1976), Dick Hebdige (1979), and Michel de Certeau (1984). Sub-cultures develop within cultures that create their own readings of popular cultural texts, and these become sites of resistance to the dominant system of meanings. Kathryn Tanner's view of culture, already noted, clearly shows that it was influenced by these ideas.

Sometimes reference is also made to "folk culture" as the simple or naïve expression of cultural values apart from elitist or mass-produced artifacts of culture. But again, the lines are slippery, and they betray value judgments that may be illegitimate; why should we assume that a cultural product is more genuine or less prone to hegemonic manipulation, simply because it precedes modern consumer capitalism (Lynch 2005: 11)? Furthermore, folk culture has subsequently been packaged for consumers outside of the cultures from which it derived, which may suggest a loss of authenticity, but it may also simply indicate another form of cultural evolution. One cannot suggest that a phenomenon is not a genuine form of culture simply because it has been modernized.

Is there then anything that we can call "popular" culture, or is there just "culture"? I would suggest that we don't need to worry very much about this, as we don't need to exclude anything from consideration based on its level of popularity or unpopularity. "Popular culture" indicates some sort of shared cultural values of a populace, or at least a set of issues around which negotiations and conflicts over meaning occur in a populace (as Tanner would say), and this may involve some elements of elite, avant-garde, or folk culture, so called; all of these may be popular with certain groups, and this is worth studying. In order to study popular culture, we don't need to restrict our study to the reception of film blockbusters; we might look at reception of cult movies or avant-garde films, and how their respective audiences construct meanings out of them. We don't need to restrict our study to the most popular music, which changes over time, after all; but we might study how different audiences relate to different forms of music and construct meaning out of them. In any contemporary city, one might find several such sub-cultures related to music. For example, the wealthier members of society may be the primary patrons of the symphony and other venues for performing classical music, and this allows them to demonstrate certain cultural values by their support of those. Avant-garde jazz fans may go to jazz festivals at universities, frequented by a small but loyal group of students and others who share this often largely academic or historical interest. There are also fans of "pop" artists who go to packed performances along with thousands of others in giant arenas, ritually celebrating yet another set of values; and the various types of popular music will attract different audiences as well. All of these groups are arguably practicing their own form of culture, or popular culture, and rehearsing certain values and preferences through their musical choices. If one of these venues has more people present at it than another, that does not mean that scholars of popular culture cannot study the others, as these also have populations involved with their activities. If we were to view some of these as *not* popular, where would we draw the line? Just how many people do I need to have involved in an activity before I can call it "popular"? It would seem foolish to refuse to call something popular just because the number of adherents drops below an arbitrary number.

So why speak of "religion and popular culture" at all? Should we just talk about religion and culture, or religion as a part of culture and in interaction with other cultural elements? We might make that argument. But most likely we will continue to use the term "popular culture" for the simple reason that it references for most of us (and not just academics) a shared set of activities and meanings which have gained a certain prominence, for some populations, either through mass media or other means of communication. Gordon Lynch defines popular culture as "the shared environment, practices, and resources of everyday life" (Lynch 2005: 14). This is broad enough to include a wide range of artifacts and activities, and not just texts or things that might be analyzed as texts, but *practices*—including all sorts of activities we might not otherwise study, such as "cooking and eating, caring for children and other dependents, spending time with work or with friends, having sex, tidying, mending or improving our homes, washing, dressing or daydreaming" (ibid.: 15). Other possibilities include watching television or movies, using the Internet or videogames, listening to or playing music, reading, shopping, clubbing or bar-hopping, and participating in or watching sports. This list may seem ridiculously exhaustive, except when one thinks of how anthropologists study other cultures, and how they pay attention to the everyday life of a people in order to understand what they value and how they make meaning (among the other purposes of anthropological research). Should we do less for the study of our own culture (or cultures)? Lynch also makes it clear that we should resist the temptation to confine popular culture to the environment, practices, and resources of everyday life for "ordinary people" in a society, as we cannot decide who is "ordinary" and who is not. We are all part of a popular culture of some sort, as noted earlier, even if it is a small counter-culture devoted to more rare practices or forms of art (like that of the avant-garde jazz musician).

What about the "and"?

In the term *religion and popular culture* there is another word we have not yet considered, which may seem so innocuous that it might be overlooked. But the conjunction is not without its own contribution to the phrase. It is precisely in the connections between these two areas of study that the overlaps and interactions occur which make the study of their interrelationship so difficult to parse and yet so fundamentally illuminating to the nature of both religion and culture. If both of these terms have referents (albeit sets of referents that are in constant flux, and constantly understood in new ways through the ever-evolving definitions of the terms), then their interactions and overlaps can be studied as well.

There are a few ways in which we might classify those interactions. Bruce Forbes and Jeff Mahan's edited volume *Religion and Popular Culture in America* (2005) organizes the contributions to the book around four basic categories: religion in popular culture, popular culture in religion, popular culture as religion, and religion and popular culture in dialogue. The first category, religion in popular culture, looks at the interpolation of religious content into the content of popular culture, such as depictions of religious figures in movies and television shows, religious imagery in music videos, and so forth. The second category flips this around; popular culture in religion looks at how religious communities have adapted the forms of popular culture to their own settings, e.g., with Christian rock, Christian Internet, and even places of worship constructed according to a model of consumer culture. While these forms seem to have adapted popular culture into religion, rather than the reverse, it is arguable that the tail may be wagging the dog, or in other words that the cultural forms and products that have been adapted in order to increase the marketability of religious forms are actually determining those religious forms.

The more one looks at these two categories, furthermore, the harder it is to tell the difference between them. One can view the same phenomenon as both a popular representation of religious content, and as an example of how religious communities utilize popular culture. Are the films of Cecil B. DeMille, for example *The Ten Commandments* (1956), to be viewed as an example of the former, but Mel Gibson's *The Passion of the Christ* (2004) as an example of the latter? Why? Because Gibson supposedly made his film for evangelistic rather than financial purposes? Did he? Can we say that DeMille did *not* make his films for evangelistic purposes? In marketing *The Ten Commandments*, DeMille installed tablets across the USA, which later became the subject of legal battles about the placement of religious content on public property (Plate 2009: 89–90). If these tablets are part of popular culture, are they an example of the interpolation of religion into popular culture by "secular"

forces, or an example of "religion" making use of popular culture for its own purposes? It may depend more on the uses to which the artifact is put—marketing, or
evangelizing in American "culture wars"—than on the original intentions of
DeMille, and this also demonstrates one of the key lessons of the study of popular
culture: we cannot determine the meaning of an object or practice apart from some
context, and varying the context or reception will change the perceived meaning.
The fact that the line between these first two categories is messy is an indication of
the ill-defined line between religion and culture; and this is another lesson, that we
cannot easily define where one leaves off and the other begins.

If the line between religion and culture is blurry, Forbes and Mahan's third category gives credence to that fact, and also echoes the approaches of the editors of this
volume, among others. I have argued (Lyden 2003) that popular films can function
religiously for populations even when this is not recognized by those populations, as
popular culture carries out functions analogous to religion by providing narratives as
expressions of worldviews (myths), moral frameworks, and rituals that connect the
consumers of popular culture with a set of beliefs and values. As such, films may
express meaning or a sense of purpose, salvation, or ritual fulfillment in experiences
of catharsis, liminality, or sacrifice. Eric Michael Mazur and Kate McCarthy's edited
volume *God in the Details: American Religion in Popular Culture* (2011) also utilizes this
viewpoint, as the contributors write about the religious function of cultural phenomena
ranging from barbecues to hip-hop. While they acknowledge that it may be problematic
to conclude that popular culture "is" a religion, they point out that popular culture may
provide "much that would ordinarily have been provided by religions, traditionally
understood" (ibid.: 10). As David Chidester has pointed out, whether we define much
of popular culture as religion, depends on how we define "religion" (Chidester 2005:
32). He notes that when we want to criticize or reject a cultural phenomenon, we often
refuse to grant it the label of "religion," preferring to label it as a "cult" (ibid.: 50).
He also sees that the conflicts between religions and popular culture themselves blur
the lines between them, making it "hard to tell where religion leaves off and popular
culture begins" (ibid.: 32). Even if we define popular culture "as" religion, we still
cannot escape the problematic questions about how we define these terms.

The last category of Forbes and Mahan is "religion and popular culture in dialogue," a category that is broad enough to allow for comparisons and exchanges,
mutual influences, and even the possibility of mutual instruction. By engaging in the
comparison, we learn more about both religion and popular culture. Sometimes this
approach is embraced by religious groups as they seek to relate better to the larger
culture by using examples from popular films or music as part of youth or adult
education; this may help people see the relevance of (e.g.) Christian categories, but
also makes people better critical consumers of culture. There may be a variety of
purposes in play by those who practice this approach: to evangelize or domesticate
popular culture, to critique or denounce it, to find areas of agreement or disagreement,
or to better understand our environment in relation to our values. This approach
has been especially utilized as a form of Christian cultural or practical theology by
scholars such as Clive Marsh (2004, 2007; Marsh and Roberts 2013), Chris Deacy
(2002, 2005, 2011), Jolyon Mitchell (2010), Robert K. Johnston (2006), Craig Detweiler
(2008; Detweiler and Taylor 2003), and Kelton Cobb (2005).

This last category has as its advantage an ability to engage in critique while also learning from its partner and not necessarily judging it before the conversation even begins. Religion gains a better understanding of popular culture, and vice versa, if both sides are willing to listen and learn. One problem with this approach is that it assumes that there are still two sides that can be defined. Once again we have to ask, where does one leave off and the other begin? If a person defines herself as a Christian, who also likes and is influenced by popular culture, is this an internal dialogue? Does the "Christian her" dialogue with the "pop culture her"? How would one define these two sides discretely? Is it not the case that one individual, or community, or a set of communities, constantly engages in a process of negotiation between conflicting or combining interests and values?

One example: Christian theology as a part of culture

Kathryn Tanner's view of culture as a dynamic process of conflicts and negotiations is here relevant once again. Although she writes on the subject of Christian theology, her points could apply equally well to any religious community engaged in a process of self-reflection. She notes that Christian theology is certainly a *part* of culture, and so is a cultural activity, which can be forgotten if we invoke the polar categories of H. Richard Niebuhr (1951) too much. Christ *rejecting* or *transforming* culture, for example, suggests some distinct entities we can identify, distinguish, and separate, as if Christianity were not as much a part of culture as the other aspects of culture with which it interacts. In fact, theology is as cultural as anything else, as religions are, as a particular version of the search for meaning which helps with "constructing a life-orienting worldview" (Tanner 1997: 64). It may seem that what distinguishes this activity is the fact that (e.g.) Christian theology operates within the context of the Christian religion; but, Tanner points out, the Christian religion is not a static entity which pre-exists theological reflection, but is a cultural process itself shaped by a variety of forces, inside and outside of what we call the Christian religion. Remembering that culture is a site of resistance and contradiction, a place where battles are fought over shared meanings, Tanner also shares a view similar to Lynch that culture refers to the "social practice of meaningful action" in the "beliefs, values, and orienting symbols that suffuse a whole way of life." Christian social practices may include prayer, confession of faith, exhortation, preaching, or lamentation (ibid.: 70). These practices are reflected upon by all Christians as they make meaning in their use, choosing the appropriate time and place to use each practice, suited to the context, and developing their own understanding of Christianity in the process. As such, theology is a feature of all Christian life, not just an academic discourse for those with higher degrees in the subject. "Everyday theology" may be distinguished from the activities of academic theology, but there must be a relationship between the two, if the academic discipline is to have any relation to the life of Christians (ibid.: 84–86).

This also means, according to Tanner, that theology is constructed in negotiation with popular practices of the social life of Christians as they exist in dialogue with other cultures and aspects of culture. Again, Christianity is not a static entity but a process of negotiations as to how to interpret its parts or weigh their respective values. Just as a poem can have multiple interpretations, so can Christianity; and further, it is not clear what lines are to be included in the poem as it does not exist as an obvious whole. We can argue that some lines should be excluded or at least reinterpreted (ibid.: 91–92). These arguments and tensions comprise the culture of Christian theology, whether at the academic or popular level. Churches argue about the content of Christianity and whether (at various times in history) it is compatible with eating food sacrificed to idols, allegiance to the Roman empire, owning slaves, serving in the military, allowing abortion to be legal, or allowing clergy to be same-sex partners in committed relationships. The central values of Christianity do not exist prior to these negotiations, but only as a process of negotiation, conflict, rejection, and affirmation.

Christian identity and theology are therefore relational, constantly changing as a result of this conflict and negotiation, which is also a negotiation with the values of the rest of culture (or other cultural values). There is in fact no fixed boundary between Christianity and culture as Christianity is in a constant process of adaptation and "poaching" of concepts and practices from the rest of culture (ibid.: 108). Tanner also echoes the Birmingham School's insistence that there is a "creativity of consumption" in the fact that we choose how to use cultural materials: "Cultural difference is more a question of *how* than of *what*; it is not so much what cultural materials you use as what you do with them that establishes identity" (ibid.: 112). She also argues that the rest of culture has already infiltrated theology and Christianity right from the start, so there is no pristine period in which Christianity exists as pure and unadulterated. Postliberal theology wrongly assumes such a state when it argues that the Christian story or code can somehow be understood apart from its borrowings from the rest of culture. Postliberals are correct, she writes, in the idea that "the identity of a Christian way of life is formed by a cultural boundary." The boundary is not fixed, but fluid and permeable:

> The boundary is … one of use that allows Christian identity to be essentially impure and mixed, the identity of a hybrid that always shares cultural forms with its wider host culture and other religions (notably Judaism). In contrast, then, to even the more moderate postliberal position, Christianity is a hybrid formation through and through … . Moreover … the distinctiveness of a Christian way of life is not so much formed *by* the boundary as *at* it; Christian distinctiveness is something that emerges in the very cultural processes occurring at the boundary, processes that construct a distinctive identity for Christian social practices through the distinctive use of cultural materials shared with others.
>
> (Tanner 1997: 114–15)

In Tanner's view, "both postliberal and correlationist theologians bring relations with the wider culture into the picture too late." These relations are not only part of the task of apologetics or application of already formed Christian perspectives, but are there "from the beginning as the materials out of which the very Christian message or lens is constructed." The boundary between Christianity and culture never existed in the first place, for it "has already been crossed in and through the very processes by which Christians come to believe anything at all" (ibid.: 115–16).

Conclusions

How might we apply Tanner's insights about Christian theology and culture to our work as those who practice the more diffuse discipline of *religion and popular culture*? I believe we can see that the lines between the terms involved are permeable, not fixed but fluid, and so subject to a process of constant change and evolution as we continually negotiate, poach, and otherwise evaluate the aspects of culture with which we interact, whether from a theological or any other point of view. We cannot precisely define where religion leaves off and culture begins, or vice versa; and that's okay. This does not erase our discipline. Rather, this reveals what we are actually doing; we are constructing our own identity out of a variety of materials, and not refusing to consider materials for being either too "popular" or too "religious." We are also willing to let those labels be slippery, and allow diverse definitions of them. This approach is not so postmodern that it prevents us from having any conclusions about our subject matter. The subject matter does exist; it is not only a figment of our imagination; but how we construct it and understand it is shaped by our imagination and our understanding. And we can engage in that task with enthusiasm and with the belief that we can gain a better understanding of ourselves, our religions, and our cultures, in the process. May the negotiations begin.

Works cited

Benedict, R. (1934) *Patterns of Culture*, New York: Houghton Mifflin.

Chidester, D. (2005) *Authentic Fakes: Religion and American Popular Culture*, Berkeley, CA: University of California Press.

Cobb, K. (2005) *The Blackwell Guide to Theology and Popular Culture*, Oxford: Blackwell.

Deacy, C. (2002) *Screen Christologies: Redemption and the Medium of Film*, Cardiff, UK: University of Wales.

——(2005) *Faith in Film: Religious Themes in Contemporary Cinema*, Aldershot: Ashgate.

——(2011) *Screening the Afterlife: Theology, Eschatology, and Film*, London: Routledge.

de Certeau, M. (1984) *The Practice of Everyday Life*, Berkeley, CA: University of California Press.

Detweiler, C. (2008) *Into the Dark: Seeing the Sacred in the Top Films of the 21st Century*, Grand Rapids, MI: Baker.

Detweiler, C. and B. Taylor (2003) *A Matrix of Meanings: Finding God in Pop Culture*, Grand Rapids, MI: Baker.

Fitzgerald, T. (2000) *The Ideology of Religious Studies*, New York: Oxford.

Forbes, B. and J. Mahan (eds) (2005) *Religion and Popular Culture in America*, 2nd edn, Berkeley, CA: University of California Press.

Godlove, T. (2010) "Religion in general, not in particular: a Kantian meditation," *Journal of the American Academy of Religion* 78, 4: 1025–47.

Hall, S. and T. Jefferson (1976) *Resistance through Rituals: Youth Subcultures in Post-War Britain*, London: Hutchison.

Hebdige, D. (1979) *Subculture: The Meaning of Style*, London: Methuen.

Hollows, J. and M. Jancovich (eds) (1995) *Approaches to Popular Film*, Manchester, UK: Manchester University Press.

Johnston, R. (2006) *Reel Spirituality: Theology and Film in Dialogue*, 2nd edn, Grand Rapids, MI: Baker.

Lyden, J. (2003) *Film as Religion: Myths, Morals, and Rituals*, New York: NYU Press.

Lynch, G. (2005) *Understanding Theology and Popular Culture*, Oxford: Blackwell.

McCutcheon, R. (1999) *Manufacturing Religion: The Discourse on Sui Generis Religion and the Politics of Nostalgia*, New York: Oxford.

——(2001) *Critics Not Caretakers: Redescribing the Public Study of Religion*, Albany, NY: State University of New York Press.

——(2003) *The Discipline of Religion: Structure, Meaning, Rhetoric*, London: Routledge.

Marsh, C. (2004) *Cinema and Sentiment: Film's Challenge to Theology*, Milton Keynes, UK: Paternoster.

——(2007) *Theology Goes to the Movies: An Introduction to Critical Christian Thinking*, London: Routledge.

Marsh, C. and V. Roberts (2013) *Personal Jesus: How Popular Music Shapes Our Souls*, Grand Rapids, MI: Baker.

Mazur, E.M. and K. McCarthy (eds) (2011) *God in the Details: American Religion in Popular Culture*, 2nd edn, London: Routledge.

Mitchell, J. (2010) *Media Violence and Christian Ethics*, Cambridge: Cambridge University.

Niebuhr, H.R. (1951) *Christ and Culture*, New York: Harper & Row.

Plate, S.B. (2009) *Religion and Film: Cinema and the Re-creation of the World*, London: Wallflower Press.

Schilbrack, K. (2010) "Religions: are there any?" *Journal of the American Academy of Religion* 78, 4: 1112–38.

Smith, J.Z. (1982) *Imagining Religion: From Babylon to Jonestown*, Chicago, IL: University of Chicago Press.

Tanner, K. (1997) *Theories of Culture: A New Agenda for Theology*, Minneapolis, MN: Fortress.

2

CONVERSATIONS AND CONFESSIONS

Who's writing about this, and why?

Eric Michael Mazur

That which hath been is that which shall be, and that which hath been done is that which shall be done; and there is nothing new under the sun.

Ecclesiastes 1:9

[R]emember, no matter where you go, there you are.

The Adventures of Buckaroo Banzai Across the 8th Dimension (1984)

In the spring of 1996, three graduate students collaborated on a proposal for a paper to be delivered at the annual meeting of the association of their intended profession. The conference "call for papers" asked for proposals investigating religion on television, and the three—who had spent the previous few years discussing (over burritos and beer) the presence and role of religion on the Fox animated television program *The Simpsons* (1989–present)—figured they had nothing to lose. To their amazement, the proposal was accepted. After spending the summer writing, one of the three delivered the paper (which they called "Franken-paper" because of how it was stitched together) that, as it turned out, was fairly well received. In the 17 years since, that paper has been published in two editions of a collection of essays on religion and popular culture (Mazur and McCarthy 2001/2011), excerpted in another (Lehman *et al.* 2005), and cited broadly in the emerging "field" of religion and *The Simpsons* (see Heit 2008; Pinsky 2001).[1]

It is probably not too surprising to learn that this is my story. I was one of those graduate students—along with Lisle Dalton and Monica Siems—but it could have been the story of almost anyone working in the field of religion and popular culture in the 1990s. Seeming to converge (or at least to coincide) in the second half of the twentieth century, a number of factors played a seminal role in the transformation of various traditional academic lines of inquiry, creating energy for the study of the relationship of religion and popular culture. Kate McCarthy and I (2011: xvi–xvii) suggest "the Marxian influence on the study of history," developments in the field of social history, and the growing interest in material culture; Lynn Schofield Clark (2008) suggests feminist studies; without a doubt there are others. In their own ways (and for their own disciplinary reasons), various areas of the academy encouraged scholars to pay greater attention to issues of class, consumerism, material culture, and cultural production, and challenged and de-centered traditional power narratives (including those about culture and cultural production), even as fields such as anthropology elevated their fascination with "the local" and others, such as media studies, emphasized the means of communicating ideas, symbols, and images of cultural authority, and recognized the role of the audience in receiving (and interpreting) those ideas.

But my story of "Franken-paper" also illuminates another important source of energy that seemed to propel the investigation of the relationship of religion and popular culture to its present state: the biographies of those working in the field.[2] This has always been the case—whether they acknowledge it or not, it is most likely that people have always been motivated to study that which has had the greatest resonance in their own minds or hearts—but what made it different this time around was the kind of experience—particularly as it relates to religion and culture in the English-speaking world, particularly in the United States—that these authors and scholars shared. Ritual theorist Catherine Bell (1992: 5) reminds us that "critical analysis of a theoretical perspective must look not only to the logic of the set of ideas under scrutiny, but also to the history of their construction," suggesting that, in addition to seeking the solution to an intellectual riddle (such as the relationship between religion and popular culture, for example), we must also ask how the riddle itself came to be formed—as she puts it, "a deconstruction of the historical definitions of the problem or issue and a delineation of the circumstances under which the problem has been *a problem for us*" (ibid.; emphasis in the original). So our immediate question is not when did the relationship between religion and popular culture develop, but why has it become such a vibrant field lately?

The question "when did this begin?"—the "first order" question one considers in investigating the relationship between religion and popular culture—produces answers that depend on the investigation's perspective. Among the chapters in this volume, contributors focusing on specific religious traditions address (in some form) when and how popular culture became a "problem" for these traditions.[3] Those focusing on specific forms of popular culture are more likely to see the "problem" as rooted in the late nineteenth and early twentieth century, with the rise of processes of mass mediation and communication.

But these two forms of analysis—the one that investigates how popular culture relates to a specific religious tradition, and the other that investigates how religion relates to a specific form of popular culture—either assume (as a given) or pass over (as too subjective) the self-reflective question posed by Bell. In the following, we will seek an answer to the question about when the relationship of (any) religion and (any form of) popular culture became an issue such that we (as a society, as a profession, or as individuals) felt the need to study it: the "second order" question about the questioning of the relationship of religion and popular culture.

A time for every purpose ...

There is a story told about atomic scientist Robert Oppenheimer who, upon seeing the mushroom cloud of the first atomic bomb being tested in New Mexico, thought to himself "I am become death, destroyer of worlds," quoting Lord Krishna from the Bhagavad-Gita (see Hijiya 2000). The fact that Oppenheimer could quote the Hindu narrative is not particularly remarkable, given his personal upbringing. What is noteworthy is that there is no record of his remembering having said this in the 20 years before 1965. While it is unlikely that this omission was made consciously, it might also be unlikely that its recollection was coincidental. But even if the story is apocryphal, it illustrates nonetheless the dramatic change that had occurred in American society between 1945 and 1965 such that—as it relates to this story—a Jewish physicist could recall in 1965 (and share with others) thinking of a line from a Hindu sacred text, when in 1945, at one of the most important moments of American scientific history (and likely, his academic career), he could not.

There is nothing particularly magical about the year 1965.[4] But there is little doubt that "the 1960s," however we define it, represent a significant period of transformation in American society. Sociologist of religion Robert Wuthnow (1998) broadly traces the changing nature of religion in American society across the twentieth century, from which we can draw three generational stages. In the first stage, Wuthnow examines the impact immigration had on American culture from the end of the nineteenth century to World War I. Migrants from largely non-Protestant, non-English speaking cultures came to this country in increasingly large numbers, transforming American cities which had only recently outpaced rural agrarian society as the engine of American culture and commerce. Forming (or enhancing) urban ethnic enclaves, these immigrants of the beginning of the twentieth century gave birth to the steady, practical-minded "dwellers" of mid-century—our second stage, the joiners who sought to remove vestiges of their ethnic heritage by blending in to American dominant (that is, largely white Protestant) culture. Their own children—our third stage, the so-called "baby boomers" of the post-World War II generation (those born between 1948 and 1963, approximately)—were not only great in number, but were financially better off than their parents (or certainly their grandparents) had been at the same age, and felt less compelled to adhere to the standards established by their government (who was sending them to Vietnam), their religious leadership (who often supported the fight against Communism, or who seemed to hesitate in the fight over changing race and gender roles), and their parents (whose "purchase" into suburban consumerism seemed spiritually bankrupt). Feeling betrayed by the traditional institutional sources of social authority, these "seekers" sought new sources of meaning-construction and maintenance. In his own investigation, Wade Clark Roof (1993) measures the impact of the 1960s on this cohort by defining them not only by their birth year but also by exposure to three types of experience he considers elemental for those transformed by this era: attendance at a rock concert, participation in a protest, and the use of marijuana. Through these experiences—the experiences of group effervescence found in a rock concert, the empowerment of social protest, and the physical (or even spiritual) liberation of getting high—the new generation of "seekers" found what they felt they needed. Coincidentally, a change in federal law permitting greater immigration from non-European countries (most profoundly India, Japan, South Korea, the Philippines, and Turkey) brought American youth face to face with leaders and practitioners of Buddhism, Hinduism, and Islam in ways that had not been possible before (Melton 1993). New sources of meaning-construction and -maintenance were, it seems, in great abundance for those who sought it in the 1960s.

Phillip Hammond (1992) chronicles how these changes in American society created an environment wherein young people felt greater freedom to distance themselves from the religious attachments into which they were born, a phenomenon he calls the "third disestablishment"; the liberation of the individual from the historic, ascriptive nature of traditional religious identity.[5] Individuals for whom Roof's indicators (rock concerts, protests, and marijuana) were of greater importance—particularly, Hammond discovers, those who (as adults) lived in larger metropolitan areas—found themselves later in life much more likely to belong to a religious community different from the one of their birth, or none at all.

For sociologists, this transformation signaled a "restructuring of American society" (Wuthnow 1988) wherein denominational allegiances were based more on ideology than theology (see Hunter 1991); for theologians, it marked either the challenge of finding God in the "secular city" (see Cox 1965), or the "death of God" (see Murchland 1967; Elson 1966). One of those "death of God" theologians, Gabriel Vahanian (1967: 4), lamented the loss of "sacramental significance" and the "transcendental dimension" in the world; philosopher Eugene Borowitz (1967: 93) concluded that "[m]odern man is secular and happily so."

But it would be a terrible mistake to see the period since the 1960s as defined by a lack of religiosity. As I have noted elsewhere (Mazur 2013: 150–51), we can find evidence of continued (or even growing) interest in things religious by examining something as mundane as the historical record of "gospel" publishing in the United States. Between 1815 and 1965, a different imprint of one of the canonical gospels (Matthew, Mark, Luke, and John) was published every year; between 1965 and 2011, that average doubled.[6] During the same period, the number of "gospels" according to entirely non-biblical figures (the Beatles, Harry Potter, Bruce Springsteen, Oprah Winfrey, etc.) exploded; six were published between 1815 and 1965 (0.04 per year), while nearly 80 were published between 1965 and 2011 (1.74 per year).[7]

Despite what some (see Carter 1993; Neuhaus 1984) have argued, what diminished was not the presence of religion in society, but the authority of a particular form of religion in society. Many (if not most) Americans remained deeply committed to institution-based Christianity, or to the religious identity of their parents (the religious identity of their youth). But the 1960s ushered in an era of religious experimentation, religious pluralism, and individual religious freedom of expression in a manner much like other periods of (American) religious revitalization (see McLoughlin 1978). What shifted (if only slightly) was the monopoly enjoyed by institution-based forms of Christianity (but also, to a lesser extent, Judaism) in the lives of many Americans. More Americans than at any time in this country's history were becoming "serially" affiliated (moving from one denomination to the next with relative ease), or institutionally unaffiliated, or were converting from one major religious tradition to another, or were non-Christian to begin with, and more Americans than at any time in this country's history were many things, or were not any one thing—what Roof *et al.* (1995: 245–46) call "cafeteria religion" or "religion à la carte"—or were not anything.[8]

In his analysis of the "death of God" theology, sociologist (and rabbi) Will Herberg (1966a: 771) argues that the theologians lamented the fact that "whatever meaning and relevance God may once have had, He has now lost this meaning and relevance for modern man." He concludes that modern man "may abandon Christian faith, and lose his Christian consciousness" (an odd lament from a rabbi, to be sure) "but that only means that the spiritual void will be filled with a legion of modern idolatries, some of them almost too weird to describe" (1966b: 840). As if in horror, Borowitz (1967: 92) exclaims: "theology threatens to become popular!"

A lot of money can be lost betting on the future of religion in America; Thomas Jefferson once prognosticated that Unitarianism would be "the religion of the majority from north to south" (Jefferson 1822). Herberg and Borowitz—probably like most religious thinkers of their era—calculated that the trends they saw in the mid-1960s would lead to religious chaos. And some of what developed was (more than likely) beyond their imagination—"too weird to describe"—or the imagination of the Christian (that is, mostly Protestant) American religious establishment. By the end of the 1960s, African-American liberation theology (Cone 1969), Latin-American liberation theology (Gutiérrez 1973), feminist theology (Daly 1973), and neo-Pagan theology (Starhawk 1979) were "popular," and within another decade, so too would be eco- and gay theology. Even mainstream theologians were getting into the act; a *New York Times* reporter specifically cited Jürgen Moltmann's *Theology of Hope* (1967) as part of the movement away from the "God is Dead" theology (see Fiske 1968).

In the world of commerce, competition flourishes in an environment where there is no monopoly. Sociologists of American religion (see Finke and Iannoccone 1993; Finke and Stark 1992), applying the same model, have provided us with a way of understanding religious growth.[9] With the removal of Christianity as the legally established religion (the "first" disestablishment, embodied in the ratification of the US Constitution's First Amendment), its subsequent loss of monopoly in social privilege (the "second" disestablishment of the late nineteenth and early twentieth centuries), and ultimately the loss of social authority for institution-based religious affiliation and identity (Hammond's "third" disestablishment), alternative forms of religion and religious expression began to flourish.[10] A common thread connecting many of these alternative forms of religious expression was the basic impulse for spiritual fulfillment—including what has often been identified as the "spiritual but not religious" phenomenon in American culture. Roof, Hammond, and others suggest that what was once a paired experience—people who were religious felt that they were spiritual, and vice versa—had for many now become separate. People who went to, affiliated with, joined, or identified with a specific (usually traditional, non-marginalized) institution-based form of spirituality were "religious"; those who did not were "spiritual." Robert Bellah *et al.* (1985) portray the ultimate "seeker" as one for whom the journey to self-discovery is the primary spiritual motivation, a position he and his co-authors identify as "Sheila-ism" (after the study subject whom they had given the pseudonym "Sheila"). These seekers became seekers of spirituality in all forms, from alternative forms of institutional religions to individual pursuits to nature to … well, almost any form of experience (see Wuthnow 1998). And these seekers became, at least initially (and, it seems, overwhelmingly), the foundation for much of the new energy in the study of the relationship between religion and popular culture.

God saw the light, that it was good ...

As difficult as it is to believe sometimes, scholars are products of the societies into which they are born—as much as those they study. This means that, at the very least, those scholars born between 1948 and 1963—particularly if they protested something, attended rock concerts, and smoked marijuana—would have been as susceptible to the cultural influences (including those on religion) as any of Roof's other "seekers," and those born later would have inherited the same world as the post-"boomer" generations ("Generation X," "Millennials," etc.). It also means that even those scholars little affected by Roof's experiential "hat trick" would still occupy—and thus be confronted with—an American society filled with those who had.

If this is the case, it may provide us with at least one possible explanation for transformations not only in religion and religious experience since the 1960s, but also in the ways in which religion and religious experience are studied—largely because those who are doing the studying have been affected by the same influences (positively or negatively) as those they study. And there is evidence suggestive of this conclusion. In 1963, the US Supreme Court ruled that not only was there a con-stitutionally significant difference between studying religion and studying about reli-gion, but there was also a lacuna in one's education if the latter was absent. As Justice Clark noted for the Court, "one's education is not complete without a study of comparative religion or the history of religion and its relationship to the advancement of civilization" (*Abington v. Schempp*, 374 U.S. 203 [1963], at 225). The following year (1964), the premier scholarly association for those engaged in the aca-demic study of religion (the American Academy of Religion) was founded, and over the course of the decade—at publicly financed state colleges and universities—so too were a number of departments of religious studies and comparative religion, dedi-cated to the academic study about religion, as opposed to the theological analysis (or confessional defense) of it.

Not surprisingly, scholarship investigating the world of religion and popular culture was strongly affected by the shifts noted above in how people approached religion and religious experience. A hint of this can be found by comparing the categories used to describe that relationship suggested in 1951 by Protestant theolo-gian H. Richard Niebuhr—"Christ against culture," "the Christ of culture," "Christ above culture," "Christ and culture in paradox," and "Christ the transformer of culture"—with those suggested in 2000 by Bruce Forbes and Jeffrey Mahan (2000: 10–18)—"religion in popular culture," "popular culture in religion," "popular cul-ture as religion," and "religion and popular culture in dialogue." Neither parallel nor in direct opposition, these terms suggest different presumptions on the part of the scholars employing them. The mid-century Protestant theologian Niebuhr is, undoubtedly, speaking theologically to a receptive (or at least familiar), primarily Christian audience; the twenty-first century scholars Forbes and Mahan—both ordained ministers, as it turns out—are likely responding to their mid-century fore-bear, but are speaking to a broader audience, using broader (and decidedly more secular) terms.

Mahan (2007: 49) identifies a specific work—from 1965, as it turns out—as one of the "precursors to the wider scholarly conversation about religion and popular culture." It was a slim volume by Presbyterian minister Robert Short, who "thought faith was best when it was subtle and most accessible when it seemed almost trivial" (Sanders 2009). Written "with the blessing of Peanuts creator Charles Schulz," *The Gospel According to Peanuts* mined the popular comic strip for common Christian themes based on the presumption that the comic was "written as moral instruction" by Schulz, and thus could be "analyzed as scriptural literature" by Short (Ahrens 1997). The work, which sold more than ten million copies in seven different languages (Sanders 2009), was not universally acclaimed at first; one contemporary reviewer noted that Short had read too much into the cartoon (Hakes 1965), and American religious historian Martin Marty noted that "this idea of mixing popular culture and the Bible" made people nervous (Sanders 2009). But the volume's introduction was written by Nathan Scott, a pioneer in the field of religion and literature whose work, according to Mahan (2007: 48–49), "drew our attention to the relationships between religion and art."[11] And its effects were long lasting; David Dobson, Short's editor, concluded that the author-theologian, who explored the theological significance of the comic, had "really invented the study of religion through popular culture" (Sanders 2009).

Ye shall know them by their fruits …

Since then, the scholarly world of religion and popular culture has grown tremendously—"almost silly with the exploration" of the topic (Mazur and McCarthy 2011: xvii). Members of the American Academy of Religion established a special unit for the study of religion and popular culture in the 1990s—as the "baby boomers" were coming into positions of institutional power—only slightly ahead of the appearance of a number of scholarly journals dedicated to the study of religion and popular culture (or some aspect thereof).[12] Work continues with great enthusiasm exploring the relationship of religion and popular culture generally, through the lens of a specific religious tradition, or through the lens of a specific form of popular culture—as our contributors map out in the other chapters in this volume.

As more work has been produced, clusters seem to have formed around three general categories. The first—from a theologically conservative perspective—consists of works that are critical of popular culture generally or some aspect of it specifically, seeing it as a threat to a particular community, or to larger society. This is the oldest model—as I noted above, the voices of the religious have long warned believers of the temptations of the world—but it is one that widened significantly in the 1980s and early 1990s with the mobilization of various "family values"-motivated organizations and individuals, including such non-religious groups as the Parents' Music Resource Center (see Persley 2007) and individual representatives such as film critic Michael Medved (see especially Medved 1992).

Not all work from a religious perspective has been critical of popular culture, however, as Short's pioneering work on the Peanuts cartoon proved. In 2000, in honor of the 35th anniversary of its initial publication, Westminster John Knox Press, the institutional descendant of the original publisher, rereleased Short's book, inaugurating a series of books exploring the "gospel according to" a wide variety of subjects, including (just from this one publisher): America, the Beatles, Bob Dylan, Bruce Springsteen, Disney, Harry Potter, Hollywood, Oprah Winfrey, science fiction, the Simpsons, *Star Wars*, J.R.R. Tolkien, and the novel *Twilight*. Works by theologians broadly representative of an academic perspective (including works by a number of contributors to this volume) rather than by those from a specifically affiliated faith community, and also by scholars with clear (but usually moderate) theological positions, have continued Short's trajectory of bringing critical but positive theological method to their analysis.

This volume (like others) amply illustrates the third category, which is populated with contributions by scholars more traditionally trained in the humanities and social sciences. These scholars have produced a steady flow of work over the past 25 years or so examining the religion and popular culture nexus motivated not only by the social changes of the 1960s, but also by many of the disciplinary shifts mentioned earlier in this chapter. Historians, sociologists, anthropologists, psychologists, and religion scholars have published work, long and short, in great abundance, in response to the expansion in scholarly interest, but also sparking it. Some of these works have found an audience in college classrooms, largely based on their ability to showcase the use of method in the service of intellectual inquiry, retain student interest based on their contemporary relevance, and appeal to instructors who feel more at home with the topic and its approach.

Standing idle in the marketplace

A 2007 essay by Lynn Schofield Clark outlining the intellectual history of the field bore the title "Why study popular culture?"—a question that those of us who have been engaged in the field have had to face regularly, from our colleagues as well as from our own consciences. Her subtitle—"How to build a case for your thesis in a religious studies or theology department"—was even more to the point. Without actually reading the essay, one becomes aware of several important aspects of the field of religion and popular culture: first, it is a relatively young field (it must be, otherwise graduate students would not need instructions for how to get their thesis proposals accepted); and second, largely because of point 1, it is still (or was still, as of 2007) a field in need of defending. In part, this is due to the social and intellectual transformations outlined above. As the years pass, more departments are supporting masters' theses and doctoral dissertations exploring the relationship between religion and popular culture; the advancing seniority of sympathetic faculty—and the eventual retirement of the unsympathetic—has certainly helped. Nonetheless, a good number of older scholars in this area of study are "second fielders"—scholars trained in other fields or specialties but more recently arrived in the field. They (we!) are either self-taught in the ways of popular cultural analysis, re-mappers of familiar method onto new data sets—I often define what I do as "spontaneous cultural archaeology"—or interdisciplinary innovators blending fields without regard to disciplinary boundaries. Nonetheless, many of us keep one foot in a field that "feels" more scholarly.[13]

It may also be that, to some extent, the study of the relationship between religion and popular culture remains in need of defending because of the existence of a fourth category of published work. This fourth category draws from the other three but also from beyond them. It also increases the visibility of materials produced in this area; that is, it drives the market as much as the theological and scholarly merit of the other three categories. I (and many others, most likely) consider it "schlock": garbage.[14] This is work with such little scholarly merit as to be unmistakably, almost objectively bad. The measure of what is or is not in this category is undoubtedly subjective, whether it is a failure to problematize, contextualize, or even adequately research a topic, or is simply a facile comparison, or a work giving little evidence of intellectual reflection. It confirms the fears of all of those who think the academic study of religion and popular culture is a waste of time. It may be that those of us who are "second fielders" are made uncomfortable with what others might see as "cutting edge," that it might push us beyond our own tradition-based, tradition-inculcated comfort levels. It is certainly the case that some of the work in this category serves as valuable primary data, even if it lacks scholarly merit.

But as intellectually vapid as some of the work in this category may be, it can be amusing. It can be fun. It can be a guilty pleasure. And it sells; it sells because we (all) read it—I'll read almost anything about the religious aspects of "Dead Elvis." As I noted earlier, members of the "baby boom" generation were, in their young adulthood, great in number, but also better off than their parents and grandparents had been at the same age. This generation was also able to exploit periods of great economic expansion, and unmoored as many of them are in terms of institutional religious attachments, in the words of the Rev. Lillian Daniel (2011), they "find themselves uniquely fascinating." What more does one need for successful consumerism? Works in the fourth category cater to this community's self-interest— their readers (like anyone would) find themselves and elements of their nostalgia to be of great interest—I remember when Elvis died, and how devastated my fourth grade teacher was; I visited Graceland, and saw the gravestone bearing the misspelled middle name, proof (to some) that the man still lives. The benefit to others has been a marked increase in interest among publishers for materials exploring the relation between religion and popular culture—particularly that which explores this relationship among those in this segment of the purchasing population—apparently whether or not this material is highly critical, profoundly theological, intensely scholarly, or fun-time leisure reading.[15] Different publishers have staked out areas of their own interest and expertise, and materials produced by religiously affiliated and "trade" publishers can be found in all three of the more academic categories. But the market in general is still populated with work of dubious value, and despite the claims of Rudyard Kipling (1922: 56), not every good cigar is a smoke—sometimes it's just a stinking mess.

Conclusion: and the whole earth was of one language

Certainly there are other factors involved in the propagation of work beyond the market impulses of the "baby boomer" generation, and the producers' willingness to address these impulses with reading materials, academic or not. At the very least, we would be remiss if we did not acknowledge the expansion of industrialization into non-Western European nations—the post-war rise of nations like Australia and (re-built) Japan, emerging nations (like Israel and South Africa), the so-called "Asian Tigers" (South Korea, the Philippines, Vietnam, and others), and the "BRICs" (Brazil–Russia–India–China)—that has created a new and expanded market not only for the products of American culture (Coca-Cola, McDonald's, Starbucks, etc.), but also for the very processes of making these products (industrialization, capitalism, commercialism), and the concomitant worldview that accompanies them (see Ritzer 1993). The cross-border realignment of cultures has generated a phenomenon Benjamin Barber (1996, 1992) calls "McWorld"—a global yet increasingly homogenous experience where one can purchase KFC in Cairo (as I have), McDonald's in India, or Starbucks in Japan (see Wade 2009). This globalization, which Roland Robertson (1985: 348) defines as "the process by which the world becomes a single place both with respect to recognition of a very high degree of interdependence between spheres and locales of social activity across the entire globe and to the growth of consciousness pertaining to the globe as such," is roughly parallel to Wuthnow's (1998) "seekers" described above: individualists who are no longer committed to specific, inherited, bounded identities, but who, for the sake of being free to define themselves, are likewise willing to accept (at face value) the self-definition of others.

On a global scale, this means that people from any of the industrialized nations could parachute into any of the others and, once language barriers are overcome, live as comfortably (intellectually, socially, and, within reason, economically) as anywhere else. In terms of popular culture, it means that these same "parachuters" can find for purchase music, films, food, clothes, or any of the carriers of personal identity that they might find at home (see Crothers 2006)—wherever that might be. And in terms of religion and popular culture, it means that many more people are engaging popular culture in ways worthy of study, and that many more are willing to read about it!

There is another aspect to globalization. As Wuthnow (1998) illustrates in the American context, there can be no "seeker" without the "dweller," the communitarian for whom identity is defined by membership in a group whose standards define its boundaries. On the global scale, these are similar to Barber's "tribalists," and while in the American context they mostly define political behavior (despite the dire rhetoric of some; see Hunter 1994, 1991), on the global stage the boundary between the two ("globalists" and "tribalists") has been the location of significant conflict (for an early exploration of the topic, see Marty and Appleby 1991). What for Wuthnow (1988) has been a "restructuring of American religion" for the world has been a restructuring of global contact, and reorganization of conflict.

As these lines get redrawn, the scholar of religion and popular culture will be increasingly confronted not only by questions about the globalization of mass produced culture and its impact on religion, but also by questions of the role of religion and popular culture in the contact and conflict of the ideologically reorganized world of "globalists" and "tribalists." What might the mass production, appropriation, commercialization, and distribution mean in this context? The answers to those questions might not be too surprising. But how might the changing context of globalization—and the reactions against globalization, and the possible calcification or irritation of the boundaries between "globalist" and "tribalist"—be affected by changing roles and meanings of religion in, and through, popular culture? Beyond the English-speaking world, these and other questions about the relationship of religion and popular culture will have increasing significance, and as historian of American religion Catherine Albanese (1996: 736) concludes in her introduction to a special issue of the *Journal of the American Academy of Religion* dedicated to the growing importance of the field, "[s]tudents of religion need to pay strenuous attention to them."

Notes

1 Unfortunately, Pinsky (2001; 2007) incorrectly cites the editors of the volume rather than the authors of the specific chapter, an error I attempt to correct in a review of Pinsky's revised edition (Mazur 2009).
2 McCarthy and I confess as much in the introduction to the first edition (2001: 7).
3 As John Lyden suggests in his chapter on definitions in this volume, depending on how one defines the terms, one could argue that popular culture has always been "a problem" for religion; religions all seem to come with scriptural and historic figures who provide stern warnings that, as the poet William Wordsworth (1889: 203) put it, "the world is too much with us, late and soon."
4 It should be noted, however, that Malcolm X, Paul Tillich, and Martin Buber died that year, and that I was born that year. But so were millions of others—for either stage of life—so you are left to draw your own conclusions.
5 Hammond here is building on the notion of the "first" disestablishment (the separation of constitutional law from religion embodied in the "religion" clauses of the First Amendment) and the "second" establishment (the beginning of the end of a mainstream Protestant cultural monopoly in American public society; see Handy 1991).
6 A similar pattern is evident for non-canonical gospels (Barnabbas, Hebrews, Judas, Mary, Philip, Thomas) as well as Bible-related gospels (Isaiah, James, Jesus, Moses, Paul, Pilate, etc.) (see Mazur 2013: 158 n11). The numbers are based on a 2011 search of the Library of Congress online catalog, which contains records for materials going back only to 1815.
7 Whether in response to the 1965 change in immigration law or not, the number of books purporting to explain the "Tao of … " or "Zen and the Art of … " has followed an identical (if slightly off-set) pattern (Mazur 2013: 158 n12).
8 In a slight bit of (likely unintentional) religion humor, members of this last cohort are often identified as "Nones," which would be the plural of their answer to the question "What is your religious preference?" (see Vernon 1968).
9 This new model has had such a profound impact on the study of religion that it has been called a "new paradigm," replacing (or at least challenging) the standard "secularization thesis" which has its roots in nineteenth century European triumphalism (see Warner 1993).
10 This is not to suggest that there were no alternative forms of religious expression before this historical point; of course there were. But the degree of diversity of expression—matched with greater social freedom to express that diversity—reached an unprecedented level after the transformations of the 1960s.
11 As if to confirm the scholarly value of Short's work, the introduction to the first Italian edition of *The Gospel According to Peanuts* was written by novelist and semiotics scholar Umberto Eco (Boxer 2000).
12 It is hardly coincidental that the *Journal of Religion & Film*, the *Journal of Religion & Theatre* (now defunct), and the *Journal of Religion & Popular Culture* were all founded around the same time, and can be located only online, in digital format.
13 As a case in point, all three who wrote the paper on religion and *The Simpsons* chose more "traditional" religious studies topics for our dissertation research: I wrote on religion and

constitutional litigation; Dalton wrote on religion and nineteenth-century pseudo-science; and Siems wrote on Native Americans and the philosophy of religion.

14 One could also argue that there is a fifth category: the study of those materials in popular culture that are entirely secular and empty of religious meaning (see Siegler 2012). There is a tendency among some theologians, scholars, and writers of schlock to see religion everywhere; works in this category—for a variety of reasons—seek to articulate clearer boundaries, or any at all.

15 Changes in the economy have also driven publishers to scale back the publication of material of "strictly" scholarly merit in favor of works that will have broader classroom or commercial appeal (see Worstall 2012; Caro 2009: 1–9).

Works cited

Abington School District v. Schempp (1963), 374 U.S. 203.

Ahrens, F. (1997) "The gospel according to 'Calvin and Hobbes,'" *Washington Post* (March 15): D9.

Albanese, C.L. (1996) "Religion and American popular culture: an introductory essay," *Journal of the American Academy of Religion* 64, 4: 733–42.

Barber, B.R. (1992) "Jihad vs. McWorld," *The Atlantic* (March 1). Online. Available: www.theatlantic.com/magazine/archive/1992/03/jihad-vs-mcworld/303882/ (accessed 1 September 2013).

——(1996) *Jihad vs. McWorld: Terrorism's Challenge to Democracy*, New York: Ballantine Books.

Bell, C. (1992) *Ritual Theory, Ritual Practice*, New York: Oxford University Press.

Bellah, R.N., R. Madsen, W.M. Sullivan, A. Swidler, and S.M. Tipton (1985) *Habits of the Heart: Individualism and Commitment in American Life*, Berkeley, CA: University of California Press.

Borowitz, E.B. (1967) "God-is-dead theology," in B. Murchland (ed.), *The Meaning of the Death of God: Protestant, Jewish and Catholic Scholars Explore Atheistic Theology*, New York: Random House, 92–107.

Boxer, S. (2000) "Charles M. Schulz, 'Peanuts' creator, dies at 77," *New York Times* (February 14): 1.

Caro, S. (2009) *How to Publish Your PhD*, Thousand Oaks, CA: Sage Publications.

Carter, S. (1993) *The Culture of Disbelief: How American Law and Politics Trivialize Religious Devotion*, New York: Basic Books.

Clark, L.S. (2007) "Why study popular culture? Or, how to build a case for your thesis in a religious studies or theology department," in G. Lynch (ed.), *Between Sacred and Profane: Researching Religion and Popular Culture*, New York: I.B. Tauris, 5–20.

——(2008) "When the university went 'pop': exploring cultural studies, sociology of culture, and the rising interest in the study of popular culture," *Sociology Compass* 2, 1: 16–33.

Cone, J. (1969) *Black Theology and Black Power*, New York: Seabury Press.

Cox, H. (1965) *The Secular City: Secularization and Urbanization in Theological Perspective*, New York: Macmillan Company.

Crothers, L. (2006) *Globalization and American Popular Culture*, Lanham, MD: Rowman & Littlefield.

Daly, M. (1973) *Beyond God the Father: Toward a Philosophy of Women's Liberation*, Boston, MA: Beacon Press.

Daniel, L. (2011) "Spiritual but not religious? Please stop boring me," *Huffington Post* (September 13). Online. Available: www.huffingtonpost.com/lillian-daniel/spiritual-but-not-religio_b_959216.html (accessed 27 August 2013).

Elson, J.T. (1966) "Theology toward a hidden God," *Time* (April 8): 82–87.

Finke, R. and L. Iannoccone (1993) "Supply-side explanations for religious change," *Annals of the American Academy of Political and Social Science* 527 (May): 27–39.

Finke, R., and R. Stark (1992) *The Churching of America, 1776–1990: Winners and Losers in Our Religious Economy*, New Brunswick, NJ: Rutgers University Press.

Fiske, E.B. (1968) "'God is dead' doctrine losing ground to 'theology of hope,'" *New York Times* (March 24): 1.

Forbes, B.D. and J.H. Mahan (eds) (2000) *Religion and Popular Culture in America*, rev. edn 2005, Berkeley, CA: University of California Press.

Gutiérrez, G. (1973) *A Theology of Liberation: History, Politics, and Salvation*, trans. and ed. C. Inda and J. Eagleson, Maryknoll, NY: Orbis Books.

Hakes, J.E. (1965) "*The Gospel According to Peanuts*, by Robert L. Short" [book review]. *Bulletin of the Evangelical Theological Society* 8, 3 (Summer): 118.

Hammond, P.E. (1992) *Religion and Personal Autonomy: The Third Disestablishment in America*, Columbia, SC: University of South Carolina Press.

Handy, R.T. (1991) *Undermined Establishment: Church–State Relations in America 1880–1920*, Princeton, NJ: Princeton University Press.

Heit, J. (2008) *The Springfield Reformation:* The Simpsons, *Christianity, and American Culture*, New York: Continuum.

Herberg, W. (1966a) "The 'death of God' theology – I: the philosophy behind it," *National Review* 18 (August 9): 771, 779.

——(1966b) "The 'death of god' theology – II: secularization and the collapse of meaning," *National Review* 18 (August 23): 839–40.

Hijiya, J.A. (2000) "The Gita of J. Robert Oppenheimer," *Proceedings of the American Philosophical Society* 144, 2 (June): 123–67.

Hunter, J.D. (1991) *Culture Wars: The Struggle to Define America*, New York: Basic Books.

——(1994) *Before the Shooting Begins: Searching for Democracy in America's Culture War*, New York: Free Press.

Jefferson, T. (1822) "To Dr. Thomas Cooper" (November 2). Online. Available: http://etext.virginia.edu/etcbin/toccer-new2?id=JefLett.sgm&images=images/modeng&data=/texts/english/modeng/parsed&tag=public&part=268&division=div1 (accessed 11 August 2013).

Kipling, R. (1922) "The betrothed," in *Rudyard Kipling's Verse*, Garden City, NJ: Doubleday, Page and Co., 53–56.

Lehman, A., J. Myers, and P. Moro (eds) (2005) *Magic, Witchcraft and Religion: An Anthropological Study of the Supernatural*, 6th edn, Boston, MA: McGraw-Hill, 477–85.

McLoughlin, W.G. (1978) *Revivals, Awakenings, and Reform*, Chicago, IL: The University of Chicago Press.

Mahan, J.H. (2007) "Reflections on the past and future of the study of religion and popular culture," in G. Lynch (ed.), *Between Sacred and Profane: Researching Religion and Popular Culture*, New York: I.B. Tauris, 47–62.

Marty, M.E. and R.S. Appleby (eds) (1991) *Fundamentalisms Observed*, Chicago, IL: The University of Chicago Press.

Mazur, E.M. (2009) "Review of *The Gospel According to the Simpsons: Bigger and Possibly Even Better! Edition*, by Mark Pinsky," *Journal of Media and Religion* 8, 1: 76–77.

——(2013) "The gospel according to comic strips: on *Peanuts*, *The Far Side*, and *B.C.*," in M. DiPaolo (ed.), *Godly Heretics: Essays on Alternative Christian Views in Literature and Other Media*, Jefferson, NC: McFarland & Co., 143–61.

Mazur, E.M. and K. McCarthy (eds) (2011 [2001]) *God in the Details: American Religion in Popular Culture*, New York: Routledge.

Medved, M. (1992) *Hollywood vs. America: Popular Culture and the War on Traditional Values*, New York: HarperCollins.

Melton, G. (1993) "Another look at new religions," *Annals of the American Academy of Political and Social Science* 527 (May): 97–112.

Moltmann, J. (1967) *Theology of Hope: On the Ground and the Implications of a Christian Eschatology*, New York: Harper and Row.

Murchland, B. (ed.) (1967) *The Meaning of the Death of God: Protestant, Jewish and Catholic Scholars Explore Atheistic Theology*, New York: Random House.

Neuhaus, R.J. (1984) *The Naked Public Square: Religion and Democracy in America*, Grand Rapids, MI: W.B. Eerdmans Publishing Co.

Niebuhr, H.R. (1951) *Christ and Culture*, New York: Harper and Row.

Persley, N.H. (2007) "A timeline of hip hop history," in M. Hess (ed.), *Icons of Hip Hop: An Encyclopedia of the Movement, Music, and Culture*, Westport, CT: Greenwood, xxi–xxx.

Pinsky, M.I. (2001) *The Gospel According to the Simpsons: The Spiritual Life of the World's Most Animated Family*, Louisville, KY: Westminster John Knox Press.

——(2007) *The Gospel According to the Simpsons: Bigger and Possibly Even Better! Edition*, Louisville, KY: Westminster John Knox Press.

Ritzer, G. (1993) *The McDonaldization of Society: An Investigation into the Changing Character of Contemporary Social Life*, Newbury Park, CA: Pine Forge Press.

Robertson, R. (1985) "The sacred and the world system," in P. Hammond (ed.), *The Sacred in a Secular Age*, Berkeley, CA: University of California Press, 347–58.

Roof, W.C. (1993) *A Generation of Seekers: The Spiritual Journeys of the Baby Boom Generation*, San Francisco, CA: Harper San Francisco.

Roof, W.C., J. Carroll, and D. Roozen (1995) *The Post-War Generation and Establishment Religion*, Boulder, CO: Westview.

Sanders, J.Q. (2009) "Theologian of Peanuts Robert Short, 76, dies," [Little Rock] *Arkansas Democrat-Gazette* (July 9): 11, 18.

Short, R.L. (1965) *The Gospel According to Peanuts*, Richmond: John Knox Press.

Siegler, E. (2012) "David Cronenberg: the secular auteur as critic of religion," *Journal of the American Academy of Religion* 80, 4 (December): 1098–112.

Starhawk [Miriam Simos] (1979) *The Spiral Dance: A Rebirth of the Ancient Religion of the Great Goddess*, New York: Harper & Row.

Vahanian, G. (1967) "Beyond the death of God," in B. Murchland (ed.), *The Meaning of the Death of God: Protestant, Jewish and Catholic Scholars Explore Atheistic Theology*, New York: Random House, 3–12.

Vernon, G.M. (1968) "The religious 'nones': a neglected category," *Journal for the Scientific Study of Religion* 7, 2 (Autumn): 219–29.

Wade, L. (2009) "The global distribution of Starbucks and McDonalds," *The Society Pages* (June 26). Online. Available: http://thesocietypages.org/socimages/2009/06/26/the-global-distribution-of-starbucks-and-mcdonalds/ (accessed 2 September 2013).

Warner, R.S. (1993) "Work in progress toward a new paradigm for the sociological study of religion in the United States," *American Journal of Sociology* 98, 5 (March): 1044–93.

Wordsworth, W. (1889) *The Poems of William Wordsworth*, London: Edward Moxon.

Worstall, T. (2012) "The coming collapse of the academic publishing model," *Forbes* (April 10). Online. Available: www.forbes.com/sites/timworstall/2012/04/10/the-coming-collapse-of-the-academic-publishing-model/ (accessed 1 September 2013).

Wuthnow, R. (1988) *The Restructuring of American Religion: Society and Faith Since World War II*, Princeton, NJ: Princeton University Press.

——(1998) *After Heaven: Spirituality in America Since the 1950s*, Berkeley, CA: University of California Press.

Part II
ENCOUNTERS WITH POPULAR CULTURE

Section A

MEDIATED ENCOUNTERS

Introduction to Part II, Section A

As we begin to examine the particular ways in which religion and popular culture interact, we first look to "mediated" encounters of the two. Modern media include a variety of forms that convey sounds and images through electronic means to a wider audience than was ever possible at previous times in human history. These media developed in the early twentieth century first with radio and movies, but have evolved into a gigantic and pervasive industry that is related to almost every activity of people living in modern technological societies. The implications of this pervasiveness are not yet fully understood, largely because of the recent and rapid nature of developments such as high-speed interactive media. What is clear is that how we communicate with each other and even how we understand community has changed greatly, and this has significant implications also for how religion is understood and conveyed.

Elijah Siegler's chapter on television (in its role as a purveyor of entertainment) examines how television has gained a kind of religious authority as a cultural story-teller. First, in its American context, it operates in a "priestly" function that ritualizes certain aspects of communal experience, reinforcing the values of the dominant religious culture of public Protestantism, often without explicit references to religion. Especially in the early days of television, non-Protestant "others" were either not shown or were depicted in stereotypical or negative ways, reinforcing the hegemony and homogeneity of Protestantism. The repetitive nature of television programs itself supports this ritual function. Second, television has had a "prophetic" function of critiquing this religious and cultural hegemony and alleged homogeneity, especially in the "second golden age" of American television that began in the 1990s. Third, Siegler argues that television also has developed a "rabbinic" function which presents the diversity of religious encounters and values to audiences for their consideration, without suggesting a particular resolution or closure. In this way, television represents the conflicts that exist within our culture and invites reflection on them. Television shows have also developed their own mythologies and religious ideas, demonstrating how the medium is not simply reflecting the religious ideas of the culture, but actively contributing to them.

Jolyon Mitchell's chapter on journalism considers how news media exert significant influence on the ways in which events are understood and interpreted, particularly events involving religion and violence. Although news producers have a great deal of control over what is covered and how it is covered, which can bias an interpretation of events, Mitchell argues that there are other factors in the historical and political context that shape how events are understood. Governments may censor coverage, and the producers of media are affected by market values that may result in a reduction of news to trivial "infotainment" that is shallow or biased. But in addition, audiences now increasingly interact with news media through, for example, online blogs or Twitter, suggesting that they are not passively accepting one version of stories but are co-creating them in their reception. He suggests that both religious communities and the creators of news media have a responsibility to reflect on how their own values affect the ways they see and interpret the news, and that journalists can hold religious and political groups accountable by seeking to illuminate what might otherwise not be seen.

John Lyden's chapter on film points out that cinema has often been pitted against traditional religions since its origin, as it was perceived as a threat to established societal values through its alleged power to influence inclination or action. In fact, films have often supported traditional religious views, but have as often critiqued them, and in this way represent the religious diversity within and between societies. Films may also be seen to have a "religious" content or significance even when it is not obvious to all viewers. The diverse ways in which religion and film interact can be seen by paying attention to the stages of the circuit of culture, in how the production, marketing, content, and reception of a particular film all express the religious values of the various parties involved in those activities. Lyden indicates how the religious values of the filmmakers, the processes of distribution and promotion, and the ways audiences react to a film all contribute to the diversity of ways in which a film may be interpreted. There is not one single popular religious culture, but rather multiple sub-cultures that exist in societies, and these sub-cultures express the diversity as well as the conflicts of values within both religion and popular culture.

Tona Hangen's chapter on radio shows how the medium helped to develop a sense of community while at the same time seeming extremely personal, as the voices of public figures were simultaneously invited into millions of homes. American religion, and fundamentalist Christianity in particular, almost immediately saw the value of this medium in spreading the word and so embraced it whole-heartedly. Concurrently, government regulation sometimes censored religious content as it sought to police what was seen as contentious or divisive to society. In some ways, this expressed the collision of religious liberalism with more strident and conservative forms of Christianity; ultimately, the freedom of religious groups to express their views on radio triumphed, resulting in a diversity of religious expressions in the medium today. Deregulation, the development of smaller stations, and online technology have made it easier for diverse religious groups to air their views, religious services, and music on radio, so that the medium continues to be an important way in which religion is communicated and understood.

Mark Hulsether's chapter on music reflects on the power of music to affect individuals and communities, and how it is often linked to religious sensibilities and choices. Both music and religion are also matters of individual taste, more so in today's pluralistic societies than ever before. He considers the multiple meanings that "music," "religion," and "popular" may have as a way to highlight the diverse ways in which these categories interact in today's societies. "Popular" music might be commercial, authentic, prevalent, hip, or counter-hegemonic, and any of these may express or critique religion. Different religious groups may adapt various types of popular music to express their own religious sensibilities, so that popular music with a religious content is found as much within as outside of religious communities. In the same way, popular songs can have multiple meanings to different audiences as they are sung seriously or ironically, used to critique or affirm religion, or found to increase or decrease political conservatism (as with, for example, contemporary Christian music). In any case, music and religion are deeply intertwined in popular culture today, and can be found to be interrelated in a multiplicity of ways.

Rachel Wagner's chapter on video- and Internet games discusses the ways in which online games, like religions, create a "magic circle" or sacred space apart from the everyday world where "sacred play" can occur. Although this play occurs in a space apart, the rituals involved still spill over into everyday worlds and influence beliefs, values, and practice. While people usually consider "religions" to be more significant than "games" in their influence, Wagner shows how online sacred space can be taken just as seriously and express or contribute to the religious values of the player. The procedural rhetoric of the game limits what can be done, but playing the game offers options within the rules wherein the players express their creativity and individuality. She also points out that when players accept the rules of an online game, they may not always realize the implications for their lives outside of the game—e.g., playing first person shooter games means operating within a violent apocalyptic and dualistic mythology that may affect how one deals with real life. In this way, online games support moral and religious values of which we should be aware, as their influence can shape culture in often unacknowledged and even dangerous ways.

Heidi Campbell and Paul Emerson Teusner's chapter on the Internet and social networking looks at another aspect of online technology and how it relates to religion. Religious communities have used the Internet not only to advertise but also to network with like-minded people and even to conduct rituals. Some religious communities only exist online, so that the Internet becomes a prime sacramental space or spiritual medium for them, in addition to a communication tool and a means of creating connections between people who never physically meet. Notions of religious authority, community, and identity are all in flux as a result of these new developments in ways that are not yet fully clear. While online technology might seem to enhance individual choice, for example, it can also support traditional authority structures for those who identify with the online communities that convey those structures. The authors conclude that our spiritual identities are increasingly formed by the technology through which we encounter the world, as our digital devices are part of our everyday lives, and therefore our religious lives as well.

Tricia Sheffield's chapter on advertising discusses how modern advertising arose in a Protestant religious context, and how it continues to be shaped by that heritage.

Specifically, she suggests that advertising is a cultural system that sacralizes objects for the consumer in order to impart meaning and a sense of community. Just as the sacraments of Christianity are viewed as a means for conveying God's grace to believers, so advertising conveys commodities that contain a value of exchange. Advertising creates a desire to participate in a commodified community that requires people to buy products that meet more of a "spiritual" than a physical need—i.e., one's self-worth is indicated by what one can buy and what one owns, even if the objects purchased are of limited usefulness. Sheffield suggests that the quest to obtain meaning in this way is ultimately unfulfilling, as it only creates a bigger appetite for commodities, and distinguishes this from the Christian hope for a society of love, peace, and justice. She also indicates that it is possible to resist the religious allure of advertising by being aware of its power and making conscious choices not to be ruled by it.

In all of these chapters, we see the tremendous diversity within the forms of modern media and the ways in which they are appropriated. Multiple religious views are represented or critiqued in all of these media, and there are multiple ways in which aspects of religion and culture interact through them. All of these chapters seek to enhance our understanding of the relationship between modern media and religion, so that we can be better educated about these influences within popular culture. We can make informed choices about what we watch, listen to, download, or play—and these choices reflect our identities and values, often with consequences for our religious or spiritual identities as well.

3

TELEVISION

Elijah Siegler

Introduction

In a book about the golden age of television, where the author, the topic, the series, and the episode being discussed are not particularly religious, Brett Martin (2013: 277) described an episode of *Breaking Bad* (AMC, 2008–13) as "one more holy object in the communal sacrament that, thanks to the gods of business, technology, and creativity, TV has become in the early twenty-first century." What is going on here? Clearly the connection between television and religion is more than an academic one; popular literature is actually ahead of scholarly literature in that regard, and until recently, the study of religion and the study of television made uneasy bed-fellows. Television studies, as part of the study of mass communication, has been most influenced by empirical sociology and psychology, as "media scholars looked largely to the social sciences instead of to the humanities for their theories, concepts, and methods" (Schultze 1990: 8); religion as a category of analysis has largely been ignored.

For example, the two most important books by two of the most important scho-lars in television studies studiously ignore religion. John Fiske (in Fiske and Hartley 2003), informed by anthropology and semiotics,[1] explores concepts of myth and ritual, but ignores religious television, religion on television, or television as religion. Similarly, *Television: The Critical View* (7th edn 2006), Horace Newcomb's essential anthology first published in 1976, has very little on religion, a lack that is especially ironic considering his own thoughtful and important pieces on religion and television (see Newcomb 2006; 1990). Or consider Mary Ann Watson's *Defining Visions: Tele-vision and the American Experience in the 20th Century* (2008), wherein each chapter focuses on a theme (race, gender, sexuality) refracted through the lens of television; mentioned in passing only a few times, religion is not one of those themes.[2]

But it is not solely the religious content of television that is ignored, but the gen-eral content as well. The result has been a greater focus on audience reception. Cultural theorist Simon During (quoted in Santana and Erickson 2008: 114–15) notes, "it is as if the programmes themselves aren't worth taking as seriously as their impact on viewers [and] it has been impossible to concentrate on close readings of TV texts or to construct a TV canon."

In the field of religious studies, television gets little respect. This is not to say that there has been no scholarship on religion and television. It is to say that most of that scholarship has not analyzed television programming as works of art with religious themes—in the way that novels, paintings, or films regularly are. Instead, TV is seen either as a cultural product, and thus viewed through the lens of "media studies" and "communications" (see Clark 2003; Hoover and Clark 2002; Hoover and Lundby 1997), or as part of "popular culture" and thus functionally equivalent to comic strips and popular music (see Mazur and McCarthy 2001; Forbes and Mahan 2000). To take one recent example, Kathryn Lofton's *Oprah: The Gospel of an Icon* (2011) analyzes its subject through a sophisticated theoretical and cultural framework, and links her to tropes in American religious history such as black women preachers and the New Thought movement. However, Lofton does not focus on *The Oprah Winfrey Show* (syndicated, 1986–2011) as television per se, but more as one part of an empire (including O magazine, a Web site, etc.), one aspect of a cultural complex.

This chapter approaches television and religion as primary phenomena. While all forms of popular culture owe a debt to the religious imagination, each has its own particular aptitude at depicting or creating an aspect of religion, its own religious genius. Scholars of religious studies regularly tease out the relationship between a cultural form and religion, however defined. The performing arts, for example, may function as ritual; the origins of theater and dance likely lie in religious performance (see Turner 1982). In the study of the visual arts—which have probably received the most attention by scholars of religion—it is a commonplace to note how certain iterations of visual art, such as Orthodox Christian icons or Tibetan Buddhist mandalas, serve as aids for prayer and meditation (see Kenna 1985 for a discussion of the former; Rambelli 1991 for a discussion of the latter). More recently, scholars have turned their attention to the role of religious images in American Protestant culture (see in particular Morgan 2005, 1998). In the area of religion and film, the last ten or 15 years have witnessed an avalanche of related research and teaching. It has become respectable for scholars of religion to treat film as a source of religious meaning, and one can now assemble a sizable shelf of books devoted exclusively to its study.

Although it may seem that TV and film are similar, their individual religious genius is very different. Movie theaters are "cathedrals of the image, where we partake in shared experiences." By contrast, televisions are "home shrines, personalized and comfortable." With the relatively recent emergence in religious studies of scholarly attention on the home as a place of important religious work, it only makes sense to recognize television as "a source of religious meaning" (Siegler 2011: 180).

This chapter examines television as a source of religious meaning without treating it merely as a subset of film.[3] Intended to be a broad survey, it will identify significant television series and scholarly sources; readers are encouraged to take over from there. We will integrate a representative and functional analysis of religion and television; in other words, we will collapse the difference between "religion on television" and "television as religion."

If television is now our "culture's central storyteller" (Nichols-Pethick 2012: 186), it has also assumed the role of a religious authority. But what kind of authority? Horace Newcomb (1990) first applied the scheme of "priestly" versus "prophetic" authority—borrowed from sociologist Max Weber—to television; the majority of this chapter uses this scheme to classify television into three loose bundles:

television in its "priestly" function, maintaining the values of public Protestantism,[4] and television in its "prophetic" function, critiquing these same values. But then we will extend Weber's original typology to include a third kind of religious function— "rabbinic"—wherein television serves as a catalyst for religious debate and religious change in the context of lived religion.

After exploring the possible religious functions of television programming, we will explore two other aspects of the "circuit of culture"—production and reception— and consider the ways in which television and broader notions of mythology interact.[5] In an increasingly diverse and non-institutional American culture, it seems inevitable that—in addition to the priestly, prophetic, and rabbinic voices television brings to its viewers—the presentation of alternative religious views and religion-like elements (particularly mythic structures) will engender conflict. But as the content that once was television's exclusive domain migrates across other and newer media, so too does its message, and its role in society.

Television's priestly function

Horace Newcomb (1990: 42) argues that television should not be criticized for being culturally conservative and repetitive—in other words, for maintaining the status quo—defending television against scholars who hope or expect television to be a vehicle for social change. Always interested in religion, Newcomb argues that television functions as a priest, not a prophet. According to Weber's canonical distinction of religious leadership, a priest's role is to comfort, to ritualize life, mark occasion, reinforce membership in a community. A prophet's is to question that community, to "speak truth to power." Watching television is expected to be a comforting ritual, not a prophetic call; like a priest, television is reinforcing and repetitive.

Writing in the late 1980s, at a time when most television was considered safe pabulum and unfit for critical analysis, Newcomb defends his chosen research subject against those who feel that the scholar's "search for the prophetic voice, for the unusual expression, and for the deep exploration of unique experience may be misplaced." To the contrary, he argues (ibid.: 43), "Television takes us into that which is already known, widely shared, meaningful in its familiarity." As an example, he points to the detective series *Magnum, P.I.* (CBS, 1980–88), set in Hawaii, and argues that its ephemeral escapism can be theologically interesting: "This series," he notes (ibid.: 38), "often explored various spiritual aspects of human experience." He also argues (ibid.: 44) that the repetitiveness of 1980s series television is its hidden strength, noting that "the deepest religious implication of television is that so long as its stories need not end, so long as it shows us the continuation and exploration of repetitive human experience, it shows us a theology of hope." Of course, Newcomb was writing this counterintuitive defense of the blandness and repetitiveness of TV before television's "second golden age" and the rise of the HBO model; with a limited number of episodes and a limited run, these series do end and often quite hopelessly.

Using less explicitly religious language, but making much the same point as Newcomb, John Fiske (Fiske and Hartley 2003: 64–65) argues that television functions as a bard in our culture: "a mediator of language, one who composes out of the available lin-guistic resources of the culture a series of consciously structured messages which serve to communicate to the members of that culture a confirming, reinforcing version of themselves." Fiske goes on to argue that television performs ritual condensation (an anthropological term describing how culture converts mental ideas into physical realities, much as religious ritual does), using the example of how a police drama converts abstract ideas about human relationships into "concrete dramatic form" (68).

Public Protestantism

Summarizing Weber, religion scholar Daniel Pals (2006: 167) notes that "the concern of priestly religious leaders with structure and stability is one source of a key devel-opment in most civilizations: the emergence of the concept of a vast cosmic order that imposes on human beings a universal ethic, or value system." In its priestly function, television—with its hundreds of thousands of hours of prime-time pro-gramming (at least pre-1990s)—accomplishes the same thing; it imposes a universal ethic based firmly in public Protestantism.

We can see this in all sorts of ways. Some of the most famous and popular chil-dren's programming was produced by Protestant denominations or organizations. A landmark is the stop-action animated series *Davey and Goliath* (syndicated, 1960–61), about a boy and his dog and their God. Produced by the Lutheran Church in America in the 1960s, it was syndicated throughout the 1960s. The more recent *Veggie Tales*, also a syndicated phenomenon, aired on various television channels but was primarily a best selling direct-to-video phenomenon. As any Jewish kid with fond memories of *Davey and Goliath*, or any Muslim parent who bought *Veggie Tales* tapes because of their emphasis on virtue, family, and faith, could tell you, these series demonstrated that "public Protestant" values on television appealed to more than Protestants.

Unlike these children's series, most programs have promoted Protestant values through regular network distribution and not via Christian media companies. One particular genre that did so quite successfully was the television western; in the late 1950s and early 1960s, it was the dominant genre of television drama. In January 1959, eight of the top ten rated programs were westerns. As Fred Macdonald (2009) argues, the western was a "relevant drama embodying the psychology of the East–West struggle," and thus "justified nationalism in terms of a moral code that may have sounded secular, but had at its base a Judeo-Christian religious heritage." Televised westerns embodied public liberal Protestant virtues such as loyalty to family, honor, and righteousness. Unlike the film western, which often complicated the western mythos and critiqued its violence (for example, *The Man Who Shot Liberty Valance* [1962] and *The Searchers* [1956]), the television western showcased comfortable American values.

A program need not be specifically Protestant to showcase the values of public Protestantism. *Bonanza* (NBC, 1959–73), which was the most watched program on American television from 1964 to 1967, and which, according to its creators, was "centered on relationships rather than good guy-bad guy gunplay," emphasizing "the values of love, respect, and family ties" while criticizing prejudice, was led by two

Jewish actors (Lorne Greene and Michael Landon), and was created by another (David Dotort). In an interview, Dotort acknowledged that he inserted into the scripts Jewish values he learned from his own father, whose name, Ben, became the name of the program's patriarchal character (Gruber 2010). No matter; in mid-century America, the values espoused by public Protestantism were equally palatable to Protestants, Catholics, and Jews (see Herberg 1955).

The western is not the only example of public Protestant values on television. Several family dramas that had generally high ratings continue to serve as cultural touchstones. Most notable are *Little House on the Prairie* (NBC, 1974–83) and *The Waltons* (CBS, 1972–81). The latter's small town Baptist values are expressed in the opening narration from "The Baptism" (aired 14 October 1976): "We were a religious people on Waltons' Mountain. The church was the center of our social, as well as our spiritual lives." Yes, religion was central to the Waltons, but not necessarily to *The Waltons*: the series did not often focus on religious issues, and when it did, it was critical of religious enthusiasm; the specific episode quoted above revolves around a "fire and brimstone" preacher whose visit disrupts the family's equilibrium. A more recent version of the Protestant family drama is *7th Heaven* (WB, 1996–2007); here the paterfamilias is actually a pastor.

The "guardian angel" drama is another genre that embodies public Protestant values in a priestly way. *Highway to Heaven* (NBC, 1984–89) and *Touched by an Angel* (CBS, 1994–2003) are among the best known, but there have been many other more short-lived series about angels, including *Down to Earth* (TBS, 1984–87) and *Twice in a Lifetime* (CTV and PAX, 1999–2001). These series have avoided denominational or theological specificity; as *Touched by an Angel* star Della Reese notes in an interview: "Religion is a man-made thing. We deal in spirituality. That's a God thing" (Watson 2008: 226).

Beyond regular programming, television's "special events" calendar is unsurprisingly Protestant in nature. The Christmas special is one of the oldest and most common (see A.V. Club 2011; Thompson 2005), while Bible stories are often presented as "special event" television, as a mini-series or a television movie. In the mid-1990s, the TNT Network broadcast a series on biblical figures, including Abraham, Joseph and Moses (see Kaye 1994). In early 2013, The History Channel aired a ten-part mini-series titled "The Bible"—produced by Roma Downey (of *Touched by an Angel*) and her husband Mark Burnett (creator of the reality show *Survivor* [CBS, 2000–present])—which, despite being critically lambasted for stultifying scripts, called itself with some justification the "#1 TV series of 2013" (see LightWorkers Media 2013).

The non-Protestant "other"

In 1990, Horace Newcomb observed:

> We have a specific set of religious signifiers: Jewish guilt and humor, often related to an individual's youthful religious experiences; the Roman collar as an acceptable signifier of religion, church, piety; the southern evangelical, Protestant in some nonspecific way, sometimes black; the Hindu guru,

almost always pathetically distracted and comic; the generalized religious "psychotic," zealous, often violent, sexually confused and repressed, and so on.
(Newcomb 1990: 33)

He was describing stereotypes "used because of their immediate visual qualities," a "shorthand" for viewers (1990: 33). Little has changed in the years since.

In the televised Protestant imaginary, Jews and Catholics are acceptably different, and represent some combination of ethnicity, working class life, and humor. The first "Jewish" American program (and the first family sitcom), depicting a family's move to the suburbs, *The Goldbergs* (radio, 1929–46; CBS, 1949–51; NBC, 1952–53; Dumont, 1954; syndicated, 1955–56), centered around Molly Goldberg (played by Yiddish theater actor Gertrude Berg) as an "ethnic"-accented matriarch in the Bronx. The series stressed all three qualities, recapitulating the processes of American Jewish assimilation. Despite *The Goldbergs'* success, there was no other "Jewish" sitcom on television until the debut of *Bridget Loves Bernie* (CBS, 1972–73), which—given its focus on the marriage of Catholic Bridget to Jewish Bernie, was also a Catholic sitcom. The series generated controversy within the Jewish community for seeming to advocate Jewish intermarriage, and was cancelled after one season (see Brook 2003).

For many years, lay Catholics in primetime television were represented as working class ethnics, policemen, or lawyers (see Siegler 2001: 203–4). *The Honeymooners* (CBS, 1955–56), another early sitcom, depicted Irish Catholic ethnic working-class New York, though to a far lesser extent than *The Goldbergs'* Jewishness. Several series also focused on Catholic clergy, where the general rule seemed to be that if nuns or priests served as window-dressing for comedy or light mystery, the show would enjoy some success, as was the case with *The Flying Nun* (ABC, 1967–70) and *Father Dowling Mysteries* (ABC, 1989–91), respectively. Television series that used Catholic clergy to focus on religious issues have been much less successful; sitcoms *Hell Town* (NBC, 1985) and *Have Faith* (ABC, 1989), and *Nothing Sacred* (ABC, 1997–98), a drama created by a Jesuit, all focused on priests in inner city churches, and all lasted one season or less (see Primiano 2009).

As one might imagine, Islam, when presented at all, is the most negatively por-trayed religion on primetime television; it is often seen as a faith whose adherents' everyday existence in America conceals a terrorist plot (see Hussain 2009: 159), where the "hidden danger of Muslim Americans" is central to the narrative. For example, billboards advertising the fourth season of *24* (FOX, 2001–10)—which fea-tured a middle-class suburban Muslim American family who were the nucleus of a terrorist cell—used the inflammatory tag line, "They could be next door" (Aleaziz 2011).

Attempts to portray Muslims in a more positive light have not had a significant impact on the culture. Lighthearted comedies such as *Aliens in America* (CW, 2007–8), about a Muslim exchange student from Pakistan, are largely forgotten. *Little Mosque on the Prairie* (CBC, 2007–12), a Canadian TV show created by a Muslim woman, deliberately depicted Muslims of a range of genders, races, ages, and degrees of piety in a small town in Canada, but was generally marred by low production values. *All-American Muslim* (TLC, 2011), a generic reality show in every way except for the religion of its protagonists, was embroiled in controversy when the hardware megastore Lowe's withdrew its sponsorship, apparently responding to anti-Muslim pressure.

Compared to the depiction of Islam, "Asian" religions have been marginalized and exoticized. The series whose representation of Asian religions has been most influential is undoubtedly *Kung Fu* (ABC, 1972–75). Jane Iwamura (2011; 2005) notes how more recent series such as *The Last Airbender* (Nickelodeon, 2005–8) and *Kung Fu Panda: Legends of Awesomeness* (Nickelodeon, 2011–present) borrow from the "Oriental Monk" trope first explored by *Kung Fu*. By comparison, the non-Asian convert to an Asian religion is a figure of ridicule in America: in *Dharma and Greg* (ABC, 1997–2002), the first of the two title characters is a middle class white woman who appropriates Asian philosophy. It is telling that one of the more nuanced portrayals of a Buddhist on American television is Lisa from *The Simpsons* (FOX, 1989–present).

Atheists and fanatics

Elizabeth Bird (2009) argues that primetime television drama favors characters who are "respectful of all mainstream faiths," are "spiritual but not religious," or practice a tradition but are not fanatics. But there are examples of the extremes, as well; one might compare the atheist who lacks empathy (such as the title character on *House* [FOX, 2004–12]; see Christina170 [2013]) to the true believer, the intolerant fanatic, or the member of a cult ("New Religious Movement," or NRM), the subject of several recent essays. Joseph Laycock (2013: 87) identifies the *Get Smart* (NBC, 1965–70) episode "The Groovy Guru" (aired on 13 January 1968), which colored its depiction of Iwamura's "Oriental monk" with contemporary concerns about brainwashing, as one of the first television programs to depict cults. Lynn Neal (2011) argues that fictional television is more influential than magazines and newspapers in its depiction of cults. Surveying several shows between 1998 and 2008, she demonstrates the common elements of the cult stereotype, which include distinct clothing, communal living practiced in an isolated setting, and holding clearly delusional beliefs. Most importantly, Neal argues that cults on primetime television are visibly marked; the oddity of a cult's rituals makes its strangeness explicit and tangible. Neal concludes that on television, cults are visualized and present, while conventional religion is usually absent or vague, yet both are invoked in larger narratives about the triumph of good (traditional religion) over evil (cult) (see also Siegler 2011).

Beyond the polar extremes of fanaticisms (atheism and cultic behaviors), it is in the marked absence of "conventional religion" that the importance of public Protestantism is clearest, and we can use Neal's thesis on the science fiction genre to demonstrate its power. For example, *Star Trek*, which was famously pitched by series creator Gene Roddenberry as "*Wagon Train* to the Stars," shares with its TV western cousins values that are rooted in American public Protestantism, as portrayed by an assimilated Jewish cast—in this case William Shatner (Capt. Kirk), Leonard Nimoy (Mr. Spock) and Walter Koenig (Ensign Chekov). However, none of the characters on *Star Trek: The Original Series* (NBC, 1966–69) are identifiably religious. In keeping with series creator Gene Roddenberry's belief (informed by secular humanism) that as humanity advances technologically and intellectually, religion will become less important, none of the characters go to religious services or pray. Several episodes of the original series have an anti-religious message, usually where the plot involves a planet whose primitive inhabitants are in thrall to a god who turns out to be a rogue computer, and the ship's crew liberates them from their imprisoning beliefs. The message here is clear: religion keeps people childish and backwards. *Star Trek: The Next Generation* (CBS, 1987–94) maintains the secularist message, but adds new age spirituality with the recurring character of Guinan (played by Whoopi Goldberg), whose race allows her to serve as an "ideological caregiver" (or "Black spiritual mammy") for the white principal characters (see Iwamura 2005: 37). Much less humanist is *Star Trek: Deep Space Nine* (syndicated, 1993–99), which provides a more complicated view of religion and politics, a complicated mythology, and a dystopian outlook. Only one regular human character on any of the *Star Trek* series has a recognizably human religious practice (as opposed to an invented extraterrestrial one): Chakotay (played by Robert Beltran), a Native American character in *Star Trek: Voyager* (UPN, 1995–2001). Still, *Star Trek* has maintained a consistent philosophy of classic liberal public Protestantism throughout its various series: the Federation represents a benevolent colonialism that practices non-interference ("the Prime Directive") unless absolutely necessary, and moral issues are dealt with as fables involving alien races.

Another influential television series is the science fiction program *Doctor Who* (BBC, 1963–89, 2005–present). The Doctor is an alien with the ability to regenerate—not only changing his appearance but also allowing 12 actors to play him over the course of more than half a century of programming. Like *Star Trek*, *Doctor Who* has a humanist outlook and rarely deals with religion directly, though there have been several plots where a fanatical cult worships a god who turns out to be an alien or a computer. Some of the original *Doctor Who*'s most notable stories include those in which the primary villain is a charismatic cult leader who brainwashes his followers and works to summon great evil, aid an alien menace, or bring about the end of the world.

From priestly to prophetic: television's second golden age

When was the "golden age of television"? The term was first used to refer to the 1950s, when TV plays, written by respected authors such as Paddy Chayefsky, were shot live-to-tape, and excelled at realistic social drama, and also included seminal comedies such as *I Love Lucy* (CBS, 1951–57) and *The Honeymooners*. Almost every decade since, argues television critic Todd VanDerWerff (2013b), has its champions who wish to identify it as "another golden age." For our purposes, we can identify the beginning of a second golden age of television in the 1990s, based not just on the exceptionally high quality acting, directing, and writing, but also as the point when many series moved away from speaking with Newcomb's "priestly voice" and began speaking with a more prophetic voice—a voice of one who, according to Daniel Pals (2006: 167), "has been specially called by either the voice of God or a vision of Truth to proclaim a life-altering message." Examples include *The X-Files*, with its distrust of government narratives, and *Homicide* (NBC, 1993–99), with its critique of criminal justice and penal systems, and its theological exploration of evil (see Siegler 2009; 2001), but there are many more.

Animated sitcoms

In the 1990s, the television genre that took religion most seriously, and voiced a prophetic critique of society in general and religion in particular, was the primetime-animated sitcom, and *The Simpsons* (FOX, 1989–present) was the first and arguably the best. It also enabled others to create sophisticated animated shows, each speaking with a different voice, but each prophetically critiquing every aspect of American life.

Much has been written on the relationship between *The Simpsons* and religion (see Feltmate 2013a; Dalton *et al.* 2011; Pinsky 2007; Turner 2004: 268–80), for good reason. At least once a season, *The Simpsons* has featured an episode that focuses exclusively on religion. One of the first is "Like Father, Like Clown" (aired 24 October 1991)—one of a surprisingly few to focus on Judaism—that reconceptualized in comic form the film classic *The Jazz Singer* (1927). Another is "Homer the Heretic" (aired 8 October 1992), which explores religious diversity, mainstream Protestantism, and religious individualism. These episodes share a tone that is both mocking and sympathetic.

The series is an intertextual and polysemic text that rewards cultural knowledge and careful viewing, especially when it comes to the religion-focused shows. One example, "The Joy of Sects" (aired 8 February 1998), portrays the Simpson family joining a new religious movement (the "Movementarians"), and plays on popular fear of NRMs in general, but also on specific aspects, drawing from contemporary NRMs such as Heaven's Gate, Scientology, the Rajneesh movement, the Unification Church, and others. The episode also satirizes the anti-cult movement (complete with a particularly violence-prone deprogrammer), NRM portrayal in the media, and (again) Protestantism.

In its early days, *The Simpsons* was criticized for being immoral; Bart Simpson's catchphrases were considered disruptive when imitated by school children, and the Simpsons' Evangelical neighbors, the Flanders, were seen as cruel stereotypes. But as the series has developed, Ned Flanders has become beloved by some Evangelicals, and the series itself is a cultural institution that, instead of being seen as an anti-"family values" program, is loved by Evangelicals and taught in some churches and seminaries (particularly "Homer the Heretic"). However, the program's most direct heir (in terms of its prophetic critique of religion), *South Park* (Comedy Central, 1997–present), is still considered offensive. This may be due to the fact that its creators, Matt Stone and Trey Parker, deliberately undermine the codes of quality television: their animation is crude, and they do most of the voices themselves (which makes them all sound alike). But *South Park* also deliberately provokes controversy in a way *The Simpsons* never has, particularly in its treatment of the Catholic Church, including the sacraments ("Do the Handicapped Go to Hell?" aired 19 July 2000), clerical abuse scandals ("Red Hot Catholic Love," aired 3 July 2002) and miracles ("Bloody Mary," aired 7 December 2005), which have raised the ire of many watchdog groups (Feltmate 2013b).

A more realistic but no less pointed satire of religion can be found on *King of the Hill* (FOX, 1997–2010), which excelled at portraying ordinary religion in suburban Sunbelt America.[6] It was particularly good at skewering Evangelical popular culture, including puppet shows for Evangelical children ("Meet the Manger Babies," aired 11 January 1998), hip skateboarding ministries for teens ("Reborn to be Wild," aired 9 November 2003), megachurches ("Church Hopping," aired 9 April 2006), hell houses ("Hilloween," aired 26 October 1997), and "re-virginizing" ("Luanne Virgin 2.0," aired 11 March 2001).

Three other primetime animated programs presenting a critique of American culture and religion—*Futurama* (FOX, 1999–2003; Comedy Central, 2008–13), *Family Guy* (FOX, 1999–present), and *Adventure Time* (Cartoon Network, 2010–present)—suggest that this genre may be particularly suited for critiquing religion (see Pinsky 2007). *Adventure Time* conjures up a wholly different kind of prophetic voice about religion. Ostensibly a children's show, it focuses on adopted brothers—a human boy named Finn and a talking, shape-shifting dog named Jake—who live in the fantasy land of Ooo. The more one watches, the more one realizes that Ooo (which may be post-apocalyptic earth, a thousand years hence) occupies a polytheist universe, with many deities odd in both name (Grob Gob Glob Grod, Prismo, Death, Cosmic Owl, Party God) and appearance.

In their treatment of religion, these animated sitcoms are far ahead of anything "non-animated" in terms of both quality and quantity. Even the more sophisticated quality sitcoms of the 2000s and 2010s (*30 Rock* [NBC, 2006–13], *The Office* [NBC, 2005–13]) generally avoided religion beyond holiday specials or weddings. One exception is *Community* (NBC, 2009–14), about a group of strangers enrolled at community college. In terms of its combination of emotion and satire, its wide range of popular culture references, and its eclectic subject matter, *Community* is more like *The Simpsons* than a typical live-action sitcom. And like *The Simpsons*, at least once a season *Community* focuses on religious issues. In the first season's Christmas episode, "Comparative Religion" (aired 10 December 2009), the central characters reveal their religious commitments: an Evangelical Protestant, a Jew, an atheist, an agnostic, a Muslim, a Jehovah's Witness, and a "Level Five Laser Lotus in my Buddhist community"—surely the most religiously diverse television ensemble ever. The series satirizes both the blandness of public institutions' acknowledgement of religion (the college's Dean dresses up as "a non-denominational Mister Winter" and wishes everybody a "merry happy" and "a sensible night, appropriate night") and the condescending and proselytizing attitude of Christians at Christmas (the Evangelical character contrasts her baby Jesus figure as the "savior of all mankind" with the Jewish character's menorah as a "trinket from your philosophy").

The rise of the anti-hero

One agreed upon date for the beginning of the golden age is the premiere of *The Sopranos* (HBO, 1999–2007) (see Martin 2013; VanDerWerff 2013b), which ushered in the age of the HBO model: a highly serialized, high quality drama with a large cast and generally ten to thirteen episodes per season. Many of the most celebrated series in this model have revolved around an anti-hero, including Tony Soprano on *The*

Sopranos, Vic Mackey on *The Shield* (FX, 2002–8), Don Draper on *Mad Men* (AMC, 2007–present), and Walter White of *Breaking Bad*. These programs (and others like them: *Dexter* [Showtime, 2006–13] and *Boardwalk Empire* [HBO, 2010–present]) have permanently enlarged the possibilities of religion on television.[7]

In all of these series, the protagonists live double lives, and act upon their darker impulses over and over again. Audiences identify with the characters but are also repulsed by them, a double effect leading them to question their own morality. The series with the greatest impact—*The Sopranos*, *The Shield*, *Mad Men*, and *Breaking Bad*—are artistic creations of the highest quality, and consistently and self-consciously probe such moral themes as the capacity for humans to change. At their heart is the question of responsibility for "evil" and where to locate it (see Kuo and Wu 2012). Yet none of the series refer to "God" or any religious tradition at all; with some notable exceptions, there is a complete absence of religion in the lives of any of the main characters. *The Sopranos*, about an Italian-American mobster, lends itself to Catholic stereotypes; one might speculate about the religious identity of the program's creator, David Chase, an Italian-American from New Jersey, or imagine the rich dialogue between Tony Soprano and a priest. But Chase was raised in a Protestant household (McCabe and Akass 2007: 191), and Tony confesses to his Italian-American psychiatrist.[8] On *Breaking Bad* and *The Shield*, none of the major or secondary characters express any religious views (positive or negative) or attend religious services. And *Mad Men* keeps religion in the background, possibly as a reflection of religious themes of the 1960s—the death of God or the hegemony of the Protestant establishment—a reading nominally supported by a comment made by Betty Draper in "The Color Blue" (aired 18 October 2009) in response to her daughter's questioning why they don't go to church weekly like their African-American maid, Carla: "we don't have to go."[9]

But what these shows do offer is a critique of moral degradation, greed, and corruption in American society. By our love for the central character we have watched for so many years, we have been made into willing accomplices. These anti-heroes are constantly justifying their evil actions to themselves and to others. Their lies also draw in the viewer, and make the audience complicit in the sin. These four series are also concerned with the fate of the central character. The audience is wishing, hoping, wondering whether they will die by the final episode, and whether that death will be seen as a punishment or a release.

Much has been written about the philosophical, moral, and spiritual aspects of *The Sopranos* (see Reinhartz 2009), but the other programs have received less attention. AMC's *Mad Men*, set in a New York ad agency in the 1960s, is built around the same tensions as *The Sopranos*: tension between home and work lives, between pursuing the American dream and the real costs of that dream, between who we pretend to be and who we really are.[10] The anti-hero, Don Draper, may not be as murderous as Soprano, but he is more of a liar. The program's prophetic critique of advertising as metonymy for America is perhaps best seen in Draper's multi-episode relationship with a lightly fictionalized version of hotel magnate Conrad Hilton. As Draper pursues Hilton's business, he must accept Hilton's folksy morality, whether he's chastising Draper for not having a Bible or a picture of his family at his desk, or calling him in the middle of the night, while sitting with a large glass of whiskey, a rosary, and a thick Bible, expressing a wish to open Hilton hotels in every country in the world, as well as the moon. Hilton's characterization seems an obvious critique for the confluence of American Christianity, capitalism, and political expansionism.

On *The Shield*, the anti-hero is Detective Mackey but, to some extent, all of the characters are corrupt—with the notable exception of Detective Claudette Wyms, the voice of morality for the duration of the series. The heart of the evil is the Strike Team: four detectives who exercise vigilante justice, cleaning up the streets and giving themselves the ability to bargain with their superiors in the LAPD, who are generally willing to look the other way. The Strike Team doesn't just bend the law; they are a full-fledged criminal enterprise that regularly engages in murder, torture, and robbery. The rotten heart of a corrupt institution is physicalized by the Strike Team's private "clubhouse" in the middle of the squad room (which is in a deconsecrated church).

Breaking Bad has been characterized as the end of the anti-hero genre, not only taking the trope as far as it can go (in Walter White's journey from mild mannered high school teacher to mass-murdering drug kingpin, all accompanied by lies and rationalization), but also rejecting the moral relativity of *The Sopranos* and *Mad Men* in favor of an uncompromising theological vision. It has been called one of "the most moral shows in the history of television" (Holmes 2013). Television critic Todd VanDerWerff (2013c) has called it "a religious show," and notes that

> Walter White isn't just a sinner. He's a man who pushes further and further into his dark heart, who unleashes all manner of destruction upon the world, both at large and in his own home. He is a murderer, many times over; he is a man who abuses his wife; and he is a force of fear for everyone who sees his true face. He is, for lack of a better word, Satan … . He gives in to his selfishness and pride, his rage and resentment. He becomes the devil, and he is punished accordingly. He lived in something like heaven, and he chose to create something far more like hell. *Breaking Bad* argues that that is a choice too many of us make, every day of our lives.

Kuo and Wu compare the series, in its philosophy of the origin of evil and its human-centered narrative, to John Milton's *Paradise Lost*, which in many ways is the ur-text of the anti-hero genre:

> Like Milton's Satan, Walt seeks to reason and justify his rebellion. He invokes art, science, free market rationality, protection of one's family … . In *Breaking Bad* the villain is not sociology, but a human being; what destroys the mortals is not a system, but a fellow mortal. This is a human-centered vision of the origin of evil. It is Old Testament at its core.
>
> (Kuo and Wu 2012)

There are other high quality hour-long dramas with strong moral visions that are not "single male anti-hero" dramas. These shows, with large casts on both sides of the law (or conflict) offer prophetic critiques of civilization itself: *Deadwood* (HBO, 2004–6), which critiques the formation of American institutions; *The Wire* (HBO, 2002–8), which critiques the systemic breakdown of American institutions; and the rebooted franchise of *Battlestar Galactica* (SyFy, 2004–9), which posits the future of our institutions. And while *The Wire* is not interested in theology per se, *Deadwood* very explicitly invokes Pauline theology (see Mitchell 2013; Newcomb 2009) and *Battlestar Galactica* is well known for its sophisticated take on religion in its depiction of a war between monotheists and polytheists (see Wetmore 2012).

Lived religion on television: television's rabbinic voice

There is another type of religious authority that Max Weber did not consider, and which might give us greater insight into how television functions religiously in our lives. In the Jewish tradition, rabbis are neither as comforting as priests nor as confrontational as prophets. Rabbis are teachers, and like teachers everywhere, rabbis are carriers of traditions. But it is the rabbi's task also to complicate that tradition and to encourage discussion about it. Whether in the famed debates between the first-century rabbis Hillel and Shammai, or in a discussion group over coffee and bagels in the conference room of the modern synagogue, rabbis facilitate arguments over culture, tradition, and values. In modern society, television has taken on this function, certainly as much as it has the function of priest or prophet. In another of the seminal articles in television studies, Horace Newcomb made a similar point (albeit without using explicitly religious language):

> In its role as a central cultural medium [television] presents a multiplicity of meanings rather than a monolithic dominant point of view. It often focuses on our most prevalent concerns, our deepest dilemmas. … The emphasis is on process rather than product, on discussion rather than indoctrination, on contradiction and confusion rather than coherence.
>
> (Newcomb and Hirsch 1983: 506)

Often this "discussion" (or, to be less charitable, "confusion") is about specifically religious issues. As I have argued elsewhere (Siegler 2011: 180), "thanks to its multiple characters and plotlines, television, more than film and perhaps more than any other art form, can represent and provoke religious debate." It might be an argument between characters, but more likely it may take the form of stories or themes that stimulate debate among viewers.

Rabbis, like priests, deal with religion as a part of everyday life. But unlike priests, who make sharp distinctions between the sacred (sacraments and sacrifice) and the profane, rabbis deal in lived religion: the everyday, the homely. It is here that we see a second rabbinic function of television. Religious studies scholar Robert Orsi (1997: 7) offers perhaps the best definition of lived religion when he writes that "religion comes into being in an ongoing, dynamic relationship with the realities of everyday life" and that "religion is best approached … by meeting men and women at this daily task, in all the spaces of their experience."

Television is the art form most uniquely bound up with lived religion (see Winston 2009)—a point we can illustrate by examining analyses of three programs written not by scholars of religion or of media, but by perceptive journalists who are also fans, suggesting that even though the phrase "lived religion" is one specific to the discipline, its meaning has been widely applied to television series. Of first responder drama *Rescue Me* (FX, 2004–11), Tom Deignan notes that the series

> most painfully mirrors Irish America's broader struggles to reconcile its Catholic heritage with a harsh, modern world. Gavin pretty much has no use for religion. Which doesn't matter because he still struggles to comprehend the ways of God, and why bad things—such as 9/11—seem to happen to (relatively) good people. ... That this vision is grim and frightening rather than soothing matters little. Tommy is televised proof that there is no such thing as a lapsed Catholic. Even if Tommy Gavin—like not a few Irish Americans—is skeptical about religion, it is still in your cultural DNA.
>
> (Deignan 2010)

Of non-traditional family drama *Big Love* (HBO, 2006–11), Donna Bowman and company (2009) call it "[o]ne of the most earnest studies of religion and morality ever to air on television," suggesting that it "deals smartly with the troubles faced by people of faith who try to seize their part of the American dream without being sullied by the secular." And of the characters in high school football drama *Friday Night Lights* (NBC, 2006–11), James Poniewozik (2013) notes that, in going to church, praying, and playing Christian rock, "faith mattered"; not a simple faith that would "magically fix anything," or which would make them superior. Rather, it was taken seriously, "matter-of-factly," and as "a major part of its characters' worldviews."

As I have argued elsewhere, part of television's unique purchase on lived religion is that it is also

> particularly good at charting long-term religious transformation in its characters, whether depicted as conversion, salvation, or disenchantment. To best appreciate how religion operates in a television series, one must first understand that a television series is not a collection of discrete moments. Television drama is an open narrative; the audience gains pleasure from viewing regular characters operating in predictable ways.
>
> (Siegler 2011: 180–81)

Whereas films typically have a defined ending, the television series has an "open narrative"; no fixed heroic ending to which all narrative and thematic elements inexorably lead. A typically complicated series will include several "journeys," offering a series of climaxes at the end of episodes or seasons. On better television series, regular characters grow and change over the seasons. The religious aspects of these characters' changes may be obvious, or they may require consistent viewing over a longer period; a television series is not just a collection of discrete moments, but requires the audience to fill in the gaps between these moments, an activity that can be deeply meaningful (not to mention pleasurable). Given that many people see their religious life as a spiritual journey (see Roof 1993), it is no wonder that television has become one of the prime creators of religious meaning in everyday life.

Meaningful story arcs can take place over many years of a long-running series. For example, in the second season of *The Simpsons*, we learn of Lisa's interest in Eastern religions; in the seventh season, she becomes a vegetarian; and in the thirteenth season, she converts to Buddhism, a religion she has continued to practice in the 12 years since. But one-hour dramas have more room for their characters' religious arcs. Fans of *NYPD Blue* (ABC, 1993–2005) must be careful readers to see the religious journey of police detective Andy Sipowicz (played by Dennis Franz). Sipowicz's spiritual journey includes alcoholism, recovery and relapse, the loss of loved ones, overcoming his racist past, and his attempts to make peace with God. Primarily expressed internally, his evolving faith is made explicit often in the show's season finales, in religious ceremonies such as confession, marriage, or baptism. The proof that religious transformation is at the heart of *NYPD Blue* lies in these moments, which give the audience a lasting image to carry with them through the summer. Of *NYPD Blue*'s first six season finales, four had explicitly religious themes and final images, and of those four, three concerned Sipowicz's spiritual journey: the confession of a murderous beat cop; a Greek Orthodox wedding; a newborn's churching ceremony; and, in the sixth season, Sipowicz praying at his bedside.

While *NYPD Blue* became less interested in religious themes and more of a conventional cop show after producer David Milch left at the end of the sixth season, the show's entire 12-season run can be seen as Sipowicz's "moral education" or spiritual journey. All of his issues ask the same question: is redemption possible? Of course, Sipowicz tells you none of this directly. Only by charting one character's lived religious journey through careful viewing across the seasons does a viewer understand how *NYPD Blue* became a stellar example of television's rabbinic function.

Televised mythologies and the "myth arc"

What is the relationship between myth and television? The answer, of course, depends on our definition of myth. Roland Barthes (1972: 127–31) defines "myth" as that which works to naturalize a particular history, and accuses television in particular of disseminating myths that promote the interests of the dominant classes, pointing to the preponderance of television series where dark-skinned characters are the villains (see Fiske 2011: 135). Here, TV works in the same way as films and other popular culture, but through the sheer repetition of television it acquires more force. Religion and media theorist Quentin Schultze (1990: 24–26), writing in the 1980s, before the rise of darker, more prophetic television series, echoes this definition, when he notes that "the tube has been formulating and reformulating at least three widely believed myths: Good will triumph over evil; evil exists only in the hearts of a few evil people; godliness exists in the good and effective actions of individuals." Taking a dim view of televised myths, he argues that because "television is probably the most popular storyteller of American society, its myths are very broadly conceived and rarely anchored in the particular religious beliefs or ethnic and racial experiences of specific social groups" (14).

Schultze's words reflect the television landscape of the mid-1980s and no longer ring true. In recent years, television has become perhaps the foremost venue in popular culture for exploring religious specificity. For example, on *The West Wing* (NBC, 1999–2006), the Catholic president curses God in Latin (see Primiano 2009); on *The Sopranos*, a Hasidic Jewish motel owner enlists Tony's help to "convince" his son-in-law to grant his daughter a *get* (Jewish divorce decree) (see Reinhartz 2009); and on *Homeland* (Showtime, 2011–present), a white convert to Islam carefully practices his ablutions and prostrations. This attention to the details of religious language, law, and ritual would have been unthinkable in the 1980s.

But leaving aside the fact that television in its "new golden age" is more aware of evil and of the particularity of religious traditions, is there a definition of myth different from that implied by the work of Schultze and Barthes? Scholar of comparative religion William Paden (1994: 73) calls myth "a definitive voice that names the ultimate powers that create, maintain, and recreate one's life … a voice that articulates the prototypical events, beings, and teachings that form the standards for all subsequent religious life." With this definition in mind, we may ask again about the relationship between myth and mass media. Many scholars have explored the relationship between film and myth (see Lyden 2003); like myth, film recreates the world in larger-than-life terms (see Plate 2008), and it often replicates the famous "hero" quest of Joseph Campbell's (1949) "monomyth," with its set pattern and characters in service to the quest. A two-hour running time seems like the perfect length for telling a tall mythic tale: departure, initiation, return; or fall and redemption; etc. But as I have argued elsewhere (Siegler 2011: 180), if film can be interpreted as a modern myth, television "does not recapitulate myth so much as complexify it."

We must take seriously the word "mythology" in the way television fan communities use it, as a reference to the overarching story arc of a series (and, if presented, its pre-series "back-story"); as a television series moves forward, it also moves back, exploring this "mythology." It is in this way that Paden's "ultimate powers" and "prototypical events, beings, and teachings" are gradually and tantalizingly revealed. The term was first used this way to apply to *The X-Files* (FOX, 1993–2002), whose episodes revolving around an alien invasion and related government cover-up were called "mythology" or "myth arc" episodes (to distinguish them from the "stand alone"or "monster of the week"episodes). Very slowly, over many years, viewers learned about abductions, secret government facilities, and conspiracies within conspiracies—a back story that informed the "reality" within which the protagonists (FBI Agents Fox Mulder and Dana Scully) operated. By later seasons, when conspiracies included super soldiers and alien hybrids, viewers complained that the mythology had become cumbersome, contradictory, and difficult to understand.[11]

Influenced by *The X-Files*, later television series became more serialized and integrated "mythology" and "monster of the week" episodes. In Joss Whedon's *Buffy the Vampire Slayer* (WB, 1997–2001; UPN, 2001–3), every season had an overarching narrative arc and an ultimate villain, known as the "Big Bad." Whedon slowly expanded his mythological world by adding classes of beings (slayers, watchers, demons, vampires); the world became known to fans as the "Buffyverse" or the "Whedonverse," which was expanded in a *Buffy* spin-off, *Angel* (WB, 1999–2004). Whedon also created some shorter-lived series in the science-fiction genre that had an equally rich mythology: *Doll House* (FOX, 2009–10) and *Firefly* (FOX, 2002–3). The latter, set on a spaceship, featured a wandering Christian missionary—a monastic who could be seen reading the Bible, praying, and offering spiritual counsel. Like the series creator, the captain of the ship was an atheist. As three-time Whedon series writer and director Tim Minear noted, "out of such smashing and bashing and chaos, universes are born. Even ordered universes. Universes in which one might find coherent strains of philosophical thought. The hidden hand of the Creator. The Creator's voice" (Kowalski and Kreider 2011: viii).

Created by J.J. Abrams, *Lost* (ABC, 2004–10) is a unique example of how a series' mythology can move from the background to the foreground. Each episode of the series (which began with a plane crash on a tropical island) explores one or more of the many characters' back stories, possible futures, and interconnections. As might be expected, a rich fan community developed around the series, focusing on theories and conspiracies and connections with real-world religions and philosophies (see Clark 2009). It is no surprise that television critic Emily Nussbaum has astutely named Joss Whedon, J.J. Abrams, and Chris Carter (*The X-Files*) "the great mythologizers" (Nussbaum 2007).

Not all mythological series are so well known or well loved. *Carnivale* (HBO, 2003–5) is an example of a series that sank under its own mythological weight. Set during the Great Depression, the series is what philosopher Eric Bronson called a "religious film noir"; one of the main characters is a priest (Justin Crowe) who has lost his God (see Sanders and Skoble 2008: 132–34). Crowe is an avatar of evil whose story runs parallel to that of Ben Hawkins, an avatar of good who is a circus hand with miraculous healing powers. The show's creator revealed, in explicitly religious terms, his inspiration for the series:

> The whole period of the '30s, that period between the two World Wars is probably a great place to build a mythology … .The idea that up until we exploded the nuclear bomb, that magic was still existent, and magic died with the burst of the bomb, and God just basically tossed us the car keys and said, 'You're on your own. You created a sun. What do you need me for?' So religion and magic being kind of intertwined …
>
> (VanDerWerff 2013a)

Religion and television production

If we can accept television as an art form that can express religious ideas, it follows that a creative individual who works mostly in television may be considered a theological artist. Scholars and critics, of religion or otherwise, rarely give attention to television artists, but if the artist and poet William Blake, the dancer Martha Graham, and the film director Ingmar Bergman can all be seriously considered as religious artists, why not an artist whose medium is the small screen?

There are at least two reasons for this inattention above and beyond the generally low regard in which television is held. First, because television is so commercialized, TV artists are seen as inherently compromised by their relationships to television networks, which are in turn motivated to achieve high ratings to appease sponsors. Thus, the argument goes, the TV artist has no venue to produce works of religious truth. But the premise of this argument is flawed. While it is true that the television industry is the most centralized and commercialized of all the culture industries—even the popular music and film industries find a space for "independent," "art," and "experimental" films or music—art has always been beholden to money and power. Even the spiritually gifted painters of the Renaissance were supported by royalty, the church, or guilds. All artists have patrons who attempt to control the content. Financial considerations do not make a piece of art trivial, as the works of Shakespeare, Mozart, and Rembrandt attest. A second reason for the lack of attention paid to the television auteur is that television is considered to be such a collaborative medium that it is often difficult to pinpoint who is the artist responsible. Film too is a collaborative medium, but since the rise of *auteur* theory in the 1940s, the director has been seen as film's primary creative artist. As I have written elsewhere (Siegler 2009: 401–2), television drama "is surely mature enough for critics and theorists to recognize that television has *auteurs*." But it isn't the series director, who is often hired to work on a "per episode" basis. One might also argue that it is the series creator, who has originally envisioned the program's premise and characters, and who does much to convince a network to buy it. But the creator is often not involved in the daily workings of the program's production. Newcomb and Alley (1983) argue that TV's *auteur* is the writer-executive producer, who is responsible for the overall development of the story, character arcs, and the "feel" of a series. He or she may or may not be credited as the show's creator but is generally known as the "show runner."

Not all *auteurs* are interested explicitly in religion. Some, such as David Simon—who created *The Wire* (HBO, 2002–8) and *Treme* (HBO, 2010–13)—have generally ignored institutional religion, or, like Alan Ball—who oversaw *Six Feet Under* (HBO, 2001–5) and the adaptation of vampire novels that became *True Blood* (HBO, 2008–14)—have expressed an identifiable if general religious sensibility (but see also Primiano 2011). But one show runner who puts a unique religious stamp on all his shows is Tom Fontana, whose treatment of religion is complex and nuanced (see Siegler 2009). He does not mine religion for topical controversy, nor for its ready-made visual iconography, and his scripts are neither "spiritually uplifting" nor moralistic. Instead, they are interested in theological issues as they are played out in people's lived experiences. These issues have remained remarkably consistent in Fontana's scripts over three decades: the search for redemption (whether explicitly sectarian or not); the nature of forgiveness and its tension with righteous anger; the danger of self-deception and pride; the slipperiness of justice; the elusive search for God; and perhaps, above all, the question of evil.

Religion and television reception

The identification of television programming—even seemingly secular series—as laden with religious meaning suggests that a critique based on religion may be expected from those for whom the religious interpretation may be incompatible with their own beliefs. According to Michele Rosenthal (2007: 29–30), midcentury Protestants did not attack, but rather looked down on television. In the 1950s, the airwaves seemed to be dominated both by Catholic media stars (like Fulton Sheen) and, less often,

Evangelical Protestants such as Oral Roberts and Billy Graham (Rosenthal 29–30). With the development of Evangelical satellite networks like Trinity Broadcasting Network (TBN) and Daystar, these same Evangelicals eventually created their own "theology of television," seeing it as a God-given gift and an aid to worldwide evangelism. As a result, Evangelicals became invested in, not alienated from, television. One byproduct of this investment was what has become known as the "watchdog group" which carefully monitors violence, sex, and anti-Christian bias on television. Such groups had existed in relation to film since its earliest years in the late nineteenth century (Ferre 1990: 101), and reached their zenith with the creation of the Hollywood Production Code—an effort led mostly (but not exclusively) by Catholics (see Black 1994; compare Romanowski 2012)—which coerced voluntary self-monitoring of the studios into the 1950s. Supreme Court rulings related to film that expanded protections for free speech in the early 1950s (for example, *Burstyn v. Wilson*, 1952), Federal Communications Commission control of the public airwaves used for television broadcasts, and network self-policing meant that religious watchdog groups did not focus on television programming until the 1970s.

But since then, the major watchdog groups—including the Parents Television Council (founded in 1995), the American Family Association (founded in 1977 as the National Federation for Decency), and the Catholic League for Religious and Civil Rights (founded in 1973)—have focused on television because of its position as the electronic hearth. The Catholic League, which is generally politically conservative and pro-censorship, has sparred with the *South Park* creators so often that League president Bill Donohue was lampooned in its "Fantastic Easter Special" (aired 4 April 2007; see Feltmate 2013b).

Major organized religious protests began in 1977 over *Soap* (ABC, 1977–81), a sitcom that parodied soap operas, but which in doing so portrayed a gay character (played by Billy Crystal) and an unwed mother in love with a priest. Catholics and Protestants joined in protest, from conservative Jerry Falwell to liberal *Commonweal*, but also (and mostly) mainstream Protestant denominations (Ferre 1990: 104). That same year, Mississippi pastor Donald E. Wildmon founded the National Federation for Decency. After Wildmon's organization threatened to call for a boycott of the program's sponsors, many ABC affiliates did not air the pilot episode, which was (in effect) the first R-rated primetime television show. Protestant watchdog groups would later rail against *NYPD Blue*—for the exposure of one male character's bare bottom, and the utterance of the word "bitch" by another—despite its concern with religious issues like redemption and grace (Nichols-Pethick 2012: 104–5). Fiske argues that this long tradition of attacks on television is part of "the nineteenth-century" middle-class attempt "to control and channel the leisure of the emerging working class into ideologically acceptable forms," itself a reflection of the Protestant work ethic and the Catholic Church's limitations on the "pleasures of the flesh" (Fiske 2011: 229).[12]

Conclusion: the end of television

While this chapter has provided an overview of subjects related to religion and television, more and more, students of religion and television must look beyond the television set itself, and extend their gaze to DVD commentaries (and other "bonus" features), Web series, YouTube channels, and on-demand programming. There is a world of regular programming beyond the scope of this chapter.

On the other hand, the programming that is (and was) on the television set remains a treasure trove of unstudied topics. Though the traditional "Big Three" networks are slowly losing ground, filling their time slots with derivative police procedurals and sitcoms, cable and satellite television providers more regularly include a number of religion-oriented channels in the upper reaches of the channel guide. Some are inheritors of PAX TV; others are more specific (Catholic or Mormon; see Santana and Erickson 2008: 114). In this regard, Canada provides an interesting contrast to the United States. With multiculturalism an official Canadian policy, Canadian religious broadcasting expresses itself through multi-faith channels, unheard of south of its own border. Along with prosperity gospel preacher Kenneth Copeland and conservative Evangelical James Robison, JoyTV broadcasts *Insight into Sikhism*, *Discovering Islam*, and *Being Hindu* (see JoyTV n.d.). Religion on television series from any of the many "golden ages" of the television cries out for religious studies analysis. In the end, religion and television remains a rich, largely unexplored territory.

Notes

1 Fiske sees dance competitions and sports as ritualized conflicts. Ritualization takes place when genuine antagonism becomes ordered, easily judged, and ceremonial (Fiske and Hartley 2003). Fiske uses 1970s British TV shows, but these insights apply easily to *Monday Night Football* (ABC, 1970–2005; ESPN, 2006–present), *Survivor* (CBS, 2000–present), and *Dancing With the Stars* (ABC, 2005–present). Other scholars have seen them as examples of collective effervescence (Dant 2012: 55–56).

2 The one exception is a detailed treatment of Bishop Fulton Sheen (*Hour of Power*, 1952–57), who lectured on TV in very specific religious trappings (full bishop's outfit including cassock, a gold cross and chain at his neck, purple cape, skull cap), and yet whose program—with its universalist message—was watched by Protestants and Jews. Sheen is the exception that proves the rule. The *Hour of Power*, along with televangelism, has become part of the standard narrative of US television history that allows historians to ignore any other religion.

3 This chapter focuses on scripted television—excluding broadcast journalism, "reality" shows, and televangelism—from the English-speaking world.

4 Scholar of American religion Catherine Albanese (2013: 276) defines "public Protestantism" as a social phenomenon in which the "majority tradition act[s] in subtle and not-so-subtle ways to wear away the sharp edges of separateness and to bring people within its scope," providing "acknowledged ways of thinking and acting supported by most institutions in society." Albanese observes that, because of the broad social construction of public Protestantism, non-Protestants (and even the unaffiliated) are strongly influenced by—and participate in—its norms.

5 Because it involves specific religious institutional mechanisms and not more subtle aspects of religious rhetoric and myth construction, we will not explore religious distribution of television. Readers interested in this topic are encouraged to start with Melton *et al.* (1997).

6 Unlike the Simpsons, who belong to a church unaffiliated with a Protestant denomination ("The First Church of Springfield"), the Hill family belongs to a Methodist church.

7 There are female anti-heroes: Patty Hewes on *Damages* (FX, 2007–10; Audience Network 2011–12); Nancy Botwin on *Weeds* (Showtime, 2005–12); Jackie Peyton on *Nurse Jackie* (Showtime, 2009–present); and Amy Jellicoe on *Enlightened* (HBO, 2011–13). All but *Damages* are 30-minute programs, a curiosity left for another time.

8 One priest, Father Phil, was a third-string character in its first season.
9 There are several anti-Semitic references, particularly in the first season, when one of Draper's lovers is a Jewish department store heiress. But these comments seem more anti-ethnic than anti-religious; no comments are made about Judaism as religious system (rituals, teachings, etc.).
10 Matt Weiner, the creator of *Mad Men*, was also a writer-producer on *The Sopranos*.
11 As it turns out, the "non-mythological" episodes were also mythological, albeit in a different form; many of the "monster of the week" plots were derived from urban legends that illuminate the deep structure of our society, as well as regional and immigrant cultures of the United States.
12 Religious studies analyses of television reception often also include an analysis of the religious dimensions of viewer fandom; space restraints make such an exploration here impossible. Readers are encouraged to see the works of Clark (2009; 2003), Santana and Erickson (2008), Porter and McLaren (1999), and Jindra (1994) for in-depth analyses of this phenomenon.

Works cited

Albanese, C.L. (2013) *America: Religions and Religion*, 5th edn, Belmont, CA: Thompson Wadsworth.

Aleaziz, H. (2011) "Interrogating the creators of 'Homeland,'" *Mother Jones* (November 4). Online. Available: www.motherjones.com/media/2011/10/homeland-season-2-claire-danes-howard-gordon-alex-gansa?page=2 (accessed 29 May 2014).

A.V. Club (2011) "TV Club advent calendar." Online. Available: www.avclub.com/features/tv-club-advent-calendar/ (accessed 16 May 2014).

Barthes, R. (1972) *Mythologies*, trans. A. Lavers, New York: Farrar Strauss Giroux.

Bird, S.E. (2009) "True believers and atheists need not apply: faith and mainstream television drama," in D. Winston (ed.), *Small Screen Big Picture: Television and Lived Religion*, Waco, TX: Baylor University Press, 17–42.

Black, G.D. (1994) *Hollywood Censored: Morality Codes, Catholics, and the Movies*, New York: Cambridge University Press.

Bowman, D., Z. Handlen, J. Modell, N. Murray, L. Pierce, N. Rabin, S. Tobias, T. VanDerWerff, and C. Zulkey (2009) "The best TV series of the '00s," A.V. Club (November 12). Online. Available: www.avclub.com/article/the-best-tv-series-of-the-00s-35256/ (accessed 16 May 2014).

Brook, V. (2003) *Something Ain't Kosher Here: The Rise of the Jewish Sitcom*, New Brunswick, NJ: Rutgers University Press.

Campbell, J. (1949) *The Hero with a Thousand Faces*, New York: Pantheon Books.

Christina170 (2013) "Gregory House on Religion," *YouTube* (February 7). Online. Available: www.youtube.com/watch?v=4AhdPLWIJ_c&list=UUMUw%C2%ADxuZB-4WHij55QG2g50w& index=1 (accessed 29 May 2014).

Clark, L. (2003) *From Angels to Aliens: Teenagers, the Media, and the Supernatural*, New York: Oxford University Press.

——(2009) "You lost me: mystery, fandom, and religion in ABC's *Lost*," in D. Winston (ed.), *Small Screen Big Picture: Television and Lived Religion*, Waco, TX: Baylor University Press, 319–42.

Dalton, L., E.M. Mazur, and M. Siems (2011) "Homer the heretic and Charlie church: parody, piety, and pluralism in *The Simpsons*," in E.M. Mazur and K. McCarthy (eds), *God in the Details: American Religion in Popular Culture*, 2nd edn, New York: Routledge Press, 237–54.

Dant, T. (2012) *Television and the Moral Imaginary*, New York: Palgrave MacMillan.

Deignan, T. (2010) "The long journey of Denis Leary's 'Rescue Me,'" *Irish Central* (30 June). Online. Available: www.irishcentral.com/story/news/sidewalks/the-long-journey-of-denis-learys-rescue-me-97484239.html#ixzz2av34nFtw (accessed 16 May 2014).

Feltmate, D. (2013a) "It's funny because it's true? *The Simpsons*, satire, and the significance of religious humor in popular culture," *Journal of the American Academy of Religion* 81, 1: 222–48.

——(2013b) "Cowards, critics, and Catholics: the Catholic League for Religious and Civil Rights, *South Park*, and the politics of religious humor in the United States," *Bulletin for the Study of Religion* 42, 3 (September): 2–11.

Ferre, J.B. (ed.) (1990) *Channels of Belief*, Ames, IA: Iowa State University Press.

Fiske, J. (2011) *Television Culture*, 2nd edn, New York: Routledge Press.

Fiske, J. and J. Hartley (2003) *Reading Television*, 2nd edn, New York: Routledge Press.

Forbes, B.D. and J.H. Mahan (eds) (2000) *Religion and Popular Culture in America*, Berkeley, CA: University of California Press.

Gruber, R.E. (2010) "Heym on the range," *Tablet* (November 4). Online. Available: www.tabletmag.com/jewish-arts-and-culture/49488/heym-on-the-range (accessed 16 May 2014).

Herberg, W. (1955) *Protestant-Catholic-Jew: An Essay in American Religious Sociology*, Garden City, NY: Doubleday.

Holmes, L. (2013) "'Breaking Bad' presents 'Ozymandias,' the great and terrible," *National Public Radio* (September 16). Online. Available: www.npr.org/blogs/monkeysee/2013/09/16/223049000/breaking-bad-presents-ozymandias-the-great-and-terrible (accessed 16 May 2014).

Hoover, S.M. and L.S. Clark (eds) (2002) *Practicing Religion in the Age of Media*, New York: Columbia University Press.

Hoover, S.M. and K. Lundby (eds) (1997) *Rethinking Media, Religion, and Culture*, Thousand Oaks, CA: Sage Publications.

Hussain, A. (2009) "'The fire next time': *Sleeper Cell* and Muslims on television post-9/11," in D. Winston (ed.), *Small Screen Big Picture: Television and Lived Religion*, Waco, TX: Baylor University Press, 153–72.

Iwamura, J. (2005) "The oriental monk in American popular culture," in B.D. Forbes and J.H. Mahan (eds), *Religion and Popular Culture in America*, rev. edn, Berkeley, CA: University of California Press, 25–43.

——(2011) *Virtual Orientalism*, New York: Oxford University Press.

Jindra, M. (1994) "Star Trek fandom as a religious phenomenon," *Sociology of Religion* 55, 1: 27–51.

JoyTV (n.d.) "Faith." Online. Available: www.joytv.ca/category/shows/faith/ (accessed 7 June 2014).

Kaye, J. (1994) "TNT's Bible studies: 'Abraham' is the first of an epic 22 testament tales," *Los Angeles Times* (April 3). Online. Available: http://articles.latimes.com/1994-04-03/news/tv-41522_1_abraham-bible-testament (accessed 1 June 2014).

Kenna, M.E. (1985) "Icons in theory and practice: an Orthodox Christian example," *History of Religions* 24, 4 (May): 345–68.

Kowalski, D.A. and S.E. Kreider (eds) (2011) *The Philosophy of Joss Whedon*, Lexington, KY: University Press of Kentucky.

Kuo, M. and A. Wu (2012) "In Hell, 'We Shall Be Free': on 'Breaking Bad,'" *Los Angeles Review of Books* (July 13). Online. Available: http://lareviewofbooks.org/essay/in-hell-we-shall-be-free-on-breaking-bad (accessed 15 October 2013).

Laycock, J. (2013) "Where do they get these ideas? Changing ideas of cults in the mirror of popular culture," *Journal of the American Academy of Religion* 81, 1: 80–106.

LightWorkers Media (2013) "The Bible." Online. Available: www.bibleseries.tv/ (accessed 1 June 2014).

Lofton, K. (2011) *Oprah: The Gospel of an Icon*, Berkeley, CA: University of California Press.

Lyden, J.C. (2003) *Film as Religion: Myths, Morals, and Rituals*, New York: New York University Press.

McCabe, J. and K. Akass (eds) (2007) *Quality TV: Contemporary American Television and Beyond*, London: IB Tauris.

Macdonald, J.F. (2009) "The TV western as political propaganda," *Television and the Red Menace: The Video Road to Viet Nam*. Online. Available: www.jfredmacdonald.com/trm/111tvwestern.htm (accessed 16 May 2014).

Martin, B. (2013) *Difficult Men: Behind the Scenes of a Creative Revolution: From The Sopranos and The Wire to Mad Men and Breaking Bad*, New York: Penguin Press.

Mazur, E.M. and K. McCarthy (eds) (2001) *God in the Details: American Religion in Popular Culture*, New York: Routledge Press.

——(eds) (2011) *God in the Details: American Religion in Popular Culture*, 2nd edn, New York, NY: Routledge Press.

Melton, J.G, P.C. Lucas, and J.R. Stone (1997) *Prime-Time Religion: An Encyclopedia of Religious Broadcasting*, Phoenix, AZ: Oryx Press.

Mitchell, M.W. (2013) "Some more light on the text: watching HBO's *Deadwood* with and without the Apostle Paul," *Journal of Religion and Popular Culture* 25, 1 (Spring): 110–19.

Morgan, D. (1998) *Visual Piety: A History and Theory of Popular Religious Images*, Berkeley, CA: University of California Press.

——(2005) *The Sacred Gaze: Religious Visual Culture in Theory and Practice*, Berkeley, CA: University of California Press.

Neal, L. (2011) "'They're freaks!': the cult stereotype in fictional television shows, 1958–2008," *Nova Religio* 14, 3: 81–107.

Newcomb, H. (1990) "Religion on television," in J.B. Ferre (ed.), *Channels of Belief*, Ames, IA: Iowa State University Press, 29–45.

——(2009) "In the beginning … *Deadwood*," in D. Winston (ed.), *Small Screen Big Picture: Television and Lived Religion*, Waco, TX: Baylor University Press, 43–68.

——(ed.) (2006) *Television: The Critical View*, 7th edn, New York: Oxford University Press.

Newcomb, H. and R. Alley (1983) *The Producer's Medium*, New York: Oxford University Press.

Newcomb, H. and P.M. Hirsch (1983) "Television as a cultural forum," in H. Newcomb (ed.), *Television: The Critical View*, New York: Oxford University Press, 561–73.

Nichols-Pethick, J. (2012) *TV Cops: The Contemporary American Television Police Drama*, New York: Routledge Press.

Nussbaum, E. (2007) "The Long Con," *New York Magazine* (June 14). Online. Available: http://nymag.com/news/features/33517/ (accessed 15 May 2014).

Orsi, R. (1997) "Everyday miracles: the study of lived religion," in D. Hall (ed.), *Lived Religion in America: Toward a History of Practice*, Princeton, NJ: Princeton University Press.

Paden, W. (1994) *Religious Worlds*, Boston, MA: Beacon Press.

Pals, D. (2006) *Eight Theories of Religion*, New York: Oxford University Press.

Pinsky, M.I. (2007) *The Gospel According to the Simpsons: Bigger and Possibly Even Better Edition*, Louisville, KY: Westminster John Knox Press.

Plate, S.B. (2008) *Religion and Film: Cinema and the Re-Creation of the World*, London: Wallflower Press.

Poniewozik, J. (2013) "History Channel's *Bible* is a hit: does that mean TV will get religion?" *Time.com* (5 March). Online. Available: http://entertainment.time.com/2013/03/05/history-channels-bible-is-a-hit-does-that-mean-tv-will-get-religion/ (accessed 15 May 2014).

Porter, J. and D.L. McLaren (eds) (1999) *Star Trek and Sacred Ground*, Albany, NY: State University of New York Press.

Primiano, L.N. (2009) "'For what I have done and what I have failed to do': vernacular Catholicism and *The West Wing*," in D. Winston (ed.), *Small Screen Big Picture: Television and Lived Religion*, Waco, TX: Baylor University Press, 99–124.

——(2011) "'I wanna do bad things with you': fantasia on themes of American religion from the title sequence of HBO's *True Blood*," in E.M. Mazur and K. McCarthy (eds), *God in the Details: Popular Culture in American Religion*, 2nd edn, New York: Routledge, 41–61.

Rambelli, F. (1991) "Re-inscribing mandalas: semiotic operations on a word and its object," *Studies in Central and East Asian Religions* 4: 1–8.

Reinhartz, A. (2009) "'Who am I? where am I going?': life, death, and religion in *The Sopranos*," in D. Winston (ed.), *Small Screen Big Picture: Television and Lived Religion*, Waco, TX: Baylor University Press, 373–400.

Romanowski, W.D. (2012) *Reforming Hollywood: How American Protestants Fought for Freedom at the Movies*, New York: Oxford University Press.

Roof, W.C. (1993) *A Generation of Seekers: The Spiritual Journeys of the Baby Boom Generation*, San Francisco, CA: HarperSanFrancisco.

Rosenthal, M. (2007) *American Protestants and TV in the 1950s*, London: Palgrave Macmillan.

Sanders, S.M. and A.J. Skoble (eds) (2008) *The Philosophy of TV Noir*, Lexington, KY: University Press of Kentucky.

Santana, R.W. and G. Erickson (2008) *Religion and Popular Culture: Rescripting the Sacred*, Jefferson, NC: McFarland.

Schultze, Q.J. (1990) "Television drama as a sacred text," in J.P. Ferre (ed.), *Channels of Belief*, Ames, IA: Iowa State University Press, 3–28.

Siegler, E. (2001) "God in the box: religion in contemporary television cop shows," in E.M. Mazur and K. McCarthy (eds), *God in the Details: American Religion in Popular Culture*, New York: Routledge Press, 199–216.

——(2009) "A television auteur confronts God: the religious imagination of Tom Fontana," in D. Winston (ed.), *Small Screen Big Picture: Television and Lived Religion*, Waco, TX: Baylor University Press, 401–26.

——(2011) "Is God still in the box? religion in television cop shows ten years later," in E.M. Mazur and K. McCarthy (eds), *God in the Details: American Religion in Popular Culture*, 2nd edn, New York: Routledge Press, 179–96.

Thompson, R.J. (2005) "Consecrating consumer culture: Christmas television specials," in B.D. Forbes and J.H. Mahan (eds), *Religion and Popular Culture in America*, rev. edn, Berkeley, CA: University of California Press, 44–55.

Turner, C. (2004) *Planet Simpson: How a Cartoon Masterpiece Documented an Era and Defined a Generation*, Toronto, ONT: Random House Canada.

Turner, V. (1982) *From Ritual to Theatre: The Human Seriousness of Play*, New York: Performing Arts Journal Publication.

VanDerWerff, T. (2013a) "Daniel Knauf opens up about Carnivàle's long, weird journey," A.V. Club (February 21). Online. Available: www.avclub.com/article/daniel-knauf-opens-up-about-icarnivaleis-long-weir-92780 (accessed 16 May 2014).

——(2013b) "The golden age of TV is dead; long live the golden age of TV," A.V. Club (September 20). Online. Available: www.avclub.com/articles/the-golden-age-of-tv-is-dead-long-live-the-golden,103129/ (accessed 15 October 2013).

——(2013c) "*Breaking Bad* ended the anti-hero genre by introducing good and evil," A.V. Club (September 30). Online. Available: www.avclub.com/articles/breaking-bad-ended-the-antihero-genre-by-introduci,103483/ (accessed 15 October 2013).

Watson, M.A. (2008) *Defining Visions: Television and the American Experience in the 20th Century*, Malden, MA: Blackwell.

Wetmore, K.J., Jr. (2012) *The Theology of Battlestar Galactica: American Christianity in the 2004–2009 Television Series*, Jefferson, NC: McFarland.

4
JOURNALISM

Jolyon P. Mitchell

Prologue

On 26 April 1937, during the Spanish Civil War,[1] a small town in the Basque Region was subjected to over three hours of aerial bombardment. More than 40 German and Italian bombers, with the encouragement of Franco's Nationalist forces, dropped high explosive and incendiary devices on the town below. It was market day in Gernika (the Basque spelling of Guernica) and many hundreds of civilian women, children, and men were instantaneously killed. Though the precise numbers of casualties are still debated, it is estimated that as many as 1,000 people died. On the days that followed, newspapers around the world ran stories about the bombing. News film reels showed shell-shocked survivors clearing rubble and making their way through the remains of devastated buildings. The story spread rapidly around Europe and beyond. For example, on the following afternoon the *Evening News* in London led with the headline: "The most appalling air raid ever known." News of this atrocity caused shock, outrage, and consternation, as this attack appeared to be directed against defenseless "innocents." It was later believed that the Nazi Air Command combined saturation bombing and machine-gun strafing both as a way to test new technologies of war and as an experiment on how to crush a civilian population. Here was a foretaste, a rehearsal, of even worse atrocities against civilians that were still to come in the Second World War.

Several pictures of corpses laid on the floor were widely circulated. A grieving woman holding her baby after the attack was captured on film. At first sight it looks a little like a nurturing Madonna, though in reality it is more like a Pietà. This woman is following the now banned custom of holding a dead infant to be photographed as if it is still alive. One famous Spanish artist living in Paris at the time, Pablo Picasso, was apparently so shocked by what he read in the news reports about this attack (and perhaps earlier bombings) that he was provoked to turn his commission for the 1937 Paris International Exposition into an expression of rage, grief, and protest.[2] In about six weeks of prodigious artistic activity he had covered nearly 30 square meters of canvas, completing one of the twentieth century's most significant pieces of art: *Guernica* (see Martin 2003).

The painting itself may now be housed in Spain, but it is widely available online. The black, white, and grey picture that is *Guernica* has become part of popular culture, with its own biography (van Hensbergen 2004). The huge picture has been

Figure 4.1 Postage stamp printed in Czechoslovakia showing *Guernica* by Pablo Picasso from Museo Reina Sofia, Madrid, Spain, *c.* 1966. © Zoltan Katona.

reduced, copied, and circulated on many different kinds of materials, including posters, shirts, mugs, and stamps (see Figure 4.1).

Disjointed shapes, figures in agony, and sharp lines recreate the devastation and the despair that the attack on Gernika caused. An impaled horse, a grotesque bull, and several faces speak of confusion and heartbreak. The body of the horse is made up of deteriorated newspaper. On the viewer's far left a female form, head arched upwards, is holding a dangling, lifeless rag-doll-like baby. It is as if the woman is screaming up toward heaven, her tongue shaped more like a dagger. For some interpreters, here is a secular Madonna placed in the center of a deeply troubling news event (van Hensbergen 2009). Religious symbols are given new meaning in a shattered landscape.

Introduction: transforming news

This story provides a starting point for analyzing the relation between news and religion, as part of popular culture. In this chapter, I outline several different elements vital for developing a critical account of the relation between news and religion. These elements are also useful to draw upon for analyzing individual news stories. First, there are various kinds of histories to be excavated. What is the evolving relation between news and religion? And what is the historical background to an individual story? To answer such questions it is useful to consider wider debates about cultural and social change. Second (and often linked with the first element), there are contexts to be mapped. What is the cultural and social context in which a story emerges, journalists operate, and news is distributed? Third, there are both news producers and actual news items to be considered. What part does a journalist, editor, or broadcaster play in shaping the contents of an actual news story? Finally, there are multiple audiences to consider. How and where do audiences interact with stories which contain a religious element? My argument is that in order to provide a rich and nuanced account of the relation between news and religion, as part of popular culture, it is vital to analyze histories, contexts, producers, contents, and audiences.

In a recent book on *Religion and the News*, I considered how approaches to understanding news about religion can be characterized by a distinct primary focal point: the journalist, the story, the context, or the audience (Mitchell and Gower 2012: 7–30). I underlined that behind every newsworthy event, or series of events, there are commonly multiple stories, contexts, journalists, and audiences. In other words, there is a multiplicity of representations, reporters, and receptions emerging out of a range of settings. These are not frozen in time, but dynamic elements within the making of news. This became clearer as I examined evolving stories, contested contexts, creative journalists, and expressive audiences in relation to the evolving Occupy St Paul's news story (Autumn 2011, through Spring 2012). My aim was to shed critical light on the coverage of religion by journalists, and on religious leaders' engagement with the news media. In this chapter, I approach the topic differently, drawing on a range of other examples. The aim is to outline several elements that are necessary for creating a rich and critical account of the relation between religion and the news, as part of popular culture. This in turn will contribute to more nuanced accounts of individual news stories.

Before turning to consider these elements, it is worth observing, as I did in *Religion and the News*, that many earlier studies on religion and the news have emerged in North America (see, for example: Winston (forthcoming); Buddenbaum 1998; Hoover 1998; Silk 1998). By contrast, European books on news, by both academics and journalists, tend either to overlook religion altogether, or to deal with it only in a cursory fashion (see, for example, Marr 2004; Tumber 1999). This is slowly changing in the UK, Europe, and other parts of the world,[3] especially following the increased interest in the place of Islam in the news (see Moore and Lewis 2008; Lynch 2008, especially Chapter 8). My intention in this chapter is therefore to contribute further to these emerging international conversations.

Histories: the evolution of news and religion

In the same way that in order to understand Picasso's *Guernica* it is useful to consider the multiple histories behind this painting, so it is helpful to reflect upon the multiple histories behind the current relationship between religion and the news. This is particularly the case because accounts of journalism can all too easily slide into ahistorical contemporary descriptions that demonstrate a lack of awareness of what has gone before. In the early modern era, both in Europe and in the United States, news coverage was commonly viewed as part of religious expression, teaching, or reflection. For many readers a news story was to be interpreted through a theologically informed lens. For example, in eighteenth-century colonial America, many people read news reports in the light of the belief that they were part of a "covenant people" living in a promised land (Copeland 2012). Religious belief and practice shaped how news, such as the conflict between the American colonies and the British government, was both reported and interpreted. Even though patterns of belief would evolve over the following two centuries, in the early twentieth century many journalists remained deferential toward both religious beliefs and religious leaders.

Almost imperceptibly this has radically changed in many parts of the news media. Among mainstream news channels in the West news is rarely, if ever, used to pro-selytize or to promote religious beliefs. Journalists have become increasingly detached in how they cover religion. In a way reminiscent of how Pablo Picasso artistically railed against the political figures (especially Franco) who brought about Gernika's destruction, so journalists in some democracies have become less subservient to and more critical of religious figures. Many journalists tend to treat religious leaders as they would political leaders or popular celebrities. In place of deference, many journalists attempt to expose or highlight weaknesses, conflict, or inconsistencies within religious groups (see Knott and Mitchell 2012).

The history of religious journalism can also be discerned in two books, both of which have the USA as their primary focus. First, it can be traced in an anthology titled *Readings on Religion as News*, containing over 100 different articles (Budden-baum and Mason 2000). Covering 300 years of American history, it is divided into four parts. The first set of stories comes from the Puritan era, when journalism was regularly used as a persuasive tool to promote visions of a "New Jerusalem." In the second section (*c.*1800–1945) it becomes clear how news about religion helped to define aspects of American culture and politics. The final two sections (post-1945 and post-1990s) provide evidence of the development to more "detached" forms of journalism. Second, this can also be discerned in the more recent *Oxford Handbook on Religion and the American News Media* (Winston 2012).[4] In particular, the first six essays, taken together, underline the radical changes in how religion has been covered in the USA over the last two centuries. While the journalistic craft has become more professional, religious leaders have become more open to challenge and criticism.

While some historians focus on precise details, specific incidents, or relatively short periods of time, others take a broader view, charting the evolution of different media. Taking a broader historical perspective, writers such as Harold Innis (1950, 1951), Marshal McLuhan (1962, 1964), and Walter Ong (1982) have developed what could be described as grand theories of media evolution. I will not attempt to follow in their footsteps and outline a grand theory of religion and news. Nor is there space here to detail other complex history of news, journalism, and media interpretation (see Katz *et al.* 2003); nonetheless, such histories offer rich insights into the relation between news and religion.

For example, there are significant differences between news about religion that is conveyed on a flimsy papyrus, a printed book, or a digital "tablet." This has impli-cations for what is communicated and what is received. Some messages may travel swiftly and then vanish, while others may hardly move from their point of origin but last many decades. Some stories may be shouted by a town crier or preached from a pulpit, while others may be inscribed on a manuscript or beaten out on the "tribal drums" of radio. Some news items may take months to reach those for whom they have relevance, while others, such as the attacks on Gernika (1937), the Golden Temple in Amritsar (1984), or the Twin Towers (2001), may be broadcast only a few hours, min-utes, or seconds after the actual event. There are clearly historical similarities and dissimilarities in how religion is covered as a news story. In an increasingly digitized and connected communicative environment, instantaneous news is commonplace. Religious leaders are now expected, like many other public figures, to be able to respond rapidly and fluently, even under the harsh glare of publicity and of live 24-hour news.

The change in the West in the manner in which religious leaders are interviewed and how stories about religion are covered is part of a wider set of social and cultural changes, one of which is the weakening of the power held by traditional institutions, such as the Church, the Judiciary, and the Legislature. Many of those working within these institutions appear to be less widely respected and can attract copious amounts of negative press coverage. The weakening of traditional institutional authority is a common observation among scholars working in the area of media, religion, and culture (see Lynch *et al.* 2012). Contemporary journalism has contributed to these changes; so too has the decline in the West of many forms of adherence to traditional forms of religious expression. New forms of spiritual expression and more outspoken attacks on religion by the so-called "new atheists" have contributed to an evolving religious landscape.

Contexts: the creation of webs of meaning

To understand this changing landscape it is worth considering a second element useful for understanding the relation between religion and news. It is commonly overlooked: the cultural context. By cultural context I am referring to the webs of meaning that can be created, inherited, and learnt in different societies.[5] Sometimes these webs are spun through different media, and therefore experienced as part of people's everyday lives (see Williams 1958: 6). As observed earlier, Picasso's painting has been translated into many different media. *Guernica* has circulated in many different forms, and continues to do so. Sometimes it is viewed in an explicitly religious context, such as when used during a sermon or religious address, while at other times it is interpreted in a non-religious setting, as a secular artifact that may have some religious resonances (Apostolos-Cappadona 1992).[6] During Franco's regime in Spain it was an offense, punishable by imprisonment, to be found with a copy of this painting, which some even saw as an indirect attack on the Catholic Church's support of the Nationalists.[7]

The communicative environment in which a story such as the Gernika bombing emerges, also contributes to a broader cultural context. Martin Minchom (2012), a cultural historian, makes a persuasive case that "it was not just the bombing of the Basque town on April 26, 1937" that contributed to the creation of *Guernica*. He argues that it is necessary to recognize a broader cultural and historical context that shaped "Picasso's earliest artistic reactions to the Spanish Civil War in late 1936 and early 1937." This means considering the kind of posters, pamphlets, and newspapers with which Picasso interacted. These would have informed him of earlier bombings on Madrid (November 1936) and the town of Durango, where a Catholic church was almost entirely destroyed. One journalist writes of the "Martyrdom of Madrid," while a French pamphlet described Durango as a "martyred town." Minchom suggests that Picasso "draws on both these sources" and the broader cultural context, transforming them into "a kind of Martyrdom of Guernica" (ibid.).

The cultural context also encircles the triangle of producers, audiences, and specific news media. Consider another example from an earlier war. In Britain during the First World War the cultural context made it difficult for the implications of news about the Christmas Truce of 1914 to be fully absorbed or acted upon. The story was not, as commonly believed, suppressed. Numerous letters from soldiers and even some photos of German and British troops together in "no man's land" were published in local and national newspapers throughout January 1915. The strict governmental control over the press ensured that in the long term this temporary peace would be downplayed as a momentary miracle instead of a sign of what could have been. This was only one story in the midst of a sea of propaganda, where Germans were demonized as an enemy who had "supposedly" amputated children's hands, bayoneted babies in Belgium, and used monks as human clappers in a monastery in Antwerp (see Mitchell 2012, especially Chapter 1). Initially the war had considerable popular support. Propaganda appears to have heightened antipathy toward the Prussians in particular. Several preachers uncritically passed on in their sermons the propaganda that they found in newspapers (Mitchell 2012: 40),[8] endorsing the image of German soldiers as "promiscuous and lecherous, and with naïve eagerness told stories of the rape and mutilation of women by the enemy" (see Wilkinson 1996: 94; Marrin 1974: 82–142). Appeals by Pope Benedict XV for an armistice fell on deaf ears, and conscientious objectors met with little understanding or sympathy throughout the war.

By contrast, the current cultural context provides a far more supportive setting for those who portray with considerable skepticism what H.G. Wells famously described as "the war to end all wars." Films such as *Joyeux Noel* (*Merry Christmas*, Christian Carion, 2005), depicting the few days over Christmas when Germans and British troops put down their guns, left their trenches, shared drinks, and even played football, not only received co-sponsorship by countries who were once on different sides—Belgium, Britain, France, Germany, Japan, and Romania—but also received positive reviews in all of these countries. The cultural context in which a film or news report is watched is as significant as the context in which it is produced. Different media can contribute to an atmosphere of hatred or provide a depiction of peaceful cooperation in the face of the madness of supposedly civilized nations at war. They can spin webs of both violent and peaceful meaning. This leads toward our third element: the producers of news, its content, and its critics.

Producers: the criticism of content

In the first half of the twentieth century not only artists such as Picasso but also scholars witnessed violence piled upon violence, leading some to conclude that news (along with other media), used as a propaganda tool, could contribute to ideological hatred and nationalistic violence. Popular culture was drawn upon for violent ends. Numerous scholars have devoted their professional lives to attempting to understand the precise extent of media effects. It is possible to draw on this research and ask: "What impact does the consumption of news about religion have upon audiences?" But my approach in this chapter is to go beyond this media effects tradition (see Gauntlett 1998) and the concern with direct impact and behavior changes, to underline instead the significance of wider historical, contextual, and critical issues. In order to develop a balanced account of religion and the news, it is useful not only to evaluate critically the practices of news producers, but also to analyze the actual content of news stories.

However much a live news broadcast might give the appearance of spontaneity, it is normally the carefully choreographed product of a stopwatch culture and high-tech production suite, where reality is put together (see Schlesinger 1992). Edward Herman and Noam Chomsky (1994) suggest that television news is part of a giant instrument of propaganda "manufacturing consent" from its viewers. They assert that "the raw material of news" invariably passes through successive filters before being presented to the public. This filtering process merits careful analysis as it influences the ways in which stories are covered and conveyed. As I have argued elsewhere, it is important to emphasize that understanding religion and news is more than simply the analysis of how a particular story relating to religion is covered; it is also about developing an awareness of why particular news stories are there (see Mitchell and Gower 2012: 7–30). In other words, it is useful to consider the journalist's background, the organization's routines, and the political economy of individual news companies, as each plays its role in the production of a story. This will enrich interpretations of stories such as the publicizing of satirical cartoons of Muhammad, the divides within religious communities over sexual ethics, and the circulation of pictures of bombings in distant cities.

The bloody turmoil through the early part of the twentieth century contributed to the development of another scholarly tradition pertinent to this discussion: critical theory. This phrase is often used synonymously with the "Frankfurt School" (see Jarvis 1998; Wiggershaus 1993; Adorno 1991; Adorno and Horkheimer 1979a; Adorno and Horkheimer 1979b). Researchers operating in this tradition analyze what they see, read, and hear as well as the institutions and structures behind these productions.[9] While the cultural context, communicative environment, and nature of the audience are important topics to analyze critically, so too is the actual content of what is produced. That is one reason why it is useful to analyze specific news broadcasts, news photographs, and films about news. Drawing upon the critical theory tradition ensures that questions will be asked about why accounts of news often overlook how women or children suffer physical or sexual abuse at home, or how ethnic minorities and the poorest groups of society are regularly overlooked by powerful multi-national news and media organizations. Critical interpreters do not stop with news texts or news audiences; they ask structural and causative questions such as "Why is this the case?" or "Which structures or lines of ownership contribute to these patterns of news production?"

More recent critics of journalistic power without accountability tend to highlight how many kinds of journalism, driven partly by economic necessity, can simplify, trivialize, or distort stories about religion to sell papers, attract listeners, or hold viewers. Culture critics such as Neil Postman, in his book *Amusing Ourselves to Death* (1985: 80), argue that television promotes "incoherence and triviality" and "is trans-forming our culture into one vast arena for show business." This includes television news, which he describes as part of the entertainment industry. His thesis has been summed up as the belief that television provides "corrosive amusement" (Jensen 1990: 44–50). Behind Postman's fear of the corrosion or trivializing of politics, education, news, and religion by television lies nostalgia for the printed word and the logical, linear world that it upheld. In Postman's eyes television, including television news, "has gradually *become* our culture, the background radiation of the social and intellectual universe." For Postman, television, including news, is "a form of graven imagery far more alluring than a golden calf" (Postman 1985: 79, 122–23). He clearly wishes to shatter that "golden calf." His primary tool is education as part of a reparative "media ecology," but he often falls into the trap of stereotyping television, and news, in order to strengthen his own case.

With the convergence of communication technologies, the growth of "citizen" and "online" journalism, and the rise of interactive forms of news, many of these comments have a dated feel, though the criticism that news has become mere entertainment or even part of the film industry is still being expressed by culture critics.[10] In the light of the *News of the World* and other newspapers' phone hacking scandal in the United Kingdom, and the subsequent Leveson inquiry examining the "culture, practice and ethics of the press,"[11] some of the criticisms directed at the apparent lack of ethical behavior in practices of financial hubs such as the City of London and Wall Street in New York might also be extended to attend to different parts of news media.

In other recent contexts, modern scapegoats are created and attacked through different news media (such as newspapers, Web sites, and broadcast news reports) as a way of deflecting attention from actual wrongdoing. The result is that victims are increasingly used not ritually to purge society of its sin, but literally to become a substitute, and a focal point for blame. René Girard's work is particularly valuable for revealing why a society's scapegoat can find itself the subject of violence (see Mitchell 2007: 219–24). Scapegoats in the news also serve a social function. Actual character assassination is found more in investigative journalism or press commentary than in feature films. Journalists justify it as a way of deconstructing carefully spun public images and unveiling the abuse of power, but it can easily slide into violent forms of expression (see Douglas 1995: 46–48; see also Jenkins 1996). Several writers have pointed out that many journalists now have considerable power but little accountability for their actions (see Curran and Seaton 1997). Reporters can justifiably expose and legitimately criticize those religious leaders who employ violent means of governance, but can equally fail to observe how some media use forms of psychological violence, or even become places of incitement toward physical attack. The precise psychological and physical impact of news about religion, and particularly the nature of "religious violence," is a highly contentious subject (see Cavanaugh 2009).

Nevertheless, vociferous critics of news can all too easily overlook the benefits to individuals and to society when reporters uncover and expose abuse or the corrupt use of power. For example, without the work of determined journalists the abuse crisis within parts of the Catholic Church could have remained largely hidden. Or in a similar fashion, the extensive embezzlement of funds by certain American televangelists during the 1980s could have gone unnoticed. Or the appropriation of biblical texts to justify acts of extreme cruelty by the Lord's Resistance Army in parts of Uganda could have remained a largely local news story. In the light of such results some celebrate journalism's revelatory power in relation to religion, arguing that certain forms of journalism can illuminate, unmask, and educate, while also entertain (see Hargreaves 2005).[12]

Consideration of the media's role in advocacy will prevent the pitfall of unreflective "journalist bashing." It recognizes that journalists can play a significant constructive role in helping to create a civil society and ensure that religious leaders and communities are held to account in public for their actions. Those concerned with how to live peacefully in a violent world have much to learn from the experiences of media professionals such as journalists, producers, and documentary makers. This assertion is partly based upon my own first-hand experience of working as a producer and journalist with BBC World Service, especially as we attempted to depict accurately the many different shades of violence and conflict. Being a journalist in one of the world's war zones is a dangerous, unique, invigorating, and some would say "addictive" occupation (Tumber and Webster 2006, especially 61–76; for a more popular account see Leslie 2006: 13). It is not something of which I had direct experience, but working alongside many of those who did further convinced me that there is much to learn from their craft and experience. Significant insights include the value of going beyond spectacular images of conflict, the importance of listening carefully to the stories of the victims of violence, and the necessity of being sensitive to the physical and psychological pressures that journalists experience when covering news about violence.

Audiences: the reception of news

In order to develop a more nuanced and critical account of the evolving relation between religion and the news, it is important to consider not only histories, contexts, and producers, but also our fourth element: audiences. Over the last three or four decades there has been a critical turn toward the audience, and an increased rigor in thinking about the nature and locations of reception. This has included news audiences. Many different theories have been developed to make sense of the unpredictable and varied interactions with various media that are found among viewers, listeners, and Web users. Media analysis and, more precisely, accounts about news, have shown how audiences are always changing, always developing. This is a significant phenomenon, which media scholars (Livingstone 2006 [2003]: 337–59), cultural theorists (Miller 2006 [2001]), anthropologists (Rothenbuhler and Coman 2004; Askew and Wilk 2002, especially 237–322), and other social scientists have mapped in detail. Drawing upon these insights, the complex activity of the audience can be taken into account. This research supports the case that audiences are by no means bound to be passive receivers of news stories, but have the potential to become dynamic respondents in the face of the stories that they see or hear.

The situation is complicated further as the communal context in which audiences watch, read, or hear the news may also be different from the professional worlds of the paid journalist and religious leader. There are inevitably points of overlap, but audiences may belong to other religious communities or to none at all. The result is that individuals can bring a new set of narratives, experiences, and beliefs to a news story that has emerged from outside their own religious tradition or worldview. This can provoke unexpected reactions. Audiences are now much more easily able to interact publicly with news stories through online posts, blogs, and comments. Audiences never were entirely passive, but now it is much simpler to express oneself to a wider public. Increasingly expressive audiences are adding to what Michel de Certeau (1984: 186) describes in another context as the "interminable recitation of stories." As stories are repeated, they are edited, adapted, and elaborated upon by audiences. As they circulate they can grow or dissipate in significance.

Nevertheless, the engagement with the painting of *Guernica* is an example of how expressive audiences may even be turning the process of "agenda setting" on its head. It is commonly claimed that news media set the agenda for public debate. Bernard Cohen (1963: 13), for instance, claimed that the press "may not be successful much of the time in telling people what to think, but it is stunningly successful in telling its readers what to think about." This quotation appeals to journalists who claim that significant power resides with their craft. In the light of active and dynamic audiences, this is open to qualification, especially with the increase of citizen journalism through Twitter, Facebook, and blogs. Even media magnate Rupert Murdoch is very aware that younger audiences (especially 19–34 years old) are increasingly turning to different parts of the Web for news. He believes that members of this age group "don't want a God-like figure from above to tell them what's important" (Allen 2010: 143). Sometimes audiences want to tell journalists which stories are significant, though whether new media actually facilitate this process is open to debate. Some stories do circulate through independent media and percolate into the public sphere in such a way as to put the issue onto the professional news journalist's agenda in an unexpected fashion. In other words, the range of agenda-setting sources has radically increased for both audiences and journalists over the last two decades. This can be observed in the multiplicity of voices that were heard in the public sphere reflecting, debating, and commenting on unprovoked attacks on civilian populations, and can be found both offline and online, in a range of alternative media; digital media—including blogs, Facebook, and Twitter—have facilitated these conversations.

In *Democracy and Tradition*, Jeffrey Stout (2004: 163, 166) suggests that "[m]ore people seek their moral edification from poems, novels, essays, plays and sermons than from moral treatises or philosophical articles," and that "[t]here is a massive modern democratic literature on character and the virtues awaiting exploration outside of the philosophical canon."[13] Stout supports his point by making imaginative use of several novels to illustrate and to develop his own argument. How far can Stout's claim be extended to go beyond the traditional communicative forms that he identifies? In other words, how far have the electronic media, such as Web sites, television, and radio programs become the places where many people consciously and subconsciously seek their "moral edification" alongside the news? Reception studies suggest that combined with the family, friendship circles, and other formative settings, such media provide audiences with a place and a set of resources for moral edification, development, and education.

Conclusion

News stories invariably take on a life of their own, reappearing in unexpected places and forms. The bombing of Gernika was no exception. News stories about this attack are mere drops in what Salman Rushdie (1990) describes as the never-ending "sea of stories." There are, in the words of Roland Barthes (1989: 89), "numberless" narratives appearing in "infinite forms" throughout human history. Why do some stories, even some explicitly religious ones, attract so much attention? Some stories have the magnetic power to stand out from other tales. Good images help. Picasso created an unforgettable picture, which is inextricably connected with what happened over 80 years ago. His picture became a powerful and memorable symbol of the impact of total war.

It is increasingly understood that the "sensational, the spectacular, the tragic, the sordid and the deviant, tend to get prominence over the orderly, the integrated, the normal and the constructive" (Neville Jayaweera, cited in Maslog 1994: 121).[14] While the bombing of Gernika was sensational, spectacular, and tragic, as we have seen it was one reader, Pablo Picasso, in particular, who would immortalize this story. Both *The Times* of London and the *New York Times* published on Wednesday, 28 April 1937, gave an understated but incisive report by war correspondent George Steer (see Rankin 2003).[15] While the English-speaking press embraced the story extensively, some parts of the French press appeared to have been more absorbed by the strength of the response in Britain and the States. Nevertheless, Steer's account was reproduced the following day (29 April) in the French Communist newspaper that Picasso read regularly, *L'Humanité*. His reading of this and other stories appears to have contributed to his haunting artistic vision, and would inspire many other audiences in the future. The way *Guernica* has been used, or even hidden, has changed over the last 70 years. For example, the tapestry copy of *Guernica* at the United Nations was famously covered over with a blue cloth just before Colin Powell began a press conference defending the proposed invasion of Iraq (January 2003; see Patterson 2007).

Picasso's painting of *Guernica* has multiple histories and contexts. It has been appropriated in different ways by a range of producers and audiences. In this chapter I used the story of *Guernica*, alongside other examples, to illustrate several different elements vital for developing a critical account of the relation between news and religion. Through this account I have suggested that in order to understand the relation between news and religion, as part of popular culture, it is vital to analyze histories, contexts, producers, contents, and audiences. Taking these elements into consideration will also enrich analysis of individual news stories, whether they explicitly deal with religious issues or simply have religious ramifications or resonances. We have seen how there are various kinds of histories to be excavated, contexts to be mapped, news producers and actual news content to be analyzed, as well as audiences' interaction with news stories to be considered.

Many scholars draw upon these and other elements to inform their research and writing. When analyzing news and religion, it would also be useful to draw upon different aspects of these four elements, particularly in relation to developing reparative patterns in a rapidly evolving communicative environment. By reparative patterns I mean practices that will contribute to enriching historical analysis, sharpening cultural criticism, improving journalistic practice, and nuancing interpretations of audience reception. This is beyond the scope of this current chapter, but it would be a valuable future research topic to consider how religious communities can, and sometimes do, play a significant role in these developments. More precisely it would be useful to consider how both religious groups and journalists covering religion can contribute to these reparative practices. Such future research could begin by investigating how celebrity journalism, simplified news copy, and spectacular popular culture events can result in making invisible, distorting, or excluding some of the many stories about religion. This could lead to a careful consideration of the practices and approaches that might transform and enrich the evolving and often complicated relations between news and religion.

Notes

1 The Spanish Civil War lasted from July 1936 to April 1939. It was fought between the Republicans and Nationalists, who were eventually led by General Franco. The Nationalist forces were ultimately successful, leading to Franco being in power for 36 years.

2 Picasso was commissioned to create a mural for the Spanish Display at the 1937 Paris International Exposition.

3 See also recent discussions of "mediatization," such as Lundby (2009) and Cohen (2012).

4 See especially the introduction and Chapters 1–6.

5 I am drawing here upon Clifford Geertz's (1973) famous definition of culture that emphasizes the practice of interpreting "webs of significance." For theological reflections on culture, see also Tanner (1997, especially 3–58); Gorringe (2004); and Gallagher (2003).

6 Apostolos-Cappadona argues that Picasso was "particularly drawn to the lamenting Magdalene in the Isenheim Altarpiece," and that examples of "the sixteenth-century German master's influence can be found in Picasso's Crucifixion drawings after 1932, as well as in Guernica."

7 The republicans, with strong communist tendencies, were commonly anti-clerical and anti-Catholic. See, for example, the photograph of the "execution of the Sacred Heart of Jesus." This photo, reproduced in the *Daily Mail* with the caption "Spanish reds war on religion," shows six men firing up at a statue of Jesus at *Cerro de los Ángeles*, near Madrid, August 1936 (see Ealham and Richards 2005: 80, 168).

8 For example, during the First World War, the Bishop of London (A.F. Winnington-Ingram) drew uncritically on stories from both *The Daily Mail* and *The Times*.

9 For a more recent appropriation of the Frankfurt School, see Lynch (2005), especially Chapters 4 and 9.

10 Such critique has a long history: see, for example, Gabler (1998).

11 Formal evidence hearings started on 14 November 2011 at the Royal Courts of Justice in London, with the formal part of the inquiry concluding July 2012. See The Leveson Inquiry (n.d.). For the report see The Leveson Inquiry (2012).

12 Hargreaves argues that "freedom of the press" and uncovering the truth remain essential goals for journalism.

13 See also how Martha Nussbaum (1986; 1990) analyzes narratives and characters in Greek tragedies and novels.

14 See Maslog (1994: 119–21) for section on "News Values."

15 It was Steer's story—published on Wednesday, 28 April 1937, in both *The Times* and the *New York Times*—that was translated into French and Spanish for dissemination in mainland Europe and beyond.

Works cited

Adorno, T.W. (1991) "Culture industry reconsidered," in *The Culture Industry*, London: Routledge, 98–106.

Adorno, T.W. and M. Horkheimer (1979a) *Dialectic of Enlightenment*, London: Verso.

——(1979b) "The culture industry: enlightenment as mass deception," in *Dialectic of Enlightenment*, London: Verso, 120–67.

Allen, S. (2010) *News Culture*, 3rd edn, Maidenhead: Open University Press.

Apostolos-Cappadona, D. (1992) "The essence of agony: Grünewald's influence on Picasso," *Artibus et Historiae* 26, 13: 31–47.

Askew, K. and R.R. Wilk (eds) (2002) *The Anthropology of Media: A Reader*, Oxford: Blackwell.

Barthes, R. (1989) *The Semiotic Challenge*, trans. Richard Howard, Berkeley, CA: University of California Press.

Buddenbaum, J.M. (1998) *Reporting News About Religion: An Introduction for Journalists*, Ames, IA: Iowa State University Press.

Buddenbaum, J.M. and D.L. Mason (eds) (2000) *Readings on Religion as News*, Ames, IA: Iowa State University Press.

Cavanaugh, W.T. (2009) *The Myth of Religious Violence: Secular Ideology and the Roots of Modern Conflict*, Oxford: Oxford University Press.

Cohen, B. (1963) *The Press and Foreign Policy*, Princeton, NJ: Princeton University Press.

Cohen, Y. (2012) *God, Jews and the Media: Religion and Israel's Media*, London: Routledge.

Copeland, D. (2012) "Religion and news in eighteenth century America," in D. Winston (ed.), *The Oxford Handbook on Religion and the American News Media*, Oxford: Oxford University Press, 23–36.

Curran, J. and J. Seaton (1997) *Power without Responsibility*, London: Routledge.

de Certeau, M. (1984) *The Practice of Everyday Life*, trans. Steven Rendall, Berkeley, CA: University of California Press.

Douglas, T. (1995) *Scapegoats: Transferring Blame*, London: Routledge.

Ealham, C. and M. Richards (eds) (2005) *The Splintering of Spain: Cultural History and the Spanish Civil War, 1936–1939*, Cambridge: Cambridge University Press.

Gabler, N. (1998) *Life the Movie: How Entertainment Conquered Reality*, New York: Vintage.

Gallagher, M.P. (2003) *Clashing Symbols: An Introduction to Faith and Culture*, rev. edn, New York: Paulist Press.

Gauntlett, D. (1998) "Ten things wrong with the 'effects model,'" in R. Dickinson, R. Harindranath, and O. Linné (eds), *Approaches to Audiences: A Reader*, London: Arnold, 120–30.

Geertz, C. (1973) *The Interpretation of Cultures: Selected Essays*, New York: Basic Books.

Gorringe, T.J. (2004) *Furthering Humanity: A Theology of Culture*, Burlington, VT: Ashgate.

Hargreaves, I. (2005) *Journalism: A Very Short Introduction*, Oxford: Oxford University Press.

van Hensbergen, G. (2004) *Guernica: The Biography of a Twentieth-Century Icon*, London: Bloomsbury.

——(2009) "Piecing together Guernica," *BBC News* (April 7). Online. Available: http://news.bbc.co.uk/1/hi/7986540.stm (accessed 12 January 2013).

Herman, E.S. and N. Chomsky (1994) *Manufacturing Consent: The Political Economy of the Mass Media*, London: Vintage.

Hoover, S. (1998) *Religion in the News: Faith and Journalism in American Public Discourse*, London: Sage.

Innis, H. (1950) *Empire and Communication*, Oxford: Clarendon Press.

——(1951) *The Bias of Communication*, Toronto, ONT: University of Toronto Press.

Jarvis, S. (1998) *Adorno: A Critical Introduction*, Cambridge: Polity Press.

Jenkins, P. (1996) *Pedophiles and Priests: Anatomy of a Contemporary Crisis*, New York: Oxford University Press.

Jensen, J. (1990) *Redeeming Modernity—Contradictions in Media Criticism*, Newbury Park, CA: Sage.

Katz, E., J.D. Peters, T. Liebes, and A. Orloff (eds) (2003) *Canonical Texts in Media Research: Are There Any? Should There Be? How About These?* Cambridge, MA: Polity Press.

Knott, K. and J. Mitchell (2012) "The changing faces of media and religion," in L. Woodhead and R. Catto (eds), *Religion and Change in Modern Britain*, London: Routledge, 243–64.

Leslie, A. (2006) "My salute to the war junkies," *Daily Mail* (May 31): 13.

The Leveson Inquiry (n.d.) *The Leveson Inquiry: Culture, Practice and Ethics of the Press.* Online. Available: www.levesoninquiry.org.uk (accessed 1 June 2012).

——(2012) *The Leveson Inquiry: Culture, Practice and Ethics of the Press. Report.* Online. Available: www.levesoninquiry.org.uk/about/the-report/ (accessed 7 January 2013).

Livingstone, S. (2006 [2003]) "The changing nature of audiences: from the mass audience to the interactive media user," in A.N. Valdivia (ed.), *A Companion to Media Studies*, Oxford: Blackwell, 337–59.

Lundby, K. (ed.) (2009) *Mediatization, Concept, Changes, Consequences*, Oxford: Peter Lang.

Lynch, G. (2005) *Understanding Theology and Popular Culture*, Oxford: Blackwell.

Lynch, G., J. Mitchell, and A. Strhan (eds) (2012) *Religion, Media and Culture: A Reader*, London: Routledge.

Lynch, J. (2008) *Debates in Peace Journalism*, Sydney: Sydney University Press.

McLuhan, M. (1962) *The Gutenberg Galaxy: The Making of Typographic Man*, Toronto, ONT: University of Toronto Press.

——(1994 [1964]) *Understanding Media: The Extensions of Man*, Cambridge, MA: MIT Press.

Marr, A. (2004) *My Trade: A Short History of British Journalism*, London: Macmillan.

Marrin, A. (1974) *The Last Crusade: The Church of England in the First World War*, Durham, NC: Duke University Press.

Martin, R. (2003) *The Destruction of Guernica, and the Masterpiece that Changed the World*, London: Plume, Penguin Books.

Maslog, C. (ed.) (1994) *Communication, Values and Society*, Quezon City, Philippines: New Day Publishers.

Miller, T. (ed.) (2006 [2001]) *A Companion to Cultural Studies*, Oxford: Blackwell.

Minchom, M. (2012) "The truth about Guernica: Picasso and the lying press," *The Volunteer* (March 9). Online. Available: www.albavolunteer.org/2012/03/the-truth-about-guernica-picasso-and-the-lying-press (accessed 7 January 2013).

Mitchell, J. (2007) *Media Violence and Christian Ethics*, Cambridge: Cambridge University Press.

——(2012) *Promoting Peace, Inciting Violence: The Role of Religion and Media*, London: Routledge.

Mitchell, J. and O. Gower (eds) (2012) *Religion and the News*, Farnham, Surrey: Ashgate.

Moore, K., P. Mason, and J. Lewis (2008) *Images of Islam in the UK: The Representation of British Muslims in the National Print News Media 2000–2008*, Cardiff: Cardiff University and Channel 4.

Nussbaum, M. (1986) *The Fragility of Goodness: Luck and Ethics in Greek Tragedy and Philosophy*, New York: Cambridge University Press.

——(1990) *Love's Knowledge: Essays on Philosophy and Literature*, New York: Oxford University Press.

Ong, W. (1982) *Orality and Literacy: The Technologizing of the Word*, London: Methuen.

Patterson, I. (2007) *Guernica and Total War*, London: Profile Books.

Postman, N. (1985) *Amusing Ourselves to Death*, London: Penguin.

Rankin, N. (2003) *Telegram from Guernica: The Extraordinary Life of George Steer, War Correspondent*, London: Faber and Faber.

Rothenbuhler, E. and M. Coman (eds) (2004) *Media Anthropology*, London: Sage.

Rushdie, S. (1990) *Haroun and the Sea of Stories*, London: Granta.

Schlesinger, P. (1992) *Putting "Reality" Together*, 2nd edn, London: Routledge.

Silk, M. (1998) *Unsecular Media: Making News of Religion in America*, Urbana, IL: University of Illinois Press.

Stout, J. (2004) *Democracy and Tradition*, Princeton, NJ: Princeton University Press.

Tanner, K. (1997) *Theories of Culture: A New Agenda for Theology*, Minneapolis: Augsburg Fortress.

Tumber, H. (ed.) (1999) *News: A Reader*, Oxford: Oxford University Press.

Tumber, H. and F. Webster (2006) *Journalists Under Fire: Information War and Journalistic Practices*, London: Sage.

Wiggershaus, R. (1993) *The Frankfurt School*, trans. Michael Robertson, Cambridge: Polity Press.

Wilkinson, A. (1996 [1978]) *The Church of England and the First World War*, London: SCM.

Williams, R. (1958) "Culture is Ordinary," in N. McKenzie (ed.), *Convictions*, London: MacGibbon and Kee, 74–92.

Winston, D. (ed.) (2012) *The Oxford Handbook on Religion and the American News Media*, Oxford: Oxford University Press.

——(forthcoming) *Heartland Religion: The American News Media and the Reagan Revolution*, Oxford: Oxford University Press.

5
FILM

John C. Lyden

Interactions between religions and film

The study of religion and film is still being developed, and yet this subfield probably has the longest history of any of the mediated encounters with religion discussed in this volume. The most obvious reason for this is that film has been around longer than most modern media (excepting print, and recorded music). In addition, the development of all other video-based technologies such as television, Internet, and computer videogames is premised on the medium of film as their predecessor and progenitor. As silent and then sound cinema developed, people learned the vocabulary of film, how to watch and understand the way it constructs narrative via image, sound, and editing; they then adapted this understanding to their viewing and consumption of newer visual technologies which employ similar narrative strategies. The development of these more recent media also makes it increasingly difficult to distinguish "film" as a medium from the others, as people watch films not only in theaters but on their home DVD players, on phones and other portable devices, and stream them via Internet services such as Netflix.

As with so many other forms of popular culture, religions have had an ambivalent attitude to film from its beginnings. Although there were violent condemnations of film and attempts to censor it from the start, it would be wrong to see this as the only way in which religions responded to film. As early as 1911, Congregational minister Herbert Jump was hailing "The Religious Possibilities of the Motion Picture," encouraging the use of the new medium by churches as a tool for evangelism, as it could convey the biblical stories visually and hence with emotion and accessibility (reprinted in Lindvall 2001: 54–77). The fact that the stories could be represented visually also meant religious leaders and educators could make a claim to verisimilitude; indeed, children might believe that a biblically recounted miracle was "true" simply because they had seen it enacted in a film, entirely missing the fact that the film was not the original but a made object (Lindvall 2007a: 129). The tendency to attempt direct representation of the sacred—and hence claim reality for it—is not confined to Western cinema, as Sheila Nayar (2012) has made clear in her recent study of how orality (and hence visual narrative) informs Hindu cinema. As she explains, filmed Hindu myths demonstrate their origins in oral rather than literary traditions by showcasing the transcendent in an obvious and accessible way, performing a "cinema of attractions" and abundance that has no qualms about portraying the sacred or the miracles of deities. Religious Hindus go to such films and experience them as religious rituals, even performing devotional acts in the theater. The Hindu experiences *darshan*—seeing and being seen by the deity through his or her image—by encountering the image of a god or goddess. Nayar points out that films have represented religious subjects from the beginning, as does Terry Lindvall (2007b), who has documented the extent to which early Western films also had religious (usually Christian) subjects. Most notably, the Oberammergau Passion Play was allegedly recreated for filming in 1898, and the life of Jesus was dramatized in early films such as *The Life and Passion of Jesus Christ* (1905) and *From the Manger to the Cross* (1912). These films were popular because they connected with religious viewers who could now see biblical stories recreated in a new larger-than-life fashion, even utilizing special effects to highlight their miraculous and transcendent nature.

At the same time, religious groups have feared the movies that could undermine traditional values by depicting immoral characters and storylines without an obvious moral message of judgment. In the USA, religious leaders pressured civic leaders to pass censorship laws, which first appeared in Chicago in 1907 and spread from there to other cities. In 1915, the US Supreme Court sided with the censors in their opinion that free speech was not guaranteed to the movies as "they may be used for evil" (*Mutual Film Corporation* 1915: 238; see also Quicke 2009). Scandals featuring Hollywood celebrities led to more calls to regulate the morality of the film industry, resulting in the formation of the Motion Picture Producers and Distributors of America (MPPDA) led by former Postmaster General Will Hays, who was to develop a series of principles governing film censorship. With the help of Protestant and Roman Catholic church leaders, he ultimately convinced the film industry to accept a system of self-regulation according to a series of rules known as the Production Code, or the "Hays Office Code" (Quicke 2009: 33–35; see also Romanowski 2012). The Production Code Administration (PCA) was overseen through much of its history by Joseph Breen, a devout Roman Catholic and anti-Semite who undertook a personal mission to combat what he perceived as an immoral "Jewish" influence on Hollywood. His work dovetailed with that of the newly formed "Legion of Decency," a Roman Catholic watchdog group that had its own criteria for censorship, and which created for Catholics its own list of acceptable and unacceptable films. Members of Catholic churches were required to sign a pledge that included a condemnation of "salacious motion pictures" that portrayed as acceptable criminal behavior and sexual impropriety, and a promise to "remain away from all motion pictures except those which do not offend decency and Christian morality" (Quicke 2009: 36).

For a variety of reasons, however, this era of censorship could not last: the Roman Catholics who controlled the process ignored Protestant opinions (as when the Legion of Decency condemned the 1953 film *Martin Luther*, which had been financed by Protestant groups); the US Supreme Court reversed its 1915 decision by upholding the right of free speech for motion pictures in decisions in 1948 and 1952; and perhaps most importantly, the criteria used by the censors were found to be subjective and constantly changing (Quicke 2009: 32–51). Modern Roman Catholic writers on film, such as Sister Rose Pacatte and Father Peter Malone, have found earlier Catholic condemnations of films to be arbitrary and sweeping in their inability to see the whole picture (often literally the case: censors did not always watch the films they condemned). These censors often failed to understand the filmic context for the allegedly objectionable images, and so missed the larger salutary messages present in the films. Pacatte (2007: 261–86) and Malone (2009: 52–71) also recognize that judgment remains a subjective matter, as what is salutary for one viewer may not be so for another. Controversies continue around films such as *Life of Brian* (1979), *The Last Temptation of Christ* (1988), *Priest* (1995), and *Brokeback Mountain* (2005).

This ambivalence toward film on the part of religion illustrates well the dynamic nature of the relationship between them. It is impossible to summarize the relationship as one of either total hostility or cooperation, although there have been times in the history of their interactions in which one or the other of these predominates. This ambivalence is further complicated by the fact that it is difficult to define when a film should be considered "religious" and when it should not. Films with obvious religious content such as the *Ramayana* or the life of Jesus may seem easy cases to judge, unless the depiction is judged "blasphemous" by religious authorities. Films have also been understood to have religious dimensions or ramifications to them even when viewers are reluctant to see them. After studying comments from British filmgoers about how they understand their viewing experiences, Clive Marsh concludes that "resistance to social control and to didacticism are so strong in Western societies that viewers are sometimes reluctant to own up to what cinema-going actually does to and for them" (Marsh 2007a: 153). Marsh (2007b, 2004) and others have argued that films can affect viewers in ways analogous to religion, even when this is not recognized by viewers (for example, see Lyden 2003). Those who are attentive to the religious content of popular culture may be more likely to view the experience of watching a movie as "spiritual" or "transformative," as when Robert Johnston, Craig Detweiler, Greg Garrett, or even Roger Ebert speak of particular film viewings as times when they encountered God or a spiritual content (Johnston 2009: 320). This demonstrates the difficulties that are inherent in trying to neatly divide "religion" from "culture" (as I noted above in Chapter 1); we cannot really define where one stops and the other begins.

Skeptics might hold that these viewers are simply seeing what they wish to see, as they were already predisposed to find religious content in films due to their own pre-existing belief structures. But the truth is that we all encounter any aspect of culture or religion with pre-existing beliefs, and in the interaction of our own views with this new content we construct meaning, which may be expressed in religious language. Gordon Lynch has noted that the increasing focus on subjective experience in modern culture is not so much a turn from religious to secular forms of experience, but rather a tendency which allows individuals to construct meaning in their own terms and often in private ways. Just as the new development of mass-produced novels in the eighteenth century led to a "cult of sensibility" which celebrated "the active cultivation of a rich inner life," so film has taken on the analogous role in contemporary society of supplying a forum for reflection on issues of values and character (Lynch 2007: 115–16, 119–20). If we understand the encounter with popular culture as one that both affectively and cognitively engages us in reflection on our lives as individuals and in community, it is not far-fetched to see this engagement as part of a search for meaning and purpose that has religious dimensions to it.

It is also worth pointing out that the complex relationship between film and religion is not limited to the encounter between Western Christianity and Hollywood movies, in the history of censorship, rapprochement, and overlap referenced above. The issues related to the representation of religion vary, depending on the cultures and the religions in question. All religions face the possibility of misrepresentation by outsiders, and in many cultures, religious or political conservatives have sought with varying degrees of success to police filmic content. Movies made in predominantly Muslim countries such as Iran have to deal with state censors, while on the other hand, the representation of Islam in Western films continues to be distorted by stereotypical images and political motivations (Hussain 2009; Ramji 2005). Jews have been the victims of stereotypical representation, most famously in Nazi propaganda films like *The Eternal Jew* (1940), but anti-Semitism also finds expression in US films, in spite of the purported influence of Jews on Hollywood (Wright 2009). The industry of Indian-made "Bollywood" films demonstrates the long and complicated relationship between Hinduism, Islam, and popular film in Indian culture and society, including a diversity of filmed versions of Hindu myths, films used as forms for ritual devotion, and films which express a secular ideology of religious pluralism and tolerance (Nayar 2012; Dwyer 2009, 2006). Buddhists have made films that demonstrate Buddhist ideals such as emptiness or the equation of nirvana with *samsara*, and have not had to wrestle with misrepresentation or censorship as much as many other religions (Cho 2009, 2003, 1999). On the other hand, new religions are almost always represented as violent "cults" involving demonic activities and brainwashing, expressing their rejection by the dominant culture (Thomas 2009).

Scholarship on religion and film has been enriched by the development of this global perspective, which has enabled researchers to look at the variety of films produced in different religious and cultural contexts and how they interact with them (e.g., Mitchell and Plate 2007; Plate 2003). At the same time, there has been greater understanding of how film technique informs the medium and the transmission of its messages, as well as more awareness of the variety of genres including both popular and "art house" films. There have also been calls to develop a cultural studies approach to religion and film (Wright 2006; Miles 1996), although this request remains largely unfulfilled. Gordon Lynch (2009: 287), a strong proponent of this method, has noted that there exists no "detailed, rigorous, and systematic analysis of an individual film across all the stages of the circuit" of culture. Although I will not attempt to remedy that deficit here, I will outline some ways in which the study of religion and film could benefit from attention to what cultural studies has called the "circuit of culture," noting in particular how the elements of this circuit and their interaction contribute to how religion and film interact and overlap. I will then briefly consider two rather different films and how the circuit of culture relates to each, in order to draw some conclusions about the connections between film and religion within popular culture.

The circuit of culture

In 1986, Richard Johnson of the Birmingham Centre for Contemporary Cultural Studies proposed the notion of the "circuit of culture" as involving a consideration of the processes by which cultural artifacts are produced and consumed by cultures. In particular, he noted that attention to the production process, the artifacts produced, the ways in which those artifacts are used, and the wider social structures related to them would all be important to a thorough understanding of a cultural artifact or text (Lynch 2009: 281). For the purposes of this chapter and in relation to religion and film, I will define the circuit of culture as involving four elements:

1 the process of creating and producing the film;
2 the marketing and distribution of the film;
3 the film itself, as an object that can be viewed and studied as a "text";
4 reception of the film by audiences, which includes fan reaction and fan culture.

How might attention to these elements help us to better understand religion and film in their interaction?

First, an examination of how the film is produced involves inquiring about the *auteurs* of the film, what their authorial intentions were, and how they hoped to realize them. They might intend to adapt a religious text to film, as when filmmakers seek to represent the Gospels or a modern religious novel like *Ben Hur*. They may start with an apparently secular subject, but invest it with religious overtones through the way in which the film is shot or edited (as when Francis Ford Coppola chose to intercut a baptism with several simultaneous murders toward the end of *The Godfather*, suggesting contrasts and connections between the two). There is also the question of how the adaptation of the text is done, or (alternatively) how an original screenplay is developed, and what decisions are made about the story, shot construction, lighting, sets, music, editing, and other production and post-production details. This involves not only the vision of the various participants in the filmmaking process (screenwriters, director, cinematographer, editors, musical soundtrack composer, etc.) but also considerations about cost, dictates from the studio, decisions by ratings board/censors, and others. In these ways, the filmmakers respond to the political and social context of their times and places, and their decisions are affected by the moral, religious, and political climate of their societies.

Second, the marketing and distribution of the film will be most affected by how much money the studio and/or the filmmakers have, and how much they are willing to put into advertising the film and making it available in theaters. Some theater chains may also be resistant to giving over screens to religious films, making them harder to see for those who are interested. But distribution of films today occurs increasingly through DVDs and online streaming video services, offering other paths for films that might otherwise have difficulty reaching a target market due to limited budgets. Films with very particular audiences (including those with specific religious preferences and sensibilities) can be seen by those audiences without the expense of theater bookings or (as was the case until recently) by stocking the shelves of video rental stores, simply by being made available through streaming systems like Netflix. In this way, distribution has become less of an obstacle for films with smaller audiences, as newer technologies have made these films more accessible. At the same time, marketing is often tied to associated products such as music, books, toys, and games that are related to the film; a film may even be created from what was first a toy, such as *Transformers* (2007). Filmmakers make money from these tie-ins just as they do from theatrical release and DVD sales and rentals, so that there is an incentive to market these as well, often before the film is even released; they can also lead to higher box office sales.

Third, looking at the film as a "text" that can be studied may seem to reference earlier approaches within religion and film studies that reduced the film to a visual novel, and analyzed the story for its religious content. But this approach has been largely superseded by newer methods that pay much more attention to film technique and how it informs the content of a film. In short, it is now increasingly recognized that film as a medium and an art form differs from literary forms due to its unique combination of visual and aural elements, structured according to the conventions of filmmaking with its distinctive vocabulary and forms. Studying the art of the film, however, still implies that there is a film to be studied, and this is worth remembering. The increasing focus on audience reception rightly points to the fact that the content of a film only exists in relation to viewers and what they find in the film, which may vary considerably from person to person. There is no content of a film that can be understood except through a particular interpretation, but this does not imply that there is no film that exists outside of the viewers. There is an actual product with particular sounds and images, viewed in a particular setting, which forms the basis for the various subjective interpretations of the viewers; they are not simply imagining their own stories in front of a blank screen, but responding to something which can therefore be analyzed and discussed. Even though two viewers may disagree about a film like *The Passion of the Christ* (2004), they did experience the *same* physical film; on the other hand, if one of them went into the wrong theater and mistakenly saw *Shrek 2* (2004) instead, their conversation would be rather different, and at some point they would realize that they had *not* seen the same film. For this reason, we cannot discard analysis of the filmic content, even though we must always be aware of the fact that this content can only be accessed in relation to the other aspects of the circuit of culture.

Finally, the reception of the film includes the diversity of audience reactions to it, but this aspect also includes fan culture and all the ways in which viewers of a film interact with it both before and after their viewing of it. As just one example of this, fans of a particular film may choose to have a "theme" wedding or bar/bat mitzvah, adopting the costumes and style of the *Matrix* films, or *Star Trek*, or *Titanic*, or *The Terminator*—ritually mimicking the characters and themes of the film in order to become part of that world for the duration of the event (Plate 2008: 80–82). It is not exactly clear why a young man would want to dress as the Terminator for his bar mitzvah, given the fact that there is no obvious relationship between the film and the Jewish ceremony for initiation into adulthood; but it appears that this sort of ritual performance has meaning for the participants in that they are allowed to play at being part of their favorite movie world, and so to leave their ordinary existence and become an admired fictional character.[1] Some may balk at reading too much into these playful events, but those who construct these rituals have invested considerable time and money into these recreations, suggesting that movies have an "afterlife" in our culture that transcends their viewing. Not only do fans dress as characters in a film and adopt their *personae*, but they also create their own art, stories, games, and toys based on the world of that film in order to bring its reality into other realms of their lives. At that point, it is clearly not "just a movie" viewed briefly for entertainment purposes—it has become the basis for meaning-making activities, and hence, could legitimately be termed "religious."

Star Wars fandom, in particular, seems to demonstrate how reception of a film can far transcend the original as it evolves into something resembling a religion. Three hundred ninety thousand people in England and Wales identified their religion as "Jedi" in a 2001 census (BBC News 2003); whether this was in some cases intended as a protest or a joke, at the very least this still signifies a conscious effort to defer to popular culture rather than traditional religions as a source of identity and meaning-making.[2] But this "religion" is not one which blindly accepts the "canon" or texts created by the *auteur*, in this case George Lucas; as I have argued elsewhere (Lyden 2012), the very fact that fans are so devoted to the films has led them into conflict with the filmmaker, arguing that they understand the "original" films better than he does. As Lucas has continually revised the original trilogy, fans believe that what they first experienced in the theater were the "actual" films, and that Lucas has changed the texts in what amounts to a heretical fashion. Fans have therefore re-edited the films in ways they find appropriate, even going so far as to re-cut the often-derided *Star Wars Episode 1: The Phantom Menace* (1999) to eliminate scenes they regard as objectionable (Wryot 2002). The fans have also created an homage somewhat ironically titled *Star Wars Uncut* (Pugh 2009), comprised of edits every 15 seconds between hundreds of fan-made film clips which mimic the scenes of the original film, shot-for-shot; this in particular highlights the ways in which interactive media have developed to the point that fans can create their own films via crowd-sourcing, showing that they are doing much more than simply passively "receiving" the film. This sort of technology allows fans to participate globally in a joint creation that reflects their involvement with the text of the film, but also alters it to bring in their own images and values.[3]

Through the following two brief case studies of two very different films—and their relationships to the circuit of culture—we can more fully appreciate how these four aspects of the circuit of culture interact in the encounters between religion and film. In each case, we can see that the processes by which the film is created, adapted, marketed, and distributed affect how it is seen and understood by viewers, and how the diversity of audience reactions suggests a plurality of communities in modern society that feel free to interpret the religious meanings of the film in a variety of ways. The differences between these two case studies also illuminate not only the differences between communities of filmgoers, but also how communities may exist in a wide variety of relationships with the larger society.

Case study: *The Passion of the Christ* (2004)

One might argue that too much has already been written and said about Mel Gibson's contentious film, but it does provide an illuminating example of how all the stages of the circuit of culture relate to the production and reception of a popular religious film.

Producing the film

When Gibson began making the film, he let it be known that he intended to make a faithful version of the biblical story of Jesus, which he regarded as historically accurate. In March 2003, Gibson stated that "we've done the research. I'm telling the story as the Bible tells it. I think the story, as it really happened, speaks for itself. The Gospel is a complete script, and that's what we're filming" (Silk 2004: 10). From a scholarly point of view, however, this is a simplification; there are multiple differences between the Gospel accounts, and conflicts between these and historical information gained from other sources (Fredriksen 2003). More significantly, Gibson drew freely on the visions of a nineteenth-century Roman Catholic nun, Anne Catherine Emmerich (1774–1824), who "saw" a variety of scenes not in the New Testament, such as the Jewish high priest Caiaphas ordering the cross to be built in the courtyard of the Temple on the night of Jesus's arrest, and Caiaphas bribing Jews to pressure Pontius Pilate to have Jesus killed (Fredriksen 2004). Although not all these elements appeared in the final version of the film, it does appear that many of the anti-Jewish elements found in it can be traced to Emmerich's visions rather than the biblical text. Even before the film was released, therefore, there was a dispute about what texts formed its basis, setting the tone for much of the controversy to follow. Gibson continued to maintain that the film was faithful to the Bible, and his supporters (especially conservative Protestant Evangelicals) believed the same. Biblical scholars who analyzed the script, on the other hand, clearly saw the elements that were non-biblical, and felt compelled to point these out.

Complicating matters further was the fact that the biblical scholars who first saw the script were connected with the US Conference of Catholic Bishops (USCCB) and the Anti-Defamation League (ADL), both of which are concerned generally about anti-Jewish elements in retellings of the death of Jesus. In the case of the USCCB, this can be traced to the Second Vatican Council (1962–65) and its efforts to improve relations between Jews and Christians. In large part, this effort took shape when the Council approved *Nostra Aetate*, a document that rejected the idea that all Jews (in any period of history) are to be held responsible as a group for the death of Jesus. Throughout history, re-enactments of the death of Jesus have often exaggerated the roles of Jewish leaders in his death beyond what is found both in scripture and in historical evidence. The Council sought to remedy this by examining presentations of the events, and making recommendations that all such presentations be purged of anti-Jewish elements, that is, that they be made more faithful to both the Bible and to history, in the process seeking to eliminate the tendency of such retellings to incite prejudice and violence against Jews (Paul VI, Pope 1965). In the wake of the Holocaust, this seemed particularly important, and by the 1960s many Christian leaders were recognizing the complicity of Christians in violence against Jews throughout history. Roman Catholic bishops have continued to develop guidelines for evaluating dramatizations of the death of Jesus (Bishops' Committee for Ecumenical and Interreligious Affairs 1988).

There was, therefore, already some disagreement about what constituted the "text" of the film even before it was released, and whether it was biblically and/or historically accurate. Although it has been stated that Gibson removed many of the offending elements, evidence still remains in the final product that they were not purged, and the debates continued between those who defended it as "biblical" (and therefore "historically true") and those who held that it was a distortion of both the biblical texts and history. On the side of the former were the unlikely partners of Protestant fundamentalists and conservative Roman Catholics, especially "traditionalist" Catholics who do not accept the decisions of the Second Vatican Council. This group of Catholics argues that there has been no legitimate Pope since Vatican II, leaving the papacy "vacant" (sedevacantism), and the efforts of the Council with regard to interreligious dialogue (including dialogue with Jews) are viewed as flawed and a betrayal of the essence of Catholicism. Mel Gibson's father, Hutton Gibson, has expressed these views, in addition to numerous anti-Jewish statements, including a denial of the Holocaust (Flannery-Dailey 2004: 13). Mel Gibson frequently stated that he did not agree with all of his father's views, but he is associated with the same group of Catholics that has rejected Vatican II, and he has been quoted as saying that the Vatican is a "wolf in sheep's clothing" (Silk 2004: 8). His own anti-Jewish views were later revealed when he was arrested while intoxicated and stated (among other things) that "the Jews are responsible for all the wars in the world" (CNN.com 2006). If the "text" of the film is indeed shaped by a group of Catholics who have repudiated the Pope and Vatican II (including its efforts to ameliorate anti-Semitism), it would seem that they do not represent most Christians, and yet the conservative Protestant population of the USA overwhelmingly supported the film as biblical, seemingly unaware of Gibson's sectarian brand of Catholicism and its effect on the screenplay.

Marketing and distribution

When the scholars who examined the script therefore found it anti-Jewish, unbiblical, and unhistorical, the reaction from Gibson's company was harsh. It was alleged that the scholars had stolen the script, and were seeking to discredit a film that was simply trying to tell the "true" story of the Bible. The USCCB apologized; the ADL and the scholars involved did not (Silk 2004: 16; Fredriksen 2003). Gibson's production company, Icon, then set out to make the most of the controversy by utilizing conservative press to support Gibson's contention that he was being attacked by those who did not want the true story of the Bible to be told (Silk 2004). The company also utilized a technique for marketing religious films that had been used since the early twentieth century, "segmentation," whereby a particular market for the film (in this case, conservative Christians) is identified and methods are used to reach them. In the case of *The Passion of the Christ*, Icon hired A. Larry Ross, head of a Christian firm that had successfully marketed to Evangelical Christians both *The Prince of Egypt* (1998) and *Jonah: A Veggie Tales Movie* (2002). Methods included private screenings to religious groups, combined with opportunities to purchase blocks of advance tickets, including "four-walling," in which churches bought out entire theaters; materials distributed to churches, including bulletin inserts and study guides; marketing tie-in products such as small crosses, books, and music; and Internet sites that specifically urged visitors to show the movie trailer to their congregations and promote it to Christian friends (Maresco 2004). US Roman Catholics and conservative Protestant groups were specifically targeted; both were likely to respond to the idea that Christian messages have been marginalized in Hollywood, and here was an effort to make them central again. In this context, Gibson was able to present himself as a rebel and Hollywood "outsider," somewhat ironically since he had starred in numerous Hollywood blockbuster movies, and was therefore well-positioned to finance the major marketing of the film. The marketing proved successful; the film generated US box office receipts in excess of $370 million, coming in as the number three film for that year (Box Office Mojo n.d.).

The film itself

As noted above, considered as part of the circuit of culture, there is no uninterpreted film; therefore, any discussion of the "film *qua* film" and the elements within it will from the outset be connected to how audiences perceive the film. This is certainly the case for *The Passion of the Christ*.

After the film's release, the background controversy regarding its anti-Semitism played a role in how it was received; conservative audiences predictably discounted it, while more liberal audiences showed greater concern. In addition, the extensive violence in the film created considerable controversy along the same lines; conservative audiences—and Gibson himself—defended this as necessary, to show the extent of Jesus's suffering for humanity in order to provoke a response of faith, while liberals saw the violence as horrific and unnecessary, particularly for children taken by their conservative Christian parents to see the film (Thistlethwaite 2006: 144). The debate extended to the theological significance of the death of Jesus, and how this should be understood; it has been argued that a focus on the "necessity" of Jesus's suffering and death to save the world may support violence rather than critique it, in that some Christian doctrines of atonement effectively sanction the child abuse of the Son by the Father and so, by extension, support similar violence among humans (Denton-Borhaug 2005). We cannot here fully engage the larger Christian theological debate about how the death of Jesus should be understood, and in what sense it is said to "save" humanity, but such theological differences certainly informed the various ways in which viewers perceived Gibson's film and its use of excessive violence.[4]

Another aspect of the film that was noticed by a much smaller group is Gibson's use of medieval and renaissance Christian art to inform the film's cinematography. This suggests a lack of historicity, particularly if the film's images suggest these later works of art rather than an accurate historical reconstruction of the first century. Nonetheless, the film's artistry *qua* film is clearly shown in its use of such images, and analysis of them yields interesting connections for those willing to look for them (Apostolos-Cappadona 2004).

Audience reception

As the previous analysis shows, it is impossible to separate the aspects of the circuit of culture in that they tend to overlap; the production of the film already implies questions about the text of the film and its interpretation, as well as about its marketing, and audience response is also to be considered throughout all these stages.

The diverse reactions to *The Passion of the Christ* testify to the stark differences between theological liberals and conservatives in the USA and elsewhere, as well as to the role played by target marketing. People generally saw what they wanted to see in the film, so that the question of whether the film was faithful to the biblical texts could not even be properly addressed by most; audiences were predisposed to answer this question in a certain way, depending on how they saw Mel Gibson, the Bible, their own religious traditions, Hollywood, and the larger society (Woods *et al.* 2004). In 2004 when the film came out, the USA was embroiled in heated partisan politics with regard to the Iraq War, and the presidential election campaign was at its height. It would be impossible to isolate discussion of the film and its religious impact from these other factors that created the context for its reception; conservatives and liberals saw themselves as involved in a battle for America, and this was one of the contested cultural texts of the time.

As of this writing, there were over 2,700 reviews on the Internet Movie Database (imdb.com), most of them from 2004. These run the gamut from those who found it "an extremely moving, emotional experience" to those who suggest "there is no justification for the pervasive level of violence in this film" which "beats you to death with its opinions and plastic message." The online debate focused primarily on the extent of the violent imagery, and whether it was necessary theologically or artistically, but there was also considerable discussion of whether the film was anti-Semitic (Internet Movie Database 2004). Predictably, the arguments mirror those that had already appeared in the press between theological conservatives and liberals, raising questions about the extent to which audience reaction was shaped even before the release of the film by the controversy related to it. Was there anyone who saw this film without having heard a great deal about it already, and perhaps having already made up her mind about it ahead of time? Do our own religious sensibilities predetermine how we view a film, shaped as we are by the communities with which we identify and the values by which we define ourselves? Could it be otherwise? The reactions to this film suggest that identities defined by society have a tremendous role in how we see the religious content of film. A film that is less well known, however, or less controversial religiously may inspire a range of reactions that are not necessarily connected as neatly with religious identity. The case of *The Passion of the Christ* may be unique, but it exemplifies how the religious and political tensions of a society can be effectively demonstrated in the reception of a major popular film. At the very least, the strong ways in which people reacted to this film suggest that such a culturally charged product can hardly be viewed as "just a movie," and an analysis of it can shed much light on the religious and cultural dynamics of societies.

Case study: *Blue Like Jazz* (2012)

The film *Blue Like Jazz* demonstrates an entirely different sort of "religious" film from Gibson's blockbuster, and is more closely related to a smaller industry of low-budget Christian films that have developed in the decade since *The Passion of the Christ*. These films also utilize market segmentation, but without most of the hype and controversy of the higher profile *Passion*.

One particularly successful team of low budget Christian filmmakers is Alex and Stephen Kendrick, two brothers who were ministers at Sherwood Baptist Church in Albany, Georgia. In 2003, they founded Sherwood Pictures and produced their first feature film, *Flywheel*. It cost only $20,000 to make, and told the simple story of how a dishonest car salesman finds Christ and undergoes moral and spiritual renewal. The film became popular with Evangelical Christians, especially through DVD sales. Three years later, the Kendrick brothers made *Facing the Giants* (2006), which cost $100,000 but made $10 million at the box office and $20 million in DVD sales. In 2008, they produced *Fireproof*, which cost $500,000 but made $60 million from box office and DVD sales combined (Parker 2012: 7). They went on to make the similarly successful *Courageous* in 2011. All of these films told stories of moral and religious conversion in contemporary settings, and all were immensely popular with conservative Christian audiences. Thanks to DVD rental services such as RedBox, the films were available nationwide, proving how a film could achieve significant distribution even when its theatrical release is limited.

Films such as these, made by and marketed to target audiences of Christians, have often flown under the popular culture radar due to their smaller budgets and distribution. Recently, scholars such as Terry Lindvall (2007b), Andrew Quicke (with Lindvall 2011), and Ryan Parker (2012) have brought more attention to this industry and its distinctive methods of production and marketing. Although Mel Gibson may have claimed to represent a non-Hollywood Christian film industry, the Kendrick brothers and others like them working with small budgets can more authentically make a claim in this regard, genuinely operating as they do outside the normal channels and markets.

Blue Like Jazz was also a low budget, independently produced Christian film, but it differs in a number of ways from films like those of the Kendrick brothers, and so demonstrates another unique cultural niche in American religion.

Producing the film

The film *Blue Like Jazz* was produced on a small budget for a distinctive religious market but, if anything, its market was even narrower than that of films targeted at traditional Evangelicals. Donald Miller's 2003 book, *Blue Like Jazz*, is an autobiographical memoir about his own experiences in college as a young man developing his religious views. The book became a bestseller, perhaps because of Miller's ability to combine fairly traditional Christian ideas with a healthy dose of self-criticism and self-effacing humor. Miller objects to the identification of Christianity with Republican (or any) political causes, and he rejects the judgmental, narrow self-righteousness he has often seen evidenced by Christians (Miller 2003: 131–32). As such, the book did not appeal to traditional Christian conservatives so much as to those who might identify with the Emerging Church movement, which is seen as dedicated to open conversation on issues of faith and morality, seeking for the truth rather than claiming to have all the answers, and avoiding traditional labels such as "conservative" or "liberal" (see e.g., McLaren 2004: 313–26).

Miller was first approached by a large studio that wanted complete control of turning the book into a film, but he rejected this offer in order to have more input in the adaptation. He met director Steve Taylor, who had already made *The Second Chance* (2006), an offbeat Christian film about a suburban minister who discovers the importance of urban ministry to disadvantaged members of society. Unlike most of the independent Christian films being made by Evangelicals like the Kendrick brothers, Taylor's film was more about the relationship of Christianity to the larger society and less about individual conversion. As such, he was a perfect partner for Miller, and they began work on the screenplay with writer Ben Pearson. Pearson and Taylor convinced Miller that in order to adapt his book of essays into a film, they needed to fictionalize certain aspects of his story to create an intelligible and effective narrative (Bluelikejazzthemovie.com 2012).

Marketing and publicity

The publicity for the film, meager as it was, was linked to the story of how the film was funded. In September 2010, without sufficient funds to make the film, the film-makers announced that they were putting the project on hold, at which point two fans of the book (Zach Prichard and Jonathan Frazier) started a Web site (Save BlueLikeJazz.com) with the goal of raising $125,000 in 30 days in order to keep the movie afloat. Utilizing Kickstarter—an online fundraising platform designed to help with the financing of independent films—they received donations totaling over $345,000 from 4,500 contributors, making it the biggest film project funded by crowd-sourcing in movie history, with an average contribution of $75 (Pattison 2010). Another backer matched the contributions obtained through Kickstarter, leaving the filmmakers with enough post-production funds to supplement the cost of marketing and distributing the film. The Internet buzz generated by the crowd-sourced funding also contributed to the film's grassroots support and publicity. A promotional bus tour followed, as did promotion from Relevant (a Christian culture media outlet), Catalyst (a Christian leadership organization), and the international aid organization, World Vision (Smith 2012). The unlikeliest of projects became a movie because a small group of people was dedicated enough to the distinctive vision of the book that they were willing individually to fund it; every contributor is listed in the credits.

The film itself

The film differs from the book in a number of respects, although all changes were made with Miller's complete support. As noted above, it was deemed necessary to create a partly fictional story for dramatic purposes and to give some shape to the film. Miller's true story of his own life, related in his book, details how he attended Reed College as a part-time student already living in Portland, Oregon, and how he became involved in a Christian group at this very secular college, ultimately embracing a much more open and socially active form of Christianity than the conservative type of Christianity he had previously experienced.

In the movie, there is considerably more dramatic tension generated by fictiona-lized events in the screenplay. Don rebels against his religious background when he realizes that his mother is having an affair with a married youth minister at his church. Struck by this hypocrisy, he chooses Reed College over the local conservative Christian college, after his father tells him that he secretly sent his son's application to Reed; not only has he been accepted, but his tuition has been paid. Don then gets in his car and drives from his home state of Texas all the way to Oregon, leaving his mother behind. The story of the film continues at Reed, as a naïve Don encounters the liberal and secular environment of Reed College, which includes student experimentation with drugs and sex. He covers up his Christian background and adopts an anti-Christian persona in an effort to fit in, and to distance himself from his past. With a militantly anti-religious friend who lampoons Christianity by always dressing as the Pope, he engages in anti-Christian acts such as placing a huge condom on a church steeple along with the message, "don't let these people reproduce." His friend Jenny turns out to be a Christian who belongs to that church, and she challenges his angry act; but when Don finds out his mother is pregnant by the youth minister, he only becomes angrier. Finally, at the Renn Fayre festival (an actual event at Reed College, involving much partying and alcohol) he becomes intoxicated and is elected the new "Pope" to replace his friend in that satirical role for the next year.

At this point in the film, however, Don realizes that his anger has been unfair to Christians like Jenny who are loving and forgiving, and that he has been hypocritical and judgmental, pretending to be morally righteous when he is not. At Renn Fayre, where he is expected as Pope to hear "confessions" from fellow students, he decides instead to confess to his friend (the former "Pope") his own hypocrisy and the sinfulness of all Christians. He also deduces that his friend's hatred of Christianity is due to his being sexually abused by a priest as a child, and tells him that he is sorry for that as well. His friend accepts his repentance as genuine, and offers Don the forgiveness he has requested.

Most of this plot is fictional. In reality, Don had not seen his father since he was a child, and his mother did not have an affair that precipitated his exodus from Texas or his questioning of Christianity. He was always involved with a Christian group at Reed, even though he sometimes questioned his own faith and beliefs, and the group was viewed with suspicion and hostility by much of the student body (Miller 2003: 42–43). Don did not have a spontaneous revelation that prompted a self-confession at Renn Fayre; rather, this was a strategy adopted by the Christian students, as they set up a "Confession" booth and then turned the tables by confessing their own sins to the students, rather than the reverse. Miller did find this a powerful and moving experience, but it was not his idea, and it was not spontaneous (Miller 2003: 116–27).

Miller consented to all of these changes in order to adapt the ideas in his book to film; it does preserve the quirky, offbeat, and iconoclastic humor of the book, Miller's honesty and humility, and the basic point that following Christ means recognizing one's own sins and seeking to do better, rather than self-righteously condemning others for their lack of morality. As such, both the book and the film provide some challenge to contemporary Christian culture, and they appealed to a smaller group of Christians more taken with the "Emerging" movement than traditional conservative or liberal Christianity.

Audience reception

Thomas Hibbs, in his review of the film, notes that *Blue Like Jazz* represents an advance on films like those of the Kendrick brothers, which are "flat and predictable, with plots that seem less the result of genuine imaginative vision than they are extended illustrations of Christian preaching." In contrast, the filmmakers of *Blue Like Jazz* know that "Christian art must engage, encompass, and transform rival worldviews and alternate artistic visions." At the same time,

> The film begins with a caricature of the Gospel, moves on to the farcical liberalism of an elite university, and ends by proposing a kind of mediation. The result for the film is the opposite of what Miller had hoped. Instead of reaching a wider audience, the film seems to have reached only a sub-culture of a sub-culture.
>
> (Hibbs 2012)

Eleanor Barkhorn's (2012) review for *The Atlantic* also contrasts *Blue Like Jazz* favorably with the films of the Kendrick brothers, as the latter simply show people "in straightforward moral dilemmas with straightforward biblical solutions," while *Blue* is more "authentic" and "unsanitized" in its portrayal of the struggles of faith. But Barkhorn also believes the film fails to achieve its object as it tries to steer a middle course between standard Hollywood films and standard Christian films, "and in the process loses everyone." It doesn't show a real witness to the distinctiveness of Christianity, but simply offers apologies for its mistakes.

The "sub-sub-culture" to which Hibbs refers might be viewed as the Emerging Christianity movement itself, seeing that it is doubly alienated from the larger culture in its self-distancing from both secular culture and conservative (or even standard forms of liberal) Christianity. Hibbs's critiques of the way in which the film expresses its message may be indicating the marginal status in American society of the audience that liked the film, but this does not in itself discredit the message. Barkhorn similarly believes that the film fails to find an audience in its attempt to present an alternative to standard secular and conservative Christian films, but she may actually be saying that the film fails to speak to mainstream culture, polarized as it is. There is a group that liked the film, and for them, the alternative to standard filmic presentations of religion was appreciated as it spoke to their own attempts to embrace a form of Christianity that differs from the norm.

Responses to the film on imdb.com (Internet Movie Database 2012) are largely from fans of the film who also frequently identify themselves as fans of the book. Most believe that it was well adapted, and that its merit is in presenting a more realistic view of Christianity:

> People talk about loving Jesus while drinking a beer, and not everyone who professes to follow Christ walks about with a pious attitude praying out loud and thumbing their Bibles incessantly. They make mistakes, hurt each other, and even cuss! In other words, it's real.
>
> (Virgil Richardson)

Blue Like Jazz is an honest look at one man's journey of faith. Don Miller doesn't write what traditional Christians want to hear. He shares openly his feelings about others and about God. He speaks with conviction that stirs in oneself the desire to take a better look in the mirror and at one's own heart and motives. It is about faith, compassion, community and giving back to others. It is about loving like Jesus.

(Bev Hayes)

Most Christian films do little more than preach to the choir. *Blue Like Jazz* goes in the opposite direction and holds up a mirror to believers and asks hard questions about how faith is lived out and what kind of effect Christians have on an unbelieving world. The film moved me in ways that I did not expect. It also depicts unbelievers not as projects for Christians to target for conversion, but as people to extend grace toward and to love unconditionally.

(elreyfeo-967-94341)

It represents the Christian message well, but doesn't get so tangled up in delivering a clean and picture-perfect message that it forgets to tell a story that is still true to life. Instead it deals with raw human emotion, which is hardly ever neat and tidy. Don struggles with things that people really struggle with. He has doubts that people like me and you really have; and he has to find his way through the external religion of Christianity to the power of a personal relationship with Christ, just like all believers have had to do. This film is going to create a new kind of discussion about faith, and one that I think is quite necessary.

(Becky Davis)

All of these writers seem to identify with the form of Christianity supported by Miller and Taylor, as a religion that has value based on its realism, honesty, and ability to embrace questioning and struggles with faith. The fact that the story was fabricated did not compromise its "realism" for most of these fans, since they believed it still expressed the genuine ideas of the book; as with *The Passion of the Christ*, we can see that filmgoers will view something as "true" because it resonates with their worldviews, although in the case of *Blue Like Jazz*, the fans know that the literal details have been changed, while fans of *The Passion* often insisted that the story was historically accurate even though it clearly contained details which were not.

Conclusions

Looking at these two case studies, we may be able to draw a few conclusions. There are numerous groups or sub-cultures within a society that may respond religiously to films in very different ways, based on how they define their own religious identities and how they choose to make meaning out of films. The diversity of (e.g.) American society with regard to religion is mirrored in reactions to popular films, and what one "sees" in a film is largely a product of the religious values and self-identifiers one brings to the film. Furthermore, there are numerous sub-cultures in relation to religion, and we cannot suggest one is not legitimate or not a part of "popular culture" simply because it is smaller than others. This means that a film's ability to find an audience is based on targeting the right groups, and this is certainly true when the film relates better religiously to some groups than others. Also, decisions made by filmmakers about how they adapt their sources do affect the finished product, but whether groups find meaning in a film may be largely unrelated to whether the film tried to be faithful to its sources or whether considerable creative license was involved in its adaptation. If the members of a group are predisposed to find meaning in a particular film due to their own religious self-identification and values, that may be a more significant factor in the film reaching that audience than the amount of money spent on its production or marketing.

Popular culture is not monolithic, but made up of multiple groups with various values making meaning in a variety of ways. Film watching, as a part of popular culture, reflects that diversity, allowing a wide range of audiences to respond to a wide variety of products. There is no single religious sensibility or single type of popular culture that is preferred in any society, but this is especially true in a modern individualistic society in which meaning making has become an intensely personal activity. At the same time, this meaning making occurs in community, just as religion always has, as fans create their own online and offline groups and support their own sub-cultures through their activities. We cannot predict all the ways in which people will find meaning in film in the future, as the medium continues to grow and change, but it is a good bet that people will continue to turn to moving images, joined to sound, story, and characters, as they search for meaning.

Notes

1 Debates about the extravagance of bar and bat mitzvahs continue, and these are often linked to the incorporation of popular culture references; e.g., Sam Horowitz's Las Vegas-type "showgirl" number (Elixir Entertainment 2012), which resulted in critique by Rabbi David Wolpe (2013a), a defense by Horowitz's own Rabbi Gershon (2013), and subsequent apology by Wolpe (2013b).
2 This is particularly evident given that "Jedi" was not one of the provided options, and therefore required an effort and an independent choice on the part of the respondents. To supplement this religious self-identification, Star Wars fans have also created a holiday: "Star Wars Day," which is celebrated on May 4—as in "May the fourth … be with you" (see Rosen 2012).
3 In 2010, Star Wars Uncut won an Emmy Award in the category of "interactive media" (Stelter 2010). As of this writing, clips for The Empire Strikes Back have been collected and are in the process of being edited for release (see Pugh 2012).
4 It does seem to be the case that conservative Christians can often accept a high level of violence in a film that appears to support their own theologies (King 2004: 155–57).

Works cited

Apostolos-Cappadona, D. (2004) "On seeing The Passion: is there a painting in this film? or is this film a painting?," in S.B. Plate (ed.), Re-Viewing The Passion: Mel Gibson's Film and Its Critics, New York: Palgrave Press.

Barkhorn, E. (2012) "Why *Blue Like Jazz* won't save Christian cinema," *The Atlantic* (April 16). Online. Available: www.theatlantic.com/entertainment/archive/2012/04/why-blue-like-jazz-wont-save-christian-cinema/255965/ (accessed 27 July 2013).

BBC News (2003) "Census returns of the Jedi" (February 13). Online. Available: http://news.bbc.co.uk/2/hi/uk/2757067.stm (accessed 10 August 2013).

Bishops' Committee for Ecumenical and Interreligious Affairs (1988) "Criteria for the evaluation of dramatizations of the Passion," National Conference of Catholic Bishops, in S.B. Plate (ed.) (2004) *Re-Viewing* The Passion: *Mel Gibson's Film and Its Critics*, New York: Palgrave Press, 181–90.

Bluelikejazzthemovie.com (2012) "About." Online. Available: www.bluelikejazzthemovie.com/about#video1 (accessed 27 July 2013).

Box Office Mojo (n.d.) "2004 Domestic Grosses." Online. Available: www.boxofficemojo.com/yearly/chart/?yr=2004&p=.htm (accessed 22 July 2013).

Cho, F. (1999) "Imagining nothing and imaging otherness in Buddhist film," in D. Jaspers and S.B. Plate (eds), *Imag(in)ing Otherness: Filmic Visions of Living Together*, Atlanta, GA: Scholars Press, 169–96.

——(2003) "The art of presence: Buddhism and Korean films," in S.B. Plate (ed.) *Representing Religion in World Cinema: Filmmaking, Mythmaking, Culture Making*, New York: Palgrave Press, 107–20.

——(2009) "Buddhism," in J. Lyden (ed.), *The Routledge Companion to Religion and Film*, London: Routledge Press, 162–77.

CNN.com (2006) "Gibson charged with drunken driving" (August 3). Online. Available: www.cnn.com/2006/LAW/08/02/gibson.charged/ (accessed 22 July 2013).

Denton-Borhaug, K. (2005) "A bloodthirsty salvation: behind the popular polarized reaction to Gibson's *The Passion*," *Journal of Religion and Film* 9, 1 (April). Online. Available: www.unomaha.edu/jrf/Vol9No1/DentonBorhaugBloodthirsty.htm (accessed 24 July 2013).

Dwyer, R. (2006) *Filming the Gods: Religion and Indian Cinema*, London: Routledge Press.

——(2009) "Hinduism," in J. Lyden (ed.), *The Routledge Companion to Religion and Film*, London: Routledge Press, 141–61.

Elixir Entertainment (2012) "Sam Horowitz—live at the Omni Hotel in Dallas," *YouTube.com* (November 26). Online. Available: www.youtube.com/watch?v=g-ByhUDUllM (accessed 10 September 2013).

Flannery-Dailey, F. (2004) "Biblical scholarship and the passion surrounding *The Passion of the Christ*," *Journal of Religion and Film* 8, Special Issue 1 (February). Online. Available: www.unomaha.edu/jrf/2004Symposium/FlanneryDailey.htm (accessed 22 July 2013).

Fredriksen, P. (2003) "Mad Mel: the gospel according to Gibson," *The New Republic* (July 28/August 4): 25–29.

——(2004) "History, Hollywood, and the Bible: some thoughts on Gibson's *Passion*," *Journal of Religion and Film* 8, Special Issue 1 (February). Online. Available: www.unomaha.edu/jrf/2004Symposium/Frederiksen.htm (accessed 22 July 2013).

Gershon, W. (2013) "A response to Rabbi David Wolpe's article in the *Washington Post*," *Scribd.com* (n.d.). Online. Available: www.scribd.com/doc/161418857/A-Letter-from-Rabbi-William-Gershon (accessed 10 September 2013).

Hibbs, T. (2012) "Not nearly blue enough and nothing like jazz," *The Catholic World Report* (18 May). Online. Available: www.catholicworldreport.com/Item/1357/not_nearly_blue_enough_and_nothing_like_jazz.aspx (accessed 24 July 2013).

Hussain, A. (2009) "Islam," in J. Lyden (ed.), *The Routledge Companion to Religion and Film*, London: Routledge Press, 131–40.

Internet Movie Database (2004) "Reviews and ratings for *The Passion of the* Christ." Online. Available: www.imdb.com/title/tt0335345/reviews?ref_=tt_urv (accessed 27 July 2013).

——(2012) "Reviews and ratings for *Blue Like Jazz*." Online. Available: www.imdb.com/title/tt1758575/reviews?ref_=tt_urv (accessed 27 July 2013).

Johnston, R. (2009) "Theological approaches," in J. Lyden (ed.), *The Routledge Companion to Religion and Film*, London: Routledge Press, 310–28.

King, N. (2004) "Truth at last: evangelical communities embrace *The Passion of the Christ*," in S.B. Plate (ed.), *Re-Viewing* The Passion: *Mel Gibson's Film and Its Critics*, New York: Palgrave Press, 151–62.

Lindvall, T. (2007a) "Hollywood chronicles: toward an intersection of church history and film history," in R. Johnston (ed.), *Reframing Theology and Film: New Focus for an Emerging Discipline*, Grand Rapids, MI: Baker, 126–42.

——(2007b) *Sanctuary Cinema: Origins of the Christian Film Industry*, New York: New York University Press.

——(ed.) (2001) *The Silents of God: Selected Issues and Documents in Silent American Film and Religion 1908–1925*, Lanham, MD: Scarecrow Press.

Lindvall, T. and A. Quicke (2011) *Celluloid Sermons: The Emergence of the Christian Film Industry, 1930–1986*, New York: New York University Press.

Lyden, J. (2003) *Film as Religion: Myths, Morals, and Rituals*, New York: New York University Press.

——(2012) "Whose film is it, anyway? canonicity and authority in *Star Wars* fandom," *Journal of the American Academy of Religion* 80, 3: 775–86.

Lynch, G. (2007) "Film and the subjective turn: how the sociology of religion can contribute to theological readings of film," in R. Johnston (ed.), *Reframing Theology and Film: New Focus for an Emerging Discipline*, Grand Rapids, MI: Baker, 109–25.

——(2009) "Cultural theory and cultural studies," in J. Lyden (ed.), *The Routledge Companion to Religion and Film*, London: Routledge Press, 275–91.

McLaren, B. (2004) *A Generous Orthodoxy*, Grand Rapids, MI: Zondervan.

Malone, P. (2009) "The Roman Catholic Church and cinema (1967 to the present)," in J. Lyden (ed.), *The Routledge Companion to Religion and Film*, London: Routledge Press, 52–71.

Maresco, P. (2004) "Mel Gibson's *The Passion of the Christ*: market segmentation, mass marketing and promotion, and the Internet," *Sacred Heart University Business Faculty Publications*. Online. Available: http://digitalcommons.sacredheart.edu/cgi/viewcontent.cgi?article=1024&context=wcob_fac (accessed 22 July 2013).

Marsh, C. (2004) *Cinema and Sentiment: Film's Challenge to Theology*, Milton Keynes, UK: Paternoster Press.

——(2007a) "On dealing with what films actually do to people: the practice and theory of film watching in theology/religion and film discussion," in R. Johnston (ed.), *Reframing Theology and Film: New Focus for an Emerging Discipline*, Grand Rapids, MI: Baker, 145–61.

——(2007b) *Theology Goes to the Movies: An Introduction to Critical Christian Thinking*, London: Routledge Press.

Miles, M. (1996) *Seeing and Believing: Religion and Values in the Movies*, Boston, MA: Beacon Press.

Miller, D. (2003) Blue Like Jazz: *Nonreligious Thoughts on Christian Spirituality*, Nashville, TN: Thomas Nelson.

Mitchell, J. and S.B. Plate (eds) (2007) *The Religion and Film Reader*, London: Routledge Press.

Mutual Film Corporation v. Ohio Industrial Commission, 236 U.S. 230 (1915).

Nayar, S. (2012) *The Sacred and the Cinema: Reconfiguring the "Genuine" Religious Film*, New York: Continuum.

Pacatte, R. (2007) "Shaping morals, shifting views: have the ratings systems influenced how (Christian) America sees movies?" in R. Johnston (ed.), *Reframing Theology and Film: New Focus for an Emerging Discipline*, Grand Rapids, MI: Baker, 261–86.

Parker, J.R. (2012) *Cinema as Pulpit: Sherwood Pictures and the Church Film Movement*, Jefferson, NC: McFarland Press.

Pattison, J. (2010) "Saving *Blue Like Jazz*: The Movie," *Relevant Magazine* (October 27). Online. Available: www.relevantmagazine.com/life/current-events/features/23281-saving-blue-like-jazz-the-movie (accessed 27 July 2013).

Paul VI, Pope (1965) *Nostra Aetate* ["Declaration on the Relation of the Church to Non-Christian Religions"] (October 28). Online. Available: www.vatican.va/archive/hist_councils/ii_vatican_council/documents/vat-ii_decl_19651028_nostra-aetate_en.html (accessed 22 July 2013).

Plate, S.B. (2008) *Religion and Film: Cinema and the Re-Creation of the World*, London: Wallflower Press.

——(ed.) (2003) *Representing Religion in World Cinema: Filmmaking, Mythmaking, Culture Making*, New York: Palgrave Press.

Pugh, C. (2012) *Star Wars Uncut: The Empire Strikes Back*. Online. Available: www.starwarsuncut.com/empire (accessed 15 August 2013).

——(ed.) (2009) *Star Wars Uncut: A New Hope*. Online. Available: www.starwarsuncut.com/newhope (accessed 9 August 2013).

Quicke, A. (2009) "The era of censorship (1930–67)," in J. Lyden (ed.), *The Routledge Companion to Religion and Film*, London: Routledge Press, 32–51.

Ramji, R. (2005) "From *Navy Seals* to *The Siege*: getting to know the Muslim terrorist, Hollywood style," *Journal of Religion and Film* 9, 2 (October). Online. Available: www.unomaha.edu/jrf/Vol9No2/RamjiIslam.htm (accessed 22 July 2013).

Romanowski, W. (2012) *Reforming Hollywood: How American Protestants Fought for Freedom at the Movies*, New York: Oxford University Press.

Rosen, C. (2012) "'Star Wars' Day: may the fourth be with you," *Huffington Post* (May 4), Online. Available: www.huffingtonpost.com/2012/05/04/star-wars-day_n_1477043.html (accessed 15 August 2013).

Silk, M. (2004) "Gibson's Passion: a case study in media manipulation?" *Journal of Religion and Film* 8, Special Issue 1 (February). Online. Available: www.unomaha.edu/jrf/2004Symposium/Silk.htm (accessed 22 July 2013).

Smith, N.M. (2012) "Roadside acquires 'Blue Like Jazz' before SXSW premiere," *Indiewire* (February 21). Online. Available: www.indiewire.com/article/roadside-acquires-for-blue-like-jazz-before-sxsw-premiere# (accessed 27 July 2013).

Stelter, B. (2010) "An Emmy for rebuilding a galaxy," *New York Times* (August 27): C1.

Thistlethwaite, S. (2006) "Mel makes a war movie," in P. Fredriksen (ed.), *On The Passion of the Christ: Exploring the Issues Raised by the Controversial Movie*, Berkeley, CA: University of California Press, 127–45.

Thomas, P. (2009) "New religious movements," in J. Lyden (ed.), *The Routledge Companion to Religion and Film*, London: Routledge Press, 194–213.

Wolpe, D. (2013a) "Have we forgotten what bar mitzvahs are all about?" *Washington Post* (August 15). Online. Available: www.washingtonpost.com/blogs/on-faith/wp/2013/08/15/have-we-forgotten-what-bar-mitzvahs-are-all-about/ (accessed 10 September 2013).

——(2013b) "The bar mitzvah, re-examined," *Washington Post* (August 20). Online. Available: www.washingtonpost.com/blogs/on-faith/wp/2013/08/20/the-bar-mitzvah-re-examined/ (accessed 10 September 2013).

Woods, R., M. Jindra, and J. Baker (2004) "The audience responds to *The Passion of the Christ*," in S.B. Plate (ed.), *Re-Viewing The Passion: Mel Gibson's Film and Its Critics*, New York: Palgrave Press.

Wright, M. (2006) *Religion and Film: An Introduction*, London: I.B. Taurus.

——(2009) "Judaism," in J. Lyden (ed.), *The Routledge Companion to Religion and Film*, London: Routledge Press, 91–108.

Wryot (2002) "The Phantom Edit," *YouTube*. Online. Available: www.youtube.com/watch?v=pfEcaH2Db1s (accessed 22 July 2013).

6
RADIO

Tona Hangen

Radio is one of the most pervasive media on earth; even in the most remote and undeveloped areas of the globe can people pull down—or send out—a radio signal and connect with the human voice. Not coincidentally, radio has been a consistent platform for religious messages since regular broadcasting began just after the First World War, and although partially transformed by digital sound technologies it remains a key site for religious popular culture. Unlike print and film media, radio is constrained by the physics of the electromagnetic spectrum. Since the overall number and types of channels are therefore limited, governments express their political and cultural priorities in setting licensing standards and allocating the spectrum for broadcast use. Radio thus magnifies broader cultural tensions and struggles because people are forced to compete for access to it. Regarding radio in the United States, Michele Hilmes writes:

> more than any other medium, radio seemed in its early days to lend itself to association with ideas of nation, of national identity, to "the heart and mind of America," its "soul"—and not just in the press releases of networks and advertisers, who might be assumed to have an agenda, but in the popular press, in sermons, speeches and songs, from radio enthusiasts' magazines to farm publications, in the opinions of factory workers and of U.S. senators.
>
> (Hilmes 1997: 1)

Michel Foucault reminds us that discourse is the mode of meaning making, enforcing and enabling some meanings and not others, especially when creating categories and definitions. Discourse is powerfully and fundamentally constructive. It literally constitutes the objects of which it speaks, thereby concealing its own genesis. Religion is, at its core, about the practices of subjectification and its cultural products aspire "to function as determinative discourses," especially through their claims of ultimate truth. Likewise, media are more than technologies or instruments, but are in fact discursive practices situated in specific historical contexts (Hoover and Kaneva 2009: 10–13).

Radio makes its meaning primarily through amplifying a single human sense: that of hearing. But radio is hardly one-dimensional; its dimension "is more like that of a geometrical plane without boundaries" (Parker *et al.* 1948: 84). Voices can sound closer or farther away; background noise or silence indicates the spatial dimensions of a studio, a stadium, or the outdoors itself. Music and other sound effects interweave to create aural landscapes that are anything but flat. Radio is populated and filled in by the listener's imagination, and conveys real places as easily as it conjures fantasy worlds. As one radio-writers' manual put it in the 1940s, "the radio program is not what is written in the script or what takes place in the studio, but what is happening in the mind of the listener" (Parker *et al.* 1948: 86). This "theater of the mind" is one of radio's inherent qualities. Listening is primal, preliterate, tapping into collective memory and emotion. Marshall McLuhan called radio "the tribal drum" harking back to "the ancient experience of kinship webs … a subliminal echo chamber of magical power to touch remote and forgotten chords" (McLuhan 1964: 263–64). Storytelling and story listening are very ancient human arts. Listening is also pleasurable and even powerful, as is eavesdropping; Susan Douglas notes that "the more we work on making our own images, the more powerfully attached we become to them, arising as they do from deep within us." She calls America in the 1920s an "odd hybrid … a modern, literate society grafted together with a traditional, preliterate, oral culture. It was an atavism Americans clearly loved. For orality generates a powerful participatory mystique" (Douglas 1999: 27–28).

Tapping the deep well of human emotion and language as radio does draws out some special considerations for religion and popular culture. Walter Ong and Mircea Eliade believed that religion was enhanced by the media, particularly in the way radio fostered the "personalist loyalties, strong social or tribal feelings and responses and special anxieties" of ancient human aural/oral traditions (Ong 1967: 257; see also Eliade 1961). Exploring media in late twentieth-century Latin America, Jesus Martin-Barbero has argued that the electronic church re-enchants and sacralizes culture, not merely by amplifying the human voice but by mediating religious experience itself, rendering it magical and ritualized. "Despite all the promise of modernity to make religion disappear," he wrote, "what has really happened is that … religion has shown itself capable of eating modernity alive and making modernity an important ingredient for its own purposes" (Martin-Barbero 1997: 112). Religious broadcasting was born along with the medium itself and has persisted throughout radio's entire history. As will be discussed, religious radio is situated between the clearly defined realms of "commercial broadcasting" designed to sell a product and "public broadcasting" to serve a nation's or community's interests. As churches, denominations, and other religious organizations adopted radio as a mode of communication, it brought religion into homes and public spaces in new and sometimes disruptive ways, and also permitted some changes in private devotional behaviors, blurring the boundaries of sacred and secular spaces.

Another of radio's inherent qualities is the immediacy and speed of its transmission and the live nature of much of its production, so that radio delivered, especially in the pre-television era, both celebratory and tragic breaking news and timely, up-to-the-minute content, becoming the audience's remote ears on the world. Like television broadcasting, radio is a precisely time-bound medium, synchronized to the clock, with hourly and daily rituals that create familiarity and segment the world into orderly slices, but always within a constant flow of sound; radio is never silent.

For audiences, radio listening has both mass and individual aspects. Listeners feel and know that they are part of a larger audience even while they generally experience radio as an individual. Listening can be active or passive (as in background, "distracted" listening). There are also different kinds or modes of listening, as Douglas observes: informational or "flat" listening to glean the facts, almost as if reading a flat page; dimensional listening, as when you mentally locate yourself in the midst of a crowd, a theater, or an athletic stadium and are following action in three dimensions; and associational listening, when you connect what you're hearing to specific personal memories. Douglas, commenting on how listening has its own set of discursive practices or rituals, identifies a "zen" of radio listening (Douglas 1999: 36).

Since radio's scale is vast but unseen, a single listener can experience it as an intimate chat. Franklin Delano Roosevelt expertly employed radio's ability to seem like a one-on-one conversation with his fireside chats. Pre-amplification oral rhetorical style favored high-volume vocal dynamics, which revival preachers in particular adopted to be heard by the maximum number of people without a microphone. In contrast, vocal personae on radio came across best as experts sitting in one's own living room. Even the voice of God, emanating mysteriously from home radio sets in the 1950 film *The Next Voice You Hear*, powerfully affects its hearers precisely because it does *not* boom forth from the sky like something out of the *Ten Commandments*. Describing why radio was effective for a religious audience, Everett Parker pointed out that "radio reaches them at home, among their most intimate and cherished surroundings. They do not have to be persuaded to go to any place. If they are willing to listen at all, they are in a receptive mood toward anything that touches their vital interests" (Parker *et al.* 1948: xiii). Radio specifically addresses our interiority (Douglas 1999: 31).

In his 1983 book *Imagined Communities*, Benedict Anderson argues that media shape modern nationalism. He is concerned with the rise of printed newspapers, but radio did this all over again in the twentieth century. It took listeners elsewhere and created new, simultaneous mass experiences, something which newspapers could never replicate. Additionally, radio allows listeners to experience something else simultaneously: "multiple identities—national, regional, local—some of them completely allied with the country's prevailing cultural and political ideologies, others of them suspicious of or at odds with official culture" (Douglas 1999: 24). However, reception theory reminds us that media messages (perhaps especially religious messages) are always subject to reinterpretation by consumers. In writing about the power found in alternative readings of cultural texts, Mark Hulsether notes that "postmodern cultural theory highlights how the residual power of religious traditions can be expressed and contested—not merely defeated and trivialized—within a society that communicates through commercial mass media" (1992: 75). Technologies like film, telephone, phonograph, and radio come to mediate human encounters in increasingly dehumanized ways, and religion could, and did, address the human condition in this new context. Even religions that identified themselves as timeless, traditional, or "old-time" readily translated onto the medium of radio, enhancing and strengthening their aural, narrative, and musical elements.

Without the institutions of modern mass culture, American religion could not have taken its present shape, and that mass culture, in turn, owes something to religion's failure to disappear in the twentieth century (Hangen 2002: 8). This is demonstrably true for American Christianity, particularly its conservative tradition, but also for other groups who jostled for access to airwaves and cultural power. Since neither modernity nor scientific rationality extinguished religion, radio was among the institutional structures in modern society that scaffolded the very environment in which religious fundamentalisms could be delineated, and against which those newly minted fundamentalisms defined themselves as the answer to the disorienting loss of solid footing. According to Hoover and Kaneva in their study of fundamentalism and the media,

> The believers who adopted the aggressive anti-modernism, reactive selectivity and dualist worldview intrinsic to fundamentalism were "framers" of the highest order … . They knew instinctively—one might say, psychologically and spiritually, how to identify, select, portray, project, and enhance the drama inherent in their supernaturalist worldview while yet retaining the modernist's faith in progress, meaning, and order.
>
> (Hoover and Kaneva 2009: 29–32)

Keeping in mind that radio always operates within specific regulatory contexts which themselves reflect cultural decisions and priorities and which have their own histories and unfolding consequences, the remainder of this chapter highlights some examples of religious broadcasting, primarily in the United States, where radio began as an undefined technology that quickly became commercialized. It became the central mass medium for decades during its "golden age," and it remains ubiquitous despite dramatic changes in the media and regulatory landscapes in the twenty-first century.

Origins

Beginning with Samuel Morse's tapped message, "what hath God wrought?" in 1837, religion over the air has been a key part of the development of broadcast media in the United States. There are records of prayers and hymn singing conveyed over the early telephone-relay wireless experiments and US Signal Corps testing in the pre-World War II era (Erickson 1992: 1). KDKA, the experimental station of Westinghouse, pioneered not only broadcasting itself—the novelty creating a demand for its radio receivers in the Pittsburgh area—but also religious broadcasting, with its simulcasts of the Sunday services in Calvary Episcopal Church starting in early 1921. Radio thus began as a marketing tool to sell radios, and quickly came under the authority of the Department of Commerce, which at first confined all broadcasting to one wavelength. Nonetheless, religious organizations were among the first licensees and station owners, some 63 of them by 1925 (Erickson 1992: 2).

It was the same decade in which Protestant liberals and fundamentalists marked cultural territory, and radio became one of the sites in that contest. Evangelists hoped to missionize the world and radio seemed a God-given method to do so; liberals hoped not to "let the fundamentalists win," in the words of Harry Emerson Fosdick (1922). In 1923, R.R. Brown in Omaha and Paul Rader in Chicago, and no doubt others, inaugurated nondenominational evangelistic ministries that included radio broadcasting, while in the same year the Greater New York Federation of Churches organized a radio division and crafted its signature program called the "National Radio Pulpit," which initially aired on an experimental hookup on New York City's station WEAF, three years before WEAF became part of the National Broadcasting Company (NBC). "National Radio Pulpit" was already part of the lineup when the new network went coast to coast in 1926 as the broadcast arm of the Radio Corporation of America.

By collapsing space with its simultaneity—whisking listeners instantly to locations both real and fantastic—radio allowed its audiences literally to constitute imagined communities. This was a genuine experience, not a merely virtual or imitative one, and those communities could be lasting rather than transitory, ritually enacted and re-enacted through the clock-bound cycles of radio scheduling. Especially in the early years, radio generated real connectivity as listeners "talked back" through letters and postcards, mail-in offers and requests. The amateur or "ham" radio sub-culture mapped new geographies with the practice of DXing ("DX" being the telegraph operator's shorthand for "distance"), in which radio operators confirmed receipt of a distant signal using mailed QSL cards that identified their frequency and location ("QSL" from the radio and telegraph "Q code" for sending messages in minimal signals).

It would take a few years before radio became something more than the dial-twiddling of amateur hobbyists, but by the mid-1920s it was already apparent that in the United States, at least, radio would not be a government-owned utility but rather a regulated market, licensing slices of the radio spectrum for commercial use. The Radio Acts of 1927 and 1934 established the regulatory standard of "the public interest, convenience and necessity" while actively discouraging "propaganda" stations such as those run by labor and educational organizations. This favored commercial broadcasters over nonprofits and created a climate in which a few very large and powerful corporations would thrive (Czitrom 1982: 73, 81; Kelman 2009: 8). Those companies would prove adept at censoring their content and creating national identity through shared consumption of corporate-sponsored programming. It seemed free to all with a receiver, but only because the real costs were hidden in the transactions between networks, sponsors, and licensees. These business decisions had an impact on American life very early on. Robert and Helen Lynd note in their community study of "Middletown" Indiana in the 1920s that radio is among the modern inventions "remaking leisure" and giving rise to "ingenious manipulative activity" and active listening (Lynd and Lynd 1929: 269).

Radio was part of the lived daily experience for much of the twentieth century, but is much more than background noise. Radio's history and meaning can be seen as a "series of small crises of cultural control," because it emerged in the context of cultural tensions over mass culture, national identity, consumption, race, gender, ethnicity, and the spheres of public and private life (Hilmes 1997: xiii). Radio tapped the "aural dimensions" of American mainstream and marginal "acoustic communities" (Kelman 2009: 14). Given all this, we can see religious broadcasting occupying a liminal space between commercial and "public" broadcasting, and so being an important shaper of the medium itself.

Some religious groups cast a wary eye on the newfangled technology, but with surprising enthusiasm most immediately saw radio's benefits for evangelism, community building, and meaning making. Even theological conservatives waxed rhapsodic about the modern technological marvel of radio. Clarence Jones, an entrepreneurial international Protestant evangelist who brought shortwave broadcasting to highland Ecuador in the 1930s, called radio and aviation the twentieth century's "twin scientific marvels. Both derive from the air sphere, releasing man from his age-long pent up restrictions of time and distance that kept him earthbound." However, he warned that "whether mankind is to be blessed or blighted by these scientific marvels of the age is chiefly a moral and spiritual question for which individual Christians and the Church of Christ do well to assume a responsible attitude" (Jones 1946: 7). Likewise, as she prepared to construct the first church-owned radio station in Los Angeles in 1923, Sister Aimee Semple McPherson told her followers that "the world" had already captured the moving pictures. "Shall we let them have the Radio too?" she asked rhetorically, "[o]r shall we say: 'No, this is Father's Air and Earth, and we will send the Message upon its breezes to spread the Gospel in this wholesale and miraculous manner'" (Hangen 2002: 68).

Part of the appeal of radio for religious messages was the potential for vast audiences, far more than could ever be gathered under a physical revival tent roof. Evangelists like Jones saw in radio a divine boost to their efforts to fulfill the "Great Commission" to teach the world about Jesus. Radio waves propagating outward from their source multiplied human effort: "a preacher of the gospel, through a radio microphone and a sufficient number of broadcast stations carrying the message simultaneously, can preach to *more people in a month* than the Apostle Paul could speak to in a life-time!" (Jones 1946: 109; emphasis in the original). Radio allowed tireless repetition of a single message, and floated over geographical and political frontiers where travel was difficult or impossible. Jones spoke for many when he claimed that "radio, the winged messenger for the gospel, has been reserved, in the providence of God, for the church of the twentieth century to employ in reaching the regions beyond" (1946: 109). His station, HCJB (which would eventually become a 10,000-watt shortwave powerhouse on the equator whose signal could be heard on every continent and ocean), pioneered radio use in international evangelism and divinity-school training. He also distributed inexpensive radio receivers pre-tuned to HCJB's frequency. His organization's latest endeavor, nearly eighty years after the installation of its first antenna, is distributing suitcase-sized low-power transmitters with portable engineering kits to help found new Christian stations in remote places around the globe (HCJB Global 2012).

The golden age of network radio

In the United States, the Radio Act of 1927 created a government agency, the Federal Radio Commission (later the Federal Communications Commission, or FCC), to regulate the emerging industry, allocate the spectrum of frequencies, and develop a core standard for broadcasting—namely, that radio must operate "in the public interest, convenience, and necessity" in order to gain and renew broadcast licenses. This established a long-running pattern in the United States in which radio would be an advertising medium with programs designed primarily to deliver ears to corporate sponsors and networks granting some public service airtime to groups they deemed appropriate. Programming that fell outside this model had a much harder time gaining a foothold, but never disappeared entirely.

During its "golden age" from 1923 to the mid-1950s, radio was the single most powerful and popular medium in America. Radio crossed social lines and, by the 1930s, could be found in nearly all homes, even those that lacked electricity or indoor plumbing. Golden age radio included news, music, variety and comedy, children's shows, soap operas, sitcoms, dramatic series, and sports, as well as religious programming. The four main radio networks and their local affiliates broadcast religious programs as either public services on "sustaining" time or by selling commercial time to churches directly. The National Broadcasting Company (NBC), the first radio network, decided early on to award its public service sustaining time solely to the Federal Council of Churches representing mainline Protestant denominations, denying commercial time to individual religious broadcasters. The Columbia Broadcasting System (CBS) developed a decorous *Church of the Air* program series that gave only well-established Protestant, Catholic, and Jewish religious bodies their turn at the microphone. The Mutual Broadcasting System in the 1940s specialized in selling airtime to Evangelical and fundamentalist Christian broadcasters outside the Christian mainstream. Some denominations and religious groups founded their own stations in the 1920s and 1930s, such as the Lutheran Church Missouri Synod's KFUO in St. Louis, and Pentecostal evangelist Sister Aimee Semple McPherson's KFSG Los Angeles, voice of the International Church of the Foursquare Gospel (Erickson 1992: 120–21; Hangen 2002: 66).

One of the cultural tensions on radio in these decades was between national identity and the standardization of tastes on the one hand, and political, ethnic, and religious diversity on the other. Even as popular entertainment on radio instructed Americans how to speak, spend, and think, and appealed to them mainly as middlebrow white consumers, the medium could not help but mirror the nation's more complex social and demographic realities. The example of Jewish radio personalities and programs might illustrate this point well. Gertude Berg developed, wrote, and starred in *The Rise of the Goldbergs*, carried on NBC from 1929 to 1934 and then on CBS as *The Goldbergs* until 1948, when it briefly transitioned to television. The popular series followed the everyday adventures of an immigrant Jewish American family in New York City, signaled on the air by their tenement neighborhood, their Yiddish-accented English, and amusing malapropisms. The show satirized and yet universalized the assimilation experience, with its exploration of universal family themes and tensions arising from the practice of Judaism in America; in so doing it introduced millions of Americans to Judaism and its traditions (Siegel and Siegel 2007: 24). NBC's stately and long-running *Message of Israel* program (1934–86) became the official voice of Reform Judaism in the United States, originating from Central Synagogue in New York City each Sunday. As Ari Y. Kelman describes, dozens of Yiddish-language educational programs, and programs of cantors singing, helped multilingual Jewish immigrants define their place in society, in part by constituting themselves as a recognizable radio audience and therefore as a distinctive American sub-culture (Kelman 2009).

Another of the tensions that religious radio programming evoked was what could (or should) be said aloud in a democratic society. By the 1930s, "controversial broadcasting" was practically synonymous with certain religious broadcasters. One notable example was John Romulus "Doc" Brinkley, who gained notoriety by promising virility through human transplantation of goat glands and who founded the rogue Mexican-border blaster megawatt station XERF, opened to a cacophony of unregulated hawkers, preachers, and hillbilly musicians. Another was Father Charles Coughlin, a Catholic radio demagogue whose "Union for Social Justice" political party and increasingly right-leaning radio screeds garnered vast audiences of conservatives outraged by what they saw as the New Deal's savaging of American freedoms. By 1939, the National Association of Broadcasters banned "editorializing" on the air, a policy upheld in the FCC's 1941 "Mayflower Decision," which stipulated that broadcasters could not advocate anything on the air. In the early 1940s, the Institute of Education by Radio opposed paid religious broadcasting of any kind, arguing that it could be dangerous, especially in wartime. In response to what they saw as the muzzling of a principled religious witness, Christian broadcasters were instrumental in founding the National Association of Evangelicals in 1942 and the National Religious Broadcasters in 1944, both of which remain important lobbying groups advocating for the freedom of religious speech (specifically, that of Christian Evangelicals) in the broadcast media. The mainline Protestant denominations likewise established their own Joint Religious Radio Committee, which in 1948 declared in its manual for religious radio writers that radio necessitated "becoming ministers to the total community" and that it needed to be used as an "agent of democracy" (Parker *et al.* 1948: ix–x).

In the 1930s and 1940s, cultural theorists and critics were also concerned about radio's reach and communicative power. Initially, they were interested in measuring radio audiences for both social scientific and marketing research. Methods of determining audience size and rating program popularity included Hooper Ratings, in which people were called on the telephone and queried about what they were listening to at that moment; Nielsen surveys, which installed an automatic device on the radio set; and Arbitron ratings, which relied on self-reported radio consumption recorded in a diary. Each of these methods was designed mainly to elicit raw data on what was being heard, but not necessarily by whom or why. Others also estimated audience size from volume of mail received, as well as gauging response to promotional offers (Parker *et al.* 1948: 20–24). In the late 1930s, the Princeton Office of Radio Research, headed by Viennese psychologist Paul Lazarsfeld, published several volumes dealing with the methodology of audience measurement and the psychology of radio listening, assessing various marketing techniques and pioneering content analysis in media studies. As Daniel Czitrom argues, their approach ("who says what to whom with what effect") became "the dominant paradigm defining the scope and problems of American communications research" (Czitrom 1982: 132).

Generated in the 1930s by the Frankfurt School of cultural theorists—including Theodor Adorno, among others—market research and audience psychology were part of a broader debate over the potential dangers both to and from the values of mass culture. Although their work was not widely available in translation until the 1960s, the Frankfurt School theorists crafted a pointed Marxist critique of commercial mass culture, especially of radio, decrying the "reign of advertising over culture" (Apostolidis 2000: 40). For Adorno, radio generated passive listening modes which inhibited resistance, ensured mass conformity, and even permitted the rise of fascism. For all his concern with the industrial underclass, Adorno was uninterested in—or not convinced of—the capacity of radio audiences to reinterpret and resist hegemonic messages, but he cogently argued that the voices of political opposition and high art should be allowed to disrupt the narcotizing commercial flow of radio.

Adorno's critiques proved all the more prescient regarding television, whose structure of commercial broadcasting and network dominance was inherited directly from radio. Network variety programming migrated to television at the same time that FM broadcasting developed, in the late 1940s; radio transitioned from being the main source of family entertainment to becoming an individual companion, the realm of national playlists of Top-40 music and "format" stations that programmed all-music, all-sports, and all-talk. It also disconnected from cabinet-style living room radios to portable transistor radios and car radios, taking advantage of post-war innovations in circuitry and plastics. The rise of television, the proliferation of format FM radio, and the post-war decommissioning of European and Asian short-wave frequencies opened up new opportunities on the AM dial for religious and paid-time broadcasters, including for-profit listener-supported ventures like KRDU in Fresno, California (1946) and KEAR "Family Radio" in Oakland, California (1958). As Hal Erickson describes, President Eisenhower's Secretary of State John Foster Dulles "gave wholehearted endorsement to high-powered, international religious broadcasts as part of his master plan to 'Christianize' Europe and deflect the influence of Communism" as one element in America's Cold War policy (Erickson 1992:10).

By the 1960s, some legal room had been carved out for religious programming, which could solicit on-air for funds and donations and advocate for one religious perspective without being subject to the requirements of the FCC's Fairness Doctrine, which required most broadcasters to cover controversial issues of public importance by airing differing viewpoints (Brennan 1989). But religious broadcasters could still overstep; in 1964, right-wing radio evangelist Billy James Hargis raised FCC ire when he accused an anti-Goldwater author of being an atheist Communist sympathizer. Denied free airtime to rebut the charges on a Pennsylvania station, the author appealed to the FCC, which ruled in his favor. The Supreme Court upheld the FCC's ruling, and the so-called "Red Lion" decision suggested that some religious broadcasting could fall under the same legal scrutiny as political speech or network editorializing (Erickson 1992: 11–12).

In fact, the only broadcaster to lose his license for violating the Fairness Doctrine was a religious one: the year was 1973, and the broadcaster was Carl McIntire of the *Twentieth Century Reformation Hour,* who had built a career and the Pennsylvania radio station WXUR around his particularly uncompromising strain of Christian anticommunism; Randall Balmer called him "the P.T. Barnum of fundamentalism." As Heather Hendershot explained:

> McIntire and his cohorts flew in the face of what the FCC and the NCC [National Council of Churches] believed to be the true purpose of religious broadcasting: explicitly, to send positive messages and promote a general

idea that religion was good, and implicitly to do public relations for a few denominations.

(Hendershot 2007: 387, 383)

Protestant fundamentalism in the 1960s and 1970s deliberately confronted the values of midcentury liberalism with the very technologies that it claimed to police in the interest of "fairness" and the public interest.

In America, the field of media theory also matured during the era of network dominance of the communication channels, especially with the work of Harold Innis and Marshall McLuhan, for whom "systems of communication were technological extensions of human mind and consciousness, and therefore the key to a civilization's value, sources of authority and organization of knowledge" (Czitrom 1982: 155). McLuhan believed the electronic media were "retribalizing" humanity; he was particularly interested in "the impact of media technology on the human sensorium" and on the complex and fecund interactions between the human and machine worlds (Czitrom 1982: 175–78). Content was less important to McLuhan; "the medium is the message," he famously (and cryptically) wrote (McLuhan 1964).

For cultural scholars, one implication of McLuhan's observations is that studying the network era of radio has meant examining the totality of the cultural text that is radio: not just the words, but the music, sound effects, vocal characteristics, rhetorical style, and qualities inherent in the medium itself and in the myriad technologies of its capture, from transcription disk to magnetic tape to digital formats. Obsolete technologies make playback and archiving critical issues as scholars seek to access and study radio's vanishing past. So much of what happened on radio happened live and unrecorded, and thus is beyond our direct grasp. Nonetheless, we can trace the many imprints it left on popular culture back when sound ruled the broadcast media.

Still speaking

Religious broadcasters moved aggressively onto cable and additional UHF channels in the 1980s, pioneering satellite broadcasting, and spawning a dramatic increase in television ministries and religious stations. Media trends of the last two decades of the twentieth century included decentralization, deregulation, audience fragmentation, media corporate mergers, globalization, and new programming strategies (Hilmes 2002: 324). Yet radio remained a vibrant space for religion of all stripes, as its airtime became more affordable relative to television and with the rise of a newly politicized Christian right in the United States adding its distinctive voice to American popular culture.

In particular, radio could amplify unpolished voices from the religious margin in search of converts, wealth, or validation. Some of this was old-timey, the aging vestiges of local-color regionalism. The rural "airwaves of Zion" serve as one example: live Pentecostal/Holiness broadcasting on local AM stations of Appalachia, predominantly on Sundays in the 1970s through the 1990s. In *Airwaves of Zion* (1993), ethnographer Howard Dorgan captured this electronic unsophisticated "folk religion" that lacked national distribution, and its untrained practitioners' "heavily provincial" theology emanating from tiny independent sects in the "Full Gospel" vein. Appalachian "Zion" programs were live, improvisational, Spirit-led, strongly personal (almost soap-opera like), and characterized by highly emotional and cathartic "kinetic expressions," like swooning, shouting, twirling, and jumping. Zion broadcasters utilized pay-for-time AM stations, financed by freewill offerings on the cheap ($25–35 per 30-minute time slot in the early 1990s). Even as he recorded their work, Dorgan recognized that such broadcasting was on its way out, both because of the aging demographic of rural Appalachian churches and because of looming changes in the broadcast industry. He saw the end of live local AM religious broadcasting in Appalachia as the passing of an era:

> the improvisational quality, the first-person intimacy, the rustic modes of speech, the immediacy of listener response, and perhaps some of the honest passion will be gone. All of this will not happen immediately. Undoubtedly there will be stations that preserve this broadcasting genre long after the main corpus of the phenomenon is dead, but for the typical Brother Roscoe Green and Sister Dollie Shirley the AM radio environment will have changed, making it much harder for them to find an airwaves-of-Zion studio from which they can send forth their "plain-folk" evangelism. When that happens Appalachia's AM airwaves may become less culturally varied and rich by the loss.
>
> (Dorgan 1993: 33)

Other programs tapped into the era's ebullient materialism, like Reverend Ike (born Frederick J. Eikerenkoetter II), a flamboyant African-American media evangelist and faith healer who preached self-actualization and get-rich theology as "mind science" for decades on both television and radio. Harking back to the messianic prosperity theology of Father Divine, Reverend Ike established the Palace Cathedral in a lavishly renovated New York movie theater, where his sermons blended scripture, motivational speaking, and unabashed celebration of the abundant life. His distinctive growly voice grooved on nearly 2,000 radio stations at his peak in the 1970s, wheedling his listeners (estimated in the millions) to "forget about pie-in-the-sky, get yours here and now" and hawking blessed prayer cloths to be mailed to donors.

Being "on the air" could afford even the most marginalized religious groups a chance to make their pitch to the public. It is worth remembering that one of the early demands of Branch Davidian prophet David Koresh—holed up with his followers, wives, and children in their heavily fortified Mt. Carmel compound in Waco, Texas, during the February to April 1993 standoff with ATF and the FBI—was that his messages be broadcast on the radio. Perhaps Koresh hoped that being granted airtime for his rambling, apocalyptic Biblical exegesis conferred a measure of legitimacy; he recorded a message from the compound that was aired in its entirety on AM-1080 KRLD Dallas, a news-talk station owned by a corporate subsidiary of a religious denomination. Recorded sound became a weapon used by both sides in that hostage standoff when the FBI blared high-volume rock music from sound trucks aimed toward the klieg-lit compound at night. Very little survived the fire which consumed the buildings and its occupants; ironically, aside from some grainy videotape, the hours of reel-to-reel spoken negotiations and sermonizing are all that remain, serving both as evidence for tactical strategists and scholars to analyze, and as a spoken eulogy to the suicidal religious far-right fringe itself.

Radio has remained important even though its cultural and regulatory environment has changed dramatically in the United States. In 1982, deregulation removed the FCC requirement for stations to report their percentage of public service programming and announcements, which further removed the incentive for both AM and FM stations to air local religious broadcasting (Dorgan 1993: 24). Five years later, the FCC declared the "fairness doctrine" unconstitutional and stopped enforcing it, finally removing it from the regulations in 2011. Rules on station ownership and market share also underwent deregulation. During the 1970s no single entity could own broadcasting and newspaper outlets in the same market, but deregulation of the 1980s and significant legal changes in the 1990s, notably the Telecommunications Act of 1996, now permit such cross-ownership.

The Telecommunications Act of 1996 was the first major rewrite of the act governing radio broadcasting since 1934. Coming 12 years after the breakup of the telecommuncations monopoly held by AT&T, the new legislation aimed to open media markets to greater competition by relaxing rules on station licensing and joint ownership of media outlets in the same markets. The new legislation had a dramatic and rapid effect on the medium of radio, resulting in a frenzy of media mergers and consolidation in the industry. Some advocacy groups, like the Future of Music Coalition, argue that the new law has accelerated consolidation by large media conglomerates, who reduce costs by running unattended operations from central offices, syndicating their products and playlists on multiple stations simultaneously (Keith 2010: 329). This robo-broadcasting, they argue, stifles truly local broadcasting and jeopardizes cultural and musical diversity on the American airwaves. In a 2006 report, they found that the top ten radio station owners claimed two-thirds of the entire listening audience and that local ownership of stations had declined by a third between 1975 and 2005 (DiCola 2006).

Between one-fifth and one-half of all radio stations in a local area can be owned by the same company, depending on the size of the market, and there are no limits on the number of stations that can be owned nationwide. The result has been massive consolidation of the radio industry, including of its religious radio segments. There are more stations than ever, occupying precisely defined demographic and format niches, but with a shrinking number of owners. In 1950, the United States had approximately 2,800 radio stations; that number grew to 6,500 in 1970 and to over 11,000 by 2009. Stations defined by the National Religious Broadcasters as full-time "Evangelical stations" continued to expand within the new regulatory structure, numbering almost 400 in 1972 but over 1,300 in 1995 (Hoover and Kaneva 2009: 70). A few very large players including Clear Channel, Cumulus, CBS Radio, and Entercom, own the vast majority of radio stations, and divide their large market shares into niche stations aimed at smaller segments of the listening audience. In the field of religious radio, the for-profit network Salem Communications is the fifth-largest radio station owner in the United States, with close to 100 high-powered

Christian stations in multiple formats on both AM and FM, airing what it describes as "family-themed content and conservative values." The company also owns the Salem Radio Network, which syndicates politically conservative talk shows and the daily or weekly shows of more than 70 Christian ministries, tied into related Internet content and magazine publishing.

One potential countertrend to radio industry consolidation is the 2000 decision by the FCC to open up the FM spectrum for low-powered (LPFM) licenses in the ten- to hundred-watt range, many of which were acquired by noncommercial religious organizations poised for a new revival of faith-based broadcasting. Triggered in part as a response to the microradio movement in the 1990s (tagged as "pirates" by the National Association of Broadcasters), these changes may allow small-wattage broadcasters to—once again—reinvent the American medium of radio.

Outside the United States, especially in developing countries, radio remains an important site of struggle between nationalism, commercialized globalism, and folk cultures. Religious movements jump borders and become "new religious movements" in fresh settings, often providing solace to followers but instability and challenge to political systems. This can be seen as audio technology (cassette tape, radio, and the Internet) fuels the growth of charismatic Pentecostalism in South America and Africa or conveys the ideas of Islamic fundamentalism to disenfranchised Arabs in diaspora around the world (see, e.g., Hackett 1998). It is remarkably difficult to block radio content; it travels readily into popular culture by car, audio player, and even cell phone, its reach extended even further (McLuhanesque) by recordings, podcasts, and filesharing technology. Radio's power to generate and maintain religious communities—and thus to reinvigorate alternative frameworks of meaning—remains undiminished in the twenty-first century.

Do we even have radio anymore?

Analog broadcasting, whether centralized or local, competes with new and emerging formats. Digital Audio Broadcasting (DAB), also called HD radio, exists but has not yet been widely adopted. It offers higher-fidelity sound quality and less interference, broader coverage, and permits up to eight additional program "side streams" emanating on the same signal. However, it requires different signaling technology and digital receivers; it remains to be seen whether it will displace or coexist with traditional radio broadcasting. Likewise, satellite and subscription direct-to-user radio (like Sirius and XM) beam radio content, including religious programming, on a potentially unlimited number of channels. Internet radio streaming, iTunes, and podcasting, not to mention filesharing programs and formats, also provide a "radio-like" experience on computers and mobile devices without being "stations" in the conventional sense. These new formats were certainly not envisioned by the 1996 Telecommunications Act and complicate the audio media environment of the twenty-first century.

Increasingly, "radio" blurs the line with multimedia digital environments. Is a Web-based service like Pandora a "radio" or a "Web site"? Are podcasts downloaded through iTunes, even if originally produced for on-air broadcasting, still "radio" productions? These transformations to radio are part of a broader digital revolution that has beleaguered "traditional" media of all kinds, and has given consumers a dizzying (perhaps even wearying) proliferation of options.

The history of how the Internet developed is quite different from the way radio developed; there are no spectrum and no "channels" on the Web, so there's no need to allocate frequencies except for wireless delivery of Internet content. The "air-waves" are clearly a public domain, but not so with the Internet, where delivery is through a complicated system of wires, cables, servers, commercial providers, and "access points." Internet production further decentralizes both production and distribution of audio content, a development that has thoroughly disrupted the music industry. Anyone with a microphone and an Internet connection can make startlingly high-quality audio programming and distribute it cheaply around the world.

It is safe to say that there will always be an audio dimension of religious life, and that both now and in the future we will see many platforms, some not yet envisioned, alongside analog broadcasting. In an increasingly fragmented media environment, even identity itself has become unstable; people negotiate and perform malleable identities in different contexts. Radio will continue to refract cultural tensions; listeners can determine meaning and resist being identified only as consumers or commodities. Lowering the threshold for radio/audio production and distribution makes room for voices of the marginalized and weak, even as corporate radio broadcasting churns out standardized, faceless, and voiceless—but slickly polished—streams of audio content. Transmission of radio far beyond its local region and beyond the reach of analog propagation may help coalesce and shape transnational identities in an increasingly globalized world.

In any case, it is critical to keep in mind that audiences are the real co-producers of radio, in that they create its meaning and its meaningfulness, whether they tune in or stream online. Even the near-total authority of "consumption" as the supreme virtue for broadcast media has never been complete, due in no small part to religious messaging and to the formation of new coalitions, lobbies, and broadcasting models (Czitrom 1982: 191). Religion overlaps with radio genres in ways that demand further study, particularly with talk radio. Format categories (like "Contemporary Christian Music") frame cultural productions in ways that religious audiences experience as both familiar and significant. In his book on radio in the global age, David Hendy (2000) argues that media do not simply report on social worlds that would be the same without them; instead, they actively constitute social worlds. Therefore, who talks, who sings, and who listens (and what they hear) remain as important as ever for scholars of media, religion, and popular culture.

Works cited

Apostolidis, P. (2000) *Stations of the Cross: Adorno and Christian Right Radio*, Durham, NC: Duke University Press.

Brennan, T.J. (1989) "The Fairness Doctrine as public policy," *Journal of Broadcasting and Electronic Media* 33, 4: 419–40.

Czitrom, D. (1982) *Media and the American Mind: From Morse to McLuhan*, Chapel Hill, NC: University of North Carolina Press.

DiCola, P. (2006) *False Premises, False Promises: A Quantitative History of Ownership Consolidation in the Radio Industry*, Washington, DC: Future of Music Coalition.

Dorgan, H. (1993) *The Airwaves of Zion: Radio and Religion in Appalachia*, Knoxville, TN: The University of Tennessee Press.

Douglas, S. (1999) *Listening in: Radio and the American Imagination*, Minneapolis, MN: University of Minnesota Press.

Eliade, M. (1961) *The Sacred and the Profane: The Nature of Religion*, New York: Harper & Row.

Erickson, H. (1992) *Religious Radio and Television in the United States, 1921–1991: The Programs and Personalities*, Jefferson, NC: McFarland & Company, Inc.

Fosdick, H.E. (1922) "Shall the Fundamentalists win?" *Christian Work* 102 (June 22): 716–22.

Hackett, R. (1998) "Charismatic/Pentecostal appropriations of media technologies in Nigeria and Ghana," *Journal of Religion in Africa* 28, 3: 258–77.

Hangen, T. (2002) *Redeeming the Dial: Radio, Religion and Popular Culture in America*, Chapel Hill, NC: The University of North Carolina Press.

HCJB Global (2012) "Radio planting and development worldwide." Online. Available: www. hcjb.org/projects/priority-projects/radio-planting-and-development.html (accessed 28 February 2013).

Hendershot, H. (2007) "God's angriest man: Carl McIntire, Cold War fundamentalism, and right-wing broadcasting," *American Quarterly* 59, 2: 373–96.

Hendy, D. (2000) *Radio in the Global Age*, Cambridge: Polity Press.

Hilmes, M. (1997) *Radio Voices: American Broadcasting, 1922–1952*, Minneapolis, MN: University of Minnesota Press.

——(2002) *Only Connect: A Cultural History of Broadcasting in the United States*, Belmont, CA: Wadsworth.

Hoover, S.M. and N. Kaneva (eds) (2009) *Fundamentalisms and the Media*, New York: Continuum International Publishing Group.

Hulsether, M. (1992) "Evangelical popular religion as a source for North American liberation theology? insights from postmodern popular culture theory," *American Studies* 33 (Spring): 63–81.

Jones, C.W. (1946) *Radio: The New Missionary*, Chicago, IL: Moody Press.

Keith, M. (2010) *The Radio Station: Broadcast, Satellite, and Internet*, 8th edition. Boston, MA: Focal Press.

Kelman, A.Y. (2009) *Station Identification: A Cultural History of Yiddish Radio in the United States*, Berkeley, CA: University of California Press.

Lynd, R. and H. Lynd (1929) *Middletown: A Study in Modern Culture*, New York: Harcourt Brace and Company.

McLuhan, M. (1964) *Understanding Media: The Extensions of Man*, New York: McGraw Hill.

Martin-Barbero, J. (1997) "Mass media as a site of resacralization of contemporary cultures," in S. Hoover and K. Lundby (eds), *Rethinking Media, Religion and Culture*, Thousand Oaks, CA: Sage Publications, 102–16.

Ong, W. (1967) *Presence of the Word: Some Prolegomena for Cultural and Religious History*, New Haven, CT: Yale University Press.

Parker, E.C., E. Inman, and R. Snyder (1948) *Religious Radio: What to Do and How*, New York: Harper & Brothers Publishers.

Siegel, D.S. and S. Siegel (2007) *Radio and the Jews*, Yorktown Heights, NY: Book Hunter Press.

7
MUSIC

Mark Hulsether

There are so many kinds of popular music, varieties of religion, and ways to write about them! It is like drinking from a fire hose to explore them in the comprehensive way that seems expected in a chapter of this kind. The issue is not solely that, if we begin such an inquiry, the task seems daunting. More troubling is that—supposing that we succeed—it is not entirely clear what we would gain. The argument would have to be so diffuse, who would be interested? What would be the takeaway argument, other than that there are many ways to think about religion and music? Who would deny that? True, teachers may want students to reflect on the complexities, and some students may be interested in small doses. Still, we need to be careful.

Thus, we open with a section that reflects on why we might care about this topic in the first place. The second section takes up problems of definition and framing raised by our inquiry. The third section makes three interpretive suggestions to orient future explorations. Since readers can make their own lists of popular musicians and forms of religion—better-textured lists than mine in the areas they most care about—we will focus on clarifying thematic and interpretive issues, which we might also imagine as strategies to manage the flow from the above-mentioned fire hose. For readers who may have hoped for a thumbnail history of US popular music or overview of global religious music, this is not an attempt to reinvent those wheels; there are fine "already-existing wheels" (e.g., Weiner 2009; Miller and Shahriari 2008; Rubin and Melnick 2007; Brackett 2004; Sullivan 1997; Cullen 1996). As you read, I encourage you to hold in mind a few songs and artists that you know well, to give concrete texture to the reflection.

Why should we care about religion and popular music?

Music is powerful. It is among the oldest and most evocative means of human communication, whether considered as a sort of language, a set of technologies to do things with groups, or raw sensual experience. If someone states "I *like* to listen to music" or "I have personal musical preferences," such words capture such a small part of music's significance that (certainly for many people and probably for everyone) they mislead as much as they clarify. They threaten to short-circuit insights needed to grasp music's depth and breadth, including effects that may be unconscious or yet-unlocked potentialities.

Music's multilayered quality gives it great density and range of expression through melody, harmony, rhythm, tone (timbre), and raw volume (amplitude)—with or without words, memories, and ritual meanings attached as they typically are. In myriad variations, music bundles the channeling of emotion, articulation of ideas, and evocation of memory (personal, collective, and evolutionary). It has remarkable capacities to move bodies (especially, although not solely, through rhythm) and connect individuals with groups. All this formidable repertoire can come into play even for one person, listening alone. Beyond this, music has deep capacities to bind listeners together if experienced collectively—not just compared to solitary listening but also to collectively hearing spoken words or viewing images (Ross 2007; Levitin 2006; Bull and Black 2004).

Suppose we turn from an inventory of music's strengths and compare it to what literacy offers as a mode of communication and experience. If so, writing words on a page and assimilating them individually through the eye seems shrunken and impoverished, even disembodied and bloodless—notwithstanding literacy's reputation as a hallmark of progress and its proven value for cultivating abstract, historical, and imaginative thought. Champions of literacy and reason are often equally attuned to sound's emotive and somatic powers, as are musicians and advocates of oral traditions—precisely because they understand that sound poses a challenge to keep in check if one valorizes linear and abstract reason (Smith 2004; Schmidt 2000). Reaching far back in time—for example, to Plato's case for musical censorship or the long-running struggle between Apollonian and Dionysian sensibilities—gatekeepers of reason have made this point as often as champions of sound. Some theorists compare cultures that stress learning through the eye—and by extension prioritizing visual metaphors like, "Can you see our point of view?"—to other cultures that cultivate sonic sensibility and favor metaphors like "Can you hear where we are coming from?" Such theorists suggest that visually oriented cultures have a more pervasive sense of distancing and abstract judgment, as opposed to cultures that stress shared participation, embodiment, and emotion.

We should not go overboard with this line of thought, since most people use both sound and sight as well as other senses including taste and smell. We can try to achieve a harmonious democracy of the senses collaborating, rather than ranking our senses hierarchically. Also, even after we note the world-historical importance of the invention of writing (extended by printing), as well as the profound differences in sensibility between European classical as opposed to blues-based African-American music—nevertheless to lump whole continents, stretches of history, and/or ethnic groups as visual or "oral" is an abstraction that may do more harm than good.

In particular there are two overstated stereotypes to keep in check. One is the "exotic Africans have rhythm but whites are square" problem, which is indeed rooted in indispensable comparative insights about orality, cultural sensibility, institutional racism, and sources of musical innovation in the Americas, yet all too often has metastasized through writing on popular music as a substitute for thinking. Another is the "religion is for exotic primitives and irrational women" problem. That is, we might wish it were obvious that religions fall at both ends of a visual/oral continuum, cultivating different parts of a larger religious repertoire. In fact, however, many people correlate literacy and rationality (seen as positive) with secularization and religious disenchantment: they correlate religion with the emotional, non-rational, feminized (in a pejorative sense), and primitive. Others presuppose the same distinction and invert the good and bad guys. It is impossible to write about religion and music without being buffeted by waves of assumptions reflecting these patterns of thought. A typical result is a discourse with more heat than light—or since we are prioritizing sonic metaphors, a dialogue of the deaf and a failure of harmony and flow.

As we try to evade these pitfalls, it remains true that humans live within cultural traditions that teach distinctive hierarchies among the senses, cultivated in variable ways in different places. In our context it is useful to revalorize sound to vie with sight as the most important sense—even for wonkish sorts of modern males who might "naturally" undervalue it. We can correct for an overstress on the visual in a culture shaped by literacy, and imagine a pendulum swinging closer to equilibrium. Moreover, although the term "postmodernity" can be associated with almost anything, scholars marching under its banner often correlate modernity with literacy, then go on to identify emerging postmodern (or late modern) trends distinguishable from classic modernity. Such thinking calls attention to our culture's ultra-mediated and highly networked quality, its orientation to spectacle and consumer choice, and the way it erodes rational deliberation about the common good since it makes decisions about what is produced (and by extension who lives and dies) through an aggregate of short-term profit calculations by those with money to spend.

Postmodern trends unsettle classic assumptions about literacy. At a minimum they suggest the value of rebranding words like "critical" and "literacy" to highlight goals like literacy in reading music videos and critical thought about social media. They may sometimes push these metaphors toward a breaking point and suggest a need for emergent concepts like "deep listening" or for reassessing what constitutes critical thought in a culture that prioritizes what comedian Stephen Colbert calls "truthiness"—assumptions about what *feels* true in one's gut—over old-fashioned warranted truth claims.

If we approach music with these ideas on board—as investigators who are theoretically self-aware and at home in postmodernity—we obviously will notice that soundscapes include more than music and that music is only one part of popular culture (however underappreciated in hybrid forms like soundtracks, ringtones, or part of the ambience of restaurants). Still, if part of our task is rethinking a hierarchy of sight over sound within postmodernity's incessant mediated flow—which in some ways seems more like traditional oral cultures than classic literate ones—there can be no doubt about the central importance of popular music, since it is among the most developed forms of sound and pervasive within our culture.

Direct participation in creating music takes us beyond what we have considered so far. In the right setting, musicians feel like a sort of vessel or instrument for mysterious creative powers channeling through them. At such times, we may think of music as quasi-religious or even quasi-mystical experience. Indeed the only reason to hesitate before dropping the qualifier "quasi" is that in some cases we need to distinguish between performances that are understood by musicians or their listeners as more religious than others, according to their own definitions. Whether we should grant that such distinctions matter much for describing the core experience is an open question.

One paradigmatic version of this mysterious experience of flow—a place where it runs deep and powerfully—comes in collective jazz improvisation with an optimum balance between structured rhythms and chords, on one side, and the opportunity for free experimentation within and against the grain of this structure, on the other. One can enter a sort of ecstatic trance in this context and feel music flowing through one's fingers as if the mind has dropped away and the body is a channel for deeper powers (Walser 1998 has many descriptions). However, non-improvising players of what we have come to call classical music (let us be clear that the categories classical, jazz, and popular have not been stable over time!) probably experience a similar sense of ordinary consciousness falling away and music flowing through them; they may go on to argue vigorously for the superior aesthetic quality of their canon compared with most jazz. Meanwhile musicians attuned to free jazz, as well as certain avant-garde composers usually lumped as classical, put less emphasis on a balance between structure and improvisation, as opposed to pushing the boundaries of structure to a point where music crosses into creative noise we have never heard before, or pure sound, or beyond. In any case, it is clear that being drawn into participatory aspects of creating music may greatly expand powers of music that were already strong.

Non-musicians can share in this phenomenon. Being swept up within music while listening—for example, keeping a beat in one's head and anticipating upcoming passages with such focus that listening and participating converge, or identifying so strongly with a song's ideas that they become building blocks for one's identity—may be comparable. Such active listening, in which "listening" is a pale word for something more like being swallowed by music, may even intensify the effect since there is less chance of being distracted by the limits of one's own musical skills. So it is possible that participatory hymn-singing, temple music, and rituals involving sacred dance—if led by skillful musicians in groups with an exemplary participatory spirit—are what truly plumb the depths of music's power. Or again, perhaps the best "non-religious" performances that build upon religious genres go yet deeper by moving beyond distractions and obstacles associated with "normal" religious contexts; we might interpret some of the best writing on religion and music as exploring this hypothesis.

If all the above layers—individual listening, collective experience, and participating in musical creation—come together in the right setting, the emotional, conceptual, and kinetic effects are among the most profound and motivating that humans can attain (see Levitin 2006). Indeed at this point we likely should expand our frame of reference beyond the human. Sadly we need an author with wider expertise to advance very far in this direction. Still we can reflect, first, on how many of our fellow creatures such as whales, coyotes, and loons use sounds that seem at least music-like, and, second, on how many esoteric philosophers (Pythagoras stands out as best-remembered in the West) treat sound and music as basic building blocks of the entire cosmos.

Thus, we arrive at a general answer to our question about why this topic matters. If we grant even a fraction of the above, could anyone *not* care about music? Can we imagine it *not* taking popular forms? Could religions possibly fail to be entangled with music—especially if they hope to become popular in a sense of thriving among ordinary people?

But wait!—someone may object—when do we get to the part about Britney Spears, Jay-Z, and the current flavor of the month like (as I write) Miley Cyrus? Aren't we discussing *popular* music, and not John Coltrane's inner ecstasies during his most sublime solos? True, we must remember that some people would not identify with much of the above—or if listening to certain artists, *any* of it. Some people discern the music with which they identify precisely in *contrast* to shallow and debased sounds brought to them by MTV, VIBE magazine, and Miller beer. Beyond this, are there not readers who have agreed with me thus far, and have been nodding along thinking about music recommended on Pitchfork.com—the only music they would ever buy or, more precisely, illegally download—but who are passionately anti-religious in their self-concept? Have they not *earned* this passion by being so profoundly bored, disgusted, or traumatized by music heard in religious institutions and on Christian radio?

When music is off-putting, its alienating effects are equal and opposite to the binding effects noted above. Can you recall an interpersonal exchange during which you thought you had shared a deep musical experience, only to discover that the other person heard nothing interesting or even something repellent? Any musician can tell stories of finding films unwatchable or restaurants intolerable due to the music, and how incredulous they felt when their non-musician companions were oblivious to the issue. Their companions may in turn complain about hypersensitive musicians obsessed with trivial preferences. The more deeply one responds to music and cares about the other people, the more such gaps are puzzling and disturbing. It can be like declaring one's love and getting a negative response.

Indeed responses to music are often part of the substance of falling in love. Couples bond through sharing music. Think of the cliché, "they're playing our song" and the filmic convention of cueing the strings—or conversely the sound that signifies a failed connection, a needle careening off a turntable. These come as no surprise when a key form of flirtation is suggesting music to share. Even without an invitation to dance that classically comes with it, this is a proxy for expressing emotion directly—like buying a Hallmark card but more robust, especially for males who have been socialized to be inarticulate about their feelings. Harnessing the affective potential of shared music and testing musical tastes for compatibility (or lack of it) may be as consequential for finding a partner as being visually attractive, smelling right, or having powerful sexual chemistry—it may accelerate a relationship or derail it.

I linger on this point because—in our cultural context that stresses voluntary self-investment in a religion that "feels right for you"—there are noteworthy parallels between finding a mate and choosing a religious practice. It is not that either side of this comparison—today's spiritual marketplace or postmodern love—reflects changeless givens of human nature. Arranged marriage was (and remains) a norm in many places, and within US history it is a fairly new (unevenly realized) phenomenon that women can choose partners while presupposing access to reliable contraceptives, economic autonomy, and a somewhat open path to choosing a partner of either sex without extreme pushback. Thus much is distinctive about how people "naturally" fall in love today, even though the trends built on evolutionary biology and postmodern youth did not invent the idea that (as Shakespeare said) "music is the food of love."

Something similar holds true for "religious preferences" today. True, as long as humans have done things that match up half-plausibly with current definitions of religion, people have exercised choice about exactly how much, in and what ways, to participate. Music and dance have been part of the equation with all their capacities noted above. Throughout history this has involved roughly the same brains and bodies responding to the same cosmos—whether people joined religious systems by being born into them (like entering arranged marriages without imagining any alternative) or by designing their own personal spiritualities like the notorious "Sheila" (from Bellah *et al.* 1985), who created "Sheilaism."

Nevertheless there are distinctive things about discerning and creating religious commitments under conditions of postmodern diversity. To whatever degree our culture valorizes personal religious choice (and however much the choice is constrained in practice), the magnetic power of music to attract—or with the polarities reversed to repel—is often as central to building religious identities as it is to courtship. The above-mentioned musician who fled an unlistenable film soundtrack and the couple who melted together as the band played their song are illuminating metaphors for whether one joins or flees a given church (or synagogue, coven, etc.). This dynamic also operates more fluidly with other spiritual self-investments. A new millennium Sheila might not seek a specific church (or yoga studio, etc.), yet her Sheilaism may be deeply shaped by music toward which she gravitates or spiritual ideas learned from her favorite musicians.

This constitutes a second argument for our topic's importance, partly entering through a back door. Musical likes (and dislikes) that create (and repel) affective bonds are major parts of spiritual-religious identity formation, especially in the current cultural context.

Working definitions to frame our inquiry

We turn to the challenge of clarifying definitions for our three terms: religion, music, and popular. Despite a risk of bogging down here, much is at stake. It is no less important for us to be pointed in the right direction as it is for travelers in an unfamiliar train station to be sure they are boarding a train headed where they want to go.

Scholarly readers may already be weary of these disputes, but for the uninitiated let us consider some representative complexities. Regarding religion, when does it cross over to not-religion? Is any practice religious, by definition, if it is deeply valued and engenders powerful attachments—so that going to dance clubs can be someone's religion and if this person were dragged unwillingly into a Baptist church it would not count (for them) as an experience with religion? Regarding the popular, what distinguishes it from the not popular? Can music that only interests a tiny subculture be popular, even if its fans call themselves a vanguard? Suppose someone takes illicit drugs and dances past dawn at an illegal rave—not a widespread practice compared to watching *American Idol*. Depending on our definitions of popular and religion, the "religion of raves" could range all the way from being paradigmatic for us to being marginal. Conversely, if Georg F. Handel's oratorio *The Messiah* is widely sold, broadcast on the radio, performed by community choirs, and used for ringtones, must we call it popular music despite it being in a category (highbrow classical) that is not ordinarily described as popular, and might even constitute what "popular" means by contrast?

Also, who defines music? The Islamic call to prayer seems clearly religious, as well as popular at least in a sense of being prevalent in many people's everyday lives. Yet suppose Muslim clerics insist, as many do, that it should not be linked with the term "music." Does this exclude it from our inquiry? What about New Age recordings of bird calls and waves, or avant-garde music like John Cage's "4' 33," with its four minutes and thirty-three seconds of silence that call attention to other sounds in the room? When do they cross over from music to mere sound or noise?

Notice how, depending on definitions, all the following examples may—but also may not—fall under an umbrella of popular religious music: the set list from a rave, folk hymns like "Amazing Grace" (if kept pure and off commercial radio), your favorite sports team's fight song, the "Hallelujah Chorus," and the Islamic call to prayer. This is only the tip of an iceberg. If we tried to address all levels of meaning in soundscapes, for all major religions, intersecting with all senses of the word "popular" in US history—that is, to map all the permutations generated by our background definitions—our discussion would become forbiddingly diffuse and abstract.

Accordingly, my top recommendation for exploring intersections among religion, music, and the popular is to delimit a universe of inquiry until it is small enough— one hopes without excluding too much of what makes our subject valuable—to find some reasonably concrete patterns and pursue a few representative cases in some depth. This advice holds true even for readers who balk at my specific suggestions for enacting it.

For current purposes, I propose to focus on recent US history. Obviously this blocks many roads not taken, both leading outward toward world musicology and backward through millennia before the rise of contemporary media. These are immensely interesting and complicated paths, certainly no less important than those left over after our cut. Importantly, this choice limits a primary focus (see Levine 1988) on how a highbrow/lowbrow distinction collapsed—how the rise of twentieth cen-tury consumer entertainment (widespread dissemination of electronic media, rise of the middlebrow, etc.) broke down distinctions between musical cultures of working people (folk music and dance) and elites.

Second, let us leapfrog over certain complications by starting from a baseline of US vernacular understandings. This approach is academically *non*-obvious—indeed dangerously uncool—and it comes with a stern disclaimer that we will not only vault over a minefield, but also skip a preparatory course in minefield safety. Nevertheless for us, today, music will not refer to all forms of patterned sound—some of which sound like *noise* to people informed by vernacular understandings, or which at least blend into wider soundscapes. Rather music will refer to ... well, the sorts of pat-terned melody, harmony, and rhythm (possibly with words) that people in today's

USA call musical. We can attend to borderline cases if needed, and work from this baseline without forgetting that the categories are fluid.

In a similar spirit we will not use the term "religious" unless we are evoking some linkage or overlap (or at least a compelling comparison) with ideas and practices associated with things that people call religious: synagogues, mosques, temples, zendos, Native American rituals—and, above all, Christian traditions which remain a strong majority option in today's USA, after having been an overwhelming majority during most years since 1492.

This does *not* mean narrowing solely to dogmas, buildings, liturgies, or formal authority structures, as opposed to wider communal traditions associated with them—vocabularies, sensibilities, rituals, prayer routines, holiday practices, and so on. What it *does* mean is caution about stipulating that religion refers, by definition, to anything whatsoever that is deeply meaningful. Down this road religion can become almost formless—such that nothing is more religious than anything else— yet also curiously narrow as in the case of the person who may not be hearing religious music in a Baptist church if she is bored. A key implication is that we will not treat any and all passionate music fandom as "its own religion." (For another approach see Laderman 2009; Sylvan 2003.) Rather we will inquire how such passions interact (as dialogue, critique, reinforcement, zero-sum competition, or messy overlap) with more focused common sense understandings of religion.

Even after this cut, the vernacular term "religious" retains ambiguities. First, although people associate it with discourse about gods, goddesses, angels, sacred places, and other superhuman entities, this pattern is not consistent enough to anchor our definition. Even in Baptist churches, not all activity is oriented to such mysteries. Cooking for potluck dinners, funding the preacher's pension, and hiring a good band are all part of Baptist lived religion. If we expand to Buddhists (often atheistic) or Native American traditions (barely distinguishing between religions and whole ways of life)—among many other possibilities—it is clear that the decisive distinction between religious and not-religious cannot simply fall between orientations to gods or not.

Second, our vernacular gives mixed messages about spirituality. People contrast religion—referencing institutions and external authorities like the Roman Catholic hierarchy with its dogmas, canon lawyers, and lobbyists—with spiritualities that are centered on internalized values and moods (typically cultivated individually) and which treat submission to external authority as something strictly optional and probably undesirable. Yet, religion does not refer solely to whatever is left after such spirituality is filtered out. There is also a vernacular category for the spiritual/religious, in which these terms blend on a shared continuum. Someone whose life is entwined with Catholic institutions (religion) would naturally have values and emotions (spirituality) informed by Catholicism (as a mode of religion/spirituality).

Given that many musicians and their fans say they are spiritual but not religious, and given our plan to focus on religion (guided by vernacular concepts), a question arises whether to include this blurred continuum under a rubric of religion interacting with popular music. I think the answer is clearly yes—and not solely because many self-styled spiritual people do not force a zero-sum choice. Also relevant is that many people underestimate how things that feel to them like mere individual taste or common sense are covertly informed by larger traditions. For example, Madonna and Oprah Winfrey model spiritualities that were shaped by Italian popular Catholicism and African-American Protestantism—whether or not fans are conscious of this. More abstractly, if we overlay core distinctions from Protestant theology (external law, work-righteousness, and ritualism versus internalized grace and the priesthood of all believers) onto a religious versus spiritual distinction, the match is too close for coincidence. In other words, to be consciously anti-religious may be the same as being formed by Protestant tradition. Perhaps we could debate whether to call this a vernacular understanding (for many Protestants it at least comes close) but in any case it suggests how spirituality and religion are entangled. If we treat the self-professed "spiritual but not religious" as religious we do foist a label on them that they may not desire—but still it is more illuminating, for understanding more people, to use an umbrella category that conflates the spiritual and religious on the same continuum, than to use spirituality to split off and marginalize religion.

To recap, as we try to clarify how religion relates to popular music, we will conceive religion broadly enough to cover many lived practices that do not necessarily refer to gods, as well as spiritualities in some tension with institutional religion. Yet we will not define it so broadly as to be untethered from broad lived traditions like Christianity and Buddhism, so that any musical sub-culture based on being fans of X may become the "religion of X" and religion can refer to almost anything but nothing in particular.

Working definitions for "popular" pose a still tougher challenge. Five common sense meanings are in play: (1) the commercial-commodified popular, (2) the authentic-folk-traditional popular, (3) the widely-prevalent popular, (4) the aesthetic-cutting-edge popular, and (5) the counter-hegemonic popular. Our challenge is that these are independent variables, and they are rarely all relevant at the same time.

Vernacular use points us toward the first sense, commercial music disseminated through electronic media to a wide audience, or at least a reasonable subcategory of such an audience. For better or worse, let us delimit our reflections mainly to this ballpark. Such a stipulation avoids certain minefields by creating others, because we are striking off in the opposite direction from a sizable body of scholarship, especially by historians, in which the term popular religion implies an authentic or folk tradition (sense 2) defined precisely by its not having been polluted by commercial popularization and electronic dissemination. If music on today's radio draws on folk roots—as of course it often does—this water becomes exceedingly muddy. Can some types of popular music (in sense 1) be more "authentic" than others (in sense 2)? Who decides? (See Miller 2010; Lornell 2002; Peterson 1997; Cantwell 1996; Frith 1996.) Nevertheless, at least in principle, we can steer toward the musical parts of the resulting mud that are in reasonably wide commercial circulation.

After bracketing this complication as best we can, the remaining discussion of commercial-popular music shades off in three directions. On one front, popular means something widely prevalent—many ordinary people consume it. Most people at a wedding dance will recognize Prince's "Purple Rain," and most (including non-churchgoers) can sing along with "Amazing Grace" because they know it from the radio (country, R&B, or gospel) or film soundtracks. In such cases the popular as commodified (sense 1) and prevalent (sense 3) coincide.

Assume for a moment that such overlap defines a sweet spot we want to identify as a paradigmatic popular (before turning to how it relates to religion). We could zero in by excluding things from two directions. Not all prevalent music is disseminated commercially—for example, "Happy Birthday to You" or songs like "Jesus Loves Me" if taught outside a nexus of consumer culture. (Since "Amazing Grace" might also be approached in this light, certain versions of it might be deemed popular in stronger senses than others.) Conversely, some commercial music is not widely prevalent. Joe Strummer, leader of The Clash, formed a band called The Mescaleros which offers a borderline example, as does Handel's *Messiah*, which here serves as an exception to prove a rule—that highbrow classical music (say, Krzystof Penderecki's "Stabat Mater") may require extreme niche marketing.

We are making progress toward a manageable focus! But a problem lurks if we concentrate on music in the overlap between commercial and prevalent populars. For example, suppose we focus on "Oops! I Did It Again" by Britney Spears over "Johnny Appleseed" by the Mescaleros, and Elvis Presley's "Heartbreak Hotel" over Bob Dylan's "In My Time of Dyin'" (with its refrain of "Jesus' Gonna Make up My Dyin' Bed," its possibly greater "authenticity"—and, fascinatingly, the same tune as "Heartbreak Hotel"). If so, we may convey—at least to discerning critics—an impression of wasting time on music that is boring, least common denominator, complicit with disturbing hegemonic trends, and/or soul-polluting. In short we may lose our focus on the music that motivated us to study this topic in the first place.

It would be complicated enough if, when critics find prevalent popular music less interesting than whatever they valorize, this solely led them to dismiss popular music and turn to highbrow music and/or more edifying religious music. Certainly such attacks form a common pattern. Clergy may decry mainstream hip-hop for pandering to promiscuity and/or misogyny; in this view popular trends are something religious people should shun. Or scholars might focus more on hymnody as opposed to mainstream hits (see Stowe 2004; Westermeyer 1993). Here again Handel's *Messiah* may pose interesting questions about boundary maintenance. Suppose it is performed at a cathedral, broadcast on NPR, and for good measure transmuted into a gospel music style. Would this be a case of the valorized highbrow being dragged toward the middlebrow and diluted by popular trends? Conversely, is it sufficiently refined to avoid the stigma attached to popular music on the radio?

In fact standoffishness toward the prevalent does not solely lead toward alternatives to popular music, but also deeper into it, toward more valorized subsets: Madonna's best videos over Miley Cyrus's worst, or Coltrane's "Love Supreme" over advertising jingles. Importantly, this road often leads toward the music and critical writing that make our inquiry most valuable. Here we broach our fourth and fifth senses of popular, the aesthetically discerning and the counter-hegemonic, and circle back to our earlier-mentioned hipsters who download music recommended on Pitchfork. Their tastes may include what they consider the best of the prevalent-popular or emergent artists that they expect to become prevalent. Frequently, however, they favor music that pushes the boundaries of the least common denominator. They may consider transgression and innovation as more aesthetically worthy than excellence in a tried and true genre, or disdain music that is embraced widely—a habit that conveniently generates cultural capital for insiders like themselves.

Many critics favor music that is popular in this sense—and *especially* favor it when superior aesthetic quality (sense 4) dovetails with counter-hegemonic cultural critique (sense 5). Here again sweet spots come together and come apart, since politically virtuous music may be more potently counter-hegemonic if it circulates widely, even at the cost of being less cutting-edge. There are many complexities because counter-hegemonic virtue comes in multiple forms.

Plenty of examples of counter-hegemonic popular music are available to construct lists that go on at length (Lipsitz 2007; Reed 2005; Werner 1999; Denning 1996; Rose 1994). Obvious choices include music that carries overt messages on its surface (e.g., "The Internationale" or "John Brown's Body") or is widely understood to be a soundtrack for a social movement. If one begins by considering a social movement important, its musical aspects become significant by extension. Conversely if one begins by finding some music (say, Bob Marley's) interesting in itself, this might help draw one into an associated social movement.

However, looking for one-to-one correspondences between music and social movements is too narrow. Music may flounder both aesthetically and as resonant critique if it is too preachy. Lyrics are equally capable of undermining a song's aesthetic or critical power and of enhancing it. Often a song's impact on both fronts is stronger if it conveys its critique through sound or becomes the soundtrack of a movement despite apolitical lyrics. Difficult to pin down, yet very important, are indirect or oblique cultural critiques carried through sounds that do not articulate overt political positions, yet have cultural-political associations. Examples include certain sounds coded "black" during the civil rights era, "punkish" in the years around 1980, or "queer-friendly" in recent years. We may also speak cautiously about a sense of possibility, or expanded imagination, which can be taught or evoked through music—a sort of cultural influence or personal formation that might be overtly politicized only in potential. Toward this outer limit, cultural politics becomes so diffuse that we cannot easily pinpoint—especially with measurable "objective evidence"—what counts as a transformative effect. Yet this is not a good reason to stop paying attention.

Sometimes it happens that counter-hegemonic music is at the same time commercially viable, widely prevalent, and aesthetically superior. It may even draw on "authentic" folk roots for a maximum 4.5-out-of-5 overlap. This is the Holy Grail pursued by many scholars of popular music—although for others, pretensions to authenticity would be a demerit and 4 would be the top score. By extension, if and when such music comes into dialogue with spiritual-religious sensibilities—fusing with them or launching resonant critiques—we have found the ultimate sweet spot for our inquiry, at least as far as such critics are concerned.

In practice, of course, Holy Grails are elusive. Music that is both aesthetically superior and counter-hegemonic is a smallish subset, at best, of commercial popular music. Precisely because this is true, people who write about music often have an edge of advocacy—they are engaged in a give and take of public contestation over what should become popular. Scholarly champions and ordinary fans of music that is popular in our fourth and fifth senses may be highly invested in *defining* this music as a paradigmatic popular, representing the exemplary articulation of a people's voice—in explicit opposition to a prevalent popular. Thus scholars (e.g., Kelley 1998;

Rose and Ross 1994; Hebdige 1979) might valorize an upsurge of a politicized reggae, hip hop and/or punk music, treated as a sort of anthem for oppositional youth sub-cultures. Or a distinction that I have tried to make non-polemically—noting that the third and fifth senses of popular are independent variables—can be made by attacking mass culture (sense 3 as the debased commercial) in defense of popular culture (sense 5 as "authentic people's music") (see Levine 1992; Hall 1981).

There is no simple way to finesse this complexity. Because five kinds of popular—commercial, authentic, prevalent, hip, and counter-hegemonic—are independent variables, tensions inevitably arise, even before we inquire how the popular (whatever subset is in focus) interacts with religion.

Because we have entered a field so broad that selectivity is inevitable, to identify a subset to explore is not a problem—provided we clarify the stakes of the choice and argue persuasively. Problems more often run in the opposite direction, when writers aspire to a neutrality and comprehensiveness that represents false objectivity. They may covertly valorize certain kinds of music, but in ways that make it difficult to perceive what is at stake. However much we pursue a Holy Grail of music that brings religion together with a maximum number of kinds of popular, the key point is to be alert to the interplay among variant meanings of our terms.

Three patterns in a field shared by music, religion, and the popular

What happens when religion, music, and the popular overlap or otherwise encounter each other? By now it should be clear that mapping all possibilities is out of the question, definitions are so slippery that it would be futile to try to quantify objective patterns, and we could extrapolate in many ways from examples already noted. Nevertheless, let us focus on three key patterns to orient further exploration.

First, we need to uproot a still-too-prevalent perception that there is fairly small overlap between mainstream commercial popular music (sometimes discussed as "secular") and music with significant religious themes and sensibilities. No one denies that they sometimes overlap (as when musicians record Christmas albums) but often people treat such cases as exceptions, proving a rule that most mainstream music is "secular" and most religious music is marginal to it. We should replace this with another rule of thumb—that overlaps are extensive, perhaps closer to defining a norm than being an exception to it.

This is a place where definitions matter. At the same time we need to conceive religion broadly—attending to the slippery distinctions between the products we consume and our religiosity, which in practice "can be described only in their infectious, ritual commingling, both in their distribution and in their consumption" (Lofton 2011: 212)—yet do so without flattening distinctions between forms of music that hold greater or lesser interest for religious issues.

As the historical rise of electronic media and consumer capitalism transformed US culture, it undoubtedly entailed some loss of power for established religious groups. Nevertheless we could overestimate how thoroughly a culture that is secular (in the vernacular sense of non-religious) displaced popular religion, and underplay how much the two converged and shaped each other. If we follow the above framing definitions, we can see that religions changed in form and interpenetrated with commercial culture more than they lost importance. Writers who assume that twentieth century popular religion became marginal and less interesting than (normal) popular culture—and who thus may assume that exploring religious aspects of popular music is like listening to mediocre Christian rock when they could be listening to cutting edge music—risk screening out a great deal. They should consider how many critically acclaimed and top-selling musicians such as Bob Dylan, Madonna, Lupe Fiasco, the Beatles, Hank Williams, Charles Mingus, Aretha Franklin, and Rubén Blades weave religious themes deeply into their music. They should reflect on how pervasively country music is infused with Protestant influences, how blues and rock are built on a foundation of African-American religious music, and so on.

Scholars may be vaguely—even acutely—aware of such things, yet discount them as exceptions or overstress one specific pattern among our meanings of popular. Many (e.g., Moore 1994) have focused on a transition—often presented as a decline by champions of religion—from our second sense (authentic popular religion inherited from the past) to the first (commercialized). They stress how such change can trivialize or marginalize religion by smoothing off its rough edges, reducing it to sound bites, and forcing it to compete with professional sports and amusement park rides as an entertainment product. This does not necessarily imply that religious practice is fading—religion may actually proliferate as private individual choice—and does not imply a position one way or the other about the separation of church and state. Nevertheless, someone pursuing this line of thought may assume that the practice of authentic religion is between a rock and a hard place: if it fails to engage with popular culture it becomes marginal—going the way of the Amish—but if it enters the cultural marketplace, the price of admission is adopting privatized consumer-friendly forms.

Although this approach is illuminating for many examples of popular music, it is often overstressed. We can find cases that fit the pattern, including a fair amount of "praise music" associated with megachurches, Contemporary Christian Music (CCM), and the ongoing rebranding of Evangelicalism to maximize its coolness (Hendershot 2004; Howard and Streck 1999). Yet this is not the sole illuminating approach, and it distracts from two key questions: what are the most prevalent forms of popular music with noteworthy religious dimensions, and which such forms (even if minority reports) make the most interesting aesthetic or counter-hegemonic interventions?

Consider the wide range of additional examples that come into view if we draw on all five senses of popular religion rather than narrowing our attention to a pattern of decline from sense two to one. Consider, also, that when religious groups promote their agendas using popular genres—responding to competition from other forms of mass entertainment by trying to beat them at their own game—this does not always represent decline for them. Often we are better off taking for granted that religion inevitably has commercial dimensions—using this as our starting point rather than using our analysis to arrive at this insight as an end point—and exploring why certain forms of commercial popular music are more prevalent than others, or counter-hegemonic alternatives to others, or more religiously interesting than others—in a context where none escape the logic of the market. If we explore within this frame, we are forced to abandon any lingering impression that religion and popular music are divergent fields with limited overlap. What is striking is how deeply they inter-penetrate, because key building blocks of US popular culture have been part and parcel of popular religion.

The rise of jazz and blues is a classic example of this dynamic, which many scholars have explored (e.g., Lipsitz 2007, 1990; Walser 1998; Small 1998; Ventura 1985; Baraka 1963). True, this music made its home in nightclubs and juke joints that some people considered the antithesis of religion. True, respectable white Protestants (as well as many black clergy) were scandalized by it. However, this music also made its home in churches in the form of gospel music, which became part of the foundation for later styles. It is much better to understand jazz and blues simply as a new style of music—one attuned to African-American sensibilities, with religious and non-religious dimensions tightly interwoven—rather than as a displacement of religious music by secular music (Pinn 2003; Reed 2003; Harris 1994).

We could not possibly provide an overview of religiously inflected country musicians, because, as its leading scholarly authority says, "a religion-shaped approach to life ... permeates the entire country music repertoire" (Malone 2002: 89–90; see also Peterson 1997; Sample 1996). A very short list of superstars known for songs steeped in Protestant ideas must suffice: the Carter family during the formative years of recorded "hillbilly" music in the 1920s; Johnny Cash's iconic career from the 1950s to early 2000s; Dolly Parton and Emmylou Harris, two of the most respected female artists of the past generation; and artists such as Ray Charles, Elvis Presley, and Bob Dylan, who blended country styles, broadly conceived, with genres such as gospel, rhythm and blues, and folk.

My point is not that all country, R&B, and jazz—among other genres—are equally indebted to religious styles and traditions, nor that they constitute "their own religion." Still, Kathryn Lofton (2011: 12) accents the nuance we need when she comments that to "force difference between [the religious and commercial popular] is to compel a false distillation from a quagmire of commingling processes."

Second, a spirituality enmeshed with popular music does not necessarily lead listeners away from institutional religion. As we hold tight to Lofton's words about collapsing distinctions between the religious and secular and make our peace with a big messy overlapping field, we should not assume—prior to case-by-case inquiries—that the default pattern within this fluid zone is people drifting away from institutional religions. Somewhat like champions of "normal" religion who are sometimes too quick to lament decline, popular music writers often overplay a liberating exodus away from the constraints of religion, in cases where they would be better off exploring mutual reinforcement.

Widely cited writers (e.g., Sylvan 2003; Ventura 1985; Marcus 1975) often assume that default forms of US religious music are held back by Western classical (as opposed to African-based) sensibilities. Frequently they associate such music with being white, individualist, emotionally inhibited, lacking in passion, and/or generally deficient in musical interest—especially insofar as one's sense of aesthetic quality stresses polyrhythms and strong communal and participatory sensibilities. Conversely, compelling popular music styles (often explained with attention to African influences) can be a vehicle, especially for generational cohorts of youth, to break away from inherited spiritual/emotional constraints toward new ways of living.

Definitely this pattern fits important cases, and many people with high standards for music and/or deep exposure to US popular music have been repelled by much religious music. If one compares mediocre music in one's local church to the best music in one's iTunes library, it is often a straightforward choice. "Church music" has earned a reputation as a "cut flower arrangement with no life left in it," linked to group singing that is "lackluster and downright awful" (Westermeyer 1993: 177).

Nevertheless this is an oversimplified "apples-and-oranges" comparison tilted to the disadvantage of churches. Notice how many factors—better understood as independent variables—cluster in the above interpretive binary. For example, it correlates being older with being Western, white, and so on, as contrasted with youth, who move beyond their parents by listening to R&B, going to raves, and so on. Yet writers in this tradition typically date a generational breakout of youth in the 1950s or 1960s, or perhaps at the foundation of punk and hip-hop in the late 1970s—that is, when the parents and grandparents of today's youth came of age. The generational implications going forward, regarding youth using R&B or hip-hop to rebel against their parents' boring music, are murky.

Other cases, too, test the limits of this binary. Suppose the youth wish to rebel against the grandparents' folk-rock liturgies or make common cause with selected parents to valorize the hip-hop aesthetic they share. What if a synagogue's cantor has musical skills superior to a singer chosen randomly from the dreck on the radio? Suppose a gospel choir is energetic and rhythmic, compared to an adult contemporary playlist that is formulaic and anesthetizing?

Importantly, if we perceive that music's full power requires participation (performing, composing, singing together), we may strongly prefer—if forced to choose—100 percent participation in religious music that only scores 75 percent on a scale of aesthetic quality, compared to passive consumption of music that scores 100 percent. And why not refuse this choice? We can hear (perform, compose, etc.) *both* music that is linked unambiguously to religious traditions, *and* music that lacks such connections. What could be less surprising than finding them dovetail? In a related context, Westermeyer (1993: 191) comments that—compared with elite trends in twentieth century classical music (he mentions Arnold Schoenberg as an example)—we could consider church music at its best to be "a prophetic witness on behalf of the human race's deepest musical longings against a derailed and esoteric twentieth-century musical culture."

Let us return to the capacity of music to move people through liminal stages involving a sense of transcendence—often harnessing rhythm and associated ritual practices to evoke an altered state of consciousness, whether described as trance-like, ecstatic, quasi-shamanic, etc. Beyond a doubt many people—and not solely youth cohorts undergoing generational upsurges—have experienced such things through listening to music influenced by Afro-Caribbean and Native American drumming, among other forms. Indeed it is hard to overestimate how profound—if one internalizes the knowledge encoded in this music—can be the rites of passage, rewiring of brain synapses, and reorganization of affective identity associated with this experience. Yet others have had comparable experiences—aesthetically distinctive but not necessarily any less profound—at religious summer camps, being swept up in folk-rock guitar music. We cannot attribute this solely to traces of African sensibility in the rock portion of folk-rock—although this is probably a significant factor to consider—because people have also had experiences in a similar vein listening to Handel's *Messiah* and traditional hymns. If our goal is to identify music with spiritual depth and potential to move a community, we can find popular forms that fall on *either* side of a distinction between African blues-based music and "Western" music heard in religious contexts.

In general we should think about the above-mentioned zone of overlap not as a one-way street channeling youth away from churches, but more like a two-way street that, for example, can also lead Bob Dylan, Johnny Cash, or various hip-hop artists turned preachers toward religion. And to imagine a street with only two directions is too narrow—this is a fluid space within which one can move in various ways. Music can deepen various existing ruts, some for formal Sabbath observances and others for one's soundtrack on other days of the week. It can remap the streets—for example, by introducing emergent musical sensibilities to a Christian liturgy, learning about Asian religion through private listening to the Beatles, blending New Age meditation with prayers taught by one's grandparents after hearing an interview with Madonna on Oprah, and so forth.

David Stowe (2011) offers an illuminating case study that documents synergies among five kinds of 1970s music with religious dimensions: stars of folk-rock-styled CCM; "praise" style pop-rock worship music associated with CCM that became prevalent in Evangelicalism; mainstream folk and/or country musicians with religious interests (especially Dylan and Cash); musicians influenced by African-American gospel (Andrae Crouch, Al Green, Marvin Gaye, Aretha Franklin, Stevie Wonder); and the musicals *Jesus Christ Superstar* and *Godspell*.

As Stowe documents the deep entanglements among these five scenes, one of his insights is that the Evangelical youth sub-culture thrived after 1970, in large part due to its synergies with artists like Dylan and Wonder, as well as the sound of its praise music that harnessed these stars' cultural capital. If there was one paradigmatic path through the zone, for Stowe, it moved secular hippies through a liminal stage toward incorporation into the Christian right—a counter-example to the above-noted hypothesis that exposure to rock-influenced music would lead youth away from organized religion. But both this hypothesis and Stowe's alternative narrative are oversimplified.

Stowe treats the California Jesus Movement as a seed from which the story grows and/or a vortex into which the rest of his protagonists (for example, Dylan) were sucked. He tracks the rise of the Evangelical Right in the 1970s, ending with Reagan reaping votes from Evangelicals who were nurtured through CCM. Many of his examples do fit this interpretation, but along the way he also offers much evidence that more complexity was in play—indeed that it would often be an insult to his musicians to conclude that they drew people rightward in any simple way. He documents Goldwater youth, who used CCM as a half-way house to mild hippiedom or Jimmy Carter Evangelicalism, people who were liberal from the start and continued on that path, and people who entered the scene from the right and exited toward the left. Read in this way, Stowe shows how the entangled CCM/folk/rock/R&B nexus (framed in the baggy way needed to grasp its lived complexity) was at least a door swinging more than one way—or, better, a zone with roads leading out in many directions. If we had more space, we could make related arguments centered on a gospel/R&B/hip-hop nexus, a country/pop/gospel nexus, and so on through many permutations.

Third, it is crucial to be skillful at reading ironies—levels of meaning that go against the grain of a text's surface meaning—to have any hope of perceiving the depth, pervasiveness, and range of religious resonances in popular music.

Expectations in the music industry have evolved such that stars feel pressure to disavow being religious, so as not to be ghettoized as substandard artists or stigmatized as right-wing cranks. This affects even artists with unambiguous religious interests. In a *Rolling Stone* interview (Sullivan 2013) Sinead O'Connor discussed plans to cut a gospel record with the Soul Stirrers and stated "I consider music a priesthood," but nevertheless trumpeted her goal of "rescuing God from religion," since "the worst thing that ever happened to God was 'religion'—especially 'religious music.'" Erykah Badu told *VIBE*, in an article dense with spiritual discourse (Buddhist, Christian, and Muslim) that "I don't think any one organization can define your relationship with the Creator … My religion, if I have one, is probably the arts" (Tate 1997: 86).

We can easily grasp the underlying code: spirituality is fine (especially in African and Asian forms), as long as one is not too religious (especially with a sense of proselytizing). We should often discount statements in this vein as disclaimers made as part of the price of admission to the business. Subtle divergences from the script hold more interest than earnest re-articulations. Thus, it was noteworthy when Katy Perry, in an otherwise generic interview, said that "speaking in tongues is as normal to me as 'pass the salt'" and told the open secret that placed this in a comparative religious context: "a lot of religions use meditation or chanting as a subliminal prayer language, and speaking in tongues isn't that different—it's a secret, direct prayer language to God" (Grigoriadis 2010). That Perry—like Aretha Franklin, Elvis Presley, Ray Charles, half of Nashville, and the list goes on—learned to sing in churches and may still be Christian in non-trivial senses is likewise an open secret, semi-disavowed by pro forma disclaimers about not "really" being religious.

Meanwhile, another cliché swings this pendulum the opposite way. Artists routinely say "God bless you" to audiences and thank God for helping them win Grammy awards, even when such utterances seem devoid of sincerity and are linked to the most self-absorbed, raunchy, and materialistic songs imaginable. To take either pendulum swing too literally is like reading without eyeglasses that are needed to correct for distortions. An ironic, not literal, approach gives the focus we need to see straight.

A second kind of irony is more subtle and important—that encoded into the music. Here we need two theoretical principles on board, both relevant not solely for analyzing music and religion but more generally (for more on theory, see Bull and Black 2004; Horner and Swiss 1999; Swiss, Sloop and Herman 1998; Morley and Chen 1996; Williams 1995). To begin, there is no single way that any music—whether a song, artist, or genre—is first created, then disseminated, later heard, and finally put to use in everyday life: perhaps through private listening in a car, in a bar, at a church, in concert, or as background music at the dentist's office. A song like "Blowing in the Wind" has circulated in all of these contexts, in dozens of styles, with implications ranging from bored complacency to mockery to deep political resonance. Theorists use shorthand terms such as "circuits of production and reception" and "indeterminacy of meaning" to discuss these points.

Even if we clarify a preferred meaning for a given song—the intended and/or likely meaning amid the range of possibilities—this best interpretation may be that the listener is expected to critique the idea stated at face value. If a rape is represented, this may glorify rape—or a psychopath might perceive it doing so—but the main point may be to condemn rape and create empathy with the victim. Simply that rape was described tells us little.

Similar things are true of the overt mention—or not—of religious ideas. One could sing about sin straightforwardly, as when a gospel singer performs "Amazing Grace" in full sincerity. But secular hippies may sing it, too, with varying degrees of irony. One can also sing songs that take pride in sinning, such as the country-pop ode to sexual transgression called "Heaven's Just a Sin Away." Or one can take this indeterminacy to the meta-level. In Merle Haggard's "Mama Tried" the song's protagonist, in retrospect, regrets that he earlier had been proud to be a sinner instead of listening to his mother. Then we can sing "Mama Tried" as an ironic joke, ad infinitum. Still, at base all three songs presuppose a recognizably Christian common sense about good and bad, even when this is partly disavowed through irony. Both the blues and country traditions can be interpreted as incessant commentaries about such things, drenched in Christian images and worldviews.

One place among many others where ironic religious motifs are pervasive is the alt. country (alternative country) movement. One critically acclaimed act, Uncle Tupelo, revived the gospel song "Atomic Power," which originally called for repentance in the context of the Cold War, which it presented as a sign of the end-times. Surely singing this means something to a hip and secular contemporary audience—but what exactly? When Uncle Tupelo recorded "Satan, Your Kingdom Must Come Down," a fan Web site commented: "Go ahead, record [the song]—if we think you mean it, we'll be off-put. If we think you're just kidding, well then, Jesus is just all right" (cited in Fox and Ching 2008: 11).

These complexities are pervasive because, for hip postmodern critics, a sincere persona associated with the 1960s folk revival or 1970s singer-songwriters—as well as many other claims to authenticity, although sweeping generalizations are hazardous—may be dismissed as flat-footed and passé. In the 2003 film A Mighty Wind, which affectionately lampoons the folk revival, performers play singers who (in the film's narrative) are mainly sincere, but this is largely a joke for the film's audience. Still the humor of its theme song—somewhat like Uncle Tupelo's recycling of gospel—makes no sense without presupposing a baseline of respect for songs like "Blowing in the Wind." In this context, one could write a song describing oneself (the song's protagonist) giving a sermon so eloquent that listeners (within the lyric) are inspired with heroic resolve and rush off to save the world. Outside this lyric, actual listeners may divide. Some may rush off to save the world, but others may be disgusted by the song's preaching, or gratified by what they interpret as a satire of do-gooders, or alarmed by the postmodern collapse of value signaled by the satire. Others may try to reassure the fourth group by pointing to the first. Importantly, the song may not circulate widely nor garner critical respect without such ambiguities built into it.

Some of this sort of ambiguity—for example, Madonna's self-promotion or some of Dylan's marketing to hip people (who without this marketing might well boycott an artist with so many misogynist and apocalyptic tendencies)—can be understood in part as strategies to create spectacles that sell, first, by being provocative, and second, through trying to be all things to all people through a plenitude of meanings. Conveniently for these artists' sales, their songs can be read at face value or as ironic provocations disavowing whatever meanings their fans dislike.

It is clear that the challenge of multiple ambiguous meanings and role of pure spectacle are not always the primary and decisive issues (for a small taste of Dylan and Madonna criticism see Cott 2006; Ricks 2003; Schwichtenberg 1992) but to whatever degree we need to focus on them, the remaining question is twofold. First, could this sort of spectacle sometimes be its own mode of spirituality, or at least reinforce more clearly religious forms? Perhaps artists may enact a sort of sublimity of spectacle for its own sake. Does religion require a degree of sincerity underlying it (is that what "depth" entails?) or could there also be something like "deep resonance of spectacle" working in other registers?

Second, for us to posit that a piece of music has serious religious interest, does this require something more than the individual appropriation of an ambiguous image? Might it be enough to say, for example, that Jay-Z and Kanye West's "No Church in the Wild" at the same time celebrates sex and cocaine (for fans who favor this reading), and *also* (for others who prefer it) critically questions the mixed benefits of unbridled sex and cocaine—holding up a mirror to it against the baseline of a church which is absent in "the wild" but definitely still haunting both the song and West's whole career—and *also* is part of a spectacular quasi-religious ritual (performed by an artist nicknamed "Yeezus") and *also* makes a satirical comment about the whole spectacle of "Yeezus-worship"—as when West raps "I am a God … hurry up with my damn croissants." Should we hypothesize that—as in advertising, so also in discourse about religion—there is no such thing as bad publicity, and that even provocative or blasphemous music with religious motifs can make interesting contributions to conversations in US religion?

Rather than offering any simple answer, I am insisting that such open questions evoke the level of complexity we must grasp. One thing clearly untrue about popular music is that its popularity is simple and one-dimensional. All too often, commentaries about it—by self-styled religious and secular critics alike—fall into a far less complex mode of reading, and thus by extension a less interesting and insightful one.

Conclusion

Recall our opening question about how to drink from a fire hose. Working on this chapter, I have often felt that any linear argument about what music does would break on the rocks of the subtleties we have considered. Yet in no way does this make music's power—when it takes deep root in listeners—any less significant. We have been thinking about one of the most compelling and motivating of all human experiences, expressed in forms circulating widely and deeply through our culture.

No doubt we could identify additional patterns in how popular music interacts with religion. However, again I recommend against a search for comprehensive coverage, because such writing typically works at levels of abstraction that offer diminishing returns, and because searching for "objective" patterns may lead to inquiries so narrow that it becomes more interesting to poke holes in the arguments—or at least ponder exceptions to their interpretive paradigms—than to embrace them.

Also, in light of all we have considered, it should be obvious that we can identify many specific examples of music worth exploring more deeply. Here is a place to return to my opening advice—to hold in mind a few songs and artists that you know well—but by now perhaps we can branch out as well. All the following themes are significant in the diffuse field where the popular, musical, and religious overlap: music with quasi-religious or spiritual-religious themes embedded—articulated directly or indirectly, lyrically or through sonic style, ironically or not; music that deepens, intensifies, or otherwise affects religious practices—inflecting worship style, reinforcing commitments, repelling people, strengthening groups, re-wiring brain synapses, etc.; music that overtly strengthens social movements and/or cultural critiques of interest to religious people; and music that has less tangible effects in reinforcing cultural critiques and utopian visions—overtly religious or not—which resonate and/or dovetail with religious values.

If we keep our antennae out for examples of any of these things, we will find more than enough cases to hold and reward our attention, and indeed to deeply enrich our quality of life.

Works cited

Baraka, Amiri [LeRoi Jones] (1963) *Blues People: Negro Music in White America*, New York: Morrow.

Bellah, R., R. Madsen, W. Sullivan, A. Swindler, and S. Tipton (1985) *Habits of the Heart: Individualism and Commitment in American Life*, Berkeley, CA: University of California Press.

Brackett, D. (ed.) (2004) *The Pop, Rock, and Soul Reader*, New York: Oxford University Press.

Bull, M. and L. Black (eds) (2004) *The Auditory Culture Reader*, New York: Berg.

Cantwell, R. (1996) *When We Were Good: The Folk Revival*, Cambridge, MA: Harvard University Press.

Cott, J. (ed.) (2006) *Bob Dylan: The Essential Interviews*, New York: Wenner.

Cullen, J. (1996) *The Art of Democracy: A Concise History of Popular Culture in the United States*, New York: Monthly Review Press.

Denning, M. (1996) *The Cultural Front: The Laboring of American Culture in the Twentieth Century*, New York: Verso.

Fox, P. and B. Ching (eds) (2008) *Politics of Alt.Country Music*, Ann Arbor, MI: University of Michigan Press.

Frith, S. (1996) *Performing Rites: On the Value of Popular Music*, Cambridge, MA: Harvard University Press.

Grigoriadis, V. (2010) "Sex, God, and Katy," *Rolling Stone* (August 19): 44.

Hall, S. (1981) "Notes on deconstructing 'the popular,'" in R. Samuel (ed.), *People's History and Socialist Theory*, London: RKP.

Harris, M. (1994) *The Rise of Gospel Blues: The Music of Thomas Andrew Dorsey in the Urban Church*, New York: Oxford University Press.

Hebdige, D. (1979) *Subculture: The Meaning of Style*, New York: Routledge.

Hendershot, H. (2004) *Shaking the World for Jesus: Media and Conservative Evangelical Culture*, Chicago, IL: University of Chicago Press.

Horner, B. and T. Swiss (1999) *Key Terms in Popular Music*, Oxford: Blackwell Publishers Ltd.

Howard, J. and J. Streck (1999) *Apostles of Rock: The Splintered World of Contemporary Christian Music*, Lexington, KY: University Press of Kentucky.

Kelley, R. (1998) *Yo' Mama's Disfunkional! Fighting the Culture Wars in Urban America*, Boston, MA: Beacon Press.

Laderman, G. (2009) *Sacred Matters: Celebrity Worship, Sexual Ecstasies, the Living Dead, and Other Signs of Religious Life in the United States*, New York: New Press.

Levine, L. (1988) *Highbrow/Lowbrow: The Emergence of Cultural Hierarchy in America*, Cambridge, MA: Harvard University Press.

——(1992) "The folklore of industrial society: popular culture and its audiences," *American Historical Review* 97, 5: 1369–430.

Levitin, D. (2006) *This Is Your Brain on Music: The Science of a Human Obsession*, New York: Penguin.

Lipsitz, G. (1990) *Time Passages: Collective Memory and American Popular Culture*, Minneapolis, MN: University of Minnesota Press.

——(2007) *Footsteps in the Dark: The Hidden Histories of Popular Music*, Minneapolis, MN: University of Minnesota Press.

Lofton, K. (2011) *Oprah: The Gospel of an Icon*, Berkeley, CA: University of California Press.

Lornell, K. (2002) *Introducing American Folk Music: Ethnic and Grassroots Traditions in the United States*, 2nd edn, New York: McGraw Hill.

Malone, B. (2002) *Don't Get Above Your Raisin': Country Music and the Southern Working Class*, Urbana, IL: University of Illinois Press.

Marcus, G. (1975) *Mystery Train: Images of America in Rock'n'Roll Music*, New York: Dutton.

Miller, K. (2010) *Segregating Sound: Inventing Folk and Pop Music in the Age of Jim Crow*, Durham, NC: Duke University Press.

Miller, T. and A. Shahriari (2008) *World Music: A Global Journey*, New York: Routledge.

Moore, R.L. (1994) *Selling God: American Religion in the Marketplace of Culture*, New York: Oxford University Press.

Morley, D. and K. Chen (1996) *Stuart Hall: Critical Dialogues in Cultural Studies*, New York: Routledge.

Peterson, R. (1997) *Creating Country Music: Fabricating Authenticity*, Chicago, IL: University of Chicago Press.

Pinn, A. (ed.) (2003) *Noise and Spirit: The Religious and Spiritual Sensibilities of Rap Music*, New York: New York University Press.

Reed, T. (2003) *The Holy Profane: Religion in Black Popular Music*, Lexington, KY: University Press of Kentucky.

Reed, T.V. (2005) *The Art of Protest: Culture and Activism from the Civil Rights Movement to the Battle of Seattle*, Minneapolis, MN: University of Minnesota Press.

Ricks, C. (2003) *Dylan's Visions of Sin*, London: Penguin.

Rose, T. (1994) *Black Noise: Rap Music and Black Culture in Contemporary America*, Middletown, CT: Wesleyan University Press.

Rose, T. and A. Ross (eds) (1994) *Microphone Fiends: Youth Music and Youth Culture*, New York: Routledge.

Ross, A. (2007) *The Rest Is Noise: Listening to the Twentieth Century*, New York: Farrar, Straus, and Giroux.

Rubin, R. and J. Melnick (eds) (2007) *American Popular Music: New Approaches to the Twentieth Century*, Amherst, MA: University of Massachusetts Press.

Sample, T. (1996) *White Soul: Country Music, the Church, and Working Americans*, Nashville, TN: Abingdon Press.

Schmidt, L. (2000) *Hearing Things: Religion, Illusion, and the American Enlightenment*, Cambridge, MA: Harvard University Press.

Schwichtenberg, C. (1992) *The Madonna Connection: Representational Politics, Subcultural Identities, and Cultural Theory*, Boulder, CO: Westview Press.

Small, C. (1998) *Musicking: The Meanings of Performing and Listening*, Middletown, CT: Wesleyan University Press.

Smith, M. (ed.) (2004) *Hearing History: A Reader*, Athens, GA: University of Georgia Press.

Stowe, D. (2004) *How Sweet the Sound: Music in the Spiritual Lives of Americans*, Cambridge, MA: Harvard University Press.

——(2011) *No Sympathy for the Devil: Christian Pop Music and the Transformation of American Evangelicalism*, Chapel Hill, NC: University of North Carolina Press.

Sullivan, J. (2013) "Q&A: Sinead O'Connor on her 'gospel sessions' and the priesthood of music," *Rolling Stone* (July 24). Online. Available: www.rollingstone.com/music/news/q-a-sinead-oconnor-on-her-gospel-sessions-and-the-priesthood-of-music-20130724 (accessed 16 October 2013).

Sullivan, L. (ed.) (1997) *Enchanting Powers: Music in the World's Religions*, Cambridge, MA: Harvard University Press.

Swiss, T., J.M. Sloop, and A. Herman (eds) (1998) *Mapping the Beat: Popular Music and Contemporary Theory*, Cambridge, MA: Blackwell Press.

Sylvan, R. (2003) *Traces of the Spirit: The Religious Dimensions of Popular Music*, New York: New York University Press.

Tate, G. (1997) "Soul sister number one," *VIBE* (August): 82–86.

Ventura, M. (1985) *Shadow Dancing in the USA*, New York: St. Martin's Press.

Walser, R. (ed.) (1998) *Keeping Time: Readings in Jazz History*, New York: Oxford University Press.

Weiner, I. (2009) "Sound and American religions," *Religion Compass* 3, 5: 897–908.

Werner, C. (1999) *A Change Is Gonna Come: Music, Race and the Soul of America*, New York: Plume.

Westermeyer, P. (1993) "Twentieth-century American hymnody and church music," in J. Dolan and J. Wind (eds), *New Dimensions in American Religious History*, Grand Rapids, MI: Eerdmans, 175–207.

Williams, R. (1995) *The Sociology of Culture*, Chicago, IL: University of Chicago Press.

8
VIDEO- AND INTERNET GAMES

Rachel Wagner

Introduction

Just as our art, culture, politics, and communications have become absorbed into wired space, so too is religion becoming wired. As Lorne Dawson (2005: 15) has observed, religion "of every kind, big and small, old and new, mainstream and more exotic, is present online, and in great abundance." Mary Hess (2008: 44) notes that today, "it makes little sense to write about media practices as separated in any way from practices of faith more generally." Leonard Sweet (2012: 122) similarly observes that technology is so "embedded" in our lives that "it no longer [can be] considered a separate category, but [is] a part of everything." A number of compelling questions emerge when religion gets wired, regarding sacred texts, sacred space, ritual experience, self, and community. But as we shall see, the most compelling and provocative point of contact between religion and wired culture is videogames, which increasingly function in ways that remarkably resemble religious practice—for good and for ill.

Sacred texting

One of the most obvious ways that religion is changing online is in our experience of sacred texts. Whereas before, the religious text was a physical object to be venerated, cared for, and protected, today's religious texts can also be experienced as digitized packets of information, accessed via iPhones, iPads, and laptops. What is lost when the physical text is replaced with a digital one? How should you treat a mobile device that carries sacred texts on it? If you purchase a Bible application ("app"), should you make sure the app and its icon aren't placed next to a less pure one? These are the kinds of new and very powerful questions that religiously minded people face in today's digital landscape.

Within the emerging debate over online religious practice, one of the most poignant questions is over the identification of authority. Religious discussion increasingly is "crowd-sourced," with anybody's opinion being treated as equal to anyone else's, provided she anchors her response in religious teachings. For example, one Reddit reader asks online Muslim readers to assess whether or not the digital deletion of a Quran is a form of "desecration." The replies generally affirm that deletion of a digital file of the Quran can be done respectfully, if the intention is honorable. They also take into account that digital files require new rules: one reader suggests that the Quran is not "holy" until it is displayed on the screen, therefore "deleting the file is not the same as destroying the book" ("needMalk" 2013).

So where *is* the Quran when it is on a digital device? Because the Quran is believed to be God's holy Word, always being recited in heaven, is the digital format just a human and temporal remnant pointing to its heavenly origin as perfectly as a physical text might? Is the Quran itself embedded in the digital file that stores it, such that the file is holy as well? At the root of all of these sticky questions is this fundamental one: where, exactly, does sacredness reside? And with the virtual world offering another mode of non-material "space," should we equate the virtual with the spiritual—with both being "non-material"—or must we deal now with three categories of existence: the material, the spiritual, *and* the virtual? There are no ancient authorities who can answer these questions; the issues are a product of a revolution in print culture, the transition from text as object to text as transient digital file.

In another recent debate about sacred texts in digital contexts, the digital device itself was the primary point of concern. In 2010, Father Paolo Padrini developed an iPad app for the Roman Missal (liturgy for the mass), sparking a number of difficult questions. Should an iPad with the liturgy loaded onto it be treated with special respect? Is using an iPad in worship a form of implicit advertising for Apple? Padrini himself claimed the app was just for occasional use, as when vacationing, and that the traditional physical book should be used when performing mass for a group in one's home church. Father Kenneth Doyle, however, writing in 2012, affirms that the practice of using an iPad for liturgical prompting is now generally accepted in the Catholic Church, even though there is a preference for physical books if they are available. If the device is used in worship, Doyle advises using a "dignified" cover to hide the manufacturer's logo (Doyle 2012). Disturbing questions about the use of corporate advertising and the reliance upon digital software, however, linger.

Another way that we can see digital environments shaping sacred texts is in the construction of religiously themed videogames, some with intentionally blasphemous purposes and others with pious intent. The online flash game *Bible Fight*, for example, takes familiar symbols and story elements from the Bible and places them in a fighting game. The game opens with hymn-like choral music, and a backstory meant to evoke religious themes but placing them within a winner–loser gaming environment:

> In the beginning, there was a contest of strength amongst the most prominent figures in scripture to determine the mightiest. The tale of this great rivalry was thought lost forever. Until now. Let there be Bible Fight!

Characters including Eve, Satan, and Jesus fight one another in tournament style matches, and a victor is determined. By transforming the context in which the characters appear, they create a new and violent mode of interaction—and in so doing, disrupt the traditional storyline to such an extent that the game may be perceived as blasphemous.

Games made by religiously motivated game creators, however, typically refuse to alter the received tradition of the text. For example, the computer game *Rashid in the World of Qur'an* (Windows, 2000) portrays a young boy traveling throughout an imagined land, learning stories from the Quran. The player accompanies Rashid, learning about established Muslim practices, hearing Quranic recitation, and learning about plants and animals through interactive games. The interactivity does not allow the player to alter the teachings or stories revealed to him or her. Instead, this is a game that confines interactivity to choices that cannot affect the integrity of the sacred stories and teachings.

A Christian game, *Bible Champions* (Third Day Games, 2007), adopts a similar tactic. Players elect to play as either a cartoon-style girl or boy, clad in first-century robes, exploring a crudely rendered digital model of ancient Jerusalem. If the player follows directions properly, he or she is rewarded with static readings of stories from the gospels. Tellingly, when these narrations occur, viewers see a frozen image of the story event on the screen, complete with a digital Bible depicted in the corner. The only "movement" comes from the female narrator, who reads the New Testament stories. There is interactivity here, to be sure, but the rules of the game allow only certain things to be changed, and none of these things includes the biblical text itself. The player can collect "faith," "hope," and "love" tokens, and is required to locate the Bible as a hovering object, in order to be rewarded with static readings from it. However, despite the interactivity allowed in collecting items and points in the game, the player is really just a passive consumer of an unaltered religious text.

Things become even more complicated when we move beyond relatively static texts to the myriad ways that digital interactivity affects faith and practice, especially in those videogames not explicitly based on religious texts. Three key concepts will help us to make sense of religion in interactive virtual reality: the magic circle, procedural rhetoric, and play.

The magic circle

The notion of the magic circle comes from the book *Homo Ludens* by Dutch cultural theorist Johan Huizinga (1872–1945). Noting the remarkable similarities between games and sacred activity, Huizinga argues that play—in both games and religion— "proceeds within its own boundaries of time and space according to fixed rules and in an orderly manner." Play "promotes the formation of social groupings which tend to surround themselves with secrecy and to stress their difference from the common world by disguise or other means" (1949: 13). That is to say, play is a means by which we interact with preconceived and separate social structures, against which we move in the creation of meaning. In all forms of play, rules adhere within the circumscribed space of play—the "magic circle"—which has the ability to offer us temporary worlds of order.

For Huizinga, sacred play and secular play are intimately connected, since sacred play is "played or performed within a playground that is literally 'staked out' … . A sacred space, a temporarily real world of its own, has been expressly hedged off for it" (ibid.: 14). If we understand the "play" of religion to be best demarcated in its rituals, then we can easily see how games and religious rituals are similar kinds of social and symbolic structures, similar modes of order-making that is taking place in worlds that are "hedged off" either by religious architecture, by sacred time, by a screened digital frame, or by any combination. Both sacred play (as ritual) and ordinary play (as game) involve entry into a "temporarily real world" that exists in a space "expressly hedged off for it." In such worlds, we follow different rules and inhabit a carefully crafted cosmos that is comprehensible and predictable. Both games and rituals invite entry into a kind of controlled space, a magic circle, wherein rules shape the possibilities of play.

But when games are over, we usually think of their effects as ending too. The game is shut down, and the magic circle disappears with it. Most game-players would suggest that afterward, the game doesn't shape the way they see the ordinary world at all. We might engage in violent or taboo behavior, the argument goes, but such behavior happens only in the realm of the game—that is, within the confines of the magic circle. Therefore, a player might argue, the unsavory behavior isn't real, and will have no effects whatsoever on everyday life. For most game-players, the magic circle of play is fixed, impermeable, a fully sealed, discrete, and separate space.

In sacred play, however, we generally want to see the effects of the magic circle experience continue. Huizinga (1949: 14) admits that despite their structural similarities, sacred play is in fact different from ordinary play, because "with the end of the play its effect is not lost; rather it continues to shed its radiance on the ordinary world outside … ." In other words, rituals are a kind of magic circle that is supposed to spill over, and in so doing, make our real lives better. As Huizinga puts it, ritual participants "are convinced that the action actualizes and effects a definite beatification, brings about an order of things higher than that in which they customarily live." The actions that take place in a magic circle of sacred play share their cosmos-constructing, order-making qualities with everyday life. This is what Huizinga means by sacred play's ability to "shed its radiance" by sharing its symbolism of order with real life.

The "magic circle" of the sacrament of communion, for example, is intended to radiate its efficacy from the altar out onto the whole world, where the "rules" of that transaction still hold. New Year's events similarly involve fixed rituals of expression, and the purity and freshness they evoke are meant to define life at large, even after the rituals themselves end. Rather than confine play to an ephemeral space and time, sacred play uses this temporary space to define how the whole of reality should be perceived. Can one argue that despite their structural and functional similarities, a videogame has an impermeable magic circle but a ritual has a permeable one? If both experiences involve symbolic areas of interactivity, and both present us with an ordered view of the cosmos, can mere intention be enough to protect the magic circle of ordinary play from also making claims on how we should see the world at large? Put differently, how can we prevent a violent game from working like a ritual? This question is even more important when we consider those experiences, like the online war game *Kuma/War*, that take real life events and present them within the rubric of a violent videogame.

One of the places where the magic circle functions in controversial ways is in the online world of Second Life. Second Life presents users with a virtual space in which inhabitants are free to digitally build anything they like, and engage in personally scripted experiences while exploring a vast world governed by very few rules. The world of Second Life exhibits some distinctive features of ritual engagement via a magic circle, in that it invites new users to pass through a sort of digital "rite of passage" upon first entering, and thus marks out the digital space as different from ordinary life. Upon entering Second Life, one chooses one's virtual appearance and learns how to navigate one's avatar. While in the magic circle of the online world, the ordinary rules of daily life are lifted, and one can engage in ritualized equalization: if you aren't popular or wealthy or sexy or beautiful in real life, you can be all of those things in Second Life. Second Life can thus be viewed as a magic circle, a space set apart from our physical daily reality.

Second Life represents a confounding kind of magic circle, however. Nested within it are more magic circles, each with their own unique sets of rules. In Second Life, one can find gaming spaces, dancing spaces, meeting spaces, educational spaces, and of course religious spaces. Normally, such nesting of the sacred within the playful is not a problem, but sometimes—as when mischievous Second Life "griefers" agitate outside a Second Life church worship service, or when Second Life inhabitants arrive for virtual worship dressed as superheroes—the placement of a religious space within a space of play becomes problematic. Do the rules of Second Life trump the rules of the worship space? Should all inhabitants of Second Life recognize that even virtual sacred spaces deserve special treatment?[1] Which "magic circle" is dominant, and how can we decide?

Religion theorist Mircea Eliade provides a means for making sense of this conundrum. Writing long before virtual reality was even a possibility, Eliade discusses how "sacred space" is constructed so that "it becomes qualitatively different from the profane space by which it is surrounded" (1959: 15). Eliade proposes that sacred space is "a strong, significant space" whereas profane spaces are "without structure or consistency, amorphous" (ibid.: 20). According to this delineation, we could see Second Life—the virtual world itself—as a kind of "sacred space," a magic circle, if you will. That is to say, virtual spaces have the capacity to act as "sacred" spaces—especially if they resemble real-life sacred spaces, borrowing the "sacredness" of the real-life spaces in virtual form. In both real-life sacred spaces and in virtual sacred spaces, areas are set apart as distinct from ordinary life, demarcated according to special rules and treated in special ways.

Eliade claims that sacred space helps us locate ourselves symbolically in a chaotic world by providing a "fixed point, the central axis for all future orientation" (ibid.: 21). Within the "chaotic" world of Second Life are orienting sacred spaces like virtual churches, synagogues, mosques, and temples, each serving as a kind of "axis" for virtual worshipers who are drawn to them. Eliade explains that within a "homogenous and infinite expanse in which no point of reference is possible and hence no orientation can be established, the hierophany reveals an absolute fixed point, a center" (ibid.). Religiously motivated Second Life residents are drawn to these spaces as virtual "hierophanies," spaces to which they can instantly teleport and find familiar people, and where they can spend time in a structure that obviously resembles religious structures they have encountered in real life. Whereas Eliade understands a "hierophany" to mark out the act of the sacred making itself manifest in the real world, in Second Life a "hierophany" is the act of the sacred manifesting in the virtual world, in the form of foundational orienting spaces, especially those that mimic real-life sacred spaces.

The lack of an easily navigable geography in Second Life makes teleporting the most practical means of moving about, so having a fixed familiar location can be crucial to feeling that you know where to go and feel welcome. Eliade describes the importance of such demarcation, using language that is remarkably reminiscent of Huizinga's description of the magic circle. Eliade uses the example of the threshold of a church, which "separates the two spaces" and "indicates the distance between two modes of being, the profane and the religious" (ibid.: 25). Sacred space in Second Life seems to serve a similar function of demarcating space in which it is acceptable to have religious conversations, or to digitally pose in prayer and meditation. However, the multiplication and nesting of multiple magic circles in Second Life leave the thornier questions of authenticity in worship practices unanswered. If the playful mood of Second Life overshadows the religious mood of a magic circle of worship within Second Life, the efficacy of religious rituals in-world suffers. Players are less apt to take in-world religious practice seriously, and more apt to "play" at religious worship as a kind of temporary game.

The notion that games can sometimes work like rituals is even more evident when we consider that rituals are typically defined in ways that highlight their performative and behavior-shaping qualities. Stanley Tambiah's definition of ritual, for example, could as easily be read as describing videogames as it could for religious rituals:

> Ritual is a culturally constructed system of symbolic communication. It is constituted of patterned and ordered sequences of words and acts often expressed in multiple media, whose content and arrangement are characterized in varying degree by formality (conventionality), stereotype (rigidity), condensation (fusion) and redundancy (repetition).
>
> (Tambiah 1996: 497)

In videogames, as in rituals, we typically observe formality (fixed patterns), stereotyping (predictable experiences or images), and redundancy (repetition). Think, for example, of how videogames require us to engage in repeated and predictable patterns of decision-making, what Tambiah calls "formality." Games also engage in digital "stereotyping," a feature that is increased by the software itself; game engines work with predesigned coding that makes the production of buildings and other structures simple by inviting "skinning" or "modding" over basic and predictable designs.

Such "stereotyping" may also involve people, who are often digitally depicted according to repetitive symbolic conventions rather than with the rich variety of everyday life—a problem not missed by contemporary theorists of race and gender, but too often necessitated to simplify coding complexities and reduce the cost of game production. Redundancy, or repetition, is also a built-in feature of most games, which are often written according to preconceived genre expectations with a pattern that quite literally invites replay to achieve success. Condensation or "fusion"—that is, the collapse between what a symbol represents and the thing itself—may also occur, especially in those videogames that purport to take real-life events and collapse them into a fixed and rigidly defined story structure, a procedural rhetoric that argues for the game's view of the world as the most accurate one.

The tension between sacred play and secular play became evident in a recent controversy involving the Sony Playstation game *Resistance: Fall of Man* (Sony, 2007; see Wagner 2012b). The game's plot involves an invasion of earth by horrifying alien creatures called the Chimera, who must be defeated, predictably, by violent gunfire in a largely individualistic messianic military fantasy. The player takes on the role of American Army ranger Nathan Hale in an alternative historical storyline, in a world in which World War II never happened. The choice of Nathan Hale is particularly poignant, since the real-life Hale is famous for saying, before being executed by the British: "I only regret that I have but one life to lose for my country." The virtual Hale, of course, can die over and over again. In the game, the player takes on the role of Hale, at one point engaging in a shootout in a digital rendering of Manchester Cathedral, an Anglican place of worship, perfectly replicated within the game's rendering of 1950s Manchester.

Because real-life contemporary Manchester has been struggling with gun violence, the virtual portrayal of violence within a sacred space of worship was extremely disturbing to officials of the Anglican Church. When its representatives complained, Sony insisted that *Resistance* was just a game, and that it projected an alternate historical perspective that rendered any violence within the digital cathedral to be pure fantasy. David Reeves, Sony's European representative, put it this way: "We do not accept that there is any connection between contemporary issues of twenty-first-century Manchester and a work of science fiction in which a fictitious 1950's Britain is under attack by aliens" (cited in Wagner 2012b). Sony was sympathetic to the Church's concerns, but ultimately insisted that they had done no wrong, because the game had no bearing on real life.

Although they didn't use this language, Sony effectively claimed that the magic circle rendered game-play completely removed from everyday life—this, they argued, was a magic circle that was not permeable. Whatever happens in the game, they said, was insulated from real life—even more so because the game took place in an alternate historical trajectory. Game designer Chris Crawford views games in a way similar to Sony's position. For Crawford, games require no external referent, since they are closed formal systems: "The model world created by the game is internally complete; no reference needs to be made to agents outside the game" (cited in Salen and Zimmerman 2004: 77). So even if a game borrows symbols or images of real people for its portrayals, the in-game experience remains insulated from the outside world.

The Anglican Church argued otherwise. The game, they said, produced a magic circle that was permeable with real life—that is to say, the game reluctantly *became* a ritual for them, one that could shed its effects onto real life by urging real-life violence. Not only that, but the "magic circle" of the Church itself was forced to compete with the "magic circle" of the game. Any spillover that takes place from ritualized activities in a cathedral should, they seemed to be proposing, adhere to religious principles and rules of the "game" of religious life—not the principles and rules implied by the videogame *Resistance: Fall of Man*. The consternation with which the Church approached this issue reveals starkly how the rules of behavior of a videogame can be perceived as applying to the real-life spaces represented digitally within them. Which one was the most defining ordered space, the Church and the "rules" of religious worship, or the videogame, and its rhetoric of violence?

Today's consumers of digital media are being asked to negotiate three complex and overlapping metaphysical ideas: material reality, spiritual reality, and virtual reality. Each of these has a unique relationship to the magic circle, and to religious belief and practice. The questions raised by the intersection between these three notions of reality are profound and important, especially with regard to the magic circle of play. The last of these three, virtual reality, is a relative newcomer, and is confounding everything we thought we knew about the sacred. So far we have considered sacred texts and sacred spaces as relatively static entities transformed within online environments. But what happens when we consider more concretely how online environments shape our behavior in terms of ritualized procedures? In other words, how is virtual reality changing our opinions about religious processes as well as about religious spaces and things? The key to making sense of this interaction is procedural rhetoric.

Procedural rhetoric

Game theorist Ian Bogost (2007: 3–5, 9) defines "procedural rhetoric" as those set processes that "define the way things work: the methods, techniques, and logics that drive the operation of systems." Procedural systems "generate behaviors based on rule-based models" and in so doing, "run processes that invoke interpretations of processes in the material world." This means that procedural representation "explains processes with other processes" (ibid.: 9). Computational processes argue things by asking us to *do* things, even if only symbolically in virtual spaces. To examine procedural rhetoric, then, is to look at how arguments are addressed to users via the things they are doing in interaction with computer programs. Procedural rhetoric determines to whom we can send a private Tweet and how many words we can use to do it; who can see our Facebook posts and how much room we have to say them; how to acquire points, badges, or "achievements" in any online environment; and what it means to "win" a videogame. Procedural rhetoric shapes digital worship too, since we are intrinsically limited by the affordances of the code in any programs we use.

For a modest example of how coding intersects with values, think about Catholic Online's *Stations of the Cross*. Users go to the site and can click through the 14 "stations" using only "previous station" and "next station" buttons. The experience itself is minimally interactive, at least so long as one mentally brackets off the ads that surround the images of Jesus. There are also additional links at the bottom for more prayers and invitations to buy Catholic paraphernalia like rosaries and crucifixes. In terms of digital processes, this set of Web pages is not theologically controversial because the processes embraced by the program closely match the real-life processes. Just as in real life, where a worshiper would move from one station to the next—in order—and reflect on what it means, so a Web surfer who uses this page for pious reflection will move through the pages in the pre-designated order. There is little interactivity here, except for guided directional navigation and related religious reflection.

Procedural rhetoric works by creating "possibility space," which Bogost (2007: 42) defines as "the myriad configurations the player might construct to see the ways the processes inscribed in the system work." Players of games assent to a limited set of choices that do not necessarily accord with similar options in real life. This means that games occupy what Bogost calls an "ontological position"; that is, games evince a "simulation gap" between "rule-based representation and player subjectivity" (ibid.: 43). We must navigate the space between what the game allows and what we assume it does not. The procedural rhetoric of the digital *Stations* is very limited—you can simply click to move forward or backward. But other instances of religiously motivated procedural rhetoric are more controversial.

When we move into the realm of mobile apps, for example, the notion of procedural rhetoric becomes central. If churches or other religious groups want to be wired today, they now have to decide if they are willing to hire a programmer to create mobile apps or other software for them, or if they'll buy predesigned software packages with predetermined procedural rhetoric. Because it is so much cheaper, most churches simply decide to import content into pre-coded app vehicles supported by third party businesses. These apps typically offer limited options like streaming videos, messaging, and information about worship times.

More creative uses, such as dynamic prayer trees or GPS-enabled software for location of church members in one's vicinity, remain beyond the budgetary reach of most churches. Paying attention to what is possible via such pre-packaged apps is important, though, since as Heidi Campbell observes (2005: 192), "there is evidence internet use may transform the ways people conceive of religious community and local church," particularly in "a new conception of religious community as social network." If churches utilize predesigned apps they will likely find their worship and community activities shaped to match what the technology allows.

Sometimes, the procedural rhetoric of gaming can work in tandem with the procedural rhetoric of religious piety, as in the game designed by Father Maxim of the Russian Orthodox Church. Father Maxim submitted a design document to a Moscow branch of the Church outlining an intended MMOG (massively multiplayer online game) in which players would "suffer hardships" for going against the faith's principles, but would be rewarded for good deeds. According to Keane Ng (2009), progress in the game would be "measured by how well you can obey the Ten Commandments." The procedural rhetoric of the game is matched by the procedural rhetoric of Russian Orthodox piety. In other words, this is a religious game at which you can "win" by doing what religious piety would similarly require. Does Father Maxim's game suggest that religion has always had gaming qualities? Or does it reflect a tendency to try to make religion seem more relevant to youth by forcing religious notions into game-style conventions?

An awareness of the ways that videogames cultivate the techniques of procedural rhetoric requires that we recognize that "meaning in videogames is constructed not through a re-creation of the world, but through selectively modeling appropriate elements of that world" (Bogost 2007: 46). The online team-based MMOG *Kuma/War* is a good example. The procedural rhetoric of the game requires that one view all other entities in the game as either a supporter of one's team in the American Army, or as enemies, who are very often represented with tropes associated with Middle Eastern identity and Islam. The game's procedural rhetoric is simple; kill one's enemies as swiftly as possible. In Mission 25, called "Najaf: al Mahdi Cemetery Battle," players are instructed to destroy Iraqi opponents, all of whom look digitally similar to one another, and who hide out in mosques or "pop up" out of tombs to attack you. The procedural rhetoric of the game, then, is laid on top of real-life war, suggesting to its players an argument about how they should view Iraqis and Muslims in real life.

Technology can also shape real worship practices by being integrated into the physical space in which they happen. At Exeter Cathedral in May 2012, self-proclaimed "geek dad" Andy Robertson helped to construct a worship experience that incorporated a Sony Playstation game called *Flower*. Worshipers passed around a joystick control, taking turns controlling the movement of wind across flower petals populating a digital landscape. The game is physically beautiful, animated, and completely without dialogue. But it did require the inclusion of a physical screen behind the minister, who conducted the liturgy for communion framed by the digital light behind him, and with worshipers focusing on him as well as on the screen and the digital device. The integration of the videogame was received relatively well in the local congregation. Robertson said of the service afterward:

> Far from being a gimmick, the video game sat comfortably in among the other elements of the service, and I have heard little feedback about its being distracting. It felt entirely appropriate. If all sorts of technology will make the crossing with us to our newly clothed world, then of course it is good to use it in meaningful ways now. It is a foretaste of what these things might become one day.
>
> (Robertson 2012)

But whether it was enjoyed or not, the integration of the Playstation introduced a new procedural rhetoric into the flow of the worship service. Thus, regardless of how they feel about its integration, worshipers should be asking to what extent the game's interface and procedural rhetoric might impose the internal values of the game onto the service. Lawrence Lessig (2006: 114) warns that with any digital medium, "code embeds values. It enables, or not, certain control. ... to the end of whatever sovereign does the coding." In the case of *Flower*, worshipers may query how the worship service's procedural rhetoric is transformed by the integration of a foreign ritual and a borrowed set of rules, complete with material objects of adoration in the form of a joystick control.

Procedural rhetoric is an unavoidable component of wired religion in all of its forms: all computer programs have purposes and limitations. Procedural rhetoric, then, is as intrinsic to coded practices as the screen itself. This means that any mode of religious engagement should inquire deliberately about what procedural rhetoric is embedded into a program's processes, and ask whether or not these accord with the procedural rhetorics of the pre-existing religious practice. One of the ways to assess an experience's procedural rhetoric is to ask about how the element of play works within the scripted experience, since play is, at root, simply a very finely tuned mode of developing procedural rhetoric.

Play

The concepts we have already considered—the magic circle and procedural rhetoric—are facets relating to another key concept that is perhaps the most important one for making sense of the relationship between religion and virtual reality. Huizinga, as we have already observed, sees play as a key feature of both games and sacred practice. In both cases, he says, play is a "stepping out of 'real' life into a temporary sphere of activity with a disposition all of its own" (1955: 8). Play is an "interlude," created within the magic circle. It is "distinct from 'ordinary' life both as to locality and duration" and is "played out within certain limits of time and place" (ibid.: 9). It's not hard to see how both games and religious activities—especially rituals—match this demarcation of play as something set apart from ordinary life. Play infuses both religious ritual and games, as both exhibit carefully scripted procedural rhetorics within defined magic circles.

But the notion of play is about more than just setting apart a space and time. It's also about the rules that govern that special place and time. Play depends upon rules even to take place. Accordingly, definitions of games are often closely related to definitions of play, since play can be seen as a clarification for how interaction with the rules of a game actually works, that is to say, how the procedural rhetoric unfolds. Games always involve play—but play doesn't always mean that a game is happening. The difference, it seems, is in how rigidly defined the rules are, whether or not there is a win-state, and how carefully one marks out the special space and time in which play happens. Although theorists disagree on the relationship between games and play, all seem convinced that games are always a form of play because of their adherence to rules as shapers of experience.

Game theorist Eric Zimmerman also defines play as a kind of rule-based movement within a more rigidly defined space:

> Play exists both because of and also despite the more rigid structures of a system … .This definition of play is about relationships between the elements of a system. Think about the use of the word "play" when we talk about the "free play" of a steering wheel. The free play is the amount of movement that the steering wheel can turn before it begins to affect the tires of the car. The play itself exists only because of the more utilitarian structures of the driving-system: the drive shaft, axles, wheels, etc.
>
> (Zimmerman 2004: 159)

The "rigid structure" is, put simply, the system of rules that define the play experience in the magic circle. The kinship between games and religion becomes even more obvious here, as religious practice, especially ritual, is in large part defined by rules—what you can and cannot do, as set within a larger, more defining structure or worldview. While it's true that games involve rules that are temporary in a space that dissolves when play is finished, and religion involves rules that are assumed to have ultimate, cosmos-shaping consequences, this distinction only enhances the fascination of the comparison. Religion may, in fact, simply be a game that lasts a lifetime and whose rules encompass all of experience, so that the "space" and "time" that are set apart for the rules of play are creation itself, with only God existing beyond the field of play.

Zimmerman's definition of play also applies to the "rules" of religious ritual and the "play" with which a practitioner engages when vocalizing a liturgy, moving the body within a ritual context, or gesturing in pre-designated ways. Play happens, Zimmerman says, in the "interstitial spaces" that exist "between and among [the system's] components." Play works against and in response to the structures of the system, but it is also "an expression of a system, and intrinsically a part of it" (ibid.: 159). Think again about the *Bible Champions* game, in which the "play" consisted of the collection of faith, hope, and love tokens—and the "road" consisted of the biblical text which provided the rigid structure against which the player was allowed to move in the game. One can think similarly of hermeneutics, the mode of biblical interpretation that lets the text serve as the rigid structure against which new meanings and developments of implications arise. In this sense, the rules of play are manifest in the emerging chain of interpretive traditions over time.

Such "play" with the system is characteristic of many forms of religious activity and of games. As Alexander Galloway (2006: 7) explains it, "[t]he imposition of constraints also creates expression." Such a rigid structure offers a reliable sense of order, even if the point is in seeing how you might bend or break them within allowable parameters. It's rules that allow the construction of a ritual or game-defined other-space, and it's rules that define the system of user or worshiper engagement. Another theorist of play, Roger Caillois, summarizes what he sees to be Huizinga's overarching argument about games, play, and culture—an argument that applies equally well to religion:

> Play is simultaneously freedom and invention, fantasy and discipline. All the important manifestations of culture are derived from it. They are indebted to the spirit of research, to the respect for rules, to the detachment that it creates and maintains. In certain respects the rules of the law, of prosody, counterpoint, and perspective, the rules for stage settings and liturgies, for military tactics and philosophical controversy, are so many rules for games.
> (Caillois 1957: 94)

In the case of religion, the rules of play tell us how to live, who can make authoritative decisions in the day-to-day world, and why. Rules dictate how sacred texts are read. Rules guide how we are supposed to act, often anchoring these prescriptions in past sets of rules, in the authority of previous rule-makers, or in the assumption that rule-based readings of texts can produce fixed rules for behavior. Rules tell us how to treat special objects, and sometimes even tell us what to say. Buying into a pre-designated set of rules can even be seen as a form of enacting belief, as a deliberate religious act.

Performance theorist Richard Schechner (2002) coined the term "make belief" to distinguish the willful act of belief from mere pretending. For Schechner, "make believe" is an imaginative act that retains the boundaries between real and play, and is denoted by merely "pretending to believe." This category, then, would encompass the attitude embraced by most players of games, including videogames. By contrast, he says, "make belief" involves an intentional blurring of these boundaries in that performers are "enacting the effects they want the receivers of their performances to accept 'for real'" (ibid.: 35). Players of alternate reality games, those games that spill over into everyday life through role play and hidden clues in the everyday world, are embracing forms of "make belief" because they have given themselves over more deeply to the experience. Play, then, can be seen as a performance as well, characterized by the choice to enter into a "make belief" space and adhere by its given rules. In both "make belief" and "make believe," adherents buy into sets of rules, enacting experience through play in response to those rules.

Belief is always performative; that is, it enacts that which it presumes to depict. By choosing to enter into the rules of the game, a player decides to act as if the given rules are the only rules that matter. This state of being can be temporarily true of games, or permanently true, in the game of religion. Schechner recognizes the role of belief in religion, and proposes that in religion, as in "other belief systems," people commit to a what-if state, buying imaginatively into a system of rules and practices:

> People make what isn't there, combine elements from fantasy, actualize situations that occur only as art or performance. These actualizations in the service of social organization, thought, ritual, or rebellious anti-structure contain, transmit, and (dare I say it?) *create* the very circumstances they purport to depict.
>
> (Schechner 1988: 220–21; emphasis in the original)

Belief is a choice, an enactment of the will, a form of play that defines behavior. The magic circle in this case is meant to absorb all of life into its bounds. Belief is something that people do, through committing to the rules of play in a given experience. And people *do* belief by deciding that the rules of the game—religious or otherwise—are worth investing in, worth abiding in. Belief is an act of faith in the game of life, the insistence that rules matter and that a specific mode of religious procedural rhetoric should define our choices.

Rules are at the root of many of the most common features of games, and rules are a key basic feature of religious practice, especially ritual (see Wagner 2012a). The "play" of religion, however, is increasingly implicated in borrowed rules, ones imported through the devices we use and the games we play. These new rules have the ability to shape our experience as profoundly at times as the original rules of the religious experience itself. Our job, then, is to be critically aware of the rules of play that we borrow from digitized experience, consciously asking ourselves how these new algorithmic rules transform traditional religious practice and belief. These changes are transformative in ways that are at times utopic and other times dismally divisive.

Digital dualism

When religion participates deeply in pre-existing programmed environments, it shares the values of the environments, whether or not these accord with a particular group's professed religious or cultural values. And some forms of digital, algorithmic experiences work against the ideals of religion at its best. That is, instead of uniting, they divide. This danger is the greatest with today's most popular mode of digital entertainment, the first person shooter videogame.

Not all games are created alike, of course. There are a number of socially positive, educational videogames meant to teach us new things about the world and to raise awareness about issues of social import. For example, in the game *Peacemaker* (2007), one can play as the prime minister of Israel and then as the prime minister of Palestine, trying to broker a plan that brings peace to the region. To "win" is to bring about an end to violence. To "lose" is to fail to bring about peace, and thus to invite another Intifada. The newly released mobile games associated with the "Half the Sky" movement were sponsored by the United States Agency for International Development. In the game *9 Minutes*, women are taught about healthy pregnancy and birth. *Family Values*, a game currently in development, is meant to teach the "value" of women in the family, and will be promoted for free in parts of the world where women struggle for basic rights. Other games similarly teach values of community, cooperation, and health. Certainly, one could critique such games for the inevitable embedded political assumptions based on the values of the creators, but even so, the games are intended to bring about a better sense of community belonging and to make for happier people.

Other games, by contrast, demonstrate that peace in the world can only be achieved through violence. Borrowing a violent apocalyptic procedural rhetoric, many of today's popular American first person shooter games teach that the world is divided into two camps: good guys and bad guys; and the goal of the game is to kill as many of the "bad guys" as possible. To "win" is to enact massive destruction while killing one's enemies, and this is usually the only path offered to victory. Cooperation does happen in multiplayer versions of game franchises, such as *Halo* (Bungie, 343 Industries), *Metal Gear* (Platinum Games), or *Gears of War* (Epic Games), but it is still frequently constrained by the procedural rhetoric of a dualistic division of the world into friends and foes, with the goal of killing as many enemies as possible to achieve peace.

Here's where an understanding of the magic circle, procedural rhetoric, and the notion of play become extremely helpful. We have already seen how religious rituals can work like games in setting apart space and time that is defined by pre-designated rules. Some modes of religious practice can even work like games in their division of the world into winners and losers, the saved and the damned. Games can exhibit a similar mode of metaphysical sorting, encouraging players to divide the world swiftly, and by first appearances, into friends and foes.

If games can work like rituals, then they too may be able to induce the kind of spillover into real life that rituals are prone to exhibit. That is to say, the magic circle of a game may be as permeable with real life as a ritual is. Both games and rituals can profoundly shape our experiences. Both can tell us how to view the world. Both can "shed" their perspective, their rules, onto everyday life. If this is true, then first person shooters represent a powerful mode of new religious ritual, a resurgence of apocalyptic, dualistic, myth-making in a new digitized mode of storytelling. At the same time that fundamentalist modes of exclusivist religious practice are on the rise, we find in many videogames a secular mode of myth-making with the same kind of apocalyptic division of people into those worth protecting and those worth killing. Such scripted behaviors are deeply damaging, and frighteningly common today. If games can work like rituals, then those urging violence against others should be viewed with a wary eye.

Any time religious groups engage with computational devices, they borrow the procedural rhetoric, the logic, of those processes. As such, any engagement with virtual reality should be carefully considered for the new limitations and affordances it engenders to religious practice. No engagement with a digital screen is free of the effects of the programming that enabled the use of the device. And, because religion itself can be seen as a kind of "programming" that is also intended to shape our behavior and tell us how the world works, religious groups should be particularly attuned to the ways in which coded processes may clash or mesh with one's original religious intentions. This is true of sacred texts, of digital depictions of sacred spaces, and also of programmed virtual environments of all kinds, including videogames. No screened environment is without its algorithmic biases.

Conclusion

The move to digitizing cultural processes has, since the 1970s, transformed our lives and "precipitated massive upheavals in the lives of individuals." Digital "acts of configuration" are increasingly "a rendering of life," says Alexander Galloway (2006). We have "submitted to a process of retaining and deployment into a new economy" that is "mediated by machines and other informatic artifacts" (ibid.: 17). Put more simply, computers are shaping us—profoundly, deeply, and perhaps irrevocably. These changes apply to all elements of life, including religion.

Because of technology's ability to link disparate parts of the globe via communications technology, some contemporary theorists have celebrated its utopic potential. Karen Parna (2010: 112), for example, argues that technology will help humanity overcome "fragility, poverty, material limitations, sickness and even death" by encouraging "brotherhood and understanding." Media theorist Kevin Kelly (2010: 358) watches technology with awe as it "wrap[s] the planet in a vibrating cloak of electronic nerves, entire continents of machines conversing with one another, the whole aggregation watching itself through a million cameras posted daily." Far from being disenchanted, the world today is filled with digital dreams, with desire increasingly transferred from the altar to the iPod, and from the pulpit to the pocket app. As we have seen, though, these dreams are guided by new algorithmic structures, processes that shape our perspectives and offer ritualized experiences that mimic religious experience, at times even absorbing existing religious practice. As Todd Gitlin (2002: 5) quips, in our hyper-wired age: "Ignorance is not bliss; information is."

But information uncritically consumed is certainly *not* bliss. Social organization and challenging interreligious or intercultural encounter can happen using coded spaces, but they may also be diluted by the cross-purposes of the media used. Today's programmed environments are increasingly restricted by authentication procedures; aggregated to suit our tastes; limited by walls that determine with whom we interact and even who we are likely to meet; and threatened by intrusive remote listening like malicious spyware and data mining. Wired spaces have always been based upon computational procedures defined by the coders more than by the users.

By exploring three interconnected tools for thinking about the intersection between virtual reality and religion—the magic circle, procedural rhetoric, and play—we have seen how religion can, at times, work like a game and that games can, at times, work like religion. Religious rituals have a particular kinship with games, since both are fixed arenas of experience that shape our behavior, and that offer temporary spaces in which fixed rules adhere. Huizinga was right in thinking that sacred play and secular play are closely aligned, and that both offer us a means of entering into an imagined, ordered cosmos. He may also be right to say that religious ritual, as a mode of play, makes larger claims about its ability to shape the whole of life, and to say something meaningful about how the cosmos works.

As we have seen, if games and religion can indeed work in similar ways, then games also have the ability to make arguments about the whole of life, and religions have the ability to reduce life to a violent winnable game. The most pertinent question, then, is not whether religion can be played as a game or whether games can work like religion. The most important question is when religion and games do work alike, what kind of cultural work are they doing? The procedural rhetoric of these programmed environments is, in its earthly form at least, in our control, since both religion and games reflect profoundly human modes of mythical play. And, like all forms of play, the rules allow for multiple modes of interpretation. This means that even if the sacred texts are fixed, even if tradition has shaped the rules of the magic circle, we nonetheless still have the ability and the responsibility to define for ourselves what it means to play to win.

Note

1 This question became vividly real for me in a classroom setting, when I had to decide whether or not to let one of my students digitally arrive in the virtual replica of Mecca in Second Life while wearing a Batman costume.

Works cited

Bogost, I. (2007) *Persuasive Games: The Expressive Power of Videogames*, Cambridge, MA: The MIT Press.

Caillois, R. (1957) "Unity of play: diversity of games," trans. E.P. Halperin, *Diogenes* 5, 19 (September): 92–121.

Campbell, H. (2005) *Exploring Religious Community Online: We Are One in the Network*, New York: Peter Lang.

Dawson, L. (2005) "The mediation of religious experience in cyberspace," in M. Højsgaard and M. Warburg (eds), *Religion and Cyberspace*, New York: Routledge Press, 15–37.

Doyle, K., Fr. (2012) "Is the use of an iPad for Mass readings appropriate?" *Catholic Courier* (August 2). Online. Available: www.catholiccourier.com/commentary/other-columnists/is-the-use-of-an-ipad-for-mass-readings-appropriate/ (accessed 1 March 2013).

Eliade, M. (1959) *The Sacred and the Profane: The Nature of Religion*, trans. W.R. Trask, New York: Harcourt, Brace & World, Inc.

Galloway, A. (2006) *Gaming: Essays on Algorithmic Culture*, Minneapolis, MN: University of Minnesota Press.

Gitlin, T. (2002) *Media Unlimited: How the Torrent of Images and Sounds Overwhelms Our Lives*, New York: Henry Holt & Co.

Hess, M. (2008) "Faith formation in a media world," *Lifelong Faith Journal* 57 (Fall): 44–47. Online. Available: www.faithformationlearningexchange.net/uploads/5/2/4/6/5246709/living_faith_in_a_media_world – hess.pdf (accessed 4 May 2013).

Huizinga, J. (1955[1949]) *Homo Ludens*, Boston, MA: Beacon Press (1949 edn London: Routledge and Kegan Paul).

Kelly, K. (2010) *What Technology Wants*, New York: Viking.

Lessig, L. (2006) *Code: And Other Laws of Cyberspace, Version 2.0*, New York: Basic Books.

"needMalk" (2013) "To the Muslims of Reddit," *AskReddit* (February 7). Online. Available: http://redd.it/182a7a (accessed 1 March 2013).

Ng, K. (2009) "Russian priest pitches idea for a religious MMOG," *The Escapist* (September 1). Online. Available: www.escapistmagazine.com/news/view/94368-Russian-Priest-Pitches-Idea-for-a-Religious-MMOG (accessed 12 March 2013).

Parna, K. (2010) *Believing in the Net: Implicit Religion and the Internet Hype, 1994–2001*. Dissertation. University of Leiden: Leiden University Press.

Robertson, A. (2012) "Not to be consoled as to console," *Church Times* (May 30). Online. Available: www.churchtimes.co.uk/articles/2012/1-june/comment/not-to-be-consoled-as-to-console (accessed 12 March 2013).

Salen, K. and E. Zimmerman (2004) *The Game Design Reader: A Rules of Play Anthology*, Cambridge, MA: The MIT Press.

Schechner, R. (1988) *Performance Theory*, New York: Routledge.

——(2002) *Performance Studies: An Introduction*, New York: Routledge.

Sweet, L. (2012) *Viral: How Social Networking Is Poised to Ignite Revival*, Colorado Springs, CO: Waterbrook Press.

Tambiah, S. (1996) "A performative approach to ritual," in R. Grimes (ed.), *Readings in Ritual Studies*, Upper Saddle River, NJ: Prentice Hall, 495–511.

Wagner, R. (2012a) *Godwired: Religion, Ritual, and Virtual Reality*, New York: Routledge.

——(2012b) "Religion and video games: shooting aliens in cathedrals," in T.R. Clark and D.W. Clanton, Jr. (eds), *Understanding Religion and Popular Culture*, New York: Routledge, 118–38.

Zimmerman, E. (2004) "Narrative, interactivity, play, and games," in N. Wardrip-Fruin and P. Harrigan (eds), *First Person: New Media as Story, Performance, and Game*, Cambridge, MA: The MIT Press, 154–64.

9
INTERNET AND SOCIAL NETWORKING

Heidi A. Campbell and
Paul Emerson Teusner

In this chapter we explore the intersection and interaction between religion and new media technologies. In the past two decades, the practice and presentation of religion has increasingly been intertwined with new media technologies. Many religious communities display Web sites about their mission and activities. Blogs have become a platform for both religious leaders and laity to reflect on their faith, and religious "apps" have enabled the faithful to make their practice of faith more mobile and digital. This embrace of digital technology has the potential to both enhance and challenge religious behavior and beliefs of individuals and groups. This is in part because the story of the Internet is a story laden with both fear and promise, from its birth in military projects under the threat of nuclear war to its public release that promised a new freedom of information and instant communication. Computers and information communication technologies carry with them certain ideological conceptions that encourage certain values (Campbell 2005a: 6–12). New media culture is characterized by key features—such as efficiency, instantaneous communication, networked interaction, and mobility—which can be seen as promoting values of efficiency, non-hierarchical authority, and individualized practice. These are values that simultaneously empower and challenge religious individuals and communities and their traditional practices or ways of life in many respects. The aim of this chapter is to explore the growth of religious Internet and new media practices as well as the outcomes and challenges of these behaviors. Furthermore, it will outline some key rhetorics of the Internet that have shaped the way people understand new technologies and use them for religious purposes.

We begin with a brief overview of the rise of religion online. Through this study, a number of key themes emerge which highlight issues and questions regarding the promises and pitfalls of practicing religion online that scholars and practitioners have debated over the past two decades. This leads to a detailed exploration of the rhetorics that new media culture seems to promote and how these relate to questions about religion online. Specific themes to be explored include how issues of identity, community, network, authority, and the blurring of online and offline contexts impact religious practice online.

Religious groups' engagement with the Internet

One way to approach the rise of religion online is to consider how different religions have engaged the rise of new media technologies. This helps create a platform for understanding common themes and questions that emerge in studies of religion online. Zaleski's *The Soul of Cyberspace* (1997) was a forerunner in comparing the use of the Internet within different religious traditions, specifically Judaism, Islam, Christianity, Buddhism, and Hinduism, and investigating how the Internet might erode hierarchy and change the ways in which different religious groups worship. Over the past two decades, we have seen a number of unique forms of religious integration with technology, from worship at cyberchurches to transporting religious prayer ritual online and creating new forms of religious interaction and community via email and social media. By looking at how religion has emerged online in the past two decades, we begin to see some shared questions and issues that the integration of the religious with the digital raises.

For almost three decades the Internet has been used as a space where spiritual rituals are conducted and traditional religious beliefs discussed. Religious use of the Internet can be traced back to the early 1980s. Rheingold (1993) documents some of the first religious-oriented activity taking place at this time on Bulletin Board Systems (BBS) under "create your own religion" on the discussion area of CommuniTree, which soon evolved into numerous BBS forums on religion. During this same period online religious discussion surfaced on Usenet. It was a time when religious computer enthusiasts began to explore "ways to use this new means of communication to express their religious interests" (Lochhead 1997: 46). For example, at this time the "net.religion" discussion list emerged as the "first networked forum for discussions on the religious, ethical, and moral implications of human actions" (Ciolek 2004: 799). Throughout the 1980s many other religious computer enthusiasts formed online groups dedicated to their specific religion, such as the first Christian email newsletter "United Methodist Information," and the "net.religion.jewish" Usenet group.

In the 1990s, increasing numbers of religious groups and mailing lists began to emerge online, such as Ecunet (www.ecunet.org, an ecumenical Christian email listserve), H-Judaic (www.h-net.org/~judaic), and BuddhaNet (www.buddhanet.net). Early in this decade, the first Christian online congregation (The First Church of Cyberspace) was established by American Presbyterians, and for over a decade they held a weekly service via Internet Relay Chat (IRC) and offered Web interaction for participants (www.godweb.org). In 1996, *Time* magazine published a special issue on religion online, highlighting the dozens of religious Web sites and resources that could be found online: from the first monastic Web site, "Monastery of Christ in the Desert" (www.christdesert.org) and Islamic e-periodical, "Renaissance: A Monthly Islamic Journal" (www.renaissance.com.pk) to the first Zoroastrian cybertemple (www.zarathushtra.com) and establishment of the "Virtual Memorial Garden" tribute to people and pets (catless.ncl.ac.uk/vmg). The special issue also proved an important landmark, highlighting media recognition of religious activity online.

Throughout the 1990s, people from traditional and non-traditional religions experimented with creating new religious resources online. For example, Gospelcom (www.gospelcom.net) provided Christians with access to online Bible study tools and various interactive devotional or fellowship groups. Others experimented with altering and adapting ancient beliefs to this digital environment, from Wicca (NightMare 2001) to new religions such as technopaganism (Davis 1998). In the late 1990s, inter-religious information hubs such as Beliefnet (www.Beliefnet.org) emerged online offering thoughts for the day from the Dalai Lama and the Pope to inspirational screensavers and access to sacred text from different traditions.

In the 2000s, religion online had become a common part of the Internet's land-scape, and as new forms and features of digital engagement began to emerge so did their religious counterparts. In the early 2000s, as blogging platforms and hosting tools such as Live Journal and Blogger.com gained popularity, so did religious blog hubs such as Jblog: The Jewish and Israeli blog network (www.israelforum.com/blog_home.php), Christian Bloggy Moms (www.bloggymoms.com), and Muslim bloggers (at hadithuna.com). The rise of podcasting also led to a revolution in "godcasting" or audio and visual broadcasting of religious-style talk shows from tel-evangelists to home school mums (see *The Godcast Network* [www.godcast.org] or *GODcasting.tv* [www.godcasting.tv]).

The rise of virtual world environments in the mid-2000s also birthed innovations in religious worship. For example, Church of Fools (www.churchoffools.com) was a short-lived online church experiment in 3D sponsored by the Methodist Church of Great Britain, and the satirical Web site Ship of Fools, and its off-shoot St Pixels: Church of the Internet offered chat rooms and a "live" online worship forum to its members. Both examples challenged the notion of what it means to be a church in a digital age. The emergence of Second Life (secondlife.com), a 3D virtual world, allowed residents to interact via a motional avatar to socialize, play, create, and do business with other virtual residents, and also enabled room for people to re-image religious location in digital. As it allowed residents to create a "second life" online, people soon began to import their religious practice into the digital space. This includes attending Shabbat services at the Second Life Synagogue-Temple Beit Israel (slurl.com/secondlife/nessus/18/146/103) and participating in a virtual Hajj (slurl.com/secondlife/IslamOnline%20dot%20Net/128/128/128).

By the late 2000s, social media had replaced email as the number one activity online, and religious users began to populate spaces such as MySpace, Facebook, and later, Twitter, using these new forms of social interaction as opportunities to publicize their faith or create novel forms of religious engagement. One can now find that Jesus, Buddha, Krishna, and Mohammed all have multiple Facebook accounts. These creations are not without controversy; debates over the imaging of the Prophet Mohammed on Facebook led to public protests, online demonstrations, and several Muslim countries threatening to ban Facebook due to such activities in 2009–10.

Some religious groups have also become concerned about the negative side of social networking: it exposes their members to secular values or problematic sexual content and promotes a trend toward the creation of religious versions of popular social networking sites, such as Jewmango for Jews (www.jewmango.com/home.php) and MillatFacebook for Muslims (www.mymfb.com). Religious versions of the video sharing Web site YouTube.com have also been launched, such as JewTube.com and Godtube.com, offering alternative venues for religious believers to participate in the same activities offered by these popular sites, but in the context of a community of like-minded believers.

Within these varieties of religious uses and adaptation we see a number of common motivations for using the Internet (Campbell 2005b). For many, the Internet is simply a functional technology, and so is viewed as an essentially useful technology, supporting the social practices or work-related tasks valuable to the religious community. Yet for some religious Internet users, the Internet is seen as a spiritual medium, facilitating spiritual experience for individuals and communities, and so it is utilized as a spiritual network or a place where spiritual encounters are made and activities performed. Other religious users see it as sacramental space that can be set aside for religious ritual or activities, so that the Internet becomes a worship environment. The Internet may also be used as a tool for promoting a specific religion or set of beliefs, and so the Internet becomes a missionary tool for making disciples or converts. For others, the Internet may be viewed as a technology to be used for affirming one's religious community, background, or theology; here the Internet can be seen as helping an individual build and maintain a particular religious identity by connecting into a global, networked community of believers. However, the Internet itself is essentially neither sacred nor secular in its character. Noting the perceptions different groups have of the Internet helps us uncover how different religious groups approach the technology.

Researching religion online

In the past two decades, scholars from different academic disciplines have focused attention on the Internet as an important sphere for investigating questions related to society, politics, culture, and even religion. A growing number of researchers have begun to focus attention on how different individuals and groups have sought to employ the Internet as a new realm in which to experience or express the spiritual dimensions of life. Much of this research has taken an interdisciplinary focus, as researchers from diverse backgrounds have often interacted and collaborated in order to investigate differing perceptions of religion online. In one of the first academic articles in this area, O'Leary and Brasher (1996) provided a foundational overview of how religion began to be influenced and manifested in online environments, followed by O'Leary's "Cyberspace as sacred space" (1996), which explored how online rituals seem to perform an important function, enabling users to import their religious sensibilities online. These articles marked the starting point for serious academic inquiry into religious engagement with the Internet. The result was a range of diverse studies looking at examples of online religious practice, such as the one conducted by Schroeder, Heather, and Lee, of prayer in a multi-user virtual reality environment (1998), and large-scale studies of religious Internet user behavior such as those undertaken by the Pew Internet and American Life Project—"Wired churches, wired temples" (Larsen 2000) and "CyberFaith" (Larsen 2001)—offering empirical evidence about the religious use of the Internet.

Since the early 2000s, the study of religion online has been taken up by scholars in sociology, religious studies, theology, communication, and other disciplines, and this has shaped the questions and approaches to the study of religion and the Internet. Sociologists of religion have provided important insights into mapping the emergence of cyber-religion (Brasher 2001), as well as helping to define the range of communal and individual religious practices online (Hennerby and Dawson 1999). For instance, Helland's (2000) popular distinction between religion-online (importing traditional forms of religion and religious practice online) and online-religion (adapting religion to create new forms of networked spiritual interactions) offered scholars a way to distinguish forms of religion in online environments and their potential impact. Recent work in sociology of religion has focused on the relationship between online and offline religious practice, in order to better understand how online presence is "often based in the conditions of offline contexts and sources" (Campbell and Lövheim 2011: 1089).

Scholars of religious studies have detailed how traditional religious rituals have been adapted or re-invented in an online environment, from online *fatwas* (Bunt 2000) to digital *puja* and cybersanghas (Prebish 2004). In a special issue of the journal *Religion* (2002), four examples helped to identify, categorize, and begin to theorize about the changing shape of religion in a wired world, as well as to inaugurate "a new sub-field of religious studies" (MacWilliams 2002: 277). Recently scholars working between religious studies and ritual studies have helped illuminate how online participants conceptually connect virtual objects and places with their offline counterparts in order to create a seamless flow between online and offline religiosity (Connelly 2012).

Theologians have been interested both in how the Internet may empower people to reconnect with spiritual beliefs in postmodern society (e.g., Cobb 1998) and in the ethical challenges posed by digital technology to religion (Houston 1998; Pontifical Council for Social Communications 2002). Work in this area has been used to critique the moral and social impact of new media on society and provide guidelines for ethical decision-making. For instance, Babin and Zukowski (2002) combine reflection from practical theology with communication theory to assess the potential ideological impact of the Internet on traditional religious practice and belief within the Catholic Church. Current theological scholars often look for links between digital culture and religious practice, such as Friesen (2009), who argues how pastors should view the church as a network of people and resources, in order to use Internetworking as a model for building relational links between people inside and outside faith communities.

Communication and media studies scholars have focused on the relationship between technology use and religion, particularly looking at correlations between religiosity and Internet use (Armfield and Holbert 2003; Hoover *et al.* 2004), the interaction of religious Internet users through the formation of online religious communities (Howard 2000; Campbell 2005a), and how religious communities negotiate and make choices about what aspects of new technologies to embrace or resist for religious usage (Campbell 2010). Such researchers have taken an interest in common patterns and trends of Internet usage for religious purposes, which have been informed by communication theory. For example, Laney (2005) applies uses and gratifications theory in order to determine the relationship between personal motive or desires, Christian Web site usage, and work done at the University of

Colorado's Center for Media, Religion, and Culture. Her research has taken the lead in investigating how the Internet acts as a "symbolic or meaning resource" and is used by spiritual seekers in contemporary society for religious orientation and formation practices (Hoover and Park 2004). Current work among new media scholars has taken up the subject of how religious institutions and leaders have responded to the ways in which authority structures and roles are clearly challenged by digital cultures (e.g., Cheong 2012).

In summing up the past two decades of research on religion and the Internet, an article in the *Journal of the American Academy of Religion* (Campbell 2012) noted several common areas of research inquiry explored by scholars. These include how the Internet contributes to the construction of religious identities, supports new forms of community, highlights changing understandings of authority, encourages the mixing of traditional and new forms of social practice, and recognizes the interconnectedness between online and offline contexts. These areas of inquiry also represent several dominant rhetorics of the Internet, highlighting important questions and challenges which digital technologies have posed to contemporary social and religious culture.

Rhetorics of the Internet

In this section, we will present a number of discussions that Internet scholars have highlighted in their exploration of the Internet and new media related to the values and ideas emerging concerning engagement with new media and its social and religious impact. We refer to these as rhetorics, in order to highlight several key discourses that have oriented scholars' investigations into new patterns of Internet usage, and illuminate the potential challenges they pose, especially to religion. These rhetorics of the Internet are situated around the perceived impact technologies have (or technology has) on our perception of identity, community, new understandings of the social world in terms of networks, authority, and the blurring of offline and online worlds.

Identity

One of the early discussions among researchers of Internet usage is how people construct their personae, or identities, online, and how these constructions have an impact on relationships they create and foster with others in online spaces. In the early years of the World Wide Web, users of chat rooms would interact only through text, unable to see the bodies of other users. This allowed people to invent or reconstruct their own identities, including aspects such as age, gender, and race through the text that they sent to these online spaces. Moreover, in these new spaces users were free to invent or reconstruct new mores of social interaction, such as greetings and expressions of emotions. In a setting devoid of social "cues" that we look for and understand in physical spaces, users were free to make their own.

Turkle's seminal work on online identity construction, *Life on the Screen* (1996), presented findings based on interviews with game users and players to propose that people experience a new relationship with their own identities when online. In the absence of social cues expected in offline settings of social interaction, users find that how they present themselves in online spaces becomes a more deliberate activity, where they are required to invent and experiment with new forms of expression in order to negotiate what are to become social norms in online spaces. Turkle sees in cyberspace a "moratorium" on traditional notions of identity. This moratorium offers a space for growth, making cyberspace a place to practice being ourselves, coming and going from an offline world where we must constantly negotiate different roles and their demands. In effect, identity construction online is a form of play. Like a child playing with costumes to invent personae, the Internet allows people to use text to experiment with new ways of presenting oneself to the online world (1996: 260–63).

Lövheim has tested Turkle's theory in relation to the performance of religious identity online. In her study of online interactions among young people, she found that cyberspace offered users a space to talk openly about religious experience, beliefs, and values, free of the constraints of offline religious community involvement. Online users felt free to ascribe new words and symbols to their own understandings of faith and religion, and present their ideas to others with a sense of impunity. For Lövheim, online interactions offered a way to "restructure" their religious identity (2005: 14). She noticed, however, that when this "moratorium" causes insecurity, users bring cues, rituals, and mores from offline social experience to compensate. Thus the lack of cues is not enough for online social interaction to make for a safe and useful "moratorium" of identity, a place for identity play. Social trust is a necessary element. Trust in the medium is not enough; Lövheim also suggests that trust in one's ability to express oneself in written language and in the conventions of interaction one expects online is important to generate enough trust to present oneself online (ibid.: 18).

As Lövheim's work suggests, the Internet's promise is to provide a space for users to effectively write themselves new identities. It attracts users to consider a potentially liberating alternative to offline religious settings for the practice of faith and sharing of ideas. Current research on religious identity online shows that the Internet has become a place for living out the religious self, which can combine both experimentation with different ways of being and evaluation and adoption of traditional identity roles (Lövheim 2012). New media provide unique opportunities for religious users to present and integrate their religious selves within their daily technology use.

Community

Traditionally, notions of community have been based on geography and, with particular respect to religious communities, defined by the locations at which people gather. As the Internet creates a space outside of physical space, the technology presents an opportunity to redefine community. "Disembedded" from any physical location, and not bounded by any real or imagined geographical lines, the gatherings of people in online locations (e.g., chat rooms, email groups, bulletin boards, etc.) are not defined as "communities" in the traditional sense.

Rheingold opened conversation and debate on theorizing online community with *The Virtual Community*, in which he attempts to define community in cyberspace as "social aggregations that emerge from the Net when enough people carry on those public discussions long enough, with sufficient human feeling, to form webs of personal relationships" (1993: 5). Since then, scholars have endeavored to define what constitutes community and by what conditions online communities evolve, knowing that they are ideally as fluid as identity, not anchored to a physical place and time but actively nurtured by the relational practices among participants in a discursively constructed online setting. Putting it more simply, online communities, not bounded by space and time, create their own identity by making their own boundaries.

Campbell's study of a community formed through email exchanges showed that its members felt a sense of belonging—though being physically distant from each other—by the recognition of a common purpose for gathering. That is, users understood and shared a common need to find meaningful connections with people outside their local church, and explore questions about faith that were not discussed in those settings. Cohesion between members of the group was fostered by the sharing of testimonials, statements of trust in each other, and statements of support between each other (2005a: 184–86). Campbell's investigation showed that the formation and definition of this online community was a discursive project, fueled and framed by ongoing conversation between emails.

That these interactions are said to be formations of community online offer the Internet a rhetoric that it is a resource for religious growth, and a source for belonging, support, and purpose. This has attracted not just individuals, but entire denominations to intentionally plant congregations in online spaces. Examples include the Methodist Church of Great Britain, which established the online church named Church of Fools (mentioned earlier), and members of the Anglican Church of New Zealand who established an Anglican cathedral in Second Life. Other religious groups challenge whether online relationships constitute legitimate religious community, without the sharing of material symbols and a shared physical presence (Hutchings 2011).

In either case, it is important to note that recent research has shown that participation in online religious communities serves more to complement than replace participation in religious groups offline (see Campbell 2005a; Larsson 2005). In some cases, involvement in a number of different groups, both online and offline, has helped people grow and develop in faith. It raises another notion worth exploring here, that of networked religion. Thus the use of new media to build community helps people of faith re-imagine their social and spiritual relationships in ways that may challenge traditional forms of religious gathering.

Network

Related to the new forms of religious community, which are facilitated by new technologies, is the emerging notion that our social world is being reconstituted in new ways in what is often described as a networked society. Since the 1970s, sociologists have come to consider a "community" as more than a spatially bound grouping of people, rather as a source of social capital (belonging, purpose, support and other nonmaterial needs) for those who belong in it. Wellman and Leighton (1979), in their study of urban patterns of social interaction, found that while urbanites look to their local community for some of these resources, personal networks beyond locality serve these needs. Personal networks, in this sense, refer to the set of connections an individual may have across a multitude of settings, communities and/ or groups.

Networked sociability refers to patterns of social interaction that extend beyond one local setting, made possible by regular migratory patterns and telecommunications (for example: work in the city center, raising children in the suburbs, meeting with friends in different places in a metropolitan area, extended family in different cities, etc.). For Castells, modern Western life has seen the rise of personal relationships outside families and embedded communities (schools, churches, sporting groups, workplaces) as a dominant pattern of sociability, leading to the embodiment of "me-centered networks" (2001: 128). That is, individual identity is defined less by one's local community than by the constellation of connections and groups with which one associates.

Castells does not blame the Internet for the rise of networked individualism, but sees that this pattern of sociability works best online, as it "provides an appropriate material support for the diffusion of networked individualism as the dominant form of sociability" (ibid.: 131). This is further fueled by Web 2.0 technologies, which enable users to create their own spaces for interaction on the Internet, not only building but displaying and promoting their own personal networks. Thus their online identity is not just expressed by their behavior in particular online spaces, but by their connections to a multitude of pages, symbols and information, to be displayed and celebrated on personal blog pages or social networking sites.

This is also seen in how new media facilitate new patterns of being for religious users. An example of this is Johns's (2008) study into the portrayal of the religious identity of Facebook users. At the time of this study, a function on profile pages on Facebook allows users to display their religious beliefs, but it is limited to a menu of choices ranging from "liberal" to "conservative" or a major religion. Yet users showed their religious affiliations by displaying on their profile page a range of Facebook groups they have joined, and pages they liked. Facebook profile pages offer a glimpse of a person's network of connections that give a sense of that person's religious interests and values. Thus we see that the presentation of religious identity becomes entwined with one's social network in new media culture.

Emerson Teusner's investigation of Christian bloggers, who write about their involvement in a global conversation called the "Emerging Church movement," also explored how the social network of religious users becomes important for establishing influence online. While these bloggers displayed their connection to the movement in a variety of ways (e.g., tagging their posts, using the name of the movement in their blog titles, etc.), they also made connections with people outside the movement, and used their blog posts to critique both attitudes within the movement and criticisms of the movement from outside. Bloggers generally tended to view themselves as being "on the margins" of the Emerging Church movement, seeing it as a resource to help them grow as Christians, but not the only source of religious information or community (2011: 285–87).

In both these examples, the notion of "networked religious identity" may be seen. Membership in a local community, or a denominational title, serves less to describe one's religious identity. What is more important are the links with a variety of people, groups and information sources to provide connection, support, and a sense of belonging. The idea of community and identity being interwoven within the network structure can present a challenge to organized religions, especially those within the West. Research into religion online notes that this decentered, non-hierarchical form of social engagement clearly challenges established forms of institutional authority. As different groups are formed both online and offline, they offer belonging and purpose, and as individuals rely less on participation in one particular group to define their religious identity, the power of institutions to define what faith is and should be, is brought into question. Thus discourse about the Internet as a social and religious network has led many to explore the implications this has for religious authority.

Authority

New media's ability to provide users with instantaneous communication, access to once private data, and greater flexibility in where and how they interact has transformed the ways we engage with information that has implications for established roles, hierarchies, and patterns of knowledge.

Consider hypertext, the name given to objects on Web pages that are embedded with a link to other objects on the same or a distant site. Through hypertext, readers have new levels of control over how they engage with a text and its interpretation. While the writer has historically been the designer of the reading project, in hypertext readers engage their own design into the reading (Burn and Parker 2003: 31–32). Hypertext, Enzensberger suggests, allows for the shift of power from producer to consumer in the creation and distribution of information. Thus new media become emancipatory, in that they free both text from the producer and people from the audience. Emancipatory media are decentralized, where each receiver is a potential transmitter (2000: 64).

This function of the World Wide Web has led many researchers to investigate the changing structure of power between those who make all types of media text, and those who receive it, not just online but in all settings, including religious ones. Dawson, for example, asserts that the "disembodiment" of religious organizations in online settings results in the removal of material sacred objects and a greater dependence on the reflexivity of identity, community, and authority (2005: 33). For example, the Internet is devoid of symbols and practices that separate clergy and laity, freeing both to explore and challenge the distinctions between them. In these assertions the writers imagine the expression of religious ideas in words and practice completely free from the rule of the church or other religious organizations.

Much of the rhetoric related to authority and the Internet suggests that embedded authority structures are primarily challenged online. However, researchers have also noted that in online settings users construct, negotiate and adhere to new patterns of authority and that patterns mirror offline experiences of authority and power (Cheong 2012). The Internet is also used by some offline religious authorities as a realm in which to solidify their position and control. This is seen in tensions within the Ultraorthodox Jewish community between religious entrepreneurs who have created Web spaces for religious dialogue and Rabbis who view these online spaces as problematic in being outside the traditional boundaries, hence undermining established patterns of authority and control (Campbell and Golan 2011).

New media culture creates opportunities and challenges simultaneously, as new forms of religious authority emerge online. Emerson Teusner's investigation into religious discourse in the blogosphere found that search engines (such as Google and Technorati) gave authority rankings to bloggers according to the numbers of hyper-text links that pointed to them from other sites. While most bloggers in his study protested against the importance people gave this ranking system, it was noted that those who had higher rankings were generally university educated (often a degree in theology), worked in a profession that afforded them time to spend blogging, were over thirty, and typically male (Emerson Teusner 2012). Thus it may be argued that the Internet reflects the conditions that favor some people over others (e.g., gender, education level, race, etc.), often present in offline religious institutions. Therefore the rhetoric of authority online demonstrates that institutional power is simulta-neously reinforced and undermined through new media, and this paradox cannot be easily overlooked.

Blurring of offline and online worlds

The proliferation of Internet-enabled mobile devices (such as smartphones and tablets) and the growing availability of 3G (and 4G) wireless data networks have made Internet access ubiquitous, to the extent that "going online" is no longer a discrete action. We acknowledge more and more that access to the Internet is with us all the time, on the periphery of our offline interactions, and that the boundary between the "virtual world" and the real world is collapsing (see Thomas 2006). Early framings of cyberspace as being a separate and distinct space we travel to have given way to an understanding that digital culture is something that is closely con-nected to our daily routines. The embeddedness of new media technologies in our everyday lives highlights an important rhetoric about the relationship and tension between our online and offline life.

The implications of this relationship for studying religion online are manifold. Initially, it challenges us to consider the context in which religious information is received and therefore experienced. An example is the availability of Bible readings on mobile devices through a Web site called the Bible podcast (thebiblepodcast.org). Through this online application, listening to scripture readings is possible while jogging or at work. The various places in which the information (i.e., scripture readings) is received will change the experience of listening. Furthermore, the information is accessible to many people at once through the Internet, but is experienced by people alone (through earphones connected to their devices).

Religious organizations that make information available, or endeavor to make connections with people online through mobile devices, must take into account that their users' connection to them is taking place in a physical context to which they have no connection. For example, a parishioner accessing a video-relay of a church-based service on her mobile phone may be alone at home, or in a public place surrounded by people who are not seeing the same video. Thus the makers of the online text have little control over the total contextual experience of their audience. For instance, makers of the Web site Prayer Buddy (www.prayerbuddy.org) are aware of this. Instead of attempting to create a discrete online community, the site facilitates connections between users in local areas, and provides resources for adopting spiritual practices in users' own offline settings.

These examples represent a challenge to rethink how we understand how religious identity and community are lived out online, and to pay attention to the offline contexts in which they may be formed. They point to a recognition that in order to understand religious practice online we must acknowledge that religious rituals are not developed in isolation online, but that there is a flow between contexts of inter-action with others, both online and offline. Scholars of religion and the Internet have placed significant emphasis on this recently, calling for more work that looks at how offline religion imprints online behaviors and how innovations in religion online may transform religious culture in the larger sense (Campbell and Lövheim 2011).

Future encounters with religion in a Web 3.0 world

Ongoing research on Internet usage is making apparent how the following rheto-rics—related to identity, community, networks, authority, and the blurring of the online–offline—have shaped our thinking about the impact new media technology is making on religion and culture. The Internet has become an important place where people are able to reflect on and reshape not only their identities, but also the ways in which they interact with each other. The connections users make with one another via these media become sources of belonging and support, from which meaningful relationships may be born and fostered. While patterns of authority emerge as communities and groups form online, these patterns are potentially in response to dissatisfactions with patterns of authority in other settings (like religious institutions). Furthermore, these connections to people and information serve to complement rather than replace other resources found offline.

Emerging forms of technology and digital culture also require further inquiry into the potential influence and challenges they pose to religious communities. In parti-cular, they challenge us to consider the connections that users have available to them at any point in space and time, particularly with respect to their participation in offline religious activities. For example, Web 2.0 calls us to consider how people interact with others in a church setting while having access to Facebook friends and information on Wikipedia through their smartphones. In this example, Internet access provides less of a "virtual reality" distinct from the real world than an "aug-mented reality" where our senses receive information not just from the world around us, but at the same time from our devices. More work is needed to explore the motivations and adaptation of visual digital media within religion online, especially in relation to how this may impact new expressions of multimedia worship. This is seen in the work done on Japanese new religious movements' use of video sharing sites and interactive Web sites and how they are being used to communicate with followers and create new digitally enhanced religious movements (Baffelli *et al.* 2011). With the rise of mobile media, work needs to be done into the impact of mobile technologies and related applications that may alter personal religious spirituality. This is seen in Wagner's research as she explores the use of smartphone mobile apps and how they can provide a means of engaging with religious ritual whenever the user wishes (2012). The rise of cloud and ubiquitous computing leads to new developments in Web design and the increase of participatory cultures, and this also calls for increased investigation into the potential social consequence of new media as personal privacy becomes a rare commodity and the rise in surveillance of specific groups creates cultural and institutional concerns about the sanctity of community boundaries and security in global society. These arising issues of inquiry, as well as the rhetorics discussed in this chapter, illustrate that new media technology is a double-edged sword, offering both promises and perils for religious individuals and institutions. Continued exploration of the impact of new media culture on religious groups and practices will be necessary to address these complexities of contemporary networked society.

Works cited

Armfield, G.G. and R.L. Holbert (2003) "The relationship between religiosity and internet use," *Journal of Media and Religion* 2, 3: 129–44.

Babin, P. and A.A. Zukowski (2002) *The Gospel in Cyberspace: Nurturing Faith in the Internet Age*, Chicago, IL: Loyola Press.

Baffelli, E., I. Reader, and B. Staemmler (eds) (2011) *Japanese Religions on the Internet: Innovation, Representation, and Authority*, London: Routledge.

Brasher, B.E. (2001) *Give Me That Online Religion*, San Francisco, CA: Jossey-Bass.

Bunt, G. (2000) *Virtually Islamic: Computer-Mediated Communication and Cyber Islamic Environments*, Lampeter, Wales: University of Wales Press.

Burn, A. and D. Parker (2003) *Analyzing Media Texts*, London: Continuum.

Campbell, H. (2005a) *Exploring Religious Community Online: We Are One in the Network*, New York: Peter Lang Publishing.

——(2005b) "Spiritualising the internet: uncovering discourses and narrative of religious internet usage," *Online: Heidelberg Journal of Religion on the Internet* 1, 1. Online. Available: http://archiv.ub.uni-heidelberg.de/volltextserver/frontdoor.php?source_opus=5824&la=de (accessed 7 September 2012).

——(2010) *When Religion Meets New Media*, London: Routledge.

——(2012) "Understanding the relationship between religious practice online and offline in a networked society," *Journal of the American Academy of Religion* 80, 1 (March): 64–93.

Campbell, H. and O. Golan (2011) "Creating digital enclaves: negotiation of the internet among bounded religious communities," *Media, Culture & Society* 33, 5 (July): 709–24.

Campbell, H. and M. Lövheim (2011) "Rethinking the online–offline connection in religion online," *Information, Communication & Society* 18, 4: 1083–96.

Castells, M. (2001) *The Internet Galaxy: Reflections on the Internet, Business, and Society*, New York: Oxford University Press.

Cheong, P. (2012) "Authority," in H. Campbell (ed.), *Digital Religion: Understanding Religious Practice in New Media Worlds*, London: Routledge, 72–87.

Ciolek, M.T. (2004) "Online religion: the internet and religion," in H. Bidgoli (ed.), *The Internet Encyclopedia*, Hoboken, NJ: John Wiley & Sons, ii: 798–811.

Cobb, J.J. (1998) *Cybergrace: The Search for God in the Digital World*, New York: Crown Publishers.

Connelly, L. (2012) "Virtual Buddhism: Buddhist ritual in Second Life," in H. Campbell (ed.), *Digital Religion: Understanding Religious Practice in New Media Worlds*, London: Routledge, 127–35.

Davis, E. (1998) *TechGnosis: Myth, Magic, and Mysticism in the Age of Information*, New York, NY: Random House.

Dawson, L.L. (2005) "The mediation of religious experience in cyberspace," in M. Hojsgaard and M. Warburg (eds), *Religion and Cyberspace*, London: Routledge, 15–37.

Emerson Teusner, P. (2011) "Networked individualism, discursive constructions of community and religious identity: the case of Australian Christian bloggers," in F. Comunello (ed.), *Networked Sociability and Individualism: Technology for Personal and Professional Relationships*, Hershey, PA: IGI Global, 265–89.

——(2012) "Formation of a religious technorati: negotiations of authority among Australian emerging church blogs," in H. Campbell (ed.), *Digital Religion: Understanding Religious Practice in New Media Worlds*, London: Routledge, 182–89.

Enzensberger, H.M. (2000) "Constituents of a theory of media," in J.T. Caldwell (ed.), *Electronic Media and Technoculture*, New Brunswick, NJ: Rutgers University Press, 51–76.

Friesen, D.J. (2009) *Thy Kingdom Connected: What the Church Can Learn from Facebook, the Internet, and Other Networks*, Grand Rapids, MI: Baker Books.

Helland, C. (2000) "Online-religion/religion-online and virtual communitas," in J.K. Hadden and D.E. Cowan (eds), *Religion on the Internet: Research Prospects and Promises*, New York: JAI Press, 205–33.

Hennerby, J. and L.L. Dawson (1999) "New religions and the internet: recruiting in a new public sphere," *Journal of Contemporary Religions* 14, 1: 17–39.

Hoover, S. and J.K. Park (2004) "Religious meaning in the digital age: field research on internet/Web religion," in P. Horsfield, M.E. Hess, and A.M. Medrano (eds), *Belief in Media: Cultural Perspectives on Media and Christianity*, Aldershot, UK: Ashgate, 126–36.

Hoover, S., L.S. Clark, and L. Rainie (2004) *Faith Online*, Washington, DC: Pew Internet and American Life Project.

Houston, G. (1998) *Virtual Morality: Christian Ethics in the Computer Age*, Leicester: Apollos.

Howard, R.G. (2000) "Online ethnography of dispensationalist discourse: revealed verses negotiated truth," in J.K. Hadden and D.E. Cowan (eds), *Religion on the Internet: Research Prospects and Promises*, New York: JAI Press, 225–46.

Hutchings, T. (2011) "Contemporary religious community and the online church," *Information, Communication and Society* 14, 8: 1118–35.

Johns, M.D. (2008) "Waving a 'hi': religion among Facebook users," unpublished paper, Association of Internet Researchers 9.0, Copenhagen.

Laney, M. (2005) "Christian Web sites: usage and desires," in M. Hojsgaard and M. Warburg (eds), *Religion and Cyberspace*, London: Routledge, 166–79.

Larsen, E. (2000) *Wired Churches, Wired Temples: Taking Congregations and Missions into Cyberspace*, Washington, DC: Pew Internet and American Life Project.

——(2001) *CyberFaith: How Americans Pursue Religion Online*, Washington, DC: Pew Internet and American Life Project.

Larsson, G. (2005) "The death of a virtual Muslim discussion group: issues and methods in analysing religion on the Net," *Online: Heidelberg Journal of Religions on the Internet* 1, 1, Online. Available: http://archiv.ub.uni-heidelberg.de/volltextserver/frontdoor.php?source_opus=5825&la=de (accessed 7 September 2012).

Lochhead, D. (1997) *Shifting Realities: Information Technology and the Church*, Geneva: WCC Publications.

Lövheim, M. (2005) "Young people and the use of the internet as transitional space," *Online: Heidelberg Journal of Religions on the Internet* 1, 1. Online. Available: http://archiv.ub.uni-heidelberg.de/volltextserver/frontdoor.php?source_opus=5826&la=de (accessed 7 September 2012).

——(2012) "Identity," in H. Campbell (ed.), *Digital Religion: Understanding Religious Practice in New Media Worlds*, London: Routledge, 41–56.

MacWilliams, M. (2002) "Introduction to the symposium," *Religion* 32, 4: 277–78.

NightMare, M.M. (2001) *Witchcraft and the Web: Weaving Pagan Traditions Online*, Toronto, ONT: ECW Press.

O'Leary, S.D. (1996) "Cyberspace as sacred space: communicating religion on computer networks," *Journal of the American Academy of Religion* 64, 4 (Winter): 781–808.

O'Leary, S.D. and B.E. Brasher (1996) "The unknown God of the internet," in C. Ess (ed.), *Philosophical Perspectives on Computer-Mediated Communication*, Albany, NY: State University of New York Press, 233–70.

Pontifical Council for Social Communications (2002) "Ethics in internet" (February 22). Online. Available: www.vatican.va/roman_curia/pontifical_councils/pccs/documents/rc_pccs_doc_20020228_ethics-internet_en.html (accessed 12 September 2011).

Prebish, C.S. (2004) "The cybersangha: Buddhism on the internet," in L.L. Dawson and D.E. Cowan (eds), *Religion Online: Finding Faith on the Internet*, New York: Routledge, 135–47.

Rheingold, H. (1993) *The Virtual Community: Homesteading on the Electronic Frontier*, New York: Harper Perennial.

Schroeder, R., N. Heather, and R.M. Lee (1998) "The sacred and the virtual: religion in multi-user virtual reality," *Journal of Computer Mediated Communication* 4, 2 (December). Online. Available: http://jcmc.indiana.edu/vol4/issue2/schroeder.html (accessed 6 September 2011).

Thomas, S. (2006) "The end of cyberspace and other surprises," *Convergence: The International Journal of Research into New Media Technologies* 12, 4: 383–91.

Turkle, S. (1996) *Life on the Screen: Identity in the Age of the Internet*, London: Weidenfeld & Nicholson.

Wagner, R. (2012) "You are what you install: religious authenticity and identity in mobile apps," in H. Campbell (ed.), *Digital Religion: Understanding Religious Practice in New Media Worlds*, London: Routledge, 199–206.

Wellman, B. and Leighton, B. (1979) "Networks, neighborhoods, and communities: approaches to the study of the community question," *Urban Affairs Review* 14, 3: 363–90.

Zaleski, J. (1997) *The Soul of Cyberspace: How Technology Is Changing Our Spiritual Lives*, San Francisco: Harper San Francisco.

10
ADVERTISING

Tricia Sheffield

Introduction: the sacramental imagination as a means of "grace"

"We're not that smart." So said my friend who works in the advertising industry after he surveyed my bookshelves full of advertising theory. He went on, "All we really want is to land the contract, keep the client happy, and sell the product so we can make some money. There's no grand cultural scheme behind it." I replied that, as true as that may be, what was interesting for me, and obviously all the authors on my bookshelves, was how advertising functioned in our culture of consumer capitalism. How do people consume advertising? What is its role, and what aspects of religion does it use to be culturally relevant in today's world of high-speed, noisy clutter? How does advertising function in American culture? I told him that there may be no grand scheme today for advertisers, but that was not always the case. In the early twentieth century, advertisers were Protestant ministers or the sons of Protestant ministers. They brought to their craft a type of Christianity that is present in modern advertising, a survival, if you will, of their understanding of what Christianity and capitalism were for the newly industrialized United States.[1] As President (and Congregationalist) Calvin Coolidge (1926) assured advertisers at the American Association of Advertising Agencies, "Advertising ministers to the spiritual side of trade. It is a great power that has been entrusted to your keeping which charges you with the high responsibility of inspiring and ennobling the commercial world. It is all part of the greater work of the regeneration and redemption of mankind."[2] Indeed, humanity thought itself redeemed with the purchase of ever more enticing products, as the United States found its foothold as an industrialized nation. It is this sense of redemption that is most compelling today in American advertising, for, as much as Americans love to hate advertising, and hate that they love it, American culture is still very much an object driven society, beholden to things that tell a story about ourselves, who we desire to be, with whom we are affiliated, and perhaps, more importantly who we don't wish to be.[3] As theologian Vincent Miller (2003: 189) states, "We expect the things we consume not only to meet the various needs of daily life in our affluent world but also to help us establish our personal identities and to signify and support our social standing."

In some ways, though, my friend was correct. There is no real insidious plan behind the advertising industry, and to be sure, enough has been said about advertising in cultural and religious theory that would assure us, in the words of the writer of Ecclesiastes, that there is nothing new under the sun. Advertising, despite the recession/depression of 2008, and the popular and hope-inspired Occupy Movement (created by Kalle Lasn, founder of *Adbusters* magazine), seems to be here to stay. But, this pesky dominance of advertising doesn't mean that one can't critically consume advertising or resist its branding of identities. If one knows what some of these cultural and religious survivals inherent in advertising are, perhaps one can resist the bombardment of 3,000 ads per day, not value another person based on what he or she owns, and work toward a future in which all will have enough food, clean water, shelter, clothing, and health care. In other words, to use the discourse of theology, one can enact a resistance against the commodification of persons as vessels of sacralized objects that then sacralize and mark the person as holy, and leave unmarked, or not holy, others who may lack said objects. To be sure, for advertising, the most holy of marked bodies are those that function to subtend the normative notions of gender, race, class, and sexual identity; in other words, the male, white, upper middle class, and heterosexual body. In our current times, these still are the bodies that advertising marks as most sacralized (see Sheffield 2006: 133–52).

This chapter is not accusing advertising of having a dastardly scheme to rule the world, nor is it another jeremiad against the evils of consumerism, but rather, it will offer a view as to how advertising functions for consumers as a cultural system that acts as the conduit, or mediator, between production and consumption, and fills an object with meaning that is then imparted to the person who consumes and displays the object. This meaning is not just product information, but is more akin to a created image of wealth and luxury, and can be thought of as a religious sacralizing process, not unlike the sacrament of the Lord's Supper wherein the Holy Spirit imparts a means of grace to the one who partakes of the sacrament. The spirit in the sacralizing moment of advertising may not be holy, but, as will be shown later, it is indeed viewed as sacred. Even though the following understanding of sacrament will resemble the Christian Reformed point of view, the sacramental survival in advertising could predate Christianity, as the sacramental often speaks to humanity's need to belong to a community and to be valued within that community.[4] In other words, the sacramental speaks to humanity's desire for grace. It is this great need for belonging, marketed now as desire for objects, that is interwoven into the fabric of American advertising and the culture of consumer capitalism and makes it recognizable, deeply felt, and intimately experienced by all those who purchase objects for conspicuous consumption.

Sacramental thought: means and methods

Sacramental thought, or the "sacramental imagination," is key to understanding how advertising functions in the culture of consumer capitalism. Some scholars, such as Sut Jhally (1989), have named such charming of objects as Karl Marx's fetishism of commodities, and I have argued in *The Religious Dimensions of Advertising* (2006: 33–51) that such objects may function in a Durkheimian totemic manner by uniting a person with a consumption clan. All of these elements may be present when a person purchases an object; all of these aspects of mediation may function in advertising. But, as Miller argues, sacramental thought has paved the way for a certain understanding of advertising and its relationship to objects and consumers. Miller (2003: 189) states, "A religious culture accustomed to seeing material things as over-determined bearers of meaning sets the stage for its members to enter the imaginative world of consumer capitalism." So, it is first necessary to understand what one means by a sacrament, especially in relation to the Lord's Supper, before making the claim of sacramental thought for the function of advertising, so as to understand the spirit being invoked not only on the object, but on the person who consumes the object.

The Spirit who guides

The *epiclesis*, or the calling down from on high of the Holy Spirit, is one of the most holy moments during the sacrament of the Lord's Supper. As holy as this particular invocation is, it also serves to remind Christians that the presence of God through the power of the Holy Spirit is always present; the Spirit does not just "pop in for a visit" when Christians partake of the Lord's Supper, but as promised to the Jewish covenant community in Exodus 33:12–17, God will never take God's Spirit from God's people. God's covenantal grace is always available for all of God's children.

From a Christian point of view, God's faithfulness is shown in the Old Testament through the various covenants that God makes with Israel—Noah, Abraham (nation and circumcision), Moses (the law), David (messianic)—and finally a new covenant given through Jesus the Christ. As stated in *The Church Speaks: The Papers of the Commission on Theology in the Reformed Church in America*, "God established a covenant with Abraham, the father of all believers, and this covenant is the background against which the drama of Israel, the ministry of Christ, and the rise of the Christian church must be seen" (Cook 1985: 60). In this covenant, we see God's *hesed* (steadfastness, faithfulness), traceable from the beginning of creation with the Divine words, "Let there be," through the history of Israel, and ending in the promise given to the people of God as foretold in Jeremiah 31:31–34 and claimed through the Great Commissioning (Matthew 28:18–20).[5] Jesus's promise, "I am with you always, to the end of the age" is God's promise, is the Holy Spirit's promise. All are one as affirmed in the Nicean Creed that the Holy Spirit proceeds from the Father and from the Son (*filioque*).[6] So, the Jesus who promises the Spirit as the advocate and comforter and who says "I am" is the same God of the covenantal community of the Old Testament; indeed, Jesus as a Jewish man is of the covenantal community.

In its enactment of the sacraments of baptism and the Lord's Supper, the Christian church is bonded to the covenant community of the Old Testament through Jewish rites, namely circumcision and Passover. Sacraments are an outward means by which God's love and grace are given to humanity.[7] They are visible signs and seals, perhaps even a modern-day type of brand, of the covenant of God as given to the church by Jesus the Christ through the power of the Holy Spirit. Sacraments express outwardly what is true spiritually (see Ursinus and Olevianus 1877 [1563]: 41, question #66; see also Calvin, IV.14.1, 1277, in McNeill 1960).

One of the sacraments in the Reformed tradition is the Lord's Supper. On the night that Jesus was betrayed, he gathered his disciples for what many believe to be a Passover supper. But what seems to have happened was more of an instructional time for the disciples. Jesus, knowing that the time when the authorities would capture him was near, left his disciples a gift of a feast, and in some ways reconfigured the Passover supper as one of bread and wine as symbols of his imminent sacrifice.

The church universal has understood the Lord's Supper in three different ways. The first is the medieval doctrine of transubstantiation whereby the substance of the bread and wine are thought to physically change into the whole substance of the body and blood of Jesus. Only the accidents of the bread and wine remain. By reciting the liturgy over the host, the priest enables the conversion of the elements through the Holy Spirit. The second theory is "real presence," constructed in opposition to the doctrine of transubstantiation. In "real presence," the substances of the body and blood of Christ along with the bread and wine "co-exist in union with each other." So, the substance of the elements does not change but is considered a shared presence with Jesus's body and blood. The third understanding of the doctrine of the Lord's Supper is that of memorial presence. That is, there is no aspect of change whatsoever, or even a shared presence, but the Supper is a liturgical action that is used to commemorate Jesus's salvific actions of death and resurrection. The bread and the wine are merely symbols for enacting the rite as a remembrance of the Last Supper.

Calvin took a different route and proclaimed that the presence of Christ was a real presence given by the power of the Holy Spirit.[8] The Lord's Supper is a sign and a seal of God's covenant with humanity. The new covenant spoken of in Jeremiah 31:31–34 is fulfilled in Christ's death and resurrection, and enacted in the Lord's Supper. Calvin states:

> For as in baptism, God, regenerating us, engrafts us into the society of his church and makes us his own by adoption, so we have said, that he discharges the function of a provident householder in continually supplying to us the food to sustain and preserve us in that life into which he has begotten us by his word.
>
> (Calvin IV.17.1, 1360, in McNeill 1960)

If the real presence of Christ

> truly represents the participation in his body through the breaking of bread, there ought not to be the least doubt that he truly presents and shows his body. And the godly ought by all means to keep this rule: whenever they see symbols appointed by the Lord, to think and be persuaded that the truth of the thing signified is surely presented there.
>
> (Calvin IV.17.10, 1371, in McNeill 1960)

The Lord's Supper is also nourishment for one's soul. One is called to live in spiritual community, as stated in Genesis 2:18. Humanity is not called to be alone, but to live in the covenantal community of God. One does not live for one's self, but must be "fed, nourished, given new life over and over again" (Guthrie 1968: 360).[9] And through the Lord's Supper, one is nourished, not just as an individual, but as the people of God who proclaim and rehearse the reign of God until it comes. In this sense, the Lord's Supper has eschatological dimensions as it is a rehearsal of the feast of God, when crying will be no more, and there will be no need of a sun, for God's glory will be the light (Revelation 21:4, 22:5). It is a joyful and justice-filled feast, available for all who come to the table.

At the table of advertising

This decidedly Reformed view of the Lord's Supper is meant to help explain where and how advertising intersects with religious discourse, picks up on the chatter of Christianity, delves into using the symbols of faith, so that advertising can make meaning of an object and be meaningful in the life of a consumer. This meaning-making of advertising and its use of religion isn't anything new. As the United States shifted rapidly from an agrarian to an industrial society, advertisers knew that consumers would need something to reference as their world of goods became confusing, with more and more choices of soap, butter, socks, cars, and furniture. Advertisers took what was familiar—traditional family values steeped in Americana and religion—and marketed objects using a tableau that would resonate with a person's deepest longing for family and belonging. Symbols in religion, specifically Protestant Christianity, such as halos, otherworldly light, radiant beams, and cups and vessels of the Lord's Supper, became established images for advertising (see Marchand 1985). Such symbols were mediators of the divine, and so, through advertising, the image was connected with the object, thus making the object and also its owner sacralized.

The Lord's Supper, as outlined in the theological discourse above, then becomes ripe fodder for advertising's own sacramental imagination, or process of image-creation. Assuredly, this analysis of sacrament is not meant to be a one-to-one correlation between advertising and the Lord's Supper; rather, my functional analysis is meant to point to certain religious dimensions that advertising uses in order to make it culturally viable for the consumer. That is to say, people "encounter religion in a commodified form, where doctrines, values, and practices are torn from their traditional, communal contexts" (Miller 2003: 6). For advertising, the process of image-making begins with an object, produced by a generally anonymous someone in a nondescript location of the world. The object has no real meaning yet, but is just a thing with a use-value. In the process of production, this use-value must be "exchanged" for something else, a deeper meaning, for although people do purchase some products just for their use, such as cleaning products, they purchase other products for their symbolic meaning. For these more symbolic purchases, "[A]dvertising encourages us to choose and to purchase but not to keep and to use" (ibid.: 142). The product is infused with an exchange value that is beyond its use-value, or even veils its use-value. The meaning that advertising gives is often vacuous and shallow, but it is still powerful. Actually, what advertising gives to the product is an image, or to use the language of sacrament, advertising imbues the product with the "real presence" of the culture of consumer capitalism. The object's "substance" isn't changed through the image-production of advertising while the accidents remain;[10] no, there is something about the presence, or the truth of the symbol that is infused into the object by advertising that is greater than a "bait and switch" tactic, or sleight of hand. There is a "truth in the thing signified," to use Calvin's terms: The "real presence" is a valuing of a person by the ability to which he or she has the sign and seal of the sacred commodities of our American society. So, the sacred is brought into the world of the profane, thus muddling the categories of sacred and profane, or perhaps even re-defining the categories altogether. As Colleen McDannell states:

> By looking at material Christianity, we will see little evidence that American Christians experience a radical separation of the sacred from the profane. If we look at what Christians *do* rather than what they *think*, we cannot help but notice the continual scrambling of the sacred and the profane.
>
> (McDannell 1995: 4; emphasis in the original)

One might argue that such a sacralization of the object and person could be considered holy, but the spirit hovering over it is not God but the spirit of consumer capitalism. This is not a spirit necessarily of new life, but of life that is pushed forward by the notion of "never enough" and insatiability (Sheffield 2006: 114).

This spirit of consumerism values a person insofar as he or she can consume/ ingest the sacred objects of consumer culture. All are certainly welcome to the table in advertising's feast of plenty, but not everyone can partake of the goods being offered. For those who can, their ability to consume/display means they have been made sacred, for they have been blessed with the "real presence" of the spirit of consumerism by their ability to own objects that have first been blessed by advertising's image-making discourse. Here is where advertising is most powerful and persuasive, and even insidious. One cannot simply partake of the communion of consumerism as an individual. Like the celebration of the Lord's Supper in a church, one's sacralization process in advertising only works if one openly displays the object that has been blessed by the spirit. For example:

> A woman can barely make her rent, and often has to choose between buying groceries or her much-needed medicine each month. Yet, she bought an iPad last week, and also has a computer at home.
>
> A man is negative in his bank account, but continues to go out to dinner twice a week in order to impress his new boyfriend.
>
> A woman overdraws her bank account, borrowing against her rent payment, so she can buy new clothes for her upcoming vacation and not look "shabby."
>
> A man who has less than $500 per month income manages to buy the latest version of the iPhone, using borrowed money.

All of these examples point to one of the main driving forces of advertising: if one does not participate in the culture of consumerism, one then does not belong in community, and this lack of participation often brings feelings of shame, or what has been called in recent years, the shame of chronic poverty. It is in the public nature of consumption that advertising is seductive and creates dependency. As the Eucharist must be celebrated in community and during worship, the consumer goes forward into the cathedrals of consumption, not only to purchase publicly the sacralized object, but then to display such an object, marking that person as part of what I have called in *Religious Dimensions*, a consumption clan. And over and over, this communion of consumerism must be celebrated; it is not enough to buy sparingly, but one should partake as often as one can of the object selected by advertising (and consumers) as worthy of being ingested. For in so doing, people are given relevance and meaning; in fact, again to use Calvin's language, people carry the sign and seal of the sacralized object. The object functions then as a means of grace, or an outward sign of an inner consumerist reality. And in the world of advertising, grace is given when the consumer reflects—shimmers and glimmers—with the sacralized image of the product. Grace is the ability to move with authority and honor in a culture that values the objects one chooses to display on one's self. Grace, in the culture of consumer capitalism, affords freedom and belonging. Grace, as bestowed by advertising's image production, dispels the shame of not belonging and therefore being considered "profane" in our culture.

Another dimension in which advertising draws from the sacramental imagination of the Lord's Supper is in the notion of rehearsal and nourishment. Christians come together to enact a collective ritual whereby they remember their baptism, that ingrafting into the covenant community, and look forward to a time of justice. It is a heightened time of faith and grace in the community, a ritual that reminds them of who they are and who they belong to. Emile Durkheim, the father of sociology, called such rituals a time of collective effervescence, a frenetic time of heightened emotion, in between the normal times of economic activity, whereby a person feels a stimulation of energies. People seek each other out, and "live differently and more intensely than in normal times" (Durkheim 1995 [1912]: 213). Advertising also has these moments of collective ritual and effervescence in the culture of consumer capitalism. We see advertising's influence in sporting events, such as the Super Bowl, in minor and major holidays, such as Valentine's Day, Mother's Day, and of course, Black Friday, the most sacred time of consumerism in the year (see Sheffield 2006: 91). These events, which have really become shopping rituals, remind individuals of their role in society; individuals are not necessarily producers anymore, as in the agrarian past, but are now consumers. Inasmuch as people can reflect their "true" nature as consumers, they are considered more relevant in the covenant community of consumerism. There is indeed a pecking order, and a person is ever more "nourished" in consumerism as they are able to be high on the hierarchical order of those who have. As individuals consume the sacralized objects of advertising, they are "fed, nourished, and given new life over and over again." But this nourishment is not sustainable; there is a planned obsolescence in advertising, so that the objects consumed must ever up the ante from the object before. Insatiability is coded into obsolescence; there is a fear lurking in the passé, and an anxiety about the not-yet of future times (see Sheffield 2006: 72–73, 109–10, 118–19). For example, even though the NYC subway requires poker faces of its riders, there is an intense scrutiny happening on the trains. People especially notice what latest technology a person is plugged into on his or her morning commute. One notes the difference between an iPhone or a Metro PCS phone. The former costs about $200 where the latter is $50 per month with no contract or credit check. The iPhone signals a type of leisure status where the PCS phone codes its owner as not having adequate financial status or credit. And if such a display is not enough, there are advertisements for Metro PCS right above the heads of the commuters to remind everyone of such a status.

Anticipation, and satisfaction guaranteed ... for a time

Advertising's produced anxiety about status and the future means that the doctrine of eschatology is implied in its use of sacramental thought. In contradistinction to advertising's use of such theological talk, the Christian community understands that whenever it gathers together around the table, it proclaims the Lord's death until God comes. Such a proclamation in the ritual of the Lord's Supper is linked to a doctrine of hope, of rehearsing the reign of God, of living between the now and not yet, and looking to a future filled with the promise of God's steadfast love and justice through the power of the Holy Spirit.

The reign, or kingdom of God, is often figured in the Old Testament as present and future, or the now and not yet. God is the ruler of the nation of Israel; indeed, ruler of all nations of the earth. God's lordship had a very real, day-to-day practicality for the covenant community, for they looked to God as their judge, ruler, and king (McKim 2001: 168). But some writers of the Old Testament, especially the apocalyptic texts such as Daniel, understood God's kingship to be a time when God would rule over all the earth through a descendant of King David, and peace would be in the land. This descendant was described as son of man, or the messiah, and the time would be a time of peace and justice for all (Micah 4:1–4; see McKim 2001: 168). McKim notes, "God will be the ultimate ruler whose presence will be the delight of the people who share in the great feast ... " (ibid.).

This soon coming reign of God was the lens through which the New Testament writers understood Jesus's ministry, death, and resurrection. To be sure, in the synoptic gospels, Jesus seems to have understood his own ministry through the lens of God's kingdom: "The time is fulfilled, and the kingdom of God has come near; repent, and believe in the good news" (Mark 1:15; Matthew 4:17, 23; Luke 9:11). Jesus's ministerial vision of the kingdom of God was one of *mispat* (justice), love, and a preferential option for the poor and oppressed of society. Jesus enacted the fast that God requires (Isaiah 58) when he healed the sick and the lame, fed the hungry, affiliated with the "lowly" of society—the tax collectors, prostitutes, and lepers. God's fast became, through Jesus's ministry, God's feast of love. The now of God's kingdom was at hand, but there was still a not yet to be fulfilled, as evidenced by the prayer that Jesus taught his disciples—"your kingdom come, your will be done, on earth as it is in heaven."[11] Through Jesus's resurrection, the not yet broke through the now, to give a foretaste of the glory that is to come in the final reign of God.[12] McKim assures us:

> Yet while the evil of the present age continues, so does the 'mystery' of the kingdom that has been disclosed to human beings in the ministry of Jesus.

The future, glorious reign of God is now at work in the world in advance of its open manifestation.

(McKim 2001: 170)

However, Jesus's imminent return and the glorious reign of God, as promised to his disciples, stretched from a few anticipated days, to months, and then to millennia. The early Christian community had to make sense of the delay of the *Parousia*, and over time, one sees the church channel its resources into other areas, such as mission, creeds, and doctrine, and move from what Rudolf Bultmann calls an eschatological phenomenon to a historical phenomenon.[13] Eschatological thinking, then, is a movement forward and a looking back; a place where the people of God and covenant live between the now and not yet. The life of the church, the invitation to the table, is a life of grace, of looking to the time when "many will come from east and west and will eat with Abraham and Isaac and Jacob in the kingdom of heaven" (Matthew 8:11).

The reign of God is about God's hope and grace for all, but within this hope is also one of judgment. The murky world of eschatology is just that—murky—and the early church up through the present day has wrestled with scriptural passages that allude to some kind of end of the world scenario. Luke 21:25–28, the apostle Paul's description of a resurrected body in 1 Corinthians 15, and the Book of Revelation (specifically 20:1–10) have provided doomsday adherents and theologians alike with plenty of material from which to make end times predictions and speculations. Most don't question if the eschaton will happen, but they do strain hard at weaving a story as to how it will happen. One of the theological responses to the last days is millennialism, or the 1,000-year reign of Christ described in Revelation.[14] Here, Jesus is thought to return to earth before the 1,000-year reign, and will rule over all the nations. Before his return, the current age will end and there will be a time of tribulation. When Jesus does return, the antichrist figure (described in 1 and 2 John) will be "judged" and the elect will be resurrected. At Jesus's second coming, Satan will be freed for a while in order to enact rebellion against the Christ, but will be finally defeated. Then, there will be a mass resurrection, where the righteous and the unrighteous are judged, and their eternal destiny of heaven or hell will be assigned.

Such millennial predictions of judgment have dominated popular culture and church life since the late nineteenth century (McKim 2001: 170).[15] Such fantastical notions can be frightening, coercive, and debilitating, for such millennial views have often been based on the fear of Christ's coming and reign, and not one of joyful anticipation and hope. But Calvin reminds us "because Christ was once for all offered for sins, 'he shall appear a second time, apart from sin … unto salvation.' Whatever hardships distress us, let this 'redemption' sustain us until its completion" (Calvin, III.25.2, 989, in McNeill 1960). Calvin's statement assures us that one of the best ways to speak about last things is to look at what God has already done so that we may see what God will do. Shirley Guthrie states,

The most certain clue to what will happen to us in the *future* is what God has been doing with us and for us all along in the past … . [W]hat we look forward to is not the destruction but the *fulfillment* of the created world and our creaturely lives in it.

(Guthrie 1968: 387, 388)

Indeed, advertising uses eschatological discourse and our need for fulfillment as it is linked to the sacramental imagination. The promise of the table in Christianity is one of bounty and plenty in the present, which points toward a future time when all will have enough. In advertising, this eschatological desire for enough is over-coupled with the desire for more and also with the notion of judgment and the shame of chronic poverty. As mentioned above, there is a shame involved in owning the Metro PCS phone as opposed to being able to afford the iPhone. The desires of hope and justice in the future reign of God are co-opted by advertising's meaning-making system, where the reign of consumer capitalism is the now. In this now, to practice deferred gratification would be anathema for advertising. M. Douglas Meeks (1989: 161) adds, "Any sense of salvation connected with repression and thus with economics has to be eliminated as irrational. Need satisfaction becomes simply a dimension of rational economic behavior." To practice deferred gratification in a Christian sense of the Lord's Supper almost queers the culture of consumer capitalism (see Sullivan 2003: 37–56).[16] Or, is this culture, by encouraging people to live in the now and practicing insatiability, queering Christianity?

As in sacramental thought, advertising uses religious symbols and dimensions from Christian eschatology that help to make it meaningful in the lives of consumers. As Miller asserts:

> Consumer desire reorients eschatological desire for justice from the outside. Imminent expectation is transformed into the endlessly deferred search for fulfillment; anguish with the injustices of the present is assimilated to the ubiquitous consumer experience of lack; the suffering of others becomes a source of intense experience; and our desire to respond is shunted into symbolic consumption.

(Miller 2003: 137)

In other words, in Christian eschatological thought, there will be a future of justice when everyone will have enough, but in advertising, the now is all there is. No one will ever have enough, and advertising functions in such a way as to conflate enough with the desire for more. For example, advertising codes needs with desire and portrays humans as naturally insatiable. Usually, needs are thought to wane as they are satisfied. In economic theory, though, needs such as thirst or hunger got coded into consumerism, and so the need for things became a part of the culture of consumer capitalism; in other words, the ownership and display of sacralized objects are part of the "natural order" of advertising.

Advertising plays into the delay of the *Parousia* by concentrating on the now, for the future not yet seems as if it will never arrive. In Christianity, the "not yet" is a time of peace and justice, but in a consumer world, "seduction … is constituted against a horizon of possibility. It is always looking beyond the present for more fulfilling alternatives. Expectation is endlessly aroused" (Miller 2003: 132). The goal of advertising's eschatological discourse is for consumers never to have enough; to be satisfied is to be unfulfilled, for "joy is sought in desire itself" (ibid.).

Memo to advertising: we're smarter than you think

> The shape and texture of consumer desire is not what it is commonly assumed to be: a shallow attachment to things. It is much more complex. It is constituted in the never-filled promise [that delayed *Parousia*] of consumption. ... It resembles more profound longings for transcendence, justice, and self-transformation enough to be able to absorb the concepts, values, and practices of religious traditions into its own forms without apparent conflict. The subversions of the mystical quest, apocalyptic longing for justice, and the radical transformation of the self live on in sedate domestication in everyday life.
>
> (Miller 2003: 144)

The long passage above may sound pessimistic, as Miller admits, but it also demonstrates that the images used in advertising draw from a deep religious well, a well of the sacramental imagination, and thus function to link individuals with some of our deepest feelings of desire, shame, belonging, and ritual. Advertising reflects the collective ritual of the Lord's Supper by infusing objects with the "real presence" of the spirit of consumerism, thus imparting to people a sense of grace with the sign and seal of the covenant of consumerism. Being sacralized by such objects is an outward sign of an inner consumerist reality.

But, I want to insist that people can resist the label of consumer given by advertising, and can enact strategies of resistance that define them once again as producers. We have seen this most recently in the Occupy Movement, a grass-roots counter-narrative to consumerism that embraced the sacramental imagination of a feast of plenty for all who come to the table, and imagined a time where all will have enough in a future of peace and justice. The lack of hope and exasperation with a culture that valued people only by what they owned was palpable down in Zuccotti Park/Liberty Square. As one moved through the park and talked with folk, over and over again, there was a discourse of resistance to the way advertising functions in the culture of consumer capitalism. One couldn't help but wonder if this was the "revolution" many had been waiting for. It seemed that as clever as advertising can be, their target market was smarter and perhaps not as gullible as previously thought. When it comes to the sacramental imagination of the people, it seems that advertising may have to realize that grace isn't cheap anymore.

Notes

1 I base my analysis of advertising on the Reformed tradition for two reasons: 1) I'm a Reformed minister, and this is the perspective from which I do theology and religious cultural analysis, and 2) when many scholars and cultural theorists write on advertising and religion, they are often employing a monolithic form of Christianity. The Christianity to which they refer tends to be generalized, obscure, or even hybridized, so that no one tradition is recognizable in the analysis. However, the most prestigious advertising agencies in the early 1900s were staffed by men who, according to Jackson Lears (1994: 154), were

college-educated, usually at prestigious Northeastern schools; Protestant, many the sons of Presbyterian or Congregationalist ministers ... [who] had a faith in inevitable progress, unfolding as if in accordance with some divine plan. They also had a tendency to cast themselves in a key redemptive role. This was a secular doctrine of postmillennialism—the belief that Christ would return after human beings had created the Kingdom of God on earth.

Thus was early advertising, which set the stage for today's advertising, informed by a very unique brand of Christianity and not a generalized form of the religion. To be sure, Christianity is not monolithic: there are the major traditions—Roman Catholic, Eastern Orthodox, and Protestant—and, within Protestantism, multiple denominations, each with its own polity, government, views of sacrament, and worship.

My essay works to correct the lack of specificity in previous analyses and to return to the ideals of those early Protestant advertisers by comparing advertising's use of the sacramental imagination with the Reformed tradition and its understanding of sacrament, so that we might have a more definitive picture of how advertising functions in American culture.

2 Twitchell (1996) places this quotation in the pages before his book's table of contents.

3 The fact that people have always used objects to convey something about their identity is nothing new. My interest is in the hyper-valuation in advertising of sacralized objects that code their owner as also sacred.

4 To be sure, there are varying points of view of the Lord's Supper. My theological discourse is from a Reformed point of view in the tradition of John Calvin.

5 God's *hesed* is not just traceable through the one covenant, but indeed through all the covenants mentioned above. Each covenant builds upon the last one given.

6 This is the Western churches' understanding of the procession of the Spirit; the Eastern churches do not accept the *filioque* (see Kelly 1978: 310–43).

7 Augustine defines a sacrament as "an outward sign of an inward grace." Reformed tradition subscribes to this definition (see McKim 2001: 135).

8 In contrast to Luther, Calvin's doctrine of real presence is one of spiritual but not physical presence. It unites the believer with Christ in heaven, but does not "drag his body" to earth (see Calvin IV.xvii.31, in McNeill 1960). It confers spiritual power and benefits (see Calvin IV.xvii.5, 11, in McNeill 1960).

9 "[A]s bread nourishes, sustains, and keeps the life of our body, so Christ's body is the only food to invigorate and enliven our soul. When we see wine set forth as a symbol of blood, we must reflect on the benefits which wine imparts to the body, and so realize that the same are spiritually imparted to us by Christ's blood" (Calvin IV.17.3, 1363, in McNeill 1960).

10 In *Religious Dimensions* (2006) I described this sacramentality as more akin to transubstantiation. Now, I view sacramentality more as a "real presence," in that there is grace given to an individual by the power of the spirit of consumerism. The presence is there with the object, and not necessarily a mystery; in fact, the presence of sacralization is very much visible for all.

11 Christopher Morse (1994: 319) asserts:

> To confess that the kingdom or dominion of heaven is "at hand" is to characterize, not the way the sky is, but the way the earth is, within the perspective of the gospel's frame of reference. Earth is not simply what is overarched by the sky; earth is what is overarched by an unimpeded dominion of love and freedom, that is "heaven." Furthermore, earth is confessed to be where this dominion of love and freedom undertakes to come at ground level: "Thy kingdom come, thy will be done on earth as it is in heaven."

12 In Christian thought, the final reign would be a restoration of a fallen world and would bring a new creation. I disagree that our world is completely fallen and instead subscribe to what Virginia Ramey Mollenkott (2001: 86) calls "creation spirituality." That is to say, there is no complete estrangement between God and creation. There is no eternal separation, but God's grace has always hovered and been present in our world.

13 Noted in Bultmann (1957: 37, 38):

> The early Christian community understands itself not as a historical but as an eschatological phenomenon. It is conscious that it belongs no longer to the present world but to the new Aeon which is at the door. The question then is how long this consciousness can remain vivid, how long the expectation of the imminent end of the world can remain unshaken … . The problem of Eschatology grew out of the fact that the expected end of the world failed to arrive, that the "Son of Man" did not appear in the clouds of heaven, that history went on, and that the eschatological community could not fail to recognize that it had become a historical phenomenon.

14 Millennial thought includes pre-millennialism, post-millennialism, and amillennialism.
15 McKim mentions the dispensationalists John Nelson Darby and C.I. Scofield.
16 In these pages, Sullivan explores a sense of the nature of queering without providing one singular definition.

Works cited

Bultmann, R. (1957) *History and Eschatology: The Presence of Eternity*, New York: Harper.

Cook, J.I. (ed.) (1985) *The Church Speaks: Papers of the Commission on Theology, Reformed Church in America, 1959–1984*, Grand Rapids, MI: William B. Eerdmans Publishing.

Coolidge, C. (1926) "Address before the American Association of Advertising Agencies," The American Presidency Project (October 27). Online. Available: www.presidency.ucsb.edu/ws/index.php?pid=412 (accessed 6 February 2013).

Durkheim, E. (1995 [1912]) *The Elementary Forms of Religious Life*, trans. K.E. Fields, New York: The Free Press.

Guthrie, S.C., Jr. (1968) *Christian Doctrine*, Atlanta, GA: John Knox Press.

Jhally, S. (1989) "Advertising as religion: the dialectic of technology and magic," in I. Angus and S. Jhally (eds), *Cultural Politics in Contemporary America*, New York and London: Routledge, 217–29.

Kelly, J.N.D. (1978) *Early Christian Doctrines*, San Francisco, CA: HarperSanFrancisco.

Lears, J. (1994) *Fables of Abundance: A Cultural History of Advertising in America*, New York: BasicBooks.

McDannell, C. (1995) *Material Christianity: Religion and Popular Culture in America*, New Haven CT: Yale University Press.

McKim, D.K. (2001) *Introducing the Reformed Faith: Biblical Revelation, Christian Tradition, and Contemporary Significance*, Louisville, KY: Westminster John Knox Press.

McNeill, J.T. (ed.) (1960) *Calvin: Institutes of the Christian Religion*, 2 vols., trans. F.L. Battles, Philadelphia, PA: Westminster Press.

Marchand, R. (1985) *Advertising the American Dream: Making Way for Modernity, 1920–1940*, Berkeley, CA: University of California Press.

Meeks, M.D. (1989) *God the Economist: The Doctrine of God and Political Economy*, Minneapolis, MN: Fortress Press.

Miller, V.J. (2003) *Consuming Religion: Christian Faith and Practice in a Consumer Culture*, New York and London: Continuum.

Morse, C. (1994) *Not Every Spirit: A Dogmatics of Christian Disbelief*, Harrisburg, PA: Trinity Press International.

Ramey Mollenkott, V. (2001) *Omnigender: A Trans-Religious Approach*, Cleveland, OH: The Pilgrim Press.

Sheffield, T. (2006) *The Religious Dimensions of Advertising*, New York: Palgrave Macmillan.

Sullivan, N. (2003) *A Critical Introduction to Queer Theory*, New York: New York University Press.

Twitchell, J.B. (1996) *ADCULT USA: The Triumph of American Advertising in American Culture*, New York: Columbia University Press.

Ursinus, Z. and C. Olevianus (1877 [1563]) *Heidelberg Catechism: Text of the Tercentenary Edition*, Cleveland, OH: German Publishing House of the Reformed Church.

Section B

MATERIAL ENCOUNTERS

Introduction to Part II, Section B

Material encounters between religion and popular culture involve physical objects: things we can play with, eat, hold, wear, or read without requiring electronic mediation. In this way, they are not new elements of culture but sometimes quite ancient. Nonetheless, they are all now created, produced, and marketed within the structures of modern popular culture, and so have evolved in distinctive ways as part of modern societies.

Jennie Chapman's chapter on popular literature notes that although literature has coexisted with religion for millennia, and they usually expressed similar values, since the time of the Renaissance literature has developed an increasingly critical relationship with religion, offering a competing set of values and beliefs. This has in some cases led to hostility or suspicion against literature on the part of religious people. But religious authors have also responded by developing their own religious popular fiction as an alternative—and this has recently become a huge and profitable industry, especially with marketing to Evangelical Christians. While some critics have dismissed such religious literature as simplistic propaganda and its readers as naïve simpletons, Chapman points out that there is a degree of diversity in religious fiction and its appropriation that resists such generalizations. Because mainstream marketing of some books has given them wider appeal, there are non-Christian readers of Evangelical fiction. There are also different groups of Christian fiction readers who may disagree on whether a particular book reflects "correct" theology, as well as readers of sub-categories such as Urban Christian or Muslim fiction which may deviate from standard assumptions regarding religious fiction. In short, there are a variety of types of religious fiction and religious readers, and this diversity shows how religious subcultures have been able to develop and support forms of popular literature that express their particular identities and views.

Christine Hoff Kraemer and A. David Lewis's chapter on comics and graphic novels shows how these forms have developed in recent decades to be a site where religious meaning is created and sustained. Like film and television, comics use images in conjunction with words to tell stories and so have an immediacy that promotes identification—and yet comics allow the reader to interact with the medium as with a book, creating a more individualized connection than the more communal consumption of film and television. Comics have proven to be a natural medium for the depiction of religious and mythological subject matter, from Bible stories to superhero tales, but they often present alternative mythologies that riff on and critique societal religious norms, freely mixing technology with magic and juxtaposing figures from various religious mythologies. Comic authors may create their own theologies in the process, and so contribute to the religious views of readers in various ways by challenging or reinforcing traditional norms and values.

Benjamin Zeller's chapter on food and cooking examines the ways in which food in contemporary societies has developed religious aspects, and how popular culture has promoted these aspects through television shows and other media. Television cooking shows offer a spectacle of performance, sacrifice, and creation that mirrors religion, and the food conveys cultural identity and transcendent meaning. Shows that save the failing restaurant convey judgment and redemption. "Foodways" like vegetarianism or locavorism also express value systems and practices that are intentionally adopted by communities as part of their identity. Foods can also express religious beliefs and identity, e.g., in kosher or halal foods, but also in "food kitsch" that is semi-serious in intent—including chocolate deities and Bible bread. Although food and practices associated with its preparation and consumption have always been an important part of religion, popular culture today adds to this through promoting and popularizing a variety of ways in which food can convey meaning—which suggests that food itself may become like a religion.

Edward Dutton's chapter on fashion examines how the ways in which religious identity can be expressed through clothing intersect with popular fashion trends. Fashion trends are defined by the cultural elites (e.g., the rich, or celebrities), and hence become desirable for others to wear or imitate in order to share in their status. But religious groups remake fashion trends to express their own values or beliefs—perhaps by wearing clothing with scriptural verses—and in this way create alternative fashions valued by their own groups. Various Christian fashion trends such as WWJD bracelets and purity rings (signaling voluntary chastity) have also become popular ways of expressing Christian identity. Some members of religious groups may also reject particular fashion trends as overly revealing or sexualized, and in this way their fashion choices express their own religious values. Westerners may also participate in fashion trends wherein they imitate the dress of non-Western cultures, thereby expressing their own values regarding appreciation and appropriation of other cultures and religions. As with other aspects of popular culture, different sub-cultures make use of diverse aspects of fashion—accepting, rejecting, or altering them, dependent on their own values and how they have chosen to express them.

Nikki Bado and Rebecca Sachs Norris's chapter on games and dolls discusses how religious toys, games, and dolls are utilized for purposes of religious education, play, and satire. Toys and games can reinforce religious values through moralistic board games that reward those who follow the rules, or dolls that dress and act chastely. Others seem to be tongue-in-cheek representations that may parody traditional religious ideas, but this can also be used by religious people as an acceptable way to engage in humor about their own traditions. Religious toys may be developed as alternatives to secular toys, or as ways to convey and sell the values of the religion.

Dolls may teach girls conservative religious values such as the submission of women to traditional gender roles, and boys' games and toys may sanction religious violence. Even though many of the values encoded in these toys may be deemed problematic or commodified, the authors argue that play is a healthy and necessary element of religion that will naturally find expression in popular culture.

Finally, Leonard Primiano's chapter on kitsch examines the ways in which this term has evolved from a judgment on popular art regarded as tacky, inauthentic, or tasteless, to an appreciation of the values of mass-produced cultural artifacts of the non-elites. Religious kitsch today embraces the value of endless repetition—with replicas of everything from the Shroud of Turin to Noah's Ark—and can be a marker for popular religious devotion that highlights the roles of materiality and sentimentality. While elite critics of art or religion may deride the simplicity of their messages, emotional excesses, and lack of originality, these artifacts function as a form in which popular religious piety is performed and communicated. They are appropriated in a variety of ways, from the serious to the ironic, but all those who embrace them show how these popular representations of religious subjects express both the ways in which modern religion is commodified and the ways in which it continues to convey meaning to people.

All of these aspects of material culture reflect how leisure and work activities are often imbued with religious qualities, as we view them as significant to our lives and values. What we eat, play with, read, or wear often hold entertainment value for us, but they also may express more profound meanings for us—which may explain why our choices in regard to them can bind us to others who share our beliefs and values, or divide us from those who do not.

11
POPULAR LITERATURE

Jennie Chapman[*]

Go into any bookstore in the USA and you will inevitably find, amid the classics, the celebrity biographies, the cookery books, and the motivational guides, a section dedicated to religion and spirituality. Every imaginable genre is represented: guides to prayer, witnessing, and charitable giving all inevitably feature, but so do rather more surprising and esoteric subjects, from biblically inspired weight-loss guides to faith-based approaches to success in the workplace (see Adams 2011; Maynard and Maynard 2010; Van Duzer 2010; Solomon 2004; Grudem 2003; Colbert 2002). Evangelical and New Age titles predominate, but readers of other faiths are catered for: there are self-help books for Muslims and marriage manuals for Jews (see Mogahed 2012; Crohn et al. 2001). The fiction sub-section is also densely populated, with a profusion of Evangelical Christian titles in particular. While other sectors struggle against the rising tide of e-books, self-publications and pirated content, religious publishers report growth and profit. According to *American Libraries*, annual sales of Christian books and products rose from \$1 billion in 1980 to more than \$4 billion in 2000 (Ralph and Larue 2005: 51). A market study undertaken in 2011 revealed that the religion category accounted for 10 percent of the overall book market, measured in sales dollars (Nelson 2011). In the rapidly burgeoning e-book market, sales of Christian fiction increased sixfold between 2010 and 2011 (MacDonald 2012). There are other indicators of the sector's accomplishments beyond sales figures and profit margins. Demand in libraries for Christian fiction is among the highest of all genres. In an interview with *Publisher's Weekly*, a Minneapolis librarian explains his policy toward Christian fiction: "if the book is with a known publisher, it's not a question of if we'll buy it, but how many copies we'll buy" (Byle 2012). In our putatively secular age, popular religious literature is not merely surviving but thriving.

Although the religious non-fiction sector is both vast and varied, this chapter will focus on religious fiction. Rather than attempting to survey every permutation of religious popular fiction—a monumental task indeed (see Mort 2002)—I will present four case studies that illustrate different facets of, and developments within, the sector. The Evangelical dominance of the sector is reflected in the case studies: three out of the four deal with Evangelical texts. However, I have sought to reflect the nuances of the market that have not been fully explored in most examinations of religious fiction. My third case study examines the emergent genre of Urban Christian fiction, written by and for African-American Evangelicals, while my fourth engages with an even newer and wholly unexamined form of religious fiction, the Urban Islamic novel.

The case studies have been chosen for what they reveal about the complex negotiations that define religious fiction: between author and audience; between faith and the marketplace; between art and didacticism; and between medium and message. Left Behind is remarkable because it succeeded commercially without compromising its Evangelical message.[1] The gamble paid off in this case, but other examples reveal the volatility of audience responses in a sub-culture whose rejection of mainstream values is predicated upon the consolidation of internal orthodoxy, and which thus often responds adversely to challenges to the status quo from within. The controversies stirred by William Paul Young's *The Shack* (2007) exemplify the powerful gate-keeping role that audiences, even more than publishers, play in staking out the limits of the genre. Audience demand also accounts for the rise of African-American Christian fiction, starting in the late 1990s. The emergence of this sub-genre reveals the complex nexus of religious and secular influences that operate in the sector and often, in their contradictory imperatives, produce tensions in the texts as they attempt to negotiate the competing requirements of genre, theology, and marketplace. In the case of the African-American genre that is Urban Christian fiction, the secular model on which it is based is—in its depictions of sex, violence, and drug use, and its use of profane language—largely incompatible with conservative Evangelical values, requiring authors and publishers to work hard to sanitize the form for a Christian readership while keeping its distinctive generic features intact. The "Urban" genre that emerged in the realm of secular popular fiction—and arguably deals with rather ungodly subjects—has also been harnessed by other religious traditions. Thus, while the primary focus on Christian (read: Protestant Evangelical) fiction in this chapter is commensurate with its dominance of the religious literature market, my final case study is the intriguing new phenomenon of Urban Islamic fiction, best exemplified by Umm Juwayriyah's *The Size of a Mustard Seed*, published in 2007. Such a text may appear anomalous in a marketplace dominated by Evangelicalism, but in its bid to give voice to an unrepresented and often misunderstood minority; its use of the mechanisms of popular culture to proclaim and affirm a deeply held personal faith; and its canny appropriation and resignification of a popular genre with quite different imperatives, Juwayriyah's novel is, in fact, as American as they come.

Religion and literature in the USA: history and scholarship

"It could easily be argued," claims cultural critic Giles Gunn (1987: 173), "that a chronicle of the relations between literature and religion, at least in the West, constitutes a history of spiritual replacements." Whereas in the period spanning classical antiquity to the Renaissance, literature functioned as a "complementary, if not deeply supportive" buttress to religious orthodoxy, by the end of the Renaissance literature was adopting a far more combative and critical orientation to traditional systems of faith that, by the time of the Enlightenment, transfigured literature itself into "an alternative to or substitute for religion" (ibid.: 182–83). Modernity, in Gunn's schema, is characterized by a series of epistemological breaks that shift truth and knowledge away from the realm of religious orthodoxy and toward the realm of literary discourse. In this model, literature cannot be viewed as anything but a threat to religion, an insolent upstart that has usurped religion's role as the culturally sanctioned repository of beauty, transcendence, and meaning. And yet, at the same time, it is also true that "[l]iterature and religion … have been historically related in fact and conceptually related in theory" (ibid.: 180). Gunn contends that "many literary genres and traditions … developed explicitly as outgrowths of religious traditions" which have left discernible "sacred traces" in even the most ardently secular of works (ibid.: 177, 176). As such, literature cannot easily be disentangled from its religious roots even as it adopts a critical, and at times condemnatory, stance toward them. The relationship between religion and literature is nothing if not fraught and contradictory.

As space does not permit an adequate examination of the historical attitudes of each major American religious tradition toward literature, I will instead focus on the most obvious case study: American Protestantism, which exemplifies precisely these contradictions and tensions between literature and religion. In terms of their attitudes toward literature—and popular fiction in particular—we might plot American Protestants along a continuum from adopters to antagonists, between which extremes lies a spectrum of ambivalences and anxieties. The most enthusiastic adopters of religious fiction are of the opinion that God approves of any and all worldly means of spreading the gospel, and that popular culture is therefore both a potent and perfectly acceptable method of reaching the unchurched. Christian journalist Belinda Elliott writes:

> Many of our friends and neighbors would never dare to pick up a Bible to read in their free time. Nor would they attend a church service where they could learn more about God. But many of them would be quick to grab a copy of the latest *New York Times* bestseller.
>
> (Elliott 2008)

Interestingly, the artistic merit of a given novel is, for these adopters, of secondary importance to the message it conveys. Fiction is simply a vehicle placed at Christians' disposal to undertake God's work on earth, which may explain the relative paucity of overtly religious novels that exhibit the thematic or linguistic sophistication that might place them in the esteemed ranks of "literary fiction."

At the other end of the continuum are those who unilaterally oppose engagement with popular culture, including (and perhaps especially) fiction, regardless of the ends to which it is put. Occupying a position that may be described as fundamentalist, these antagonists resist cultural accommodation as a sullying compromise with a world that is irremediably fallen and corrupt (see Marsden 2006). To not merely tolerate, but actually adopt as tools of witness, cultural artifacts such as popular fiction is to capitulate to a degenerate world in which the saved should take no part. Such wholesale rejections of fiction are increasingly rare in the contemporary era, however; more common is the strict monitoring of purportedly religious fiction for content that may be deemed unorthodox, unbiblical, or of dubious moral value, and the loud denunciation of material found guilty of any of these transgressions. The controversy evoked by *The Shack* stands as a prime example of the enduring anxieties that attend the combination of religion and fiction even in an age in which it is commonplace.

Scholarship that aims to trace the contours and analyze the effects of Evangelical cultural production is a relatively novel phenomenon, though by no means a wholly niche or esoteric one. The emergence of the Religious Right as a powerful political force in the late 1970s precipitated a surge of academic interest in this hitherto neglected demographic (see Bellah *et al.* 1996; Hunter 1983; Lienesch 1993; Wilcox 1992; Diamond 1990; Liebman and Wuthnow 1982; Zwier 1982). While a number of important studies focused on the politics of Evangelicalism, others began to consider the cultural dimensions of born-again America (see Chidester 2005; Mazur and McCarthy 2001; McDannell 1998). For these scholars, culture was the arena where Evangelical identities were forged, galvanized, and reproduced. Evangelical popular literature, music, film, television, and art held up an affirming and flattering mirror to Evangelical culture. While the ostensible aim of many cultural products was to evangelize the unchurched, in many cases it was apparent that this was popular culture created by Evangelicals for Evangelicals: a validation of their faith and the sense of cultural and social identity that it generated.

In many ways it was the Left Behind phenomenon that instigated the now thriving field of popular religious literature studies, though there were a few trailblazers who took note of the genre prior to this. Jan Blodgett's *Protestant Evangelical Literary Culture and Contemporary Society* (1997) appears to be the first sustained examination of Evangelical popular literature on its own terms, though the genre had been noted in some earlier studies of Evangelical popular culture in a broader sense, notably Randall Balmer's 1993 ethnography, *Mine Eyes Have Seen the Glory*. Blodgett's study offers a survey of Evangelical fiction publishing from 1972 to 1994, spanning eight genres (biblical; romance; fantasy/science fiction; spiritual warfare; historical novels; westerns; action/adventure; and mystery). The scope of the study, encompassing 60 novels in total, means that there is little space to develop sustained textual analyses of the novels; rather, Blodgett identifies recurring themes and motifs that work to express and entrench shared values and established norms of behavior. At the same time, Blodgett finds that fiction can provide a space in which orthodoxies might be tested, though rarely challenged outright. The Christian fiction of the 1980s and 1990s reflects, for example, the growing (if at times grudging) acceptance of principles of gender equality within Evangelicalism (Blodgett 1997: 155).

Blodgett's study is also instructive in revealing the dramatic developments that have taken place in the Christian fiction market since its publication in 1997, many of which have been prompted or influenced by what we might call the "Left Behind effect." But other calibrations of the market may also be observed. For example, every novel in Blodgett's survey has a white author. Only a tiny number feature African-American or other ethnic minority characters; indeed, race and racial issues are rendered invisible by the vast majority of the titles surveyed.[2] Had Blodgett's investigation been conducted ten years later, it would have been remiss of her to discount the dozens (if not hundreds) of Christian novels written by and for African Americans which have come to constitute a genre in their own right. Nevertheless, little if any scholarship has been undertaken on this emergent literature.

Anita Gandolfo's *Faith in Fiction* (2007) reflects a changed religious literary landscape, dedicating a full (albeit uncomplimentary) chapter to the Left Behind phenomenon, as well as examining in detail other emergent trends such as Christian "chick-lit" and Christian young adult fiction. Still, African-American titles remain overlooked, as do religious fictions representing other faiths, with the exception of Jewish author Anita Diamant's *The Red Tent* (1997). Instead, Gandolfo explores how "serious" writers who refuse the label of "Christian author," from Frederick Buechner to John Updike, nonetheless incorporate religious concerns into their work. In so doing, Gandolfo usefully troubles the rather reified, and often unquestioned, distinction between "Christian fiction" and "secular fiction." This is an important intervention given the sets of assumptions that attach themselves to each category: "Christian fiction" is formulaic, didactic, facile, propagandistic, and medieval; while its secular counterpart, a precocious child of the Enlightenment, is intellectual, complex, profound, serious, and modern. Rather than interrogating these value judgments, however, Gandolfo's study often re-inscribes them: consumers of Christian fiction are denigrated as "unsophisticated," "inexperienced," or "naïve" readers who cannot but "unconsciously absorb" the "radical, political ideology" masquerading as harmless fiction in books such as the Left Behind series (Gandolfo 2007: 103, 105).

Such generalizations about audiences are indicative of a pervasive tendency toward oversimplification and category errors when attempting to describe a realm of the popular that is extraordinarily heterogeneous. Most commentators, for example, are wont to indiscriminately label as "Christian fiction" that which might be more properly named "Evangelical fiction." John Mort's guide to Christian fiction, although intended primarily as a reference for librarians rather than a detailed scholarly analysis of the genre, is laudable in its resistance to such easy conflations of terms. "[T]here are many fiction writers who don't fit the evangelical mold and yet are clearly Christian writers," he observes, though he concedes that "when readers ask for Christian fiction, most of the time what they mean is evangelical fiction" (Mort 2002: 1, 2). Mort's guide includes the most extensive surveys of Catholic, Mormon, and even Amish, Mennonite, and Quaker fiction in the field (see ibid., particularly Chapters 12–14); nonetheless, the Evangelical tradition continues to predominate. Perhaps more problematic is the prevailing omission from the scholarship of religious literature by writers of color. While religious publishing inarguably remains a white-dominated industry, African-American authors and African-American-led publishing houses such as Baker, New Hope, and Walk Worthy have made significant inroads. I have therefore sought in this chapter to unsettle the hegemony of white Evangelicalism in studies of religion and popular culture.[3]

Religious fiction as cultural phenomenon: the Left Behind series

No discussion of religion and popular literature in the contemporary period could ignore the Left Behind series (1995–2007)—not least because these novels are largely responsible for the academic discourse that now circulates around Christian fiction, and in which this chapter participates. My discussion of the series here will be less concerned with an analysis of the texts themselves (see Chapman 2013; Shuck 2005; Gribben 2004; McAlister 2003), than with an examination of Left Behind's reception and circulation in the larger context of religious popular fiction in the USA, and the powerful effect that the series' commercial success has had upon the sector.

The story conveyed by Left Behind will be familiar to many: the dispensational theology that informs it was once the exclusive province of fundamentalist and Evangelical churches, but is now, in the USA at least, a cultural commonplace, thanks in part to Tim LaHaye and Jerry Jenkins's novels. The narrative begins with the sudden, inexplicable disappearance of millions of individuals who leave only their clothes and personal effects behind. It soon transpires that these disappearances have been caused by the rapture: the snatching up of born-again Christians to heaven so that they may be spared the wrath of the Tribulation, during which the Antichrist will institute a despotic global dictatorship and God will pour out his wrath in an attempt to convert the unrepentant before the final judgment. The series follows the fortunes of a group of characters who, despite being left behind, quickly see the error of their ways and convert to Evangelical Christianity, determined to resist the Antichrist as the earth enters into its final days.

The story of Left Behind's unprecedented success is almost as renowned as the eschatological mythos it propagates. When the first Left Behind novel was published in 1995, it was given a modest initial print run of 150,000; by 2000 and the publication of the eighth installment, this had risen to 2.5 million (Forbes 2004: 6). To date, the series has sold upwards of 65 million copies—remarkably, these official figures do not include purchases made in independent Christian bookstores which, the publishers claim, account for around one third of total sales (Gribben 2009: 131; Forbes 2004: 8). The last six books all reached the number one position on US bestseller lists including *New York Times*, *USA Today*, *Publishers Weekly* and *The Wall Street Journal* (Forbes 2004). A study undertaken in 2006 made the astonishing discovery that one in five Americans has read at least one of the Left Behind novels (Bader *et al.* 2006: 19). The reasons behind the extraordinary success of Left Behind are manifold and complex. Timing undoubtedly played a part: the series was launched five years prior to the turn of the millennium, a date that for some carried apocalyptic significance. But perhaps the most salient event to elicit a wider interest in the end-times narrative that Left Behind delineates took place not on 1 January 2000, but a year and nine months later, when hijacked planes collided with the World Trade Center and the Pentagon. LaHaye and Jenkins's Manichean narrative, which pits good against evil and self against other, resonated with readers trying to make sense of the 9/11 terrorist attacks. It promised that even in times of trauma and loss, God is in control, and that justice will be restored. It is perhaps unsurprising that a survey conducted by the Evangelical Christian Publishers Association found that, in the eight weeks following the atrocities, sales of Left Behind leapt by 71 percent compared with the eight weeks preceding them (Sack 2001).

But the wild popularity of Left Behind cannot be exclusively attributed to the need for consolation in times of catastrophe. In many ways the series owes its popularity to the robust cultural networks that bind the Evangelical community. Amy Frykholm (2004: 47) argues that "[t]he reading of *Left Behind* and the functioning of the church community are often mutually supportive and constitutive of one another." In the conservative Evangelical world in which Left Behind circulates, popular religious literature operates as part of a much more extensive cultural complex. Left Behind, then, does not and could not function independently of the extensive circuits of culture that call forth an Evangelical universe unto itself. We might envisage the cultural complex that engenders and supports Left Behind in terms of a nodal network. At the center of the network is the Left Behind series itself. Connected to this center are multiple nodes that further extend and consolidate the network of signification. One node represents the non-fiction prophecy guides written by LaHaye and Jenkins and their associates that cite the original novels as something akin to proof texts, thus re-inscribing their authority. Another represents the Left Behind films; another the series for children; another the videogame (see Sarin 2000; Corcoran 2002; Baxley 2005).[4] Farther away from the center are nodes representing other examples of prophecy fiction by different authors, and Evangelical novels in other genres. All of this extra-textual apparatus works to consolidate the series' cultural dominance. This arterial complex of culture is dependent on perpetual circulation if it is to remain vital and relevant; indubitably, it is the interconnected grassroots network of Evangelical churches, Bible studies, and Christian festivals, supplemented in the virtual realm with blogs, forums, and online publications, that permits this complex to thrive.

We can see, then, how this cultural complex works to inaugurate an enclosed, self-sufficient system that tends to turn its gaze inward rather than outward, thus engendering a self-referential circuit of signification. However, while Evangelical culture may look very much like a sovereign "parallel universe," as Daniel Radosh (2008) describes it, closer scrutiny reveals a porous, permeable membrane between the Evangelical culture and the cultural mainstream against which it defines itself. While commentators often note the extent to which Evangelical popular culture appropriates secular forms—Left Behind may have looked quite different had Tom Clancy never put pen to paper—cultural osmosis in the opposite direction is less frequently acknowledged, yet clearly takes place. The Left Behind phenomenon attests to this: no piece of fiction becomes a number one bestseller by appealing to only one demographic, however populous that demographic might be. Left Behind attracted a core readership of Evangelicals, but also reached beyond its implied audience to entice book buyers who did not identify as Evangelical or even Christian. A Barna survey conducted in 2001 indicated that

> nearly one-tenth of the audience for the series are atheists and people associated with non-Christian faiths … while more than two million of the readers are individuals who consider themselves to be Christian but have never accepted Jesus Christ as their savior.
>
> (Barna Group 2001)

The pervasive influence of end-times theology is registered throughout American culture: apocalyptic films such as *The Book of Eli* (2010), novels featuring rapture-like disappearances such as Tom Perotta's *The Leftovers* (2011), and Left Behind spoofs in *The Simpsons* (FOX, 1989–present) and *American Dad!* (FOX, 2005–present) all indicate the degree to which "rapture culture," as Frykholm (2004) describes it, cannot be delimited to a clearly defined Evangelical demographic. The binary formula of belief/non-belief fails to account for the variety and subtlety of faith in America: other, more nuanced models are called for. Paul Boyer (1992: 2–3) suggests that we visualize the realm of Christian prophecy belief as "a series of concentric circles." At the center is a "core group of devotees" who take biblical prophecy extremely seriously and whose behavior is shaped by this knowledge. Then, in the next circle are individuals "who may be hazy about the details of biblical eschatology, but nonetheless believe that the Bible provides clues to future events." The outer circle comprises "superficially secular individuals ... whose worldview is nevertheless shaped to some degree by residual or latent concepts of eschatology, the theology of last things." By piquing the interest of this outer circle, LaHaye and Jenkins were able to produce something of a crossover product that, while appealing primarily to Evangelical readers, also mobilized other reading publics, with extraordinarily profitable results.

Controversies in Christian fiction: *The Shack*

First published in 2007, William Paul Young's *The Shack* is among the most successful and prominent Christian novels to emerge in the wake of Left Behind. A story of terrible loss that precipitates a crisis of faith and, eventually, a personal redemption, Young's novel departs from the apocalyptic action thrillers of LaHaye and Jenkins, rendering a personal God of love and friendship in place of Left Behind's imperious and wrathful deity. It tells the story of Mackenzie "Mack" Philips, a seminary graduate whose relationship with God is tested to its limit when his six-year-old daughter Missy is abducted and murdered by a serial killer during a family holiday. Having labored under the weight of a grief that he describes as "the Great Sadness" for three-and-a-half years, Mack finds his life transformed by a note—intriguingly signed by "Papa," Mack's wife's affectionate name for God—inviting him to the last place on earth he wishes to revisit: the shack where Missy is presumed to have been killed. Surrendering to his curiosity, Mack goes to the shack to find a large black woman who calls herself Papa, a Jewish man going by the name of Yeshua, and a small Asian woman called Sarayu; or, to give them their theological names, the Father, the Son, and the Holy Spirit. During his time with the trinity at the shack, Mack regains his faith and begins to come to terms with the loss of his daughter.

The Shack's inauspicious origins as a self-published text—according to the author, "secular publishers didn't want it because it had too much Jesus," while "it was too edgy for faith-based publishers"—did not impede its progress toward the bestseller lists where, at the time of writing, it remains a fixture after 191 consecutive weeks in the charts (Nelson 2011).[5] Interest in the novel was generated primarily via word-of-mouth recommendations—a particularly powerful form of knowledge exchange in the close-knit Evangelical sub-culture—and within a year *The Shack* was the most hotly discussed novel among Evangelicals, thus attracting the interest of publishers. This culminated in a deal with the FaithWords division of the major (and, notably, secular) publishing group Hachette in 2008, after which sales increased exponentially.

There are currently more than eighteen million copies of *The Shack* in print; taking into account typical Evangelical reading practices in which a single copy of a favored text is circulated among several individuals via congregational networks, the author has extrapolated from this figure an overall readership of some one hundred million (Elliott 2012). Countless readers have testified that the novel has had a transformative effect upon their lives. According to *USA Today*, "Young gets nearly 100 e-mails a day from readers saying they found solace and inspiration in his novel" (Grossman 2008).

But the success of *The Shack* is by no means uncomplicated. Praise for the novel has been counter-balanced by a powerful antagonism among the more conservative wings of American Evangelicalism. Perhaps unsurprisingly, given its portrayal of God as an African-American woman, Jesus as a large-nosed man in a plaid shirt, and the Holy Spirit as an Asian sylph, detractors accuse the novel of promulgating an unorthodox understanding of the trinity, eschewing biblical accuracy in favor of emotional catharsis, and even promoting heresy.[6] Glenn R. Kreider, a theology professor at Dallas Theological Seminary, describes "the author's portrayal of God [a]s confusing at best and untrue at worst" (Kreider n.d.). James De Young, a former personal friend of the author, has authored a book-length riposte entitled *Burning Down "The Shack"* that, according to the subtitle, fulminates on "How the 'Christian' Bestseller is Deceiving Millions." De Young points to the author's alleged dabblings in universalist theology in order to "lay the groundwork for the plausibility of uncovering errors" (Wooding 2010). Several Internet commentators have identified a more nefarious hidden intent at work in the narrative, branding it a satanic expression of "New Age heresy" that beguiles and deceives the spiritually naïve (Keller 2008; Smith 2008), a theme developed at length by the president of the Southern Baptist Convention, Albert Mohler. "This book includes undiluted heresy. It is a deeply troubling book," he asserted in a radio program dedicated to a point-by-point refutation of *The Shack*'s theology. Like other critics, Mohler views *The Shack* as a potent threat to orthodoxy whose malignant influence should not be underestimated. "There is danger here, especially for people who don't know anything about Christian doctrine," he opines. "It is a very subversive, even seductive story." But for Mohler, "one of the larger points" that the success and controversy of *The Shack* raises is "the danger of this category of Christian fiction" as a whole (Mohler 2008).

Mohler's paranoid perspective on the Christian novel is predicated on a facet of fiction that seems especially problematic for biblical literalists who encounter the Bible as the inerrant and infallible word of God. Fiction is, by nature, literally "untrue"; taking this line of thought to its next logical stage, one might infer that it is therefore deceptive. Mohler's denunciation not only of Young's novel, but "this category of Christian fiction" in broad terms, as "dangerous," "subversive," and "seductive" issues from precisely this position. Such commentators participate, then, in a long-established discourse about fiction that imbues it with mysterious, transgressive, perhaps diabolical powers to deceive and dissemble. If Christianity is about truth and light, then it cannot be compatible with a discursive form that at best cloaks the literal truth in metaphor, symbol, and allusion, and at worst falsifies and distorts.

Indeed, the most interesting—and contentious—aspect of *The Shack*, from both a literary-critical perspective and within the context of contemporary Christian fiction, is its tolerance of doubt and its refusal to provide the reader with definitive answers or narrative closure. A sense of contingency clings to its very form: though seemingly a third-person omniscient narrative, the story is in fact a first-person frame narrative relayed by a narrator named Willie—presumably a surrogate for the author—whose own voice can be discerned in the foreword and afterword that enclose the main plot. The conceit used by Young here is that "Mack is not comfortable with his writing skills ... . So he asked if I would ghost-write this story—his story" (Young 2008: 12). This framing allows the author to qualify, and perhaps establish some critical distance from, the controversial theology that underpins the subsequent story. It undercuts the narrative's (and the author's) claim to authority—the reader engages with Mack's story second-hand, via the mediating voice of the narrator, to whom the story has putatively been told, thus attenuating any final claim to absolute veracity. Hence, the foreword functions as a hedge to any totalizing assumptions regarding the absolute truth of the narrative: "It's a little, well ... no, it is a *lot* on the fantastic side. Whether some parts of it are true or not, I won't be the judge" (12). In the afterword this sentiment is reiterated: "I am sure there will be some who wonder whether everything really happened as Mack recalls it, or if the accident and morphine made him just a little bit loopy" (247). Furthermore, while the narrator states "I want all of it to be true," he is alert to the varieties of truth—literal, metaphorical, allegorical, emotional, psychological—with which Evangelical authors are often reluctant to engage. "Perhaps if some of it is not actually true in one sense, it is still true nonetheless—if you know what I mean" (ibid.). This circumlocution undoubtedly lacks sophistication, and is not developed in a way that might facilitate a more penetrating discourse on epistemology, but even this ultimately evasive construction stands in remarkable contrast to the bombastic certainties of the Left Behind novels.

The Shack's strategic ambiguities and refusals indicate that there is another way to conceive the relationship between faith and fiction, one that proponents of the contemporary religious novel have articulated in its defense. Belinda Elliott, writing for the Christian Broadcasting Network, posits an intrinsic and abiding relationship between Christianity and imaginative narrative:

> Jesus told parables and used metaphors to grab the attention of his listeners, explain spiritual concepts, and sometimes shock people out of their comfort zones. Why would we think that God would be offended by people in our culture using the art of storytelling in much the same way?
>
> (Elliott 2008)

Elliott's vindication of fiction recognizes storytelling as a form of discourse that does not fit easily into a binary model that simplistically categorizes utterances as true or false. Rather, narrative bears important functions—explanatory, rhetorical, and affective—not fulfilled by other species of language precisely because it is not transparently and literally "true." In its evasion of dogma and disregard for orthodoxy, *The Shack* may appeal to Christians for whom doubt is an essential part of faith, while those who conceive of their convictions as a means to unassailable certitude view the novel's questioning posture as egregious, irreverent, and indeed, heretical.

"Our new underground railroad": African-American Christian fiction

To read the extant scholarship on contemporary Christian publishing is to encounter a world dominated by white conservative Evangelicals, from the perspective of both production and consumption. But there is another story to be told about religious popular literature. According to publishing editor Rebecca Irwin-Diehl, "[t]he African-American market has become so established we no longer refer to it as developing" (Kiesling 2008: S3). Since its inception in the early 1990s, the African-American Christian Market (AACM) has blossomed into a thriving and lucrative industry whose operations are nevertheless largely self-contained and self-sustaining. Fiction has proven especially viable, with contemporary romances and "Urban" novels predominating. Authors including Victoria Christopher Murray, Jacquelin Thomas, ReShonda Tate Billingsley, and Kimberla Lawson Roby have enjoyed considerable success with novels that address subjects that Evangelical publishers—and audiences—have historically found unpalatable, including divorce, sexuality, infidelity, and suicide. By taking cues from the graphic and gritty world of African-American Christian fiction, these authors push against the established boundaries that exert a powerful influence on Christian literary expression. In so doing, they are reconfiguring the parameters of a genre whose success is predicated on maintaining an optimal tension between accommodations to and separation from the secular "mainstream."

The reasons behind the triumph of AACM in the early twenty-first century are inevitably complex, variously bound up with issues of identity and the representation of minorities in literature and culture; the buying behavior and reading practices of the demographic at which its products are targeted; and the increasing specialization of the publishing industry at large. Several figures in the industry claim that the success of the genre emerges out of African-American readers' desire to see themselves represented in literary genres that have traditionally marginalized black characters. As Joyce Dinkins, a managing editor, explains, "I went to school with Dick and Jane and Beatrix Potter, whom I loved, but when did I ever see my picture? Never" (Kiesling 2008: S2). The problem of non-representation or under-representation of people of color undoubtedly afflicts the Evangelical fiction sector disproportionately, as Blodgett's survey of 60 titles by exclusively white American authors (only a few of which feature non-white characters) demonstrates. The dearth of black authors who might represent black characters in a non-tokenistic manner generated such a degree of "pent-up demand," as Dinkins describes it, that once readers discovered fiction that filled this void "[they] wouldn't be able to get enough of it, and [they]'d tell all [their] friends" (ibid.). In this reading, African-American Christian fiction functions as a fulfillment of long-frustrated desire whose eventual consummation led to a frenzy of voracious purchasing.

Other commentators point to the particular vicissitudes of African-American history in their narratives of the genre's genesis. Tony Rose, the founder of the African-American Pavilion at BookExpo America, the US publishing industry's largest trade fair, suggests that the emergence of AACM can be traced back through the inter-connected histories of enslavement, segregation, the black church, and black entre-preneurialism; in this sense, the genre is less a novel phenomenon than the culmination of long-established practices of black self-sufficiency and self-expression:

> Frederick Douglass and other writers used the church as a vehicle to sell their books and pamphlets, and they self-published through their churches. African-Americans always wrote, always read—we had to write about our plight, whether it was slavery or Jim Crow or some demeaning situation. What we're seeing now is an extraordinary re-emergence of this self-publishing movement ... and religion is leading the pack.
>
> (Kiesling 2008: S4)

Rose's understanding of AACM in terms of historical resistance to white hegemony and oppression is shared by others in the industry. Alluding to the network of men and women who assisted escaped slaves on their journeys to the free North and to Canada, Pam Perry, whose public relations firm promotes AACM titles, evocatively describes black Christian fiction as "our new underground railroad" (ibid.).

Drawing on powerful narratives of black self-determination and self-representa-tion, African-American Christian fiction thrives by targeting a specific, racially homogenous audience that feels alienated from a "mainstream" Evangelical popular culture that often turns upon and thus entrenches ethnocentric notions of white normativity. However, the isolation of AACM from other genres and sectors within religious publishing, while ensuring its distinctiveness and engendering a loyal read-ership, is not without its problems. Some authors perceive a pernicious form of segregation at work that serves not only to reify the racial divisions that remain operative in American religious practice (one author echoes Rev. Martin Luther King, Jr., in her observation that "this country is largely segregated and unfortunately most segregated on Sunday mornings"), but also to shut out or put off potential readers (Lewis 2009). According to *Publisher's Weekly*,

> some black writers looking to attract nonblack readers feel stuck in a double bind, noting that often those readers are not only turned off by the "Christian fiction" label but sometimes feel uncomfortable looking for titles in the African-American section of the book store.
>
> (Sanders 2011)

The positioning of African-American Christian titles in a bookstore is a bone of contention for some authors. "Why am I 'limited' to the multicultural Christian genre?" asks *My Soul Cries Out* (2007) author Sherri L. Lewis. "[W]e have to find some way to bridge cultural gaps in Christian fiction" (Lewis 2009). The myriad categories that operate in this highly specialized and fragmented market do not favor authors whose work cuts across generic or, indeed, racial lines.

The problems of market positioning and the demands of an audience that will not hesitate to reject (and vociferously denounce) a book that does not meet its standards in terms of theological fidelity, adherence to orthodoxy, and its depiction and promotion of Evangelical social and moral mores, are extraordinarily acute in the genre to which I now turn: Urban Christian fiction. Influenced by the secular African-American publishing phenomenon of Urban fiction (also known as Street Lit), Urban Christian fiction is a fascinating example of the negotiations and accommodations Evangelical writers and readers undertake in their quest to produce literature that is at once culturally relevant and theologically and morally palatable. According to Wanda Brooks and Lorraine Savage, Urban fiction has typically conveyed "ultra-realistic tales of urban living rife with explicit language and street slang told through characters who [a]re often pimps, prostitutes, and drug dealers" (Brooks and Savage 2009). Clearly, then, both the stylistic conventions and the narrative content of Urban novels are at profound odds with the modes of representation that are deemed acceptable and appropriate in conservative Christian publishing. And yet, Urban Christian fiction has emerged as a sub-genre within AACM that attempts to marry the gritty and controversial issues that propel the secular form with a "clean" Evangelical aesthetic that promotes moral rectitude and an abstinent, godly lifestyle. How did this unlikely hybrid come to be?

Sherri L. Lewis's *My Soul Cries Out* provides an apt example of an author attempting to negotiate the contradictory generic imperatives of Urban fiction on the one hand and the AACM aesthetic on the other, and in doing so, questioning and unsettling the boundary between the acceptable and the anathema in Christian fiction. The novel's opening anagnorisis is enough to raise eyebrows: the first few pages of the novel witness the protagonist, Monnie, returning home to find her husband, Kevin, in bed with another man. The ensuing drama sees Monnie draw upon the strength her faith and church provide her to come to terms with her husband's homosexuality. Importantly, while the novel explicitly identifies homosexual behavior as a sin, it does not distinguish that sin from others, such as premarital sex, the consumption of alcohol, and, notably, intolerance. Indeed, one of the readers' group discussion points that appear at the end of the text suggests that "judging people struggling with homosexuality is just as much of a sin as homosexuality itself" (Lewis 2007: 452). From a liberal secular point of view this perspective is problematic—homosexuality is positioned as a disorder that individuals must "struggle with" in order to be "freed" of their "sin." But in the context of contemporary Christian fiction, the fact that homosexuality has been depicted at all, let alone in a non-judgmental manner, is groundbreaking. Though attitudes toward homosexuality among Evangelicals vary widely—from straightforward acceptance among progressives, to the view that while Evangelicals must "hate the sin" they are nonetheless called upon to "love the sinner," to the conviction that homosexuality is a depraved scourge upon society that will incur divine wrath—there is no doubt that it is deeply controversial in Evangelicalism. Erring on the side of caution, most writers and publishers have avoided the subject altogether. Where gay characters appear, they are usually stereotypical and unsympathetic: Left Behind's only lesbian character is a "militant" hard-nosed journalist (LaHaye and Jenkins 1995: 411) who wears "sensible shoes" (LaHaye and Jenkins 1996: 13); its token gay man, meanwhile, is an "outrageous and flamboyant" sculptor whose art is "laughably gaudy and decidedly profane" (LaHaye and Jenkins 2000: 44, 60). Lewis's Kevin, in contrast, is a fully realized and sympathetic character rather than an object of repugnance or ridicule.

The depiction of Monica is also important. *My Soul Cries Out*, like many other Urban Christian novels, features a female protagonist who is saved but nonetheless flawed. In contrast to the idealized, model Christians who populated earlier fictions in the genre, such as those by Janette Oke and Francine Rivers, Urban narratives show characters struggling with what Evangelicals often describe as their "walk"—their journey through faith and their attempts to stay on the path of righteousness—and behaving in ways that have rarely been depicted in more typical examples of the genre. In the wake of her marital troubles, Monnie struggles with her weight, she drinks, and she even smokes marijuana. Lewis has not made her an archetype of perfect saved behavior: on discovering Kevin's infidelity, she "unleashe[s] [a] spray of foul language" before threatening to physically attack her husband with a golf club (Lewis 2007: 4). There is, of course, a degree of censorship at work here—the reader is not privy to the specific foul language that Monnie verbalizes—but the mere depiction of an Evangelical character cursing, even in such testing circumstances as these, breaks a taboo that is difficult to appreciate unless one is familiar with the genre and the cultural mores it both reflects and legitimates.

This is not to say that readers of secular Urban fiction would recognize its Christian equivalent as part of the genre. They would likely view the latter as tame and sanitized, and certainly from a non-Evangelical reading perspective these texts appear exceptionally bowdlerized. To this extent, the usefulness and accuracy of the "Urban" classification is open to question. But context is key here: while readers outside the sub-culture would view Urban Christian novels as gentle and innocuous, Evangelical readers used to the vanilla romances of Oke and Rivers may well find much that is provocative and risqué in these narratives. Urban Christian fiction is thus defined by often-contradictory generic and stylistic imperatives, of which many in the industry are acutely aware. As AACM promoter Pam Perry explains,

> Some [religion] houses are promoting authors who are trying to reach the urban lit genre of readers, with gritty story lines and "real" characters, but without all the trash, and they have a dilemma. It looks like a very urban street-lit novel [intentionally], but they're between a rock and a hard place. It's too Christian for some of the basic bookstores and too gritty for the CBA [Christian Bookstore Association] bookstores.
>
> (Kiesling 2008)

Perry's observation speaks to the dexterity required to appropriately position a book within this most sensitive and volatile market, and the powerful role that grassroots gatekeepers play in rendering a book a success or a failure. That which is acceptable to some readers is too "gritty" for others, and while some find the "real"-ness of the Urban genre refreshing in a literary landscape that is often highly sanitized, others perceive Urban Christian fiction as a risky venture into a depraved secular world from which the devout reader might not emerge unscathed.

Emerging audiences, emerging genres: popular Islamic fiction

In 2007, American Muslim author Umm Juwayriyah published *The Size of a Mustard Seed*, the story of an American Muslim woman of blended heritage attempting to negotiate the demands of faith, work, and love in the shadow of 9/11. Like many a romantic heroine, Jameelah Salih seems to have it all: she is a talented stylist at a Muslim beauty salon, a successful graduate who is about to complete her second degree, and has a marriage offer from one of the most respected men in the community. But her life is far from perfect. She "passionately loves Allah" but often struggles to live up to her own ideals of a faithful life. "You didn't think you were reading about the life and times of a super-righteous Muslimah?" she chides the reader (Juwayriyah 2007: 10). "Point blank, I have a bad attitude, but I'm far from terrible. I'm like you: a struggling Muslimah with a lot of faults" (11). Like African-American Urban fiction, *Mustard Seed* reassures the implied female reader that it's okay not to be perfect: that "real women" of faith are flawed, frail, but trying to be better. This is not to say that the personal journeys of the protagonists across these genres are undifferentiated: Jameelah's struggle is particularized by her circumstances, and is framed by one event in particular. "New York City wasn't the only city affected by 9–11," she explains. "My city and every other city on earth changed. People changed. I changed too" (12). A formerly confident young woman, Jameelah becomes terrified of the outside world as reprisal attacks against Muslims sweep her city.

But discrimination in the novel does not only appear in the form of Islamophobia. Juwayriyah also delicately explores the latent prejudice that exists in parts of America's multicultural Muslim community. As a child of blended heritage—her father is Indonesian, her mother African-American—Jameelah discovers that some of her brothers and sisters in Islam view her hybridity as a problem. One character attributes the rise in divorce among Muslims to interracial marriages, and urges Jameelah to marry an Indonesian man in order to efface her mixed ethnicity and "bring [her] closer to [her] Indonesian roots" (239). Jameelah's resistance to such logic—by the end of the narrative she is happily engaged to a white "revert" (to use the novel's preferred terminology) to Islam, with the full blessing of her family—affirms her independence and agency, positioning her in deliberate contrast to the stereotype of the passive and subjugated Muslim woman. At the same time, Jameelah remains a devoted and dutiful daughter who practices Islam rigorously. Juwayriyah's novel attempts to show that it is possible to do both: to enjoy the freedoms and opportunities that contemporary America offers without adopting the moral positions associated with secularism. This is especially pertinent with respect to gender: in the novel, Jameelah and her female friends cover their hair and are forbidden from being alone with men unchaperoned; at the same time, they choose their own husbands, are financially independent, and highly educated. Like American Evangelicals, they are in the world, but not of it.

In its depiction of an urban, multicultural, modern, yet devout Muslim community, *The Size of a Mustard Seed* inaugurated what the author describes as "a new era of fiction" (Juwayriyah 2007).[7] Juwayriyah's claim is not as hyperbolic as it initially appears: popular, didactic Islamic fiction is an extremely recent phenomenon, emerging only in the first decade of the twenty-first century. At the time of writing, the genre remains nascent, with only a handful of novels to its name, but it is undoubtedly a growth industry. In 2005, the Islamic Writers' Alliance (IWA) was founded with the aim of "defining Islamic fiction and determining the criteria to establish it as a fiction sub-category of Adult and Juvenile fiction" (IslamicFiction Books.com n.d.a). The IWA's first Islamic Fiction Awards took place in 2009, following the success of its awards for poetry inaugurated four years previously.[8] Difficulties in placing didactic Islamic novels with mainstream publishers led to the formation of Muslim Writers Publishing in 2005, an affiliate of the IWA that provides a platform for the dissemination of Islamic fiction. The sector has some distance to travel before it matches the extraordinary sales (and profits) of the now firmly ensconced behemoth that is Evangelical publishing; nonetheless, the emergence of the genre is indicative of what one blogger described as a "burst of creative energy within an Islamic cultural context" (Whitaker 2007).[9]

As an emerging genre, popular Islamic fiction is undergoing the same phase of dynamic self-fashioning in an attempt to define its imperatives and parameters that mainstream Evangelical fiction underwent in its incipient stages during the 1980s. As interested parties seek to stake a claim in the formation of the genre, competing visions regarding its proper intentions and principles emerge. The reader-response page on the IWA-affiliated Islamic Fiction Books Web site reveals a wide variety of perspectives regarding the genre's purpose, but the most common paradigms might be classified as *normative*, *outreach*, and *alternative*.

The first view of Islamic fiction perceives it as a positive space where different stories about Muslims from those circulating in the dominant discourse might be told. Commentators on the IWA Web site observe that Muslims are either excluded from mainstream cultural representations, or represented in a negative light. As American author Najiyah Umm Waheeb observes,

[o]ur society at large is diverse and includes Muslims; however its cultural knowledge-base does not include Muslims. Libraries are full of stories about other cultures and faiths, and Islam needs to be represented as it is part of the mosaic of the American landscape.

(IslamicFictionBooks.com n.d.b)

Stories of the pernicious negative stereotyping of Muslims post-9/11 are legion: in their study of Muslim women in the USA, Yvonne Haddad, Jane Smith, and Kathleen Moore (2006: 28) observe that "[p]opular movies and television fare have portrayed Muslims as religious fanatics and terrorists." Responding to such stereotypes, supporters of Islamic fiction regard it as a space where alternative narratives might be forged. One commentator, Omair Ali, puts it exuberantly: "Let's get some stories where the Muslims are not cutting off hands or burning flags. Have a story of some Muslims baking cookies. YAY!" (IslamicFictionBooks.com n.d.b). Ali's alternative vision of domestic normalcy is intended as a powerful antidote to the stories of fundamentalism, terrorism, and barbarism that circulate in the dominant cultural discourse. In this reading, fiction is imbued with an extraordinary power to challenge and overturn entrenched cultural perceptions and presumptions. Islamic fiction, in the words of another commentator on the genre, "normalizes faith and makes Islam as regular and ordinary as apple pie" (Quraishi 2012).

The normative imperative that some proponents ascribe to Islamic fiction is somewhat connected to another, nevertheless distinct, position that values its potential as a tool for cross-cultural outreach. IWA founder Linda Delgado states that "[t]his genre of literature can make positive inroads into the non Muslim's [sic] understanding of Muslims and Islam" (IslamicFictionBooks.com n.d.b). This view would imply that one intended audience for popular Islamic fiction of the kind that the IWA endorses is that composed of non-Muslims. Nevertheless, the example of Evangelical fiction shows that while such novels may declare a proselytizing or educational imperative, their primary appeal lies with the already converted. Authors of overtly religious fiction must therefore attempt to strike a balance between the distinctive languages of the ingroup and the outgroup if their work is to speak effectively to both. Many popular religious fictions operate inside this tension, albeit with varying degrees of success; non-Evangelical readers of Left Behind interviewed by Amy Frykholm complained of the novels' pervasive employment of "Protestant-ese," complaining that "they use phrases, they use sentence constructions, they use words in ways that other people won't understand" (Frykholm 2004: 72). *The Size of a Mustard Seed* reveals a keen awareness of the ingroup/outgroup conundrum. It makes pervasive use of language that would likely be unfamiliar to a non-Muslim reader. Characters greet one another with "as salaamu alaikum wa rahmatullah," preface their exclamations with "insha'Allah," ponder on the rectitude of their "deen," and offer "dua" in their prayers. But these concepts are explained to the reader at appropriate intervals in the narrative: a person's *deen*, we discover, is his or her "way of life" (Juwayriyah 2007: 30); *dua* consists of supplication to Allah (20). The extensive inclusion of such language speaks to a Muslim reader who will perhaps notice his or her own idioms and speech patterns in the narrative, thus creating the sense of recognition that functions as a powerful affective force in popular religious texts. At the same time, those outside the faith are not excluded from the potentially alienating webs of significance spun by the novel's pointedly religious consciousness.

A third perspective posits Islamic fiction as a necessary alternative to mainstream publications. One commentator on the IWA Web site, Shahida, states: "My kids need quality Islamic fiction! Or else they might keep reading the fictions [sic] which does not teach any morals in fact which influences kids to lose morality" (IslamicFictionBooks.com n.d.b). Like many readers of Evangelical fiction, Shahida regards Islamic books as safe substitutes for other fiction that may be deemed incompatible with Muslim values. Whereas those who occupy the normative and outreach category positions view fiction as a positive catalyst for cultural empathy and enlightenment, those who posit Islamic fiction as an alternative tend to perceive fiction *per se* as transgressive and threatening, thus echoing the fears of those Christian readers who condemned *The Shack*. If fiction has the power to alter cultural perceptions and countermand ethnic and religious stereotypes, it also has the potential to damage its readers spiritually and morally. The dangerous possibilities that fiction encompasses are registered in the IWA's ambivalence about the form even as it seeks to promote it: it is anxious to warn that "not all of the Islamic content in these books will be considered factual or acceptable by all Muslim readers" (IslamicWritersAlliance.net 2005). As such, the term "Islamic fiction" is necessarily contested and problematic; and furthermore, if the genre is to thrive it will remain so. If Evangelical fiction can be taken as a reliable precedent, it is precisely the variety, rather than the homogeneity, of audiences that fuels demand for diverse fictions that cater to progressives and conservatives, traditionalists and modernists, the erudite consumer of fiction and the rookie reader. Furthermore, as with all forms of popular religious fiction, it is ultimately readers, not publishers, authors, or advocacy groups, who will be the final arbiters and gatekeepers of the genre.

Conclusion: the futures of religious fiction

At a moment when the entire publishing industry stands at a crossroads, the route that religious fiction will take through the brave new world of e-books, flash fiction, self-publishing, and digitization remains open to speculation, though the patterns of the past can tell us much about the shape of things to come. If history tells us anything, it is that religious Americans are nothing if not innovative. Such ingenuity has been notable in the Evangelical community, but is by no means limited to it: in many respects, the Evangelical example has been held up by other religious groups as a model of what can be achieved by embracing popular culture. A petition launched by the IWA calling for the publication of more Islamic fiction states that "[t]he immense and ever growing Christian fiction industry should serve as an example to the Muslim book industry. Fiction has the potential to alter lives" (Taylor 2006).

As faith continues to assert itself as a defining—and increasingly culturally legitimate—marker of identity, the popular fiction market will respond to the needs of readers who want their reading material to reflect their religious realities; it is already changing from one almost exclusively populated by novels aimed at white Evangelicals to a far more heterogeneous arena that caters to the needs of diverse audiences. Such diversity has its drawbacks as well as its advantages, of course: while specialization means that more audiences may be reached, those audiences will inevitably become smaller in numbers as the market fragments. Such fragmentation is also, ironically, an effect of the sector's growth: the exponentially increasing volume of religious fiction expands consumer choice but contracts the potential for an individual novel to achieve massive sales. Janette Oke's success in the 1970s might be attributed in part to the lack of anything else in the market that fulfilled the same cultural function, but as the genre moves toward saturation point, an individual author's chances of producing a hit like Left Behind or The Shack become infinitesimal. The fragmentation of religious fiction may also have a negative effect on the cultural groups to which it caters. In the Evangelical context, fiction has worked as a social glue, binding congregations and communities together as well as defining and re-inscribing those groups' definitions of orthodoxy that underpin identity. The increasing specialization of religious fiction to reflect various theological and denominational positions, as well as genres and styles, may negate fiction's capacity to generate and regenerate what Stanley Fish calls "interpretive communities" based on shared frames of reference (Fish 1980). It may also further fortify the barriers between different faith groups that authors such as Sherri Lewis have already noted: if every permutation of a given faith tradition is catered to by a specialized sub-genre of fiction, then fiction's capacity to provide a gateway to unfamiliar worlds that furnish different perspectives to those held by the reader is effaced. This prognostication may appear excessively pessimistic; the other side of the story of specialization is that conveyed by the example of AACM, which appeals powerfully to readers who until recently had almost no representation in an ethnocentric marketplace. The recent developments in religious fiction reveal a profound democratizing impulse, even as the sense of belonging that it fosters can inadvertently reinforce divisions between groups rather than heal them.

In terms of the academic study of the phenomenon, the question of what gets included and excluded from the category of "religious literature" will also surely remain a pressing problem and, as literary scholars become increasingly concerned with the religious inflections of putatively secular narratives (see Hungerford 2010; Fessenden 2007; McClure 2007), will perhaps become even more so. Even novels written by authors who deny the existence of God cannot be excluded from the realm of the religious: Arthur Bradley and Andrew Tate contend that the philosophical and ontological positions adopted by "New Atheist" writers and thinkers such as Martin Amis, Ian McEwen, Philip Pullman, and Salman Rushdie evince a transcendent "faith in fiction" that undercuts New Atheism's privileging of hard rationalism, empiricism, and skepticism (Bradley and Tate 2010). If the fiction of avowed atheists can be read "religiously," then it might follow that the designation of religious fiction obscures more than it illuminates. Scholars are instead concerned with the porous and nebulous nature of the boundary that separates the religious and the secular, the sacred and the profane. Even a novel that appears unproblematically "religious" to a secular reader, such as *The Shack*, can, in another frame of reference, be deemed heterodox and heretical. Whatever the academic debates, the slipperiness of religion as a category has not hindered the progress of religious literature: on the contrary, it has served to energize and stimulate its production. It is precisely the diversity and malleability of American religious belief, its contents, and discontents that have engendered the extraordinarily dynamic popular literary culture we see today.

Notes

* I would like to thank Jo Metcalf for her helpful comments on this chapter.
1 I do not italicize Left Behind in order to differentiate the whole series from the first novel in the sequence, also titled *Left Behind*. I follow Crawford Gribben and other commentators in this formulation.
2 One author in Blodgett's study who does engage with racial discrimination is Boedie Thoene, whose historical novels address slavery, Klan violence, and anti-Semitism. Kathleen Karr's *The Promised Land* (1993) depicts the disenfranchisement of Native Americans.
3 The necessarily brief discussions of African-American Christian fiction and popular Islamic fiction presented here are among the first to appear in the scholarship. These are rich and untapped genres that no doubt will be subject to more extensive investigations in future.
4 Jerry B. Jenkins and Tim LaHaye's Left Behind: The Kids series comprises 40 novels pub-lished between 1998 and 2004; the Left Behind videogame, *Eternal Forces*, was released in 2006, followed by sequels *Left Behind: Tribulation Forces* (2010), *Left Behind 3: Rise of the Antichrist* (2010) and *Left Behind: World at War* (2011).
5 At the time of writing, *The Shack* ranked #150 on the *USA Today* list of best-selling books (USA Today.com 2013).
6 The problematic racial stereotypes evoked by Young's depiction of Jesus have not gone unnoticed by more thoughtful commentators on *The Shack*. In the novel, Jesus tells Mack:

"I am Jewish, you know. My grandfather on my mother's side had a big nose. In fact, most of the men on my mom's side had big noses" (113). The novel posits this racial essentialism uncritically; however, while some internet reviewers identify such stereotypes as emanating "straight from anti-Semitic writings" (Sherwood 2012), the majority of commentators do not appear to find such depictions troubling or, at least, worthy of remark (see "RodtRDH" 2011).

7 The quote appears on the book's back cover.

8 Links to a list of poetry and fiction contest winners can be found on the IWA Web site (www.islamicwritersalliance.net/home.html).

9 The specific comment was made by "zahed" (a reader), and posted at 7:16 a.m. on 20 March 2007.

Works cited

Adams, E. (2011) *Jesus Was Thin so You Can Be Thin too: Seventh-day Adventist Edition*, Bloomington, IN: iUniverse.

Bader, C., K. Dougherty, P. Froese, B. Johnson, F.C. Mencken, J.Z. Park, and R. Stark (2006) *American Piety in the 21st Century: New Insights to the Depth and Complexity of Religion in the US*, Waco, TX: Baylor Institute for Studies of Religion.

Balmer, R. (1993) *Mine Eyes Have Seen the Glory: A Journey into the Evangelical Subculture in America*, New York: Oxford University Press.

Barna Group (2001) "Different groups follow Harry Potter, Left Behind and Jabez," (October 22). Online. Available: www.barna.org/barna-update/article/5-barna-update/61-different-groups-follow-harry-potter-left-behind-and-jabez (accessed 21 November 2012).

Baxley, C.R. (dir.) (2005) *Left Behind: World at War*.

Bellah, R.N., R. Madsen, W.M. Sullivan, A. Swindler, and S.M. Tipton (1996) *Habits of the Heart: Individualism and Commitment in American Life*, 2nd edn, Berkeley, CA: University of California Press.

Blodgett, J. (1997) *Protestant Evangelical Literary Culture and Contemporary Society*, Westport, CT: Greenwood Press.

Boyer, P. (1992) *When Time Shall Be no More: Prophecy Belief in Modern American Culture*, Cambridge, MA: Belknap Press.

Bradley, A. and A. Tate (2010) *The New Atheist Novel: Fiction, Philosophy and Polemic after 9/11*, London: Continuum.

Brooks, W. and L. Savage (2009) "Critiques and controversies of Street Literature: a formidable literary genre," *ALAN Review* 36, 2 (Winter): 48–55.

Byle, A. (2012) "Helping librarians crack the cover," *Publishers Weekly* (May 21): S4–S5.

Chapman, J. (2013) *Plotting Apocalypse: Reading, Agency, and Identity in the Left Behind Series*, Jackson, MS: University Press of Mississippi.

Chidester, D. (2005) *Authentic Fakes: Religion and American Popular Culture*, Berkeley, CA: University of California Press.

Colbert, D. (2002) *What Would Jesus Eat? The Ultimate Program for Eating Well, Feeling Great, and Living Longer*, Nashville, TN: Thomas Nelson.

Corcoran, B. (dir.) (2002) *Left Behind II: Tribulation Force*.

Crohn, J., H.J. Markman, S.L. Blumberg, and J.R. Levine (2001) *Beyond the Chuppah: A Jewish Guide to Happy Marriages*, San Francisco, CA: Jossey-Bass.

Diamond, S. (1990) *Spiritual Warfare: The Politics of the Christian Right*, Montreal: Black Rose Books.

Elliott, B. (2008) "What's so bad about 'The Shack?'" CBN.com (n.d.). Online. Available: www.cbn.com/entertainment/books/ElliottB_TheShack.aspx (accessed 2 January 2013).

Elliott, T. (2012) "Exclusive interview with best selling author WM Paul Young," *Life on Overflow* (November 23). Online. Available: http://lifeonoverflow.com/2012/11/23/exclusive-interview-with-best-selling-author-wm-paul-young/ (accessed 8 January 2013).

Fessenden, T. (2007) *Culture and Redemption: Religion, the Secular, and American Literature*, Princeton, NJ: Princeton University Press.

Fish, S. (1980) *Is There a Text in This Class? The Authority of Interpretive Communities*, Cambridge, MA: Harvard University Press.

Forbes, B.D. (2004) "How popular are the *Left Behind* books … and why? A discussion of popular culture," in B.D. Forbes and J.H. Kilde (eds), *Rapture, Revelation and the* Left Behind *Series*, New York: Palgrave MacMillan, 5–33.

Frykholm, A. (2004) *Rapture Culture: Left Behind in Evangelical America*, Oxford: Oxford University Press.

Gandolfo, A. (2007) *Faith in Fiction: Christian Literature in America Today*, Westport, CT: Praeger.

Gribben, C. (2004) "Rapture fictions and the changing evangelical tradition," *Literature and Theology* 18, 1 (March): 77–94.

——(2009) *Writing the Rapture: Prophecy Fiction in Evangelical America*, Oxford: Oxford University Press.

Grossman, C.L. (2008) "'The Shack' opens doors, but critics call book 'scripturally incorrect,' 'subversive,'" *USA Today* (May 29): D1.

Grudem, W. (2003) *Business for the Glory of God: The Bible's Teaching on the Moral Goodness of Business*, Wheaton, IL: Crossway.

Gunn, G. (1987) *The Culture of Criticism and the Criticism of Culture*, New York: Oxford University Press.

Haddad, Y.Y, J.I. Smith, and K.M. Moore (2006) *Muslim Women in America: The Challenge of Islamic Identity Today*, New York: Oxford University Press.

Hungerford, A. (2010) *Postmodern Belief: American Literature and Religion since 1960*, Princeton, NJ: Princeton University Press.

Hunter, J.D. (1983) *American Evangelicalism: Conservative Religion and the Quandary of Modernity*, New Brunswick, NJ: Rutgers University Press.

IslamicFictionBooks.com (n.d.a) "As salaam'Alaykum and welcome to Islamic fiction books." Online. Available: www.islamicfictionbooks.com/index.html (accessed 3 January 2013).

——(n.d.b) "What Muslim readers say about Islamic fiction books." Online. Available: www.islamicfictionbooks.com/muslimreaderssay.html (accessed 3 January 2013).

IslamicWritersAlliance.net (2005) "Islamic fiction: defining Islamic fiction." Online. Available: www.islamicwritersalliance.net/islamicfictionbooks.html (accessed 7 January 2013).

Juwayriyah, U. (2007) *The Size of a Mustard Seed*, Tempe, AZ: Muslim Writers Publishing.

Keller, B. (2008) "*The Shack* is NOT a Christian novel, but simply more New Age heresy," LivePrayer.com (October 7). Online. Available: http://liveprayer.com/ddarchive3.cfm?id=3473 (accessed 3 January 2013).

Kiesling, A. (2008) "African-American market comes of age," *Publishers Weekly* (September 1): S2–S5.

Kreider, G.R. (n.d.) "A review of The Shack: *Where Tragedy Confronts Eternity*," *Insight for Living*. Online. Available: www.insight.org/library/articles/review/the-shack.html (accessed 2 January 2013).

LaHaye, T. and J. Jenkins (1995) *Left Behind: A Novel of the Earth's Last Days*, Wheaton: Tyndale House.

——(1996) *Tribulation Force: The Continuing Drama of Those Left Behind*, Wheaton: Tyndale House.

——(2000) *The Indwelling: The Beast Takes Possession*, Wheaton: Tyndale House.

Lewis, S.L. (2007) *My Soul Cries Out*, Deer Park, NY: Urban Christian.

——(2009) "Bridging the multicultural gap," *Christian Fiction Online Magazine* (January). Online. Available: http://christianfictiononlinemagazine.com/jan-09-best_multicultural.html (accessed 5 January 2013).

Liebman, R.C. and R. Wuthnow (eds) (1982) *The New Christian Right: Mobilization and Legitimation*, Hawthorne, NY: Aldine Press.

Lienesch, M. (1993) *Redeeming America: Piety and Politics in the New Christian Right*, Chapel Hill, NC: University of North Carolina Press.

McAlister, M. (2003) "Prophecy, politics and the popular: the *Left Behind* series and Christian Fundamentalism's new world order," *South Atlantic Quarterly* 102, 4 (Fall): 773–98.

McClure, J. (2007) *Partial Faiths: Postsecular Fiction in the Age of Pynchon and Morrison*, Athens, GA: University of Georgia Press.

McDannell, C. (1998) *Material Christianity: Religion and Popular Culture in America*, New Haven, CT: Yale University Press.

MacDonald, G.J. (2012) "In digital Christian fiction, pluses and perils," *Publishers Weekly* (February 13): S12–S13.

Marsden, G.M. (2006) *Fundamentalism and American Culture*, 2nd edn, New York: Oxford University Press.

Maynard, P. and A. Maynard (2010) *The Jesus Diet: An Easy Way for Christians to Lose Weight*, Bloomington, IN: CrossBooks.

Mazur, E.M. and K. McCarthy (eds) (2001) *God in the Details: American Religion in Popular Culture*, New York: Routledge.

Mogahed, Y. (2012) *Reclaim Your Heart*, San Clemente, CA: FB Publishing.

Mohler, A. (2008) *The Albert Mohler Program* (November 4). Online. Available: www.sbts.edu/media/audio/totl/2008/AMP_04_11_2008.mp3 (accessed 2 January 2013).

Mort, J. (2002) *Christian Fiction: A Guide to the Genre*, Greenwood, CO: Libraries Unlimited.

Nelson, M.Z. (2011) "Christian fiction going strong," *PublishersWeekly.com* (July 20). Online. Available: www.publishersweekly.com/pw/by-topic/industry-news/religion/article/48057-christian-fiction-going-strong.html (accessed 27 January 2013).

Quraishi, A. (2012) "Noor Kids: must-have books for children," *Illume Magazine* (August 27). Online. Available: www.illumemagazine.com/zine/articleDetail.php?Noor-Kids-Books-for-Muslim-Kids-14079 (accessed 3 January 2013).

Radosh, D. (2008) *Rapture Ready! Adventures in the Parallel Universe of Christian Pop Culture*, New York: Scribner.

Ralph, P. and J. Larue (2005) "Christian fiction labels: help or hindrance?" *American Libraries* 36, 11: 50–51.

"RodtRDH" (aka "Rod the Rogue Demon Hunter") (2011) "Sex in the Trinity: Wm. Paul Young's The Shack, p2/6," PoliticalJesus.com (June 5). Online. Available: http://politicaljesus.com/2011/06/05/sex-in-the-trinity-wm-paul-youngs-the-shack-2/ (accessed 13 February 2013).

Sack, K. (2001) "Apocalyptic theology revitalized by attacks," *New York Times* (November 23): A33.

Sanders, J. (2011) "Christian fiction for African-Americans: a dilemma," *Publishers Weekly* (December 12): 24.

Sarin, V. (dir.) (2000) *Left Behind: The Movie*.

Sherwood, R. (2012) "Analysis of 'The Shack'; by William P. Young: or, why 'The Shack' sucks, pt. 2," *Yahoo Voices* (2 April). Online. Available: http://voices.yahoo.com/analysis-shack-william-p-young-11186214.html?cat=38 (accessed 13 February 2013).

Shuck, G.W. (2005) *Marks of the Beast: The* Left Behind *Novels and the Struggle for Evangelical Identity*, New York: New York University Press.

Smith, W. (2008) "*The Shack* and its New Age leaven: God in everything?" *Herescope* (June 21). Online. Available: http://herescope.blogspot.co.uk/2008/06/shack-its-new-age-leaven.html (accessed 2 January 2013).

Solomon, L.D. (2004) *Evangelical Christian Executives: A New Model for Business Corporations*, Piscataway, NJ: Transaction Publishers.

Taylor, P. (2006) "Call for English language Islamic fiction," *Bureau of Petitions* (July 21). Online. Available: www.petitionspot.com/petitions/islamicfiction (accessed 20 January 2013).

USAToday.com (2013) "Best-selling books." Online. Available: http://books.usatoday.com/list/search-results?t=title&k=the+shack (accessed 2 January 2013).

Van Duzer, J. (2010) *Why Business Matters to God (And What Still Needs to Be Fixed)*, Downers Grove, IL: IVP Academic.

Whitaker, B. (2007) "Punk Muslims," *Guardian* [London] (March 19). Online. Available: www.guardian.co.uk/commentisfree/2007/mar/19/sexdrugsanprayer (accessed 4 January 2013).

Wilcox, C. (1992) *God's Warriors: The Christian Right in Twentieth-Century America*, Baltimore, MD: The Johns Hopkins University Press.

Wooding, G. (2010) "New book 'Burning Down "The Shack"' exposes great deception lurking in church's blindside," *Christian News Wire* (May 6). Online. Available: www.christian newswire.com/news/6057113838.html (accessed 2 January 2013).

Young, W.P. (2008) *The Shack*, London: Hodder & Stoughton.

Zwier, R. (1982) *Born-Again Politics: The New Christian Right in America*, Westmont, IL: InterVarsity Press.

12
COMICS/GRAPHIC NOVELS

Christine Hoff Kraemer and A. David Lewis

The past seven years have seen a rush of scholarship on the subject of religion and comic books. Comics already had an established place in popular culture studies, partly because of the increasing recognition of comics as a sophisticated artistic medium and partly because of the importance of the superhero genre, which has offered scholars powerful insights into American history and culture (especially regarding the World War II and post-war periods). The recent explosion of religion and comics scholarship, however, seems to recognize that comics do not merely reflect the culture they inhabit. Comics are instead a place where culture is being *created*: tools in the hands of religious and spiritually-oriented people for spreading their ideologies, educating readers in their practices, and at times, even seeking participants for their rituals or groups. For traditional religious groups, comics have long been used for educational and missionary purposes, in the belief that a medium that combines text with visuals is more accessible than text alone. But contemporary comics have also attracted a number of creators who are passionate about their religion or spirituality, or about their opposition to organized religion. For some creators, concerns about religion are expressed through satire of religious imagery and institutions. For others, however, comics are a vehicle for theologically innovative thought. Particularly for alternative religious groups and for the growing body of individuals who consider themselves "spiritual but not religious," theologically experimental comics can offer springboards for thought and discussion about religion, and even opportunities for spiritual experiences.

Comics need not be explicitly theological to be implicated in readers' religious thought and practice. Scholars have observed that pop culture consumption and participation in fandom can perform a function that simulates religion. Adam Possamai has coined the term "hyper-real religion" for this phenomenon. As he explains,

> Hyper-real religion refers to a simulacrum of a religion, created out of, or in symbiosis with, popular culture, which provides inspiration for believers/ consumers. The most commonly known twenty-first century examples are Jediism (from the *Star Wars* films) and Matrixism (from the *Matrix* films). However, this phenomenon is not limited to full-blown cases and can also involve people being religiously inspired by popular culture[.]
>
> (Possamai 2012: 2)

Drawing on the work of Jean Baudrillard, Possamai sees popular culture as being dominated by signs whose meanings are derived only from their relations to each other, rather than from some independently existing reality. A hyper-real religion is one in which there is no perceived ground or origin of meaning outside of culture. The narratives of popular culture, therefore, are up for grabs to be used by anyone seeking to create meaning. Comics fandom may constitute a hyper-real religion in that it provides ritual practices, community, mythological narratives, and beliefs (though perhaps not a systematic theology) to comics readers.[1] Although comics fans are most likely to understand their consumption of comics as a secular activity, in many ways fandom serves needs once tended by mainline churches.

As a form of sequential art, the comic book medium has specific advantages when communicating religious ideas.

Accessibility. Illustrated narratives have been used around the world to inspire devotion and teach morality, with stained glass cathedral windows depicting the lives of Jesus and the saints being the best-known example of this art form in the West (McCloud 2012 [1993]: 10–17; Orcutt 2010: 96). Sequential art has often been used to educate an illiterate or semi-literate population in the religious narratives of their culture (or, in the case of pre-literate cultures, sequential art was a primary method for recording narratives). This accessibility is one of comics' advantages for communicating ideas. Although sequential art requires a certain level of visual literacy to interpret—and contemporary comics can be quite sophisticated in the way they visually convey meaning—text-image hybrids are widely thought to be easier to understand than text alone.

Emotional engagement. Viewer-response theory provides a framework for understanding the powerful emotional impact that religious sequential art can have. Scholars such as David Freedberg and David Morgan have observed the intense engagement that viewers often have with images, which may be perceived as having the power to induce religious passion—or, more dangerously, passions of an erotic kind. Freedberg describes a cross-cultural history of people attempting to engage images devotionally, erotically, and sometimes violently (Freedberg 1989: 2–8). In contemporary culture, this belief in the power of images has often emerged in censorship movements, some of which have been directed against comics. In the 1950s, for example, psychologist Fredric Wertham's vitriolic arguments for the negative impact of comic books on children's cognitive skills and social mores convinced the public that comics were a dangerous influence. Wertham's campaign and publications led to the establishment of the Comics Code Authority (CCA), a stricture that the budding industry imposed on itself, but which stifled the creativity of the American comics market for the next several decades (Daniels 1971: 83–90; see also Nyberg 1998). The relationship between the viewing of violent images and actual violence is still unclear, and the relationship between sexual images and violence is even more in doubt. However, the belief that images have a visceral impact on the viewer that is far more invasive than text is common in Western culture.

Participation. Because sequential images give an impression of movement and therefore life, they have an immersive or participatory quality. The sense that images are provocative, potentially reaching out to produce a bodily response in the viewer, is responsible for the emotional reactions they have produced in individuals, and these reactions can be positive as well as negative. For example, Morgan suggests that the sense of personal relationship that images can offer to the viewer is responsible for their religious impact (Morgan 1998: 23–24). This effect is most pronounced with anthropomorphic images, such as images of deities or saints. The frequency of "breaking the fourth wall" in religiously and spiritually oriented comics can be read as evidence of creators' attempts to personally contact the reader through sequential art. Comics creators may have characters speak directly to the reader (for example, see Kraemer and Winslade 2010: 283–87), or encourage the reader to include herself in the narrative through physical participation. As Darby Orcutt describes, one popular Evangelical tract by Jack Chick promotes identification with the main character through the physical act of reading. When the protagonist of the comic begins to read the Chick tract that will save his soul, a pair of thumbs appears on the edges of the page, overlapping the areas where the reader's thumbs most likely rest (Orcutt 2010: 101). Through this technique, Chick coaxes the reader to take the images of conversion from the comic narrative and make them part of his own reality—to literally become the person being saved.

Comics function religiously in a way that has considerable overlap with film. Both sometimes express traditional religious narratives and values in order to inspire or reinforce an existing religious practice. In both film and comics, images create opportunities for emotional engagement and can provide a sense of immersion or participation. Both mediums convey narratives that function as modern myths, providing secular and religious audiences with ideological stories that help them to articulate ethical positions and form individual and collective identities. Film and comics also share an overlapping community of consumers, some of whom gather at festivals or conventions for ongoing discussions of their favored works. There are some obvious differences between the two, however. Comics readers do not experience the *communitas* that John Lyden assigns to the film experience (Lyden 2003: 96–97). If a comic provides an emotional rollercoaster or a spiritual transformation, it is undergone alone, not in a theater where one might share in the cheers or tears of an enthusiastic audience. Isolation is so much a part of the comics-reading experience, in fact, that creator Warren Ellis used the title "Come in Alone" for his column on the medium. Ellis suggests that comics are cut off from the cultural mainstream, and that it is rare to be able to enter into a casual workplace conversation about a comic or hear about a comic on television (Ellis 1999). Enforced isolation can be a strength, forcing the reader to absorb the work "clean," without assumptions about its meaning (or at least, far fewer assumptions than one has when viewing a much-hyped film). The nature of comics fandom has changed since the time of Ellis's writing, however. In an era where communications technology is ubiquitous, the conversation of kindred spirits is never more than a click away; some comics fans are engaged in community discussion about their favorite medium on a daily basis. Nevertheless, the act of reading itself remains a solitary pursuit.

Although film and comics both have an immersive, participatory aspect, in the actual act of consumption, comics reading is arguably the more active of the two.[2] During home viewing, film viewers have the ability to pause, fast forward, or rewind the film according to their interest. Once a film starts rolling, however, it usually plays through to the end regardless of whether the viewer is raptly attentive, distracted by another activity, or fast asleep. Comics require the active interpretation of the reader, not just in the physical act of turning the pages, but also in providing the movement of time. As seminal comics theorist Scott McCloud observes, in comics, space and time are equivalent; the passage of time in the narrative is experienced through the movement of the reader's eyes over the page (McCloud 2012: 94–117). Further, the reader must fill in the gaps in action in the "gutters," the spaces between panels. In McCloud's well-known example, a two-panel sequence shows an angry figure raising an axe over another character, then a night-time cityscape torn by a scream. The sequence is easily interpreted as portraying a murder (McCloud 2012: 68). Yet, explains McCloud, the murder is never explicitly shown—the meaning of the sequence is provided by the reader. One might even argue that without the reader to fill in the gaps in action, no action occurs; the comic positions the reader to supply the murder herself. As comics theorist Robert Fletcher remarks, the comics medium "calls attention to its fictionality by displaying its narrative seams," constantly implicating the reader in the act of interpretation (Fletcher 1998: 381). Whereas film can often appear seamless—a window onto a perfectly rendered otherworld—comics instead call attention to the process of narrative creation.

In *Mutants and Mystics* (2011), religion scholar Jeffrey Kripal points out that the self-consciousness of the comics medium lends itself to the expression of certain religious and spiritual philosophies. One recurring trope in comics is the notion that reality itself is a narrative being actively written, either by a divine personality, or collectively by all beings in the universe. Kripal sees this narrative as a spiritual opportunity for the reader, a moment to claim the ability to radically self-define:

> This insight into the realization that we are being written matures in the even more stunning idea that we can do something about this, that we can write ourselves anew. … We do not need to be puppets at the mercy of some neurological programmer, or for that matter some faithful believer in the dictates of some authoritarian sky-god. We can become our own authors[.]
>
> (Kripal 2011: 28)

Kripal sees references to reality as narrative in comics—and to comics artists as divine creators—as encouraging belief in this theology (Kripal 2011: 254–91).[3] Additionally, Kripal's observations support the idea that, because the reader provides the mechanism by which time passes in a comic, she is encouraged toward certain insights about time's holistic nature. Kripal quotes major comics creators Alan Moore and Grant Morrison on their experiences of time as unitary and non-linear. The two report a belief that from a particular perspective, all events in time are occurring simultaneously (Kripal 2011: 16, 19). Both authors have attempted to encode this experience into their productions, often using the structure of the comics form to express the point. For example, in one sequence in Moore's *Promethea*, an FBI agent suddenly finds herself outside of time, looking back at her life as a series of static comics panels (Moore et al. 2005: #28). The series also represents time achronologically with circular mandalas and even a Moebius strip (Kraemer and Winslade 2010: 283–86; see also Di Liddo 2009: 95). Comics provide unusual opportunities to gaze simultaneously at multiple moments as if they were a whole (Orcutt 2010: 99).

The study of the unique advantages of the comics medium for portraying religious concepts represents one of the most exciting directions for current religion and comics criticism. Religion scholars wishing to pursue this method will be well served by existing comics studies scholarship, which provides rich resources for visual/ textual analysis (see Harvey 1996; Klock 2002; Cohn 2003; Groensteen 2007; Wolk 2007). At present, much of the scholarship on religion and comics is still directed toward the superhero genre. *Super Heroes: A Modern Mythology* (Reynolds 1994) was the first to address at length the links between superheroes' adventures and myth. Author Richard Reynolds notes how the 1939 narrative tone of Superman's origin mimics that of the King James Bible, and he ties the crucial pieces of the superhero's back-story to that of both Greco-Roman and Christian godhood. *The Gospel According to Superheroes* (Oropeza 2006) and *Up, Up, and Oy Vey!* (Weinstein 2006) employ decidedly Christian and Jewish perspectives on the genre (see also Baskind and Omer-Sherman 2008; Buhle 2008; Kaplan 2008). Something more of an inter-religious and even occult approach to these comics comes in *Our Gods Wear Spandex* (Knowles 2007) and *Superheroes and Gods* (LoCicero 2007). These two works suggest that superheroes are symbols for divine impulses dating back to pre-history. Published that same year, *Disguised as Clark Kent* (Fingeroth 2007) makes a case for the superhero as an empowerment fantasy of disenfranchised, immigrant religious communities, while the rereleased edition of *Holy Superheroes!* (Garrett 2008) claims that it is the visual nature of these superhuman demigods that gives them their cultural potency. More recent publications expand the source and impact of the superhero beyond exclusively Western, monotheistic religions (see McLain 2009; Lewis and Kraemer 2010; Chopra 2011; Morrison 2011; Saunders 2011).

Although the importance of the superhero is undeniable, the dominance of the genre in religion and comics scholarship represents missed opportunities. Some existing pieces of scholarship, however, outline potential growth areas for religion and comics scholarship. *The World of Chick?* (Fowler 2001) and the documentary film *God's Cartoonist* (Kuersteiner 2008) only begin to explore the role of comics in traditional Christian communities, where comics have been used both for missionary work and for education within the group. Kraemer and Lewis's collection *Graven Images* (2010) addresses that gap with articles on comics in Evangelicalism and Catholicism, and expands beyond the common focus on superheroes and Western monotheisms to a variety of independently published comics and non-mainstream religious traditions. *Graven Images* also sketches out how religion and comics scholars might deepen their analyses by focusing not on "religion" as a broad category, but rather on more specific religious or theological issues. The tropes with which comics represent deities, clergy, or the afterlife can tell us a great deal about popular religious culture—and in the hands of the most skilled creators, innovative uses of the comics form can compellingly challenge the religious status quo.

For the remainder of this chapter, we have divided the subject into three sections. In the first, we examine the use of comics by traditional religious groups for educating adherents or potential adherents. Although many Americans are familiar with Bible comics received in Sunday school or the Evangelical tracts used in missionary work, Hindu groups in the United States and India have also published explicitly religious comics for the education of young people, as have Japanese artists with Buddhism and Shinto. The topic of manga (Japanese comics), however, is too large to deal with effectively here. Manga are produced in a significantly different cultural and religious context, in which what appears to be religious practice is nigh universal, but religious belief in the Western sense is relatively rare. Further, manga reading in Japanese culture includes readers of every class, age, and gender; in contrast, comics reading in the USA is by far most popular among single, white, college-educated adult males (Carlson 2007). Since the subject of manga and religion deserves its own article, we will limit ourselves to comics published in English or in English translation for Western markets, focusing particularly on comics that are produced by or for religiously affiliated institutions.

In the second section, we engage comics that could be said to appropriate religious content rather than necessarily be driven by it. Although these comics, and the activity of comics reading, are generally understood as secular by consumers, they are an important arena in which readers engage in considerations of ethics, meaning, and values. In particular, superhero comics are examined for their use of religious material. Superhero comics is the genre of comics most widely consumed, and they have gained even greater exposure through the recent deluge of television and film adaptations, as have a variety of independent comics titles in other genres. However, these purportedly secular comics may also serve as the apparatus through which ideas about the supernatural and other meaning-creating myths are bubbling to the surface, bypassing—and, indeed, criticizing—institutionalized religion while addressing their ideological concerns.

Finally, our third section engages those publishers and artists who are self-consciously creating idea-driven and theologically innovative comics. These experimentally minded creators are among the most likely to innovate with the comics form, and it is here that the formal potential of comics for spiritual exploration can be seen most clearly. Although many of these creators resist the term "religious" for their comics, they often accept the terms "spiritual," "philosophical," or sometimes "magical" for their comics work. Accordingly, such comics are popular among those who consider themselves "spiritual but not religious," as well as among readers identifying with various new religious movements.

Explicitly religious comics in historical context

A large number of comic books predate the 1938 publication of *Action Comics* #1, the debut of Superman, but they have retroactively been assigned the status of "Platinum Age" titles because Superman's arrival began the so-called "Golden Age."[4] Though the word *superhero* was already in existence, prior to Superman it did not yet refer to a genre of stories. While Superman, in the words of comics scholars Randy Duncan and Matt J. Smith, "was and still is the purest embodiment of the superhero," much of what constituted his story can be found in earlier pulp and mythic American heroes, such as Natty Bumpo and Daniel Boone (Duncan and Smith 2009: 218); Danny Fingeroth additionally names Doc Savage, The Shadow, and Ka-Zaras as the pulp heroes who prefigured Superman and Batman (Fingeroth 2004: 16). Creators copied the Golden Age mold of Superman and, shortly thereafter, Batman, and the proliferation of characters gradually led to the genre's cohesion. As publishers developed superheroes of every variation, however, the eventual glut led to a falling-off of publication after World War II (Wright 2009: 50; Sabin 1996: 66).

Before the implementation of the Wertham-triggered Comic Code Authority (CCA) in 1954, only the Superman, Batman, and Wonder Woman titles had remained in continual publication (Hendrix 2007; Jourdain 2010). Following the CCA's crackdown on the more popular genres of the time, particularly crime and horror, superheroes resurged, starting with a re-imagining of the Flash. These newer models of the heroes were customized to fit the CCA's conventional standards (Nyberg 1998: 136, 158–59). As more of these code-sanctioned characters came back into print, they were often teamed together for greater sales. This practice led Martin Goodman, publisher of upstart Marvel Comics (née Timely Comics, Atlas Comics), to solicit the 1961 inaugural issue of the superhero team comic *Fantastic Four* from Stan Lee. The new title offered revolutionary feet-of-clay superheroes, setting off the supposed "Silver Age" (Nyberg 1998: 137).[5] By the "Bronze Age" of the 1980s, the cracks in the superheroes' moral façades would crumble to reveal dark anti-heroes afflicted with major psychological distress, pioneered by Alan Moore's *Watchmen* and Frank Miller's *Batman: The Dark Knight Returns* (Versaci 2007: 9–10). This metamorphosis may also have been influenced by the underground "commix" movement of the 1970s, where creators like R. Crumb and Art Spiegelman engaged in unflinching satire, edgy cultural commentary, and sometimes outright pornography beyond the reach of mainstream publishers.

The mental collapse of superhero characters was echoed by the genre's narrative collapse: as Geoff Klock puts it, "After sixty years and hundreds of titles, the DC Universe, for example, stops making sense" (Klock 2002: 125). Superheroes had moved from refreshingly imperfect in the early 1960s to disturbingly grim by the late 1980s. Moore and Miller's deconstruction of the superhero temporarily synched the characters to the new era, but as other creators rushed to imitate their innovations, the genre itself became destabilized, necessitating yet another paradigm shift (Klock 2002: 39). One could tie the build-up to the early 1990s recession—and the growing bubble in the comics market—to this trend: an over-juicing of the superhero. In the 1990s, characters with unwieldy back-stories were streamlined and rebooted with the latest superhero sensibilities, and the speculation market in comics finally fell. The as-yet-unnamed present period has featured not only a return to more inspired superhero fare but also the resurgence of other genres, particularly autobiographical memoir.

Across these would-be ages, various creators and organizations have engaged the medium to serve religious communities. Much scholarly ink has already been spilled on the largely Jewish make-up of the early American comic book publishing industry. These artists include the creators of Superman: Jerry Siegel and Joe Shuster; the creator of the Spirit and early proponent of the graphic novel: Will Eisner; the creator of Batman: Bob Kane (with Bill Finger); and the creators of Fantastic Four, X-Men, and Iron Man: Stan Lee (Stan Lieber) and Jack Kirby (Jacob Kurtzberg).

Since that era, a number of other notable Jewish creators have made their mark in the field, among them Stan Goldberg (*Archie*), William Gaines (*MAD*), Art Spiegelman (*RAW*), Harvey Pekar (*American Splendor*), Joe Kubert (*Sgt. Rock*), Trina Robbins (*Wimmen's Comix*), Howard Chaykin (*American Flagg!*), and Peter David (*The Incredible Hulk*). Although these men (and very few women) were ostensibly not producing these works with the goal of Jewish education in mind, many scholars have pointed out the noticeable impact of Jewish religion and culture on the comics industry (Buhle 2008; Fingeroth 2007; Kaplan 2008; Weinstein 2006).

American Christian groups seemed initially reticent to make full use of comics during the Golden Age (Netzler 2010: 219–21). This uneasiness has long since been overcome, however, not only by Jack Chick but also by the Community Comics group of Christian creators, the PowerMark Adventure series from the Assemblies of God ministries, and the Zondervan Publishing's Z Graphic Novels imprint. Additionally, the Christian scriptures have been graphically interpreted dozens of times, and include *The Comic Book Bible* (1995), *The Illustrated Bible: Complete New Testament* (1997), *The Picture Bible* (1998), *The Lion Graphic Bible: The Whole Story from Genesis to Revelation* (2004), and *The Manga Bible* (2008), as well as more innovative and deliberately interpretive adaptations such as Steve Ross's *Marked* (2005) and *Blinded* (2008). Portions of the Hebrew Bible have also been turned into graphic novels, such as *Samson: Judge of Israel* (2002), *Testament* (2003), *Daniel: Prophet of Dreams* (2006), and *Megillat Esther* (2006). Religious comics also include offerings from creators of minority and non-Western faiths. Most popularly known for his superhero work on *X-Statix*, Mike Allred has been producing *The Golden Plates*, a comic book account of the Book of Mormon, ongoing since 2004. Islamic English-language works have made their way into the US market courtesy of the Egypt-based AK Comics and Dr. Naif Al-Mutawa's Teshkeel Comics, and stateside creators such as G. Willow Wilson (*Cairo*, 2008) and Toufic El Rassi (*Arab in America*, 2008) have also engaged Muslim themes. In the area of Eastern religions, Osamu Tezuka's eight-volume story of *Buddha* has been translated from its original Japanese into English by publisher Vertical (2006–7), while Virgin Comics has released lavishly illustrated tales of Hindu gods and goddesses as the series *India Authentic* (2010).

Although faith-based comics are a well-established niche in the comics industry, little research has been undertaken to poll comics readers' demographics or personal views, particularly their religious sensibilities. Yet some population of religiously devout comic book readers must exist, given the demonstrable sale of books targeted at religious groups. Specifically, the sales figures for varieties of Christian comics uphold the contention that comic book readers are not solely secular. Documentary maker Kurt Kuersteiner reports that over three-quarters of a billion copies of proselytizing Chick tracts have been distributed worldwide (Kuersteiner 2008), while magazine-turned-Web site *Christian Comics International* lists sales totals extending into millions of copies for some of their titles (Christian Comics International n.d.). In research surveys of religious populations, reading habits and their potential impact on the individuals reporting are rarely assessed. Over the last several years, the Pew Research Center has released several reports on religious knowledge and affiliation among younger Americans. Though none of these track reading or its impacts, the reports do suggest that the newest generation of single, college-educated adults—demographics that overlap with those of comic book readers—are less affiliated with particular faiths and less likely to attend services, yet more likely than their elders to believe in interactions with the deceased, multiplicity in the interpretation of scripture (Pew Research Center 2010a), and a mixture of traditionally Eastern and New Age ideas (Pew Research Center 2009). Combine these trends with religious knowledge being tied to individual levels of education (Pew Research Center 2010b), and a likely relationship between comics readers and the rising generation of religious practitioners, mainstream Christian or otherwise, emerges.

Secular comics and appropriation of the religious

Not all of the religious material that appears in comics is employed for religious purposes. In fact, it is common for creators to appropriate religious narratives and symbolism for provocative narrative content rather than for their theological or ethical messages. For instance, the small press Archaia Entertainment has released several works among its other fantasy and genre titles that re-read the Bible as a literary document and a source of rich mythology: *The Lone and Level Sands* (2009), a telling of Exodus from the Egyptian royal family's point of view; *The Secret History* (2010), the story of ageless immortals living through biblical into modern history; and *Some New Kind of Slaughter* (2010), a cross-cultural compilation of flood myths. The publisher has also produced titles based on Greek mythology, *Hybrid Bastards* (2010), and Mayan and Aztec apocalyptic lore, *The Long Count* (2007–9). Similarly, Image Comics features several series that employ religious content primarily for known, pre-established characters and themes, and only secondarily (and often belatedly) for spiritual commentary (e.g., the 1990s–2000s' *Proposition Player*, *Spawn*, and *Strange Girl*).

Some comics also utilize religious material for satirical or irreverently sacrilegious stabs at faith. Take, for instance, Robert Kirkman and Tony Moore's series *Battle Pope* (2006–7), which titillates readers with sexual promiscuity, obscene language, vulgar depictions of both Jesus and Mary, and an apostatic papacy. In the comic, a highly heretical Pope Oswald and his inept sidekick Jesus are left behind after the Rapture to defend the less-than-virtuous from demons. The Rapture is also the setting for Jim Munroe and Salgood Sam's *Therefore, Repent!* (2008), a graphic novel that originally appears to be faithfully aligned with the principles of Christian apocalypse but then sharply deviates, suggesting the whole catastrophic affair is of extraterrestrial origin. What had been an authentic Pre-Tribulationist snapshot morphs into a New Age exploration of how the Christian mythos is imprisoning the planet. In a similar reversal, Garth Ennis and Jacen Burrows's *Chronicles of Wormwood* (2003) follows an attempt to thwart Revelation's prophesies by the unlikeliest of protagonists, the Antichrist. Rooting for the spawn of Satan against Satan (and God!) places the reader in a theologically dicey position, especially when the title's hero is accompanied by—in a move akin to *Battle Pope*—an addled, reborn Jesus. These titles do not offer alternative theologies or spiritualities, however; instead, religious imagery is appropriated for sensationalistic and often raunchy entertainment, which sells well to the comics industry's base demographic.

Yet comic creators' attraction to religious content and images—even if the corresponding beliefs are simultaneously criticized or jettisoned—is unquestionable, particularly when it comes to the superhero genre. Part of that attraction may come from the easy visual shorthand that faith traditions offer: horns represent the demonic, a cross-legged sitting posture suggests meditative reflection, and crucifixes allude to a morally righteous ultimate sacrifice. Comics theorist Peter Coogan cites the superhero chevron, the personal insignia representing a character, as an essential element of the genre (Coogan 2006: 33), and this iconic use of symbols dovetails with iconic representations of religion: the Jewish star of David, the yin-yang of the Tao, the moon and star of Islam, etc. Comics and religion engage in similar semiotic methods, making the adoption of content from the latter enticing to the former (see also Orcutt 2010: 95–97).

In superhero comics, religion is often conflated with the supernatural, which functions as a conveniently dogma-less, flexible belief system with overt visual/physical results. Plot lines often center on characters drawn from religious narratives. In addition to Neil Gaiman's rendering of Lucifer in *Sandman* (1989–96), the major superhero publishers throughout the 1990s and into the twenty-first century have employed a multitude of Satan-like characters (e.g., Mephisto, Neron, Blaze, Satannish, Hades, Satanus, Malebolgia, Hela, etc.), all of whom occupy a realm not unlike hell. Angels also play roles in the superhero genre, from adversaries (e.g., The Saint of Killers in *Preacher*) to allies (Zauriel in *Justice League of America*) to weapons (The Punisher in *Punisher*, 1998–99). When religious elements appear, they are most often characterized as practices, not as part of a belief system—as sorcery or witchcraft that empowers would-be heroes like Ghost Rider, Zatanna, Jason Blood, The Doctor of *The Authority*, and so forth. These portrayals sometimes reduce the religious to a form of esoteric science: the engagement of tamable energies and laws just beyond modern scientific investigation. Through this brand of over-encompassing inclusion, a Norse god such as Thor can fight alongside a magic practitioner such as the Scarlet Witch, a technological Iron Man, and a devout Catholic such as Dagger, all against an emissary of a monotheistic divinity (e.g., the recurring Marvel universe character The Living Tribunal).

A number of fictional religions populate the superhero genre, operating variously as stand-ins for real-world religions, as politically correct straw men, as easy targets for ideological vilification, and occasionally as serious explorations of organized religion's cultural impact. In the 1970s, Marvel writer-artist Jim Starlin developed a malevolent incarnation of his Christ-figure Adam Warlock into the leader of the Universal Church of Truth (a storyline pursued in both *Strange Tales* and *Warlock*). Using this alternate version of Warlock (now dubbed the Magus), Starlin comments on the errant nature of institutionalized or papal Christianity. Elsewhere in the Marvel universe, the Triune Understanding stands in for the Church of Scientology in Kurt Busiek's *Avengers* run (1998–99). Though responsible for the empowerment of the Avengers' ally Triathlon, the Triune Understanding is linked to a pernicious alien race, making the group's motives dubious. This skepticism toward organized religion is common in Marvel titles, where religion is often the main impetus for alien aggression (for example, that of the shape-shifting Skrulls, whose attempted infiltration of earth is prophesied by their scripture). The DC Comics universe has also developed its own fictional deities and religions, most notably around Jack Kirby's New Gods. Though the New Gods were initially portrayed in the early 1970s as a powerful pantheon of warring aliens, they have taken on much more cosmically divine features in later interpretations. Religious warfare is also a theme in the DC mini-series *The Rann-Thanagar War* (2005) and its sequel, *The Rann-Thanagar Holy War* (2008).

Given the sheer volume of content, imagery, and *faux* zealousness being appropriated by the superhero genre from religious sources, is there some particular, innate relationship between the two? Scholars have suggested that the comic book superhero is tied to religious thought in significant and inextricable ways. Like Kripal, esotericism scholar Chris Knowles argues that the genre's philosophical elements are grounded in over a century of Western occult thought (Knowles 2007). Further, following theories articulated by Northup Frye, Joseph Campbell, and C.G. Jung, a number of contemporary writers have described the superhero genre as a modern expression of cross-culturally valid myths and archetypes (Reynolds 1994; Saunders 2011; Morrison 2011). These mythological approaches to superheroes see the genre as optimistically prefiguring humankind's evolution toward higher levels of consciousness and transcendence of the physical. In short, superhero narratives may frequently overlap with religious ones because they both focus on human potential, potential that cannot be achieved through science alone, but which requires a leap of the immeasurable spirit.

Theologically innovative comics

Of the comics that creators and readers understand as explicitly "spiritual," "philosophical," or alternatively "religious," a significant number were published or rereleased under DC Comics' Vertigo imprint. Advertising its comics as "for mature audiences," Vertigo's titles often contain sexual situations, violence, and profanity, and many are written in the fantasy and horror genres. Although these sensationalistic elements have made Vertigo titles popular among adolescent and college-age readers, Vertigo has also developed a reputation for edgy, sophisticated storytelling and has helped make famous a number of experimental British-born creators. The imprint was the brainchild of editor Karen Berger, who initially recruited Neil Gaiman (*The Sandman*), Peter Milligan (*Shade: The Changing Man*), and Grant Morrison (*Animal Man*, *The Invisibles*) for DC Comics in the late 1980s. Along with Alan Moore (*Saga of the Swamp Thing*) and Garth Ennis (*Preacher*), these creators formed the core of the new imprint at its 1993 launch. The imprint's flagship title *Hellblazer*, featuring a character initially created by Moore in *Swamp Thing*, has been written and drawn by a variety of creators, and in addition to spawning the feature film *Constantine*, it is the only title from Vertigo's initial launch that is still being published (as of 2012).

These titles all engage issues of what theologian Paul Tillich might refer to as ultimate human concern. Gaiman's *Sandman* universe (original series 1989–96) anthropomorphizes primal forces into beings such as Dream and Death, two of the series' main characters. Although *Sandman* takes the reader on a whirlwind tour of world religions and their deities, including visits to the Western heaven and hell, ultimately the human characters provide grounding for the plot and for all-too-realistic considerations of ethics and mortality. Milligan's *Shade* (1990–96) and Morrison's *Invisibles* (1994–2000) explore the nature of the self and of reality, and both are touched by psychedelics culture; Morrison additionally pulls in his studies of Western ceremonial magic, and at one point he even invites readers to join him in an act of auto-erotic group spell-casting to prolong the life of the series (Goodwin 2010: 268–69). Moore's *Swamp Thing* (1984–87) is permeated by a holistic ecotheology that sees all living things as interdependent, and it devotes a significant plot arc to exploring the nature of good and evil. Finding a basis for ethical choices is also a significant issue in *Hellblazer* (1988–present), where main character John Constantine finds himself challenging spirits and gods and performing acts of dubious morality, usually in the hope of achieving a larger good. Ennis's *Preacher* and the later Vertigo title *Lucifer* (a *Sandman* spin-off written by Mike Carey, 2000–2006) put forward humanistic, non-theistic theologies that reject Western notions of God. In *Preacher* (1995–2000), God is assassinated in the name of human freedom; *Lucifer*'s plot arc is more complex and involves the creation of alternate universes and creator deities, one of them originally a young girl. Although *Preacher* ends on a note of infinite possibilities, *Lucifer* goes on to explore the obligations and difficulties of being able to self-create without restriction, as well as the ethical dilemmas inherent in having responsibility for others. Following the success of *Lucifer*, Vertigo also released Carey's series *Crossing Midnight* (2007–8), in which divine forces from Asian traditions clash in a modern-day conflict. In 2010, Vertigo became a creator-owned imprint, and all titles that had originated in the DC universe were moved back to DC, with the exception of *Hellblazer*. Since conflicts over intellectual property rights have driven some of the most cutting-edge writers away from DC (particularly Alan Moore), this move may help to sustain a space for strong, innovative voices in comics under the DC umbrella.

Alan Moore and Grant Morrison are the two creators most famous for producing explicitly spiritual comics while working with a mainstream publisher. Lavishly rendered by artist J.H. Williams, Moore's *Promethea* (1999–2005) is functionally a superhero comic, but its ultimate purpose is to educate its audience in Western esotericism. *Promethea*'s story arcs include explorations of the neoplatonic elements, Tarot (a card-based system of divination), the chakras of the human body, and hermetic *kabbalah*, a metaphysical system derived from Jewish mystical texts. Additionally, the series has a distinctive theological viewpoint that resonates with progressive theologies of the erotic in Christianity and Contemporary Paganism (Kraemer 2012). Although Moore sees *Promethea* as a philosophical and magical text that can be relevant to practitioners of many religions or of none, contemporary Pagans have embraced Moore as one of their own and are using *Promethea* to help educate new practitioners (Kraemer and Winslade 2010: 288). *Promethea* has also been praised for its formal innovations, which include the use of fine-art styles to create immersive, meditative tableaux; visual portrayals of time as non-linear; and even a cut-and-paste activity meant to highlight the way human consciousness creates meaning. Moore plans to continue to develop such magical education tools in *The Moon and Serpent Bumper Book of Magic*, a combination grimoire and activity book forthcoming from Top Shelf Productions.

Moore and Morrison also share a perspective similar to process theology, in that human beings are thought to be actively participating in the ongoing creation of the universe (and may themselves be part of an immanent deity). In his take on Western esotericism, Morrison focuses on the linguistic nature of reality and has his *Invisibles* characters employ occult ritual techniques from his own practice (Goodwin 2010). Morrison also draws parallels between the artistic creative process and the divine process of creation in *Animal Man* (1988–90), as does Moore in *Promethea*. As previously mentioned, Kripal argues that this blurring between reality and narrative is part of a consistent belief system appearing in contemporary pop culture, particularly in works of speculative fiction (Kripal 2011: 26–28). With its connections to progressive theological movements in traditional religions, as well as to gnostic, tantric, and other mystical philosophies from the world's religions, Kripal sees this theology of self-authorship as having enormous significance for the future of religion. While he may overstate the coherence and consistency of these ideas in science fiction, Kripal is right to identify comics as one important site of these theological innovations.

Independent publishers are also producing theologically challenging new works in genres other than science fiction and fantasy. Craig Thompson's autobiographical graphic novel *Blankets* (2003) explores an erotic theology rooted in biblical Christianity. Like Moore and Morrison, Thompson identifies artistic creation with divine creation, and the book makes use of full-page panels that can serve a meditative or devotional function. In *Habibi* (2011), Thompson explores spirituality and eroticism in a dreamlike Islamic culture where the characters find their sexual desires inherently compromised by economic and religious structures. As in *Blankets*, *Habibi* plays with words as being images themselves, as well as with the act of writing and drawing as a way of participating in divine process. Thompson works in black and white, a creative choice that has also been employed effectively by others exploring religion in comics. In Marjane Satrapi's *Persepolis* (2000; English translation 2003, 2004), stark visual contrasts are employed to address the rigidity of Muslim fundamentalism; Moore and Eddie Campbell's *From Hell* (1991–96) uses hauntingly scribbled lines to explore links between sexism, racism, classism, and Western religion in a patriarchical Victorian culture; Steve Ross's *Marked* (2005) retells the book of Mark in a barren, postmodern future; and R. Crumb's *The Book of Genesis* (2009) delivers an uncomfortably literal rendering of the Bible in art reminiscent of religious woodcuts.

Other non-mainstream comics that challenge traditional theologies or attempt to articulate new ones include underground works by Jack Jackson (*God Nose*, 1964) and Justin Green (*Binky Brown Meets the Holy Virgin Mary*, 1972), whose satires of traditional Christianity also open up possibilities for spiritual alternatives; comics great Will Eisner's *A Contract with God* (1978), which explores the struggle to maintain faith in the Jewish tenements of early twentieth-century New York City; anime filmmaker Hayao Miyazaki's *Nausicaä of the Valley of the Winds* (1982–94), which combines Buddhist, Shinto, and messianic themes; Carla Speed McNeil's *Finder* (1996–present), whose "Sin Eater" story arc explores issues of sacrifice and ritual scapegoating; Arvid Nelson's *Rex Mundi* (2003–9), an alternate world Holy Grail quest/murder mystery that portrays a sympathetic Judas; and Linda Medley's *Castle*

Waiting (1996–present), which includes a story arc focusing on a convent of patriarchy-defying bearded nuns. Now marketed toward audiences that see comics as a potentially serious art form, independent works such as these provide substantial material for spiritual thought and discussion. Those in autobiographical or historical genres were some of the first to cross over to mainstream bookstores, as opposed to being exclusively available in comics specialty shops (Art Spiegelman's *Maus* [1980–91], a graphic novel of the Holocaust, being the most famous example). Today, some have become the subject of philosophically oriented discussion groups or are assigned as texts in college classrooms next to novels and films.

Conclusion

As many scholars of religion and comics have already argued, comics have a unique potential to convey religious concepts—and perhaps even religious experiences—through the unusual vehicle of a visual/textual medium that demands reader participation. The distribution of millions of copies of Christian comics suggests that Evangelicals are confident about comics' power to persuade and convert, and those participating in minority or new religious movements have also employed comics to teach their religious beliefs. As scholars bring increased attention to the narratological features of the comics form, the special mechanisms that can make comics religiously persuasive will only become clearer.

But when speaking of comics reading outside of religious communities, the question remains: do comics alter the religious beliefs and practices of those who do not read them in an explicitly religious context? For example, the narrative innovations of the comics form easily support the concept of a multiple rather than unitary self, as A. David Lewis argues (2012); but do these representations cause readers to question traditional Western notions about the self or the soul? Or, can the lushly visual nature of comics also influence an audience to embrace progressive new theologies of the erotic, as Steve Jungkeit suggests (2010: 341–43)? Reader-response analysis of religion and comics would benefit enormously from ethnographic and sociological studies of comics readers. This territory has been pioneered by Matthew Pustz in *Comic Book Culture* (1999), which examines the ritualistic aspects of comics fan culture. Although Pustz does not explicitly identify comics fans as engaging in religious behavior, he portrays the comic shop as a place of pilgrimage, the comics as sacred artifacts, and the fans as "true believers" and custodians of special knowledge. Even as annual comics conventions and online Web communities proliferate, Pustz's observations of the brick-and-mortar spaces continue to hold. The comics medium has a fandom and network of members that could be said to resemble an extended faith community.

Thus far, however, little scholarly research has been undertaken to poll readers' religious demographics. Some comic book companies have privately conducted informal censuses, with only some of their results being made public; as previously mentioned, the data show that the majority of North American comic book readers are male, single, college-educated, and adult aged (Carlson 2007; see also Schenker 2011). Comics readers' personal views and beliefs are almost entirely uncharted territory. However, a semi-formal survey conducted by Lewis in 2005 suggests a

CHRISTINE HOFF KRAEMER AND A. DAVID LEWIS

correlation between committed consumption of the superhero genre and a decreased fear of death (relative to more casual readers of the genre) (Lewis 2006). If confirmed by formal research and compared with religious attitudes among non-comics readers, such findings could teach scholars a great deal about the relationship between comics reading and postmodern religiosity.

Possamai's notion of "hyper-real religion" suggests that popular culture is a source of religious inspiration for an increasingly large percentage of consumers, especially among the younger generation. Comics inhabit an ever more significant place in that culture. Due to greater acceptance of the comics medium as a serious art form, trade paperback "graphic novels" are now enjoying widespread distribution in bookstores and libraries; gone are the days when most comics could only be acquired from specialty shops. Additionally, multiple mainstream (and some independent) films based on comics are being released every year, many to considerable financial success. Under these conditions, comics have the opportunity to reach a much more diverse demographic than ever before—and, potentially, to impact their religious thought. In this context, scholars would do well to focus on comics as an essential area of inquiry in the study of religion and popular culture.

Notes

1 We rely here on Catherine Albanese for a definition of religion (1999: 8–11) and Matthew Pustz's *Comic Book Culture* (1999) for analysis of ritualistic behavior around comics fan culture. Kripal's *Mutants and Mystics* (2011) argues that comics and science fiction *do* have a coherent, consistent theology, a narrative Kripal calls "the Super-Story." Kripal's claims are so broad, and the book attempts to synthesize so many works, that it is difficult to fully evaluate them. Nevertheless, he makes an intriguing case for comics and science fiction as providing a theological context for paranormal experience.
2 Film events that include a performative aspect, such as *Rocky Horror* or *Hedwig* shadow casts, are a notable exception (Kraemer 2008: 119–82).
3 For additional examples of comic book characters confronting their creators, see Tripp 2010: 114–15, Mohapatra 2010: 128–29; for discussions of reality as linguistic and therefore alterable by the magico-religious use of language, see Goodwin 2010: 258–73, Kraemer and Winslade 2010: 283–84.
4 In the parlance of comic book collectors and retailers, particular eras of production are referred to as "ages." This nomenclature focuses heavily on the formation and fortunes of the superhero, and it often leads to the neglect of comics' many other genres (e.g., romance, western, historical, religious, etc.). Nevertheless, no other major system has addressed the inherent weakness of the "ages," and so they will be utilized briefly here to outline the medium's history in the American market.
5 Nyberg also credits the *Batman* television show with cementing this new superhero craze of the 1960s.

Works cited

Albanese, C.L. (1999) *America: Religions and Religion*, 3rd edn, Belmont, CA: Wadsworth Publishing Co.
Baskind, S. and R. Omer-Sherman (eds) (2008) *The Jewish Graphic Novel: Critical Approaches*, New Brunswick, NJ: Rutgers University Press.

Buhle, P. (ed.) (2008) *Jews and American Comics: An Illustrated History of an American Art Form*, New York: The New Press.

Carlson, J.D. (2007) "Superhero comic reader stats," *Comics Worth Reading*. Online. Available: http://comicsworthreading.com/2007/05/10/superhero-comic-reader-stats/ (accessed 18 September 2012).

Chopra, D. (2011) *The Seven Spiritual Laws of Superheroes: Harnessing Our Power to Change the World*, New York: HarperOne.

Christian Comics International (n.d.) "Notable comics of the 20th century." Online. Available: www.christiancomicsinternational.org/series_details.html#anchor-notablecctop-2010 (accessed 18 September 2012).

Cohn, N. (2003) *Early Writings on Visual Language*, San Diego, CA: Emaki Productions.

Coogan, P. (2006) *Superheroes: The Secret Origin of a Genre*, Austin, TX: Monkeybrain Books.

Daniels, L. (1971) *Comix: A History of Comic Books in America*, New York: Bonanza Books.

Di Liddo, A. (2009) *Alan Moore: Comics as Performance, Fiction as Scalpel*, Jackson, MS: University Press of Mississippi.

Duncan, R. and M.J. Smith (2009) *The Power of Comics: History, Form and Culture*, New York: Continuum.

Ellis, W. (1999) "Come in alone" #2, *Comic Book Resources*. Online. Available: www.comicbookresources.com/?page=article&id=13138 (accessed 18 September 2012).

Fingeroth, D. (2004) *Superman on the Couch*, New York: Continuum.

——(2007) *Disguised as Clark Kent: Jews, Comics, and the Creation of the Superhero*, New York: Continuum.

Fletcher, R.P. (1998) "Visual thinking and the picture story in *The History of Henry Esmon*," *PMLA* 113, 3: 379–94.

Fowler, R.B. (2001) *The World of Chick?* San Francisco, CA: Last Gasp.

Freedberg, D. (1989) *The Power of Images: Studies in the History and Theory of Response*, Chicago, IL: University of Chicago Press.

Garrett, G. (2008) *Holy Superheroes!: Exploring the Sacred in Comics, Graphic Novels, and Film, Revised and Expanded Edition*, Louisville, KY: Westminster John Knox Press.

Goodwin, M. (2010) "Conversion to narrative: magic as religious language in Grant Morrison's *Invisibles*," in A.D. Lewis and C.H. Kraemer (eds), *Graven Images: Religion in Comic Books and Graphic Novels*, New York: Continuum, 258–73.

Groensteen, T. (2007) *The System of Comics*, trans. B. Beaty and N. Nguyen, Jackson, MS: University Press of Mississippi.

Harvey, R.C. (1996) *The Art of the Comic Book: An Aesthetic History*, Jackson, MS: University Press of Mississippi.

Hendrix, G. (2007) "Out for justice," *The New York Sun*. Online. Available: www.nysun.com/arts/out-for-justice/67866/ (accessed 18 September 2012).

Jourdain, B. (2010) "75 years of DC Comics!" *The Golden Age of Comic Books*. Online. Available: http://goldenagecomics.org/wordpress/2010/02/19/75-years-of-dc-comics/ (accessed 18 September 2012).

Jungkeit, S. (2010) "Tell-tale visions: the erotic theology of Craig Thompson's *Blankets*," in A.D. Lewis and C.H. Kraemer (eds), *Graven Images: Religion in Comic Books and Graphic Novels*, New York: Continuum, 323–44.

Kaplan, A. (2008) *From Krakow to Krypton: Jews and Comic Books*, Philadelphia, PA: The Jewish Publication Society.

Klock, G. (2002) *How to Read Superhero Comics and Why*, New York: Continuum.

Knowles, C. (2007) *Our Gods Wear Spandex: The Secret History of Comic Book Heroes*, San Francisco, CA: Red Wheel/Weiser.

Kraemer, C.H. (2008) *The Erotic Fringe: Sexual Minorities and Religion in Contemporary American Literature and Film*, unpublished Ph.D. dissertation, Boston University.

——(2012) "The undying fire: erotic love as divine grace in *Promethea*," in T.A. Comer and J.M. Sommers (eds), *Sexual Ideology in the Works of Alan Moore: Critical Essays on the Graphic Novels*, Jefferson, NC: McFarland, 150–62.

Kraemer, C.H. and J.L. Winslade (2010) "The magic circus of the mind: Alan Moore's *Promethea* and the transformation of consciousness through comics," in A.D. Lewis and C.H. Kraemer (eds), *Graven Images: Religion in Comic Books and Graphic Novels*, New York: Continuum, 274–91.

Kripal, J.J. (2011) *Mutants and Mystics: Science Fiction, Superhero Comics, and the Paranormal*, Chicago, IL: University of Chicago Press.

Kuersteiner, K. (dir.) (2008) *God's Cartoonist: The Comic Crusade of Jack Chick*, Tallahassee, FL: Achingly Beautiful Film Company. DVD.

Lewis, A.D. (2006) "The ever-ending battle research project on comics and mortality," *Caption Box*. Online. Available: http://captionbox.net/eeb (accessed 17 November 2014).

——(2012) *The Superhero Afterlife Subgenre and Its Hermeneutics for Selfhood through Character Multiplicity*, unpublished Ph.D. dissertation, Boston University.

Lewis, A.D. and C.H. Kraemer (eds) (2010) *Graven Images: Religion in Comic Books and Graphic Novels*, New York: Continuum.

LoCicero, D. (2007) *Superheroes and Gods: A Comparative Study from Babylonia to Batman*, Jefferson, NC: McFarland & Co., Inc.

Lyden, J.C. (2003) *Film as Religion: Myths, Morals, and Rituals*, New York: New York University Press.

McCloud, S. (2012 [1993]) *Understanding Comics: The Invisible Art*, Northampton: Tundra Publishing.

McLain, K. (2009) *India's Immortal Comic Books: Gods, Kings, and Other Heroes*, Bloomington, IN: Indiana University Press.

Mohapatra, S. (2010) "Echoes of eternity: Hindu reincarnation motifs in superhero comic books," in A.D. Lewis and C.H. Kraemer (eds), *Graven Images: Religion in Comic Books and Graphic Novels*, New York: Continuum, 121–32.

Moore, A. (writer), J.H. Williams (penciller), and M. Gray (inker) (2005) *Promethea, Book Five*, La Jolla, CA: America's Best Comics.

Morgan, D. (1998) *Visual Piety*, Berkeley, CA: University of California Press.

Morrison, G. (2011) *Supergods: What Masked Vigilantes, Miraculous Mutants, and a Sun God from Smallville Can Teach Us about Being Human*, New York: Spiegel & Grau.

Netzler, K. (2010) "A hesitant embrace: comic books and Evangelicals," in A.D. Lewis and C.H. Kraemer (eds), *Graven Images: Religion in Comic Books and Graphic Novels*, New York: Continuum, 218–29.

Nyberg, A.K. (1998) *Seal of Approval*, Jackson, MS: University Press of Mississippi.

Orcutt, D. (2010) "Comics and religion: theoretical connections," in A.D. Lewis and C.H. Kraemer (eds), *Graven Images: Religion in Comic Books and Graphic Novels*, New York: Continuum, 93–106.

Oropeza, B.J. (2006) *The Gospel According to Superheroes*, 2nd edn, New York: Peter Lang Publishing.

Pew Research Center (2009) "Eastern, New Age beliefs widespread," *Pew Forum*. Online. Available: www.pewforum.org/Other-Beliefs-and-Practices/Many-Americans-Mix-Multiple-Faiths.aspx (accessed 18 September 2012).

——(2010a) "Religion among the Millennials," *Pew Forum*. Online. Available: http://pewresearch.org/pubs/1494/millennials-less-religious-in-practice-but-beliefs-quite-traditional (accessed 18 September 2012).

——(2010b) "U.S. religious knowledge survey," *Pew Forum*. Online. Available: http://pewresearch.org/pubs/1745/religious-knowledge-in-america-survey-atheists-agnostics-score-highest (accessed 18 September 2012).

Possamai, A. (2012) "Yoda goes to Glastonbury: an introduction to hyper-real religions," in *Handbook of Hyper-real Religions*, Boston, MA: Brill, 1–22.

Pustz, M.J. (1999) *Comic Book Culture: Fanboys and True Believers*, Jackson, MS: University Press of Mississippi.

Reynolds, R. (1994) *Super Heroes: A Modern Mythology*, Jackson, MS: University Press of Mississippi.

Sabin, R. (1996) *Comics, Comix & Graphic Novels: A History of Comic Art*, New York: Phaidon.

Saunders, B. (2011) *Do the Gods Wear Capes? Spirituality, Fantasy, and Superheroes*, New York: Continuum.

Schenker, B. (2011) "Comic book fans on Facebook – May 3, 2011," *Graphic Policy*. Online. Available: http://graphicpolicy.com/2011/05/03/comic-book-fans-on-facebook-may-32011/ (accessed 18 September 2012).

Tripp, A. (2010) "Killing the graven god: visual representations of the divine in comics," in A.D. Lewis and C.H. Kraemer (eds), *Graven Images: Religion in Comic Books and Graphic Novels*, New York: Continuum, 107–20.

Versaci, R. (2007) *This Book Contains Graphic Language: Comics as Literature*, New York: Continuum.

Weinstein, S. (2006) *Up, Up, and Oy Vey!: How Jewish History, Culture, and Values Shaped the Comic Book Superhero*, Baltimore, MD: Leviathan Press.

Wolk, D. (2007) *Reading Comics: How Graphic Novels Work and What They Mean*, Cambridge, MA: Da Capo.

Wright, N. (2009) *The Classic Era of American Comics*, New York: Prion.

13

FOOD AND COOKING

Benjamin E. Zeller[1]

"I think a lot about food. ... It's been a culinary journey for sure, and also a spiritual one all wrapped up in one." With these words, television food personality Alton Brown, host of the Food Network hit shows *Good Eats* and *Iron Chef America*, penned the opening of his musings on food and spirituality. Brown explained that "I'm always talking about the physics of cooking, but I'm also into the metaphysics of it. A good meal should offer both physical and spiritual nourishment" (2006). That Brown finds spirituality in food should not surprise. Many people do. Cooking, eating, watching programs about cooking on television, journeying on food pilgrimages, and sharing table fellowship centered on eating are all examples of the ways in which contemporary people have found spiritual value in food, cooking, and eating.

The study of religion and popular culture offers many avenues for research and study, a great many of which are considered in the present volume. The preparation, viewing, and consumption of food offer particularly apt areas for this research for several reasons. First, it is truly universal, since everyone eats. Second, making and eating food is both quotidian and completely mundane, but also an arena in which individuals and groups have engaged in extensive work to define and delineate ritual, boundaries, meaning, practice, and beliefs. Among religious movements, consider the cases of Jewish *kashrut*, Muslim halal, Christian feasting and fasting, Mormon food preservation and prohibitions against certain "hot beverages," Buddhist mindful eating, and various religious forms of vegetarianism (Zeller *et al.* 2014). Outside of religion, one finds food in play to define cultural boundaries—the French eat "French food," Finns eat "Finnish food," etc.—as well as individual identity—vegetarianism, veganism, raw food, etc. (Counihan and Van Esterik 1997). Food is central to most civic and religious holidays, and at family gatherings in most cultures. There is much to consider.

This chapter primarily considers the way in which food functions as a form of religion—what I have elsewhere called a "quasi-religion" since it looks quite akin to religion, but does not contain some of the elements traditionally associated with religion, such as gods, spirits, or beliefs about an afterlife (Zeller *et al.* 2014). However, many aspects of religions are present in the ways that people engage food in popular culture. These include rituals, spectacles, texts, conversion and apostasy to new forms of eating, communities, and senses of identity and morality. Within the world of food, religion, and popular culture, several loci present themselves as fruitful avenues for investigation. Here I consider cooking shows, which emphasize religious spectacle, alternative ways of eating such as vegetarianism that become something akin to religion (quasi-religions) to those who adhere to them, and various forms of foods that themselves embody popular religion.

Cooking shows as religious spectacle

In medieval Europe the most important public events, with the exceptions of political and civic events such as coronations, were often religious spectacle (Hanawelt and Reyerson 1994: xviii). These ranged from processions to Advent celebrations to public penitence to saints' days festivals (Hanawelt and Reyerson 1994). Morality plays, passion plays, Pentecost plays, and nativity dramas all served the role that television and film do for today's audiences (Davidson 1988). To take one famous example, the passion play in Oberammergau, Bavaria (in present-day Germany), features a five-hour long performance of not only the passion of Christ, but various biblical scenes from the Hebrew Bible that its authors believed prefigured the story of Christ. Like many spectacles, Oberammergau includes a combination of vivid imagery, physicality, moral teachings, and spiritual value (Shapiro 2000). For most consumers today, television and film have replaced such performances as their source of entertainment. Yet the spectacle remains, particularly when it comes to television cooking shows.

Dramatist and theater theorist Baz Kershaw describes spectacle as the essence of performance. It captures the audience and demands attention. Spectacle engages sensitive topics and uses this engagement to enrapture its viewers.

> Spectacle seems always aimed to produce excessive reaction—the WOW! factor—and at its most effective it touches highly sensitive spots in the changing nature of the human psyche by dealing directly with extremities of power: gods, monarchy, regicide, war, terrorism, catastrophe, apocalypse now.
> (Kershaw 2003: 592)

Some spectacle takes the form of activism and promotes specific commentary on those extremities of power, whereas in other cases the activism is beneath the surface or implied. The spectacles of television cooking shows implicitly invoke issues of abundance in a world where many people suffer from hunger and malnourishment. American cooking shows in particular display conspicuous and copious consumption when much of their audience suffers from obesity and eating disorders. While seldom explicit, the contours of power are not far submerged under the succulent dishes presented to the television cameras. Television cooking shows do not explicitly offer religious meaning, but it is nonetheless present. They offer an implicit statement that food itself is a religion, and judgments about what sort of food and consumption is appropriate within that religion of food. Within the cooking show universe, food and eating offer ultimate meanings, value, purpose, and identity.

The best example of television food show as religious spectacle is the Japanese series *Iron Chef* and its subsequent international versions. In each of the episodes of the various *Iron Chef* series, contestants challenge a master chef in a battle over "whose cuisine reigns supreme." Each battle centers on a theme ingredient, often but not always a protein or vegetable. In the context of the show, the ingredient is not mere food, but rather a fetish in the traditional Durkheimian sense of a central object both venerated and set apart, but also invoked and utilized (Durkheim 2001 [1912]). It is butchered, cooked, manipulated, extolled, explained, viewed, and dissected. The entire show centers around this ingredient, and the show's hosts and commentators spend a great deal of time explaining every nuance of the ingredient. Crucially, the initial revelation of the theme ingredient occurs on what *Iron Chef* calls an "altar." The altar is precisely that: a raised platform at the front and center of the television studio, a spatial *axis mundi* of not just the soundstage/kitchen, but the *Iron Chef* universe itself.

The revelation of the theme ingredient—called the "secret ingredient" in the US-based *Iron Chef America*—is religious theater at its best. In a press release for a publicity event entitled "The Next Iron Chef Experience," the producer of the American version of the program that airs on Food Network referred to this event as "the iconic 'secret ingredient' altar reveal moment" (Awai 2011). Like the pivotal moment of a Catholic Mass wherein the priest intones the ritual words that transubstantiate the wine and wafer into the blood and body of Christ, so too the host of *Iron Chef*, the mysterious "chairman," reveals the secret ingredient. Like a priest, the chairman wears vestments of his trade. Rather than a cassock or stole, the chairman of *Iron Chef America* dresses in a casual business suit, permitting him to engage in spectacles of martial arts. The chairman in the original Japanese *Iron Chef* wore vestments that blurred the lines between a cabaret performer, Liberace, and the Sun King Louis XIV of France. Yet in each case, the chairman's dress signaled him as special performer and ritual specialist who inaugurated the spectacle of the television show. Further, in the context of the show's narrative, it is the chairman's largess that makes *Iron Chef* possible. He is both priest and monarch (and performer), and his ritual actions and presiding words inaugurate the sacred drama of *Iron Chef*.

The actual unveiling follows the pattern of pre-conciliar Catholic liturgy by invoking the language of God in a ritual moment of revelation. In pre-conciliar Catholicism, this was Latin, the language of the Church as Bride of Christ. In *Iron Chef*, it is French, the language of *haute cuisine* and famous gastronome Jean Anthelme Brillat-Savarin, who nearly single-handedly reshaped high food culture, and whose words begin every episode of the original *Iron Chef* series. Rather than the phrases of Catholic consecration, the *mysterium fidei* originally spoken in Latin that transform the host into body and blood, the chairman intones an oddly constructed French phrase, "Allez cuisine!" (Go kitchen!). Native French speakers scratch their heads, since the phrase is so strange. However, the meaning of the words is irrelevant, just as they were for generations of Catholics who heard Mass in Latin. Rather, the words function to enact a moment of transformation when the materials on the altar change from being mere food to something greater.

Iron Chef is most certainly a spectacle. Its producers have carefully designed the show to invoke awe, which is also one of the key elements of religious spectacle. In her comparative study of medieval and contemporary portrayals of the crucifixion, religious studies scholar Alison Griffiths roots the religious spectacle in just this sense of awe, calling it one of the essential design aspects of religious spectacle (2007: 9). *Iron Chef* is filled with awe-inspiring camera shots of spectacular food, cooking, and eating. As media studies scholar Mark Gallagher notes of the original Japanese series, the episodes "offer spectacle through close-ups of completed dishes, kitchen footage of expert food preparation, and occasionally, views of restaurant interiors and urbane or picturesque vacation destinations" (2004: 181). It has been called "food porn" for similar reasons, since the show emphasizes explicit imagery of food designed to both arouse and satisfy desire and craving. This begins in the introductory phase of the program before the "iconic altar reveal," to use the producer's terminology. The original Japanese *Iron Chef* generally featured montages of nature images interspersed with images of succulent dishes being prepared by the contestant. The show invoked samurai-style martial imagery and generally indicated the lineage of the chefs, their training, and the sort of blades that they utilized (Lukacs 2010). *Iron Chef America* tends to favor shots of frenetic kitchens, with steam and fire spurting hither and thither. It eschews the samurai approach of the original, but replaces it with a sense of rugged American manliness expressed through action scenes, fire, and sweat. In both cases, the show offers vivid imagery of succulent foods, but also positions the subjects as a spectacle (Gallagher 2004). This is done in ways culturally appropriate to Japanese or American audiences, and *Iron Chef* is inserted into a dialogue about the nature of culture and the meaning of cooking within that culture.

I am not the first person to recognize something quasi-religious in *Iron Chef*. *Time* magazine featured the show in its article "Kitchen Gods," wherein the author Lisa Abend (2010) identified *Iron Chef* as one among several cooking shows "making food a spectacle." The article focused on the celebrity nature of television chefs, who Abend identified as the eponymous "kitchen Gods." Abend did not indicate what qualified such chefs as divinities, but the comparison is apt. This begs the question: what makes *Iron Chef* religious, at least in terms of the religion of popular culture? Fundamentally, it is so because it bestows transcendent meanings into food. Food comes to represent culture, tradition, ethnicity, land, morality, and community. The Japanese series featured an extended culinary war between the "Óta faction" of traditional Edo-style Japanese cooking—who the show's writers refer to as "Óta's Party of Heaven and Earth," highlighting the religious ramifications of this made-for-TV conflict—and iron chefs Rokusaburo Michiba and Masaharu Morimoto, proponents of neo-Japanese cooking that adopts Western techniques. Óta and Michiba/Morimoto differed over the fundamental nature of what it means to eat Japanese food, and by extension to be Japanese. The Óta group invoked the Shinto tradition and on one occasion even brought a Shinto priest onto the studio set. The spectacle of Japanese chefs parading in traditional garb, complete with ritual objects drawn from Shinto, Japan's native religious tradition, revealed how strongly *Iron Chef* infused higher meanings into food.

The American series invokes transcendental themes as well, though less explicitly. America does not lack a civil religion akin to Shinto, as Robert Bellah—himself a scholar of Japanese religion as a young man—has indicated (1967). Rather, the American civil religion centers on the nation-state and civic holidays such as the Fourth of July and Thanksgiving. *Iron Chef* commemorates and reinforces that American civil religion by elevating the culinary traditions associated with its holidays and rituals, most importantly its quintessential holiday, Thanksgiving. Anthropologists Melanie Wallendorf and Eric J. Arnould argue that Thanksgiving reveals "how Americans use ritual consumption to construct culture," specifically as "a collective ritual that celebrates material abundance enacted through feasting" (1996: 537–49). It is at the heart of the American civil religious calendar, and a central ritual that shows how Americans define themselves through culinary culture. *Iron Chef America* has featured three episodes entirely devoted to Thanksgiving: a "First Thanksgiving" episode commemorating the foods associated with the "original meal" (as it has been constructed and remembered) in Plymouth in 1621; a "Traditional American Thanksgiving"—to quote the show—centering on turkey and various fixings; and a less structured Thanksgiving battle. In each case, *Iron Chef* reinforced a set of prescribed values: to be American, one celebrates Thanksgiving. To celebrate Thanksgiving, one cooks and eats. To cook and eat for Thanksgiving, one eats particular foods, namely those drawn from a prescribed list of dishes such as turkey, duck, potatoes, yams, stuffing, and corn.

While *Iron Chef America* does not harp on the politics of power present in its presentation of the Thanksgiving feast, it nevertheless functions to establish boundaries of the meaning of "Americanness" within the American civil religion, and a prescribed way of following the Thanksgiving cooking and eating ritual. Anthropologist Janet Siskind argues that

> Thanksgiving far more subtly [than other holidays] expresses and reaffirms values and assumptions about cultural and social unity, about identity and history, about inclusion and exclusion. Thanksgiving is highly structured and emotion laden, with its celebration of family, home and nation.
>
> (Siskind 2002: 41)

Iron Chef America encapsulates these values and assumptions, and as such transforms food from mere material to the conduit of absolute values. While certainly the television show is not the same type of religion as one finds in a church or synagogue, nor the food on *Iron Chef* the same (theologically speaking) as the host in a Catholic Mass, it does similar religious work. It conveys meanings and values about community, identity, and belongingness.

Cooking shows as prophetic religion

Iron Chef is not the only cooking show on television, although it is one of the most popular, and in many ways represents all of the competitive reality-based television food shows that fill the airways. Another type of television food show is the "flawed restaurant" show wherein a celebrity chef dispenses wisdom to the owners and operators of a failing restaurant. The two best examples of these prophetic cooking shows are *Restaurant: Impossible*, hosted by Chef Robert Irvine, and *Ramsay's Kitchen Nightmares* (alternatively, called simply *Kitchen Nightmares* in its American incarnation), hosted by Gordon Ramsay. Such shows are prophetic in approach, since they position the celebrity chef as a prophet offering both the direst of warnings and a chance for redemption. In the Hebrew Bible, prophets functioned in precisely this role. They pointed out social flaws, made dire predictions of what would follow if the flaws were not fixed, and offered a chance for the people to repent of their failings and create a new order. As Shalom M. Paul and his co-authors have described it,

> the prophet is neither a philosopher nor a systematic theologian, but a mediator, often a covenantal mediator, who delivers the word of God to his people in order to shape their future by reforming their present. He is not the ultimate source of the message nor its final addressee; he is the middleman who has the overpowering experience of hearing the divine word, and who must perform the onerous task of bearing it to a usually indifferent if not hostile audience.
>
> (Paul 2007: 568)

Neither Gordon Ramsay nor Robert Irvine are prophets in the strict biblical sense, since they do not (as far as I know) claim to speak for the divine. Yet they clearly function as prophets of culinary religion, bringing the Word of foodie culture to recalcitrant restaurant owners whose culinary sins include poor hygiene, outdated menus, rude servers, incompetent chefs, and just plain bad food. They mediate between the restaurant owners and managers—nearly always blind to their own failings and sometimes, like the biblical audience of the prophet, quite hostile—and the expected norms of restaurants as expressed by the public, members of which are quoted by the program to show their disapproval of the current state of the restaurant.

In both *Restaurant: Impossible* and *Ramsay's Kitchen Nightmares*, the prophetic call for fixing the failing restaurant is also a chance to exult in spectacle, just as is the case in *Iron Chef*. Kershaw argues that spectacle portrays the object of either curiosity or contempt. This is certainly true in the case of these types of cooking shows, which alternate between projecting images of succulent abundance and repugnant foulness. As Kershaw indicates, "[t]here is a strong dynamic in this view of spectacle because it suggests—despite the binary assumptions of that either/or—that the same display of excess can be the subject of rapture and disgust" (2003: 593). *Restaurant: Impossible* and *Kitchen Nightmares* highlight kitchens with unsanitary conditions, spoiled ingredients, and poorly executed dishes. Irvine and Ramsay seem to compete in their two television shows to reveal the more disgusting broken restaurant and make the most fuss over the nasty products therein. In the first episode of the British incarnation of the program, the foul-mouthed kitchen prophet Ramsay holds aloft a container of an unknown brown speckled substance snatched from a filth-strewn refrigerator, as he declares "[i]t looks like sheep turd that's been infested by ants" (Hall 2004). In an episode of the American series, Ramsay holds a dead rodent by its tail while scolding the restaurant's owners for their ignorance of hygiene. Irvine is no less prone to histrionic displays of revulsion toward the unsanitary and unpleasant conditions of the kitchens he visits. In one episode he scrapes the congealed oil off a ceiling tile, only to deposit it in the palm of the appalled owner (Hilgedick 2011). In another, he displays filth and fungus that have overrun the tubing of a soda machine (Recht 2011). Perhaps the most scandalous and graphic spectacle is the third episode of the first season, where Irvine visits a failing restaurant only to find it overrun with filth: dead rats, rotten meat, copious flies, and cluttered garbage. Never afraid to include a bit of melodrama, at one point Irvine puffs out his cheeks and runs out of the back door, making retching sounds as he does so. The audience is left to assume the details (Cornwall 2011).

In true prophetic form, Irvine and Ramsay expose the rot at the core of the restaurants—sometimes literally!—and propel the owners, managers, and chefs toward resolving the underlying problems. Like Elijah, they sometimes work miracles, conjuring outside consultants, guest chefs, or professional cleaning crews to solve seemingly insurmountable problems. They speak words of wisdom, offer solace and advice, and threaten doom and despair unless the restaurants' management turns around. Their jeremiads usually work, and ultimately the two television shows are able to offer their viewers spectacles of a different variety. In their closing montages, *Restaurant: Impossible* and *Kitchen Nightmares* feature visions of succulent food produced by the kitchens after the hosts have assisted their flawed owners and chefs. The shows' final segments show diners gushing over the final dishes as if they worked for the Michelin ratings board or the Zagat guide. Well-framed camera angles focus on food as delightful to the viewers' eyes as the dishes are assumed to be to the imbibers' tastebuds.

One cannot forget that these shows, like *Iron Chef*, are ultimately theater. Restaurant owners whose establishments have been featured admit that shows are scripted, and that the producers intentionally introduce scenes meant to heighten the spectacle. In some cases, much of it is façade. The owner of the aforementioned filth-ridden restaurant featured in *Restaurant: Impossible* noted that

> employees working on the show moved old equipment and bags of trash to make it seem as though the restaurant's patio was piled with garbage. He said show employees sprinkled caraway seeds on the floor to look like mouse droppings and that another employee heated and exploded coffee in a microwave and left the oven dirty ... a producer wouldn't allow him to clean it before filming took place.
>
> (Talorico 2011)

One cannot say which elements of the spectacle were invented and which were not, but this is hardly the point. The prophet does not let details such as this prevent the message from sinking in. These shows are fundamentally religious dramas about sin and salvation, about the prophetic call for repentance and the need to return to the Church of High Cuisine.

Religious devotion to foodways

Thus far we have focused on the visual performative elements of food as religion as a way of considering the intersection between food, cooking, religion, and popular culture. Viewers of cooking and food shows "consume" them as visual culture, and as such they consume the messages these television shows implicitly project about good food, bad food, real food, etc. Yet there is far more to the nexus of food, cooking, religion, and popular culture. One of the most important ways that individuals express food as religion is through a religious (or quasi-religious) devotion to specific foodways. "Foodway" is a term invented by folklorists to refer to the collective food practices and worldviews of a culture or sub-culture, akin to the earlier term "folkways" (Yoder 1972). We often associate foodways with ethnic identity, and speak of Italian foodways or Korean foodways. Yet foodways are also present within sub-cultures, and they are in constant flux as new ones are developed. Some of the most religious levels of devotion to foodways in the West occur among those dedicated to the new foodways of vegetarianism, organic food, veganism, slow food, local food (locavorism), raw food, and the paleo-diet.

While those foodways vary significantly, they possess definite thematic overlaps. Each emerged or re-emerged recently, as contemporary people sought to reconnect themselves to the land, environment, community, and rituals of eating. Each thrives among middle class individuals—especially British, Canadian, and American—for whom individualism and individual foodway choices are paramount, and are part of a consumer culture taken for granted by most North Americans (and Westerners more broadly) wherein one's consumer choices define oneself. Each of these foodways emphasizes control and limitation over what one eats, as a way of exercising control over the self, the body, and one's relationship with the world. Finally, all are totalistic, meaning that each seeks to do more than just list what foods one eats and does not eat. These foodways-as-religions make transcendent claims just like other religions.

Before the advent of the modern industrial economy, most people grew their own food, and those who did not generally had a fair idea of what was involved in the process, since most people were farmers. Prior to refrigeration, people ate food in tune with the seasons out of necessity, and since only the richest could afford transported foods, most people ate locally produced foods. It goes without saying that food was what we would today call "organic," since petroleum-based pesticides and fertilizers did not yet exist. Nor did "processed foods" exist, and with a few socio-geographic exceptions, no one had access to highly refined sugars or grains. The actual act of eating was generally set within a familiar or communal structure, and food was generally consumed in the home unless one was traveling.

One must be careful not to romanticize pre-modern foodways. Many people suffered from malnutrition, and famine was common. Since medicine had not yet developed disease theory, there was little awareness of hygiene. The work required to produce, prepare, and store food dwarfed that required today. Difficulties in transportation and a general lack of infrastructure meant that only the richest people could afford to eat a variety of different foods. Most individuals generally ate the same meals every day, with occasional breaks for holidays and festivals. The lack of globalization meant that some products simply did not exist outside of limited geographies. It was no food Eden. Yet proponents of today's quasi-religious foodways look to these pre-modern foodways as a sort of paradise lost, configuring them as a time when people ate good, fresh, wholesome food among family and friends without the mediation of corporations or chemicals.

Today's foodways that attract the most religious devotion are ones that re-imagine pre-modern foodways, investing them with senses of purpose and value akin to religion. Proponents of the Slow Food movement, for example, look to the pre-modern production and consumption of food as marking decline of culture and the mechanization of humanity. Their 1989 "Slow Food Manifesto" called for returning to pre-industrial patterns of eating, "by advocating historical food culture and by defending old-fashioned food traditions." A quasi-religious current runs through Slow Food and its manifesto, at least if we understand religion to refer to transcendental truths and purposes. Their manifesto declares, "Homo sapiens must regain wisdom and liberate itself from the 'velocity' that is propelling it on the road to extinction. Let us defend ourselves against the universal madness of 'the fast life' with tranquil material pleasure." The manifesto clearly invokes language marking Slow Food as not just a culinary choice, but a quasi-spiritual one as well. Eating in accordance with Slow Food brings "liberation" and "wisdom." Elsewhere, the manifesto refers to Slow Food as a "way of life." Failure to adopt Slow Food's approach may lead to "extinction." These are not minor claims, and not merely culinary ones. Slow Food's manifesto makes broad claims about the nature, value, and purpose of human existence, and as such it has tread into the territory of religion (Slow Food International 1989).

Vegetarianism offers one of the best examples of how foodways can become religious, and how individuals can treat foodways in religious ways. Numerous varieties of vegetarianism exist, with some vegetarians abstaining from all animal products (veganism), some permitting dairy (lacto-vegetarianism), and others allowing dairy and eggs (lacto-ova-vegetarianism). Proponents of each variety of vegetarianism marshal a variety of rationales and supports for their positions but generally they fall within a few groupings: moral/ethical opposition to animal suffering or death, environmental or ecological sensitivity, or bodily purity or health. In each case, vegetarians utilize a foodway to establish boundaries and order in their lives, and as such this foodway looks a lot like a form of religion.

All known religions demand specific limits on behavior and practice, ranging from the well-known strictures—such as the Ten Commandments, Laws of Manu, Five Precepts—to unwritten codes of conduct among non-textual religious groups. Such limitations establish order within communities, indicating the bounds of appropriate behavior and how one ought to act in both daily life and special ritual occasions. Such limitations form and support communities, since they establish boundaries of who does or does not belong. They also function among individuals to create a sense of order and appropriateness. As part of his famous definition of religion, anthropologist Clifford Geertz has written that this aspect of religion functions to "establish powerful, pervasive, and long-lasting moods and motivations in men by formulating conceptions of a general order of existence" (1977: 90). This general order of existence functions to assuage the "metaphysical anxiety" of an unordered and completely relative cosmos wherein no ultimate differentiations or distinctions exist. According to Geertz, this aspect of religions allows followers to know right from wrong, respond to the problem of suffering, and delineate meaning from meaninglessness (1977: 100–108). Vegetarians use limitations on eating to establish similar boundaries and limitations, and to explain what is right and wrong. Though not quite a religion in the formal sense of Geertz's definition, vegetarianism functions like one.

Beyond the theoretical similarities, numerous examples exist of vegetarians using religious language to describe their foodways, especially in the most influential books written in support of this foodway. Consider how Frances Moore Lappé frames the issues in her *Diet for a Small Planet* (1971), one of the foundation texts for contemporary vegetarianism. Lappé situates her contention that people could live without meat as a form of "heresy" and her discourse as "heretical" (1971: xv). Since heresies necessarily imply an orthodoxy, Lappé names that as well: "the great American Steak Religion" that preaches the need to eat meat every day in order to retain health, suitable manliness (at least for males!), and patriotism (1971: 92–95). Instead, Lappé offers "a new myth of being" predicated on vegetarianism.

As an explicit work of ethics and the most popular book on vegetarianism of the past four decades, Peter Singer's *Animal Liberation* (1975) also treads on religion's ground. Singer does not base his argument on theology, but on philosophy (although both answer fundamental questions about the nature of self, being, eternity, society, and the cosmos). He avoids direct references to God or the supernatural, but otherwise offers an approach to vegetarianism that one could easily imagine being sounded from a pulpit. Singer roots his ethics in universal morality and a set of fundamental truths that point to an eternal and intrinsic Justice that all must follow. This "fundamental moral principle of equality" functions as a basic "golden rule" against which all other morals and ethics are judged (Singer 2002: 213). Singer considers Jewish, ancient Greek, and Christian (primarily Thomistic) alternatives, and rejects all three (2002: 186–212), explicitly developing a "rational argument" that does not consider souls, creation, or divine justice. This does not make Singer's work irreligious, just religious in a different sense. He still appeals to absolute sets of morals, justice, and purpose of living in the universal ethic of eating that he develops.

In a series of oral history interviews that I conducted in 2009, I asked proponents of vegetarianism to narrate their trajectories into this foodway, to explain their rationales for practicing vegetarianism, and to talk about what it meant for them. The oral histories that these vegetarians produced were explicitly religious in character, even without any prompting from me. Many of the vegetarians discussed their foodways with reference to transcendental truths. Harriet, who had been a vegetarian for decades—ever since she attended college—explained, "something always felt wrong about eating meat. … It isn't normal to eat meat. Being vegetarian, it was a reclamation and empowerment of the real me." Gillian, who had become a vegetarian in 2001, was even more explicit: "vegetarianism chose me. It was more [on] a spiritual than a conscious level. … It was like an enlightenment. Like waking up." Such vegetarians claim that their foodway is self-evidently true, and that it represents not mere culinary choices but aligning oneself with correct morality, correct order, and a correct way of living. Douglas, who had more recently become vegetarian, explained to me that "all living things are related," and as a "matter of conscious [sic]" people should not eat other animals. He cited books about ethics and moral philosophy during our conversation, and made it clear that he considered vegetarianism not only a moral requirement, but the ultimate foodway for humanity.[2]

Religions always include practices, and quasi-religious foodways are no different. From the perspective of the study of religion and popular culture, the most obvious examples of such practices derive from proponents of foodways engaging in acts of proselytizing and evangelization. Proselytization possesses a rich history within religious traditions, with most religions accepting or promoting the gaining of converts at some time in their histories. While some traditions currently frown on such practices—most notably Judaism, Hinduism, and traditional Chinese religions—that has not always been the case for them. And it certainly is not the case among the largest world religions (Christianity, Islam, and Buddhism), each of which claims to offer an absolute truth for the entire world. Proponents of foodways as religions often make the same claim, particularly those associated with vegan, organic, or local eating. Upholders of these foodways believe that if the entire world were to practice their foodway, all would be better off, and they seek to spread their perspectives as widely as possible. Vegans are perhaps the most noteworthy (or notorious, depending on one's perspective) because of the overtly confrontational tactics of their international umbrella group, People for the Ethical Treatment of Animals (PETA).

PETA's approach to evangelism roughly parallels that of the early Church, when leaders highlighted attention-grabbing forms of public proselytizing despite the legal consequences. PETA's evangelists picket businesses associated with the meat industry, hold sit-ins to protest meat-eating and perceived instances of animal abuse, and engage in other forms of civil disobedience in order to evangelize. The organization has clearly oriented many of its tactics—such as naked protests against the fur industry, the use of animal costumes, parading with models of skinned dead animals, and covering nearly naked men and women in vegetables—to gain publicity. PETA also engages in the more usual forms of evangelism, such as distributing tracts and leaflets at major events, holding informational sessions on college campuses, and informally seeking converts through direct encounters between friends and colleagues.

The very act of proselytizing is itself religious, since it effectively conveys the assumption that the potential convert does not possess access to the appropriate eternal truth and requires assistance from one of the already saved. It is also an essential part of religious psychology. Sociologist Leon Festinger found in his study of an American new religious movement (pseudonymously called "the Seekers") that gaining new converts served as an essential means of reassuring current members that they had made the correct decision in joining the movement, and that they possessed the correct transcendental truth (Festinger *et al.* 1956). Certainly Paul of Tarsus (né Saul) offers another example.

Religious proselytizing results in conversion, and proponents of quasi-religious foodways such as vegetarianism and locavorism (local eating) also talk about their trajectories into these foodways in terms of conversions. In the twenty oral histories that I collected, the majority of the subjects described their experiences using traditionally religious language of conversion. They described feeling that something was wrong in their lives, that they somehow were missing something important and had erred in some way. Most had become "foodway spiritual seekers," investigating or even trying different food practices. Finally, they encountered a text, individual, or movement associated with vegetarianism or locavorism that led them to convert to the new foodway.[3] Nearly every individual with whom I spoke recognized "conversion" as the proper term for their experience, and saw the religious analog. "That comparison makes sense. It was definitely a conversion moment," noted one of my subjects. Again, these alternative foodway practices function like religions.

Religious food kitsch: the case of chocolate deities

As we move from the preparation, consumption, and spectacle of food to food itself, we can find ample evidence of a rich intersection of food, religion, and popular culture at any well-stocked grocery store. There are several types of religious food. The most obvious type is food that is prepared in accordance with the ritual laws of one religious group or another. Kosher food—including its subtype, food that is also kosher for Passover,[4]—halal meat, ayurvedic food, and vegetarian food (for a Buddhist or Hindu) all serve as examples. These are certainly religious food in one sense, since they help consumers to follow religious regulations, but they are generally not what we mean when we think about religion, food, and popular culture. A tomato, for example, fits within all of those strictures and therefore merits the designation of this first type of "religious food." Yet there is nothing about a tomato to particularly mark it as religious, just as a kosher hot dog is not particularly religious either (even though its package may bear a *hekshur* [marked symbol] that signifies it as kosher). Certainly the consumers of the tomato or hot dog might purchase these products rather than other ones because of religious reasons, but others will consume them without much thought or even awareness of the "religious" nature of the foodstuff. Kosher salt, so named because observant Jews use it to *kasher* (make kosher) meat by draining away blood, offers another example. Yet kosher salt is merely normal table salt produced with a specialized grain size. Chefs and home cooks make frequent use of kosher salt without any thought to its name referencing a religious practice.

A second type of religious food is food marketed for particular religious observance, such as Easter candy, Hanukah *gelt* (chocolate coins), or Diwali sweets. These are certainly also religious, and represent an instance of religion within popular culture. Consumers generally purchase these products for particular observances, and while the actual foodstuffs may not vary significantly from non-religious equivalents, marketers recognize that labeling these foods as intended for a specific religious occasion helps to sell them. Such foods do not serve ritual functions—for example, they are not communion wafers, Passover matzah, or Hindu prasadam—but they nevertheless are "religious" in that individuals use them to mark religious observance. While these products generally attract consumers who intend them for such observances, this is not always the case. In some cases, people outside of the religion purchase such foods too. Many Christians buy the chocolate coins known as Hanukah *gelt*, and non-Christians certainly purchase Easter candies, particularly (as Jewish and Buddhist friends of mine do) when they go on sale after the holiday. Such food is also religious, in a sense, but again not generally what we mean when we think about religion, food, and popular culture.

The most interesting type of religious food is what I call "religious food kitsch." This is food that is self-evidently religious, but not designed for specific religious use. It bears no obvious ritual function or purpose, and in fact its manufacturers seldom foresee any interest in the use of such products for religious practices or observances. It tends to be somewhat kitschy, meaning that these types of religious foods blur any distinction with being simply tacky, lowbrow, aesthetically questionable, and even religiously offensive. Chocolate deities, beer bottles shaped like the Buddha, Easter butter lambs, and crackers marketed as "Bible Bread" all represent this category. Such religious food kitsch appeals to sentimentality, humor, and a sense of irony, depending on the consumer. But what makes them so fascinating is that they invoke taste in multiple ways. As foods, they possess taste. But as popular culture, they embody everything from good to bad to questionable taste.

While numerous examples of religious food kitsch exist, Jeanne Fleming's chocolate deities, which she sells from her Web site (chocolatedeities.com), offer a clear example of the vagaries of taste within food kitsch (Fleming 2006). When I first encountered the chocolate deities Web site in 2006, I was teaching a class on religion and food. I spent several minutes staring at the screen trying to decide if this product was "serious" or not. In one sense, the chocolate deities seem comical. Available in dark, milk, or white chocolate, they can be purchased as molded chocolates shaped like everything from the famous Venus of Willendorf fertility figure, to the Buddha (three different varieties of Buddhas, actually), to Ganesh, to the Sacred Heart of Jesus. Munching down on Christ's Sacred Heart would seem vaguely heretical to many Christians, and while Hindus have a rich tradition of food offerings, actually consuming an image of Ganesh or Krishna is also outside the norms of most forms of Hinduism. On the other hand, one can easily imagine atheists or ex-adherents of various religious traditions gleefully consuming chocolate icons of the world's major religions. From this perspective, therefore, the chocolate deities are not "serious" and are meant to poke fun at religion.

From another perspective, the chocolate deities are quite serious. Fleming's Web site indicates how she envisions consumers actually using the chocolate icons:

> chocolate … is the food of the gods in that it induces and celebrates love, which brings you into relationship with all living things; helps to heal a broken heart; brings joy, which helps your spiritual journey; calls forth peace and compassion; lowers stress, which helps you on your inner journey; carries anti-oxidants, which help you on your healing journey; has aphrodisiac qualities which enlarge and foment fecundity; stimulates the imagination, and according to the ancient Aztecs who first discovered it, provides strength and wisdom. Chocolate Deities are: offerings; prayers and wishes; food stuffs; love objects; altarpieces; spiritual chocolates, kitchen art of the highest order and yummy chocolate gifts.
>
> (Fleming 2006)

From this perspective—that of the producer of these foods—the chocolate deities in fact embody real religious values, and she intends their consumers to utilize them in accordance with actual religious practice. Fleming envisions her chocolate deities as part of individuals' spiritual quests, healing practices, devotional acts, creations of sacred spaces, and spiritual explorations. These are explicitly religious functions. Yet within Fleming's description there exists a tension. While she notes the value of her chocolate deities for offerings and altar pieces, the Web site's longer description of the items' value actually describes not the deities themselves but the substance of chocolate. Here it is not the form that the chocolate takes but the substance that embodies the sacred, and that therefore merits the designation as a religious food-stuff. This looks quite similar to the other forms of food, religion, and popular culture where the food itself becomes the religion. As Fleming's Web site indicates, "chocolate has powers to transport and inspire beyond other mere consumables" (2006). That is certainly a transcendental claim beyond that of mere nutrition or even sensual enjoyment.

Religion and beer

In some cases, religion and food intersect in the realm of marketing, rather than function or performance. Alcoholic drinks seem to serve a special arena for the use of religious imagery for styling and marketing purposes. Since the Western brewing and winemaking traditions developed so closely in tandem with religious institutions, this is hardly surprising. In fact, the beer industry features religious imagery in particular prevalence. Of course, this is most evident among beers brewed in monastic fashion, specifically Belgian abbey-style ales. Considering only such Belgian beers, one finds examples aplenty. The use of pictures of monasteries on the labels of abbey-style beers is common. Brasserie Caulier's "Abbaye Cistercienne Paix-Dieu" takes its name from a famous Cistercian monastery. Its label features a woodcut picture of the monastery, projecting an image of rootedness in medieval religious, artistic, and brewing traditions. Abbaye du Val-Dieu brewery also features its eponymous monastery on its bottles, as does Artevelde Frand Cru. Other beers swap an image of a monk for the monastery; for example Broeder Jacob's "Frère Jacques," Brasserie Leroy's "Het Kapittel Watou ABT" and "Kapittel Watou Prior," Bavik's "Petrus Gouden Tripel" (whose monk holds a beer glass in one hand, and a cross in the other!), St. Bernardus's entire line of beers, and Slaghmuylder's "Witkap" line. Monks do not brew any of these beers, yet each utilizes monastic images in order to convey a sense of continuity with the monastic brewing tradition, an air of authenticity, and an aesthetic of monastic flavor.

Moving outside the realm of traditional Belgian beers, one finds ample evidence of the use of religious imagery to position and market beers. In many cases, these beers also inhabit the realm of religious food kitsch. Québécois brewer Unibroue sports a line of beers including "La Fin du Monde" (End of the World), "Don de Dieu" (Gift of God) and "Maudite" (Damned). California's Russian River Brewing Company features beers named "Beatification," "Consecration," "Supplication," "Sanctification," "Benediction," "Temptation," "Redemption," and "Damnation," meaning that one can drink one's way from sainthood to hellfire in a single sitting. (They also feature "Defenestration," though being hurled from a window seems less religiously relevant.) The labels on the bottles bear little relevance to the names, and one suspects that brewer Vinnie Cilurzo chose names for his beers somewhat tongue-in-cheek. In fact, his rationale derived from a quirk of brewing history, as he named his beers in homage to one of the foremost Belgian breweries, Duvel ("Devil," named for its high alcohol content), but was also inspired by a bit of musical popular culture. As Cilurzo recounts,

> I had been home-brewing that beer for about three years, and I was on my way home when this Squirrel Nut Zippers song came on the radio in my car called "Hell." In the song, they spell out the word damnation, and I knew that was going to be the name. By the time I got home I figured I had to also make a beer called Redemption, and then my buddy suggested Salvation and Temptation as well.

(Anderson 2008)

Devil-themed beers are quite popular, with most indeed paying homage to Duvel and its distinctive Belgian style. Het Anker's "Lucifer" beer, Riva's "Lucifer," and De Block's "Satan" are all Belgian abbey-style brews that invoke the irony of demonically labeled monastic beers. Stone Brewing's entire line of beers features demonic imagery on its labels, with a winged devil looming over the beer's name and description of their yearly and seasonable products (www.stonebrew.com/home.asp). Such beers not only tip their metaphoric hats to the original devil-named Duvel beer, but also play at the borders of the social taboos against alcoholic consumption, demonic iconography, and religion.

In addition to such demonic oriented beers, other beers utilize religion for the kitsch factor. The Jewish founded and owned Schmaltz Brewery crafts a line of beers they call "He'Brew: The Chosen Beer." Playing at popular associations with Judaism and a series of horrendous puns, the brewery features beers named "Messiah Bold," "Genesis," "Jewbelation," and "Rejewvinator," and adorns its packages with images of a beer-toting Hasidic hipster. He'Brew moves beyond kitsch to shtick, the Yiddish sense of humor implying contrived and often self-deprecating comedy. With its motto of "Shmaltz Brewing Company is Dedicated to Crafting Delicious Beer and Delicious Shtick … L'Chaim!" ("L'Chaim," literally "to life," is a traditional Jewish toast), and the brewery's official name (shmaltz, Yiddish for "rendered animal fat," but also implying anything campy or over-dramatic), He'Brew playfully engages Jewish humor and a sense of literally consuming culture in the form of a religio-ethnicity. The brewery has even featured a gift set to allow drinkers to construct their own Hanukah menorah of beer bottles. Unlike the Belgian monastic beers, the case of Schmaltz indicates how religion is used not to convey the authenticity of a specific brewing tradition, but the qualities of a culture. Using un-translated Yiddish words (kvell, mishpukah, etc.) and referencing Jewish practices (Passover, circumcision, bar mitzvahs), the brewery clearly seeks to market itself as a "Jewish beer." The brewery's marketing approach mirrors the development of identity politics, wherein one's cultural identity serves as a central means of engaging the world and constructing a worldview.

One finds similar self-referential jokes predicated on self-depreciating humor drawn from a specific religious sub-culture within the brewing industry in geographic regions dominated by the Church of Jesus Christ of Latter-day Saints (the Mormons). Wasatch Beer Company's "Polygamy Porter" and Epic Brewing Company's "Jack Mormon Coffee Stout" both reference recognized elements of Mormonism within popular religious culture, namely the LDS Church's past practice of polygamy, and the Mormon dietary prohibition—rooted in the text called the Word of Wisdom—against both coffee and beer. Naming a beer after these now prohibited practices of polygamy, and coffee and beer consumption marks a certain Mormon sense of humor for these two Utah-based breweries.

Conclusion

This chapter has considered various ways in which religion intersects with food, eating, and images of food and eating. We have seen that food and the ways people relate to food bear certain similarities to religion, or what one might term quasi-religion, since some aspects traditionally ascribed to religion seem absent (divinity, etc.). Yet many other aspects are present, and these include rituals, spectacles, texts, conversion and apostasy to new forms of eating, communities, and senses of identity and morality achieved through consuming food or images featuring food, as in cooking shows.

Studying food and religion actually gives us traction to better understand both of these concepts. Food is not mere foodstuff, but a set of meanings embedded in physical objects, including conflicting notions of culture and ethnicity, absolute values about life, and sentiments about personal identity. Consumption of food is therefore far more than the mere addition of nutrients to the body, a fact that even a precursory examination of the food industry and its advertisements reveals. Rather, food is a central nexus of how communities and individuals identify themselves. The study of religion and food also challenges what we think we mean when we talk about religion. Though certainly lacking some elements of what most people mean when they say "religion," practices and beliefs related to food reflect many of the same qualities and functions as other religions. Spectacles of abundance, morality tales, sacred texts teaching morals and ethics, ritual objects meant for adoration or meditation, and kitschy items used to negotiate one's identity vis-à-vis cultural groups are all present in food as religion. If this is the case, then is the "quasi" in quasi-religion really necessary when studying food? Or ought not the category of religion be construed much more broadly so as to include the religious experience of architecture, music, art, and politics? Since the birth of the academic study of religion, scholars have tended to foreground theology and liturgical practices and leave popular and quotidian religious practices as afterthoughts. As numerous scholars have noted, this replicates Protestant religious norms, with the result that the religious engagement with food has tended to be ignored within the academic study of religion (Fitzgerald 2003). So too the possibility of food functioning as a form of religion. In the end, religion and food offers an opportunity to reassess what we mean when we study culture.

Notes

1 I wish to acknowledge the Wabash Center for Teaching and Learning in Theology and Religion, which provided funding for the oral history project; the participants of the 2012

Åboagora Symposium in Turku, Finland, where I presented an earlier draft of this paper; Jon Zeller for selflessly braving the capital of Belgian monastic beer to bring me research material; my various friends on social networks who have given me suggestions and feedback; and colleagues at Åbo Akedemi University where I was a visiting Fulbright Scholar in Fall 2012, and where this research project was a frequent topic of conversation over coffee and chocolate.

2 These responses were part of an oral history project I conducted in Asheville, NC, and edited in 2009. All of the names have been changed to protect the identities of those interviewed.

3 Here I found a distinction between some individuals who saw their conversion as an active choice, and those who had a more passive view that it "happened to them," mirroring the distinction within Christianity between Arminian and Calvinist views of conversion (see Zeller 2014).

4 Food that is "kosher for Passover" must not only be kosher according to traditional standards for consumption year round, but also must contain none of the foods deemed prohibited for consumption during the eight days of the holiday of Pesah (Passover), including grains and leavening agents.

Works cited

Abend, L. (2010) "Kitchen Gods," *Time* 175, 24: 62–66 (June 21). Online as "The cult of the celebrity chef goes global." Available: www.time.com/time/magazine/article/0,9171,19958 44,00.html (accessed 17 October 2012).

Anderson, L. (2008) "Vinnie Cilurzo gets funky: the daring beers of Russian River Brewing Company," *Chow: The Blog* (September 8). Online. Available: www.chow.com/food-news/ 54702/vinnie-cilurzo-gets-funky/ (accessed 17 October 2012).

Awai, J. (2011) "Kitchen Stadium hits the streets at the New York City Food & Wine Festival's Next Iron Chef Experience," *The Daily Meal* (September 30). Online. Available: www.thedailymeal.com/kitchen-stadium-hits-streets-new-york-city-food-wine-festivals-next-iron-chef-experience-0 (accessed 1 July 2012).

Bellah, R. (1967) "Civil religion in America," *Daedalus* 96: 1–21.

Brown, A. (2006) "Food for thought," *Guideposts*. Online. Available: www.guideposts.org/ celebrities/alton-browns-food-thought (accessed 25 May 2012).

Cornwall, R. (dir.) (2011) "Rascal's BBQ & Crab House," *Restaurant: Impossible* (aired 2 February 2011). Television. Food Network.

Counihan, C. and P. Van Esterik (eds) (1997) *Food and Culture: A Reader*, New York: Routledge.

Davidson, C. (1988) *Festivals and Plays in Medieval Britain*, Hampshire, UK: Ashgate.

Durkheim, É. (2001 [1912]) *The Elementary Forms of Religious Life*, trans. Carol Cosman, New York: Oxford University Publishing.

Festinger, L., H.W. Riecken, and S. Schachter (1956) *When Prophecy Fails*, Minneapolis, MN: University of Minnesota Press.

Fitzgerald, T. (2003) *The Ideology of Religious Studies*, New York: Oxford University Press.

Fleming, J. (2006) "Chocolate deities: chocolate gods and goddesses, chocolate Buddha, spiritual chocolates." Online. Available: www.chocolatedeities.com/deities.php (accessed 17 October 2012).

Gallagher, M. (2004) "What's so funny about *Iron Chef?*" *Journal of Popular Film & Television* 31: 176–84.

Geertz, C. (1977) *The Interpretation of Cultures*, New York: Basic Books.

Griffiths, A. (2007) "The revered gaze: the medieval imaginary of Mel Gibson's *The Passion of the Christ*," *Cinema Journal* 46: 3–39.

Hall, C. (dir.) (2004) "Bonaparte's Restaurant," *Ramsay's Kitchen Nightmares* (April 27). Television. Fox Network.

Hanawelt, B.A. and K.L. Reyerson (1994) "Introduction," in B.A. Hanawelt and K.L. Reyerson (eds), *City and Spectacle in Medieval Europe*, Minneapolis, MN: University of Minnesota Press, ix–xx.

Hilgedick, E. (dir.) (2011) "Flood Tide," *Restaurant: Impossible* (aired 2 March 2011). Television. Food Network.

Kershaw, B. (2003) "Curiosity or contempt: on spectacle, the human, and activism," *Theatre Journal* 55: 591–611.

Lappé, F.M. (1971) *Diet for a Small Planet*, New York: Ballantine Books.

Lukacs, G. (2010) "*Iron Chef* around the world," *International Journal of Cultural Studies* 13: 409–26.

Paul, S.M. (2007) "Prophets and prophecy," in M. Berenbaum and F. Skolnik (eds), *Encyclopaedia Judaica*, 2nd edn, Detroit: Macmillan Reference USA, 566–86.

Recht, G. (dir.) (2011) "McShane's," *Restaurant: Impossible* (aired 9 November 2011). Television. Food Network.

Shapiro, J.S. (2000) *Oberammergau: The Troubling Story of the World's Most Famous Passion Play*, New York: Pantheon Books.

Singer, P. (2002 [1975]) *Animal Liberation*, New York: Harper Collins.

Siskind, J. (2002) "The invention of Thanksgiving: a ritual of American nationality," in C.M. Counihan (ed.), *Food in the USA: A Reader*, New York: Routledge, 41–58.

Slow Food International (1989) "Our philosophy." Online. Available: www.slowfood.com/international/2/our-philosophy (accessed 17 October 2012).

Talorico, P. (2011) "'Restaurant: Impossible' experience not a happy one, New Castle restaurateur says," *Delaware Online* (January 25). Online. Available: http://blogs.delawareonline.com/secondhelpings/2011/01/25/restaurant-impossible-experience-not-a-happy-one-new-castle-restaurateur-says/ (accessed 14 October 2012).

Wallendorf, M. and E.J. Arnould (1996) "Consumption rituals of Thanksgiving Day," in R.L. Grimes (ed.), *Readings in Ritual Studies*, New York: Prentice Hall, 536–51.

Yoder, D. (1972) "Folk cookery," in R.M. Dorson (ed.), *Folklore and Folklife*, Chicago, IL: University of Chicago Press, 325–50.

Zeller, B.E. (2014) "Quasi-religious American foodways: the cases of vegetarianism and locavorism," in B.E. Zeller, M.W. Dallam, R.L. Neilson, and N.L. Rubel (eds), *Religion, Food, and Eating in North America*, New York: Columbia University Press.

Zeller, B.E., M.W. Dallam, R.L. Neilson, and N.L. Rubel (eds) (2014) *Religion, Food, and Eating in North America*, New York: Columbia University Press.

14

FASHION

Edward Dutton

During my fieldwork with Evangelical Christian students at British universities, how the students dressed was one of their most salient points of differentiation. Occasionally, such as during their annual "Mission Week" (a highly organized effort to evangelize on campus) they chose to use their clothes to conspicuously advertise both their Christian identity and their ongoing Evangelical activities. They did this by wearing specially produced "hoodies" which included the Mission's name, a Bible quote and other relevant information. However, most of the time, the use of fashion to foster an Evangelical Christian sub-culture was somewhat subtler. Some Christians would wear bracelets advertising their faith, such as the well-known "WWJD" ("What Would Jesus Do?") wristband, "FROG" ("Fully Reliant On God"), or simply "JESUS." But, in most cases, members of the Christian Union, and particularly the females, would dress in a manner that was subtly different from that which constituted mainstream student fashion during my fieldwork period of 2002 to 2005 (see Dutton 2008).

Many religious groups differentiate themselves, to varying degrees, using their clothes. Most obviously, the Amish are strongly defined by the eighteenth-century costumes that they continue to wear. Likewise, some conservative followers of immigrant religions in Europe and the USA, such as Muslims, almost completely reject fashionable clothing in favor of a specific form of dress. This chapter, however, will focus on those religious groups who make use of popular fashions and how they do so as well as on the way in which popular fashion has been influenced by religious groups. I am far from the only researcher who has noted the way in which many religious groups do not simply mark themselves out, through clothing, as conspicuously "different" through rejecting popular fashions. Rather they concomitantly express both a sense of mainstream and counter-cultural identity by embracing popular fashions while using them as a means of differentiating themselves and expressing their religious identity. This chapter will begin with an overview of the research on religion and popular fashion, also providing a definition of "fashion." It will then examine how these fashions are produced, sold and received by religious communities. The chapter will illustrate the processes involved using a number of examples but it will focus mainly on my own experiences with British, Evangelical undergraduates. It will then look at the way in which fashionable clothing itself, in the West, is influenced by various Eastern religious traditions and ultimately may reflect a form of replacement religiosity that prizes these traditions.

Fashion and religion: an overview

Many anthropologists have observed the way in which religious groups employ clothing as one of the most obvious symbols of group membership. Linda Arthur (1999) argues that though a conservative religious group can never fully know whether a member is genuinely committed, the manner in which they dress is a useful shorthand. Their modes of dress will express, to varying degrees, the extent to which they are prepared, with regard to an important symbolic discourse, to conform to the group's norms of behavior, something understood to be a significant part of group membership. Thus, as Douglas (1970) argues, the more tightly controlled an organization is, the more it will stamp this control on the bodies of its members through demanding conformity to its behavioral norms. And, indeed, the closer to the group's power center a particular member is, the more important their behavioral conformity—such as their dress—becomes.[1] Thus, clothing is controlled such that the individual expresses the group of which he is a member, and even his place in it, by means of his body. Secondly, Arthur (1999) observes that clothing is a particularly useful canvas through which a religious group can express the degree to which they are differentiated from the societal mainstream. They may, as with some conservative Muslims, opt to dress in a markedly different manner or, as with many Sikh males, dress as non-members do but with a significant extra marker of differentiation, in the form of a turban (see Abbas 2005; Singh and Tatla 2006, especially Chapter 4).

Nevertheless, there is a body of research in the social sciences on the way in which fashion is employed to express social identity and police group borders. Roach-Higgins and Eicher (1992) have looked at the way in which dress is a vital means of non-verbal communication, establishing the social identity, with various degrees of specificity, of the subject. It has been widely argued that dress is one of the most visible means of expressing cultural, and therefore sub-cultural and religious and social identity (see Davis 1989; Hall 1993; Lipp 1989). Equally, many scholars have focused on the way that dress is employed, in particular, as a means of controlling females, with evaluations of them being heavily influenced by their perceived deviation from expected norms in terms of dress (Workman and Johnson 1994). Likewise, Micklin (1977) has found that many societies have a low tolerance of deviant dress among women because such dress is perceived to reflect a failure to conform to society's norms, something that is seemingly deemed more important in relation to women.

Research into specific counter-cultural religious groups has, likewise, found that conformity in terms of dress is one of the most important dimensions of group membership because dress is of such symbolic significance. Those who dress differently are seen as deviant. Thompson's (1986) research into American religious groups such as the Amish found that it was Amish dress, more than anything else, which caused them to be regarded as deviant. Poll (1962) noted that clothing conformity was an essential means of being accepted as a Hasidic Jew because clothing conformity was understood to symbolize broader religious conformity within the community. Equally, Arthur (1999) notes, in her research into Mennonite women, that her informants were unable to articulate why they chose to still dress as their ancestors had 200 years ago. She argues that this is because the need to conform in terms of dress is so deep and ingrained in human group dynamics. Arthur terms their use of outdated clothing as a religious marker as "fossilized fashion."

Indeed, the edited volume *Religion, Dress and the Body* is one of the few recent books to specifically deal with the relationship between "religion" and the use of clothing, though the relationship with popular fashion is not dwelt upon. Graybill and Arthur (1999) look at the way in which clothing is used in Mennonite communities to control the female members. The typical female dress expresses the group's religious value system—including the need for "modesty"—and any deviation from it is thus evidence of deviation from the group's norms. Similar points are made with regard to the Amish (Hamilton and Hawley 1999) and the use of clothing to express identity and conformity to a sub-culture and its beliefs is examined in relation to various other religious groups (for example, see Goldman Carrel 1999 on Hasidic Jews).

Defining fashion

In order to understand the way in which certain religious groups employ fashionable clothing it is important to be armed with a working definition of what constitutes fashion. Generally, the accepted definition of fashion is a relatively intuitive one. Something is "fashionable" if it is popular at a given time and there is the implication that it might not be popular in the future. Thus, the *Oxford English Dictionary* defines "fashion" broadly, as being "a popular trend." Accordingly, the special costumes of specific religious organizations—such as a priest's robes—do not constitute "fashion" (or they constitute it within the very limited parameters of the priestly sub-culture). Second, "fashion," though it might refer to ornament, speech patterns or even behavior, is commonly employed to refer primarily to clothing and some lexical definitions emphasize this. In common English usage, if a person is described as a "fashion expert" it is usually assumed that their area of expertise is contemporary clothing. New York Fashion Week focuses on clothing and so does the degree in "Fashion" that it is possible to study at Southampton Solent University in the south of England. A number of fashion theorists, such as Entwistle (2000: 3), have pondered the relationship between "fashion" and "clothes," arguing that fashion is an idealized concept that trickles down to popular clothing in a diluted form.

Third, another nuance to the term "fashion" is that it refers to clothing popular among trend-setters; that is to say among the (often youngish) elite within a particular culture.[2] In this regard, there is a power-dynamic to fashion and Entwistle (2000: 3) observes that there is a distinction between "fashion" and everyday "dress." A particular example of clothing is fashionable if members of the elite wear it. A number of sociologists have noted that the nature of this elite has become more complex and multifaceted, especially as Western societies have become more meritocratic and more celebrity-oriented (e.g., Wouters 2007). But generally, researchers in this area agree that elite status is accorded by virtue of ancestry, talent (including education) and money. Many researchers, such as Veblen (1925) or Bourdieu (1984), have argued that it is this elite who will tend to innovate that which is then deemed fashionable. Following Simmel's (1957) "Trickle Effect," these fashions will be imitated—often poorly—by those further down the social scale who will intermix this fashion with their own particular penchants and financial limitations. Eventually, the elite will innovate something else and the original innovation will be "unfashionable"; preserved among the lower classes, the elderly and those who are not as fashion-conscious. It has been pointed out that one difficulty with this model is that there are different dimensions to status and their importance in different societies varies (see Morris 2002: 178; Fox 2004). Another problem is that increased communication has led to a separate "celebrity class" within the elite who are a particularly pronounced object of imitation (see Gitlin 1998). A person may be a celebrity because of their talent, wealth, or ancestry, or any combination of these; though normally, they would have talent and wealth. Accordingly, lower social classes no longer imitate the upper class but, rather, celebrities, who may be from a variety of social backgrounds (see Argyle 1994; Wouters 2007). However, it might be countered that becoming a celebrity—usually through talent—initiates your entry into an elite based to a great extent on ancestry and money, though it may also include talented people. The lower class styles may then be imitated by this elite—among whom there are now talented lower class people—who are, in turn, imitated by those below them: people who, independently of this, also imitate the celebrities. But what becomes clear is that there is a power dynamic to "fashion." Something is fashionable because the elite wear it and, indeed, there is research looking at the way that, in Britain, one of the dimensions which marks out the "Chav" underclass is the supposedly pathological manner in which they dress, vulgarly attempting to imitate black rappers, for instance (see Hayward and Yar 2006).

Fourth, it follows that that which is deemed "fashionable" is only so within a specific cultural context. It is fashionable—because it is popular—in Finland for women to wear very thick-rimmed spectacles but it is not fashionable in England. Equally, the sari may be regarded as "fashion" in India but it is not so in Iowa. However, in common usage the word "fashion" refers to what is fashionable in terms of clothing within Western societies. As these societies might be regarded as the world's dominant societies, this is congruous with the view that "fashion" emanates from an elite. This is evidenced, for example, in the way that "fashion history" almost always focuses on Europe (see, for example, Welters and Lillethun 2011, Part 1). "Fashion," as a global phenomenon, involves exporting Western "fashions" around the world though, as we will see below, it is sometimes influenced by Eastern clothing styles. So, in the following discussion of religion and fashion, in the context of popular culture, we are focusing on Western culture and on clothing that is "popular" but ultimately popular among the elite within this culture. We will look at how religious groups make use of such clothing and also how religion influences such clothing.[3] Finally, many fashion theorists such as Barnard (2002) and Leopold (1992) have emphasized that "fashion," as a discipline, combines various elements such as sociology, psychology and economics. In understanding the relationship between religion and fashion, therefore, we must bear in mind the methods of analysis that inform any study of fashion.

"Christian" clothing

As already noted, there are methods by which Evangelical Christians differentiate themselves using fashion. The first is to deliberately produce their own clothes—sold through Christian shops and usually with an Evangelical bent—and the second is to use certain kinds of fashion and to wear them in certain ways. Let us begin with the first method.

An example is the company Christian Clothing Alliance, which is based in the United Kingdom (Christian Clothing Alliance n.d.). The company's slogan is "Where Fashion, Flair and Faith Collide" and the business is mainly Internet-based, though it also sells at Christian concerts and through some churches. Evangelical in focus, the company's "For Women" section produces T-shirts and hoodies with some kind of Christian image or message. T-shirts and hoodies are both relatively fashionable and they are thus being used as a means of evangelism and identity-expression. The range includes two "retro" zipped jackets (one red, one blue), on which is written the word "washed." The word "retro" is interesting in itself. It has been fashionable for at least two decades, in the United Kingdom, to wear retro clothes (e.g., Kley 1998) and, in particular, 1970s clothes or clothes which look like they're from the 1970s. Increasingly, it is some 1980s fashions that are now being recycled (e.g., Mail Online 2009).

A black hoodie also displays the word "washed." However, this is a lampoon of the washing labels that are found inside clothes. Beneath the standard pictures found on these labels are the words: "100% Authentic Unique Creation/ Washed in the blood of JC/ All Colours Washed together/ Do Not become lukewarm/ Soak in Holy Spirit/ Will be Pressed/ Will not Tumble." As I will discuss below in relation to the Christian use of "normal" fashion, this is not only a means of showing your commitment to the group but also, from the wearer's perspective, a method of evangelism. (As an aside, it might be noted at this point that the model, in addition to the advertised top, wears blue jeans—just as many "non-Christian"[4] females do— and some makeup. But there is a high-cut T-shirt beneath her jacket so that no cleavage is exposed.) In addition, other models advertise hoodies with the words "Love," "Hope," and "Internal Light" on them. The latter is printed beneath an image of a light bulb.

The T-shirts and the vest which are available are very similar in content to the hoodies and jackets. But, in addition, there is a T-shirt with a cross on it and a quotation from Romans 8, another with a so-called "Adam" Plant Design, T-shirts with cross-based coats of arms and one stamped with the words "Paid in Full" across an image of some blood. One of the ladies models a vest and, again, it is a highcut one so that no cleavage can be seen. The men's clothes are the same as the women's ones, though sometimes in darker colors. It may also be noteworthy that none of the men have long hair and none of the women have short hair. In my own research, I found that very few Christian men had long hair and very few Christian women had short hair, although it didn't seem to be deemed unacceptable to trans-gress this habit. Also, there are men's T-shirts with somewhat more macabre designs than the women's ones, such as a cross that is covered in thorns. This might be interpreted as reflecting traditional, Christian gender models, though I appreciate that this is purely speculation. Obviously, I have not conducted any work with this organization, which makes it difficult for me to know why it makes particular fash-ion decisions. Usefully, it does have "testimonies" on its Web site from satisfied customers. One customer writes:

The item that made me realize that I am glad that I was brought on board was the Romans T-shirt … . This item of clothing not only subconsciously shaped my mind, but spiritually gave me wings so that I could lift to the skies and closer to God [sic].

(Christian Clothing Alliance n.d.)

It should also be observed that such clothing seems to specifically be fashionable among young Christians. Older female informants have told me that they regard such clothes as "studenty" and would not, in their thirties, wear them, even though they wore them when they were younger.

Christian students and fashion[5]

My own fieldwork with Christian Unions involved discussions both of specifically "Christian" clothing and of the Christian use of broader fashion trends. In particular, I conducted fieldwork with the Christian Unions at Aberdeen University (AUCU—Aberdeen University Christian Union) in Scotland and Oxford University (OICCU—Oxford Inter-Collegiate Christian Union) between 2002 and 2005.[6] I observed a number of members of OICCU, although by no means the majority, wearing tops that indicated clearly, either to the other Christians or to the outside world, that they were Christians. I observed a number of other T-shirts and sweaters of Christian origin. Among OICCU members, I also observed the wearing of T-shirts bearing references to Word Alive, Soul Survivor, and Greenbelt. These events are Evangelical gatherings. Soul Survivor, for example, is an annual festival of Christian music and especially Christian popular music. When I asked members about these clothes, many commented, at first, that they just happened to "like them." However, many eventually commented that wearing them was "a way of starting a conversation," particularly in the case of WWJD ("What Would Jesus Do?") bracelets.

Another "Christian" marker has been the "silver ring." I have never observed any Christian student wearing one of these at either Oxford or Aberdeen. However, when I was an undergraduate at Durham University I did observe two female undergraduates wearing them. Moslener (2011) has looked in some detail at the "silver ring" movement, which began in the United States in about the year 2000. In purchasing one of the rings, which occurs at live Evangelical events, adolescents are supposed to commit to sexual abstinence until marriage, at which point they take the ring off. Moreover, they pledge themselves to Jesus. However, another movement—"True Love Waits"—popularized so-called "purity rings" as early as 1993. Again, the aim of such dress, in terms of social science research, is to express Christian identity to the supposedly non-Christian world but also to show to the group of which one is a part that one is committed to the group. Thus, in Douglas's (1970) terms the "silver ring" involves imprinting the ideology of the group on the body of the member. The member is using her body to evidence, in symbolic terms, her commitment to the group. As discussed, the items in question are produced by Christian organizations and distributed through Christian bookshops, Web sites and through stalls at Christian events.

In general, though, I observed very little difference between the manner in which Christians dressed and the way in which most Oxford students dressed. However, there were certain subtle differences. I observed that male members dressed in a conventional manner in almost all cases. The hair would be relatively short, the clothes relatively fashionable. I observed no male who might be termed unconventionally dressed in OICCU. It was among female members that I found the greatest differences in clothing style. Though it now seems to have passed, it was fashionable among young females at the time to wear "revealing" clothing. By this I mean the exposing of their midriffs while also wearing "hipsters" and, in so doing, often exposing the rim of their underwear (e.g., Barbieri 2004). I would argue that this is "revealing" because it nearly shows a part of the body that is generally understood to be sexual—i.e., the buttocks or the area just above the pubic hair. Often, the underwear would be a thong, meaning that part of the buttocks was exposed. Indeed, when females who dressed in this way happened to bend down, the top of their buttocks were sometimes visible. However, with regard to female members of OICCU, I observed the wearing of crop tops or at least high cut T-shirts but I did not observe the wearing of hipsters at all. In other respects, the clothing worn by female OICCU members did not appear to be especially differentiated from that worn by non-members. Like many of their non-Christian counterparts, I observed female CU members wearing trousers and, in the warmer months at least, tops which revealed the arms, shoulders and, occasionally, some breast cleavage, though never much. However, the hipster brand of trouser was not observed. A possible reason for this absence is the seemingly sexual nature of such a form of dress. To dress in such a manner reveals the midriff. Hence, we might understand such a fashion to be suggestive and thus the rejection of it by female CU members might appear to be congruous with the attitudes of such members toward sex.[7] Equally, I also did not observe among OICCU females the then-contemporary fashion for leaving the top of their panties exposed and we might explain such an absence in a similar fashion to that of hipsters. When I questioned female members as to why this was, the response, in most cases, was that they felt this fashion to be "too sexual" and that they wanted to dress "modestly." A few said they had no difficulty with it but made remarks like, "I don't have the figure for it" or "If only!" However, after further discussion, it was found that female members did not think it was appropriate for them to wear such clothing. Many commented that it was "provocative" and, as such, was "unhelpful,"[8] particularly at a CU meeting. They commented that it had negative "associations" and, as such, was "not good witness." One girl even commented that, "I wouldn't want people to think I was a slut! It's just not helpful. It's just not the right thing for me to wear."

I also asked female members whether they felt the use of such clothing would be acceptable to the broader group. Most felt that it would not be. They were correct in this feeling. All members to whom I spoke felt that it would be unacceptable for members, whether at CU meetings or in general, to wear "revealing" and "provocative" clothes. Many had difficulty in defining precisely where they would "draw the line" but certainly suggested that the hipster and crop-top fashion would not be "helpful." When I mentioned another fashion among young women of wearing trousers such that the upper half of their bottom is revealed and then wearing a wide belt around the waist, most members just laughed. A small number commented, "I've never seen that!" They did not find such a fashion acceptable. The male members did not seem to find it acceptable either. Almost all male members whom I interviewed in both groups responded to the initial question about hipsters and crop-tops with some kind of joke: "Depends what their figure's like!" "Well ... as long as I can watch!" "I'm sure I'd be interested," and so on. Further discussion, however, seemed to indicate a distaste for such clothing if worn by CU members. Members felt that such clothing was provocative, would prevent concentration if actually worn at CU, would distract people from Christianity, was "unhelpful," was "bad witness," or was "not really appropriate." Male members felt that they would have no problem with a non-Christian wearing such clothes even at a CU meeting. Members felt that they were inappropriate and "unhelpful" for a CU member. Even having said this, some members felt it necessary to make jokes.

So, we can see the way in which fashionable clothing is employed in these Evangelical groups to demonstrate conformity to the group's perceived mores with regard to sexuality. Interviews and surveys indicated, indeed, that both groups were relatively conservative in their attitudes to sexuality. Sex before marriage was almost totally unacceptable as was "snogging" (tongue kissing) outside of the context of some kind of committed relationship. It was very interesting, in this regard, when I conducted fieldwork with an Evangelical student group at Leiden University in the Netherlands, who we will call CSL (Christian Students Leiden). The group had a generally more liberal attitude to sex—reflected in the numbers who admitted having already had sex despite not being married (it was nil in the other groups)—and this was reflected in their attitudes to female dress. Among women, the kind of clothing was perhaps in general more conservative in terms of the exposure of flesh and so forth than among other Leiden students. The majority, though perhaps not a large majority, did not wear what we might understand as revealing fashions. When I spoke to them about this, they explained it in a similar way to their British colleagues. Some said such fashions were "too sexual" and immodest while others became embarrassed and made jokes such as "Perhaps I need to lose a little weight to wear such clothes!" or "I do not have the figure for such clothes" or "They would not look good on me!" But in contrast to the situation among female members of OICCU, the rest did wear such fashions. I regularly observed female members to be wearing hipsters and crop-tops together, although I only observed one female member reflect the fashion of deliberately exposing the top of her panties. When I asked her about this and informed her that I had not noted such a fashion before in other such groups the woman concerned was amazed. She felt there was nothing "un-Christian" about it and that how a person dressed had nothing to do with what they believed. Others who wore hipsters said they were just ordinary people who happened to be Christians and as such wore clothes that everyone else wore.

Female members tended to agree that highly provocative fashions were not appropriate for Christian women but they did not feel that the wearing of the kind of fashions to which I referred were sufficiently provocative. They did, however, agree that the (albeit very rare) kind of fashion in which part of the female's bottom is left exposed was not appropriate and was indeed too provocative. Male members to whom I spoke seemed to agree with their female counterparts. None of the members to whom I spoke seemed to believe that the hipster with crop-top fashion was inappropriate for Christian girls. Many remarked that such a style was simply "fashionable." Neither did any male members hold any objection to female members wearing very short mini-skirts although I never observed any female members doing this. Male members again emphasized that clothing which was "very sexual" was not appropriate but they found it difficult to articulate precisely what that was. One member joked, "Perhaps if they walk around and they are naked then this is not good!" He then thought about this remark and decided that nudity was probably preferable to revealing forms of clothing because it was not necessarily trying to be seductive. When I suggested the kind of highly revealing fashion to which I have previously referred, many members laughed and all seemed to agree that such a fashion would not be approved of. So, we can see that this religious group is less differentiated in terms of ethics from average students and dress requirements are less differentiated accordingly. It was also less differentiated theologically, with more members accepting evolution than in the other groups, where it was almost always rejected.

I specifically asked some female British Christians if there were any clothes shops that they would avoid. They had all kinds of reasons for avoiding certain shops—"I don't shop at Karen Millen, I haven't got the figure for it!"—but none of these seemed to relate to their religiosity. The only shops, which also happened to sell clothing, which Christians said that they would avoid were "pagan" or "New Age" shops, and they would also avoid the fashions associated with this sub-culture. But here there were differences. In the Dutch group, there was a female student whose dress sense was, to some extent, "goth" and members there did not consider this to be a problem.

Finally, it has been argued that in the United States, where the Evangelical movement is strong, Evangelical Christian fashion is effectively influencing what non-Christians wear. It does this, though the influence does not seem to be substantial, by exerting lobbying pressure on fashion retailers, meaning that fashions begin to reflect the kind of "modesty" which such groups prize (see Michelman 2003). Clearly, whenever a group with conservative attitudes to sex becomes powerful it may begin to influence "fashion" among those who do not accept its views.

Religious influence on mainstream fashion

So far, we have examined the way in which religious people—focusing on Evangelical Christians—make use of contemporary secular fashions. However, we have noted the way in which the reverse can be true in a context in which the "religious" have power. Another significant issue is the way in which people who do not significantly identify with a particular religion make use of forms of dress commonly associated with religion. In looking at this issue, it would be useful to briefly pause to discuss the nature of religion. In this chapter, I am drawing upon what might be called the "lexical" definition of religion: the one commonly found in the dictionary which defines "religion" as involving membership of a group which believes in gods or spirits, or membership of a particular world faith. This is useful when making a distinction between worldviews based around spiritual beliefs and worldviews not based around these but it is problematic in that it draws a clear line between pre-Enlightenment and post-Enlightenment ideologies, implying that they are fundamentally different. It might be suggested that they are not. "Religion" can also be defined in broader terms with regard to how it functions. Broadly speaking, "religion" involves fervent belief, regardless of the evidence, in certain dogmas or ritual practices coupled with a belief in some kind of agency behind empirical events (see Dutton 2012). Such a definition includes traditional religions but also various ideologies that, it has been argued (e.g., Scruton 2000), have effectively come to replace Christianity in the West, such as nationalism or Marxism. In general, these ideologies find their roots in the Romantic movement in which city life is rejected as superficial, unjust (due to inequality) and vain, just as Christianity is seen to reject wealth. The life of the peasant or tribesman is prized as genuine, honest, equal, and something to return to, just as Christianity advocates the Kingdom of Heaven in which the last shall be first. Accompanying this is a belief in a kind of destiny—that the "Will of the People" will triumph, for example—and a strong group identity which rejects as "other" those who do not accept the essential doctrines of the group and its will (Popper 1966). This might be compared to Christianity believing that history follows God's will and rejecting dissenters as in league with the Devil. Thus, Romantic nationalism prizes peasant life, Marxism prizes the worker, and multiculturalism prizes the primitive or non-Western culture, including its religiosity, and it rejects as "racist" (implicitly immoral) outgroups those who dissent (see Dutton 2012; Gottfried 2004; Ellis 2004; Sandall 2001).

This romantic prizing of non-Western cultures—including their religiosity—is clearly influential in the Western world and has led to fashion sub-cultures that imitate, in their dress, other cultures. This could be observed among Westerners—who might dress like Turks, for example—even in the nineteenth century. The most obvious contemporary manifestation is the style of dress best summarized as "hippy" or even "ethnic" (see Hebdige 1979). Both involve using articles of clothing worn in Eastern countries, ultimately for religious reasons. When I was an undergraduate, for example, there was a fashion, among male students who broadly adopted this style, of wearing the kind of headscarves favored by Palestinians but wearing them as neck scarves. Others wore the kind of long shirts favored by men in Muslim cultures such as Pakistan. The Web site "Ethnic Fashion" provides a broad array of "ethnic" clothing for those with an "ethnic" style. Their products include the "Kaftan" (a shirt with origins in Persia), a Kurta (a traditional, long shirt worn in India), granddad shirts (collarless shirts, also popular in India), a pashmina (scarves, worn by Indian and Nepalese women), a traditional gypsy skirt, and a sarong (a kind of kilt worn in South East Asia) (see Ethnic Fashion UK n.d.). However, there is no need to shop at "Ethnic Fashion" to acquire these items. "Ethnic style" is now so mainstream that it can be purchased at Marks and Spencers, a British department store that is commonly regarded as purveying only the most mainstream of fashions.

The popularity of these clothes can be looked at in two ways. On the one hand, as already indicated, it evidences the influence of "religion" on mainstream fashion. That which some religious people wear is imitated by those who are not especially religious. On the other hand, though with caution, it can be analyzed in much the same way as we have the Christian use of certain contemporary fashions. By dressing in this way, people are evidencing their conformity to an albeit very broad and loosely structured religious group, namely multiculturalism. This is especially pertinent if they are part of an identifiable organization—such as a left-wing political organization——to which this ideology is central. Proponents of multiculturalism argue that all cultures are equal but that the purest cultures are ethnic (non-Western) and tribal cultures. These cultures enrich Western culture, which has been responsible for terrible atrocities such as colonialism, and should be prized, imitated and encouraged by Westerners (see Sandall 2001; Gottfried 2004). Accordingly, by dressing in an "ethnic" way, a person is implicitly involving themselves in what has been argued to be, in the West, the most dominant replacement religion. They are stamping their religiosity upon their bodies, and demonstrating their orthodoxy to those who police the boundaries of the, albeit vaguely structured, latter-day religious organization. It is important in stating this to draw a distinction between people who might be best characterized as "religious" (in the operational sense) and those further away from the center of the essentialist category of "religion" who are simply inclined to follow trends.

Following an operational definition of religion, philosophers such as Karl Popper (1963) have noted that one of the important factors that distinguishes a religious (and thus tribal) organization from one focused on science is the attitude to the past. Tribal organizations look to the past as a golden era and use it as a source of inspiration with regard to how they should live in the present (though, in some cases, they also look to a future utopia, sometimes based around aspects of this past). Accordingly, they are strongly attached to the traditions and ways of the past. By contrast, civilizations, in the scientific spirit, are focused on constantly developing in order to better control their environment. They are happy to abandon long-held beliefs and long-employed practices in the pursuit of this goal and, accordingly, a civilization is constantly innovating. In this regard, we might consider the current "postmodern" fashion of recycling fashions from decades earlier as evidence of the pervasive influence of Romanticism—and postmodernism has been argued to ultimately have its intellectual roots in the Romantic movement (see Scruton 2000). In postmodern terms it would not necessarily involve nostalgia for the past so much as an expression of the confused nature of the postmodern condition, a critique of the "progress" of modernism. Of course, it could also involve nostalgia for the aspects of that period's fashion that might be seen as congruous with postmodern thinking, such as fashions that challenge traditional male hegemony. Since around 1990, in Britain, fashions popular 30 years earlier have become mainstream fashion once again. Thus, in the 1990s, the fashions of the 1960s once more became mainstream, and by the 2000s this was changing to become the 1970s' ways of dressing. It seems that in the early 2010s the 1980s are once again fashionable among trendsetters (see Guffey 2006). This is despite the fact that in the 1990s, the fashions of the 1970s were widely ridiculed, as were the fashions of the 1980s around ten years later.

In addition, there are other increasingly mainstream movements that involve reviving even older forms of dressing. For example, in July 2011, the fashion magazine *Vogue* reported that it was now fashionable for women to wear updated versions of clothes that were popular in the 1940s:

This autumn/winter 2011–12, designers (…) have ushered in a season of sheer Forties glamour, complete with furs, pearls, gloves and shrugs—all revolving around the pencil skirt. Hemlines have dipped to a strict—yet feminine—on-the-knee length that is at once conservative and very alluring. "This collection was about the empowerment of women," says Donna Karan in the August 2011 issue of *Vogue*. "Their words of wisdom and their ability to be strong and take a stand without giving up their femininity."

(Smith 2011)

Amongst men, fashions from the 1940s and 1950s considered laughable for young people in the 1990s and 2000s—such as cravats—are also making a comeback, as is the use, with various modern twists, of the kind of tweed country casuals stereotypically worn by the English aristocracy (e.g., Neel 2011). Again, for some people, perhaps the trendsetters, this might also be seen in latter-day religious terms. Such dress may, in some cases, reflect a nostalgia for a more distant past in which Britain was clearly British, in which there was an empire, strong codes of politeness, and national unity caused by the Second World War.[9] Accordingly, it might be regarded as congruous, I stress for some users, with a kind of nostalgic, Romantic nationalism.

Conclusion

In this discussion we have examined the relationship between religion and fashion in two key ways. Defining "fashion" as popularly employed clothing that ultimately spreads through the populace by means of imitation of a perceived elite, we have noted the way in which religious groups use clothing as a means of expressing their sense of differentiation from the mainstream. Equally, we have observed that as religious groups tend to control the bodies of their members, fashion can also be used as a means of policing the boundaries of the group. Some religious groups reject almost completely clothing that would be regarded as "fashionable." However, many members of religious groups make use of mainstream fashions in order to express a small degree of differentiation. In this regard, we have looked at Evangelical Christians and observed that they have their own specifically manufactured "Christian clothing" which is an obvious means of identity expression and evangelism. But it tends to reflect broader fashionable styles, within certain limitations, as does their "non-Christian" clothing. In particular, we have noted that Christian women reject fashionable styles that they regard as immodest and styles which they associate with Paganism of various kinds. We have noted that there are variations in this regard, based on the degree to which the group is differentiated in terms of sexual morality, but it broadly holds and is reflected in interviews with group members.

The second relationship we have examined is the influence of religious clothing on mainstream Western fashion. We have argued that the Romantic movement—and the movements which it has spawned—prized non-Western cultures and that unlike in the post-Enlightenment West such cultures involve no clear division between "religion" and "culture." We argued that the Romantic movement is effectively a replacement religion in the West. Accordingly, the contemporary fashion for ethnic clothes involves an influence of religious items on Western fashion. For some ardent multiculturalists, the use of such clothing might be analyzed in the same manner in which we analyzed clothing among Evangelical students. Revivals of historical fashions might also be seen in these latter-day Romantic terms. This raises the central question of how religion should be defined but as long as we are clear about how we are defining religion in a specific set of circumstances and why we are using the definition we are using, there is no need for this to lead to confusion.

Notes

1 Though it has been noted that those at the center of power are, to a certain extent, above the rules. As we will see below this provides them with a greater freedom to innovate (see Dutton 2007). In addition, it might be argued that those furthest from the power center might, in some respects, be more controlled in what they can wear than those above them as dress can be used as a means of playing for status and thus challenging the system of order. This is exemplified in the sometimes violent reaction to the African-American use of "zoot suits" in the Deep South during segregation (see Alvarez 2008).

2 I use the word "elite" in Argyle's (1994) sense to refer to members of the "upper class"— that is to say the old aristocracy, the new rich and, to a lesser extent, those with cultural influence, such as celebrities, who may not necessarily be wealthy.

3 There is an ongoing debate with regard to how the word "fashion" should be defined and even a postmodern critique of the concept, arguing that it is a means of imposing Western hegemony on the rest of the world. See, for example, Lillethun (2011). For an analysis of the postmodern critique of such categories see Dutton (2012, Chapter 2).

4 The binary division of the world implied in this term would seem to indicate a strong degree of group identity.

5 Parts of this section were originally published in Dutton (2005).

6 For other fieldwork on youthful religious people and their fashions, see also Anijar 1999; Tarlo 2000; Shirazi 2000.

7 Almost all members whom I interviewed were opposed to premarital sex (see Dutton 2008).

8 This was an interesting word and, to some extent, an example of Christian Union "restricted code" (see Douglas 1970). It meant "unhelpful" to the CU's purpose of preserving Christians as Christians and bringing non-Christians to Christ. But this didn't need to be explicitly stated because, from an in-group perspective, the meaning was so obvious. Douglas notes that a high level of restricted code tends to denote a tightly structured organization with strong boundaries. "Witness" is another such word, used idiosyncratically by CU members to mean "evangelize to," in this case by means of behavior.

9 This is especially so among those who are part of a tongue-in-cheek "movement" known as "Chappism" active in the United Kingdom. With their own regular magazine (*The Chap*) and events in the UK, they call for a "Tweed Revolution" and a "Call to Charms." See Temple and Darkwood (2001).

Works cited

Abbas, T. (2005) "British South Asian Muslims: state and the multicultural society," in T. Abbas (ed.), *Muslim Britain: Communities Under Pressure*, London: Zed Books.

Alvarez, L. (2008) *The Power of the Zoot: Youth Culture and Resistance During World War II*, Berkeley, CA: University of California Press.

Anijar, K. (1999) "Jewish genes, Jewish jeans: a fashionable body," in L.B. Arthur (ed.), *Religion, Dress and the Body*, Oxford: Berg, 181–200.

Argyle, M. (1994) *The Psychology of Social Class*, London: Routledge.

Arthur, L.B. (1999) "Dress and the social control of the body," in L.B. Arthur (ed.), *Religion, Dress and the Body*, Oxford: Berg, 1–8.

Barbieri, A. (2004) "A brief history of bare midriffs," *New Statesman* (November 15): 20.

Barnard, M. (2002) *Fashion as Communication*, London: Routledge.

Bourdieu, P. (1984) *Distinction: A Social Critique of Judgment and Taste*, London: Routledge.

Christian Clothing Alliance (n.d.) Online. Available: www.christianclothingalliance.co.uk/ (accessed 24 September 2011). [Web site down as of 12 October 2012.]

Davis, F. (1989) "Of maids' uniforms and blue jeans: the drama of status ambivalences in status and fashion," *Qualitative Sociology* 12, 1: 337–55.

Douglas, M. (1970) *Natural Symbols: Explorations in Cosmology*, London: Routledge.

Dutton, E. (2005) "Crop-tops, hipsters and liminality: fashion and differentiation in two Evangelical student groups," *Journal of Religion and Popular Culture* 9 (Spring). Online. Available: www.usask.ca/relst/jrpc/art9-fashion.html (accessed 30 August 2010).

——(2007) "'Bog off dog breath! You're talking pants!' Swearing as witness evangelism in student Evangelical groups," *Journal of Religion and Popular Culture* 16 (Summer). Online. Available: www.usask.ca/relst/jrpc/art16-swearing.html (accessed 30 August 2010).

——(2008) *Meeting Jesus at University: Rites of Passage and Student Evangelicals*, Aldershot: Ashgate.

——(2012) *Culture Shock and Multiculturalism: Reclaiming a Useful Model from the Realm of Religion*, Newcastle: Cambridge Scholars Publishing.

Ellis, F. (2004) *Political Correctness and the Theoretical Struggle: From Lenin and Mao to Marcus and Foucault*, Auckland: Maxim Institute.

Entwistle, J. (2000) *The Fashioned Body*, Oxford: Wiley-Blackwell.

Ethnic Fashion UK (n.d.) "Ethnic fashion," Online. Available: www.ethnic-fashion.co.uk/ (accessed 2 September 2012).

Fox, K. (2004) *Watching the English: The Hidden Rules of English Behaviour*, London: Hodder and Stoughton.

Gitlin, T. (1998) "The culture of celebrity," *Dissent* 45 (Summer): 81–83.

Goldman Carrel, B. (1999) "Hasidic women's head coverings: a feminized system of Hasidic distinction," in L.B. Arthur (ed.), *Religion, Dress and the Body*, Oxford: Berg, 163–80.

Gottfried, P. (2004) *Multiculturalism and the Politics of Guilt: Towards a Secular Theocracy*, Columbia, MO: University of Missouri Press.

Graybill, B. and L.B. Arthur (1999) "The social control of women's bodies in two Mennonite communities," in L.B. Arthur (ed.), *Religion, Dress and the Body*, Oxford: Berg, 9–30.

Guffey, E. (2006) *Retro: The Culture of Revival*, London: Reaktion Books.

Hall, E.J. (1993) "Waitering/waitressing: engendering the work of table servants," *Gender and Society* 7, 3 (September): 329–46.

Hamilton, J. and J. Hawley (1999) "Sacred dress, public worlds: Amish and Mormon experiences and commitment," in L.B. Arthur (ed.), *Religion, Dress and the Body*, Oxford: Berg, 31–52.

Hayward, K. and M. Yar (2006) "The 'chav' phenomenon: consumption, media and the construction of a new underclass," *Crime, Media and Culture* 2, 1 (April): 9–28.

Hebdige, D. (1979) *Subculture: The Meaning of Style*, London: Routledge.

Kley, E. (1998) "Fashionable fashion," *PAJ: A Journal of Performance and Art* 20, 3 (September): 26–30.

Leopold, E. (1992) "The manufacture of the fashion system," in J. Ash and E. Wilson (eds), *Chic Thrills: A Fashion Reader*, Berkeley, CA: University of California Press, 101–17.

Lillethun, A. (2011) "Fashion theory: introduction," in L. Welters and A. Lillethun (eds), *The Fashion Reader*, 2nd edn, Oxford: Berg, 117–24.

Lipp, S. (1989) "Racial and ethnic problems: Peru," *International Journal of Group Tensions* 19, 4: 339–48.

Mail Online (2009) "Pixie Geldof rocks the retro 80s look with backwards baseball cap and chunky black boots" (29 May). Online. Available: www.dailymail.co.uk/tvshowbiz/article-1189459/Pixie-Geldof-rocks-retro-80s-look-backwards-baseball-cap-chunky-black-boots.html (accessed 31 August 2012).

Michelman, S. (2003) "Reveal or conceal? American religious discourse with fashion," *Etnofoor* 16, 2: 76–87.

Micklin, M. (1977) "Anticipated reactions to deviance in a South American city: a study of social control," *Pacific Sociological Review* 20, 4 (October): 515–35.

Morris, D. (2002) *People Watching*, London: Vantage.

Moslener, S. (2011) "'Don't act now!' Selling Christian abstinence in the religious marketplace," in E.M. Mazur and K. McCarthy (eds), *God in the Details: American Religion in Popular Culture*, 2nd edn, New York: Routledge, 197–218.

Neel, J. (2011) "Tartan army," *Vogue* (July 7). Online. Available: www.vogue.co.uk/fashion/trends/2011–12-autumn-winter/tartan-army (accessed 31 August 2012).

Poll, S. (1962) *The Hasidic Community in Williamsburg*, New York: Glance Free Press.

Popper, K. (1963) *Conjectures and Refutations: The Growth of Scientific Knowledge*, London: Routledge, Kegan and Paul.

——(1966) *The Open Society and Its Enemies II: The High Tide of Prophecy: Hegel, Marx and the Aftermath*, London: Routledge, Kegan and Paul.

Roach-Higgins, M. and J. Eicher (1992) "Dress and identity," *Clothing and Textiles Research Journal* 10, 4 (June): 1–8.

Sandall, R. (2001) *The Culture Cult: On Designer Tribalism and Other Essays*, Oxford: Westview Press.

Scruton, R. (2000) *Modern Culture*, London: Continuum.

Shirazi, F. (2000) "Islamic religion and women's dress code: the Islamic Republic of Iran," in L.B. Arthur (ed.), *Undressing Religion: Commitment and Conversion from a Cross-Cultural Perspective*, Oxford: Berg, 113–30.

Simmel, G. (1957) "Fashion," *American Journal of Sociology* 62, 6: 541–58.

Singh, G. and D.S. Tatla (2006) *Sikhs in Britain: The Making of a Community*, London: Zed Books.

Smith, Z. (2011) "Forties glamour," *Vogue* (July 7). Online. Available: www.vogue.co.uk/fashion/trends/2011–12-autumn-winter/forties-glamour (accessed 31 August 2012).

Tarlo, E. (2000) "Sartorial entanglements of a Gujarati wife," in L.B. Arthur (ed.), *Undressing Religion: Commitment and Conversion from a Cross-Cultural Perspective*, Oxford: Berg, 147–67.

Temple, G. and V. Darkwood (2001) *The Chap Manifesto: Revolutionary Etiquette for the Modern Gentleman*, London: Fourth Estate.

Thompson, W.E. (1986) "Deviant ideology: the case of the Old Order Amish," *Quarterly Journal of Ideology* 10, 1 (January): 29–33.

Veblen, T. (1925) *The Theory of the Leisure Class*, London: Allen and Unwin.

Welters, L. and A. Lillethun (eds) (2011) *The Fashion Reader*, 2nd edn, Oxford: Berg.

Workman, J. and K. Johnson (1994) "Effects of conformity and non-conformity to gender-role expectation for dress: teachers versus students," *Adolescence* 29, 113 (Spring): 207–23.

Wouters, C. (2007) *Informalization: Manners and Emotions Since 1890*. London: Sage.

15

GAMES AND DOLLS

Nikki Bado and Rebecca Sachs Norris

> "I think every Barbie doll is more harmful than an American missile."
>
> Iranian toy seller (quoted by BBC News, 5 March 2002)

Introduction

Mormonopoly and Job-with-boils action figures: these were our passports and intro-
ductions to a magical and occasionally disturbing kingdom filled with improbably
cute and cuddly Jesus, Buddha, and Kali dolls, board games with celestial weapons
and eternal treasures, Passover plague toys, and Resurrection eggs. Modestly attired
and religiously sanctioned anti-Barbies occupy one corner of the kingdom, with
pocket Goddesses, karma cards, and endlessly turning *BuddhaWheels* occupying
others. There are practical religious tchotchkes as well as toys and dolls. Jesus ban-
dages protect and soothe minor scrapes and cuts, while the Holy Toast blesses
breakfast by stamping an image of the praying Virgin Mary on bread.

Welcome to the world of religious games, toys, and dolls—a world filled with artifacts
of material culture that have delighted, intrigued, captivated, and occasionally confounded those exploring the connections between religion and play. The interweaving
embodied by these items illustrates the complexity and non-dualism of religions as
they are lived in the everyday, challenging a tendency in Western scholarship to divide
the world too neatly between things sacred and profane, or spiritual and secular.

Not only are play and playfulness intimately intertwined with most (if not all) of
the world's religions, but their connections are indeed quite ancient. They are also at
times quite problematic. Despite its entertaining and humorously playful nature, the
world of religious games and dolls can be equally filled with deeply troubling issues of
politics, consumerism, commodification, competitiveness, gender stereotyping, indoctrination, and economic exploitation. For example, talking Jesus, Moses, and the modestly dressed Virgin Mary and Esther dolls provide children with wholesome toys
that quote bits of biblical scripture. But they are accompanied on the same Web site by
impressively muscular Samson action figures designed to fight for children's souls in a
militaristic and apocalyptic "Battle for the Toybox." While these themes are common
in the marketing of boys' toys, some may find them unsettling, and even divisive.

261

One point on which the Abrahamic traditions do seem to agree is the need to provide modestly dressed dolls as correctives to the ubiquitous influence of Barbie. While Christian girls have talking Mary and Esther, Jewish girls can play with Gali girls, which resemble the wholesome-looking American Girl line of dolls. Their Muslim counterparts have an assortment of modestly dressed dolls, from the American-produced Razanne to the extremely popular Syrian doll Fulla, which out-sells Barbie in the Middle East (MacKinnon 2005). "Immoral" Barbies and apocalyptic battles for children's souls are only two of the many social and political issues we discovered. Religions and toy manufacturing corporations are actively competing for converts and profits; one of their primary battlegrounds is what children do on the field of play (Bado-Fralick and Norris 2010: 43).

During our research, we found a surprising diversity and abundance of board games, many with variations on popular and familiar family games such as *Monopoly*, *Risk*, or *Trivial Pursuit*, employing a "race game" style of play in which being the first person to reach a goal means winning the game.[1] Christianity is well represented here, as in *Monopoly*-type games such as *Catholicopoly*, *Episcopopoly*, and *Bibleopoly*, in addition to *Mormonopoly* (produced by the Church of Jesus Christ of Latter-day Saints). *Mortality* (see Figure 15.1) is another LDS produced game, a spin-off of the *Game of Life*. *Missionary Conquest*, a game in which players build missions in foreign lands, is a cross between *Risk* and *Monopoly*, and clearly not intended as a game of ecumenical goodwill (see Figures 15.2 and 15.3).

There are complicated educational games such as *Divinity*, the only game we found with the papal *imprimatur*, the Catholic Church's official seal of approval. There is also *Vatican: The Board Game*, a game in which boys (and girls!) compete to become the Bishop of Rome by answering questions with complex global social and political implications for the Church, while moving cardinal figures (including one with trendy sunglasses) around the board, ever closer to the papal prize. Nuns form their own large and imaginative subgroup of Catholic toys, from boxing nun hand pup-pets and nun Barbie dolls to *Nunzilla*, a wind-up nun toy that walks and spits fire, and Nun-chucks, which, yes, chuck nuns.

If your game-playing taste runs more to adventures in the ancient world, there is *Journeys of Paul*, set around 60 CE, or *Settlers of Canaan*, a variation of the recent award-winning *Settlers of Catan* game, demonstrating that game manufacturers are quick to take advantage of current trends in the industry, as well as current trends in popular religious thought. For example, *Iron Age—Council of the Clans* is an educa-tional board game designed to appeal to Contemporary Pagans, while the best-selling "Left Behind" novels have inspired both a board- and videogame involving players in religiously themed adventures in connection with the apparently highly anticipated second coming of Christ.

The other branches of the Abrahamic tradition are also well represented in popular culture by board games, toys, and dolls. For example, there is *Race to the Kabah*, *Mecca to Medina*, *Exodus* (complete with a "wheel of plagues"), and *Kosherland*, a takeoff of *Candyland*. There are plush Torahs, hijab-clad Muslim dolls designed for very young girls that teach useful Arabic phrases (see Figure 15.7), and even an Orthodox Jewish doll that prays when his four-fingered hand is pressed.[2]

Figure 15.1 Mortality: A Mormon version of Hasbro's *Game of Life*. (Photo courtesy of Courtney Cutler.)

Eastern religions also have a place in the world of religious games and toys. The *Buddha Board* demonstrates Zen-like concepts of impermanence and change, allowing you to draw on it with a water-dipped brush and then watch as the image fades away. It now comes as an iPhone application so that Zen-mind can accompany you anywhere. Educational games such as *BuddhaWheel* and *Karma Chakra* teach the Dharma, and *Leela*, a New Age version of *Snakes and Ladders*, reinforces proper actions. *Snakes and Ladders*—known in the United States as *Chutes and Ladders*—is a game with indeterminant origins—ancient Hindu or Buddhist—that comes in many versions: Christian, Jewish, Muslim (traditional and Sufi), and Sikh.

Commercially manufactured religious games are not new, and have been produced in the United States since the early nineteenth century. Games such as *Bible Characters* and *Mansion of Happiness* date back to the 1800s, and were meant to instill moral values. It is surprising, then, that there is so little scholarship in the field addressing the connections between religion—particularly Western religions—and play. While there are certainly folklore studies of children's games, nothing really

Figure 15.2 Missionary Conquest board game. (Photo courtesy of Courtney Cutler.)

Figure 15.3 Missionary Conquest game, detail. (Photo courtesy of Courtney Cutler.)

connected those games with religion, let alone acknowledged the possibility of experiences of play and fun at the core of religious practice. These many interesting and varied items of religious material culture have flown almost entirely under the radar.

There is clearly something about the ways in which the field of religious studies is constituted in the West that ignores these connections. The division between religion and play in much of religious studies scholarship is not a reflection of religions as they are lived now, nor as they have been lived throughout history. This is part of the larger story of Western scholarship, which is all too often prone to dichotomous thinking and compartmentalization, making neat divisions in scholarship where none exist in the far messier world of embodied and lived reality.

Today the attention of religious studies scholarship to play and playfulness in religion is somewhat improved. We are seeing a growing interest in the subject of games, play, and religion, as newly collected bodies of research are presented at academic conferences such as the American Academy of Religion, the American Folklore Society, and the Anthropological Association of America, to name a few. Journal articles are being written on the subject, expanding studies to include videogames as well as board games and other forms of popular religious culture. In addition to our own work (Bado-Fralick and Norris 2010), a wide-ranging anthology of writings by European scholars (Bornet and Burger 2012) is a useful sourcebook for scholars researching the relationships between religion and play. Another recent book (Raj and Dempsey 2010) focuses on play rather than games, as is the case with most scholarship in this area. Additionally, we are seeing a growing interest in the pedagogic use of religious games and toys, not only in learning how to be religious, but also in the religious studies classroom.

Games and religion in history

Archeological evidence suggests that games have always been an important part of religious life. Game boards, dolls, and other kinds of toys were buried in ancient tombs in Egypt, Greece, and Rome, and painted in murals on temple walls. Archeologists have discovered game boards dating from the sixth millennium BCE in Jordan (Rollefson 1992: 1) and from 3500 to 4000 BCE in Egypt (Murray 1951: 12).

Some of the earliest known game boards are seen in Egyptian pyramids, including *Mehen*, a game shaped like a coiled snake, dating from between 3200 and 2250 BCE, and *Senet*, which resembles backgammon. While it is hard to say exactly how these ancient games were played, their presence in the tombs suggests that they were religious artifacts. Game playing is portrayed in the Egyptian *Book of the Dead*, "where the soul of the departed plays a game in the other world." Egyptian gods and goddesses also played games; one painting shows the pharaoh Rameses III playing a game with Isis (Murray 1951: 14). Even ancient games such as chess and the Chinese game *Weiqi*, known in Japan as *Go*, have their roots in cosmological play, as does the ancient Aztec ball game *ullamaliztli* (Fox 2006: 110–17).

Games of chance—including dice, cards, and even sports—provide one of the strongest historical connections between religion and play, and were often used for ritual divination. From the earliest ninth century BCE Akkadian dice to the more recent and (presumably satirical) *God-Jesus Robot* of Japan, people have used games and toys to divine the will of the Gods. The history of games is intimately inter-woven with religious rites and practices. Games were an integral part of religious life, and the movement of games from place to place may have accompanied the spread of religion, as through the dissemination of Buddhism from Northern India (Murray 1951: 229). When religious people traveled, games accompanied them, even in Islam, where (according to most official early interpretations) the Quran forbade game playing as a form of gambling (Murray 1951: 230).

As artifacts of everyday life, games and toys reflect cultural as well as religious attitudes that are easily disseminated through travel and the meeting of cultures. Because they are fun to play, games also transmit religion intentionally, and are a natural resource for people who wish to teach religious values. Their playfulness also lends them to satire and parody, such as in the religious games *Nuns on the Run*, or *Fleece the Flock*. Illustrating the games' liminal position in Western culture, many people—including ministers and religious studies scholars—cannot tell at first glance whether they are serious or satire, for children or adults.

Games, children, and education

The late seventeenth- and eighteenth-century invention of the notion of childhood as a discrete time of life is one reason for the lack of scholarship on play and religion. With the invention of childhood, play becomes something that *children* do. It becomes trivialized and therefore seen as unworthy of the kinds of rigorous scho-larly examination and analysis that something as apparently serious as religion deserves.[3]

Western scholarship tends to divorce religion and spirituality from play and fun, even though festivals, games, and play are integral parts of religious life. Many reli-gious traditions honor and acknowledge the importance of play. From Beltane to Purim to Holi, religious festivals can hardly be ignored. And their playfulness runs the gamut, from lighthearted innocence to bawdy ribaldry. While scholars of religion can't entirely disregard play, they usually emphasize the festivals' more "serious" pedagogical or social goals.

Contemporary religious games and dolls also mingle the playful and serious by teaching through fun and play. This approach to learning is not new; Plato argued that "[w]e learn through playing, and only through playing" (Ardley 1967: 234). Religious games use a number of devices to enculturate children, by emphasizing knowledge, using moral conduct cards, and providing spiritual game rewards.[4] Most of the Muslim games, as well as some Christian and Jewish ones, are *Trivial Pursuit*-type games, which require knowledge of ritual, religious history (and the like) to move forward in the game. The *Hajj Fun Game*, for example (see Figure 15.4), asks questions of varying levels of difficulty, e.g., "Where is the birthplace of the prophet Mohammad?" or "What is Rukn Aswad?" Moral conduct cards are common in many games, with the level of the ethical issue based to some extent on the recom-mended age for the game. For example, a card in the *Armor of God* game (Christian,

Figure 15.4 Hajj Fun Game. (Photo courtesy of Courtney Cutler.)

ages 5–9) states: "You are tempted to lie about the lamp you broke, but you tell the truth instead." In some games, moral conduct cards will move you forward or back; in this game, having told the truth the player gets a spiritual reward: the Belt of Truth, one of the *Armor of God* playing pieces needed to win. Event cards may also have moral implications; picking the wrong Career Event card in the *Vatican* game will land you in the Cesspool of Sin. Similarly, some games have spiritual rewards such as Eternal Treasures (*Richest Christian Game*), or Celestial Weapons (*Mahabharata Game*). These symbolic elements can evoke the mystery of myth and the sacred.

Religious games use various styles of imagery as well, in order to appeal to children. *Karma Chakra*, a Buddhist game, is almost completely abstract, with intensive thought put into each color and element (Ghartsang 2007), while the *BuddhaWheel* board is the Wheel of Life. Muslim game boards may have images of mosques, but for the most part are simple and abstract, likely because of Islamic restrictions on sacred images. Judaism has similar restrictions, but many Jewish games, such as *Kosherland*, *Let My People Go*, or *Exodus*, aren't bound by Orthodox concerns and have bright colors and human images, including nasty-looking pharaohs.

Christian boards display the most variety, in part because there are more Christian games in general, a natural result of the history of Christianity and commerce in the United States, as well as the Christian call to spread the gospel in any way possible (Bado-Fralick and Norris 2010: 78). *Vatican: the Board Game* uses geometric symbolism with different sections of the board representing steps on the way to becoming pope. The historical *Journeys of Paul* game board employs a map of the

Mediterranean around the time of Paul, along with cartoon-style realism on the event cards. *Bibleland* uses children's cartoon images even for the crucified and resurrected Christ, who does not look like he is suffering very much on the cross—how could he be when he is so cute and chubby-cheeked? (See Figures 15.5 and 15.6.)

The use of cartoon images is natural for artifacts that merge religion with popular culture, but this raises a number of interesting questions about what effects these images will have on religious life. Certainly graphic images are powerful, as demonstrated by religious efforts to control them, from Jewish and Islamic restrictions on images of God or Muhammad, to Reformation iconoclasm, to the Taliban's destruction of Buddhist statues. Being less able to work with abstract concepts than adults, children are especially vulnerable and highly responsive to graphic imagery (Kline 1993: 187). These images construct associations that inform our religious identities and experience (Norris 2005). In other words, games convey ideals and values through their graphic style as well as structure. And given the limitations of game structure and the influence of popular culture on the imagery, we might well question the nature and scope of knowledge conveyed (see also Norris 2011).

Religion, games, and commerce

To successfully compete with widely advertised and readily available popular toys, religious toys must be visually appealing and fun to play with. One way to do this is to make religious games mirror popular games, replacing secular terms with religious

Figure 15.5 Bibleland. (Photo courtesy of Courtney Cutler.)

Figure 15.6 Bibleland, detail. (Photo courtesy of Courtney Cutler.)

ones, as in *Catholicopoly*. Religious dolls exhibit much of the same mirroring to compete with their popular rivals. But using popular culture and images to attract young people can create uncomfortable combinations of ideas and goals. For example, games are marketed as fun, even though the relation of fun to religious practices such as *salat* (prayer, one of the five pillars of Islam) in *Madinah Salat Fun Game*, seems uneasy at best. Many of the games suggest that to be fun, a game must also be easy, and a number of Christian games even reassure us that no Bible knowledge is required.

Another import from popular culture is the "warm and fuzzy" approach to religion, which sacrifices accuracy on the altar of approachability. For example, the Holy Huggables talking Esther doll speaks "actual scripture verses to introduce children of all ages to the wisdom of the Bible" (SpiritoftheBible.com 2009). But while her sound bites may be derived from scripture, "My natural beauty won the king's heart" is barely recognizable as Esther 2:12–17. Their talking Jesus doll does not fare much better. While his scripture quotes may be more accurate, few of his phrases are from the Bible; "'I love you and I have an exciting plan for your life" is not in any version of the New Testament of which we are aware. The creators of some of these toys are clear that they are not aiming for textual accuracy. They are more interested in the relationship between the child and the doll, a "faith-based and wholesome alternative to teddy bears and stuffed animals" that can "give kids a special source of comfort" (WDC Media News 2007). (See Figure 15.7.)

Figure 15.7 Talking dolls: (from left) Holy Huggables Jesus, Little Farah doll (teaches Arabic words and phrases), Holy Huggables Esther. (Photo courtesy of Courtney Cutler.)

The need to create appealing religious toys requires entering into a marketing mindset based on a business model. For many Westerners, this creates friction; religion/commerce is another dichotomy made clearly visible through the lens of religious toys. American perspectives on the relationship between religion and money range from one extreme to the other—from "profound discomfort" (Carrette and King 2007: ix) with the connection between religion and commerce to the idea that religious consumerism is "liberating and democratic" (Twitchell 2000: 290). In between is a range of diverse views, including some seeking to mediate between religion and consumer society, usually seen as naturally antagonistic to one another, in spite of the fact that the relationship between religion and commerce has always been present, and even thrived.

In the United States, religion and commerce are closely interwoven. American religious history is primarily a story of Protestant Christianity, which shaped American business practices and consumerism. Contemporary religious games and toys stem from the same source; as a result most of them are Christian (Bado-Fralick and Norris 2010: 71–72). One element in the connection between religion and commerce in the United States is the need for institutional growth driven by the separation of church and state, which gave rise to practices that led to consumerism itself. Many of the competitive methods developed by various Protestant denominations to attract new members form the core of consumer marketing today.[5] Evangelism and proselytizing are, after all, ways of selling Christianity to people.

These themes also play themselves out in contemporary religious games. According to media scholar Heather Hendershot (2004: 20–21), Christian toys emerged from a long history of Christian retailing and the development of a commercial approach to evangelism. Even targeting children was a logical approach, since they were considered "the group most vulnerable to the lure of secular culture's pleasures" (ibid.: 34).

But as natural as the evolution may be, the strength and tone of religious toy marketing sometimes appears contradictory and even counterproductive, revealing an effort to serve too many masters. One issue is whether contemporary religious toys are superficial innovations resulting from a consumer culture that trivializes religion, as in games intended to teach Christian values that are marketed as fun and easy—"No Bible Knowledge Required!" Other aspects of marketing seem intrinsically contradictory. Religious toy promotional materials often endorse ecological awareness and compassion, yet these commodities add to the very problem, as in the heavy promotion of plastic toys on religious Web sites. These issues are particularly poignant when considering that we are discussing the manufacture of children's toys and games, created and marketed in order to teach ethical behaviors.

The politics of dolls

Toy makers have nevertheless decided that dolls and games are effective and lucrative vehicles for transmitting parts of a religion's tradition, giving rise to a global industry whose products are easy to find online if not in retail stores during peak holiday seasons. In fact, the Christian company one2believe made news internationally in 2007 with their release of talking Jesus and other religious dolls in Wal-Mart stores throughout parts of the USA, demonstrating the receptivity of the marketplace to "God-honoring toys" that reflect Christian values (Smith-Spark 2007). These dolls are part of their *Messengers of Faith* series and recite small bits of scripture—usually about 60 or 70 seconds of sound bites—that children are expected to absorb (see Figure 15.8). While designed to make scripture "fun to learn," they raise the question of what is being learned in 70 seconds of decontextualized (and possibly inaccurate) text. Biblical stories take place within larger historical and cultural contexts that change and develop nuanced meanings whose richness, range, and multiple levels of interpretation cannot be captured by a 60-second sound bite.

Although this is not likely to be the only time these children are exposed to scripture, it can be argued that such reduction ill serves children who learn from an early age to treat text one-dimensionally and literally, missing entire swatches of meaning. Compounded in modern culture by a widespread tendency to communicate in ever shorter and more superficial sound bites, an inability or unwillingness to read—and read deeply—materials that are complex and multidirectional in their layers of meaning takes hold, affecting everything from education to religion to government.

In addition to scripture, religiously themed dolls are designed to transmit the religion's values with respect to gender roles and behavior, providing an interesting and often problematic intersection of religion with identities of race, gender, sexuality, and politics. The female body and sexuality are particular concerns of doll

Figure 15.8 Messengers of Faith talking Jesus doll. (Photo courtesy of Kevin Salemme.)

designers, especially in terms of portraying the right kinds of female bodies and sexuality. Not surprisingly, all three of the Abrahamic traditions have developed dolls that use dress and body proportion to display proper and religiously sanctioned images of the female body and sexuality.

Modesty is a critical and overarching theme for girls' dolls, connecting dress with sexual behavior across the Abrahamic traditions. Popular secular dolls such as Barbie, and her now-defunct rival Bratz dolls, are frequently targeted as unacceptably slutty, trashy, and morally lax—a veritable missile of promiscuity. To be sure, Barbie's effects on children have been studied by everyone from psychologists to advertisers, and she has been accused of everything from promoting anorexia to sexualizing young girls (see Bado-Fralick and Norris 2010: 57–66). As a result, some doll designers actively market their toys as anti-Barbies in order to emphasize their products as wholesome alternatives that promote proper values in young girls.

The Jewish *Gali Girl* is one such line of dolls. On the company's Web site, an amusing video depicts "Bubbi," a worried Jewish grandmother who fears her granddaughter will grow up to be like that "trashy, scantily clad" Barbie she always plays with. *Gali Girls* come to the rescue, bringing modesty and appropriate role models for nice little Jewish girls. These dolls resemble the wholesome-looking *American Girl* dolls and come complete with back-stories. Their accessories—sold separately—include Shabbat kits, books, jewelry, and clothing sized for both dolls and little girls, so that life really can imitate art, or at least dolls.

While not explicitly marketed as "anti-Barbies," the talking Mary and Esther dolls also are consciously crafted to reflect wholesome models for young girls. In an interview with the BBC, one2believe founder David Socha spoke about the "revealing clothes" and "G-string underwear" of girls' dolls, which he saw as "promoting promiscuity to very young girls" (Smith-Spark 2007). In stark contrast, Esther and Mary look like average human women, reasonably proportioned and modestly attired in presumably traditional articles of clothing.

One2believe's Esther and Mary join their other line of girls' dolls to communicate something more than simply how appropriately to dress the female body in order to defuse the promiscuity of Barbie dolls. Called the *P31 Series*, these dolls are based on the teachings of Proverbs 31 and are designed to encourage young girls to pursue "biblical womanhood" by exhibiting the characteristics of a virtuous wife or ideal woman.[6] These dolls—Abigail, Leah, and Elisabeth—reinforce the message of appropriate and modest little-girl femininity. Like *Gali Girls*, they resemble *American Girl* dolls and come with a modest and contemporary outfit and accessories, including a Bible lesson based on Proverbs 31:20, two cookie cutters, and a cookie recipe (Livingston n.d.). Talking about the valuable lesson they provide to young girls, Socha said

> [G]irls today are influenced by their surroundings, and when a girl spends a lot of time with a doll that looks like she belongs in a brothel … we have problems. In creating the P31 dolls, our goal is to give young girls positive, contemporary dolls that instill values that girls will carry with them their entire lives.
>
> (ibid.)

Proverbs 31 Ministry makes clear what is meant by "biblical womanhood." Started in 1992 by Lysa TerKeurst and Renee Swope as a monthly newsletter, it is now a comprehensive online ministry growing in popularity among a segment of Christian women. The ministry provides a list of services, including a selection of speakers, courses, books, a radio show, magazine, and even holiday tips and recipes—cooking apparently being one of the virtues of biblical womanhood.

Another online P31 ministry, "The Virtuous Woman," started in 2001 by Melissa Ringstaff, provides advice to both girls and women about the ten (up from seven) attributes of and spheres of activity for a proper woman, including faith, marriage, mothering, health, service, finances, industry, homemaking, time, and beauty (Ringstaff n.d.). Among other things, these ministries emphasize that women can be warriors and soldiers for Christ—an important theme we shall get to shortly—while nevertheless remaining completely feminine and not exhibiting any unattractive tomboyish behavior.

What implicit or covert meanings might these religious dolls carry that are perhaps not intended by their designers? In particular, Esther represents an interesting and potentially positive teaching moment for children—as well as students of religious studies—by providing a text in which a woman's heroic actions are highly valued.

Women's roles in the Bible, as in many religious texts, are largely ignored if not erased by androcentrism, and the talking Esther doll provides a glimpse into at least one small chapter of their stories.

Like Jewish and Christian parents, Muslim parents want wholesome toys and dolls for their children that emphasize religious values and counteract negative influences in secular culture. There are a number of Muslim dolls that fit the bill, including Razanne, a Muslim American doll produced in Michigan by NoorArt, Inc. (see Figure 15.9). As might be expected, Razanne comes modestly dressed in a *hijab*, but other accessories include high heels, makeup, and a sleeveless dress for private or family gatherings. The doll is available in a variety of ethnicities, and also includes specialty outfits, such as a Girl Scout uniform, making her fit—modestly and wholesomely—into normal American life.

Like the *Gali Girls*, Razanne is marketed as a doll that represents qualities other than external beauty. According to the founder of NoorArt,

> The main message we try to put forward through the doll is that what matters is what's inside you, not how you look. … It doesn't matter if you're tall or short, thin or fat, beautiful or not, the real beauty seen by God and fellow Muslims is what's in your soul.

(El Tablawy 2003)

Reflecting these high goals, the Online Islamic Store describes Razanne as "[T]he perfect gift for all Muslim girls! Builds Muslim identity and self-esteem. Provides

Figure 15.9 Razanne dolls with accessories. (Photo courtesy of Courtney Cutler.)

Islamic role models. Promotes Islamic behavior. Shapes interactive play" (Online Islamic Store n.d.). Quite a lot to expect from a toy!

Expectations are even higher for Fulla, one of the most popular and interesting of the Muslim anti-Barbies. Created in Syria by NewBoy, the doll is extremely popular with Muslim parents and children, outselling Barbie in Damascus toy stores by about forty-to-one, and selling over two million dolls since her creation in 2003 (MacKinnon 2005). In sharp contrast to Barbie, that "immoral whore" with her "improbably pneumatic curves and lanky legs," Fulla comes modestly dressed in *abaya* or *hijab* (O'Loughlin 2005). Described as "honest, loving, and caring," she "respects her father and mother" (Zoepf 2005). Fulla is "popular because she's one of us. She's my sister. She's my mother. She's my wife. So as a parent, I'd like Fulla for my daughter" (Nelson 2005). Ironically, the bodies of female religious dolls reveal their highest moral value in what it is they most conceal—the form of the female body itself, usually by covering it with cloth.

From this description, one might think that Fulla and Barbie look drastically different from one another, yet both dolls are made by the same Chinese subcontractor using the same plastics and basic molds. Barbie and Fulla are the same height with the same tiptoe feet designed for high-heeled shoes. There is one measurable difference: Barbie's less-than-modest breasts are flattened out to produce Fulla (MacKinnon 2005). Here the presence of positive moral values is again ironically expressed through absence—in other words, in terms of what is lacking or missing in comparison with Barbie: the size and display of the breasts (see Bado-Fralick and Norris 2010: 63).

Although described as being worlds apart, Barbie and Fulla share something other than production facilities: both dolls are equally invested in consumerism and advertising strategies. Barbie and Fulla use slick Western-style television advertising methods to create an audience of young girls who clamor for the latest products. Their marketing enthusiastically uses the "razor and razor blade" strategy, an approach used by Ruth and Elliot Handler of Mattel (Handler 1994: 4–5) in which the doll is analogous to the razor, while the accessories are razor blades that continue to sell long after the doll. Once a doll is purchased, the consumer has an enormous variety of accessories to choose from—each sold separately. Fulla has a full range of merchandise almost rivaling Barbie's, including lunch boxes, silverware, stationery, backpacks, luggage, and an extensive line of clothing designed and sized for both dolls and little girls.

Not every religious doll participates in this business strategy. Talking Virgin Mary and Esther dolls do not come with additional outfits or accessories. It is difficult to imagine accessories for the Virgin Mary—certainly nothing on the order of Barbie's "Malibu Beach House" or Fulla's trademarked pink luggage. In fact, the Mary doll's scripted and biblically historicized nature not only limits the range of accompanying product, but also limits the field of creative play.

This is another important feature that Barbie and—to a lesser extent—Fulla share: status as cultural icons (Bado-Fralick and Norris 2010: 59). Cultural icons are open-ended and ontologically empty artifacts that become the medium for fantasy and play (Rogers 1999: 2). Dolls such as Barbie might have a back-story to go with particular accessories, but Barbie the doll may become anything—a racecar driver, a teacher, a doctor, a princess, or an astronaut—accessories sold separately, of course.

Ruth Handler, the creator of Barbie, has always insisted that the doll is a canvas on which children paint dreams of their own futures as adult women (Handler 1994: 3). As a cultural icon, Barbie participates in the infinite dreams, multiple meanings and endless stories of play.

Successful dolls allow for the magic of play, the ability for children to create and tell their own stories. Even though Fulla is promoted as the "moral Muslim choice" for young girls, she has a limited amount of open-endedness built into her marketing. Fulla occupies herself at home and shops, but also has some career options, including dentist and teacher.

In contrast to Barbie and Fulla, the talking Virgin Mary doll has a significantly reduced and highly scripted storyline. That Barbie is a more successful icon than Virgin Mary points to an interesting conundrum. Religious doll makers count on the power of dolls to influence behavior and instill religious values. Yet the more dolls are used to script the behavior of children through a limited and rehearsed notion of play, the less likely it is that the dolls will succeed—and the more likely that children will deviate from the script.

While one might expect politics to play some role in the anti-Barbie discussion, one might be surprised at the extent to which governments and even police have interfered with the marketing and selling of dolls. Saudi Arabian religious police have implemented bans on Barbie and removed her from store shelves in an attempt to eradicate what they see as a "Jewish doll, whose revealing clothes and shameful postures ... are a symbol of the decadence of the perverted West" (for example, see CBSNews.com 2009).

Saudi Arabia is not the only country to perceive Barbie as a threat. Iranian officials at The Institute for the Intellectual Development of Children and Young Adults, affiliated with its Ministry of Education, launched their own modestly attired anti-Barbies, Sara and Dara. So have Arab League officials in Cairo. Russia has attempted to ban Barbie "on the grounds that she has harmful effects on the minds of young girls." According to Eric Clark, Barbie "has been accused of awakening sexual impulses in the very young and encouraging consumerism among Russian infants" (Clark 2007: 101).

Curiously, Fulla's marketing of religious values can be problematic, and she has had her own share of problems. While some see her as a wholesome influence, others are worried she encourages a conservative and repressive form of Islam. In September 2006, Tunisian security forces removed Fulla from stores because of her *hijab* (Al-Hamroni and Al-Humaidy 2006). Since her creator, NewBoy, is based in Syria, she was on the State Department's terrorist list and not allowed in US markets; a revisionist history relocating her creation to Dubai has enabled an evasion of the ban.

The battle for the toybox

While girls' religious dolls are marketed to promote a certain kind of embodied morality, boys' dolls are marketed as healthier alternatives to toys that embody darker or even demonic themes. The Job-with-Boils Christian action figure, formerly available from Train up a Child, Inc., came with realistic sores to tempt little boys who would otherwise play with godless mutant mummies or alien zombie action figures.

Boys' dolls are almost always referred to as "action figures," a term coined in the 1960s by G.I. Joe creator Don Levine as a way to avoid the "feminizing stigma" of little boys playing with dolls (Bado-Fralick and Norris 2010: 48–50). Levine has gone on to develop his own line of gender specific Old Testament action figures called the *Almighty Heroes* collection, complete with appropriate accessories and Bible stories. "Action figures" Samson, Joshua, Noah, Moses, David, and Goliath come with a plastic sword for little boys. "Fashion dolls" Queen Esther and Deborah the Warrior come with a charm bracelet for little girls.

Advertising, like sports, has many militaristic narratives, especially in the marketing of toys for boys. According to Eric Clark's *The Real Toy Story*, "good fighting evil is a major psychological element in boys' play" (2007: 166), making violence "common in ads for boys' toys" (2007: 186). Military and apocalyptic themes abound in religious games and dolls, especially in boys' "action figures." As noted earlier, the militaristic theme includes young girls, who are encouraged to be good (albeit feminine) Christian soldiers. One2believe's Web site is dedicated to winning the "Battle for the Toybox"—a relatively recent militaristic narrative. Their most current Web site includes a handy downloadable poster portraying wrestling hypermasculine *Spirit Warrior Action Figures* who encourage the reader to "join the battle for the toybox" and ask "which side are you on?" (one2believe 2013).

As we noted in our earlier work, this raises a critical question: "Are toys like the *Spirit Warriors* or *Almighty Heroes* harmless and wholesome alternatives to even more destructive toys, or are they helping to prepare children for religiously sanctioned violence against those 'left behind'?" (Bado-Fralick and Norris 2010: 51). This issue has been raised most recently with products connected to the Christian dispensationalist "Left Behind" novels of Tim LaHaye and Jerry B. Jenkins, which describe the end of the world and the epic battle between good (the members of the Tribulation Force) and evil (the Antichrist and his Global Community). Beginning as a series of novels, the franchise has expanded to include films, board games, and videogames. The toys-and-games market is multidirectional, its merchandise overlapping and tightly knit with products targeted to as many ages as possible.

Not surprisingly, a wide cross-section of people—including educators, psychologists, scholars, theologians, and religious people of all kinds—are concerned about the level of violence in religious toys and games. Some object to the glorification of violence in the name of God and the gory sensationalizing of death and destruction; others point to disturbing themes of Protestant theocracy and spiritual warfare: the mission "to convert or kill Catholics, Jews, Muslims, Buddhists, gays, and anyone who advocates the separation of church and state—especially moderate, mainstream Christians" (Hutson 2006). These increasingly violent and militaristic narratives from the Religious Right produce a disturbing combination of the themes of war, religion, and play (see Bado-Fralick and Norris 2010: 51).

Religion, games, and play

Just as there are concerns about the mix of religion with commerce, ethics, gender, and politics, there are also concerns about religion and fun or play—mostly within the Abrahamic traditions. Ministers (and academics) wonder whether it is appropriate to use fun to teach religion, whether it harms spiritual development to give a child a cuddly Jesus doll, and whether games somehow contradict the very nature of religion. Religions outside the Abrahamic traditions don't have the same difficulty; for instance, consider the Hindu concept of play (*lila*). Even in the Abrahamic traditions the relationship between religion and play is not necessarily as rigid as assumed, as seen, for instance, in the Jewish customs of Purim, or the *hadith* noting Mohammad's playfulness with children and the essential place of play in children's lives.

But when it comes to marketing, the use of fun in religious games can strike an odd chord. For example, the *hajj* or pilgrimage to Mecca is one of the five pillars of Islam, required at least once of all able-bodied Muslims. It is a serious and sacred obligation that expiates sin and brings the pilgrim closer to Allah. Although the impulse to educate children about the rituals and meaning of *hajj* is understandable, the word *fun* in the title of the *Hajj Fun Game* seems unfortunate, or even sacrilegious (see Figure 15.4).

Tension between religion and fun or play is still evident in Western culture. The association of religion with play is problematic for those religious authorities who depend on control and power to make their institutions thrive; fun and play often involve releasing control, and even subverting power. Some of these authorities fear that fun and playfulness somehow dilute or distort morality, emphasizing trivial rather than profound issues. A hierarchical distinction between textual and popular religion, prevalent among Western academics and traditional religious authority figures alike, underlies their concerns about religious toys and games. For those literate elite who view text as the only true religious authority, games may appear frivolous, misleading, or even a corruption of doctrine and values.

Although there are worries that religious toys somehow separate religion from its central importance in human life, the industry's growth can be interpreted as a sign of a revitalization of religion. If religion is no longer as controlled by institutional monopolies, individuals are freer to practice and express religion in a "deregulated" market (Miller 2003: 76). People practice religion in new ways, reflecting their needs in contemporary contexts. The increase in the number and availability of popular religious games, toys, and dolls is not a sign of over-commodification or deterioration, but a natural result of the interplay between religion and all aspects of contemporary culture. Religious toys and games are examples of contemporary lived religion, reflecting practices taking place in the home, among friends or family, and with familiar materials and modes of representation. Parents have a natural desire to pass on their traditions. Given the emphasis in contemporary culture on fun and entertainment, what better way to transmit religious values and beliefs than through fun, games, and dolls?

Notes

1 Even this seemingly innocuous play type can become problematic when mixed with religion. In *Bibleland* (a Christian version of *Candyland*) the winner gets to Heaven, but none of the other players do.
2 In deference to prohibitions against making "graven images," Orthodox dolls cannot look completely human.

3 Colleagues often ask us about our research on childhood and religion, which not only illustrates this understanding of toys as children's playthings, but also ignores the quantity and role of adult play in culture and religion.
4 There are many other types of religious educational toys available as well, including puzzles and Shabbat play sets.
5 "In the 1920s and 1930s, fundamentalists energetically embraced the business ethos with its secular values of organization, efficiency, consumerism, promotionalism, and emphasis on size and numbers. To evangelize and build institutions, they tapped innovative modern strategies and technologies, such as advertising, magazines, and radio … . When President Coolidge in a famous dictum of the 1920s compared a factory to a temple and its workers to worshipers, he reflected an affinity between business and religion that fundamentalists also celebrated, sometimes to embarrassing extremes" (Abrams 2001: 11–12).
6 Proverbs 31:20 (KJV): "She stretcheth out her hand to the poor; yea, she reacheth forth her hands to the needy." Not coincidentally, the passage is in the middle of a reading (Proverbs 31:10–31) known as the "Eshet Chayil" (often translated as "A woman of valor") sung by traditional Jewish husbands to their wives every Friday evening at the beginning of Shabbat.

Works cited

Abrams, D.C. (2001) *Selling the Old-Time Religion: American Fundamentalists and Mass Culture, 1920–1940*, Athens, GA: University of Georgia Press.
Al-Hamroni, M. and U. Al-Humaidy (2006) "Hijab-clad Fulla 'wanted' in Tunisia," OnIslam. net (September 22). Online. Available: www.onislam.net/english/news/africa/422811.html (accessed 20 March 2013).
Ardley, G. (1967) "The role of play in the philosophy of Plato," *Philosophy* 42, 161: 226–44.
Bado-Fralick, N. and R.S. Norris (2010) *Toying with God: The World of Religious Games and Dolls*, Waco, TX: Baylor University Press.
BBC News (2002) "Muslim dolls tackle 'wanton' Barbie" (March 5). Online. Available: http://news.bbc.co.uk/2/hi/middle_east/1856558.stm (accessed 20 January 2013).
Bornet, P. and M. Burger (eds) (2012) *Religions in Play: Games, Rituals, and Virtual Worlds*, Zürich: Pano Verlag.
Carrette, J. and R. King (2007) *Selling Spirituality: The Silent Takeover of Religion*, London: Routledge.
CBSNews.com (2009) "Saudis bust Barbie's 'dangers'" (February 11). Online. Available: www.cbsnews.com/2100–2202_162–572564.html (accessed 13 March 2013).
Clark, E. (2007) *The Real Toy Story: Inside the Ruthless Battle for America's Youngest Consumers*, New York: Free Press.
El Tablawy, T. (2003) "Muslims' answer to the over-sexy Barbie," *Canberra Times* (September 29): A9.
Fox, J. (2006) "Students of the game," *Smithsonian* 37: 110–17.
Ghartsang, C.T. (2007) Unpublished interview (March 16), Toronto, ONT.
Handler, R. (1994) *Dream Doll: The Ruth Handler Story*, Stamford, CT: Longmeadow Press.
Hendershot, H. (2004) *Shaking the World for Jesus: Media and Conservative Evangelical Culture*, Chicago, IL: The University of Chicago Press.
Hutson, J. (2006) "The purpose driven life takers" (part I), *Talk to Action* (May 26). Online. Available: www.talk2action.org/story/2006/5/29/195855/959 (accessed 13 March 2013).
Kline, S. (1993) *Out of the Garden: Toys, TV, and Children's Culture in the Age of Marketing*, London: Verso.

Livingston, J. (n.d.) "P31 dolls teach young girls attributes of a true American girl," Christian News Wire. Online. Available: www.christiannewswire.com/news/281032011.html (accessed 13 March 2013).

MacKinnon, M. (2005) "Barbie meets her Muslim match," *Globe and Mail* [Canada] (October 27): A1.

Miller, V. (2003) *Consuming Religion: Christian Faith and Practice in a Consumer Culture*, New York: Continuum.

Murray, H.J.R. (1951) *A History of Board Games Other Than Chess*, Oxford: Clarendon.

Nelson, C. (2005) "Modest Fulla doll displaces Barbie in Mideast toy stores," [San Diego] *Union-Tribune* (November 20). Online. Available: www.utsandiego.com/uniontrib/20051120/news_1n20fulla.html (accessed 13 March 2013).

Norris, R.S. (2005) "Examining the structure and role of emotion: contributions of neurobiology to the study of embodied religious experience," *Zygon: Journal of Religion & Science* 40, 1: 181–99.

——(2011) "The battle for the toybox: marketing and fun in the development of children's religious identities," in S. Ridgely (ed.), *The Study of Children in Religions: A Methods Handbook*, New York: New York University Press, 189–201.

O'Loughlin, E. (2005) "Fulla has the Mid-East doll market covered," *Sydney Morning Herald* (December 23): 12.

one2believe (2013) "Battle for the Toybox." Online. Available: http://one2believe.com/battleforthetoybox.asp (accessed 13 March 2013).

Online Islamic Store (n.d.) "Razanne: The Muslim Doll." Online. No longer available: http://onlineislamicstore.com/razmusdol.html (accessed 28 February 2009). Snapshot of Web page available: http://web.archive.org/web/20080315095322/http://onlineislamicstore.com/razmusdol.html (accessed 24 March 2013).

Raj, S. and C. Dempsey (eds) (2010) *Sacred Play: Ritual Levity and Humor in South Asian Religion*, Albany, NY: State University of New York Press.

Ringstaff, M. (n.d.) "10 virtues of the Proverbs 31 woman," *A Virtuous Woman*. Online. Available: http://avirtuouswoman.org/10-virtues-of-the-proverbs-31-woman/ (accessed 13 March 2013).

Rogers, M. (1999) *Barbie Culture*, London: Sage Publications.

Rollefson, G.O. (1992) "A Neolithic game board from 'Ain Ghazal, Jordan," *Bulletin of the American Schools of Oriental Research* 286 (May): 1–5.

Smith-Spark, L. (2007) "Faith-based toys to hit US stores," BBC News (July 30). Online. Available: http://news.bbc.co.uk/2/hi/americas/6916287.stm (accessed 13 March 2013).

SpiritoftheBible.com (2009) "Talking Esther doll." Online. Available: www.spiritofthebible.com/site/1627494/product/773–7992347 (accessed 14 January 2010).

Twitchell, J. (2000) "Two cheers for materialism," in J. Schor and D. Holt (eds), *The Consumer Society Reader*, New York: The New Press, 181–90.

WDC Media News (2007) "New 'Holy Huggables' plush dolls pack fun and faith into one lovable kid-sized package." Online: www.wdcmedia.com/newsArticle.php?ID=1769 (accessed 14 January 2010; no longer available).

Zoepf, K. (2005) "Bestseller in the Mideast: Barbie with a prayer mat," *New York Times* (September 22). Online. Available: www.nytimes.com/2005/09/22/international/middleeast/22doll.html?_r=0 (accessed 13 March 2013).

16
KITSCH

Leonard Norman Primiano

Introduction

- A store for Catholic religious goods in suburban Philadelphia filled with inexpensive, mass-produced plastic and resin images of Jesus, Mary, and the pantheon of saints in all sizes and colors. (Figure 16.1)
- The Mustard Seed Christian Books and Gifts in Parsons, Kansas, offering word-centered scriptural plaques and wall clocks, resin figures knelt in prayer, images of a kindly Jesus, and bracelets asking: "What would Jesus do?" (Figure 16.2)
- A Lisbon tourist shop selling a statuette of a Catholic monk with a pull-string raising the figure's carved wooden penis into a state of erection under his green robe. (Figure 16.3)
- A kitchen in Latvia containing a box of wooden matches with a depiction of Jesus as the "Divine Mercy" and the Polish words: "Jezu, ufam Tobie" ("Jesus, I trust in You"). (Figure 16.4)
- The official Thomas Kinkade Web site, offering for the purchaser's consideration an "inspirational print" of the sentimental, bucolic "Forest chapel," by the self-proclaimed "Painter of light."
- A north-west England newspaper's death announcement and "In Memorium" pages in the 1960s offering as a public remembrance an often-used twee verse:

  Trumpets Sounded
  A Voice Said Come
  Pearly Gates Opened
  And in Walked Mum

- A cup of green tea in Lisbon, served in a cup and saucer at the Bellisimo Café, emblazoned with God the Father and Adam from Michelangelo's Sistine Chapel ceiling.
- A book titled *Look It's Jesus: Amazing Holy Visions in Everyday Life* (2009): not a scholarly exploration of expressions of vernacular religion, but a novelty book of vernacular photography highlighting "dozens of documented religious visions" of Jesus, the Virgin Mary, even the Buddha appearing in sandwiches, wood grain, trees, gems, furniture, and the sky.

Figure 16.1 Small statues of holy figures (plastic), St. Jude Shop, Havertown, Pennsylvania, 2014. (Photograph by Leonard Norman Primiano.)

- *The Life of Pope John Paul II* illustrated in a publication from Marvel Comics.
- A solid, semi-sweet chocolate "Voodoo Doll" in a cardboard presentation box with the following product description: "Voodoo is an ancient mystical practice that can bring spectacular gifts and rewards to those who believe. Chocoholics Chocolate Voodoo Doll is even better because, whether you believe or not, you will be rewarded with a darkly delicious chocolate treat."

While the examples above are all drawn from the last 50 years of Christianity (or a religion with a relationship to it), they illustrate a worldwide religious phenomenon, one found in all world religious traditions: religion and kitsch.[1]

Any handbook of religion and popular culture must include the materially abundant, scholarly contentious, but still enormously significant, subject of religious kitsch. A recent issue of *Material Religion* dedicated to "Key Words in Material Religion" (Meyer *et al.* 2011) contained discrete essays on such terms as "Sign," "Thing," "Icon/Image," and "Display," but no separate consideration of "kitsch", a highly important modern expression of religious artfulness—sometimes verbal, often material and visual—in the lives of many religious individuals in nineteenth-, twentieth-, and twenty-first-century society. This chapter will specifically examine "kitsch": defining the term, discussing the scholarly debates it has inspired, and highlighting its energetic employment and influence within the vernacular religious lives of humans around the globe, with specific emphasis on the Christian tradition.[2]

Figure 16.2 "What would Jesus do" cotton wristbands, 2014. (Photograph by Leonard Norman Primiano.)

Definition

David Dutton begins his assessment of kitsch in *The Dictionary of Art* by citing Harold Rosenberg who, in his book *The Tradition of the New* (1970), associates it with sentimentality when it is found in popular arts and entertainment. Reflecting on the past usage of the term "kitsch," Dutton clarifies:

> although many popular art forms are cheap and somewhat crude, they are at least direct and unpretentious. On the other hand, a persistent theme in the history and usage of "kitsch," going back to the word's mid-European origins, is pretentiousness, especially in reference to objects that simulate whatever is conventionally viewed as high art.
>
> (1996: 100)

Figure 16.3 Monks and other items on display in Lisbon tourist shop, 2014. (From the collection of Leonard Norman Primiano. Photograph by István Povedák; used with permission.)

Sentimentality, pretentiousness, and imitation are just some of the qualities associated with the term.

The *Oxford English Dictionary* (*OED*; Oxford Dictionaries Online n.d.), explaining that the word can be used as both a noun and an adjective, defines kitsch as: "art, objects, or design considered to be in poor taste because of excessive garishness or sentimentality, but sometimes appreciated in an ironic or knowing way." It lists as derivatives "kitschiness" and "kitschy."

Figure 16.4 Divine Mercy of Jesus image on matchbox, 2014. (Photograph by István Povedák; used with permission.)

This definition is fascinating because it refers specifically to kitsch as art—that is, to human creative skill and imagination expressed or applied in various forms. While a thesaurus might suggest "fine art" as a synonym for "art," it seems doubtful that it would likewise offer "kitsch." Yet, for those individuals open to its evocative value as an artistic expression, kitsch represents human artistry in quite a different sense: as an expression of popular culture. Generally, both positive and negative interpreters have seen kitsch as a cultural response to the problems of modern social and personal life (Binkley 2000: 134). Its usage is almost exclusively pejorative, as its synonyms—tacky, tawdry, showy, gimcrack, gaudy, cheap, tasteless, vulgar, camp, clinquant, corny, twee, affected, artificial, Daliesque, gimmicky, mod, ostentatious, posturing—suggest (Kipfer 2013).

The *OED* definition also refers to kitsch as something "considered" poor in quality, with stress on the act of consideration by a critic. In the end, kitsch is a word of evaluation and criticism. A picture, a word, or an action may be considered inappropriate because it is excessive in some way, whether such excess connotes the sentimentally overwrought, the cheaply produced, the deceptively imitative, or the emotionally bankrupt. The association of the word "tawdry" is useful in appreciating kitsch. "Tawdry" is

> short for *tawdry lace*, a fine silk lace or ribbon worn as a necklace in the sixteenth–seventeenth centuries, [itself a] contraction of *St. Audrey's lace*: Audrey was a later form of Etheldrida (died 679), patron saint of Ely, England, where tawdry laces, along with cheap imitations and other cheap finery, were traditionally sold at a fair.
>
> (Oxford Dictionaries Online n.d.)

Another wonderful and rarely used word also associated with kitsch is "gimcrack," which refers to an object that is flimsy or poorly made, but deceptively attractive.

The *OED* definition concludes with a reflective coda about the act of appreciation of kitsch by individuals who recognize and disparage its excess, but at the same time comprehend it "in an ironic or knowing way." Such individuals have partnered with the expression of kitsch by placing themselves as critics of its tastelessness and unacceptability, while at the same time winking knowingly in strange appreciation of its garish power.[3]

Etymology of kitsch

The term "kitsch" was popularized in the twentieth century, but its linguistic origins are uncertain. Literary critic Matei Calinescu reveals that kitsch came into usage "in the 1860s and 1870s in the jargon of painters and art dealers in Munich, and was employed to designate cheap artistic stuff" (1987: 234; see more generally 232–37), specifically rapidly produced merchandise for voracious British and American tourists (McDannell 1995: 164). Aesthetician and art critic Gillo Dorfles's widely read 1969 edited volume, *Kitsch: The World of Bad Taste* elucidates that some commentators link "kitsch" to the English word "sketch," while others trace it to the German phrase *etwas verkitschen*, "to knock something off cheaply" (1969: 4), a verb Colleen McDannell ascribes to the Mecklenburg dialect (1995: 164). Another philosopher of aesthetics, Ludwig Giesz, is credited for attributing kitsch to *kitschen*, "meaning *den Strassen-schlamm zusammenscharren*, literally 'to collect rubbish from the street'" (Dorfles 1969: 4). This etymological interpretation is closest to the concept of "artistic rubbish" and bears a striking resemblance to the term "junk art" (Dorfles 1969: 4). Philosopher of art Tomas Kulka adds that "there have been speculations that *kitsch* comes from the inversion of the French *chic*" (1996: 19); art historian

Whitney Rugg (2002) suggests the possibility that kitsch is a derivation of the Russian *keetcheetsya*, to be haughty or "puffed up." Whatever its linguistic origin, Kulka (1996: 18) notes that the word entered international usage by the end of the 1920s. Regardless of its linguistic origins, kitsch is a word that has carried with it onerous connotations whether applied to buildings, landscape design, domestic interiors with their decoration and furnishings, painting, sculpture, music, film, television, or literature—"virtually anything subject to judgment of taste" (Calinescu 1987: 235). Just as there are divisions regarding the exact etymology of "kitsch," there are serious divisions among scholars about its conceptual significance, historical influences, and meaning, creating a rather dynamic "kitsch debate" (Olalquiaga 1998: 39, n.8).

The history of kitsch as a concept

When approaching the subject of kitsch—and certainly before considering its relationship to religion (be it institutionalized religion, a world religious "tradition," or an individual's vernacular religiosity; see Primiano 1995, 2012)—one must be mindful that for many individuals, kitsch is a technical term. It is scholarly jargon that emerged out of a critical cultural analysis of consumer society and describes what has been recognized as a phenomenon of the industrial revolution: mass-produced, often marketed, commercialized, material culture. For others, however, especially those eager to arbitrate matters of aesthetics and in so doing distinguish themselves from the "undiscerning" masses, "kitsch" takes on a Bourdieusian aggressiveness; it becomes a term not only for objects or literature or behavior, but an expression which both describes and dismisses the "taste" of common people.

How old is the concept of kitsch? Did past cultures maintain a concept of art or craft that was in some way distasteful within their lived contexts of beauty or functionality? As a concept regarding art, artistic production, and artistic consumption, kitsch has a rather formidable history, and is a source of much debate among scholars from a variety of disciplines including aesthetics, philosophy, art criticism, art history, sociology, folklore, religious studies, and cultural studies. Tomas Kulka probes the issue of whether kitsch, not as a term but as an idea, could be applied to art and artfulness throughout human history. If kitsch is equivalent to issues of taste, and the concept of bad taste is not a modern innovation (a point argued in Dorfles 1969: 9–12, who defines kitsch as "really bad taste" [10; "*vrai mauvais gout*" in the 1968 French edition (19)]), but "like poor judgment in general, is … a universal human feeling … " then "it is difficult to imagine that [bad taste] could have appeared only some one hundred and fifty years ago" (Kulka 1996: 16). The issue of "taste" will arise repeatedly in discussions of kitsch, but arguably the impact of what has been described exclusively as kitsch can be traced to the period following 1850.

In the early twentieth century, the idea of kitsch's development was observed not by sociologists, but by critics and supporters of Modernism (in art and thought) assuming postures as social analysts. These critics elaborated on what they noted was an endemic behavioral problem among the working and middle classes in post-industrial revolution European and American society. Namely, these "masses" uncritically embraced a commercial culture of unlimited choices and demonstrated a consumer enthusiasm for domestic and decorative goods often imitative of the luxury products and the visual and material art available to wealthier classes.

Two influential voices in the development of this critical perspective were the Modernist Austrian writer Hermann Broch and the American art critic Clement Greenberg. Broch in 1933 wrote in moralistic terms of the "producer of kitsch," who is not an artist but an imitator using "set recipes." He continues, "This never-ending sentimentalization of the finite, this gazing at 'the beautiful,' imbues kitsch with a false element behind which one can sense ethical 'evil'" (Broch 1969 [1933]: 76). Ludwig Giesz beautifully summarizes Broch's story of kitsch's cultural evolution as "vulgarized Romanticism plus the emancipation of the petit bourgeoisie" (1969: 156). Commenting on the debate over the influence of Romanticism on the advancement of kitsch, Tomas Kulka concurs: "One can hardly deny that Romanticism, with its emphasis on dramatic effects, pathos, and overall sentimentality, displays intrinsic affinities with kitsch" (1996: 15). Succeeding and influenced by Broch, the American visual art critic, Clement Greenberg, wrote a 1939 essay in the *Partisan Review*, "Avant-Garde and Kitsch," a Marxist-influenced defense of avant-garde art and an attack on art that he perceived as mired in "realistic imitation." One of the most influential essays critiquing kitsch and with it twentieth-century culture, Greenberg's work appropriates the word "kitsch" to describe perfectly "the culture of the masses ... everywhere ... " (in Dorfles 1969: 122). Kitsch, he declares:

> is a product of the industrial revolution which urbanized the masses of Western Europe and America and established what is called universal literacy. ... The peasants who settled in the cities as proletariat and petty bourgeois learned to read and write for the sake of efficiency, but they did not win the leisure and comfort necessary for the enjoyment of the city's traditional culture. Losing, nevertheless, their taste for the folk culture whose background was the countryside, and discovering a new capacity for boredom at the same time, the new urban masses set up a pressure on society to provide them with a kind of culture fit for their own consumption. To fill the demand of the new market, a new commodity was devised: ersatz culture, kitsch, destined for those who, insensible to the values of genuine culture, are hungry nevertheless for the diversion that only culture of some sort can provide.
>
> (Greenberg 1939: 39)

Kitsch for Greenberg epitomizes a real stagnation of the progress in social thought represented in avant-garde art. In his view, kitsch is a mass-produced corruption of art, a debased copy of culture, a "faked sensation" of emotion and intellectual reflection, a defiler of individual artistic inspiration or new visions of traditional artistry resulting in a watered-down, lessened, diluted object (ibid.: 40). Kitsch is essentially the embodiment of all that is false and inauthentic in modern society.

The understanding of kitsch as a flaccid cultural expression—a stagnation in human progress found in the culture of modernity and post-modernity—is the conceptual inheritance of Broch, Greenberg, and other early advocates of the term, and continues to be propagated in the twenty-first century by scholars, the media, and individuals who are familiar with it (see Dorfles 1969; Kjellman-Chapin 2013). Of course, what is truly stagnating is how such a conceptualization carries with it a perception of society in which there is "the denial of the possibility of cultural production of any significant value [occurring] anywhere but at the top" (Kirshenblatt-Gimblett 1991: 125).

Significantly, in the last twenty years, a recovery project of sorts concerning kitsch as a useful concept for describing authenticity and even agency in post-modernity has been underway, as suggested by cultural studies scholar Sam Binkley (2000) and especially in the scholarship of the critic of postmodernism Celeste Olalquiaga (1992a; 1992b; 1998). Such reclamation has been attempted in incisive recognition that the term was used previously to rank levels of culture and taste. Exposing the deficiencies found in previous explorations of kitsch, Olalquiaga specifically criticizes Broch and Greenberg for the use of "exclusive social formulae which base their power on the belief that a certain class, race, or gender is privy to a real or supposed purity which bestows on it a degree of superiority" (1992b), along with an associated sensibility of art or taste hierarchically and intrinsically richer or of a greater aesthetic quality. Binkley clarifies that "the implicit aesthetic, moral and political criteria that served to separate high culture from low, art from kitsch, have been effectively dismantled in much sociological and historical work" (2000: 132). Aware of these critiques, some writers in the social sciences and humanities have dropped the word kitsch from their scholarly vocabularies and forged new appreciation of the patterns of taste distinctions through the articulation of terms such as "taste cultures" (Gans 1974) or "cultural boundaries" (Lamont and Fournier 1992). Both Binkley and Olalquiaga have applauded the removal of two-tiered models for taste, models that limited kitsch's usefulness as a category in postmodern aesthetics. At the same time, they have worked to rethink the qualities of kitsch that make it a useful category and have recognized its significance as a descriptor of consumer products that play a dominant role in world culture and everyday life. "Might," Binkley asks "the term kitsch still offer some theoretical and empirical assets to the study of material culture and the consuming habits of modern people?" (2000: 132).

In his 1996 aesthetic consideration of kitsch, Tomas Kulka poses three questions which both Olalquiaga and Binkley valuably attempt to answer: Is kitsch worthless? What is the mass appeal of kitsch? and What makes kitsch work? (1996: 19–22). Olalquiaga's response is key to her understanding of kitsch as expressing a sensibility of loss and an intrinsically human need to connect with nature: "Deeply embedded in the processes of industrialization and mechanical reproduction that made it possible in the first place, kitsch, with its love of imitation, artifice and repetition, can be finally appreciated as the foremost representative of a modernity whose official emblem was for too long the quest for originality" (1992b: 22). This analysis is also central to her understanding of how kitsch works so well in the contemporary practice of religion.

Kitsch and religion: one man's kitsch is another woman's religious aesthetic

In a thoughtful discussion of the "Five Faces of Modernity," Matei Calinescu describes kitsch and reflects on the word's relationship with "modernity":

Modernity and kitsch—the notions might seem mutually exclusive, at least insofar as modernity implies antitraditional presentness, experiment ... commitment to change, while kitsch—for all its diversity—suggests repetition, banality, triteness. But in fact, it is not difficult to realize that kitsch, technologically as well as aesthetically, is one of the most typical products of modernity ... . Once kitsch is technically possible and economically profitable, the proliferation of cheap or not-so-cheap imitations of everything—from primitive or folk art to the latest avant-garde—is limited only by the market. Value is measured directly by the demand for spurious replicas or reproductions of objects whose original aesthetic meaning consisted, or should have consisted, in being unique and therefore inimitable.

(Calinescu 1987: 225–26)

Soon after reading this assessment by Calinescu in May of 2013, I rather ironically and serendipitously received a telephone call from a representative of a new company called "Artifactory" located in Boyertown, Pennsylvania, about 45 miles from where I teach. This representative asked for an appointment so that she could familiarize me with the various objects, or as she called them, "religious replicas" and "archeological products," that Artifactory was producing for sale. One can only imagine my delight at the prospect of communicating with someone responsible for the production of such religious products. Eagerly, I examined the company's Web site. Included in their current and future offerings were a replica of the Shroud of Turin in various sizes; replicas of the implements used in the crucifixion of Jesus; a mold of a dinosaur track and a human foot to appeal to creationist Evangelicals; a replica of Noah's Ark; and what Artifactory describes as a "Vampire Killing Kit" in deluxe, standard, and wall display models. I entered this world of object production and distribution through an interview with the owner and developer of this company and product line. A former Roman Catholic and now "born-again" Evangelical, Steve Dymszo sees these objects as serving religious, pedagogical, and inspirational purposes. In his view, their price at several hundred dollars each removes them from the realm of "kitsch." He explains:

I tend to think of [kitsch as] less expensive ... more lighthearted type pieces. Some of the pieces are like that, some are deeply religious. I don't know if you can give a blanket one-word definition—"kitsch"—to everything. The vampire killing kit is kitsch; I would not say the Shroud of Turin is. People in my office start to cry when they see the Shroud of Turin, including the pastor of my Evangelical Baptist Church. We don't believe these products to be in bad taste.

(Interview with the author, 10 June 2013)

Mr. Dymszo's candid assessment of his company's religious products, directed at both the Roman Catholic and Protestant Christian market, describes his sense of the usefulness and power of these objects in the lives of his customers. His reflection speaks volumes about a wider, ongoing debate.

Matei Calinescu offers that for him, the determination of "whether an object is kitsch always involves considerations of purpose and context" (1987: 257). Scholars of religion and religious culture are faced with a fascinating set of quandaries regarding religious objects prone to classification as kitsch in whichever sensory form they take—from Artifactory's three sizes of the Shroud of Turin to the dozens of different incense sticks and resin images of the Buddha in a Chinatown shop. If perceived or labeled as kitsch—whether by scholars, functionaries, or practitioners of a given religious tradition—are such objects irreparably condemned as cultural refuse, the vacuous frills of religious life, items to be disdained or at least dismissed from serious consideration? Can kitsch be salvaged as a valid term, used to reference significant textual and material elements of contemporary religiosity? If kitsch is maintained as a productive concept, should it function strictly as a name for religious expressions of questionable taste in the post-industrial world, or might its usage be retrofitted to earlier eras, in deference to kindred sensibilities or classifications that may have existed for as long as people themselves have been religious and expressed themselves religiously?

These questions stimulate intellectual reflection, certainly, but they also foreground issues of taste, issues that figure centrally in the work of American religious historian Colleen McDannell. McDannell is one of the most frequently cited scholars whose work justifies the serious analysis of what many across taste communities would consider kitsch. In her book *Material Christianity*, McDannell outlines three approaches to the study of kitsch: the cultural, the aesthetic, and the ethical (1995: 164–67). McDannell herself takes what could best be described as a cultural/historical approach, but as she admits, often the boundaries of these categories blur. In the chapter "Christian kitsch and the rhetoric of bad taste," McDannell points to a fascinating emic debate within American Christianity, a debate that took shape in the first half of the twentieth century and that might best be summarized as: "One man's kitsch is another woman's religious aesthetic." Considering published debates as well as material evidence from church architecture and popular imagery within the Roman Catholic and Protestant traditions, McDannell argues that within dominant aesthetic judgments of religious art, one frequently finds messages about masculinity and femininity expressed by these belief systems. McDannell, therefore, provides readers with a fascinating "gendered" critique and analysis of the influence of what she identifies as kitsch in the architectural, ritual, and devotional culture of Catholics both pre- and post-Vatican II. For her, such a critique has deeply ethical implications and ramifications for women and men, Catholics and non-Catholics, alike.

With strong influences from the Greco-Roman world, Christianity developed as a tradition with a profound attraction to art. Its material culture centered on visual and material representations of the sacred, all related to a belief in the blessed character of creation and its potential for resplendent goodness. As the sect grew over the centuries into a Church, so too did the material accoutrements supporting both its normative worship in ecclesiastical structures and the vernacular worship of wealthier and not-so-wealthy Christians (see Bowes 2010; Luria 2010; Mentzer 2010; Pitarakis 2010; Talbot 2010; Trout 2010; Webb 2010). A major component of this material tradition in the Western Church was the development of the cult of the martyrs and saints. The veneration of such personages centered on a reverence for their physical remains. Known as relics, these remains were stored in churches and less often in homes, in receptacles known as reliquaries (see Brown 1981 for a nuanced discussion of these complex developments; see also Bagnoli *et al.* 2010). The salient display of relics concretely reminded the faithful of their spiritual connection to the martyrs and other sacred dead in the early centuries after the first evangelists spread the religion through the Mediterranean. Even in the twenty-first century, one merely has to set foot into a historical Catholic church in Europe to see the conspicuous display of relics on main and side altars, often physical fragments as dramatic as large bones and skulls. Such displays are reminiscent of the early Christian custom of celebrating the liturgy quite literally over the burial places of the martyrs. Felt affection for the saints led to strong personal and institutionally sanctioned expressions of devotion especially evidenced in the art and other decorative embellishments placed in church sanctuaries. The practice—beginning in the third century and made optional only after the Second Vatican Council of 1962–65—of placing an "altar stone" with a physical fragment of a saint into a cavity in the eucharistic altar of every Catholic church underscores what was once the unmitigated commitment of the Church hierarchy to the communion of saints. During the Counter Reformation, St. Charles Borromeo (1538–84) accentuated the transubstantiated, "Real Presence" of the reserved eucharistic host by promoting the introduction of center altar tabernacles. In addition to glorifying the eucharist, many church sanctuaries also carried material reminders of the other sacraments, of purgatorial beliefs, and of associated devotions—not as significant as the Divine Liturgy of the Mass—called paraliturgies. Complementing the very physical presence of the holy found in tabernacles and reliquaries came an assortment of other artful objects in churches to guide devotionalism and intercessory prayer. Known as "sacramentals," these objects included statues of Jesus, the Virgin Mary, and the saints; stained glass windows; holy water fonts; votive candles; monstrances for eucharistic adoration outside of the liturgy, and more. The sacramentals formed a visual geography receptive to the objects that the faithful themselves gradually acquired—especially as they became more economically affordable—and brought into churches: objects such as rosaries, missals, Bibles, scapulars, holy cards, and medals. It is the multiple layers of material culture found within church buildings that Colleen McDannell chooses to emphasize in her book and to trace against considerations of kitsch.

McDannell identifies the strong association of the term kitsch with objects massproduced for Catholic consumption, and specifically with a particular type of religious artifact first manufactured in the 1800s in Europe and the United States, but especially in France. By the end of the nineteenth century, the Parisian neighborhood of Saint-Sulpice was famous as the birthplace of a form of painted plaster statue whose aesthetic would become "the international style of Catholic church art" (1995: 170). Noting the instant appeal and financial accessibility of the "Sulpician" statues pouring into the hands of consumers and into sanctuaries worldwide, McDannell writes: "From Ireland to Mexico to India to the United States, local art was replaced by goods either imported from France or copied from French standards" (ibid.). By the end of the nineteenth and the early twentieth century, Catholic forms of devotion, already highly material in orientation, readily adopted these new colorful and literal depictions of Jesus, Mary, and the saints. They were easily obtained and incorporated within personal paraliturgical devotion in homes and in churches, along with other forms of decoration and ornamentation (see McDannell 1986; Taves 1986; Kane 2013: 208–9). "For at least a hundred years, from 1840 to 1940, Catholic devotionalism and *l'art Saint-Sulpice* were closely aligned" (McDannell 1995: 170), but criticism of the style had already begun in the 1870s. Then, in the early twentieth century in Europe and the United States, a counter-movement (led by scholars, theologians, and critics) known as *l'art sacré* took root with the aim of simplifying church décor. The Liturgical Movement for reform of worship in the Catholic Church, a more visible crusade, was also soon aligned with *l'art sacré*'s critique of Catholic liturgical environments. For liturgical reformers, excesses in Marian and hagiographic devotionalism and their accompanying material culture undermined the preferred emphasis on the eucharistic celebration. Scholars and clergy criticized the Sulpician art as promoting a "tasteless" aesthetic which was extravagantly representational, sentimental, and ornamental. In some cases, churches in the 1950s were renovated—their plaster statues removed, their altars transformed, their ornamentation painted over. After the Second Vatican Council, a plain aesthetic became even more common in Catholic churches as altar rails, votive candles, and statues of saints were removed. Following the new order for the liturgy promulgated by Pope Paul VI in 1969, altars were brought out away from walls, in some cases to the middle of sanctuaries, in what became common renovations so that priests could face the congregation during prayer and especially during the consecration of the bread and wine.

While this history of the relationship of mass-produced religious objects to Roman Catholic devotionalism is itself fascinating, McDannell forges through her research of this period of artistic and liturgical reforms a further and arguably more significant insight. In letters and published sources, she uncovers a direct association of the Sulpician aesthetic on the part of church reformers not simply with "bad taste," but more critically with what such reformers identified as the excessive devotional practices of Catholic women. Deeming a great many of the religious objects found in Catholic churches to be cloying, decorative, and weakly theological, these reformers (both men and women) characterized religious kitsch as essentially *feminine* in nature. Articles of kitsch in their view were in danger of undermining the profoundly intellectual—and properly masculine—underpinnings of Catholicism and, thereby, feminizing the Church itself. McDannell argues:

> It is my contention that Catholic art reformers employed a rhetoric that equated *l'art Saint-Sulpice* with feminine characteristics and *l'art sacré* with masculine ones. ... What was at stake was not merely art or kitsch, the mass or devotions to the saints, but whether the church was to be masculine or feminine, a place for men or for women.
>
> (McDannell 1995: 174)

Catholic art reformers moved to eliminate the clutter of statues, papers, and other paraphernalia in Catholic sanctuaries which "emphasized artifice, duplication, ornamentation, grandeur, and devotionalism" (ibid.: 173). They worked to effect, in ecclesiastical architecture and decoration, a new Catholic aesthetic which emphasized simplicity and ostensibly more "masculine" forms to represent the power of God. It is for this reason, according to McDannell, that more abstract or masculinized images of Jesus appeared on mass-produced Catholic art such as holy cards, starting in the 1950s.

Though based on textual sources alone without the benefit of ethnographic corroboration, McDannell's diachronic study of Catholic kitsch is an important attempt to see how the perception of such objects by the faithful and the hierarchy have changed over time. Through this fascinating interpretation, McDannell introduces an appreciation of "the feminine gender of Catholic kitsch" (ibid.: 174) as a key to understanding "Christianity and the Problem of Women" (ibid.: 193). While I see the gendered, liturgical, and spiritual issues McDannell broaches as far more complicated in the Catholic context (see Primiano 1997; 1998), her serious analysis of religious kitsch as one means of exploring the liturgical, sexual, and devotional politics of the Church makes a powerful case for the scholarly treatment of such seemingly insignificant objects. McDannell deftly continues her narrative of the history of religious kitsch in twentieth-century Christianity by declaring that the same debates over art and religion that Catholics experienced happened for liberal and conservative Protestants as well. Among Protestants, accusations of "Bad taste ... reflected not class differences or aesthetic ignorance but moral and spiritual weakness"—any art that feminized the divine became theologically untenable (1995: 188–89). In a somewhat ironic development, as Catholics began using fewer objects due to the de-emphasis on personal devotions in the wake of the Second Vatican Council, the material culture of contemporary Protestants kept expanding in a multimillion dollar Christian retailing business, the origins of which McDannell traces to the Victorian period (ibid.: 223–46).

Another prominent approach to religious kitsch has been taken by the historian of American religion, art, and culture, David Morgan, in his 1998 *Visual Piety: A History and Theory of Popular Religious Images* (among many other publications). Morgan offers readers a clear differentiation of kitsch when considering it religiously rather than artistically. Reflecting on the reception of what he calls "popular religious images" such as lithographs or colorful chromolithographs, he notes that

> the popularity of these images is based on the way they answer to the needs of the devout, replying in a voice that is not grandiose, imposing, authoritative, or impersonal, but tailored to the stature of the believer's life. ... Usefulness, though, conflicts at the most fundamental level with the traditional definition of aesthetic values. Unlike objects created for disinterested or 'aesthetic' contemplation, designed to celebrate craft and the history of stylistic refinement, popular iconography is thoroughly "interested," "engaged," functional and extrinsically purposive ... taste is misbegotten if it neglects the existential benefits of the imagery.
>
> (Morgan 1998: 22–25)

Acknowledging criticism of certain forms of kitsch as somehow lessening the quality and maturity of faithful Christian commitment ("inexpensive, mass-produced broadside print, pilgrimage medal or other item, dashboard saint, and offset-lithographic reproduction," ibid.: 24), Morgan asks for a more balanced view of the place of sentiment in the practice of religion, drawing on the insights of philosopher Robert C. Solomon (1991). He demands too a recognition of the complex, nuanced, unique, and distinctive religious literacy associated with the devout collection and use of mass-produced imagery. Morgan's emphasis, therefore, on the intimate and particular value of kitsch in the everyday lives of believers is certainly a retort to those scholars who feel that mass-produced religious objects are mere junk and of no value historically or ethnographically. Morgan has spent much of his career identifying the power of mass-produced imagery and objects and other forms of media on the personal religious lives of American Christian and sectarian believers. He traces the means by which believers as consumers use such forms to create their own religious identities and environments. Such elements of religious culture, therefore, need to be considered for their contribution to religion in American life, for "these images and the emotions they engender are an essential component of popular piety" (Morgan 1998: 24). Morgan sees in what some term kitsch a central fiber of American religiosity, one that has contributed in positive and negative ways to nation-building, ethnic divisions, and religious tensions. A part of the power of religious kitsch for many is its relationship to "the quest for release" from life's many exigencies. As Morgan explains, "The lure of images resides not only in their promise of continuity or renewal, but also in transformation. In every case, the lure answers to a deep longing, which is the underlying business of religious belief to engage" (2007: 261). There is agency in these objects and the ways that they interact with believers and the ways believers interact with them.

This sensitivity to read in kitsch clues to human needs is also found in another valuable interpreter of specifically religious kitsch, cultural historian Celeste Olalquiaga. Her book *The Artificial Kingdom: A Treasury of the Kitsch Experience* (1998) relates kitsch to a cultural sensibility of loss, tracing to the nineteenth century the relationship between such artistic forms and the phenomenon of living in a vicarious, indirect way. Presenting kitsch as the ambivalent crystallization of the lost experience of pre-industrial life and the attempt to recover emotional intensity in the face of technological dehumanization, *The Artificial Kingdom* explores this sensibility through the objects and narratives that industrialization produced, in particular those related to the popular underwater imagery of the time: aquariums, paperweights, the myth of Atlantis, and Jules Verne's *20,000 Leagues Under the Sea*. But it is in her 1992 study *Megalopolis* that Olalquiaga offers a typology of religious kitsch in the chapter, "Holy Kitschen: Collecting Religious Junk from the Street." Within post-modernity, Olalquiaga believes that different iconographies fight for hegemony, and that three degrees of Catholic kitsch have come to overlap in time and space: "First-degree kitsch" is represented by the imagery and objects available for sale or for the taking at church entrances and botanicas, articles which have technically been produced simply and cheaply. For believers, such kitsch represents a "relationship between object and user" which "is immediate," and one of "genuine belief." For believers, she states, "kitsch objects are meaningful even when they are used ornamentally" (1992a: 43) (see Figure 16.5). An example of first-degree kitsch would be the mass-produced colorful saints' candles sold in supermarkets, botanicas, and even novelty stores that are purchased by the faithful for a multiplicity of domestic vernacular religious uses.

These same objects are observed and even treasured, but at a distance, by what Olalquiaga terms "kitsch aficionados." These individuals achieve vicarious pleasure

Figure 16.5 Our Lady of Guadalupe belt buckle, late twentieth century. (From the collection of Leonard Norman Primiano. Photograph by Ben Danner; used with permission.)

by collecting kitsch objects. For "first-degree believers," attachment to an image or object of kitsch is directly related to the devotional meaning of the iconography. For aficionados, however, this meaning is secondary; what matters is not what the images represent, but the intense feelings they inspire, for example, those of hope, fear, and awe. There is no religious attachment for aficionados, but rather a fascination with and attraction to the rawness of emotion that first-degree kitsch symbolizes and makes available for recovery.[4]

"Second-degree kitsch" is for Olalquiaga a category of empty icons—mass-produced religious products sold in specialized shops selling any number and variety of souvenirs or "novelties." Devoid of the emotional intensity that aficionados seek, such objects and images are bland reproductions that exist primarily as toys to pass on. A popularization of camp sensibility, they are designed as commodities for playful exchange, the fodder of "gag" gifting. An irreverent symbol of a supposedly "mysterious" and "exotic" Caribbean religious culture, the chocolate "Voodoo" doll mentioned at the beginning of this chapter, serves as a fine example of Olalquiaga's categorization of second-degree kitsch, as does "NunZilla," a toy evocation of twentieth-century Catholic parochial education—at times staffed by stern religious sisters—combined with an homage to Japanese cinematic science fiction (see Figure 16.6).

Figure 16.6 "NunZilla" (plastic), 2010. (From the collection of Leonard Norman Primiano. Photograph by Ben Danner; used with permission.)

In "third-degree kitsch," Catholic iconography is invested with a new or foreign set of meanings generating a hybrid product. Such hybridization represents an active transformation of kitsch objects and environments by fine artists in a revalorization of Catholic iconography. Through their efforts, such artists are attempting to change the value of what for believers is an already priceless religious asset. Olalquiaga specifically mentions the art of photographer Dana Salvo as an example of this artistic encounter with kitsch. Salvo is an artist who has taken as his inspiration and subject matter the contexts of vernacular religion such as the home altars of women in Mexican rural communities or of the wives of Sicilian migrant fishermen in Gloucester, Massachusetts (see McNiff 1999; Salvo 1997).

Any discussion of approaches to kitsch by more recent scholars such as McDannell, Morgan, and Olalquiaga must, of course, include mention of the deeply influential work of French sociologist Pierre Bourdieu. Bourdieu's *Distinction: A Social Critique of the Judgment of Taste* (1984) stands as one of the most incisive treatments of the social logic of aesthetic discernment ever written. Working to expose the technologies of domination effected by judgments of "taste," Bourdieu's analysis masterfully dissects the distancing strategies and hidden pleasures inherent in the wielding of terms like "kitsch," terms that demonstrate a "disgust for the 'facile'" (1984: 486). What may uncritically be experienced as one's own "good" or "pure" taste is more than likely:

> based on [a] disgust that is often called "visceral" (it "makes one sick" or "makes one vomit") for everything that is "facile" ... . The refusal of what is easy in the sense of simple, and therefore shallow, naturally leads to the refusal of what is facile in the ethical or aesthetic sense, of everything which offers pleasures that are too immediately accessible and so discredited as "childish" or "primitive" (as opposed to the deferred pleasures of legitimate art). ... "Vulgar" works, as the words used to describe them indicate—"facile" or "light", of course, but also "frivolous", "futile", "shallow", "superficial", "showy", "flashy", "meretricious", or in the register of oral satisfactions, "syrupy", "sugary", "rose-water", "schmaltzy", "cloying"—are not only a sort of insult to refinement, a slap in the face to a "demanding" (*difficile*) audience which will not stand for "facile" offerings ... they [also] arouse distaste and disgust by the methods of seduction ...
>
> (Bourdieu 1984: 486)

The establishment of "superior" taste, in other words, depends perhaps more on what it loathes than on what it likes. Indeed, "Taste classifies, and it classifies the classifier" (ibid.: 6). According to McDannell, "Kitsch for Bourdieu has no intrinsic value or meaning of its own" (1995: 165). The classification of art as kitsch, however, like "cultural consumption ... fulfill[s] a social function of legitimating social differences" (Bourdieu 1984: 7). The question of how to approach art that is religiously powerful for thousands while squarely located for thousands more within the paradoxical realm of dependency and disgust can be prominently confronted through consideration of the creative production of the American artist Thomas Kinkade. Once deemed the "king of kitsch" by journalist Cahal Milmo (2001), Kinkade and his work provide one of the most provocative late twentieth- and early twenty-first-century case studies for discussing the difference between art and kitsch and the relationship of taste to religious devotionalism (see Thomas Kinkade Company n.d.).

Thomas Kinkade (1958–2012) is one of the most recognizable American artists of the last 30 years. His medium was painting, and his business the sale of high-quality prints of those paintings. His prints were often embellished with highlights either painted by the artist himself or by other trained artists. Acknowledged by the media as one of the most collected artists in United States history, Kinkade represents a dream example of the challenges for a cultural analysis of essentially mass-produced, merchandised, and mediated religious art. Kinkade's art offers an excellent opportunity for a discussion of the central issues of what defines art as art, religious art as art, and religious art as kitsch.

"To his critics," writes Alexis Boylan in *Thomas Kinkade: The Artist in the Mall*, an anthology dedicated to a consideration of the artist and his output, "Kinkade's work does not stimulate the audience toward complex, ambiguous, or subversive understandings of our world" (2011: 2) in the same way that "fine art" or a movement like Pop Art has (see Botz-Bornstein 2010). His work resorts to cloying color schemes and formulaic landscape tropes that borrow heavily from Hudson River school artists and impressionists, but do neither source justice in terms of technique, originality, or innovation … . Likewise, the work does little to question his role as an artist or our role as audience.

(Boylan 2011: 2)

A self-professed "born-again Christian" and master marketer, Kinkade certainly swam in the conservative and Evangelical currents found in America in the 1990s and into the new millennium. Fascinatingly, he described his paintings as "messages of God's love" even though his art was rarely specifically religious in theme. David Morgan, tracing this lineage and noting Kinkade's place in American Protestant visual culture, attributes the popularity of Kinkade's landscape imagery to his "ability to intermingle piety with national pride by envisioning landscapes that are glorious and inviting, magnificent and intimate" (2007: 260). Kinkade loved commodifying his art, as much as he seemingly enjoyed contesting the established system of museums, galleries, critics, and educational institutions. Operating outside the world of fine art, he established an enormous following and demand for his sentimental, ephemeral, didactic art. If one can accept Kinkade as a religious artist, as his admiring audience certainly does, how should his work— described by critics as kitsch—be evaluated? Artistically? Theologically? Both?

In a short essay entitled "Religious Trappings" in his 1969 anthology of kitsch critiques, published many years before the career of Thomas Kinkade, Gillo Dorfles voices a rather predictable conclusion about the stagnation of both "contemporary sacred art" and religious people:

> What unfortunately must inevitably make a considerable part of religious art kitsch, if not all of it, is that it is usually aimed at a public who, it is thought, ought to be fed with inferior products rather than with products of any artistic merit, for fear that anything "new" in art may lead the faithful away from religion (or rather away from the "old" element in religion).

(Dorfles 1969: 141)

This statement is a prelude in this volume to German Catholic writer Karl Pawek's essay on "Christian Kitsch," wherein Pawek delivers a classic elitist opinion:

> When you consider what a high percentage of the population—judging by the windows of shops selling furniture, lamps, wallpapers and china—live in tasteless surroundings, it is not surprising that the religious pictures and objects which Christians have on show are also tasteless. … From the point of view of taste, Christian kitsch does not pose a specific problem. Most of what is produced and offered for consumption today is tasteless … . What is unique about Christian kitsch is that there is more to it than a purely stylistic deficiency. A kitsch flower-vase does display a stylistic deficiency, but a kitsch statue of the Sacred Heart displays a theological deficiency. … We might allow them their Christian kitsch if this would not at the same time indicate a vast theological loss of substance, as it were.

(Pawek 1969: 143, 145)

Here again are aestheticians commenting on the general state of religious affairs. What we have not really encountered is a theological approach to the role of kitsch in the lives and worship of religious people. Such a perspective has been taken by professor of religion and the arts Frank Burch Brown. Brown's book *Good Taste, Bad Taste and Christian Taste* focuses on the division of sacred and profane kitsch. His suggested definition is not revolutionary:

> Kitsch can be regarded, broadly and simply, as that kind of successful work which most educated and disciplined artists in a given medium would be embarrassed to have produced, and which most established art institutions ... would be embarrassed to display or perform—because, to them, its success seems somehow cheap. Theologically speaking, it is art that educated, disciplined religious artists and their publics might be able to enjoy "in God," but only with some sense of embarrassment and with apologies to the Deity ... just as theologies can have characteristic inadequacies (and embarrassments), so can tastes.
>
> (Brown 2000: 146)

Brown offers three case studies of Christian kitsch that are useful to consider because they are not all object-centered; two engage literature. His first case study addresses Carthage, Missouri's Precious Moments Chapel, an American giftware catalog's company "sanctuary," featuring wall paintings and stained glass windows where children or childlike characters are posed as angels, Biblical figures, or actors from the parables of Jesus.[5] Brown then turns his analysis to *Saving Grace*, Lee Smith's novel of Christian witness with the dramatic moment of self-revelation taking place at a Christian-themed miniature golf course. Finally, he tackles a group of contemporary Christian novels: the "Left Behind" series, which centers on the apocalyptic event known as "The Rapture," and the best-selling New Age novel *The Celestine Prophecy* and its sequel *The Tenth Insight*, both by James Redfield. Brown, like other aesthetic evaluators of kitsch before him, is haunted by the specters of value, excellence, quality, taste, judgment, and appropriateness. He does admit that the quality of a work of art is a matter of the viewer's perspective. With his three case studies in mind, he remarks that the taste for religious kitsch "is a major component of specifically Christian taste and (arguably) a significant force in shaping and expressing contemporary Christian faith" (ibid.: 137).

Complementing Brown's approach of reflecting on kitsch from a perspective of faith is Christian artist Betty Spackman, who seeks to understand as a faithful Christian "often garish visual representations of Christianity" which she playfully refers to as "faith in drag" (2005a; 2005b). Not willing to discard as religiously insignificant the poorly made, Christian-themed imagery merchandised throughout the Evangelical Protestant world, Spackman proclaims that the omnipresence of such imagery marks a significant shift in post-Reformation Christianity. By the later decades of the twentieth century, "a point in history" had been reached "when the Protestant West really embrace[d] the arts for the first time since the iconoclasm of the Reformation" (2005b: 408). The recognition and classification of objects as kitsch "was not just a matter of taste. It was more about intellectual and spiritual arrogance."

Organized Protestantism fears, she speculates, the agency that believers generate from the "opportunity for personal ownership of materially motivated worship ... objects of faith in the home take focus, and even authority, away from the institutional church" (2005b: 410). Evangelicals acting as consumers and as makers of religious images and objects arguably reflect the growing need for an *embodiment of faith* among contemporary Protestants more generally. Needed too, from an academic perspective, is the interpretation of such images and objects by the individuals who create them, by those who consume their creativity, and by the churches working to interpret the Christian message in it all.

Expectations

New religious histories are being forged as scholars probe and artists ask about the place of objects produced in quantity—whether locally or imported from distant markets. Most scholars have been careful not to identify such objects as kitsch, but as materials used in many contexts to forge an expressive religious culture. Important ethnographic treatments of Catholic vernacular materiality include research into the vital life of popular devotional prints in the domestic environments of such diverse locations as Hungary and Newfoundland in the nineteenth and twentieth centuries (Barna 1994; Pocius 1986). Unexpected and especially exciting for scholars as well as the faithful is work on Protestant contexts not known for their iconographic tradition, but still surprisingly rich with artifacts and ephemera. Art historian John Harvey's scholarship on the material religious culture of Nonconformists (Calvinistic Methodist Christians) in Wales since the 1800s (Harvey 1995; 1999) presents vitally significant and transformative research into the function of material culture in the daily religious life of a seemingly iconophobic denomination. American folklife scholar Don Yoder's work on the centrality of paper ephemera in the daily life of Pennsylvania Germans traces the value of religious broadsides, house blessings, and heaven-letters in a variety of sacramental rites of passage (2005; see also Primiano 2007) within those transplanted European Protestant "church" and "sectarian" traditions. Also working with the transformative power of images is Monique Scheer. Using both historical and ethnographic methodologies, Scheer has clarified how the public face of a private apparitional experience comes into being, resulting in an iconic image which is then mass produced as a medium of devotion. "Iconization" is "the process of finding a single public face for an apparition" (2013: 454), a form of Catholic apparitional branding, if you will, necessary for the proper development of an appreciation by the faithful of a new saint or Blessed Virgin devotion. Studying the apparitional culture of Medjugorje in Bosnia-Herzegovina, the most significant Marian apparition in the last twenty years of the twentieth century, Scheer notes that the properties of radical visual innovation are limited. The Marian images of Medjugorje follow the "internalized" iconography of nineteenth-century visual templates. Scheer highlights how the process of communicating an acceptable image is accomplished so that the narrative of the apparition site can be told with a common visual theme, both locally and internationally.

Beginning at the end of the twentieth century as decorations on the graves of children, the use of kitsch objects such as teddy bears, T-shirts, and greeting cards as material declarations of memory and loss has become a widespread tradition in the public enactment of ritual mourning. Visual culture scholar Marita Sturken (2007) sees this vernacular use of commercial objects as emblematic of a complex objectification of grief, fear, and naïve politics by Americans following national tragedies such as the Oklahoma City Bombing and the terrorist attacks of 9/11. Used in such instances of public memorialization, consumer items and associated tourist practices have been identified by Olalquiaga as "melancholic kitsch" and "nostalgic kitsch," two distinct kinds of "memory kitsch" meaningfully expressing the experience of loss. She explains:

> Kitsch is the attempt to repossess the experience of intensity and immediacy through an object. Since this recovery can only be partial and transitory, as the fleetingness of memories well testifies, kitsch objects may be considered failed commodities. However in this constant movement between partially retrieving a forfeited moment and immediately losing it again, kitsch gains the potential of being a dialectical image: an object whose decayed state exposes and deflects its utopian possibilities, a remnant constantly reliving its own death, a ruin.
>
> (Olalquiaga 1998: 291)

The dialectical and multivalent nature of mass-produced objects is an important quality of their postmodern aura, an effect addressed in the work of Birgit Meyer, scholar of global Christianity and material religion.

Birgit Meyer's fascinating ethnographic work in Ghana highlights the efficacy of mass-produced Christian imagery in developing Christian environments in Africa. In this lively religious marketplace where Roman Catholic, Evangelical, and Pentecostal Christianities vie for believers' affiliation and affections, mass-produced "Jesus pictures" pervade private domestic settings as well as public spaces, if rarely Protestant churches. Meyer's scholarship tracks an important distinction in the understanding and function of these pictures in the vernacular religion of different Ghanaian Christian communities. While some groups maintain an ocular-centric focus on such pictures, understanding them to be visual representations of the holy, others focus on the agency and power of the pictures themselves as material objects. Meyer urges scholars to be conscious of any religious context in which a mass-produced image or object is indeed considered "more" than itself. In Catholic homes, pictures of Jesus on calendars and other domestic objects remain central, sacred images enhancing prayer and devotion to Christ. In Pentecostal circles in Ghana, however, such images open the door for the direct entrance, not of goodness or grace, but *evil* into the everyday lives of the people who purchase, display, or carry them. Meyer observes that many Ghanaian Pentecostals have come to associate mass-produced pictures of Jesus and other products of modernity with the work of the devil. For them, the sacramental nature of Jesus pictures has been trumped by a greater and specifically wicked power. Their discomfort with these pictures does not involve belief in the falsity of iconophilic aesthetics, but stems rather from faith in the literal ability of the devil to occupy and lend objects a malevolent agency. The Pentecostal belief that diabolical influences can enter an individual's life through the eyes of a picture of Jesus recalls for this reader, at least, the "ethical evil" lurking behind sentimental kitsch for Herman Broch. What is especially valuable about Meyer's ethnography is the way it complements, from an African Christian perspective, David Morgan's work on the tradition of visual piety in American Protestantism. As Meyer herself acknowledges, "Interestingly then, by contrast to Morgan's analysis in which Jesus pictures function in the context of certain religiously authorized practices of looking, the Pentecostal suspicion vis-à-vis pictures suggests an understanding of pictures as potentially prone to 'going wild.' Pictures, in this view, cannot be fully contained and easily act out their excessive potential" (2012: 316). The views many Ghanaian Pentecostals hold about "Jesus pictures" reflect the influence of early Protestant missionaries. These missionaries were deeply critical both of Catholic sacramental iconography and of indigenous African religions that engaged objects in their practice. Fascinatingly, for most Ghanaian Pentecostals, film in its various forms is not open to demonic inhabitation like mass-produced chromolithographs of Jesus. In her study, Meyer is working to answer a question insightfully asked by religious studies scholar Graham Harvey when studying "animist worldviews and lifeways" and the way "things act" in the context of North American indigenous religions (2012: 194). Harvey's question about material culture generally could naturally be applied to the study of religious kitsch: "What difference would it make if instead of … us … [considering] 'material culture' we thought about the 'culture of things'? What if these objects are not simply present but actively participate?" (ibid.: 209).

Coda: a tale of two objects: contemporary visual religious literacy and kitsch

Let us conclude by considering two examples of Christian religious material culture. They are both representations of Jesus Christ as an adult. They are both colorful. They are both contemporary pieces produced in the decades after the turn of the new millennium. They are each a representation of a popular devotion in Roman Catholicism: Sister Margaret Mary Alacoque's vision of the "Sacred Heart of Jesus" which originated in France in the seventeenth century (1673), and Sister Mary Faustina Kowalska's vision of the "Divine Mercy" (1931) which began in Poland in the twentieth century.

The first object (Figure 16.7) is decidedly "postmodern," what Olalquiaga would classify as second-degree kitsch, in its ironic, and arguably offensive, take on Catholic devotionalism. Purchased from the now defunct Border's bookstore chain, it is a purple, glittery "Sacred Heart of Jesus" money bank, an object that rather curiously links devotion to a Catholic apparition to monetary gain or hoped-for prosperity. In contrast, the second object (Figure 16.8) was designed ostensibly to support or inspire more sincere devotional practices. It features a non-whimsical representation of Jesus with a miniature "Divine Mercy," the apparition of Jesus described by Sister Faustina. Jesus's image is glued into the center of a clear basket filled with bright

Figure 16.7 Sacred Heart of Jesus bank (plastic with purple glitter), 2011. (From the collection of Leonard Norman Primiano. Photograph by Ben Danner; used with permission.)

pink flowers and moss at the Savior's feet. This all-plastic shrine was given to me by Deborah Ann Bailey, a public sector folklorist in Missouri who collected it at a religious gathering of Vietnamese-American Catholics in that state. It was in fact made by blind Vietnamese children who are taught the craft to support themselves and their Catholic orphanages in Vietnam.

Both of these objects would certainly be recognized by those familiar with the tradition as examples of Catholic culture. Both feature well-known, international apparitions of Jesus. The question is, which object, if either, could be described as an example of Catholic kitsch? As we have seen, scholarly approaches to questions such as this one lead us down various avenues of consideration.

Figure 16.8 Divine Mercy of Jesus shrine (plastic), 2013. (From the collection of Leonard Norman Primiano. Photograph by Ben Danner; used with permission.)

In this matter, I have found it useful to invert the ideas of engineer and philosopher Abraham Moles, who asserts that "kitsch is essentially an aesthetic system of mass communication." Moles speculates that kitsch allows the masses to pass "from sentimentality to sensation" (1971: 74, as quoted in Calinescu 1987: 258), from mere pleasure to the "genuine" experience of art. The communicative power of Catholic kitsch is perhaps better understood through an inversion of Moles's proposal. Rather than pleasure in material objects giving way to higher, more sophisticated or "genuine" realms of experience, ardent religious commitment might result in the active transformation of cheap or aesthetically suspect objects into cherished instruments of authentic vernacular worship.

The argument has already been noted that art for one person can represent kitsch to another. Certainly what I would identify as a folkloristic approach to the study of religious objects would root itself in the recognition that every social group and, in fact, every individual has an artistic sensibility—an often diverse and creative system of vernacular aesthetics with its own internal logic. Scholars regardless of discipline should not judge a group's or individual's taste in religious material culture from the etic perspective of a critic (see Primiano 1999: 197–98).

One of the ways in which ethnologists of religious materiality and concerned others can "read" kitsch is at the level of the object itself. In this sense, one at least is extending to items of "religious kitsch" the same level of integral reading that scholars afford so-called "high" or "elite" or "formally-wrought" objects of art. One would assume that producers of religious objects typically do not see it in their best business or religious interest to categorize their artifacts as "kitsch," as in the case of Steve Dymszo, but I wonder what the manufacturer of the Sacred Heart of Jesus bank had in mind. Is the bank mocking Catholicism or inviting those familiar with it to enjoy the idiosyncrasies of the tradition? As cultural critic Anne Rowbottom noted in a June 2013 personal communication: "One of the most liberating things about post-modern society is that you can embrace kitsch. You can embrace it as playful irony and that is what makes it so acceptable."

Any comprehensive consideration of kitsch asks us to reflect on this question: is kitsch always in the mind of the beholder, or is the re-presentation of the world through cheaply produced reproductions by now so complete that it negates the designation of any given object as kitsch? Indeed, can any one object be called Catholic, or Protestant, or Orthodox kitsch from an ethnographic perspective?

After I purchased the purple Jesus bank and displayed it in my office, a colleague commented that it was obviously an object made for "young people." This remark prompted me to wonder whether, in this "post secular" society, young Catholics actually possess a sufficiently rich religious frame of reference to understand what a piece of so-called Catholic kitsch is actually communicating, expressing, or signifying. While *religious* illiteracy (by which I mean content knowledge of the world's religious traditions) is on the rise (see Prothero 2007), an equally significant *visual* illiteracy is characteristic of many young Catholics, especially those I have observed in American contexts (see Primiano 2011a, 2011b). While the pervasive digital conveniences of twenty-first-century life enable some to locate and research traditional Catholic imagery, many young Catholics possess little knowledge of the context and meaning of such imagery, even when it is brought dramatically into focus in their everyday lives in the tattoos some have etched on their bodies. How is the changing level of familiarity with Christian religious symbols and material culture, regardless of its narrative of production, brand of distribution, or situation of circulation, affecting the vernacular religious sensibilities of "spiritual Christians"—that is, individuals who self-identify as Christians, but who do not desire to participate in any formal relationship with an institutional church? How is the changing literacy about religion and religious symbols and material culture going to affect the way "spiritual Catholic, Protestant, or Orthodox Christians" relate to all forms of religious art: from what is identified as folk or vernacular art to the mass-produced religious objects they encounter most frequently in their lives?

Value and meaning are reproduced at the confluences of everyday life, Joseph Sciorra notes in *Built with Faith: Italian American Imagination and Catholic Material Culture in New York City* (2015). In this book, Sciorra constructs a strong case for the place of kitsch religious objects and kitsch environments in the creation of the unique style of urban vernacular architecture emblematic of this ethnic community. Yard shrines, outdoor Christmas displays, indoor *presepio* manger scenes, and many other forms of creative, ceremonial display are interpreted as public and private expressions of faith, ethnicity, and artistry. The complexities involved in understanding, appreciating, and analyzing the internal dimensions of these sites of religiosity are like learning a language of its own. Kitsch has been characterized in all of its garish, overwrought, repetitive glory as both affirming and threatening, particular and universal, deceptive and spiritual. It has been called a power, a pawn, a scapegoat, a weapon, a commodity. It has been deemed both a mirror and a manipulator of reality, active in both "high" and "popular" culture. It can be designed, distributed, and sold by an entrepreneurial company or "transfigured" and exhibited by a "great" artist. It is the postmodern art of the people and possibly in the words of performance studies scholar and folklorist Barbara Kirshenblatt-Gimblett "an affirmation of the possibility of creative expression in all quarters" (1991: 125). It will prove exciting to continue to observe and study how individuals incorporate what many identify as religious kitsch (see Figure 16.9)—religious objects of all shapes and sizes and quality—into the articulation of their vernacular religious expressions in the twenty-first century.

Figure 16.9 "Jesus is my coach" ice hockey Jesus (molded resin image), 2014. (Photograph by Maria C. Monastra; used with permission.)

Notes

1 Versions of the material in this chapter were presented at the 2013 meeting of the International Society for Ethnology and Folklore (SIEF), Tartu, Estonia; 2013 meeting of the American Folklore Society, Providence, Rhode Island; 2014 Conference of the International Society for Ethnology and Folklore (SIEF) Working Group on Ethnology of Religion, Lisbon, Portugal; and as a 2014 lecture at the Elphinstone Institute, University of Aberdeen. I thank Thomas A. McKean for arranging that occasion. I wish to thank Mavis Aitchison, Barbara Ambros, Deborah Ann Bailey, Marion Bowman, Daniel Cheifer, Steve Dymszo, J. Gregory Garrity, Cécile Guillaume-Pey, Jeffrey Hamburger, Kim Kennedy, Nicolas Le Bigre, Laura S. Levitt, Sabina Magliocco, E. Ann Matter, Maria Santa Montez, Deborah Dash Moore, Takemi Odajima, Andrew Owen, István Povedák, Lisa Ratmansky, Nicholas Rademacher, Anne Rowbottom, Clara Saraiva, Matthew Serfass, Joseph Sciorra, David Simonowitz, Matthew Slutz, Tamarah Smith, Irina Stahl, Joseph Tissot, Kay Turner, Joanne Punzo Waghorne, Roger S. Wieck, as well as Jen Hasse and especially Anne Schwelm of Cabrini College's Holy Spirit Library for their assistance. I am grateful to Kathy McCrea, Patti Stocker, and Ben Danner for their technical assistance; Anne Skleder and Jeffrey Gingerich for their support; and to John DiMucci, and Nancy Watterson, who read drafts of the article. Laura Sauer Palmer read final drafts with great dedication and care. I am continuously grateful to Eric Michael Mazur for his unfailing support.
2 Kitsch can be appreciated locally as a part of a community that shares a common ethnic, gendered, occupational, age, religious, or other identity; or it can maintain a more universal level of recognition, especially when it relates to material representations of well-known touristic places such as the Statue of Liberty, the Taj Mahal or St. Peter's Basilica, or to such internationally recognized historical figures such as Jesus or the Buddha. This chapter emphasizes my specific area of research and knowledge: the Christian tradition. There is ample work on the study of kitsch—even if the concept is not so identified—in other world religious traditions: Judaism (Loewy 1997; Friedlander 2000; Bennett et al. 2005; Neulander 2006; Shandler 2008); Islam (Roberts et al. 2003; Leaman 2004; Gorlée 2011; Allan 2011; Khosronejad 2012; Gruber and Haugbolle 2013); the religions of India (Kapur 1993; Pinney 1995; McDermott 1996; Mankekar 1999; McDermott 2003; Lutgendorf 2006; McLain 2009; Ramachandran 2014). There is nothing specifically on kitsch in Japanese religions, although there is literature on Japanese religion and pop culture that examines the culture of cuteness (for example, see Morean 1993; Buckley 2002; Reider 2003; Miller 2011; Occhi 2012).
3 Such a wink can also be applied to the idea of "camp" identified by Susan Sontag in her "Notes on camp" (1961/1968), and others (Shugart and Waggoner 2008) who have extended its appreciation from simply Sontag's camp sensibility to being an aesthetic of its own.
4 Some of the objects that I describe at the beginning of this chapter—the Pope John Paul II comic book and the Sistine Chapel teacup and saucer—I have collected in the role of aficionado that Olalquiaga describes.
5 Jennifer Rycenga's critique of the Precious Moments Chapel is insightful: "Precious Moments intends to celebrate the private and the personal," she writes. "But it can only do so through the public mediation of the market" (2011: 146).

Works cited

Allan, J.W. (2011) *The Art and Architecture of Twelver Shi'ism: Iraq, Iran and the Indian Sub-Continent,* London: Azimuth Editions.
Bagnoli, M., H.A. Klein, C.G. Mann, and J. Robinson (eds) (2010) *Treasures of Heaven: Saints, Relics, and Devotion in Medieval Europe,* New Haven, CT: Yale University Press.

Barna, G. (1994) "Objects of devotion or decoration? the role of religious objects in everyday life in the nineteenth and twentieth centuries," in N.A. Bringeus (ed.), *Religion in Everyday Life*, Stockholm, Sweden: Kungl. Vitterhets Historie och Antikvitets Akademien, 105–20.

Bennett, R., N. Kroll, and J. Shell (2005) *Bar Mitzvah Disco: The Music May Have Stopped, But the Party's Never Over*, New York: Crown.

Binkley, S. (2000) "Kitsch as a repetitive system: a problem for the theory of taste hierarchy," *Journal of Material Culture* 5, 2: 131–52.

Botz-Bornstein, T. (2010) "The aesthetics of frozen dreams: kitsch and anti-kitsch in Jeff Koons and Mariko Mori," *Art in Society* 9 (n.d.). Online. Available: www.art-in-society.de/AS9/TBB_Koons-Mori.html (accessed 22 November 2014).

Bourdieu, P. (1984) *Distinction: A Social Critique of the Judgment of Taste*, trans. Richard Nice, Cambridge, MA: Harvard University Press.

Bowes, K. (2010) "Personal devotions and private chapels," in V. Burrus (ed.), *A People's History of Christianity: Late Ancient Christianity*, Minneapolis, MN: Fortress Press, 188–210.

Boylan, A.L. (ed.) (2011) *Thomas Kinkade: The Artist in the Mall*, Durham, NC: Duke University Press.

Broch, H. (1969) "Notes on the problem of kitsch," in G. Dorfles (ed.), *Kitsch: The World of Bad Taste*, New York: Bell Publishing Company, 49–76.

Brown, F.B. (2000) *Good Taste, Bad Taste, and Christian Taste: Aesthetics in Religious Life*, New York: Oxford University Press.

Brown, P. (1981) *The Cult of the Saints: Its Rise and Function in Latin Christianity*, Chicago, IL: The University of Chicago Press.

Buckley, S. (2002) "Kawaii" [cuteness], in S. Buckley (ed.), *Encyclopedia of Contemporary Japanese Culture*, New York: Routledge, 250.

Calinescu, M. (1987) *Five Faces of Modernity*, Durham, NC: Duke University Press.

Dorfles, G. (1969) *Kitsch: The World of Bad Taste*, New York: Bell Publishing Company.

Dutton, D. (1996) "Kitsch," in J. Turner (ed.), *The Dictionary of Art*, 18, London: Macmillan, 100–101.

Friedlander, S. (2000) *Reflections of Nazism: An Essay on Kitsch and Death*, Bloomington, IN: Indiana University Press.

Gans, H.J. (1974) *Popular Culture and High Culture: An Analysis and Evaluation of Taste*, New York: Basic Books.

Giesz, L. (1969) "Kitsch-man as tourist," in G. Dorfles (ed.), *Kitsch: The World of Bad Taste*, New York: Bell Publishing Company, 156–74.

Gorlée, D.L. (2011) "Orientalized kitsch," *American Book Review* 32, 6: 21–22.

Greenberg, C. (1939) "Avant-garde and kitsch," *Partisan Review* 6, 5 (Fall): 34–49.

Gruber, C. and S. Haugbolle (eds) (2013) *Visual Culture in the Modern Middle East: Rhetoric of the Image*, Bloomington, IN: Indiana University Press.

Harvey, G. (2012) "Things act: casual indigenous statements about the performance of object-persons," in M. Bowman and U. Valk (eds), *Vernacular Religion in Everyday Life: Expressions of Belief*, Sheffield, UK: Equinox, 194–210.

Harvey, J. (1995) *The Art of Piety: The Visual Culture of Welsh Nonconformity*, Cardiff, UK: University of Wales Press.

——(1999) *Image of the Invisible: The Visualization of Religion in the Welsh Nonconformist Tradition*, Cardiff, UK: University of Wales Press.

Kane, P.M. (2013) *Sister Thorn and Catholic Mysticism in Modern America*, Chapel Hill, NC: University of North Carolina Press.

Kapur, A. (1993) "Deity to crusader: the changing iconography of Ram," in P.G. Pandey (ed.), *Hindus and Others*, New Delhi, India: Viking, 74–107.

Khosronejad, P. (ed.) (2012) *Art and Material Culture of Iranian Shi'ism: Iconography and Religious Devotion in Shi'i Islam*, London, UK: Tauris.

Kipfer, B.A. (2013) *Roget's 21st Century Thesaurus*, 3rd edn, New York: Dell.

Kirshenblatt-Gimblett, B. (1991) "Who's bad? accounting for taste," *Artforum International* 30, 3: 119–25.

Kjellman-Chapin, M. (ed.) (2013) *Kitsch: History, Theory, Practice*, Newcastle upon Tyne, UK: Cambridge Scholars Publishing.

Kulka, T. (1996) *Kitsch and Art*, University Park, PA: The Pennsylvania State University Press.

Lamont, M. and M. Fournier (eds) (1992) *Cultivating Differences: Symbolic Boundaries and the Making of Inequality*, Chicago, IL: The University of Chicago Press.

Leaman, O. (2004) *Islamic Aesthetics: An Introduction*, Notre Dame, IN: University of Notre Dame Press.

Loewy, P. (1997) *Jewishness*, Munich: Gina Kehayoff Verlag, 1997.

Luria, K.P. (2010) "Rural and village piety," in P. Matheson (ed.), *A People's History of Christianity: Reformation Christianity*, V, Minneapolis, MN: Fortress Press, 48–69.

Lutgendorf, P. (2006) "All in the (Raghu) family: a video epic in cultural context," in J.S. Hawley and V. Narayanan (eds), *The Life of Hinduism*, Berkeley, CA: University of California Press, 140–57.

McDannell, C. (1986) *The Christian Home in Victorian America, 1840–1900*, Bloomington, IN: Indiana University Press.

——(1995) *Material Christianity: Religion and Popular Culture in America*, New Haven, CT: Yale University Press.

McDermott, R. (1996) "The Western Kali," in J.S. Hawley and D.M. Wulff (eds), *Devi: The Goddess in India*, Berkeley, CA: University of California Press, 281–313.

——(2003) "Kali's New Frontiers: A Hindu Goddess on the Internet," in J. Kripal and R. McDermott (eds), *Encountering Kali: At the Margins, at the Center, in the West*, Berkeley, CA: University of California Press, 273–95.

McLain, K. (2009) *India's Immortal Comic Books: Gods, Kings, and Other Heroes*, Bloomington, IN: Indiana University Press.

McNiff, S. (1999) "Celebrations of memory: Dana Salvo and the Mother of Grace Club." Cultureport.com. Online. Available: http://168.144.121.83/cultureport/artists/salvo/index01.html (accessed 24 July 2014).

Mankekar, P. (1999) "Mediating modernities: the *Ramayan* and the creation of community and nation," in P. Mankekar (ed.), *Screening Culture, Viewing Politics: An Ethnography of Television, Womanhood, and Nation in Postcolonial India*, Durham, NC: Duke University Press, 165–204.

Mentzer, R.A. (2010) "The piety of townspeople and city folk," in P. Matheson (ed.), *A People's History of Christianity: Reformation Christianity*, Minneapolis, MN: Fortress Press, 23–47.

Meyer, B. (2012) "'There is a spirit in that image': mass-produced Jesus pictures and Protestant-Pentecostal animation in Ghana," in D. Houtman and B. Meyer (eds), *Things: Religion and the Question of Materiality*, New York: Fordham University Press, 296–320.

Meyer, B., D. Morgan, C. Paine, and S.B. Plate (eds) (2011) "Introduction: key words in material religion," *Material Religion* 7, 1 (March): 4–8.

Miller, L. (2011) "Tantalizing tarot and cute cartomancy in Japan," *Japanese Studies* 31, 1: 73–91.

Milmo, C. (2001) "Kinkade, king of kitsch, coming to a home near you," *Independent* (May 5): 11.

Moles, A.A. (1971) *Le kitsch: l'art du Bonheur*, Paris: Mame.

Morean, B. (1993) "Synderella Christmas: kitsch, consumerism, and youth in Japan," in D. Miller (ed.), *Unwrapping Christmas*, Oxford: Clarendon Press.

Morgan, D. (1998) *Visual Piety: A History and Theory of Popular Religious Images*, Berkeley, CA: University of California Press.

——(2007) *The Lure of Images: A History of Religion and Visual Media in America*, London: Routledge.

Neulander, J.S. (2006) "Tchotchkes: a study of popular culture in tangible form," in L. J. Greenspoon and R.A. Simkins (eds), *American Judaism in Popular Culture*, Omaha, NE: Creighton University Press, 175–200.

Occhi, D.J. (2012) "Wobbly aesthetics, performance, and message: comparing Japanese kyara with their anthropomorphic forebears," *Asian Ethnology* 71, 1: 109–32.

Olalquiaga, C. (1992a) *Megalopolis: Contemporary Cultural Sensibilities*, Minneapolis, MN: University of Minnesota Press.

——(1992b) "The dark side of modernity's moon," *Agenda* 28 (November): 22–25. Online. Available: www.celesteolalquiaga.com/moon.html (accessed 14 July 2014).

——(1998) *The Artificial Kingdom: A Treasury of the Kitsch Experience*, Minneapolis, MN: University of Minnesota Press.

Oxford Dictionaries Online (n.d.) "Kitsch." Available: www.oxforddictionaries.com/us/definition/american_english/kitsch (accessed 14 July 2014).

Pawek, K. (1969) "Christian kitsch," in G. Dorfles (ed.), *Kitsch: The World of Bad Taste*, New York: Bell Publishing Company, 143–50.

Pinney, C. (1995) "An authentic Indian 'kitsch': the aesthetics, discriminations and hybridity of popular Hindu art," *Social Analysis* 38: 88–110.

Pitarakis, B. (2010) "Objects of devotion and protection," in D. Krueger (ed.), *A People's History of Christianity: Byzantine Christianity*, Minneapolis, MN: Fortress Press, 164–81.

Pocius, G.L. (1986) "Holy pictures in Newfoundland houses: visual codes for secular and supernatural relationships," in P. Narvaez and M. Laba (eds), *Media Sense: The Folklore-Popular Culture Continuum*, Bowling Green, OH: Bowling Green University Popular Press, 124–48.

Primiano, L.N. (1995) "Vernacular religion and the search for method in religious folklife," *Western Folklore* 54: 37–56. [Japanese Translation: *Annual Journal of Tohoku Religiology* 3 (2007): 129–53.]

——(1997) "Colleen McDannell, *Material Christianity: Religion and Popular Culture in America*" [review], *The Records of the American Catholic Historical Society* 108: 83–87.

——(1998) "'I hate that book because it does not change and I do': recent books on vernacular religion," *Critical Review of Books in Religion* 11: 193–209.

——(1999) "Post-modern sites of Catholic sacred materiality," in P.W. Williams (ed.), *Perspectives on American Religion and Culture*, Malden, MA: Basil Blackwell, 187–202.

——(2007) "Don Yoder, *The Pennsylvania German Broadside: A History and Guide*" [review], *Pennsylvania Magazine of History and Biography* 131: 214–16.

——(2011a) "'I wanna do bad things with you': fantasia on themes of American religion from the title sequence of HBO's *True Blood*," in E.M. Mazur and K. McCarthy (eds), *God in the Details: American Religion in Popular Culture*, 2nd edn, New York: Routledge, 41–61.

——(2011b) "Catholiciana unmoored: ex-votos in Catholic tradition and their commercialization as religious commodities," in J. Sciorra and R. Briscese (eds), *Graces Received: Painted and Metal Ex-votos from Italy*, New York: Calandra Institute Press, 8–37.

——(2012) "Manifestations of the religious vernacular: ambiguity, power, and creativity," in M. Bowman and U. Valk (eds), *Vernacular Religion in Everyday Life: Expressions of Belief*, Oakville, CT: Equinox Publishing, 382–94.

Prothero, S. (2007) *Religious Literacy: What Every American Needs to Know—And Doesn't*, San Francisco, CA: Harper San Francisco.

Ramachandran, T. (2014) "A call to multiple arms! protesting the commoditization of Hindu imagery in Western society," *Material Religion* 10, 1: 54–75.

Reider, N.T. (2003) "Transformation of the oni: from the frightening and diabolical to the cute and sexy," *Asian Folklore Studies* 62, 1: 133–57.

Roberts, A.F., M.N. Roberts, G. Armenian, and D. Gueye (2003) *A Saint in the City: Sufi Arts of Urban Senegal*, Los Angeles, CA: UCLA Fowler Museum.

Rosenberg, H. (1970) *The Tradition of the New*, New York: Da Capo Press.

Rugg, W. (2002) "Kitsch," *The University of Chicago Theories of Media Keywords Glossary* (Winter). Online. Available: http://csmt.uchicago.edu/glossary2004/kitsch.htm (accessed 14 July 2014).

Rycenga, J. (2011) "'Dropping in for the holidays: Christmas as commercial ritual at the Precious Moments Chapel," in E.M. Mazur and K. McCarthy (eds), *God in the Details: American Religion in Popular Culture*, 2nd edn, New York: Routledge, 140–53.

Salvo, D. (1997) *Home Altars of Mexico*, Albuquerque, NM: University of New Mexico Press.

Scheer, M. (2013) "What she looks like: on the recognition and iconization of the Virgin Mary at apparition sites in the twentieth century," *Material Religion* 9, 4: 442–67.

Sciorra, J. (2015) *Built with Faith: Italian American Imagination and Catholic Material Culture in New York City*, Knoxville, TN: University of Tennessee Press.

Shandler, J. (2008) *Adventures in Yiddishland: Postvernacular Language and Culture*, Berkeley, CA: University of California Press.

Shugart, H.A. and C.E. Waggoner (2008) *Making Camp: Rhetorics of Transgression in U.S. Popular Culture*, Tuscaloosa, AL: University of Alabama Press.

Solomon, R.C. (1991) "On kitsch and sentimentality," *Journal of Aesthetics and Art Criticism* 49, 1: 1–14.

Sontag, S. (1961/1968) "Notes on camp," in *Against Interpretation and Other Essays*, New York: Dell, 275–92.

Spackman, B. (2005a) *A Profound Weakness: Christians and Kitsch*, Carlisle, UK: Piquant.

——(2005b) "Reconsidering 'kitsch,'" *Material Religion* 1, 3: 404–16.

Sturken, M. (2007) *Tourists of History: Memory, Kitsch, and Consumerism from Oklahoma City to Ground Zero*, Durham, NC: Duke University Press.

Talbot, A.M. (2010) "The devotional life of laywomen," in D. Krueger (ed.), *A People's History of Christianity: Byzantine Christianity*, Minneapolis, MN: Fortress Press, 201–20.

Taves, A. (1986) *The Household of Faith: Roman Catholic Devotions in Mid-Nineteenth Century America*, Notre Dame, IN: University of Notre Dame Press.

Thomas Kinkade Company (n.d.) "Thomas Kinkade: painter of light." Online. Available: www.thomaskinkade.com/magi/servlet/com.asucon.ebiz.home.web.tk.HomeServlet (accessed 24 July 2014).

Trout, D. (2010) "Saints, identity, and the city," in V. Burrus (ed.), *A People's History of Christianity: Late Ancient Christianity*, Minneapolis, MN: Fortress Press, 165–87.

Webb, D. (2010) "Domestic religion," in D.E. Bornstein (ed.), *A People's History of Christianity: Medieval Christianity*, Minneapolis, MN: Fortress Press, 303–28.

Yoder, D. (2005) *The Pennsylvania German Broadside: A History and Guide*, University Park, PA: The Pennsylvania State University Press.

Section C
LOCATIVE ENCOUNTERS

Introduction to Part II, Section C

There is an aspect of the physical that goes beyond the material aspect of the relationship between religion and popular culture: namely, the encounter of the two in defined space, at a definite (if not always defined) time. What we see in these "locative" encounters, however, is more than just a specific location that houses the encounter, but—for each of the contributors to this section—the deconstruction, reconceptualization, and reconstruction of what both "religion" and "popular culture" mean as a result of the encounter. None of the following chapters examines anything approximating a tradition-based religious location; from the shopping mall to the National Mall, from an electronic dance music event to a sports spectacular, these chapters examine how collective and individual experience of space is integral to the collective and individual construction of place. In other words, the physical space takes on meaning beyond the component parts, beyond (but not absent) an elite narrative. It is in this way that these locations focus our attention on the relationship between religion and popular culture; aspects of individual investment are affirmed in religion-like fashion.

It is to our first—and likely most seemingly mundane—location that Sarah McFarland Taylor takes us in her chapter, "Shopping and consumption." We begin to see here the physical nature of the locative encounter emerge from the mediated and material encounters previously explored, still closely related, and at times even dependent, but increasingly distinct. There is something particularly modern going on at the mall, it seems, and it is to be expected that a reader might conjure Max Weber's linking of capitalism to Protestantism. But of course, in the modern (or even postmodern) world, there is more to the relationship between shopping and capitalistic consumption than just Calvinist ideology. In the mall—itself a distinctly modern phenomenon—we see an intentionality in the design and use of space that constructs for all people a sacred space of shopping, and affirms—it does not create—a very religious-like devotion to consumption, both physical and spiritual. But in the twenty-first century, such devotion is more than just a locative experience; it is also the personal experience of the acquisition of the material through the mediated, be it via point-and-click shopping or devotional inspiration from the mediated deities of consumption. Tradition-based religion like Weber's Protestantism may be present, and it may even benefit (at times), but religion is for the most part simply the conceptual framework to explain to the individual any meaning inherent in shopping and consumption.

In his chapter, "Electronic dance music events," Graham St John reminds us that music may be produced by some, and transmitted by others, but it is heard—and, just as importantly, experienced—by others, and those others give it a meaning of their own. Going beyond humming or toe-tapping, the music experience of the electronic dance music (EDM) event is—according to those devoted to its production, performance, and encounter—transformative, and emphasizes a liminal, transitional state that is also foundational in religious ritual. In the hands of the "technoshaman"—the DJ who does more than simply play music—the EDM event participant encounters a blend of sensual experiences beyond the aural that is intended to enhance the sense of spiritual liberation. Not quite as "popular" an event as shopping, the EDM event illustrates the use ("consumption") of popular culture for distinctly religious (or at least religion-like) purposes.

Jeffrey Scholes takes us into the world of sport, examining how it and religion interact both instrumentally and as presumed equals. Religious athletes who acknowledge the Divine for their successes—or even religious figures who explain their world through sports metaphors—provide a quick glimpse into the ways religion uses sport, or sport uses religion to convey meaning or to secure a place in society. But in contemporary society, the significance of sport may be better understood if it is seen as providing in the lives of those who partake of it an equivalence (if not identity) to religion. Scholes takes us into the world of the sports location— the stadium—to provide evidence of this equivalence, examining how owners, fans, and players construct, maintain, and perpetuate meaning in this space that marks it as different, ritualized, and significant, elevating it to a level of sacrality comparable to spaces considered sacred in the more tradition-based sense. But its significance also reveals the stratification—economic, temporal, and functional—that is the mark of contemporary society, where popular functional equivalents mirror cultural institutions (including religious ones).

Darryl Caterine's examination of "Monuments of civil religion" explores (in the American context) the ways in which intentional locations of collective transcendence have been transformed into intentional locations of individual memory and emotion. Starting from the New York site of national tragedy that occurred on September 11, 2001—oddly and yet appropriately nicknamed "Ground Zero"— Caterine takes us back in time to the American Puritans, Protestants who were rebelling not only against Catholic notions of sacred space and time, but also against similar conceptualizations as they were expressed and put into operation by the Church of England. A history of warfare (domestic and foreign) and invention (railroads and automobiles) served as the catalyst for a nationwide expansion of "American sacred space," with its sacred center firmly located in the nation's capital. Transformations in American society, however, threatened society-wide meaning (or the presumption of it), and the monuments of American civil religion—the celebration of "great [white, wealthy, Protestant] men"—ultimately lost favor to the memorials to the emotions of any (and each) person, becoming sites of popular (rather than elite) meanings.

In all of these we are encouraged to consider the psychic effect of the encounter between religion and popular culture. Not only is there a borrowing of a bit of one for the purposes of the other, but a powerful new hybrid is also created, a form of being religious that is not tradition-based, and a use of popular culture that is not always popular. Inevitably, each of these chapters requires us to reconsider not just how religion and popular culture interact in the physical, location-specific (that is, "locative") encounter, but what it is about this encounter in physical space that creates these results.

17

SHOPPING AND CONSUMPTION

Sarah McFarland Taylor

Introduction: exploring the féerie and phantasmagoria of the arcade

Cultural critic and theorist Walter Benjamin (1892–1940) was fascinated with the "shopping malls" of his time. Captivated by the sharp contrasts of light and shadow in the glass-roofed Parisian "arcades," he saw these as enchanted replicas of the "world in miniature" (Benjamin 1999: 31). For more than a decade, Benjamin kept a series of folders (or "Convolutes") containing scraps of notes with quotations, ideas, citations, images, and observations that became known as *The Arcades Project*. Legend has it that when Benjamin committed suicide in exile in 1940, a briefcase belonging to him went missing: it contained a completed manuscript drawn from the voluminous material related to the project (Taussig 2006: 9). Benjamin's notes on the arcades are filled with the use of religious idiom. He refers to the arcades as "temples of commodity capital" and characterizes the structure of the arcade as "a nave with side chapels" (1999: 37). He calls the arcades "dream houses" or "dream cities"—glass-and-iron-trimmed rows of stores, enclosed and lit from above, filled with luxury goods and utopian promise. Piecing together Benjamin's fragments, Margaret Cohen marks a transition from the earlier period of the project, when Benjamin cast the arcades as a kind of féerie or enchanted world of supernatural creatures and magical objects (Cohen 2004: 203). A theatrical genre popular in France, the féerie used special effects and dreamy aesthetics to draw audiences into a mystical world of fantasy creatures and otherworldly events. In the latter years of Benjamin's project, his theatrical cognate for the arcades had become much darker and shifted from the image of the féerie to the phantasmagoria (ibid.: 207). Like the féerie, the phantasmagoria used special effects and the projection of light and shadow to create illusion, but instead of faeries, the phantasmagoria woke the dead, conjuring demons and ghosts. With the use of lanterns, candles, smoke, and mirrors, the phantasmagoria projected frightening images of a shadow world haunted by terrifying specters. For Walter Benjamin, the arcade housed both these cultural expressions of the mystifications of capitalism.

A critical look at religion, consumption, and shopping culture in the USA illustrates the complex interplay of religious symbolism and capitalism of which Benjamin

317

was so keenly aware. The prolific use of religious idiom to talk about things like "shopping" evokes both the féerie and the phantasmagoria of Benjamin's analysis. From the Mall of America to the Apple Store, and from Oprah to child-star "Honey Boo Boo Child," the projections of both the féerie and the dark phantasmagoria are alive and well, together producing dreamlike cultural expressions of hope and horror. To explore these, Benjamin's arcade itself provides an ideal structure. In the sections below, think if you will of moving through a series of compartmentalized and yet connected retail spaces, punctuated by mirrors, enclosed by glass, and linked by walkways. Each one is filled with tempting offerings and expertly framed by "authentic" faux foliage illuminated by carefully staged lighting. What do we ultimately come away with from our sojourn into the arcade?

Temples of consumerism

Are shopping malls sacred spaces? Is shopping a religion? Whatever the answer may be to each of these questions, the fact that so many commentators on culture (both academic and non-academic) speak of consumption and shopping in terms of religious language should make us sit up and take notice. What does it mean to call arcades or, in this case, contemporary shopping malls "temples"? How things get categorized and classified matters. That religious idiom is repeatedly used to express the nature of institutions, environments, and experiences related to shopping signals that these things are being given a certain weight or seriousness. It communicates a degree of intensity or commitment to shopping, a heightened degree of what Ann Taves would term as "specialness" to shopping, a degree of ritual import to shopping, and it even connotes a supernatural aspect to shopping (Chidester 2005: vii) which contests its otherwise commonplace secular categorization.

In the 1980s, Ira Zepp, Jr. produced the first phenomological religious studies analysis of enclosed shopping malls in the USA. In *The New Religious Image of Urban America: The Shopping Mall as Ceremonial Center* (1997), Zepp looked at shopping mall architecture and floor plans much in the way that Mircea Eliade had analyzed sacred cities of the world in his books on comparative religion (Zepp 1997: 51–53). Zepp theorized that planners filled the central mall atrium with beautiful displays of water and idyllic vegetation to recreate an Edenic world of perfect blissful reflection. The mall center, comments Zepp in Eliadean fashion, "with all the paths leading to the middle, is a replication of the primordial world in all its harmony and pristine order" (ibid.: 51). Frequently, points out Zepp, this "miniature world" features some sort of world tree or world center. A more recent example of such a feature, since the publication of Zepp's book, would be the two-story-high oak tree at the center of Northbrook Court Mall in Northbrook, Illinois. When the deteriorating mall was remodeled in the 1990s to "revitalize" it, a gigantic tree was added in the atrium, complete with a tree house for children to climb into. Although the Northbrook mall features installations of idyllic gardens and fountains, the colossal faux "world tree" provides the distinct center of mall community and activity. Eliade termed this kind of symbolic sacred center an "ompholos" or "world navel" and associated it with the presence of an "axis mundi" or "world axis," which he theorized provided a point of sacred connection between the human world and the world of the gods

(Eliade 1987: 36–47). Whether strategically and centrally placing Edenic fountains, cosmic mountains, or world trees, Zepp argues that mall designers "do as the gods did in the beginning," engaged in an *imitatio Dei* by crafting an idyllic environment designed to elicit feelings of sacredness and perfection (Zepp 1997: 33–35). Malls had become the new "temples of worship." What's more, for Zepp, they possess a distinct advantage over more traditional religious spaces: "The shopping mall, open almost every day from 10 A.M. to 9 P.M. ... is a more inclusive and egalitarian center [than] most churches" (ibid.: 80).

Looking at descriptions and photographic images of turn-of-the-century department stores in the USA, religious historian Leigh Schmidt analyzes very explicit church features and aesthetics found in grand department stores, such as Philadelphia's famous Wanamaker's (Schmidt 1995: 159). Using historical examples of popular material culture, Schmidt shows how, during the holiday season especially, these stores became magical wonderlands, "enchantments of consumer culture" and "Christmas cathedrals" that fostered the convergence of shopping with Protestant church aesthetics. The 1911 installation of an ornate organ in the splendid marble-trimmed atrium of Wanamaker's completed the picture of a store that was a church and its customers the faithful. Wanamaker's was eventually subsumed under other department store names, and the latter part of the twentieth century marked the decline of stand-alone department stores, but stores such as Macy's and Bloomingdale's took on new roles as "anchor" stores on either side of large-scale enclosed malls. Inside these climate-controlled retail terraria, anchor department stores (for a period of time) regained some of their mystical aura.

In *Enchanting a Disenchanted World: Continuity and Change in the Cathedrals of Consumption* (2010), sociologist George Ritzer points to the mechanisms by which shopping malls serve to "re-enchant" a "disenchanted" world:

> Shopping malls have been described as places where people go to practice their "consumer religion." It has been contended that shopping malls are more than commercial and financial enterprises; they have much in common with the religious center of traditional civilizations. Like such religious centers, malls are seen as fulfilling people's need to connect with each other and with nature (trees, plants, flowers), as well as their need to participate in festivals. Malls provide the kind of centeredness traditionally provided by religious temples, and they are constructed to have similar balance, symmetry, and order. The atriums usually offer connection to nature through water and vegetation. People gain a sense of community as well as more specific community services. Play is almost universally part of religious practice, and malls provide a place (the food court) for people to frolic. Similarly, malls offer a setting in which people can partake in ceremonial meals. Malls clearly qualify for the label of cathedrals of consumption.
>
> (Ritzer 2010: 10)

As a scholar of design, Lisa Scharoun, much like Benjamin, looks at the construction of malls as "dream spaces"—as mirrors of utopian longings rife with salvific imagery and supernatural intimations. Unlike Zepp, who sees malls as largely supplanting in function more traditional religious spaces, Scharoun points to more of a convergence.

In *America at the Mall: The Cultural Role of a Retail Utopia* (2012), she draws less distinction than do other analysts between malls as enchanted secular spaces and more traditional religious spaces, chronicling a variety of religious communities that have now infiltrated mall space (52). Zepp had featured the Mall Area Religious Council (MARC), a conglomeration of 25 religious groups in the area of the Mall of America that works to create connections between religious groups and mall spaces, and Scharoun further points to the blurring of these boundaries. With the growing popularity of religious storefronts in malls, rather than competing against malls as "cathedrals of consumption" that siphon off the faithful, savvy religious groups have instead integrated their storefronts and chapels into these spaces, occupying retail space where they, like their retail neighbors, capitalize on "foot traffic" and "window shopping." To use R. Laurence Moore's (1994) phrase, when "selling God," as with any other retail enterprise, the three most important things are: "location, location, and location."

All that glitters is not gold for Lutheran theologian Jon Pahl, whose *Shopping Malls and Other Sacred Places* (2009) sees more sinister ghosts than magical faeries lurking in the mall. Both Ritzer and Scharoun point to malls, despite their dreamy aesthetics, as providing real and important community functions. In contrast, Pahl contends that shopping malls such as the Mall of America, in all their fantastic attributes, simulate the Kingdom of God, infusing the mall with a palpable feeling of grace that is powerful yet ultimately *false*. The mall promises its pilgrims pure happiness and fulfillment through consumption—shopping as a path to salvation—intoxicating the consumer with the euphoric prospect of a better life free of pain and discomfort. Yet, at some point, Pahl claims, these promises do not deliver and leave consumers feeling depressed and haunted by their own empty hearts. Highly critical of the mall's glittering artifice that promises salvation but delivers none, Pahl anxiously urges a reorientation instead toward "real" spaces in nature that offer authentic and sustainable spiritual nourishment.

Pahl's mistrust of the mall's apparent enchantments echoes the earlier pop-culture critique made by independent filmmaker George Romero, who intertwines the sublime and the horrific in his apocalyptic cult classic, *Dawn of the Dead* (1978). The film's protagonists seek refuge from a zombie outbreak in the local shopping mall, which subsequently becomes both sanctuary and prison as the zombies relentlessly try to fight their way in. Matthew Walker examines Romero's depiction of zombies as the ultimate consumers, and observes how zombies are indeed all around us, and the specter of a "zombie outbreak" hardly fictional: "Doubt it? Go and you'll see them shuffling down the aisles, staring vacantly into space, consuming without end. At Christmastime, you'll find them pressed against store windows, hell-bent on hot bargains" (2010: 81). Julie Corman's science fiction horror film, *Chopping Mall* (1986), drives home similar themes, casting shopping malls as places of cleverly masked horror and unseen violence. In the opening sequence, Corman's mall initially appears as a kind of idyllic 1980s American sanctuary, complete with modern glass ceilings, pristine potted trees and plants, beauty queens, and even the most technologically advanced "security mall robots." When the robots go out of control and become "killbots," the veneer of "security" peels away, revealing the real horrors and carnage of consumption, both of which are predicted in the film's bloody tagline: "Where Shopping Costs You an Arm and a Leg."

Malls littered with butchered corpses, as in Corman's film, or infested with the "Undead," as in Romero's, presage the current fascination with the study of so-called "dead malls." A subject of fascination for retail historians, artists, videographers, and even ghost hunters, "dead malls" are eerie ghost towns of abandoned retail space. Trespassing "explorers" with cameras who wish to investigate the mall's dark and empty corners, collecting data to document its history and death, have become numerous enough to pose a significant security problem at "dead and dying malls" around the country. Investigators can log their data-collecting experiences and videos at Deadmalls.com, a virtual phantasmagoria of ghosts and shadows. In a somewhat ironic twist to cultural commentators who have fretted about the seductive enchantments of the mall supplanting American churches, as it turns out, a number of these "dead malls" are being purchased and assimilated by religious organizations. After the Forest Park Mall in Illinois "died" in the 1990s, Living Word Christian Ministries bought and took over the 33-acre mall in 1998 (Working 2007). The defunct Forest Park Mall has since been resurrected as Forest Park Plaza and houses the Living Word Worship Center, the Living Word Bible Training Center, and the Living Word Mission Center, among Christian retail shops, a Christian bookstore, and a Christian café. The once-deserted auditorium is now filled with high-definition Jumbotrons for worship services, and the once-still corridors now boom with the sounds of Christian rock bands performing live at the mall's center. Forest Park Plaza's updated slogan reads: "A place where the integrity of God creates a lasting foundation for success and changes the economic destiny of the people." Here, once again, we see promises of salvation and altered destinies—visions of economically successful futures and transformed lives made possible by a worship and practice in which God has taken over the mall, and presumably has been a better business marketer and manager than the previous owner. Instead of analyzing malls as "temples" or "cathedrals of consumption" that threaten to displace traditional religious institutions, a new wave of scholarship might instead examine malls themselves as "consumed" spaces, devoured and assimilated by religious institutions.

MRIs and Black Fridays

Beyond the discourse on shopping malls as the new "temples" or "cathedrals," religious idiom also pervades critiques of shopping fervor. A series of shopping-crush deaths in 2005 prompted business writer Julian Baggini of the *Guardian* to publish a widely circulated article asking whether shopping might not be "the new religion and Mammon our new God" (Baggini 2005). Baggini asserted, "The kind of 'must have' mania that infects some shoppers as they close in on a good deal is more akin to the imperatives of religious devotion than those of personal finance." For Baggini, this kind of shopping hysteria is a disease that "infects" shoppers, presumably much like the transmission mechanism for religious fanaticism. Crazed shopping is thus cast as both new "religion" and a dangerous pathogen. Baggini is certainly not the first to equate religion with "disease." In the sixth century Heraclitis of Ephesus, according to a number of sources, is supposed to have called religion "a disease," albeit a noble one.[1] Sigmund Freud, most notably in *The Future of an Illusion* (1989: 54–56), pathologized religion in light of psychoanalytic theory and the notion of neurosis. More recently, Darrel Ray (2009) has written about "the God virus" and the ways in which "religion infects our lives and culture." So, in Baggini's commentary, religious devotion makes a good analogy for shopping "mania" because it, like infectious disease, is communicable, invades its host, causes nasty systemic problems or disorders, and can be "tough to get rid of."

In the 2011 documentary *Secrets of the Superbrands*, BBC filmmakers Adam Boome and Alex Riley made the link between the disease of religion and the disease of shopping even more explicit by subjecting both "maladies" to high-tech medical diagnostic testing. Riley keenly observed an example of shopping "mania" when filming the opening of a new Apple store in London's Covent Garden. Riley writes, "The scenes I witnessed at the opening of the new Apple store in London's Covent Garden were more like an evangelical prayer meeting than a chance to buy a phone or a laptop." Riley and his producers followed up their filming by asking one ecstatic Apple devotee, who had made pilgrimage to 30 different Apple store openings around the world, to submit to an MRI diagnostic brain scan. In the film, a team of neuroscientists places the Apple fan inside the MRI scanner and shows him images of Apple's logo and products. They then record his physiological responses and report that "the results [suggest] Apple was actually stimulating the same parts of the brain as religious imagery does in people of faith" (Riley and Boome 2011). This is an "ah-hah" or "gotcha" moment in the film, the link being scientifically drawn using medical equipment designed specifically to diagnose *disease*.

In an article titled "America's real religion: shopping," history professor Lawrence Wittner echoes these asserted links between religious devotion and shopping fanaticism (Wittner 2012). Commenting on the mob violence associated with "Black Friday" (the day-after-Thanksgiving's official start of the Christmas shopping season), Wittner observed: "The frenzied participants were not starving, impoverished peasants or product-deprived refugees from Communist nations but reasonably comfortable, middle-class Americans. Their desperation was not driven by hunger. They simply wanted … more!" Wittner blames churches for "not opposing the corporate cultivation of untrammeled greed among Americans." In so doing, he argues that "churches have left the door open to the triumph of America's new religion—not liberal secularism, but shopping" (ibid.).

Across a variety of platforms, expressions of popular culture diagnose shopping "mania" as the equivalent of religious fanaticism. What does this tell us? Is this a way to communicate irrationality, intense emotion, unhealthy obsession, extremism, and ultimately something dangerous and out of control? What's more, cultural observers evoke the specter of "real" or "authentic" religion being subsumed or taken over by a virulent consumerism run amok. Even Sharon Zurkin (2005), in her sociological history of how shopping has changed American culture, sounds the death knell for religion: "We shop because we long for value—for a virtuous ideal of value that we no longer get from religion, work, or politics" (8). No longer relevant, religion is replaced by shopping, the "new religion," as Wittner calls it. Russell McCutcheon points out that "'religion' is a wonderfully useful rhetorical tool that packs a significant rhetorical punch" (McCutcheon 2004: 179). Classification matters.

The fact that shopping is classified by a variety of public cultural commentators in a variety of media contexts as being "a religion" signals something very important about perceptions of shopping, the societal role it plays, anxieties about the place of religion and its power in society, as well as fears about religion's potential demise.

Shopalujah!

Two weeks after the horrific events of September 11, 2001, as the USA headed into war, then-President George W. Bush urged families to head on "down to Disney World" and to keep spending money. In a later speech, Bush lamented that some Americans "don't want to go shopping for their families" and feel intimidated to do so. A number of political pundits interpreted the administration's message as one that promised America salvation through consumption. If Americans stopped shopping, then the terrorists had "won." Sociologist Andrew Weigert has written about this kind of mentality as the American "ethic of consumption" that expresses itself best through Evangelical popular culture. Ironically, says Weigert, it is not "this-worldly asceticism … but this-worldy consumerism" that is a sign of salvation. It is the American Protestant televangelist who most skillfully hammers home this message: "consuming, or helping their televangelist to consume, signals salvation, and thus provides that supreme motive that all believers seek" (Weigert 1991: 111). This "most American of messages, salvation through consumption," says Weigert, goes beyond the televangelist and audience and permeates American culture. In so doing, it effectively "takes [sociologist Max] Weber's thesis and stands it on its head" (ibid.). Although President Bush did not use the exact words, as some have claimed, "Go out and shop!", his phrasing at a time of extreme crisis about a way to salvation through Disney vacations and family shopping trips evoked, especially for those who share Bush's Evangelical faith, a resonant call to this "ethic of consumerism." The most powerful and efficient route to vanquishing the dark ghosts lingering amid the mangled iron and shattered glass of the World Trade Center would be a trip to the féerie and utopian enchantments of Disney World, "the happiest place on earth."

If anyone "gets" the tensions between the ethereal aura of corporate retail "dream worlds" and their darker masked specters, it is New York performance artist and street theater activist Bill Tallen. Taking on the messianic street-corner evangelist personality of "Reverend Billy," he inserts himself into the smoke and mirrors that veil the layers between the féerie and the phantasmagoria. In Reverend Billy, there is much of what David Chidester (and Lowenthal 1992, Trilling 1972, and Baudrillard 1983 before him) analyzes as "authentic fakes," the play and improvisation of religious forms in popular culture that nonetheless do "real religious work" (Chidester 2005: 2–3). Reverend Billy and his "Church of Life After Shopping" (formerly the "Church of Stop Shopping") stage public shopping "interventions" at corporate retailers like the Disney Store, Starbucks, and Wal-Mart (Lane 2002: 70). In these acts of what his group calls "ritual resistance," they exorcise cash registers, illuminate the environmental impact and labor practices used in manufacturing various products, and "snap people out of the hypnosis" or the magical enchantment they feel while shopping (Reverend Billy: The Church of Stop Shopping n.d.). Although they identify themselves as a "post religious church," Reverend Billy and his "Earthalujah Choir" persistently pose the moral question to consumers, "What would Jesus buy?" In the 2007 documentary film of the same name, produced by Morgan Spurlock, Reverend Billy prophesies the "shopocalypse," a prophecy that the Reverend says has now come to fruition. That is, we are literally "shopping ourselves to death," as rampant capitalism and obsessive consumerism have intensified climate-change-related natural disasters such as the 2012 hurricane "Sandy." Marking the Mayan calendar doomsday, Reverend Billy and the Life After Shopping Church held an "End of the World" ritual in Times Square, seeking to "turn back the devils of debt and destruction, rallying those of radical faith to save themselves and save us all." Reverend Billy also offers exorcism services to cast the shopping demons out of "shopaholics," who like many Americans "walk in the valley of the shadow of debt." He has also performed exorcisms directly on credit cards and investment bankers and has attempted to cast the "evil spirits" and "dark soul" out of British Petroleum following the oil disaster caused by its leaking oil well in the Gulf of Mexico. In 2008, Billy's church held a candlelit prayer vigil in the parking lot of the Long Island Wal-Mart, where employee Jdimytai Damour was trampled to death on Black Friday by "out-of-control" shoppers who broke down the store doors at five in the morning and stepped over Damour's dead body in order to make their way to discounted plasma television sets. As Wal-Mart employees informed shoppers over the PA system that an employee had been killed and they would have to leave, shoppers yelled back that they had been in line since Friday morning, they would not leave, and they kept on shopping (Mallia and Chayes 2008). The death of Damour by shopper stampede came just two months after one of the worst death tolls ever recorded from religious stampede, as 224 pilgrims were trampled to death when 25,000 worshipers rushed the doors of the Chamunda Devi Temple in northern India during the 2008 Kumbh Mela festival (*Hindustan Times* 2013).

Bethany Moreton, author of *To Serve God and Wal-Mart: The Making of Christian Free Enterprise* (2009), may not be surprised by the juxtaposition of these two stampedes and the comparison between "religious temples" and "retail temples." In her history of Wal-Mart, Moreton tells the story of how Evangelical values and frameworks came to be embedded in Wal-Mart's corporate structure and management strategies. Notions of "Christian service" and male-led family "headship," concepts that employees practice in their own homes and churches, came to define Wal-Mart's workforce. Moreton observes: "Drawing on the new relationships among managers, employees, and customers in its stores and on the regional evangelical revival, the company's emerging service ethos honored [employees] as Christian servants" (Moreton 2009: 89). Wal-Mart stores became inscribed or encoded with a language, imagery, and personnel dynamic that "read" like both "Christian home" and "church" to its Evangelical patrons. Unlike the luxurious ornamentation of Philadelphia department stores, such as Wanamaker's, that simulated the aesthetics of elite Protestant churches, Wal-Mart's stripped-down frugal "warehouse" aesthetic felt more like the modest contemporary rural and/or storefront churches its Evangelical customers associated with worship. Operation Rescue founder and Christian

Coalition director Ralph Reed once famously advised political strategists: "If you want to reach the Christian population on Sunday, you do it from the church pulpit. If you want to reach them on Saturday, you do it in Wal-Mart" (ibid.: 90). In this way, says Moreton, Wal-Mart came to sanctify "Christian free enterprise," "servant leadership," folksy frugality, while (in a twist on Adam Smith) exalting the gospel of God's invisible hand in the sanctity of neoliberal globalization.

As with "dead" malls, however, Wal-Marts that have expanded too quickly, in a shrinking economy, themselves are becoming consumed and transformed into sites of conversion. In 2012, the Cornerstone Church took over the Wal-Mart in Marion, IL, and turned it into an unconventional 120,000 square-foot worship space (Fox News.com 2012). In the same year, Evangelical megachurch purchases of Wal-Mart retail stores for conversion into worship space ranged from Wisconsin, Indiana, Illinois, and Nebraska to Florida and Louisiana (see Ford-Stewart 2013; Lostroh 2012; OnlineAthens 2011; Hovey 2011; Moore 2011). When giving a media tour of Church of Eleven22's newly converted Wal-Mart home in Jacksonville, Florida, Senior Pastor Joby Martin pointed out to camera crews that the congregation's new children's safari-themed "worship center" sits right on the spot where he used to purchase his shotgun shells at Wal-Mart. "Little did Sam Walton know that when he was putting a Wal-Mart here, he was actually part of building the Kingdom of God," expounded the pastor (see FirstCoastNews.com n.d.). Bethany Moreton's research for her book on Wal-Mart and the Walton family suggests otherwise—that Sam Walton might be anything but surprised by connections between his commercial endeavors and efforts to hasten the Kingdom of God's arrival.

In the Church of Life After Shopping's tours across America's heartland, Reverend Billy has performed numerous "exorcisms" in Wal-Mart parking lots as well as inside the retail space, charismatically casting demons out of the register with his most exuberant preacherly flair. Reverend Billy is not the only one, however, doing battle with the "demons of shopping." Estimates of Americans with diagnosed "compulsive buying disorder" cite around 18 million afflicted (Workman and Paper 2010: 89). Founded in 1968, Debtors Anonymous (DA) holds more than 500 weekly meetings in 15 countries and identifies itself as a "fellowship" for compulsive spenders (DebtorsAnonymous.org 2011). Following the structure and process of 12-Step programs and modeled with some modification on Alcoholics Anonymous, DA testimonials frequently recount how fellowship members came to terms with their "disease." One anonymous member recalls: "I gradually came to realize my debting disease manifests every time I assume that I am so special I can have whatever I want, whenever I want it, without having to earn it or pay for it" (Anonymous n.d.). Although DA is not a religious organization per se, as with AA, belief in a "higher power" is key, and those in recovery frequently characterize their struggle to deal with their disease in spiritual terms. In Debtors Anonymous, the strands of disease, shopping, and religion once more intertwine, an entanglement that has been reinforced through recent popular cultural expressions. Sophie Kinsella's bestselling "Shopaholic" novel series—made into the 2009 film Confessions of a Shopaholic— brought the "disease" of compulsive spending and debting into more widespread popular consciousness, employing both comedic and serious portrayals of real addiction. Shopaholic "Rebecca's" retail conquests are ecstatic experiences that she has longed for since childhood, when she would gaze into the "dreamy world of perfect things" inside shop windows. There, we are told, she would see "grown-up girls, like faeries or princesses, getting anything they wanted" because they had "magic cards" (Hogan 2009). Rebecca's entrancement with the retail "faery world" is finally broken by the stark consequences of credit card debt and the prospect of homelessness in New York City. Like the 12-steppers in DA, Rebecca goes on a "spiritual journey" where she must confront the demons that lurk underneath pretty silk scarves and sparkling Jimmy Choo shoes. Rebecca does not quite exclaim "Revolujah!" in Reverend Billy fashion, but she does see the error of her ways and struggles to vanquish her "shopping demons."

Rebecca's road to recovery from "shopaholism" and academic analyses of shopping malls, like the Apple Store fanatic MRI, Reverend Billy's street theater activism and, of course, Benjamin's reading of the Parisian arcades all still focus on "brick and mortar" retail spaces. How fascinated Benjamin might have been by today's virtual arcades on eBay, Amazon.com, or Zappos.com. What might he have made of "Cyber Monday," the "point and click" shopping component to the ceremonial holiday retail triptych: Black Friday, "Shop Local Saturday," and now, "Cyber Monday"? And what of the new ritualistic culture of online shopping and "shop and tell" social media, in which the posting of so-called "haul videos" post-consumption has become a form of evangelizing or witnessing to other potential shoppers? As of 2012, YouTube hosted more than a quarter of a million "haul videos," in which shoppers display their shopping hauls, including product details and prices. The videos receive tens of millions of hits and create their own "haul" celebrities with their own passionate "vlogger" (video blogger) followings.

HBO's drama series *Big Love* (2006–11) offers audiences a reading of contemporary online and cable shopping "addiction" that specifically draws parallels between religious "fanaticism" and fanatical consumption. The story of *Big Love* centers on a family of independent fundamentalist polygamous Mormons. The family's patriarch, "Bill Henrickson," had once lived as a young boy on a fictitious polygamous compound ("Juniper Creek") similar to those associated with the real-life Fundamentalist Church of Latter-day Saints (FLDS). Bill's second wife, "Nicki," who has lived most of her life on the compound with few modern conveniences and in a milieu of relative material deprivation, is the daughter of the religion's central prophet. In Season One of the series, Nicki develops a serious online and cable "home shopping addiction." The narrative portrayal of Nicki's addiction juxtaposes her indoctrination as a child into extreme religious practice and her now-adult compulsive shopping behavior. As Nicki's new marital situation transports her off the fundamentalist compound and into "mainstream" suburban life, the narrative suggests that one form of religious fervor replaces another, exchanging or transferring "addictions." When Nicki's sister wives discover that she has incurred over $60,000 of credit card debt, thus compromising the financial security of the entire family, they realize she is "unwell," much in the way outsiders cast the "cult-like" activity on the fundamentalist compound as a "disease."

First sister wife "Barb's" own mother and sister, who are members of the more mainstream Church of Jesus Christ of Latter-day Saints (LDS), treat her as though she has fallen under an evil spell or has been brainwashed to maintain her continued loyalty to Bill and their polygamous life. Like Nicki and her shopping addiction, Barb is "unwell." Later in the series, Bill's third wife, "Margene," develops a devoted following as a popular home shopping network retail personality, and then finds herself sucked into a retail pyramid marketing scheme, having fallen under the spell of a charismatic guru-like leader who hawks energy drinks. At various points in the series, the writers prompt the viewing audience to question what gets "read" or classified as "addiction," "illness," "religion" and/or "cult" and why. The sister wives are not the only ones who struggle with compulsive behavior. Bill himself is simultaneously consumed by the capitalist drive to build his financial empire at all costs, while obsessed with consolidating his authority as a religious entrepreneur and new church founder. As Bill deals with the moral dilemmas and questions raised in both of these realms, he is increasingly haunted by visions of Joseph Smith's ghost and that of his wife, Emma. In the end, it is Bill who becomes a ghost as he occupies his old chair at the family table and watches as his wives take up and run both the family's financial and now religious empire.

Retail gods

In *Gods Behaving Badly: Media, Religion, and Celebrity Culture* (2011), Peter Ward observes that at its root, popular culture "draw[s] us into a conversation about what we do and do not value" (2). Analyzing the phenomenon of "celebrity worship," Ward contends that religious analogy is the closest one can come to adequately characterizing the kind of relationship fans have toward celebrities. He writes,

> Celebrities are routinely called idols, or icons, and from time to time they are called "divine" or even referred to as "gods." Fans are said to be devoted to celebrities, to adore them, and in many cases the behavior of fans is likened to "worship."
>
> (Ward 2011: 3)

For fans, many celebrities take on supernatural qualities and, as Gary Laderman says, "arouse the religious passions of followers in modern society who find spiritual meaning, personal fulfillment, and awe-inspiring motivation in the presence of these idols" (Laderman 2009: 64). In the tradition of *imitatio Dei*, fans do as the gods do, especially in the realm of retail. Because most fans cannot spend $3,000 to $5,000 on handbags or afford $900 Manolo Blahnik shoes, fan magazines like *Us Weekly* and *In Touch* regularly run "Get That Look!" features, in which the magazine suggests more financially modest "knock offs" for fans to dress like the gods and thus capture some of their supernatural resplendence. Not just clothing accessories, but pricey bodily modifications become highly organized ritual attempts at celebrity imitation. For devotees who cannot afford the high cost of a plastic surgeon, cheaper alternatives become a path to "get that look." In imitation of reality TV-star Kim Kardashian's famous posterior silicone injections, "pumping parties" (wherein unlicensed "Madames" inject partygoers' backsides with cheap industrial silicone, Super Glue, and Fix-A-Flat tire sealant) became all the rage among Hollywood wannabes until partygoers began bringing home sepsis, fatal allergic reactions, and multi-organ and lung failure as "party favors" (Broach 2013; Nelson 2012).

Still, the pull to imitate the idol or "celebrity god" through imitative consumption is a powerful devotional call. In her chapter on "Practicing purchase" in *Oprah: The Gospel of an Icon*, Kathryn Lofton illuminates the "spiritual capitalism" of Oprah Winfrey and her peddling of a "good news materialism" through purchasing recommendations and directives issued to what Lofton calls her "congregants" (Lofton 2011a: 22). For Lofton, Oprah's approach to her television audience, magazine readership, and online community is catechistic. Consuming the "right goods" becomes a pathway to personal growth, spiritual improvement, and a meaningful, purposeful life. Lofton explains that, "In Winfrey's capitalist modernity, this materiality is *spiritual* practice" (ibid., emphasis in original), and what "separates Winfrey's work is the soul-saving signification attached to her recommendations" (ibid.: 23). Oprah's congregants

> are told that their purchasing power is correlated to their moral merit. Individual shopping choices offer moments of possible piety: "Our simplest shopping decisions can protect the environment, save family farmers, lift villages from destitution, and restore dignity to war-torn communities."
>
> (ibid.: 35)

If Oprah's mantra is "Behave your way to success" (ibid.: 24), "reality" TV's sassy Honey Boo Boo's mantra is "Misbehave your way to success." One might reasonably assume that successful business woman and media empire mogul Oprah Winfrey and small-town pageant princess Honey Boo Boo would have little in common. And yet, Honey Boo Boo's fans, like Oprah's congregants, also demonstrate a devoted practice of purchase. Dubbed alternately the "Redneck Messiah" and the "White Trash Messiah," Honey Boo Boo (whose real name is Alana Thompson) first rose to fame on The Learning Channel's (TLC) controversial series *Toddlers and Tiaras* (2009–11). The program showcased little girls whose mothers go to extreme measures to transform their daughters into heavily made-up adult-looking contestants. The average cost to families for each pageant, including dresses, travel costs, hair, makeup, spray tans, padded bras, jewelry, coaches, and false teeth, is between $3,000 and $5,000. The program tallies this competitive consumption, often undertaken by contestant families of meager financial means, as it documents the ritual of pageant preparation and performance (Blue 2012).

Honey Boo Boo both charmed and captivated audiences (in a train wreck way) not only with her transmogrification from a wisecracking scruffy "redneck kid" to a painted child-woman princess, but also with her startling performance of stereotypical "strong Black woman" vernacular and gesture. Part Lolita, part Martin Lawrence in drag, Honey Boo Boo's minstrel-esque monologues are a surrealistic study in "redneck Ebonics," as she wags her finger at the camera with a scowl, bobs her head of blonde curls from side to side, and proclaims "no she di'n't" (see Andrews 2012). So captivated were audiences that in 2012, TLC contracted with her and her family to do their own spin-off program called *Here Comes Honey Boo Boo*. In Season One of the new show, viewers watched seven-year-old Honey Boo Boo drink pageant "Go Go Juice" (a potent cocktail of Mountain Dew and Red Bull), down 15 bags of "pageant crack" (pixy sticks of sugar), and eat road kill served to her by "Mama June," her overbearing pageant mother. Critics howled, raised questions of child abuse, and chastised TLC for exploiting Honey Boo Boo for financial gain. However, the online "Hillbilly Gossip" site, the *Hillbilly Times*, and many other media outlets, including the *Washington Post*, sang Honey Boo Boo's praises for ministering to our times, "a Shirley Temple for this ceaseless Great Recession" (Oldenburg 2012).

What does it mean to call Honey Boo Boo the "Redneck Messiah," and what sort of *salvation* is being offered? In her home state of Georgia, Honey Boo Boo began to be regarded as an economic savior of sorts, single-handedly boosting the fortunes of beleaguered small rural businesses as fans flocked to anywhere that Honey Boo Boo had shopped. As with Oprah, an endorsement from Honey Boo Boo became the Midas touch. After one episode aired that showed Honey Boo Boo shopping at a local boutique, Lucy Lu's in Douglas, Georgia, the store was mobbed with local viewers. A tiny business struggling to keep afloat, Lucy Lu's sold out its stock and moved more than three hundred Honey Boo Boo T-shirts in just a week (Proud 2012). Each time Honey Boo Boo was scheduled for a local publicity event, fans would travel hundreds of miles to make what press called "sacred pilgrimage," thus boosting local economies in small depressed Georgia towns. "As far as we know," reported one pundit, "Honey Boo Boo did *not* multiply the loaves of bread—but we're guessing that local Wal-Marts reported record low numbers that day" (The Daily Scandal n.d.; emphasis in the original).

Like Oprah, Honey Boo Boo's "favorite things" provide her fans with a way to practice their devotion to her through consumption. What's more, the influence of both Oprah and Honey Boo Boo extends beyond the realm of entertainment and shopping to serving as a source of political authority. Indeed, in 2012, when Honey Boo Boo Child publicly endorsed Barack Obama on *Jimmy Kimmel Live* (ABC, aired 15 October 2012), her endorsement received far more press coverage than did Oprah's endorsement. Winfrey, who grew up a poor bare-foot girl on a "red dirt road in Mississippi" (Lofton 2011a: 24) struggled up and out of the poverty, racism, and sexual abuse of her childhood to become a self-made billionaire, a virtual Cinderella story of self-improvement, right thinking, hard work, and the powers of purchase. Roadkill-eating Honey Boo Boo, hailing from a poor, white, uneducated family in rural Georgia has also "made good." Mama June gambled that grueling pageants, necessitating thousands of dollars in costumes and "Go Go Juice" for stamina, and the rebranding of daughter Alana into the commodity that has become "Honey Boo Boo," would all pay off, magically turning her daughter (financially at least) into the enchanted princess she performs as for the pageant judges. Whether messiah or fairy princess, Honey Boo Boo's episodes of prancing about in grown-up makeup and sexy outfits also conjured the dark specter of six-year-old beauty pageant queen JonBenèt Ramsey, who was strangled to death in 1996. Honey Boo Boo had become the newest model for the kind of child sexploitation blamed for JonBenèt's widely publicized murder. Since her death, JonBenèt, on a much smaller scale than Honey Boo Boo, has also been a "reality" TV money-maker, as shows like TruTV's *Haunting Evidence* (2005–8) sent paranormal investigators and a medium to the Ramsey home to connect with JonBenèt's ghost ("Inside the Ramsey House" 2008), while more recently various "ghost-hunting" cable programs have tried to make contact with her petite poltergeist.

For all of Honey Boo Boo's moxie, unlike Oprah, she is *not* a powerful adult but still a vulnerable child at the mercy of her parents' judgment (or lack thereof). In August 2012, after receiving a video of Honey Boo Boo being paid to "table dance" for frat boys at a college bar, Child Protective Services began to investigate the child star's family. By the fall of 2012, a full-time body-guard had been posted to Honey Boo Boo in response to kidnapping threats and an attempted home invasion by a suspected pedophile. Around the same time, media blogs began to refer to the beauty queen *cum* "Redneck Messiah" as the latest "sacrificial lamb" to greed-driven "reality" TV profits, while the alternative rock band WAN released a concept album called *Honey Boo Boo: Human Sacrifice* (2012).[2] Mandy McMichael, a scholar of religion at Duke University who conducts ethnographic research on beauty pageants in Alabama, says: "When I tell people that I study religion and beauty pageants in America, they usually ask, 'What do beauty pageants have to do with religion?' 'Everything,' I reply" (McMichael 2010).

Conclusions: *consumo ergo sum*

In "Convolute N" of *The Arcades Project*, Walter Benjamin writes:

> Method of this project: literary montage. I needn't *say* anything. Merely show. I shall purloin no valuables, appropriate no ingenious formulations. But the rags, the refuse—these I will not inventory but allow, in the only way possible, to come into their own: by making use of them.
>
> (Benjamin 1999: 460)

Benjamin becomes a master at juxtaposing a series of dialectical images and quotations, assembling "large-scale constructions out of the smallest and most precisely cut components" (ibid.: 461). The experience of moving through the arched corridor of the arcade is itself an experience of montage, where shops with fancy ladies' hats appear next to dusty "tabacs," and spools of delicate lace next to racks of glistening knives.

In 2009, the creative agency Digital Kitchen was nominated for an Emmy Award for the powerful title sequence montage they designed for the HBO series *True Blood*, a series that explores the drama that ensues in the small rural Louisiana town of "Bon Temps" when vampires admit publicly that they are "real" and have existed all along among humans. Digital Kitchen's title sequence provides an arc into the world of America's rural South through a montage of complex images that evoke ecstatic religion, sex, violence, addiction, racism, and death: Pentecostal enthusiasm and topless dancing, a preacher healing and a carnivorous Venus fly-trap, a striking snake and a barfly constricting a drunk trucker between her thighs, a woman in black lace panties sinking sensually down onto a bed and two church ladies rocking in devout prayer, strawberry-eating children and children dressed up in KKK robes, a rotting fox and a midnight river baptism.

True Blood producer Alan Ball, who previously won acclaim for his disturbingly beautiful and violent portrayal of American suburban life in the 1999 film *American Beauty*, creates in *True Blood* a phantasmagorical world of supernaturals: vampires, faeries, werewolves, maenads, shape-shifters, Voodoo queens, shamans, and witches. In the world of *True Blood*, vampires have "come out of the coffin" and begun to "mainstream" now that the Japanese have invented a synthetic (albeit untasty) blood substitute called "True Blood" that meets all their nutritional needs. As with the greater availability of foods such as Tofurky and seitan (wheat gluten) that technically satisfy humans' nutritional needs and thus render human consumption of animal protein unnecessary, vampires no longer need to consume humans to survive. More socially conscious "True Blood"-drinking "vegetarian" vampires practice "temperance," pay taxes, and agitate for civil rights to marry whom they please. The source of conflict in much of the first season is between bloodthirsty merciless vamps (who continue to kill and consume humans) and series hero "Vampire Bill," a respectable (khakis-and-button-down-wearing) vampire who cultivates self-restraint as he tries to figure out the ethical limits of desire. Bill struggles to restrict his diet, feeding only (at first) consensually from his girlfriend "Sookie," but even this limited temperance becomes unbearable since it turns out that Sookie is a human/faery hybrid, thus endowing her with irresistible faerie blood—the vampire version of "crack." Human citizens of Bon Temps also struggle with the desire to consume, as they develop intense addictions to vampire blood or "V," a drug that functions like a combination of XTC and Viagra, leaving the user with a voracious appetite for more. Both humans and vampires are consumed with the desire to consume, a not-so-subtle comment on America's own vampire-like consumerist addictions.

In the series, "Russell Edgington," the once vampire "king" of Mississippi, articulates most directly the ways in which humans' inability to temper consumption makes them effectively no different from vampires. Edgington commandeers a television news anchor desk and proclaims on "live" TV to the nation: "We [vampires] are narcissists, we care only about getting what we want no matter what the cost, *just like you*. Global warming, perpetual war, toxic waste, child labor, torture, genocide. That's a small price to pay for your SUVs and your flat screen TVs, your blood diamonds, your designer jeans, your absurd garish McMansions—futile symbols of permanence to quell your quivering, spineless souls" ("Everything is Broken," aired 15 August 2010). Vampire, faery, or human, *True Blood* illuminates the compulsion to consume as powerful, erotic, ecstatic, and deadly. What's more, in the fifth season of *True Blood*, we learn that consumption also constitutes a *religion*. Russell Edgington is part of a larger movement of vampires called the "Sanguinistas," religious fundamentalists who oppose "mainstreaming" into human culture, read the *Vampire Bible* literally, and regard vampires' consumption of human blood as a divinely endowed gift. The *Vampire Bible* states that humans are "no more than food" and that humans were created for the specific purpose of vampire consumption. According to the Sanguinista fundamentalists, vampires thus have divinely granted dominion over humans and can use them as they wish, farming them like veal, if they choose.

Benjamin's dream houses, temples of utopian possibility framed in iron and glass. The World Trade Center's remnants of dark twisted iron and shattered glass. The enchanted Edenic spaces of the American mall, promising kingdoms of bliss and fulfillment. The mildewing abandoned retail cubicles of the defunct mall, enticing to urban archeologists and ghost hunters alike. Reverend Billy's playful "Shopalujah!" street spectacles and Jdimytai Damour's trampled corpse. *Big Love* and Black Friday. Wal-Mart's Christian service altar call and cash-register exorcisms. Kim Kardashian's silicone-pumped backside and Debtors Anonymous. Honey Boo Boo's world of painted fairy princesses and JonBenèt Ramsey's tortured ghost. A peculiar and probing parataxis.

Secrets of the Superbrands film directors Boome and Riley go to great effort to employ the highly advanced diagnostic technology of the MRI to probe the Apple Store fanatic's brain, seeking scientifically, objectively, and anatomically, to "confirm" the active presence of *religion* in his grey matter as he ecstatically views Apple icons and products. But the mystical dimensions of capitalism and the dialectics of the féerie and the phantasmagoria, the "religious" and the "secular," are as close as the "reality" TV show, the YouTube "haul" video, the supermarket celebrity tabloid, the mall down the street, or the veins on our necks.

Notes

1 Betrand Russell attributes this to Heraclitis, as do others. Max Mueller writes that there is no proof Heraclitis ever actually said this, but that it certainly "sounds" a lot like something he would say (see Mulford 1885: 46).
2 In a treatment of similar sacrificial dynamics in the media consumption of child star Britney Spears, Kathryn Lofton (2011b: 351) observes of Spears's myriad dramas played out in the public eye: "The circle of paparazzi creates a fishbowl for viewers and readers to watch the banal, tortuously slow procedure of the kill. It is, then, a religious violence conducted under the guise of media consumption." I am indebted to Lofton for her comments on an earlier draft of this article.

Works cited

Andrews, H. (2012) "Honey Boo Boo? Honey, Please," *The Root* (August 15). Online. Available: www.theroot.com/views/honey-boo-boo-child?page=0,0 (accessed 10 March 2013).

Anonymous (n.d.) "An erstwhile underearner discovers the real meaning of recovery," Debtors Anonymous.org. Online. Available: www.debtorsanonymous.org/Erstwhile.htm (accessed 10 March 2013).

Baggini, J. (2005) "G2: Inside story: assembly required: the astonishing scenes at the opening of a branch of Ikea yesterday were a kind of religious frenzy, says Julian Baggini—but worshipping at the altar of Mammon needn't be all bad," *Guardian* [London] (February 11): Features 4.

Baudrillard, J. (1983) *Simulations*, trans. P. Foss and A. Beil, New York: Semiotext(e).

Benjamin, W. (1999) *The Arcades Project*, trans. H. Eiland and K. McLaughlin, Cambridge, MA: Harvard University Press.

Blue, A. (2012) "Princess by proxy: when child beauty pageants aren't about the kids," *University of Arizona News* (October 26). Online. Available: http://uanews.org/story/tiaras-0 (accessed 10 March 2013).

Broach, J. (2013) "Pumping parties: a dangerous way to get curves," WMCTV.com [Memphis] (February 6). Online. Available: www.wmctv.com/story/20969435/a-look-ahead-pumping-partiesa-disturbing-beauty-trend (accessed 9 March 2013).

Chidester, D. (2005) *Authentic Fakes: Religion and American Popular Culture*, Berkeley, CA: University of California Press.

Cohen, M. (2004) "Benjamin's phantasmagoria: the Arcades Project," in D. Ferris (ed.), *The Cambridge Companion to Walter Benjamin*, New York: Cambridge University Press, 199–220.

The Daily Scandal (n.d.) "Honey Boo Boo, Redneck Messiah." Online. Available: www.daily scandal.net/honey-boo-boo-redneck-messiah (accessed 10 March 2013).

DebtorsAnonymous.org (2011) "About Debtors Anonymous." Online. Available: www.debt orsanonymous.org/about/about.htm (accessed 10 March 2013).

Eliade, M. (1987) *The Sacred and the Profane: The Nature of Religion*, trans. W.R. Trask, New York: Harcourt, Inc.

FirstCoastNews.com (n.d.) "Local Wal-Mart converted into a church." Online. Available: www.firstcoastnews.com/video/1852847623001/51325884001/Local-Wal-Mart-converted-into-a-church (accessed 10 March 2013).

Ford-Stewart, J. (2013) "Old Greenfield Walmart's transformation into church begins," Green fieldNow.com (February 5). Online. Available: www.greenfieldnow.com/news/old-greenfield-walmarts-transformation-into-church-begins-nm8l440–189904121.html (accessed 9 March 2013).

FoxNews.com (2012) "Illinois church finds new home in old Walmart" (August 26). Online. Available: www.foxnews.com/us/2012/08/26/illinois-church-finds-new-home-in-walmart/ (accessed 9 March 2013).

Freud, S. (1989) *The Future of an Illusion*, ed. and trans. J. Strachey, New York: W.W. Norton and Company.

Hindustan Times (2013) "Deadly stampedes at religious events in India since 2008" (February 11). Online. Available: www.hindustantimes.com/India-news/NewDelhi/Deadly-stampedes-at-religious-events-in-India-since-2008/Article1–1010208.aspx (accessed 9 March 2013).

Hogan, P.J. (dir.) (2009) *Confessions of a Shopaholic*. Touchstone Pictures.

Hovey, A. (2011) "Seward church plugging away at Walmart conversion" [Lincoln, Nebraska], JournalStar.com (July 3). Online. Available: http://journalstar.com/news/local/seward-church-plugging-away-at-walmart-conversion/article_8c56cabd-e28e-5675-8243-dd9ba03cd867.html (accessed 9 March 2013).

"Inside the Ramsey House" (2008) *Haunting Evidence* (truTV, aired 4 October). Online. Available: www.trutv.com/shows/haunting_evidence/index.html (accessed 21 June 2013).

Laderman, G. (2009) *Sacred Matters*, New York: The New Press.

Lane, J. (2002) "Reverend Billy: preaching, protest, and postindustrial flanerie," *Drama Review* 46, 1 (Spring): 60–84.

Lofton, K. (2011a) *Oprah: The Gospel of an Icon*, Berkeley, CA: University of California Press.

——(2011b) "Religion and the American Celebrity," *Social Compass* 58: 346–52.

Lostroh, T. (2012) "Church gives new life to Walmart," Omaha.com (March 26). Online. Available: www.omaha.com/article/20120326/NEWS01/703269957 (accessed 9 March 2013).

Lowenthal, D. (1992) "Counterfeit art: authentic fakes?" *International Journal of Cultural Property* 1: 79–103.

McCutcheon, R. (2004) "Religion, ire, and dangerous things," *Journal of the American Academy of Religion* 72, 1 (March): 173–93.

McMichael, M. (2010) "A bikinied Muslim Miss USA," *Christianity Today* (May). Online. Available: www.christianitytoday.com/women/2010/may/bikinied-muslim-miss-usa.html (accessed 10 March 2013).

Mallia, J. and M. Chayes (2008) "Wal-Mart worker dies in Black Friday stampede," *Newsday* (November 28). Online. Available: www.newsday.com/long-island/nassau/wal-mart-worker-dies-in-black-friday-stampede-1.884298 (accessed 9 March 2013).

Moore, M. (2011) "Valley church buys old Walmart for new building," MyWabashValley. com (September 2). Online. Available: http://mywabashvalley.com/fulltext?nxd_id=206417 (accessed 9 March 2013).

Moore, R.L. (1994) *Selling God: American Religion in the Marketplace of Culture*, New York: Oxford University Press.

Moreton, B. (2009) *To Serve God and Wal-Mart: The Making of Christian Free Enterprise*, Cambridge, MA: Harvard University Press.

Mulford, E. (1885) *Republic of God: An Institute of Theology*, New York: Houghton Mifflin.

Nelson, L.J. (2012) "Desperation for beauty turns fatal; a quest for larger hips and buttocks leads to silicone 'pumping parties,' sometimes with tragic results," *Los Angeles Times* (October 9): A6.

Oldenburg, A. (2012) "Honey Boo Boo Child—charming or disturbing?" *USAToday* (August 9). Online. Available: http://content.usatoday.com/communities/entertainment/post/2012/08/ honey-boo-boo-child – charming-or-disturbing/1 (accessed 10 March 2013).

OnlineAthens [Georgia] (2011) "Athens church work begins in old Walmart" (January 23). Online. Available: http://onlineathens.com/stories/012311/bus_774790748.shtml (accessed 9 March 2013).

Pahl, J. (2009) *Shopping Malls and Other Sacred Places: Putting God in Place*, reprint edn, Eugene, OR: Wipf & Stock Publishers.

Proud, A. (2012) "The Honey Boo boom effect: Georgia store enjoys record sales after their tribute T-shirts to the star are features on show," MailOnline (October 14). Online. Available: www.dailymail.co.uk/tvshowbiz/article-2217784/Honey-Boo-Boo-Georgia-store-enjoys-record-sales-tribute-T-shirts-featured-show.html (accessed 10 March 2013).

Ray, D. (2009) *The God Virus: How Religion Infects Our Lives and Culture*, Bonner Springs, KS: IPC Press.

Reverend Billy: The Church of Stop Shopping (n.d.) "About us." Online. Available: www. revbilly.com/about-us (accessed 10 March 2013).

Riley, A. and A. Boome (2011) "Superbrands' success fuelled by sex, religion and gossip," *BBC News Business* (May 16). Online. Available: www.bbc.co.uk/news/business-13416598 (accessed 9 March 2013).

Ritzer, G. (2010) *Enchanting a Disenchanted World: Continuity and Change in Cathedrals of Consumption*, 3rd edn, Los Angeles, CA: SAGE Publications.

Scharoun, L. (2012) *America at the Mall: The Cultural Role of a Retail Utopia*, Jefferson, NC: McFarland and Company.

Schmidt, L. (1995) *Consumer Rites: The Buying and Selling of American Holidays*, Princeton, NJ: Princeton University Press.

Taussig, M. (2006) *Walter Benjamin's Grave*, Chicago, IL: The University of Chicago Press.

Trilling, L. (1972) *Sincerity and Authenticity*, Cambridge, MA: Harvard University Press.

Walker, M. (2010) "When There's No More Room in Hell, the Dead Will Shop the Earth: Romero and Aristotle on Zombies, Happiness, and Consumption," in R. Green and K. Mohammad (eds), *Zombies, Vampires, and Philosophy: New Life for the Undead*, Chicago, IL: Open Court Press, 81–90.

Ward, P. (2011) *Gods Behaving Badly: Media, Religion, and Celebrity Culture*, Waco, TX: Baylor University Press.

Weigert, A. (1991) *Mixed Emotions: Certain Steps Toward Understanding Ambivalence*, Albany, NY: State University of New York Press.

Wittner, L. (2012) "America's real religion: shopping," *Huffington Post* (December 12). Online. Available: www.huffingtonpost.com/lawrence-wittner/americas-real-religion-shopping_b_222 8617.html (accessed 9 March 2013).

Working, R. (2007) "Church ownership is a miracle for mall," *Chicago Tribune* (May 28). Online. Available: http://articles.chicagotribune.com/2007-05-28/news/0705280088_1_shopping-center-church-business-school (accessed 9 March 2013).

Workman, L. and D. Paper (2010) "Compulsive buying: a theoretical framework," *The Journal of Business Inquiry* 9, 1: 89–126.

Zepp, I. (1997) *The New Religious Image of Urban America: The Shopping Mall as Ceremonial Center*, 2nd edn., Niwot, CO: University Press of Colorado.

Zurkin, S. (2005) *Point of Purchase: How Shopping Changed American Culture*, New York: Routledge.

18
ELECTRONIC DANCE MUSIC EVENTS

Graham St John

Introduction: sampling religion

That electronic dance music (EDM) events have been popular contexts for the expression of religious sensibilities worldwide is a circumstance recognized among scholars. The "religious," "spiritual," or "tribal" character of momentous events is asservated across a spectrum of genres, from early disco and house to hip-hop, acid house, techno, hardcore, trance, and dub. The enchantment of raving in dedicated urban clubs or forest hinterlands; the transfiguring impact of ecstatic dancing with strange compatriots and expatriate strangers at times in-between and beyond the law aided by digital, cyber, and chemical technics; the declaration of clubbing and other events as "shamanic," "devotional," "sublime," and otherwise "life changing:" all are commonplace in the reports of those native to global EDM scenes. That these scenes are as much contexts for appropriations of religious symbolism as they are contexts for inspirational experiences, often facilitated by psychoactivating compounds, suggests that this field is cross-cut with religious s[t]imulation—the simulation and/or stimulation of religious sensibilities. That participants "sample" religion speaks to the technologics endogenous to EDM, where sampling technics are deployed to remix existing sounds in dance tracks performed for populations in a multitude of social dance contexts. But sampling does not mean that the outcome is simply a "copy," nor EDM duplicitous, for found sounds are typically adapted to forge novel works performed within unique phenomenal events—dance floors at parties, clubs, and festivals—where individuals interface with the music and one another in contexts where they claim to "feel more alive" than at any other time in their lives. This chapter explores this innovative and interactive experience with attention to what I call "media-shamanism" within psychedelic trance (or psytrance) culture. That is, it investigates how the remix is purposed to liminal design imperatives and thus to an acutely transitional project within an EDM movement. I offer specific attention to processes by which vocal content from film and other popular cultural sources is reconfigured by psytrance DJ/producers within a media ecology that services a liminal atmosphere and potentiates mystical states of consciousness in which gnostic "truths" are revealed.

Demonstrating that this super-liminalization possesses objectives in common with the Human Potential Movement, the chapter contributes to the study of the remix as a core component of spiritual experience among participants in late modern culture.

EDM cultures, religion, and remixticism

Popular music has been recognized as an integral resource and context for religious sensibilities and cultural movements (e.g., Sylvan 2002; Gilmour 2005, 2009; Bossius *et al.* 2011) and the study of EDM cultures offers much to this discussion. The growing interest in the religio-spiritual characteristics of EDM cultures is characterized by a diversity of analysis and debate. That these cultures contextualize collective alterations of consciousness, especially among adolescents, has drawn conflicting responses: from moral panics like that expressed by Christian fundamentalists,[1] the zealous architects of the so called "RAVE Act" (2003) in the United States,[2] or the Zionist reaction to transnationalizing youth culture in Israel (see Meadan 2001), to prophetic statements and declarations of self-awakening (Spurgeon n.d.) produced by raving evangelists (see Fritz 1999). In diverse scholarship researchers identify scenes as contexts enabling an immediate and extraordinary sociality approximating a religious or spiritual experience for its participants (St John 2004a; see also St John 2006). A variety of insights have been forged, for example, about ritual and the sacred (Gauthier 2004; Gerard 2004; Sylvan 2005), New Age and alternative spirituality (Partridge 2006a; D'Andrea 2007), and millenarianism and revitalization (Olaveson 2004; St John 2004b).

A recurrent approach is that which recognizes the use or repurposing of technology for religious or spiritual ends, a practice especially embodied in the DJ. Entries abound on this popular figure as a religious specialist or technoshaman (see Hutson 1999; Takahashi 2005), a master motif played, for instance, in a range of feature films and scene documentaries such as *Groove* (Harrison 2000), *Liquid Crystal Vision* (Rood and Klimmer 2002), *Welcome to Wonderland* (Short 2006), and *God Is My DJ* (Goeijers 2006). The West Coast New Edge rave scene has recently been explored as a vehicle for "gnostic clarity" via two interrelated paths. That is, an assemblage of computers and psychedelics are found to enable *disassociation* or deconditioning processes revealing the "chaos" beneath routine lies and deception, and facilitate *augmentation* techniques enabling "order" and wholeness amid the anxieties of modern life (Zandbergen 2011). Otherwise, while the spiritual function of a host of technics has been taken up by various authors (see Young 2002), and the important re/uses of technics by Afro-diasporic populations has been addressed (see van Veen 2013), the field remains under-analyzed. Take, for instance, headphones, devices that are, as Nye (2011) points out, repurposed in EDM from their function as instruments in command-and-control and space aviation environments. Headphones are a defining feature of the DJ. The headphones-equipped (and most often male) DJ uses them to select and queue the "track" subsequent to that amplified in an ideally seamless "set" of selections. Often alone on stage, the DJ becomes a medium for transmissions to which he (or occasionally she) alone is privileged (until the clubbing crowd becomes exposed as the new sound is mixed). It is a compelling image. In dedicated milieus where participants convene before figures renowned for their abilities to transport habitués from the mundane into ecstatic and often transpersonal realms, headphones are sacralized technics. Since their operation sees users channel sound from the beyond, animating bodies in dance, there's little wonder they have become fetishized, iconic of the DJ and his/her reputed shamanic function. The lone figure with the phones manipulating sound performance technology on stage is commonly construed as a religious specialist in possession of a unique relationship with the divine, whose ministrations are performed in venues sometimes reckoned as places of "worship."[3] This is something other than parody or hyperbole since, adorned with efficient removable headphones, the figure of the DJ becomes a ubiquitous medium of the divine in the everynight life of the contemporary. And as a popular "hyper-apparent" medium (see Meyer 2011), users gain immediate access to and control over "the source" transmissions, an empowering privilege which, I suspect, motivates many to become a DJ, and which motivates the phenomenon of the "fetishized stereo necklace" (Nye 2011: 87).

In other research (see Lynch and Badger 2006), clubbing has been found to exemplify the turn to "spiritualities of life," which Paul Heelas observes downstream from the "revolutionary" turn to the subjective or "expressive life" in the 1960s (Heelas 1996, 2008; Heelas et al. 2005). While that period is known to be important to the spiritual turn, the role of psychoactivating compounds in this development is routinely neglected within academia. LSD achieved popular circulation in the 1960s and 1970s, with a prodigious influence on aesthetics and culture despite prohibition, and yet it has been the subject of a professional oversight that appears to be the norm within disciplines like sociology, cultural studies, and religious studies. A 40-year moratorium on research into psychedelics subsequent to prohibition has given rise to a silence found in the often-times deficient heuristics inherited by scholars struggling under the constraints of an institutionalized taboo. The socio-aesthetic party "vibe" recognized as native to EDM events and addressed by numerous commentators (see Fikentscher 2000: 80; Taylor 2001; Takahashi and Olaveson 2003: 81; Gerard 2004: 178–79; Olaveson 2004: 90; Rill 2006; St John 2008; St John 2009) has been circumscribed by one such dominant heuristic—Victor Turner's concept of "spontaneous communitas," where, in tribal healing cults, Catholic pilgrimage, hippy happenings and other social liminal occasions, participants may experience a spontaneous "flash of mutual understanding on the existential level, and a 'gut' understanding of synchronicity" (Turner 1982: 48). The Turners (Victor and Edith) employed a policy of avoidance when it came to the psychoactives—again notably LSD—that were proliferating at the time they were adapting the concept of "communitas." The circumstance has incited modified heuristics such as "psychedelic communitas" (Tramacchi 2000), in research subsequently ignored by E. Turner (2012). However, with the acknowledgement of the role of empathogens, principally Ecstasy (MDMA), in fueling the vibe, the empathetic sociality of the "neotribal" dance club is held to offer an interstitial context for vitality, belonging, and identification (Malbon 1999). Such cults of vitality may operate outside the "dictated life" of primary institutions in ways reminiscent of the sociality of "secondary institutions" (Luckmann 1967; see Lynch and Badger 2006). Yet given the potency of such events in the lifestyles of participants often-times facilitated through "chemical intimacy" (Jackson 2004: 163) or "neural tuning" (Takahashi 2004), where habitués become frequently altered together—not simply "being together" to note the language of Maffesoli (1996) partly inherited from Durkheim—a case could be argued for the primary stature of these institutions in which altered conditions of selfhood are paramount and far reaching. These associations echo the modern primacy of the self, albeit in de-individualized contexts removed from traditional sources of belonging (family, church, state), and where technics (digital, cyber, pharmacological) have augmented spiritual endeavors.[4]

Dissatisfied with early cultural Marxist perspectives which held youth (sub-)cultural expressions as ineffectual and tragic (e.g., Clarke *et al.* 1976), with postmodernist approaches (e.g., Baudrillard) beholding rave as an "implosion of meaning" (Melechi 1993), and with heuristics (e.g., Bourdieu) weighted toward distinction over experience (Thornton 1996), ethnographic scholarship of the past 15 years has recognized EDM as a primary source of identification for participants, holding significance often connected to the interwoven causes of gender, sexuality, and ethnicity performed within social dance contexts (e.g., Malbon 1999; Pini 2001; Buckland 2002; Madrid 2008). This chapter builds on this research by illustrating the importance of repurposed technology and remixed media in meaning-making activities with attention to the immersive media ecology in which participants sample religion and experience spirituality. This approach takes the artifice of the remix as its central concern. Using a variety of hardware and software, EDM producers/DJs select, record, edit, and process sonic material, sampling practices through which novel works are recreated as resources for other DJs and subsequent producers (Rodgers 2003). Sampling is the means of making meaning through the appropriation and fusion of extant sources, a process rapidly augmented by the Internet (e.g., peer-2-peer networks). Whether sampling bass lines, melodies, scripted dialogue, or film scores, the pirating and re-editing of found sound is endemic to EDM, where sound sequences are selected and synthesized in production, and/or modulated in performance to fashion new works. Sample-based music, along with sound amplification, intelligent lighting, and spatial design, offers an assemblage designed to *move* people, primarily expressed in dance, a functional circumstance unrecognized in some approaches to the remix (see Navas 2010). As Butler (2006: 47) has noted, dancers are performers and not simply an audience. These assemblages cannot simply be regarded as "texts" or "entertainment" but are designed to elicit a response, and not uncommonly a sense of "connection" rarely known outside that environment. Here we approach the phenomenal atmosphere that incites the experienced to return time and again to the scene of the sublime. A mystical technics may then be identified in the remix, where connectedness and at-one-ment relies upon cut-ups and disassembly, and thus the evolution of new forms from destruction and breakdowns—a practice that has drawn inspiration from the Jamaican dub "versioning" tradition which bore a heavy influence on punk, disco, and hip-hop (Hebdige 1987; Partridge 2010), as well as on the cut 'n' paste practices of syncretic esotericists (St John 2012a). The artifice dedicated to optimizing mystical states of consciousness is what I call *remixticism*.

Digital culture has facilitated popular cultural religions pre-Internet. In the Discordians and Temple of Psychic Youth, Kirby (2012), for instance, has identified exemplars of Lessig's (2008) "read/write generation" wresting popular cultural and traditional religious content from their moorings, and creating new spiritual works, howsoever absurd, from the resultant bricolage. The resistance to consumerism and traditional religious options implicit to the motivations of such new movements has certainly been facilitated by information communication technologies, but also by alternative festivals where researchers have found diverse cultural and religious traditions artfully recombined to forge individualistic and immediate "DiY ["Do it Yourself"] spiritualities." In research on the Burning Man festival, Gilmore (2012: 51) identifies art forms and community rituals that "deliberately blur the lines between irony and spirituality, thereby destabilizing normative assumptions about religious structures, religious behaviors, and religious experience." With the digitalization, networking, and immediate use of religious and other content sampled and remixed by consumers, the latter are more accurately prosumers, a process hyperactivated within EDM and at sites like Burning Man, which, while not an EDM event, is flush with the sounds of electronic music (St John 2014a). In rave, techno, and psytrance, for example, there is a prevailing tendency toward the consumption of experience (e.g., parties) that users themselves are involved in creating. Participants are more accurately curators than audiences, an empowerment that sees the development of independent music, festivals, and art, and a rapid formation of iterated aesthetics and their associated scenes, with *prosumption* complicating "circuit" models of culture. Among DJs, digital and communications media are assembled and purposed to establish control over the means of production, distribution, and perception to an extent unlike that found in most other forms of popular music. In the age of digital reproduction, "performance" and "production" have become indistinct practices, giving rise to new understandings of "liveness" and authenticity in music performance (see Théberge 1997; Miller 2003a, 2003b). At the same time, risk of abuse is reduced and wellbeing maximized through increased awareness of the psychopharmacological status and effects of drugs to which participants are exposed (see Hunt *et al.* 2007)—informed awareness enabled by the World Wide Web and "harm minimization" campaigns. These concurrent processes facilitate gnostic and social liminal contexts in which the individual becomes exposed to universal truths and potential self re-evaluations. The experimental remix is integral to these contexts, a circumstance captured by Australian producer Merkaba, who on "Epic Life" (*Rediscovery*, 2011), samples a spokesman commenting:

> We don't live in a democracy any longer, we live in a mediocracy. Our media is creating and perpetuating a cultural trance that we all subscribe to. The task today for the person who wants to live awake, to be fully awake, is to break free of that cultural trance that is perpetuated by consumerism and by mechanization. We have forgotten how to live an epic life.

Psytrance, media ecology, and liminal experience

At the intersection of popular culture and religion, psytrance is an intriguing subject not so much in its popularity but in its absorption of popular culture for religious ends. Psytrance is a cultural movement cultivating the transfiguring experience inherent to the corporeal interfacing of individual participants with deejayed music in optimized conditions. It shares heritage with "psychedelic" or "cosmic" music styles—e.g., cosmic jazz, garage rock, ambient, dub, space disco, cosmic techno—that have been shaped or enhanced by psychoactive drugs, including LSD, psilocybin-containing mushrooms, and perhaps most pervasively cannabis. That is, the milieu is thoroughly impacted by the sensual alterity and phenomenally transitional (i.e., liminal or in-between) condition of the dance floor, a liminality that permeates the scene's sensory artifice—pharmacological, sound design, décor and installations, visionary art, pragmatic and scintillating fashion design—designed to enhance liminal conditions. In this milieu, trance enthusiasts, label managers, research chemists, party collectives, and event organizers are dedicated to optimize the party vibe, fashioning a superliminal zone for the mind, body, and spirit, which may be at its most advanced in major international festivals such as Portugal's Boom Festival and Hungary's Ozora. Boom is especially important in this development as it is host to the Liminal Village, a dedicated area for lectures, workshops, panels, films, and visionary art which adopts the language of initiation from anthropological discourse to forge a consciously liminal—and thus transitional—space (see St John 2012a).

From overnight parties to week-long festivals like Boom, psyculture events have been held inside disused warehouses or in dedicated urban clubs, and more favorably in bushland, forests, beaches, deserts, and other open-air locations where enthusiasts hold them to mark seasonal transitions or celebrate celestial events. As a remote, idyllic, and protected location hosting full-moon parties since the late 1960s, the former Portuguese colony of Goa, India, was formative to this development. Populated by privileged self-exiled travelers seeking freedom from a variety of oppressions in the lands of their upbringing, and following the alternative spiritual projects popularized by the likes of Timothy Leary, Ram Dass, the Beatles, and Osho (Bhagwan Shree Rajneesh)—whose *sannyasins* would later be implicated in the circulation of MDMA in Goa and elsewhere (see D'Andrea 2006)—these parties were spearheaded by Goa Gil, a Californian expatriate who arrived in Goa in 1970, later becoming a *sadhu*, and more recently Shri Mahant, advocating "re-creating ancient tribal ritual for the 21st century" (McAteer 2002: 29; see also St John 2011). Through the 1970s and 1980s, from psychedelic rock to DJ-mixed electronica, Goa became the seasonal context for autonomous experiments in music, dance, and sociality forged by "expressive expatriates" mobilized across physical and metaphysical space (see D'Andrea 2007). Two-stepping through palm trees and among one another through to sunrise on Anjuna beach and elsewhere, travelers forged a trance dance ritual that by the early 1990s had informed the sound structures and aesthetics of the emergent music genre, Goatrance, infusing subsequent parties and festivals worldwide (see Rom and Querner 2011; St John 2014b). The event-culture arising in the aftermath of the Goa scene carries its legacy, reproducing its hallmark artifice: the sanctified passage from night to day, the transit from the shadows into light, a movement which signifies illumination and the ostensible dawning of consciousness. This gnostic trend redolent in esoteric, fantasy, and New Age fiction where, having transited from the darkness, avatars become exposed to "truths" that are integral to self-transformation, infuses psychedelic trance praxis. Evident in events held overnight in open-air locations, this revelatory gestalt is far removed from, for instance, the "dark" dystopian sensory aesthetic of drum 'n' bass born in working class raves and clubs in London and south-east England (Christodoulou 2011). Following the successes of Goatrance in the mid-1990s, buoyed by the end of the Cold War, premillennial excitement, and the emergence of the World Wide Web, the genre saw the development of various sound aesthetics—including "progressive" and "dark."

Integral to the sub-genres arising in this wake is an Orientalist legacy in which Eastern timbres and tropes have flourished, echoing memories of India, and leading to efforts among music producers, label houses, and party organizations to create a transposable aesthetic from the Goa "state of mind." Hindu symbology is a pervasive feature, found for instance on the artwork accompanying the first Return to the Source compilation, *Deep Trance and Ritual Beats* (1995), which featured a booklet with stylized images of the elephant-headed Ganesh (son of Shiva and Goddess Parvati), and the sitar-playing Hindu muse Sarasvati. In the Goatrance diaspora, the Hindu sacred syllable *Om*—and its Devanagari sign ॐ—remains iconic. In efforts to induce Visions of Shiva, the name Paul van Dyke chose for his outfit formed in 1992 with Harald Blüchel (aka Cosmic Baby); to project *The Colours of Shiva*, the compilation series produced by Tua Records (1997–1999); or to reduce the *Distance to Goa*, the successful compilation series released by French label Distance (founded in 1995), promoters, producers, and designers fashioned label aesthetics, album cover art, track titles, music structures, and festival concepts saturated with soft Orientalism. At the same time, it should be recognized that Yoga and meditation, for example, pervade the movement as indicated by "lifestyle" zones found at many festivals, serving as a reminder of the influence of non-dualistic thought and practice, and the quest for spiritual evolution. And thus psychedelic trance can be regarded as not unrelated to the Human Potential Movement which had been inspired by syntheses of Eastern and Western philosophy, notably through the works of Sri Aurobindo (see Kripal 2007). The metagenre is infused with evidence of this influence, as found in the Buddhist lessons programmed in music. For instance, on the ethno-tribal "Indian Summer" by Monkey Machine (*Closed Caption Radio*, 2011) the sample states: "This life is full of pain. And this world is full of suffering. The cause of suffering is craving, self-love and attachment. The remedy for suffering, is the systematic destruction of craving."

While Orientalist essentialism is recognizable in the appropriative and reappropriative practices of Goatrance artists and their progeny, in accordance with the endogenous ontology of the remix, a cornucopia of spiritual, cultural, and popular cultural influences have shaped the psychedelic trance aesthetic. Yet, despite the profusion of influences, there remains a persistent motivation throughout the psychedelic trance development, across sub-genres, and to which diverse resources are devoted: the achievement of mystical states of consciousness within the context of ecstatic dance. While there is much evidence that many (especially older) participants seek to rejoin social contexts and "just have fun," recurrent events suggest that a gnostic commitment remains telling. Radically different from everyday consciousness, transpersonal experience is typically aroused within such environments through the recombination of alterity: native, outlaw, monstrous, metaphysical, hyperspatial. Exemplary UK-based psybient act Shpongle are renowned for deploying diverse material from world regions, exotic instruments, tribal chants, nature sounds, and textual references to primitivity as well as the "hyperspace" associated with the consumption of tryptamine such as DMT. The audio feast, like that served up on Shpongle's *Nothing Lasts ... But Nothing Is Lost* (2005), caters to the appetites of enthusiasts bent on the timbres of the ethnic, the Orient, the tribal, and the cosmic. These and other "global fusion" artists, like French-based duo Entheogenic

(Helmut Glavar and Piers Oak-Rhind), use exotic soundscapes to forge tableaux of difference. With inheritance from such diverse influences as the Theosophical Society, Surrealism (see Tythacott 2003), Carl Jung, the Human Potential Movement (Kripal 2007: Chapter 4), science fiction, and psychonauts like Tim Leary and Terence McKenna, for these and many other artists, the Other is devised as a source of self-discovery, with gnosis of origins, destiny, and one's relationship with the cosmos to be revealed to, or uncovered by, the trance "initiate." Travelers—i.e., those who are mobilized across physical sites and inner space—are tasked to uncover hidden secrets, to awaken from the dark, to find the key that will unlock their potential, to become whole, and to evolve consciousness, the promised land that lies beyond the maladies of modern life.

As is evident in psytrance album concepts and the ubiquitous sampling of McKenna in music productions, the increased popularity of ayahuasca, DMT, magic mushrooms, and other substances commonly held to be "entheogens" (tools that awaken the divine within) is consistent with remixticism where sources are recombined in alchemical syntheses to produce effects that are literally mind blowing.[5] Not unrelated to the "sampling" (ingestion, smoking) of these substances themselves, this use demonstrates commitment to transpersonal states of consciousness, often achieved via experiments with blends and infusions, as evidenced by the preparation and smoking of *changa*.[6] While these plants, compounds, decoctions, and blends may be valorized in accordance with their association with Amerindian shamanic practices—as may explain concomitant interest in tipis, the Mayan calendar, and other artifacts and icons evidencing soft primitivism—the fact that they are mixed and synthesized to often uniquely transfiguring effects improves our understanding of the function of the remix in contemporary spiritual life (see St John 2013).

Occulture and media shamanism

Over the last decade, researchers have reflected on the interweaving of religion and popular culture. In his *The Re-Enchantment of the West*, Chris Partridge (2004, 2006b) has drawn on "mystical religion" (as understood by Ernst Troeltsch) and "cultic milieu" theorist Colin Campbell to argue that a popular occult, or what he calls "occulture," flourishes in film, music, literature, and the popular imagination. More recently Roeland, Aupers, and Houtman (2012) discuss fantasy and conspiracy narratives prevalent in literature and cinema as expressions of discontent with what Weber had earlier recognized as processes of "disenchantment" and the dissipation of meaning—a product of the "mass manifestation of Romanticism" evident in the counter-culture of the 1960s and 1970s. The authors recognize that this dissatisfaction shaped prevailing critical socio-cultural theory, most evidently Theodore Roszak's (1995) critique of a dehumanizing "technocracy." This cultural discontent has given rise to proliferating alternative worlds and efforts to uncover the "truth" within popular culture, a cultural re-enchantment further evident in the turn to Eastern religion (Campbell 2007), the cultural permeation of magic and Paganism (Bennett and Weston 2013), "dark green" religion (Taylor 2009), digital religion (Aupers and Houtman 2010), and the cultural influence of Aleister Crowley (Bogdan and Starr

2012). Nodding to the agency in which consumers are offered the choice of taking the "blue pill or the red pill," Roeland *et al.* (2012: 419) conclude that "in an increasingly disenchanted world, it is likely … that meaning will assume dramatically new shapes and that popular culture will play a vital role in its articulation, so as to enable its appropriation by its audiences."

Partridge specifically comments on psytrance as an occultural vehicle (2004: 166–75), a thesis allowing for the recognition of direct experience with the divine in circumstances that may otherwise be held as simulacra—i.e., through a thinly adapted Baudrillardian lens (see Possamai 2012). Free from the obfuscations of postmodernist theory, Partridge's approach offers a useful heuristic, though the sensory techniques facilitating occultural experience require closer scrutiny—e.g., the liminal states of consciousness that are cultivated and revisited within optimal events allegorized and amplified with the aid of a variety of sources. As the occultural media ecology of psychedelic trance is noisy, attention to what I call "nanomedia" assists purchase. Audio material sampled from popular cultural sources by electronic musicians has become integral to the sonic fictions embraced by natives of the digital age. If "mass media" consists of regional and national print and television news, "niche media" includes scene specific publications, "micro media" includes event flyers and album cover art, and "social media" refers to the Web-based and mobile technologies enabling interactive dialogue and user-generated content, then the sampling of popular culture using the medium of the programmed music itself is nanomedia: fleeting, heavily edited sound bites, entire film scripts condensed into a few carefully chosen lines on long tracks that are mixed and performed for dance floor habitués at events worldwide. A component of the sampledelic apparatus of the electronic musician and expressive of the compositional character of identity in late modernity, nanomediations are purposed to religio-spiritual ends. Vocal sampling possesses numerous guises and intentions within EDM and other scenes. For instance, Rose (1994) addresses the aural message in the sampling culture of hip-hop. Sampling can be deployed to effect intentionally political, transgressive, or ludicrous outcomes. While elsewhere I have addressed, for instance, the role of sampling in "agit-house" (St John 2010) and psychedelic warriorhood (St John 2012b), here I illustrate how media are used specifically for spiritual ends.

In conjunction with other scene visual media, including event visual design, and notably the visual media sampled and edited by VJs (video jockeys) in a live artifice complementary to that of the DJ (but also album art, promotional materials, Web site designs), nanomedia are componential to what Kodwo Eshun (1998) identified as "conceptechnics": technics shaping the aesthetics of EDM cultures and the "new sensory experience" of their participants. Moreover, these technics shape subjectivities within the optimized socio-aesthetics of the dance floor. Remixed audio-visual media are compelling within this context since participants, unlike those audiences seated in cinemas or before television and computer screens, are intercorporeally animated. These sites of reception are also sites of performance (in dance). Programmed into tracks, often used sparingly, with the same line frequently repeated in 7–9 minute compositions (when used at all), narratives appropriated from cinema, TV, radio, computer games, documentaries, news reports, and countless spokespersons, are then uniquely performed, embodied in moves, and recognized in glances and other interactions. I do not focus on this detail to suggest that it is has greater significance than the rhythm structures, bass lines, and melodies of the music, but that it is a component of it. A density of programmed audio-fragments made available to interpreting minds and bodies enables those who may have arrived at transcendent states to integrate the experience.

This is a complex field. Many tracks and entire artist albums do not possess vocal samples at all, many DJs will not select tracks with vocal samples in their performed sets, and furthermore, there is no guarantee that dancers will receive the material in the way intended by music producers, perhaps due to textual polysemy, muted narrative, or misrecognition. Each participant is exposed to the media-ecology of a dance floor carrying a unique set of knowledge (e.g., about music and drugs), intentions, and expectations. This diversity in reception renders debatable the oft-repeated des-ignation of DJs as "technoshamans," unless they are comporting themselves as ritual specialists dedicated to transformative outcomes, as is evident in the intent of Goa Gil (McAteer 2002), Ray Castle (Gaffney 2001), and DJ Krusty (Gaffney 2008), though the perplexing question of interpretation remains. Regardless, as a specific recogni-tion of the enduring presence of redeployed datafacts, DJ/producers can be viewed as media shamans, new technicians of the sacred who remix media to orchestrate (i.e., imitate and initiate) liminality. That is, as "cutters 'n' pasters" of pop-cult detritus, they select content to decidedly liminal specifications. While the transformation one might expect in traditional rites of passage or therapeutic rituals is here uncertain, the experience of the being-in-transit is typical. Psytrance demonstrates consistency with the techno-logic of other EDM styles such as disco, house, and techno, where the techniques of trance inducement are more important than any symbolic-ideational content. Across these functional art forms, we find the operation of a noetic logic— the feeling of revelation, and the process of knowing itself—an artifice optimized within psytrance where the feeling of transit is orchestrated within a superliminal atmosphere engineered by countless artists, technicians, and designers working in diverse industries, among whom we can certainly count producers such as Simon Posford (notably as Hallucinogen), Ollie Wisdom (Space Tribe), Astral Projection, and Bill Halsey (Cosmosis), whose remystical endeavors have provided participants with the means to access and integrate transpersonal experience (for more detail, see St John 2012a). Here we are firmly in the realm of "self-shamanism" (Tramacchi 2006: 34), where not only molecules and compounds but a bristling array of convergent technics are developed to manifest a media ecology grown to maximize self-potential and cultural change. Removed from the professionally minded religious practitioners identified by Eliade (1951)—i.e., those whose ritual "techniques of ecstasy" and "soul-flights" allowed them interaction with the spirit world on behalf of the com-munity of believers especially for the purpose of healing—and in the landscape of media shamanism, the responsibility for transit is passed to individual participants.

Experience, of course, may fall short of ideals as excesses and abuses can lead to unexpected outcomes, including extraordinarily "bad trips." In any case, the study of such re-mediations and its transformative or therapeutic potential is in its infancy. While film and television have been recognized as popular media through which religious sensibilities are expressed and received (e.g., Martin and Ostwalt 1995; Cowan 2008, 2010; Lyden 2003, 2009), how EDM performs this function through the iteration and recomposition of media content (such as film scripts) is little understood. Complex interactive, polysemous, and highly idiosyncratic contexts pose a challenge for researchers, not least because music aesthetics shift rapidly. That said, despite internal variation, Goa/psytrance has demonstrated a progressive humanistic sensibility broadly consistent with the goals of the Human Potential Movement and transpersonal psychology. While in the interactive theater of the dance floor, a carnival of spoken *dadafacts*—e.g., monsters, aliens, outlaws, and natives—deriving from science fiction, horror, fantasy, New Age, and other sources are part of the aural experience, and a progressive project forms amid the noise of symbols, texts, and images. Betraying a progressive evolutionary telos also located in cosmic rock, initiatives such as The Infinity Project, Akasha Project, the original Etnica Project, Sun Project, Astral Projection, and Antaris Project evoke the intent of seminal psychedelic artists and events to orchestrate transformative outcomes, often by way of the disintegration and reintegration of the self, a project ever-reliant upon an achievable and integral end-state: wholeness.

The trance project

Films like *Waking Life*, *Dune*, and *The Matrix* have been popular resources for this project. On Israeli group Astral Projection's "Back from Hell" (2004), Captain Morpheus from *The Matrix* announces to the massive: "I believe this night holds for each and every one of us the very meaning of our lives." Deploying samples evoking the unveiling of the vital data-lode—invocations of pure process—productions are consistent with the functionality of techno. Sampling from 1960s TV series *The Outer Limits*, SFX (an early incarnation of Astral Projection) stated their purpose: "We Are Controlling Transmission" (1998).[7] Key musical texts amplify fixation with the noetic sensation of revelation, with transmission over transmitted content, with the feeling of knowing. But in the evocation of the threshold across which an adept passes and gains insight, producers do not simply effect, but are affecting, religious experience. The Infinity Project's psybient masterwork *Mystical Experiences* (1995) is a seminal achievement in this development. Dropping the words of Aldous Huxley, the title track on the album conveys its producers' intimacy with "a feeling of one-ness with the world." On Juno Reactor's classic *Transmissions* (1993); in the work of Chi-A.D. (on whose "The Flame of Eternal Life" [*Anno Domini*, Velvet Inc., 1999] a woman announces: "I will show you what no other living mortal has seen"); and among countless other more recent artists like Chilean Ovnimoon (Hector Stuardo Marileo), whose epic "Galactic Mantra" and other material on *Magnetic Portal* (2011) are permeated with audio-koans suggestive of universal energies, light sources, and dream states, access is given to that which will enable mutation toward optimal conditions of self. As one of the most popular figures in the neognostic movement, the voice of McKenna is repeatedly sampled to promote the "shamanic plants" and compounds that are adopted as tools to achieve understanding of one's own divine nature. For instance, on Streamers' "Power and Light" (*Goa Trance Volume Nineteen*, 2012), McKenna speaks: "We have no idea what it would mean in our own lives if we could throw off the notion of ourselves as fallen beings. We are not fallen beings.

When you take into your life the gnosis of the light-filled vegetable. ... the first thing that comes to you is: you are a divine being. You matter. You count. You come from realms of unimaginable power and light, and you will return to those realms." In these works, an occultural database is curated in which vocal fragments are unarchived and reanimated from countless sources and played to dance floor occupants. While DJs/producers edit and mix occultural texts already in circulation—e.g., a phantasmagoria of alien abduction narratives, fantasy like *Lord of the Rings*, conspiracy theories, and other esoteric phenomena—other sources are totally repurposed to the revelatory ambiance desired.

Adapted from NASA radio dialogue, sci-fi cinema and television series, outer space travel motifs are especially prominent throughout the Goatrance development and its progeny. These motifs serve to allegorize self-transcendence, inner travail, and the gnostic encounter with one's other-self storied via the poached figure of the alien. For instance, in their 1995 release "Hypersphere," pioneering French outfit Transwave analogized the journey into innerspace via the launch into aerospace anticipated in the repeating announcement from *Dune*: "31 seconds and we're going for auto-sequence start." The pervasive use of Apollo Program countdown sequences through the psytrance development narrativize quantized rhythms intended, with the assistance of carefully measured micrograms of psychedelics, to effect consciousness alteration: lift off. The result is immeasurable: "Boy, it's just beautiful up here looking out the window—it's just really fantastic."[8] The psychedelic gnosis can be located in The Infinity Project's *Time and Space* EP which possesses an untitled track ("B2") featuring space-avatar Dave Bowman's eureka moment from Arthur C. Clarke's epic novel and unedited versions of Stanley Kubrick's concurrent 1968 classic *2001: A Space Odyssey*: "My god, it's full of stars!" That the gnostic payoff of twentieth-century space exploration continues to be adapted to twenty-first-century contexts is apparent on Re:Actor's "Spirit Poem" (2010), where a sample conveys "the soaring spiritual high" of the "central revelation" of Carl Sagan's TV series *Cosmos: A Personal Voyage* (first broadcast in 1980): "our oneness with the Universe. ... Through the searching of 40,000 generations of our ancestors we have come to discover our coordinates in space and in time." On another track, Cosmosis (the UK's Bill Halsey) drops the payload, again care of Sagan: "We journey from ignorance to knowledge. Growth reflects the advancement of the species. The exploration of the cosmos is a voyage of self-discovery."[9]

The figure of the alien is prolific in visual art, event promotions, and sonic graffiti. They are typically benevolent messengers, bearing Tao-like koans of truth grafted to the objective of self-discovery and the evolution of consciousness, a development consistent with Helena Blavatski's ascended "Venusian masters" which Partridge (2003) argues has been the basis for the varied presence of aliens as "super-gurus" in UFO religion. In Cosmosis's oeuvre—especially 2002 album *Contact*—alongside the popular UFO contactee and alien abductee narratives programmed into countless tracks, the sagacious alien is a provider of sound counsel, expander of consciousness, guide to inner peace and becoming. Here, as in rave culture (see McLeod 2003), the alien is a potent icon of wisdom, hope, and unity. Indeed, as symbols of freedom from a multitude of existential, social, and political concerns, extraterrestrials form an iconography ideal for the pursuit of alternative modes of subjectivity.

Yet the "alien" is not always the bearer of good tidings, a perhaps stridently optimistic theme counterweighted by dark trance. Also called "darkpsy," sometimes "horror trance," and more recently just "night music," dark trance emerged in the post-Iraq invasion period as a distinctly faster and darker style of psychedelic trance performed during the nocturnal hours. Psychosis and death are prevailing themes. Many artists in this development poach lines from religious-oriented horror films where discomfort of the greatest magnitude (i.e., terror) resides in a secularized universe where the divine order has lost its significance (Cowan 2008). German artist Xenomorph (aka Mark Petrick) was a pacesetter, early submitting a sonic jeremiad on a world gone mad, as captured on "Abominations" (*Cassandra's Nightmare*, 1998), which stepped off the precipice with a reading from the work of Lovecraftian novelist Sutter Cane: "Trent stood at the edge of the rip, stared into the inimitable gulf of the unknown, the Stygian world yawning blackly beyond" (from John Carpenter's *In the Mouth of Madness*, 1994). Foretelling a world in crisis, the track also used a harrowing line from *Exorcist III* (1990): "God is not with us now, there is only the darkness here, and your death." Malevolent aliens, corrupt humans, serial killers, evil robots; a host of monstrous figures lifted from horror cinema have run rampant through the soundscapes of darkpsy. While many examples could be given of the dark influences and schizoid states invoked in this development, Dark Soho's sample from *The Wolf Man* (1941) is evocative: "even a man who is pure in the heart and says his prayers by night, may become a wolf when the wolfsbane blooms, and the winter/autumn moon is bright" ("Depth of Emotion", *Sun Spot*, 2000). As many producers deploy material signposting cinema's horrific metataxis which derives from the inversion or invasion of established religious order, a conscious interest in the liminal device of the monster emerges. For Goa Gil, the monstrous is pressed into the service of an overarching commitment to transformation—on personal and wider cultural levels (see St John 2011). Gil has selected and mixed dark trance in 24-hour trance rituals mounted in locations worldwide for the past 25 years. In these overnight open-air events participants are exposed to ego-shattering practice. This is the basic view of Gil, who is well read in the world literature on rites of passage, and who orchestrates an infernal trial for his "initiates," furnishing an apocalypse of the self in which symbolic death precedes rebirth, where the darkness precedes dawn, where chaos is integral to evolution, and where terror is hyperbolized with the assistance of sampled horror cinema.

Goa Gil has been a principal agent in the development of dark trance, forming his own production outfit The Nommos. Evolving in tandem with the "progressive" sound, the dark trance aesthetic is characterized by a frenetic pace, and determined efforts to destabilize minds affected by a cacophony of muffled TV news bites and radio broadcasts, with countless spokespersons issuing a white noise of unintelligible communications. The frisson was worked, for instance, by Australian Adam Walter (aka Scatterbrain), whose proto-dark trance album *Infernal Angel* (2003) hosts the brooding "Possessed" in which Professor Pacoli from Besson's *The Fifth Element* is heard to announce that "when the three planets are in eclipse, the black hole like a door is opened. Evil comes spreading terror and chaos." The mood is then upstaged by Darth Vader, who drops the heavy wood: "If you only knew the power of the dark side." Using recognizable motifs, artists have sought to exploit themes like evil and hopelessness. And so, within the dread caterwauls Demonizz (on "Aknofobia", *Contagion Vol. 1*, 2008) bursts out with Pinhead's immortal retort from Clive Barker's *Hellraiser* (1987): "Do I look like someone who cares what God thinks?" Amid the godless ambience, a little girl breathes: "My mommy said there were no monsters. No real ones. But there are, aren't there?" To which Ellen Ripley (from James Cameron's 1986 film *Aliens*) responds: "Yes, there are" (sampled on Chi-A.D.'s "Monsters", *Neighbourhood*, 1999). Many darkpsy producers dwell on the discord of the gothic liminal. At its extreme edge, producers seek to expose consciousness to the ultimate unknowability of "reality," offering a dark romantic and sometimes brutal counterpoint to the strident optimism of Goatrance. Yet, playful exaggerations of monstrous human potential blasting out over the darkest hours of events are not inconsistent with the project of trance already outlined as progressive. For the dark recesses of the night give way to the sun, and in the Goa tradition, dawn signifies awakening and the illumination of consciousness.

Conclusion

EDM cultures and their events have grown as popular occasions for religio-spiritual experience, as has been observed by a variety of commentators. In this chapter we have explored one EDM event-culture holding the stature of a movement more than a moment. Specifically, psytrance has been identified as an industrious assemblage of the remix, an artifice that has developed as a technics for spiritual evolution. Part of a broader project investigating the spiritual technologies of EDM and the means by which religious sensibilities are imitated and initiated among participants, we have examined how producers and DJs in psytrance appropriate and edit texts from diverse religious and popular cultural resources reconfigured to maximize liminality—and human potential—and thus echoing the transformational goals of the Human Potential Movement and transpersonal psychology.

While there are many aspects of the liminal assemblage that a host of artists and technicians within this movement have helped optimize, I have addressed scripted and other vocal floating signifiers selected, treated, and performed by technicians of the sacred I have referred to as media shamans. From the Goatrance period onwards, artists in the psychedelic trance tradition have recombined elements from a cornucopia of popular cultural resources—science fiction and horror cinema, TV, documentary, computer games, political commentary, NASA radio dialogue—to effect and affect transition, to inaugurate mystical states of consciousness in which gnostic "truths" about one's self and one's place in the universe can be accessed. There is no question that this can be the case, since the assemblage to which these technicians are dedicated ordinarily facilitates non-ordinary states of consciousness. Re-mediated media are integral to the innovative aesthetics in which transnational populations draw meaning, fashion identity, and connect with communities across the world. As components in an assemblage of audio-visual media, remixed content is important to the signifying capacities of psytrance and other EDM participants, with attention to nanomedia enabling insight on the recomposition and re-enchantment of subjectivities in contemporary cultural life.

Psytrance is a liminal culture. It is mobilized to maximize potential which it achieves in its seasonal event culture. Here we have seen that the assemblage in which textual re-mediations circulate is designed not so much to orchestrate the transformation in being and status that is the common objective of rites of passage, but the superliminalized state of being-in-transit, an experimental field of experience optimized by technicians of the *limen*—the Latin term (meaning "threshold") that is the source of the word "liminal"—and event habitués themselves. On the dance floor of global psytrance events, the threshold is cultivated through optimal music, architecture, and psychoactives. Carefully remixed popular culture augments the noetic feeling of knowing which draws from traditions that enable individuals to unravel mysteries that lie within, to unlock their potential. Detailed ethnographic analysis of the production, performance, and reception of occultural and neognostic texts will shed further light on the artifice and efficacy of the remix—especially within global dance music movements whose participants seek meaning and belonging beyond traditional religious frameworks and ethnonational identifications. Such research is necessary as the recombination of popular culture in global EDM produces sonic fictions that enervate, enchant, and inspire the lives of millions.

Notes

1 For example, a now-removed fundamentalist Christian Web site "Truthaboutrave.com" purported to reveal the "awful truth" that raves are "a means of the devil to solicit worship."

2 "RAVE" is an acronym for "Reducing America's Vulnerability to Ecstasy," the apparent vocation of then-Senator Joe Biden (D-DE) and Senator Chuck Grassley (R-IA). An update on the repressive "crack-house" laws extended to temporary, one-off, and open-air events, the "Rave Act" legislation was embedded in the *Child Abduction Protection Act of 2003*.

3 For example, *Last Night a DJ Saved My Life* is the title of a popular history on DJ culture (Brewster and Broughton 2000).

4 However, some scholars have addressed the appropriation of EDM within Christian contexts (see Till 2006; Sai-Chun Lau 2006).

5 Ayahuasca is a psychoactive brew prepared from the *Banisteriopsis Caapi* vine typically mixed with the leaves of dimethyltryptamine (DMT)-containing species. DMT is also smoked or vaporized (most effectively through the use of a glass pipe) with a commonly profound effect lasting 15–30 minutes.

6 Invented in Australia, *changa* is described as "revolutionary plant alchemy … a smoking mixture which contains Ayahuasca vine and/or leaf, an intelligent combination of several admixture herbs and naturally sourced DMT that has been infused into those herbs" (Palmer 2011/12: 98).

7 Recorded in 1993 and released on *SFX: The Unreleased Tracks—89–94* (1998).

8 Apollo 16 Commander John W. Young, sampled on The KLF's "What Time is Love? (Live at Trancentral)" (1990).

9 Carl Sagan, on the TV series Cosmos, sampled on "Self-Discovery" by Cosmosis (2009).

Works cited

Aupers, S. and D. Houtman (eds) (2010) *Religions of Modernity: Relocating the Sacred to the Self and the Digital*, Leiden: Brill.

Bennett, A. and D. Weston (eds) (2013) *Pop Pagans: Paganism and Popular Music*, Sheffield: Equinox.

Bogdan, H. and M.P. Starr (eds) (2012) *Aleister Crowley and Western Esotericism*, New York: Oxford University Press.

Bossius, T., A. Häger, and K. Kahn-Harris (eds) (2011) *Religion and Popular Music in Europe: New Expressions of Sacred and Secular Identity*, London: I.B. Tauris.

Brewster, B. and F. Broughton (2000) *Last Night a DJ Saved My Life: The History of the Disc Jockey*, New York: Grove Press.

Buckland, F. (2002) *Impossible Dance: Club Culture and Queer World-Making*, Middletown, CT: Wesleyan University Press.

Butler, M.J. (2006) *Unlocking the Groove: Rhythm, Meter, and Musical Design in Electronic Dance Music*, Bloomington, IN: Indiana University Press.

Campbell, C. (2007) *The Easternization of the West*, Boulder, CO: Paradigm Publishers.

Christodoulou, C. (2011) "Rumble in the jungle city, place and uncanny bass," *Dancecult: Journal of Electronic Dance Music Culture* 3, 1: 44–63.

Clarke, A.C. (1968) *2001: A Space Odyssey*, New York: New American Library.

Clarke, J., S. Hall, T. Jefferson, and B. Roberts (1976) "Subcultures, cultures and class," in S. Hall and T. Jefferson (eds), *Resistance Through Rituals: Youth Subcultures in Post-War Britain*, London: Hutchinson & Co., 9–74.

Cowan, D.E. (2008) *Sacred Terror: Religion and Horror on the Silver Screen*, Waco, TX: Baylor University Press.

——(2010) *Sacred Space: The Quest for Transcendence in Science Fiction Film and Television*, Waco, TX: Baylor University Press.

D'Andrea, A. (2006) "The spiritual economy of nightclubs and raves: Osho Sannyasins as party promoters in Ibiza and Pune/Goa," *Culture and Religion* 7, 1: 61–75.

——(2007) *Global Nomads: Techno and New Age as Transnational Countercultures in Ibiza and Goa*, New York: Routledge.

Eliade, M. (2004[1951]) *Shamanism: Archaic Techniques of Ecstasy*, Princeton, NJ: Princeton University Press.

Eshun, K. (1998) *More Brilliant than the Sun: Adventures in Sonic Fiction*, London: Quartet.

Fikentscher, K. (2000) *"You Better Work!": Underground Dance Music in New York City*, Middletown, CT: Wesleyan University Press.

Fritz, J. (1999) *Rave Culture: An Insider's Overview*, Canada: Smallfry Press.

Gaffney, E. [aka DJ Krusty, Eugene ENRG] (2001) "Psychic sonics: tribadelic dance trance-formation," in G. St John (ed.), *FreeNRG: Notes from the Edge of the Dance Floor*, Melbourne: Common Ground, 157–69.

——(2008) "Trance and dance: bush doofs and the shamanic vision," *Undergrowth*. Online. Available: http://undergrowth.org/bush_doofs_by_dj_krusty (accessed 21 September 2012).

Gauthier, F. (2004) "Rapturous ruptures: the 'instituant' religious experience of rave," in G. St John (ed.), *Rave Culture and Religion*, London: Routledge, 65–84.

Gerard, M. (2004) "Selecting ritual: DJs, dancers and liminality in underground dance music," in G. St John (ed.), *Rave Culture and Religion*, London: Routledge, 167–84.

Gilmore, L. (2012) "Burn-a-lujah! DIY spiritualities, Reverend Billy and Burning Man," in G. Lynch, J. Mitchell, and A. Strhan (eds), *Religion, Media and Culture: A Reader*, London: Routledge, 49–58.

Gilmour, M.J. (2009) *Gods and Guitars: Seeking the Sacred in Post-1960s Popular Music*, Waco, TX: Baylor University Press.

——(ed.) (2005) *Call Me the Seeker: Listening to Religion in Popular Music*, New York: Continuum.

Hebdige, D. (1987) *Cut 'N' Mix*, London: Comedia Books.

Heelas, P. (1996) *The New Age Movement: The Celebration of the Self and the Sacralization of Modernity*, Oxford: Blackwell Publishing.

——(2008) *Spiritualities of Life: From the Romantics to Wellbeing Culture*, Oxford: Blackwell Publishing.

Heelas, P., L. Woodhead, B. Seel, B. Szerszynski, and K. Tusting (2005) *The Spiritual Revolution: Why Religion Is Giving Way to Spirituality*, Oxford: Blackwell Publishing.

Hunt, G.P., K. Evans, and F. Kares (2007) "Drug use and meanings of risk and pleasure," *Journal of Youth Studies* 10, 1: 73–96.

Hutson, S. (1999) "Technoshamanism: spiritual healing in the rave subculture," *Popular Music and Society* 23: 53–77.

Jackson, P. (2004) *Inside Clubbing: Sensual Experiments in the Art of Being Human*, Oxford: Berg.

Kirby, D. (2012) "Occultural bricolage and popular culture: remix and art in Discordianism, the Church of the SubGenius, and the Temple of Psychic Youth," in A. Possamai (ed.), *Handbook of Hyper-Real Religions*, Leiden: Brill, 39–57.

Kripal, J. (2007) *Esalen: America and the Religion of No Religion*, Chicago, IL: University of Chicago Press.

Lessig, L. (2008) *Remix: Making Art and Commerce Thrive in the Hybrid Economy*, New York: Penguin Press.

Luckmann, T. (1967) *The Invisible Religion: The Problem of Religion in Modern Society*, New York: MacMillan.

Lyden, J.C. (2003) *Film as Religion: Myths, Morals, and Rituals*, New York: New York University Press.

——(ed.) (2009) *The Routledge Companion to Religion and Film*, New York: Routledge.

Lynch, G. and E. Badger (2006) "The mainstream post-rave club scene as a secondary institution: a British perspective," *Culture and Religion* 7, 1: 27–40.

McAteer, M. (2002) "'Redefining the ancient tribal ritual for the 21st century': Goa Gil and the trance dance experience," unpublished paper for Division of Philosophy, Religion, and Psychology, Reed College. Online. Available: www.goagil.com/thesis.html (accessed 21 September 2012).

McLeod, K. (2003) "Space oddities: aliens, futurism and meaning in popular music," *Popular Music* 22: 337–55.

Madrid, A. (2008) *Nor-tec Rifa! Electronic Dance Music from Tijuana to the World*, New York: Oxford University Press.

Maffesoli, M. (1996) *The Time of the Tribes: The Decline of Individualism in Mass Society*, London: Sage.

Malbon, B. (1999) *Clubbing: Dancing, Ecstasy and Vitality*, London: Routledge.

Martin, J.W. and C.E. Ostwalt, Jr. (eds) (1995) *Screening the Sacred: Religion, Myth, and Ideology in Popular American Film*, Boulder, CO: Westview Press.

Meadan, B. (2001) *TRANCENational ALIENation: Trance Music Culture, Moral Panics and Transnational Identity in Israel*, Raleigh, NC: Lulu.com.

Melechi, A. (1993) "The ecstasy of disappearance," in S. Redhead (ed.), *Rave off: Politics and Deviance in Contemporary Youth Culture*, Aldershot: Avebury, 29–40.

Meyer, B. (2011) "Mediation and immediacy: sensational forms, semiotic ideologies and the question of the medium," *Social Anthropology* 19, 1: 23–39.

Miller, G. (2003a) "The real deal: toward an aesthetic of authentic live electronic dance music," *Stylus Magazine*. Online. Available: www.stylusmagazine.com/articles/weekly_article/the-real-deal-toward-an-aesthetic-of-authentic-live-electronic-dance-music.htm (accessed 12 September 2012).

——(2003b) "The real deal: toward an aesthetic of authentic live electronic dance music, pt. 2," *Stylus Magazine*. Online. Available: www.stylusmagazine.com/articles/weekly_article/the-real-deal-toward-an-aesthetic-of-authentic-live-electronic-dance-music-pt-2.htm (accessed 12 September 2012).

Navas, E. (2010) "Regressive and reflexive mashup in sampling culture," in S. Sonvilla-Weiss (ed.), *Mashup Cultures*, Vienna: Springer, 157–77.

Nye, S. (2011) "Headphone-headset-jetset: dj culture, mobility and science fictions of listening," Dancecult: Journal of Electronic Dance Music Culture 3, 1: 64–96.

Olaveson, T. (2004) "'Connectedness' and the rave experience: rave as new religious movement?" in G. St John (ed.), *Rave Culture and Religion*, London: Routledge, 85–106.

Palmer, J. (2011/12) "Changa," *Entheogenesis Australis Journal* 3: 98–101.

Partridge, C. (2003) "Understanding UFO religions and abduction spiritualities," in C. Partridge (ed.), *UFO Religions*, London: Routledge, 3–42.

——(2004) *The Re-Enchantment of the West: Alternative Spiritualities, Sacralization, Popular Culture and Occulture*, vol. 1, London: T & T Clark International.

——(2006a) "The spiritual and the revolutionary: alternative spirituality, British free festivals and the emergence of rave culture," *Culture and Religion* 7, 1: 41–60.

——(2006b) *The Re-Enchantment of the West: Alternative Spiritualities, Sacralization, Popular Culture and Occulture*, vol. 2, London: T & T Clark International.

——(2010) *Dub in Babylon: Understanding the Evolution and Significance of Dub Reggae in Jamaica and Britain from King Tubby to Post-punk*, London: Equinox Publishing Limited.

Pini, M. (2001) *Club Cultures and Female Subjectivity: The Move from Home to House*, Hampshire, UK: Palgrave Macmillan.

Possamai, A. (ed.) (2012) *Handbook of Hyper-real Religions*, Leiden: Brill.

Rill, B. (2006) "Rave, communitas, and embodied idealism," *Music Therapy Today* 7, 3: 648–61.

Rodgers, T. (2003) "On the process and aesthetics of sampling in electronic music production," *Organised Sound* 8, 3: 313–20.

Roeland, J., S. Aupers, and D. Houtman (2012) "Fantasy, conspiracy and the romantic legacy: Max Weber and the spirit of contemporary popular culture," in A. Possamai (ed.), *Handbook of Hyper-real Religions*, Leiden: Brill, 401–22.

Rom, T. and P. Querner (2011) *Goa: 20 Years of Psychedelic Trance*, Solothurn (Switzerland): Nachtschatten Verlag.

Rose, T. (1994) *Black Noise: Rap Music and Black Culture in Contemporary America*, Middletown, CT: Wesleyan University Press.

Roszak, T. (1995) *The Making of a Counter Culture*, Berkeley, CA: University of California Press.

Sai-Chun Lau, S. (2006) "Churched Ibiza: evangelical Christianity and club culture," *Culture and Religion* 7, 1: 77–92.

Spurgeon, R. (n.d.) "Rave—the awakening." Online. Available: www.rave-theawakening.com (accessed 15 September 2012).

St John, G. (ed.) (2004a) *Rave Culture and Religion*, London: Routledge.

——(2004b) "Techno millennium: dance, ecology and future primitives," in G. St John (ed.) *Rave Culture and Religion*, London: Routledge, 213–35.

——(2006) "Electronic dance music culture and religion: an overview," Culture and Religion 7, 1: 1–26.

——(2008) "Trance tribes and dance vibes: Victor Turner and trance dance culture," in G. St John (ed.), *Victor Turner and Contemporary Cultural Performance*, New York: Berghahn, 149–73.

——(2009) *Technomad: Global Raving Countercultures*, London: Equinox.

——(2010) "Making a noise—making a difference: techno-punk and terra-ism," *Dancecult: Journal of Electronic Dance Music Culture* 1, 2: 1–28.

——(2011) "DJ Goa Gil: kalifornian exile, dark yogi and dreaded anomaly," *Dancecult: Journal of Electronic Dance Music Culture* 3, 1: 97–128.

——(2012a) *Global Tribe: Technology, Spirituality and Psytrance*, Sheffield: Equinox.

——(2012b) "Freak media: vibe tribes, sampledelic outlaws and Israeli psytrance," *Continuum: Journal of Media and Cultural Studies* 26, 3: 437–47.

——(2013) "Indian spirit: Amerindians and the techno-tribes of Psytrance," in J. Mackay and D. Stirrup (eds), *Tribal Fantasies: Native Americans in the European Imagination, 1900–Present*, New York: Palgrave Macmillan, 173–95.

——(2014a) "Begoggled in the theater of awe: electronic dance music culture at Burning Man," in S. Krukowski (ed.), *Playa Dust: Collected Stories from Burning Man*, London: Black Dog Publishing, 144–59.

——(2014b) "Goatrance travellers: psytrance and its seasoned progeny," in S. Krüger and R. Trandafoiu (eds), *The Globalization of Musics in Transit: Musical Migration and Tourism*, New York: Routledge, 160–82.

Sylvan, R. (2002) *Traces of the Spirit: The Religious Dimensions of Popular Music*, New York: New York University Press.

——(2005) *Trance Formation: The Spiritual and Religious Dimensions of Global Rave Culture*, New York: Routledge.

Takahashi, M. (2004) "The 'natural high': altered states, flashbacks and neural tuning at raves," in G. St John (ed.), *Rave Culture and Religion*, London: Routledge, 145–64.

——(2005) "Spirituality through the science of sound: the DJ as technoshaman in rave culture," in M.J. Gilmour (ed.), *Call Me the Seeker: Listening to Religion in Popular Music*, New York: Continuum, 239–66.

Takahashi, M., and T. Olaveson (2003) "Music, dance and raving bodies: raving as spirituality in the central Canadian rave scene," *Journal of Ritual Studies* 17, 2: 72–96.

Taylor, B. (2009) *Dark Green Religion: Nature Spirituality and the Planetary Future*, Berkeley, CA: University of California Press.

Taylor, T.D. (2001) *Strange Sounds: Music, Technology and Culture*, New York: Routledge.

Théberge, P. (1997) *Any Sound You Can Imagine: Making Music/Consuming Technology*, Middletown, CT: Wesleyan University Press.

Thornton, S. (1996) *Club Cultures: Music, Media and Subcultural Capital*, Cambridge: Polity.

Till, R. (2006) "The nine o'clock service: mixing club culture and postmodern Christianity," *Culture and Religion* 7, 1: 93–110.

Tramacchi, D. (2000) "Field tripping: psychedelic communitas and ritual in the Australian bush," *Journal of Contemporary Religion* 15, 2: 201–13.

——(2006) "Vapours and visions: religious dimensions of DMT use," unpublished thesis, University of Queensland.

Turner, E. (2012) *Communitas: The Anthropology of Collective Joy*, New York: Palgrave.

Turner, V. (1982) *From Ritual to Theatre: The Human Seriousness of Play*, New York: PAJ Publications.

Tythacott, L. (2003) Surrealism and the Exotic, New York: Routledge.

van Veen, t. c. (ed.) (2013) "Vessels of transfer: allegories of afrofuturism in Jeff Mills and Janelle Monáe," *Dancecult: Journal of Electronic Dance Music Culture* 5, 2: 7–41.

Young, R. (ed.) (2002) *Undercurrents: The Hidden Wiring of Modern Music*, New York: Continuum.

Zandbergen, A.D. (2011) "New Edge: Technology and Spirituality in the San Francisco Bay Area." PhD Dissertation. Leiden University.

Discography

Chi-A.D. 1999. *Anno Domini*. Velvet Inc. CD, Album: NTD 92511–22.

Cosmosis. 2002. *Contact*. Transient Records. CD, Album: TRANR640CD.

——2009. *Fumbling for the Funky Frequency*. Holophonic Records. CD, Album: HOLO 606.

Dark Soho. 2000. *Sun Spot*. Sphere Records. CD, Album: SPHCD004.

Infinity Project, The. 1993. *Time and Space*. Dragonfly Records. Vinyl, 12-inch, EP, White Label: BFLT 9.

——1995. *Mystical Experiences*. Blue Room Released. CD, Album: BR005CD.

Juno Reactor. 1993. *Transmissions*. NovaMute. CD, Album: NoMu 24 CD.

KLF, The. 1990. *What Time Is Love?* (Live at Trancecentral). KLF Communications. Vinyl, 12-inch, 45 RPM: KLF 004 X.

Merkaba. 2011. *Rediscovery*. FLAC Album. Not on label.

Monkey Machine. 2011. *Closed Caption Radio*. Altar Records. CD, Album: ARCDAP02.

Ovnimoon. 2011. *Magnetic Portal*. Ovnimoon Records. CD, Album: OVNICD014.

Re:Actor. 2010. ... *Soulscript* ... Digital Reality. CD, Album: DRRCD003.

Scatterbrain. 2003. *Infernal Angel*. Digital Psionics. CD, Album: DPSICD07.

SFX. 1998. *SFX: The Unreleased Tracks—89–94*. Phonokol, CD, Album: 21152.

Shpongle. 2005. *Nothing Lasts ... But Nothing Is Lost*. Twisted Records, CD, Album: TWSCD28.

Transwave. 1995. *Hypnorhythm*. Matsuri. Vinyl, 12-inch, EP: MP08.

Xenomorph. 1998. *Cassandra's Nightmare*. Koyote. CD, Album: KRCD007.

Various. *Contagion Vol. 1*. 2008. Dead Tree Productions. File FLAC (Comp): DTP002.

Various. *Deep Trance and Ritual Beats*. 1995. Return to the Source. CD (Comp): RTTSCD1.

Various. *Goa Trance Volume Nineteen*. 2012. Compiled by DJ Tulla. Yellow Sunshine Explosion. CD (Comp): MillYSE 277-CD.

Various. *Neighbourhood*, MIDIJUM Records. CD (Comp): MD CD 002.

Various. *Psytisfaction*. 2004. Phonokol. CD (Comp): 22992.

Filmography

Barker, Clive. 1987. *Hellraiser*. Cinemarque Entertainment BV.

Besson, Luc. 1997. *The Fifth Element*. Gaumont.

Blatty, William Peter. 1990. *Exorcist III*. Morgan Creek Productions.

Cameron, James. 1986. *Aliens*. 20th Century Fox.

Carpenter, John. 1994. *In the Mouth of Madness*. New Line Cinema.

Goeijers, Carin. 2006. *God Is My DJ*.

Harrison, Greg. 2000. *Groove*. 415 Productions, Groove LLC.

Kubric, Stanley. 1968. *2001: A Space Odyssey*. MGM, Stanley Kubrick Productions.

Linklater, Richard. 2001. *Waking Life*. Fox Searchlight.

Lynch, David. 1984. *Dune*. De Laurentis.

Rood, Billy, and Torsten Klimmer. 2002. *Liquid Crystal Vision*. US.

Sagan, Carl. 1980. *Cosmos: A Personal Voyage*. KCET, Carl Sagan Productions, BBC.

Short, James. 2006. *Welcome to Wonderland*. Short Documentaries.

Wachowski, Andy, and Lana Wachowski. 1999. *The Matrix*. Warner Bros., Silver Pictures Production.

Waggner, George. 1941. *The Wolf Man*. Universal Pictures.

19
SPORT

Jeffrey Scholes

Sport occupies a vast expanse in today's popular culture landscape. Four of the top five most-watched programs in the history of American television are sporting events (Eames 2012). The scandals of Tiger Woods and Lance Armstrong lead the national nightly news. Yet rarely do people link sport and religion. But from the ancient Olympic games to the recent prayer-filled rituals of football player Tim Tebow, a relationship between the two most certainly exists. The intersection of religion and sport, though, is a strange one—what could athletic activity possibly have to do with spiritual matters? One might argue that sport has been thoroughly secularized; religion still deals with sacred things. It is therefore not surprising that statements about a relationship between religion and sport generate more questions than they do answers: "Are Sports Good for the Soul?"; "Does God Care Who Wins the Super Bowl?"[1] But another set of questions emerges: How does religion relate to sport, if at all? Is sport a religion, or does the one have nothing to do with the other? And if there is a connection, what might it tell us about how they intersect as an expression of popular culture?

Sampling from the wide range in recent scholarship, one can discern a variety of interpretive models used in the analysis of religion and sport: sport enacts religious myths on a secular stage; sport is a transmitter of religious values and/or an expression of divine will; or sport uniquely reveals divine will, stages miracles, and sanctifies certain athletes who perform at the highest levels. Yet most of them avoid the production of a blended religion and sport phenomenon in (primarily American) culture.

Religion and sport: theoretical approaches

In this chapter, we will examine one particular site where the sacred is produced in sport: the stadium. It is impossible to separate the modern stadium from the "profane" world of commerce, meaning that any discussion of religion and sport, especially as it is situated in a stadium or arena, must acknowledge the interdependence of sacred and profane culture-making processes. First, we shall survey alternative ways of interpreting the relationship between religion and sport. One may investigate the relationship's *instrumentality*, or how they use each other for their own purposes; or one may investigate the relationship's *equality*, in which sport is identified as a religion, or as having religious characteristics. Both assume a separation that presumes that sport is no longer a religious ritual but has become secularized (Guttmann 1978: 26). Along with such social institutions as the state, work, education, science, and others, sport can be performed without recourse to religion to legitimize it.

The instrumental model flows in two directions: religion using sports and sports using religion. Perhaps one of the most well-known examples of religion using sports in Christianity comes from St. Paul's first letter to the Corinthians, in the New Testament:

> Do you not know that in a race the runners all compete, but only one receives the prize? Run in such a way that you may win it. Athletes exercise self-control in all things; they do it to receive a perishable wreath, but we an imperishable one. So I do not run aimlessly, nor do I box as though beating the air; but I punish my body and enslave it, so that after proclaiming to others I myself should not be disqualified.
>
> (1 Corinthians 9:24–27, NRSV)

Here, Paul uses the sports metaphor of the foot race to transmit a religious truth. Notice, though, that Paul does not equate the race and the spiritual journey—the race for eternal rewards is more important than the one for a laurel.

Sport-as-instrument to reveal religious truths is similarly displayed by the early twentieth-century evangelist Billy Sunday, who would sometimes wear his professional baseball uniform to preach. Muscular Christianity—an Anglo-American Protestant movement with roots in the late 1890s (see Putney 2001)—portrayed Jesus as a strong, athletic man, and athleticism became essential to sanctification for those churches that preached this Christology. Movies like *Chariots of Fire* (1981)—in which Muscular Christianity is explored—and organizations such as the Fellowship of Christian Athletes and Promise Keepers—based upon this philosophy—make explicit the connection between faith and athletic prowess. Some athletes readily appropriate the image of Jesus as a strong, macho warrior, drawing on the principles of Muscular Christianity. As Robert Higgs (1995: 311) notes, "Just as religion has been warped to justify sports, so sports have been warped to assist in preparation for war and the waging of it, as a technique in the training of soldiers but mainly as a reinforcing symbol of manliness and knighthood." Muscular Christianity arose (in late nineteenth-century Britain and the United States) to combat the image of the meek, feminized boy raised in the church to sing hymns, also emphasizing sport's character-building aspects: work hard, follow the rules, and respect your opponent.

Many contemporary athletes—such as Tim Tebow, Albert Pujols, or Jeremy Lin—link their performance to "the Glory of Christ," meaning that their faith gives them the strength to compete not just to the best of their ability, but in ways that reflect positively on their religious beliefs. But there is presently the risk of believing that, somehow, the Christian savior is in any way specifically interested in the exploits of one player or team. Shirl Hoffman (2010: 162) is highly critical of these notions of "Christ as brawny jock, impelled by self-interest and team spirit, capable of shutting down feelings for others when the whistle blows, loving it when he comes out ahead of others," and identifies the use of "a meek and gentle Jesus whose mission exemplified servanthood, peace, and reconciliation," as a form of what theologian H. Richard Niebuhr called "personifications of abstractions," in this case an "unlikely model" for modern, often violent athletes.

Others use religion in ways that seem less theologically suspect, and do not seem to threaten core religious principles. In her "Church of Baseball" monologue in the movie *Bull Durham* (dir. Ron Shelton, 1988), Annie Savoy (Susan Sarandon) expressed a need for "church" more than for baseball, but it is baseball that she needs to be her church.[2] Today, "Faith Night" transforms some Major League ballparks into makeshift churches after the game, with players giving testimony and fans wishing to stick around singing praise songs. Frank Deford (1976: 59) derisively calls the practice of using famous sports figures to promote and sell religion "Sportianity." Churches and para-church organizations that exploit the fame of Christian athletes and coaches to spread the Gospel are, according to Deford, debasing both religion and sports. "Sport is the converse of religion," he writes, hence the latter should not misuse the former in order to convey its truths.

In all of these examples, sport is needed but is clearly in the service of religion. This subordination is similarly reflected in the work of scholars who claim that, despite appearances, sport embodies deep religious values and principles. From a theological point of view, Greg Smith (2010) argues that athletic ability is a gift from God, and cites biblical passages as proof of the theological import of sports. Here, sport becomes a kind of litmus test that reveals who is squandering their talent, as well as a lens into the nature of divine gifts (a sentiment recently expressed by professional football player Tim Tebow [Tebow and Whitaker 2011: 173]). From a sociological perspective, D. Stanley Eitzen and George H. Sage (1978: 127) and Steven J. Overman (2011) contend that modern sport draws on the legacy of a Calvinist work ethic, and mirrors Protestant values. Others argue that the principles that undergird the games themselves—and the way they are played—are religious principles that sport happens to express well.

By contrast, when sport uses religion, religion justifies, legitimates, clarifies, or promotes sport in some way. The most direct (perhaps theologically crass) way of expressing this type of relationship is to claim that God (or a supernatural force) acts to guide the outcome of sporting events. When an athlete credits God for a win or, more controversially, for guiding a ball into the basket, the supernatural is clearly being exploited to explain natural events. Less crass is the use of superstition and belief in curses to assist with performance or explain events on the field. It seems less crass because the athlete's admission of ritual behavior that is superstitious, such as baseball's Wade Boggs's habit of eating chicken before every game, is usually stated tongue-in-cheek. Michael Jordan would no doubt minimize the significance of wearing his college uniform shorts under his professional uniform—but he wore them just in case (Murphy n.d.). The superstitious rituals performed in the movie *Major League* (1989) are contrasted with the more traditional ways of getting religion involved in sport, such as prayer—even though the superstitions seemed to produce better results. Religion is often employed to explain an unlikely series of events, as with the "Curse of the Billy Goat," which some claim is the cause of the 100-year championship drought endured by the Chicago Cubs (see Juffer 2006: 292–93). Not unlike crediting God for a Super Bowl win, superstitions and curses are based on the logic that spiritual forces either explain or legitimate action on the field, even though the degree of belief in supernatural intervention may vary.

Novels such as *A River Runs Through It* (Maclean 1976) or *The Brothers K* (Duncan 1992), and movies such as *The Natural* (1984) or *Angels in the Outfield* (1994) cloak sport with a religious aura that endows athletic activity and the fans' experiences with metaphysical import. Underlying the "sports using religion" model is an acknowledgment that sport can produce experiences of transcendence that often defy ordinary explanation. Rather than reducing these experiences to material causation, religion furnishes sport with a vocabulary that may correspond more closely with the emotions felt. In similar fashion, religious terms, themes, and stories are often used in sports discourse. From Al Michaels's famous exclamation at the end of the improbable American victory over the Soviets in the 1980 Olympic hockey semifinals—"Do you believe in miracles?" (see Posnanski 2010)—to the Chicago White Sox use of the band Journey's hit, "Don't Stop Believin'" (1981) to motivate their World Series run in 2004 (Merkin 2005), religion helps in ways that the X's and O's of game planning cannot. Lance Armstrong, according to most pundits, was seeking redemption with his *mea culpa* to Oprah Winfrey regarding his use of performance enhancing drugs (see Day 2013). Trips to Lambeau Field in Green Bay, Wisconsin, or to the baseball Hall of Fame in Cooperstown, New York, are frequently thought of as pilgrimages by the "pilgrims" who go there (see Gammon 2004). On the level of discourse, religious concepts are needed to convey a seriousness with which we approach and think about our sports.

The second general way that religion and sports are related is in their equation. Sport may function like religion, but rarely is religion equated to sport—usually the comparison is made in the other direction. Robert Bellah's foundational 1967 essay on civil religion enabled comparisons of religion to responses to powerful symbols, including sport. For Bellah, many beliefs held by citizens about their nation are bolstered by powerful symbols, are a bonding agent for a national consciousness, and therefore function as a type of religious belief without resorting to a church for support. For Craig A. Forney (2007: 14–18), the development of football, baseball, and basketball dovetailed with national cultural trends in the twentieth century to form their own kind of civil religion in the United States. Michael Novak takes it a step farther and claims that sport is a religion because of what it draws out of our human nature:

> sports flow outward into action from a deep natural impulse that is radically religious: an impulse of freedom, respect for ritual limits, a zest for symbolic meaning, and a longing for perfection. The athlete may of course be pagan, but sports are, as it were, natural religions.
>
> (Novak 1976: 19)

Fans may experience sport as a natural religion too, as exemplified in *Field of Dreams* (1989), in which Roy Kinsella hears voices and feels compelled to carve a baseball diamond out of his Iowa cornfield.[3]

Unlike Novak, James Mathisen (1992: 19) refuses to reduce what he holds to be the religious component of sport to mere human instinct, but instead sees it as an institution that organically emerges from the grass roots of a community, and which is able to "provide social integration and the legitimation of American values." In other words, sport is a folk religion for Mathisen that

> encapsulates, magnifies, and reflects back to us the primary beliefs and norms of the surrounding American culture ... . At the same time, sport raises up particular values and myths of its own and projects them onto the culture with a normative certitude. It is this authority that emphatically characterizes sport as a folk religion.
>
> (ibid.: 22)

Lastly, Charles Prebish (1993: 68–69) moves beyond a functional equating of religion and sport by boldly claiming that sport is a religion in every sense of the word. Not only are rituals, saints, and worship to be found unadulterated in sports, but ultimate reality can be experienced through it. He replaces functional similarity with substantive identity.

Both models of framing religion and sport—the instrumental and the equation—are important tools for understanding their relationship. Yet often, these models assume a static relationship between religion and sport; they may individually undergo change, but the basic contours of their relationship do not. But what if that which we consider "religion" were produced or destroyed at a secular site, through secular means? Might this not make the two more dependent than even the instrumental model admits? Spaces often maintain a tenuous hold on their sacredness, especially when it has been humanly constructed; they depend on the production and destruction of the sacred. When that space is operating in a secular setting, a new way of understanding the relationship between the sacred and the secular presents itself.

Production of the sacred in the stadium

One site of cultural production that brings religion and sports together is the sports stadium, which may be endowed with ethereal qualities. For example, in his effort to equate religion and sports, Prebish compares the stadium to the "traditional house of worship," describing it as

> set apart from the ordinary, profane world. Consequently, a series of rituals is required as one crosses the threshold, the boundary between chaos and cosmos, for purification is required of all entrants to the consecrated place ... . What we are indicating here is that the sport structure, no less than the traditional religious edifice, is infused with sacredness as a result of its location as the meeting point between earth and heaven, the location from which the experience of ultimacy becomes more readily accessible.
>
> (Prebish 1993: 73)

While Prebish's model suggests that the stadium is "infused with sacredness,"— suggesting a kind of static, divinely sanctioned status—it is imperative to explore the way in which the stadiums themselves help produce as well as destroy the sacred. For all who participate, the experience of the sacred (or the profane) is generated through the geography of the stadium, the social relations that manifest there, and the specific activities taking place within it. So while the instrumental and equality models demonstrate how religion and sport relate, a closer examination of their means of production in culture—both through human agency and the human response to external forces—will necessarily ground these models.

American sports stadiums stick out, attract attention, and have the power to alter cityscapes like few other edifices—the kind of physical power that most modern churches can only dream about. In addition, sports stadiums provoke intense emotions and religious devotion as much as a childhood home or church (Trujillo and Krizek 1994: 315–18). There are also visual aspects of a stadium reminiscent of religious spaces: the pitcher's mound in the center of a baseball diamond may remind one of Black Elk's mountain lookout, while the bronze busts of players on display at the National Football League (NFL) Hall of Fame might be seen to resemble the saints frozen in stained glass illuminating many Catholic churches, or their statues populating church grounds. Many stadiums themselves resemble religious institutions: Fenway Park in Boston sneaks up on you, and then overwhelms you like a neighborhood temple, while Cowboys Stadium in Arlington, Texas, glistens in the sun like Robert Schuller's former headquarters, the Crystal Cathedral (now owned by the Catholic diocese of Orange County, California). Yet appearance alone does not endow buildings with sacredness; skyscrapers inspire awe, too. Making connections between the look of religion and of sports, while important observations they may be, does not actually move us closer to an understanding of how sports stadiums become sacred spaces.

From the father of sociology Emile Durkheim to the dean of the history of religions Mircea Eliade, the sacred has been considered nothing if it was not set apart from the profane and ordinary in some way. The difference between the two is "absolute," they "are different in kind," and "have nothing in common" (Durkheim 1995: 36). Yet this approach to the relationship between the sacred and the profane often artificially demarcates the two with clean, thick lines. Scholars David Chidester and Edward Linenthal (1995) suggest that the conversation should focus on the "production of the sacred," and rely on anthropologist Arnold van Gennep's (1961: 12) image of "the pivoting of the sacred" to argue that sacredness is an attribute of the productive process, and not an absolute that is inherently attached to things, including spaces. This means that the concept of "the sacred" is fluid and applicable to a variety of spaces; it can flow into a space as quickly as it can flow out (or become profane). As Jonathan Z. Smith concludes, "there is nothing that is inherently or essentially … sacred or profane. There are situational or relational categories, mobile boundaries which shift according to the map being employed" (1978: 291).

The means by which the "set-apartness" of sacred spaces is produced—and the map employed to track its production—is crucial to understanding its sacredness. In the case of sports stadiums, from the moment that an enterprising businessman saw that people wanted to watch games played in public parks, fields became enclosed and admission tickets were sold. Sociologist John Bale highlights three historical stages of what he calls "territorialization" that set the sports stadium apart: first, "playing space" is "separated from spectating space so that a segmented but mono-cultural sport-place was established"; second, the crowd is "segmented"; and third, sport is separated "from non-sportive space by the establishment of 'sport estates' or specialized sport zones in particular parts of the city." Today, new stadiums built in urban environments often include surrounding developments (both commercial and residential) to create a larger "sport estate" (Bale 1994: 74), suggesting that the line between the stadium and the non-stadium is less distinct today than it was when stadiums were built without these considerations. Bale is quick to point out that all three stages of territorialization are the result of the exertion of power by certain groups of people over other groups, noting that "the growth of commerce in the late eighteenth and nineteenth centuries led to restrictions on public access to places like the commons and the streets," linking the stadium inextricably with the mechanisms of capitalism (1993: 123–24).

The ability of a stadium to convey the sacred and generate human experience with the sacred cannot simply be reduced to the financial interest in constructing the building. Chidester and Linenthal (1995: 9–16) highlight the three levels on which space becomes sacred. First, sacred space must be ritual space, a place where actions are endowed with extra significance, performed routinely, and in this specific space. Second, sacred space must be significant space, in that it focuses attention on what it means to be a human being. Third, sacred space must be contested space, where the question of ownership over meaning, capital, and status is heightened, revealing both the sacredness of the battle and the stakes for winning it.

While a complete analysis of the relationship between religion and sport would also include the players' experiences, the neighborhood ballpark, and non-American sports, in the following analysis we will focus on the fans' experience in major American sports stadiums, which can serve as a significant lens through which to examine the relationship between religion and sport, and the way that the sacred is produced there.

Ritual space

For Chidester and Linenthal, sacred space is a ritual space or "a location for for-malized, repeatable symbolic performances" (1995: 9). Sacred space does not merely provide the environment for any repetitious action. Action in a sacred space must, by its performance, represent and fulfill a function that transcends the physical action itself. Sacred spaces are able to endow ritual behavior with this kind of sig-nificance, in part, by virtue of the separation of the space from ordinary, mundane space that surrounds it. Cross the threshold into one of these spaces, and rituals can become "extra-ordinary." Chidester and Linenthal (1995: 9) add that the ordinary/ extraordinary binary expresses a kind of "is/ought" dynamic. In a sacred space, rituals "act out and embody perfectly the way things 'ought to be,'" and are hence always in tension with the way things are. It is for this reason that the role that rituals play in the production and maintenance of sacred space is "in conscious ten-sion with the way things are normally perceived to be in the ordinary world." Sacred spaces insulate, thereby generating symbolic acts while in a dialectical relationship with the ordinary ("real") world that is outside the space.

Sociologist Randall Collins (2004: 48) identifies four elements needed for what he calls an "interaction ritual" to result in the kind of collective effervescence that Durkheim associates with the sacred. First, two or more people share the same physical space, whether they are aware of it or not. Second, boundaries are maintained preventing outsiders from participating. Third, the group focuses its attention on a common object or activity, and by communicating this focus to each other become mutually aware of each other's focus of attention. And fourth, they "share a common mood or emotional experience." Marci Cottingham (2012: 176) has no problem finding all four elements among Pittsburgh Steelers fans at a home game in 2008. Interestingly, she finds that some of the same rituals performed in the stadium spilled out into the tailgating section in the parking lot and into local sports bars, though they were more "muted and uncoordinated" (ibid.). The power of the stadium extends into other venues and even into homes, but is diminished when it is appropriated anywhere but inside the stadium.

The rituals that take place in stadiums are either prescribed, obligatory, conspicuous, and long-standing rituals or subtle and situational rituals in which not all participants partake. Among the former, perhaps the singing of the national anthem before a game is the ritual most common to all American sports, and perfunctorily performed in most stadiums. In addition, rituals such as the "seventh-inning stretch" (baseball), the "wave" (football), and attempts by basketball fans to distract an opposing player shooting free throws are widely performed by fans across the country.

There are also team-bound rituals designed to mark and protect home territory. The Denver Broncos' fans yell "Incomplete!" after each missed pass thrown by the opposition (see Adams 2008). Some of the Detroit Red Wings' fans throw dead octopi on the ice during the playoffs (see Bradsher 1996). Boston Red Sox fans sing Neil Diamond's "Sweet Caroline" in the middle of the eighth inning (see Vosk 2005). And "Cameron Crazies"—fans sitting in the student section of the Duke University Cameron Indoor Stadium—shout "whoosh" after their player makes a free throw (see Heinen 1995). At Texas A&M University's Kyle Field, there is an elaborate system of call-and-response, practiced at midnight before each football game, involving yell leaders and fans, and intended to support the Aggies on the field while intimidating the opposition. Each class has its own yell to follow the one screamed by all (Texas A&M University 2013).

The rituals are grounded in the spatial arrangement of the stadium that partitions off areas for home fans, visiting fans, yell leaders, students, and the players, especially at college events. This, in turn, helps release latent territorial instincts (which could otherwise manifest in violence, and at times do) through sublimation. Home fans mimic players: "This is our house," they claim, creating a kind of united front against threats. The lines separating fans economically, racially, ethnically, or by gender outside the stadium are temporarily blurred in this communal act of solidarity. Likewise, spatial distance between like-minded fans in the stadium is narrowed—the fan in the upper level yells the same cheer at the same time as the fan in the luxury box. Other rituals symbolically attach fan to player when vocal chants are directed to the field, breaching the otherwise sacrosanct white lines separating the action on the field from the stands. As with the fleeting but profound unity experienced by disparate fans through common rituals, the chasm between fan and player is crossed through supportive and ritualistic cheers (and boos).

Through ritual behavior, the sports stadium furnishes the space for fans to lay claim to territory, though certainly not in a proprietary sense—a reality made abundantly clear as they are forced to exit at the game's conclusion. The unity experienced by fans—whether by all in such rituals as the national anthem or by respective teams through representative cheers—stands in marked contrast to the disunion that exists outside the stadium, conveying a utopic way things "ought to be" in contrast to the way things actually are in the economic and social hierarchy that describes much of ordinary life. Fan rituals symbolize and act out an ideal that, while only temporarily realized, helps produce a collective sense of the sacred by way of contrast to the ordinary world on the outside.

Significant space

For Chidester and Linenthal (1995: 12), sacred space is significant because it "focuses crucial questions about what it means to be a human being in a meaningful world." In other words, a sacred space heightens our attention to a worldview even as that worldview is subject to interpretation. Specifically, Chidester and Linenthal highlight two aspects of a worldview grounded by sacred space: the classification of persons, and general orientations in space and time. Sacred space becomes significant space when it is able to situate entrants in a way that foregrounds questions about classification and orientation as well as provides provisional, but no less important, answers to those questions.

As noted above, people in stadiums are distinguished in three ways: by role (fans versus players), by team allegiance, and by economics. While rituals can demarcate as well as blur these classifications, the structural features of many sports stadiums serve to magnify their significance, and in so doing, forge identities based on the status assigned to the space. Discussing religion and boundaries, Catherine Albanese notes that

> [b]y searching for identity and finding it, individuals metaphorically establish inner boundaries, discover through testing who they are not, and begin to affirm who they are. In the process, each individual finds that these personal boundaries overlap with those of others, so that there can be a free process of exchange. In other words, a person locates those who occupy the same inner territory and, because of the shared internal space, feels at one with them and their concerns. This is the meaning of identification with others.
> (Albanese 1992: 5–6)

Team loyalty is the most obvious area of overlap between fans that may share nothing else; the stadium most easily puts people into exchanges based on a similar "inner territory" occupied by the same team spirit.

This shared interest may facilitate exchanges between people of different social classes. Sociologist Nick Trujillo (1994: 312) tells a story of Jimmy and Bobbie Jo

Fowler, long-time fans of the Texas Rangers baseball team, who, because of their limited funds, sat in some of the worst seats in the park. Trujillo recounts how Jimmy proudly recalled that the general manager of the Rangers once trekked up into the stands to thank them for their support, and even wrote Jimmy a get-well letter during a hospital stay (Trujillo and Krizek 1994: 312). This exchange between "this blue-collar couple" and the white-collar administration, unlikely as it would be absent the relationship forged in the stadium, is initiated by the team's general manager, who crossed a boundary to reach out. Did a connection to the team bind them together, or did the general manager simply want the couple to buy season tickets at the new stadium about to be built? In either case, it is the stadium that facilitated such boundary crossings.

Stadiums also reinforce boundaries based on team allegiance, thus brokering exchanges of an altogether different variety. In college sports, "visiting" fans usually sit in a designated block in a less-than-desired section of the stadium or arena, and team colors worn by fans help identify visually the "home" and "visiting" blocks. In this way, the stadium quickly focuses on the question of identity: "protector" or "invader." One's identity will be, in this respect, determined by the results on the field, court, or rink, but until that point one's identity is dictated, in part, by fan seating distribution. When college games are played at neutral sites, such as the "Red River rivalry" between the universities of Texas and Oklahoma (played at the Cotton Bowl in Dallas, Texas), such demarcation is visibly split down the middle, with one half of the stadium adorned in burnt orange and the other in crimson red (see Betsill 2012; Carlton 2012). "Neutrality" here is determined by the fact that Dallas is almost exactly equidistant from both universities. No "home field advantage" means that the contested element of sacred space is removed, making the contest among fans and players particularly acute, as can be seen in downtown Dallas the night before the game (for example, see Ricciardi 2012).

At professional sporting events, fans are not usually so obviously segregated. Unlike college games where institutional rules generally dictate who sits where, in the professional venue the market assigns seats. This means that the visiting fans rarely sit in a large block, but are dispersed throughout. Lacking the protection afforded a large, cohesive group, visiting fans must either amplify their fan-ship (like a peacock in danger) or blend in with the home fans and cheer privately (like a chameleon).

And when the cost of a ticket determines seating, classification runs largely along economic lines. The most expensive tickets—whether season tickets or tickets for a single game—are closest to the court/rink, are behind home plate, or are at mid-field. Fans can certainly camouflage their real wealth in the stadium; fans often spend beyond their means, and season ticket holders with good seats often sell them for individual games to make up for the exorbitant cost. Similar class distinctions are visible elsewhere—on airplanes, for example, or in nightclubs—but with all of the fans watching the same action and cheering in unison, distinctions such as these may be briefly obscured.

The location of luxury boxes relative to the rest of a stadium's seats is more difficult to disguise. Here, spectators are enclosed in glass and have optimum views of the action, getting their food and drinks delivered to them while perched above fans in the stands. Technically, those enjoying the game from one of these boxes are in the stadium, but they occupy a separate territory within the building that has been carved out and rented at a premium. Some team owners sit in a box, some sit in the stands; both express a relationship with fans that relates back to the fan's self-identification, now including notions of whether "my owner" (and hence, "my team") is "one of the people" or not.

Interestingly, many teams (half of all NFL teams and an increasing number of teams in other sports; see Kaszuba 2012) are striking a middle ground between the luxury box and the seat in the stands. Such teams offer "personal seat licenses" (PSLs) which generate millions of dollars for the team, but prevent anyone but the very wealthy from holding season tickets. The purchase of a PSL gives the seat owner the opportunity to purchase a ticket (for that seat) for any event in the stadium, including (but not limited to) season tickets for the team that plays there. The annual cost of a PSL varies from stadium to stadium, but at Cowboys Stadium, which hosts big boxing matches, concerts, and the Super Bowl (in 2010), they can cost up to $150,000, an amount that even the fan who can afford season tickets might find prohibitive. *New York Times* reporter Toni Monkovic (2008) identified a New York Giants football fan (whose family had held season tickets since 1961) who earned "a very average salary" but would now have to pay what he estimated to be "about a third of his salary." Noted another fan "I think it's a knock on the true fan." So constructed, the stadium begins to resemble a neighborhood where some rent houses and some buy. The indicators dividing the PSL owners, the "mere" season ticket holders who attend all the games, and the single-ticket buyer may not be as obvious to see as the differentiation created by the luxury box, but stadiums are slowly dividing classes on a more permanent, yet subtle economic basis.

The economics of the stands notwithstanding, perhaps the most significant dividing line in a stadium is the white line separating fans from the players. Fans are positioned to center their attention on the players, but players need not reciprocate. "Look but don't touch" is the intractable rule. On the occasion that a fan runs onto the field, an unwritten rule permits a player to do almost anything in his or her power to subdue the fan, including the use of excessive force. After a father and son duo ran onto the field and attacked the Kansas City Royals baseball team coach, not a single team member—who kicked and punched them in response—was arrested, or even criticized (see SI.com 2002). Interestingly, different sports have different attitudes about the line, and different ways of enforcing its integrity. The Green Bay Packers football team (and the referees) allows a player to jump into the stands after scoring a touchdown, though only after the play is over (see Bondy 2012). The Dallas Cowboys installed a "players' tunnel" that connects the locker room to the field, enabling fans to line the path and reach out to touch the players as they pass by.

Baseball stadiums define the boundaries between fans and players differently, with an ambiguous space between them limited by how far a player can reach (or jump) to catch a ball. In this space—at least according to the rules—the authority of the fan is equal to that of the player; a fuzzy area rather than a clear white line, where each can reach for the ball. This liminal space is, according to Victor Turner (1997: 95), "neither here nor there," but is "betwixt and between the positions assigned and arrayed by law, custom, convention, and ceremonial." The ambiguity can be a space of progress (as in a rite of passage), but it is, by definition, a dangerous place, as Chicago Cubs fan Steve Bartman learned when he reached for a foul ball while seated in the ambiguous "zone" (see Johnson 2011). Had his action assisted "his" team's efforts, he would have been considered a hero; but his actions interfered with "his" team's progress, and he was roundly criticized for breaching the fan/player barrier.

How does the classification of people in the stadium generate and direct significant religious questions? And what are the questions? In all three social divisions, the sports stadium amplifies the question of identity, in reality and as an ideal. In the stadium, the "home" fan is restricted within the same space as the "visiting" fan, and locked in a kind of struggle. But unlike a physical war, the stadium struggle (usually) ends peacefully. Grievances are aired, territories are staked out, but after the game, these are (usually) put aside. While a stadium is stratified along economic lines, it can also equalize fans, if only for the time spent in the building. And through a process of democratization, the kinds of exchanges to which Albanese refers are made possible with those "who occupy the same inner territory" (Albanese 1992: 6). With the expressed shared purpose of "defending" the stadium, these inner territories overlap. The stadium becomes a sacred space—the sacred is produced in this place—when those entering into these kinds of exchanges, exchanges that normally do not occur in ordinary social life, cross these boundaries and experience a collective effervescence.

Alternatively, the relationship forged between fan and player at a game is one that is characterized by limits. Even though the stadium brings fans into a shared space with their athletic heroes which is not possible while watching on television, there is maintained nonetheless a strict boundary between them. This tension between the closeness to—and yet distance from—that which is ultimately and literally untouchable resembles that experienced by religious believers. Reminiscent of Charles Prebish's conception (noted above), the stadium functions like the "traditional religious edifice," uniquely putting the entrant into relationship with what Rudolph Otto (1958) calls "the Holy": it is fascinating and attractive, and yet simultaneously powerful and dangerous.

The second way that the sacred is produced by way of making a space significant is through the orientation of participants to experiences of time. Sports and the spaces that house them raise temporal awareness by operating asynchronously with the outside world; as Michel Foucault (1986: 26) put it, they "open onto what might be termed … heterochronies." For Foucault, the space "begins to function at full capacity when men arrive at a sort of absolute break with their traditional time." In football, basketball, and hockey, the game's length is of limited duration; in baseball, golf, and tennis, it is virtually limitless; and in swimming and track, the timer is the primary aspect of the drama that unfolds. Those in a stadium who are paying attention to the game operate on "sports time," while "real" time plods on outside the stadium. This stadium "time warp" enables a suspension of flowing, unstoppable (lived) time and invites new, freeing ways to experience the past, present, and future.

Many stadiums house statues of the past greats who played there. Lining some stadium walls are names in "Rings of Honor" (literally signs, banners, plaques, and other memorabilia encircling the stadium), the jerseys of players whose numbers have been permanently "retired," and championship banners. Yankee Stadium contains "Monument Park," a museum just beyond center field enshrining past Yankee greats. Fans who step into the stadium are not only reminded of the past but, because of the game that is about to start, are also encouraged to think about how the past has a bearing on the present (both good and bad).

Beyond historic past and temporal present, time within the stadium (and for most sports) is punctuated, managed, and even slowed down during the game. There are layers of time: internal clocks framed by the main game timer that count down the time needed to take a shot (basketball), initiate a play (football), or sit in the penalty box (hockey). In many sports, time can be stopped with a time out, an injury, a penalty, a "dead" ball (that has gone out of bounds, for example), or at pre-designated breaks in the game. A coach or player who "manages the clock" knows exactly what needs to be accomplished in the time remaining, when to call a time out, and how to run a play. Athletes who are playing at a peak athletic level often experience "time slowing down" (Shainberg 1989). They are moving in regular time, but they feel that they can anticipate future action because it seems like everyone else is in slow motion. In many sports, time is ultimately the master—legendary football coach Vince Lombardi is reported to have said that he never lost a game, he just ran out of time (Lombardi 2001: 235)—but it can be a servant of human agents during a sporting event.

Even in an untimed sport like baseball, this relationship between time and agency is present, but is experienced differently. The pitcher cannot hold the ball for an inordinate amount of time, and the breaks in the game are determined by the inning's end, not by a timer. Theoretically, a baseball game can go on for ever, and one's sense of time has no regular, consistent punctuation; only the passage of innings indicates where (or when) you are in the game. Instead of two "games" (the play on the field and the race against the clock), there is just the one, giving a baseball game a freeing, ethereal, and even eternal feel. As essayist Roger Angell (1987: 25) puts it: "Since baseball time is measured only in outs, all you have to do is succeed utterly; keep hitting, keep the rally alive, and you have defeated time. You remain forever young."

Each inning will end (as will the game), but no clock can predict when that will be. The timeless environment of a baseball game dramatizes the interplay between experiences of the finite and the infinite, mimicking dynamics present in many religious lives. Whether it be binaries of natural/supernatural, flesh/spirit, earth/heaven, body/mind, or material/spiritual, the ballpark contains a similar schema not found in many other locations.

Hence the sports stadium is a sacred space by being a significant space. It is where one's identity can be cast in light of social positioning uniquely established there. And through the alteration of a temporal orientation, everyone in a stadium can challenge measured time that is traditionally beyond manipulation and limited. If religion, as Chidester (2005: 149) has defined it, "is about human identity and orientation, about what it is to be a human person in a human place," then religion is at work in the sports stadium because of its ability to trouble profane, mundane, ordinary experiences and recast them in expansive, yet still human ways.

Contested space

A third quality explicitly involved in the production of sacred space is conflict over space. Just because a space is contested this does not necessarily make it sacred. Battles over where a demarcated space should be, who has access, and what should go on there disclose that such a space is important, whether it is a convenience store in a strip mall or a Wal-Mart in a suburban neighborhood. But contests over sacred space involve a "site of negotiated contests over legitimate ownership of sacred symbols" (Chidester and Linenthal 1995: 15). Ownership—the processes of both acquisition and retention—involves power. But ownership of a publicly accessible sacred space (and its contents) is more ambiguous than that of private spaces, where ownership is unambiguous. As Chidester and Linenthal (ibid.) contend, "since no sacred space is merely 'given' in the world, its ownership will always be at stake. In this respect, a sacred space is not merely discovered, or founded, or constructed; it is claimed, owned, and operated by people advancing specific interests." Who actually owns a space, confounded by questions of who should own that space, characterizes the "contest" that may make space sacred.

What sacred symbols are retained by those who, in a legal sense, have no ownership stake in a stadium? For some, it is the game, and the "home" team, of which the fan is part owner. For others, it is the stadium, at which important family relationships (often a father and son) are grounded, and memories solidified. For yet others, it is the material symbols within the stadium, such as the "Green Monster" (the left field wall, which is high and painted green) at Fenway Park, or the "Touchdown Jesus" ("Word of Life") mural on Hesburgh Library, overlooking the University of Notre Dame football stadium, that are sacred. And for still others, it is the one historic game at a particular stadium, one that generated an intense experience for those in the stadium witnessing it, that becomes an extraordinary event, even a sacred one. It is these and other symbols or symbolic experiences that bind the fan and athlete to a stadium, and often produce a strong sense of ownership.

Some stadiums reveal their status as contested spaces with the anticipation of change. The naming (or renaming) of a stadium is a particularly acute change that raises the issue of ownership. Dispute can be avoided if a stadium is named for someone (or something) clearly associated with the team, such as an owner (Joe Robbie Stadium, near Miami), the location (Candlestick Park, in San Francisco), the team itself (Tiger Stadium, Detroit), or a famous athlete with ties to the city or team (Joe Louis Arena, also in Detroit). Yet to raise additional revenue, stadium owners often sell the naming rights to private corporations, a perfectly legal but often unpopular act. A survey of students at the University of Kansas found that a hypothetical renaming of Allen Fieldhouse (named for legendary coach Phog Allen) to something corporate would "result in greater perceived loss of team distinctiveness and anger" (see Reysen *et al.* 2012: 352). The loss is related to the perceived ownership of not only the name of the stadium but also the traditions associated with the University of Kansas basketball team and to the edifice that houses them. Allen Fieldhouse expresses its distinctiveness and proximity to these home grown traditions; "Verizon Fieldhouse" would not.

In the same way, it is this sense of ownership that is challenged when a corporation's name is added to the name of a stadium. The Celtics' Boston Garden was changed to the Fleet Center and Lincoln Financial Field followed Veterans Stadium as the home of the Philadelphia Eagles. These corporations are seen by some as interlopers exploiting the team without investing in the community that supports it. Anger stemming from corporate naming, however, can be mitigated. If a new stadium is built to replace the old one, fans may "relinquish" ownership of the new stadium that has a corporate name—they may still feel that they own the old one. In Denver, the owners of the professional football team realized that replacing the old stadium (Mile High Stadium) with a new one with a corporate name (Invesco Stadium) would incite a fight with the public that they did not wish to engage. But needing the money that corporate sponsorship would bring, they reached a compromise—"Invesco at Mile High" (see Moore 2002). Power relations were reinforced: the owners still got the corporate name on the stadium in the first position, but the final name nonetheless reveals the negotiations between interested parties, and the compromise that was reached. The use of a hybrid name may satisfy all parties. And if the corporation naming the stadium has historical, financial ties to the city—Heinz Field in Pittsburgh, or Coors Field in Denver—the "interloper effect" may be diminished.

Structural alterations to stadiums are also occasions for contestation. In 1988, when the owners of Wrigley Field (home to the Chicago Cubs) decided to put up lights in order to play night games for the first time in club history, a battle ensued (Thomas 1987). On one side, the traditionalists (and even purists) claimed that lights at Wrigley would break with a daylight tradition that, among professional baseball stadiums, only their ballpark still kept. Some cited with pride a 1938 game that was almost postponed due to darkness right before a crucial home run was hit, helping the Cubs win the league pennant. Lights, they argued, would eliminate such heroics, and minimize the stadium's distinctiveness. On the other side, the team's owners and executives cited new rules that required some playoff games to be played at night on primetime television, and made it clear that Wrigley would either have lights or never host another Cubs game. This firm (and probably exaggerated) stance changed the debate, and even the most ardent opponents began to relent. Unlike in Denver, in this contest the actual (that is, legal) owners won, the strong sense of ownership shown by fans notwithstanding. As Chidester and Linenthal (1995: 16) note, "Sacred places are arenas in which power relations can be reinforced, in which relations between insiders and outsiders, rulers and subjects, elders and juniors, males and females, and so on, can be adjudicated. But those power relations are always resisted." With Wrigley field and the fight over lights, the hierarchical relationship between owners and fans was reinforced by the power struggle over who had the authority to alter the ballpark.

Sometimes, the very existence of the stadium is at stake, tending to set off greater pitched battles between interested parties. When a stadium is threatened with a newer "better" replacement or (worse) relocation to another city, battles become entrenched warfare, and the question of ownership divides the warring factions. Who gets to decide the fate of a stadium when it is publicly owned—that is, subsidized by state or local taxes—and privately owned? Unlike most public/private hybrid buildings, sports stadiums bring with them another element of ownership; fans, especially long-time fans, of a team come to think of the team and stadium as theirs. Razing a stadium to build a new one, or completely relocating the team, is not as simple as a calculated business decision made in a boardroom. When large sums of public money (either in the form of higher taxes or ticket prices) are required for renovation or replacement, the stadium becomes the focus of a political contest between competing ideologies. Spending millions on a fancy new stadium may seem foolhardy when a municipality has other, more pressing needs. Then again, stadiums bring jobs, can rejuvenate blighted areas of a downtown, temporarily guarantee the team's immobility, and even create community solidarity.[4]

Little resistance may be raised by the public in cases where a stadium is in disrepair. But the type of renovation, and/or the look of the new stadium, depend on the connection of a stadium to its community. Convincing Texas Rangers fans to tear down a shoddily built stadium built in 1971 and replace it with a new one was less contentious in 1994 than replacing the "House that Ruth Built" (Yankee Stadium) in 2009 (for example, see O'Connor 2006). The case of the Cleveland Browns demonstrates the role a stadium plays in cementing a fan base to its team, a team to its city, and an owner to his or her primary interests. The Browns had played in their stadium since 1955 and had generated intense fan loyalty and allegiance from the small-market through the years. In 1995, after of a series of bad financial decisions and with the team and stadium losing money, owner Art Modell secretly began the process of moving the team to another city while publicly promoting an initiative to raise tax dollars to refurbish the stadium. Soon after, he announced the team's relocation to Baltimore, where city officials were offering money to build a new stadium. In desperation, the Cleveland voters overwhelmingly endorsed the tax measure, but it was too late (Harris 1995).

Here, as with the controversy over naming a stadium, the result is a reinforcement of power dynamics, and money usually trumps popular consensus. The damage to the Browns fans in the wake of Modell's decisions parallels cases of corporations closing American factories to relocate overseas. Yet the stadium controversy reveals its significance because the struggle over its location is almost existential and not just financial. Ownership of a stadium is an open question; if it were not, the Cleveland fans quietly would have resigned themselves to the harsh reality. They did not, and continued pressure after the incident resulted in the arrival of an expansion team in 1999: the Cleveland Browns "2.0."[5]

Stadiums elicit symbolic as well as legal conceptions of ownership unlike other structures, and express their sacrality through the commitment of all participants to secure the ownership of sacred symbols, however ownership is understood. When proprietary interests conflict, we see the stadium not only at the center of the contest, but as the environment that contains and guides the struggle. In most contests over stadium ownership, the battle begins when there is a sense that something sacred will be "profaned," be it by opposing fans or "opposing" investors.

Encroachment of the profane

Sports stadiums are sites where the sacred is produced through rituals, meaning making, and contestation. They are also popular cultural artifacts accessible to all, either through attendance, via television, or local and personal folklore. And while the contests over meaning performed through ritual produce the sacred, the involvement of capitalism often prevents the sacred (in the stadium) from being protected from the profane (outside the stadium). That is, if a stadium is commercially valuable, it can retain its sacredness by resisting the profanation accomplished through commercial contests over legal ownership.

Some stadiums retain a sense of distinction through a connection to tradition. Is it possible, then, for a stadium to become so indistinct that it is no longer able to produce the sacred? Brent Mayne, head of Center Operating Company at the American Airlines Center in Dallas, suggests that recent trends encourage stadium designers to add amenities—"more opportunities for sponsorship"—to produce more revenue. "It's much better," he concludes, "than the concrete and brick concourses of the past" (Lamberth 2006: 6). In other words, for those seeking to make a profit from the stadium.

Some stadiums will never have to go out of their way to appeal to consumers. Historic ones like Wrigley Field and Lambeau Field (in Green Bay, Wisconsin) are icons in the world of American sport, and attract tourist/pilgrims without needing to attract ticket buyers. Most stadiums do not enjoy this luxury, and find themselves adding features to the stadium experience (in addition to the game) in order to sell tickets. Some of these are episodic and inexpensive—such as "theme nights" at minor league baseball parks. Some are more permanent; many stadiums now allow fans to watch (on their cell phones) instant replays of the game (Michaels 2012).

The new (or significantly remodeled) stadium must now provide all manner of amenities to compete with the abundance of entertainment options available to fans. The epitome is Cowboys Stadium (outside Dallas), built in 2009 and cynically called "JerryWorld" for the team's owner Jerry Jones, who is also the majority owner and designer of the stadium. Cowboys Stadium effectively blurs the line between sports stadium, sports bar, nightclub, living room, museum, and shopping mall. The stadium has platform cages for female "cage dancers," is adorned with commissioned art, and has a Victoria's Secret store. For less than the cost of an actual ticket, fans can buy a "party pass" which allows them entry into two upper concourse areas (one on each end of the stadium), neither of which has a view of the field; you are at the game and not at the game at the same time. Those with a ticket can watch the action on the largest high definition television screen in the world (60 yards x 30 yards), which presents the game with more clarity than one could get by watching the action on the field unmediated.

No doubt, technological features (like personalized cell phone replays and structural modifications that create shorter lines for concessions) will please most who attend these modern venues. However, the stadium's attempt to please the fan is most often realized by blurring the line between the world outside the stadium and the world inside it; the HD screen extends the living room into the stadium; the "no line" bathroom mimics one's experience at home. Even the advertisements decorating the stadium resemble a highway littered with billboards. Fans now get many services in the stadium that can be acquired elsewhere. The line is blurred; you are in the stadium, and yet you are not.

These changes may alter a stadium's ability to convey sacredness. Rituals are still performed, significance is still built through classification and orientation, and contests between people still occur there, but the more the "profane" world of revenue is insinuated into the stadium, the more difficult it may be for the participants to experience transcendence. Why?

The collective effervescence, the blurring of social class, the transcending of measured time—all are predicated on the excitement that comes with the uncertain outcome of the event. Were the outcome known in advance, as with a movie, the rituals, contests, and their significance in the stadium would not move participants into states of transcendence. The stadium acts as the set-apart space that fosters these experiences.

The sense of a slow encroachment of the outside world can serve to lessen the effect of spontaneity, uncertainty, and hence the sense of sacredness. Fans do not gain more insight into who will win a game just because they are watching replays on a high-definition screen above the field, or because a new set of luxury boxes is installed in a stadium. But the incorporation of more accoutrements may negatively affect the ability of a stadium to be a truly contested space. The uncertainty that breeds excitement is increasingly framed by a different story unfolding before fans' eyes—the colonization of the stadium by corporations and private interests in the service of the bottom line. If a contest over ownership of meanings is crucial to the production of sacred space, and the participants perceive that the deck is stacked against them, then the active participation necessary to maintain the presence of the sacred may be sacrificed to the passive enjoyment of mere entertainment.

Conclusion

The emphasis on the production of the sacred and the encroachment of the profane in the modern stadium brings religion and sports into a different relationship than just instrumentality or equality. While acknowledging a stadium's economic function keeps it from being perceived as absolutely sacred space, it is clearly not just profane space, as the presence of ritual, the focusing of significance, and the contests over meaning strongly suggest.

The processes of cultural production mean that the relationship between religion and sports is fluid, not static; separating one from the other, or setting them in opposition, may impede our understanding them as cultural expressions. And while an examination of the relationship between religion and sports on the cultural plane may threaten to defile sacred spaces, it also allows for the examination of the production of the sacred in places such as sports stadiums, through efforts to protect what is considered worth protecting. In this way, religion—as expressed through sacred symbols—is made manifest through sport, which can then be better understood through the use of religious language. Conversely, examining the profane, ordinary aspect of sports challenges the argument that sport is religion, or that it possesses some religious essence. Tracking their relationship requires close attention to the forces that produce each, and not just taking their respective cultural expression as pristine, finished products.

Notes

1 These questions were posed on the covers of *Newsweek* (January 11, 1971) and *Sports Illustrated* (February 4, 2013), respectively.

2 "I believe in the Church of Baseball. I've tried all the major religions and most of the minor ones. I've worshiped Buddha, Allah, Brahma, Vishnu, Siva, trees, mushrooms, and Isadora Duncan. I know things. For instance, there are 108 beads in a Catholic rosary and there are 108 stitches in a baseball. When I learned that, I gave Jesus a chance. But it just didn't work out between us. The Lord laid too much guilt on me. I prefer metaphysics to theology … . I've tried them all, I really have. And the only church that truly feeds the soul day in, day out, is the Church of Baseball."

3 Any who are in doubt about the power of constructed sacred space in sport should visit the baseball diamond built for the film, and extended facility built for the tourists who have visited there since the film opened (see Belson 2011).

4 Not surprisingly, Rick Eckstein and Kevin Delaney (2002) suggest that, despite these kinds of arguments made by stadium investors to communities, beneath the promise of increased "community self-esteem or collective conscience" is a motive to collect large sums of public money for private interests.

5 Though now a common nickname, the term is often attributed to "Tuesday Morning Quarterback" writer Gregg Easterbrook (for an early example, see Easterbrook 2001).

Works cited

Adams, S. (2008) "'In-com-plete' chant may de-part," *Rocky Mountain News* (30 August). Online. Available: www.rockymountainnews.com/news/2008/aug/30/adams-in-com-plete-chant-may-de-part/ (accessed 6 August 2013).

Albanese, C.L. (1992) *America, Religions and Religion*, Belmont, CA: Wadsworth.

Angell, R. (1987) "The interior stadium," in J. Thorn (ed.), *The Armchair Book of Baseball II*, New York: Scribner, 415–23.

Bale, J. (1993) "The spatial development of the modern stadium," *International Review for the Sociology of Sport* 28: 121–33.

——(1994) *Landscapes of Modern Sport*, Leicester, UK: Leicester University Press.

Bellah, R. (1967) "Civil religion in America," *Daedalus* 96, 1 (Winter): 1–21.

Belson, K. (2011) "New dreams for field," *New York Times* (October 30): SP1.

Betsill, J. (2012) "Oklahoma destroys Texas in 2012 Red River Rivalry in Dallas," DFW.com (October 14). Online. Available: www.dfw.com/2012/10/14/696181/Oklahoma-destroys-texas-in-2012.html (accessed 6 August 2013).

Bondy, F. (2012) "It's time for the NFL to jump all over the Green Bay Packer's Lambeau Leap celebration," *New York Daily News* (January 12). Online. Available: www.nydailynews.com/sports/football/giants/time-nfl-jump-green-bay-packers-lambeau-leap-celebration-article-1.1005465 (accessed 6 August 2013).

Bradsher, K. (1996) "When octopuses are flying in Detroit it's … ," *New York Times* (April 14). Online. Available: www.nytimes.com/1996/04/14/us/when-octopuses-are-flying-in-detroit-it-s.html (accessed 3 August 2013).

Carlton, C. (2012) "Texas' DeLoss Dodds says Red River Rivalry won't leave Dallas any time soon," DallasNews.com (October 10). Online. Available: www.dallasnews.com/sports/college-sports/texas-longhorns/20121010-carlton-texas-deloss-dodds-says-red-river-rivalry-won-t-leave-dallas-any-time-soon.ece (accessed 6 August 2013).

Chidester, D. (2005) *Authentic Fakes: Religion and American Popular Culture*, Berkeley, CA: University of California Press.

Chidester, D. and E.T. Linenthal (eds) (1995) *American Sacred Space*, Bloomington, IN: Indiana University Press.

Collins, R. (2004) *Interaction Ritual Chains*, Princeton, NJ: Princeton University Press.

Cottingham, M.D. (2012) "Interaction ritual theory and sports fans: emotion, symbols, and solidarity," *Sociology of Sport Journal* 29: 168–85.

Day, P.K. (2013) "Lance Armstrong admits doping to Oprah, but not after 2005," *Los Angeles Times* (January 17). Online. Available: http://articles.latimes.com/2013/jan/17/entertainment/la-te-st-lance-armstrong-oprah-winfrey-interview-20130117 (accessed 5 August 2013).

Deford, F. (1976) "The world according to Tom," *Sports Illustrated* (August 26): 58–65.

Duncan, D.J. (1992) *The Brothers K*, New York: Doubleday.

Durkheim, E. (1995) *The Elementary Forms of Religious Life*, trans. K.E. Fields, New York: The Free Press.

Eames, T. (2012) "Super Bowl XLVI becomes most-watched TV program in US history," DigitalSpy.com (February 6). Online. Available: www.digitalspy.com/tv/news/a364251/super-bowl-xlvi-becomes-most-watched-tv-program-in-us-history.html (accessed 4 August 2013).

Easterbrook, G. (2001) "Atsah defeat Sange, 20–26, as McNabb stars," Slate.com (December 18). Online. Available: www.slate.com/articles/sports/sports_nut/2001/12/atsah_defeat_sange_206_as_mcnabb_stars.html (accessed 4 August 2013).

Eckstein, R. and K. Delaney (2002) "New sports stadiums, community self-esteem, and community collective conscience," *Journal of Sport and Social Issues* 26: 235–47.

Eitzen, D.S. and G.H. Sage (1978) *Sociology of American Sport*, Dubuque, IA: William C. Brown.

Forney, C.A. (2007) *The Holy Trinity of American Sports: Civil Religion in Football, Baseball, and Basketball*, Macon, GA: Mercer University Press.

Foucault, M. (1986) "Of other spaces," *Diacritics* (Spring): 22–27.

Gammon, S. (2004) "Secular pilgrimage and sport tourism," in B.W. Ritchie and D. Adair (eds), *Sport Tourism: Interrelationships, Impacts and Issues*, Buffalo: Channel View Publications, 30–45.

Guttmann, A. (1978) *From Ritual to Record: The Nature of Modern Sports*, New York: Columbia University Press.

Harris, R. (1995) "Voters extend 'sin tax' to rehab Browns' stadium," *Associated Press* (8 November). Online. Available: www.apnewsarchive.com/1995/Voters-Extend-Sin-Tax-To-Rehab-Browns-Stadium/id-161b5e024f7ef2ec2046bf1e5d6b368c (accessed 4 August 2013).

Heinen, D. (1995) "Blue Devil athletics steeped in countless traditions," *Chronicle* [Duke University] (September 19). Online. Available: www.dukechronicle.com/articles/1995/09/20/blue-devil-athletics-steeped-countless-traditions (accessed 3 August 2013).

Higgs, R. (1995) *God in the Stadium: Sports and Religion in America*, Lexington, KY: University of Kentucky Press.

Hoffman, S.J. (2010) *Good Game: Christianity and the Culture of Sports*, Waco, TX: Baylor University Press.

Johnson, K.C. (2011) "The invisible fan: scapegoat Bartman has managed to remain undetected for 8 years," *Chicago Tribune* (September 26). Online. Available: http://articles.chicagotribune.com/2011-09-26/sports/ct-spt-0927-bartman-chicago–20110927_1_cubs-five-outs-scapegoat-bartman-alex-gibney (accessed 4 August 2013).

Juffer, J. (2006) "Why we like to lose: on being a Cubs fan in the heterotopia of Wrigley Field," *South Atlantic Quarterly* 105, 2 (Spring): 289–301.

Kaszuba, M. (2012) "Seat license fees are prevalent in the NFL," [Minneapolis] *Star Tribune* (November 15): 1A.

Lamberth, C.R. (2006) "Trends in stadium design: a whole new game," *Implications* 4, 6: 1–7.

Lombardi, V., Jr. (2001) *What It Takes to Be #1: Vince Lombardi on Leadership*, New York: McGraw-Hill.

Maclean, N. (1976) *A River Runs Through It, and Other Stories*, Chicago, IL: The University of Chicago Press.

Mathisen, J. (1992) "From civil religion to folk religion: the case of American sport," in S. Hoffman (ed.), *Sport and Religion*, Champaign, IL: Human Kinetics, 17–33.

Merkin, S. (2005) "Sox hope journey doesn't stop," MLB.com (October 20). Online. Available: http://mlb.mlb.com/news/article.jsp?ymd=20051020&content_id=1255934&c_id=cws (accessed 6 August 2013).

Michaels, P. (2012) "Let's go to the replay: Stanford beams in-game action to fans' phones," Macworld.com (January 10). Online. Available: www.macworld.com/article/1164705/lets_go_-to_the_replay_stanford_beams_in_game_action_to_fans_phones.html (accessed 3 August 2013).

Monkovic, T. (2008) "Personal seat licenses: Jets to Giants, you first," *New York Times* (June 27). Online. Available: http://fifthdown.blogs.nytimes.com/2008/06/27/personal-seat-licenses-jets-to-giants-you-first/?_r=0 (accessed 26 June 2013).

Moore, P. (2002) "A controversial deal in 2001: Invesco buys naming rights," *Denver Business Journal* (March 3). Online. Available: www.bizjournals.com/denver/stories/2002/03/04/focus10.html?page=all (accessed 4 August 2013).

Murphy, R. (n.d.) "10 Most Superstitious Athletes," Men'sFitness.com. Online. Available: www.mensfitness.com/leisure/sports/10-most-superstitious-athletes (accessed 3 August 2013).

Novak, M. (1976) *The Joy of Sports: End Zones, Bases, Baskets, Balls, and the Consecration of the American Spirit*, New York: Basic Books.

O'Connor, I. (2006) "Groundbreaking for new Yankee Stadium a step back for history," *USA Today* (August 16). Online. Available: http://usatoday30.usatoday.com/sports/columnist/oconnor/2006-08-16-oconnor-yankee-stadium_x.htm (accessed 6 August 2013).

Otto, R. (1958) *The Idea of the Holy*, London: Oxford University Press.

Overman, S. (2011) *The Protestant Ethic and the Spirit of Sport*, Macon, GA: Mercer University Press.

Posnanski, J. (2010) "10 interesting facts you may not know about the Miracle on Ice," SI.com (February 22). Online. Available: http://sportsillustrated.cnn.com/2010/writers/joe_posnanski/02/22/miracle.on.ice/index.html (accessed 3 August 2013).

Prebish, C.S. (1993) *Religion and Sport: The Meeting of Sacred and Profane*, Westport, CT: Greenwood Press.

Putney, C. (2001) *Muscular Christianity: Manhood and Sports in Protestant America, 1880–1920*, Cambridge, MA: Harvard University Press.

Reysen, S., J. Snider, and N.R. Branscombe (2012) "Corporate renaming of stadiums, team identification and threat to distinctiveness," *Journal of Sport Management* 26: 350–57.

Ricciardi, T. (2012) "Red River rivalry parties, celebrities in Dallas," GuideLive.com (October 10). Online. Available: www.dallasnews.com/entertainment/state-fair-of-texas/headlines/20121010-red-river-rivalry-parties-celebrities-in-dallas.ece (accessed 6 August 2013).

Shainberg, L. (1989) "Finding 'the zone,'" *New York Times Magazine* (April 9). Online. Available: www.nytimes.com/1989/04/09/magazine/finding-the-zone.html?pagewanted=all&src=pm (accessed 6 August 2013).

SI.com (2002) "'I was stunned': Royals first base coach assaulted by father-son duo" (September 19). Online. Available: http://sportsillustrated.cnn.com/baseball/news/2002/09/19/royals_white sox_ap/ (accessed 6 August 2013).

Smith, G. (2010) *Sports Theology: Playing Inside Out*, Indianapolis, IN: Dog Ear Publishing.

Smith, J.Z. (1978) *Map Is Not Territory*, Chicago, IL: The University of Chicago Press.

Tebow, T. and N. Whitaker (2011) *Through My Eyes*, New York: HarperCollins.

Texas A&M University (2013) "Midnight Yell," *Traditions of Texas A&M*. Online. Available: www.tamu.edu/about/traditions.html#midnightYell (accessed 6 August 2013).

Thomas, K.M. (1987) "Opposition to Wrigley Field lights still burns bright," *Chicago Tribune* (November 16). Online. Available: http://articles.chicagotribune.com/1987-11-16/news/8703 260241_1_amendment-bernard-hansen-night-games (accessed 3 August 2013).

Trujillo, N. and B. Krizek (1994) "Emotionality in the stands and in the field: expressing self through baseball," *Journal of Sport and Social Issues* 18, 4 (November): 303–25.

Turner, V. (1997) *The Ritual Process: Structure and Anti-structure*, New York: Aldine De Gruyter.

van Gennep, A. (1961) *The Rites of Passage*, Chicago, IL: The University of Chicago Press.

Vosk, S. (2005) "Another mystery of the Diamond, explained at last," Boston.com (May 29). Online. Available: http://boston.com/sports/baseball/redsox/articles/2005/05/29/another_mystery_of_the_diamond_explained_at_last/ (accessed 3 August 2013).

20
MONUMENTS OF CIVIL RELIGION

Darryl Caterine

Introduction: land of the pilgrims' pride, land where my fathers died

There was never really a question that Ground Zero would receive some kind of memorial. Less than six months after September 11, 2001, New York Governor George Pataki, New York City Mayor Michael Bloomberg, and the Lower Manhattan Development Corporation announced the building of an interim site. By April, 2003, a selection jury for a permanent memorial had been formed, and general guidelines were publicized for anyone wishing to submit a concept. These included "convey[ing] the magnitude of personal and physical loss at this location," "evok[ing] the historical significance of the worldwide impact of September 11, 2001," and "creat[ing] an original and powerful statement of enduring and universal symbolism" (Lower Manhattan Development Corporation n.d.: 19). In January of the following year the jury announced "Reflecting Absence," designed by architects Michael Arad and Peter Walker, as the winner. Now known as the National September 11 Memorial and Museum, it is laid out like a park, complete with paths and swamp white elms, designed to allow visitors to take in the sheer absence of the Twin Towers that once stood here. The only reminders of their former existence are two, one-acre, granite-lined reflecting pools where the foundations of the skyscrapers once stood. These are continuously replenished by water which runs down their sides in gentle cascades. Etched into the stone barriers that surround them are the names of those who perished here in the September 11 attacks. The space is clean and relatively unadorned, allowing visitors to develop their own relationships both to the site and to the historical event that it marks.

Construction of the memorial began in March of 2006; the site was opened to the public on September 22, 2011. The National September 11 Memorial and Museum will soon become a very important addition to the vast array of statues, obelisks, historic sites, monuments, heritage sites, and national parks commemorating the individuals and events that have shaped America's destiny. At least as long as eyewitnesses are alive to remember them, the attacks of September 11 will loom large in the nation's memory as life-changing events, both for individuals and for the public as a whole. For this reason alone, New York has deemed it fit to set aside more than four acres of premium Manhattan real estate for the purposes of commemoration. In Judaism, the Hebrew word translated into English as "holy," *quadosh*, also means "set aside" or "distinct." But beyond this linguistic turn, does the setting aside of the former site of the World Trade Center—or Civil War battlefields, or military cemeteries, or the sculpted likenesses of former military and political leaders—warrant their designation as "religious" places?

At first glance, there would seem to be countless precedents in world religions for making comparisons between the sacred places of religion and sacred national sites like the National September 11 Memorial and Museum. Certainly there are countless examples in world religions for setting aside certain public spaces for remembrance in perpetuity. One thinks, for example, of the Bodhi Tree in Bodh Gaya, where Siddhartha Gautama attained enlightenment to become the Buddha, or perhaps of the Via Dolorosa, the road in Jerusalem along which Jesus carried his cross on the way to Golgotha. In fact, by definition, every place of religious pilgrimage is a place set aside and designated for memorializing. But it is misleading to equate the notions of memory in religious and modern national contexts. The National September 11 Memorial and Museum reflects a radical departure not only from traditional religious strategies of memorializing, but even from older methods of preserving memory in the American national context.

The novelty of national monuments and memorials can easily be glossed over in scholarly discussions of American "civil religion." This latter concept originally appeared in Jean Jacques Rousseau's *The Social Contract* (1762), but was reanimated within religious studies by sociologist Robert Bellah in his 1967 essay, "Civil religion in America." Bellah referred to a "collection of beliefs, symbols, and rituals with respect to sacred things and institutionalized in a collectivity [namely, the American nation-state]" (Bellah 1967: 8). Drawing examples from a number of presidential speeches, Bellah suggested that "behind the [American] civil religion at every point lie biblical archetypes: Exodus, Chosen People, Promised Land, New Jerusalem, and Sacrificial Death and Rebirth" (ibid.: 18). Inspired by these insights, a number of scholars in the field of American religion subsequently documented the very real influence of colonial Puritan theology on the early formation of America's national mythology.

Notwithstanding the conclusions of this scholarship, however, religious and national notions of memorial space remain quite distinct. In order to show why this is so, in the following pages I will discuss a pre-national commemorative ritual, the New England Puritan observance of the Sabbath in the public meetinghouse, highlighting the distinctive conceptions of space, time, and community that it reflects. I will continue by presenting an overview of the strategies that Anglo-Europeans used to memorialize the nation from the time of the Revolution until the early twentieth century, clarifying the important differences between civil religion and its religious antecedents. Focusing on the development of Washington, DC as the symbolic center of the United States, we will see that national monuments failed to evoke a sense of American unity until the construction in 1901 of the National Mall, a space reflecting new understandings of space, time, and community that contrasted with those of pre-modern religions. Finally, in the concluding section of the chapter I will return to the latest instantiation of memorializing in the United States, in which the September 11 Memorial and Museum derives its meaning.

This new era, inaugurated in 1982 by Maya Lin's Vietnam Veterans Memorial, represents an even further departure from religious strategies of memorializing in its rejection of late-nineteenth- and early-twentieth-century monuments. The Vietnam Veterans Memorial was built neither to glorify "great men who make history" nor to celebrate the nation as an abstract collective. Lin designed the memorial as an "anti-monument," geared toward evoking highly personal experiences and interactions with the space, and intended to heal the nation rather than to glorify it.[1] Although I will use the terms "memorial" and "monument" interchangeably throughout this chapter, architects, artists, and planners following in Lin's footsteps have increasingly kept these terms quite distinct. In current parlance, a memorial signifies a physical site or artifact designed to bring participants into a highly individualized and experiential relationship with the imagined community of the nation, while a monument signifies those earlier places and spaces intended to symbolize a consensual and "official" version of national history (Doss 2010: 38).

"Reflecting Absence" incorporates many of the concepts pioneered by Lin, who was in fact a member of the 13-person jury that chose Arad's and Walker's memorial to commemorate the September 11 attacks. As one scholar has observed, the emphasis on individual emotional experience reflected in America's latest kind of memorials echoes the sensibilities of nineteenth-century republicans who tried in vain to prevent the building of national monuments altogether. Paradoxically, however, the Vietnam Veterans Memorial seems to have set in motion a new wave of memorializing that Erika Doss has characterized as "memorial mania." The plethora of memorials now rising up throughout the American landscape in many ways represent the antithesis of Bellah's notion of a single, unified civil religion, although it is questionable whether or not there ever was any "religious" dimension—civil or otherwise—to national monuments in America before the Vietnam Veterans Memorial.

From Puritan to national memory

The New England Puritans are the customary starting point for most discussions of American civil religion in its various manifestations, as most of the nation's mythology derives from their self-understanding as a people set apart from the rest of the world, and chosen to complete a divine mission during the last days of salvation history (see Bloch 1985; Mead 1977; Richley and Jones 1974). The Puritans understood the events of both the Old and New Testaments as foreshadowing their own migration to America. As the Israelites had escaped from bondage in Egypt, wandered for 40 years in the wilderness of Sinai, and eventually arrived in Israel to build a society in accordance with the Laws that God had revealed to Moses, so too did Puritans see themselves as having broken free of England's religiously corrupt society, and as restoring the primitive church in the "wilderness" of New England. As Robert Bellah made explicit, American political history is replete with speeches invoking these and other biblical tropes. The United States is thus rendered the modern institutional heir of Puritan mythology. From the time of the Revolution until today, Americans have perennially proclaimed their ostensibly secular nation to be a community set apart from the rest of the world, and destined to carry out a divine mission during the last days of human history.

There are fundamental differences, however, between invoking Puritan mythology in the modern context (either the political or the scholarly one), and the former acts of remembrance in the seventeenth-century colonial context. If and when *we* remember the Puritans, we imaginatively envision them as existing "in time"; and if and when we mythologize the Puritans as America's sacred ancestors, we remember them as prototypes or models for whatever present-time national decisions or actions we wish to valorize. But when the Puritans wished to evoke memories of the past for their own purposes, it was not simply time and precedent that they were recalling. Rather, they were evoking the laws and events related in God's Word, which was understood to be articulating truths that exist outside of time altogether. Historian of religion Mircea Eliade referred to the actions recounted in religious myths as unfolding *in illo tempore*—"in that time," an eternal realm imagined completely outside or before human time (Eliade 1954: 3–5). In the Puritan understanding of scripture, biblical tales of ancient Israel and the early church transpired within an overarching mythos that was the same in their day as it was thousands of years earlier. As far as they were concerned, not everything under the sun was new.

Eliade also noted that pre-modern societies routinely commemorated sacred stories at special places understood to be thresholds between heaven and earth, or eternity and time, which he termed *axes mundi* (singular: *axis mundi*), or "centers of the cosmos" (ibid.: 12–17). Indeed for the Puritans, any place in New England could become an *axis mundi* if God's providential hand was discerned in the events unfolding there. Wars waged with Indians, unsuccessful harvests, successful harvests, and the safe arrival of ships are just a few of the more common examples of events that spurred Puritans to pray for or rejoice in the intervention of a wrathful but forgiving God who watched over the founding of a Protestant theocracy in the biblical wilderness of Massachusetts, just as He had led the ancient Israelites, and guided the apostles of Jesus.

Within this general understanding of New England as the American Holy Land, the Puritan meetinghouse was regularly set apart as a particularly sacred place. Unlike most other places of worship, the meetinghouse served as a secular as well as a religious building—with heads of wolves killed for bounty hanging from its exterior walls, and barrels of gunpowder stored inside (see Fischer 1989: 117–25). Nevertheless, the meetinghouse was also where the Word of God came alive—in sermons delivered during spontaneous days of thanksgiving and public humiliation, or routinely during weekly Sunday observances of the Sabbath. On the one hand, Puritans followed in the footsteps of other Protestants in denouncing the sundry *axes mundi* of the English and continental countryside—places such as holy wells, saints' shrines, monasteries, and even churches—as so many legacies of Catholic "pagano-papism." The consecration of these sites was an affront to Christian faith, so they reasoned, because human beings could neither limit nor control God's sovereign power. On the other hand, as soon as English Puritans had migrated to New England, they proceeded to build their townships according to the time-honored custom of setting aside a sacred center in the middle of their settlements—the meetinghouse—around which all other buildings and cultivated lands were organized. Reviewing the conceptions of town planning that guided this practice, Belden C. Lane has summarized:

[The] paradigmatic townscape [of Puritan New England consisted] of six concentric circles set within a six-mile square. Optimally every Puritan village would be laid out in this manner. At the innermost circle would be the meetinghouse where the faithful gathered regularly to worship. As towers and spires were added to the simple New England churches after 1699, this symbolism of the church as ancient roland or *axis mundi* would be enhanced even further. In the second concentric circle, surrounding the meetinghouse on its village green, were the houses of the congregation members, "orderly placed to enjoy comfortable communion." This proximity to the house of meeting and to each other was considered crucially important on both social and theological grounds. Reverence for communal authority and respect for the Body of Christ could be nourished, it was thought, only by physical closeness to the symbolic center of God's rule.

(Lane 2002: 140)

Beyond these two circles the Puritans concentrically arranged a ring of common fields, a circle of larger lots for "men of great estate," a ring of free-standing farms for the public food supply, and finally an outer ring of "swamps and rubbish waste grounds" demarcating the boundary between cosmos and chaos (ibid.: 140–41). Lane draws attention to "the hierarchical and centripetal notion of space that characterized the early New England mind," which in turn reflected the implicit theological notion of space as organized around an *axis mundi* (ibid.: 138).

In their strict observance of the Sabbath, the Puritans broke once again from continental Reformers' condemnation of religious ceremonialism. In their explications of Christian doctrine, both Martin Luther and John Calvin had qualified the meaning of the fourth commandment of the Decalogue to "remember the Sabbath day and keep it holy." Luther taught that the new covenant had set Christians free from what he saw as the ritualism of Jewish Law; he recommended Sunday observance as a sound Christian practice, but also taught that no particular day of the week was more sacred than any other. In Calvin's more conservative interpretation of the fourth commandment, Christians were required to set aside Sunday as their Sabbath "to hear the word of God, to celebrate the sacraments, and engage in the regular prayers" (Calvin 1545). But Calvin also took pains to clarify that the sanctity of the day derived from the piety of its observers, rather than its inscription in any ritual calendar.

As the theological heirs of Calvin, English Puritans were appalled by what they saw as a lapse of piety regarding the observance of the Lord's Day among Anglicans, and called for its strict enforcement as part of their ecclesiastical reforms. Quite unlike either Luther or Calvin, however, Puritans came to understand the weekly structuring of time into six days of labor and one of rest as reflecting the cosmic structure of time, as it came to be *in illo tempore* recounted in biblical Creation myths. The "Westminster Confession of Faith," a seventeenth-century summary of principles upheld by England's Calvinist dissenters, made the point explicit:

As it is of the law of nature, that, in general, a due proportion of time be set apart for the worship of God; so, in His word, by a positive, moral, and perpetual commandment, binding all men in all ages, He hath particularly appointed one day in seven for a Sabbath, to be kept holy unto Him; *which, from the beginning of the world* to the Resurrection of Christ, was the last day of the week; and from the Resurrection of Christ was changed into the first day of the week, which in Scripture is called the Lord's Day, and is to be continued to the end of the world as the Christian Sabbath.

(Westminster Assembly 1646, Chapter 21,
paragraph 7, emphasis added)

English Puritans brought this understanding of the Sabbath with them to New England, observing the Lord's Day much like Jews observed Shabbat. From sundown on Saturday through sundown on Sunday, they abstained from all work whatsoever—making exceptions only for acts of necessity and charity—subordinating ordinary to cosmic time. Despite the Puritans' denouncement of Catholic ritual, the entire performance reflected a powerful, though unconscious, continuation of Medieval Christian practice.

It is important to recall also that the Puritans did not distinguish between sacred and secular political authority. John Winthrop's famous image of New England as the "City Upon a Hill" referred to the ideal of a Protestant theocracy in which individuals were expected to prioritize the welfare of the community, understood as the "body of Christ," through various acts of Christian charity. Their conception of political community, no less than their notion of space, was a centripetal and therefore hierarchical one—notwithstanding their proto-democratic vision of the church as a "priesthood of all believers." In their role as preachers, Puritan ministers stood at the religious and social center of society as the "ambassadors of Christ," living thresholds between eternity and time.

While it remains true that the founders of the United States borrowed mythic themes from Puritan sermons and literature, their understandings of space, time, and community were fundamentally different from those of their colonial predecessors. In *Sons of the Fathers: the Civil Religion of the American Revolution*, historian of religion Catherine L. Albanese has provided an illuminating account of the first Revolutionary memorials in the "liberty trees" around which patriots spontaneously gathered as they broke away from the English Crown (Albanese 1976: 46–80). On August 14, 1765, a few protestors against the recent Stamp Act hung two effigies, one of the stamp master and another of his assistant, from the limbs of the first liberty tree in Boston. Later in the day, it was cut down and carried in a procession, followed by crowds of people shouting "liberty and property forever, no stamps" (Ramsay 1811: i, 89). As news of the protest spread, other New England towns quickly followed suit, setting aside their own liberty trees, or in some cases liberty poles, as symbolic rallying points for the new revolutionary society. The British were quick to notice the ritual significance of the trees, taking care to raze and burn them in attacks against the patriots. The decoration of liberty trees continued as a political ritual for several decades after the American Revolution. Supporters of Andrew Jackson, for example, erected hickory poles on the eve of the presidential election to celebrate their candidate's republican ideals (Albanese 1976: 66).

But the religious symbolism of the liberty trees was ambiguous. Albanese notes that, to a partial extent, they resembled the sacred trees found throughout the world's religions connecting the earth to heaven. Quite unlike *axes mundi*, however, the liberty trees were "self-conscious, historicized symbols," marking the humano-centric orientation of America's fledgling nationalism (ibid.: 59). What the original liberty trees marked off as "sacred" were the awe-inspiring events of revolutionary society—not the ahistorical events *in illo tempore* of the Bible. Despite their naturally occurring verticality, the liberty trees were more like mirrors, figuratively reflecting the early modern American collective back to itself.

The humanocentric orientation of American nationalism reflected a constellation of Enlightenment assumptions about the structure of ultimate reality. The notion of "empty and homogenous" time—in which the events of human history supposedly unfold in linear succession—had by the late 1700s come to eclipse the concept of archetypal time in large part embraced by the Puritans.[2] Relatedly, the Revolution-aries imagined the American landscape as consecrated only to the extent that the deeds of "great men" set it apart as noteworthy, and in this belief they turned away from the older organization of space around an *axis mundi*. The very ideal of democracy, furthermore, came to replace the centripetal and hierarchical social vision of the New England Puritans. Notwithstanding this modern orientation, however, revivalist ministers of the First Great Awakening had provided eighteenth-century Americans with a new theological language through which they could still relate the Revolution to biblical events. Evangelical Calvinists understood themselves as "making history" in response to the guiding hand of Providence, and they cele-brated the new democratic *polis* as a social order that made manifest God's will—even if it did not quite reflect a celestial archetype. Summarizing the civil religion of the American Revolution, Albanese concludes that it "'flatten[ed]' transcendence with-out obliterating it"—investing human acts and deeds with a mythic significance of their own, while appropriating Calvinist themes within a modern context (ibid.: 18).

Consecrating national space

The problematic task of creating a political center that could symbolize the entire nation fell to the immediate heirs of the Revolution. In 1791, a year after Congress approved the construction of the federal capital along the banks of the Potomac River, George Washington appointed the French-born architect and engineer Pierre (Peter) Charles L'Enfant to design plans for the new city of Washington, DC. L'En-fant's master plan proposed building a constellation of politically symbolic sites throughout the city. These included a house for the president and the Congress—today's White House and Capitol building, respectively—as well as a series of "sta-tues, columns, and obelisks" commemorating Revolutionary heroes remembered in each state (Savage 2005: 30). Based on a modification of these plans, construction of the capital began in 1792. The President's house was completed in 1800, and the Congress house in 1811, but it would not be until after the Civil War that anything close to a city resembling today's Washington—a veritable city of monuments and memorials—would come into being. Well into the nineteenth century most of the capital city languished as an undeveloped badland, with its local economy largely dependent on the trading of slaves.

Throughout the antebellum period, two conceptual obstacles stood in the way of building a capital capable of memorializing the American nation as a whole. Planners of Washington, DC, continued to conceptualize the city in pre-modern terms, as the centripetal hub symbolically consolidating power into a single center. Federalists advocating a strong national government invariably supported this vision, while Republicans, who triumphed a loosely knit confederation of states, opposed it. The partisan disagreement over urban planning came to a head over a Federalist proposal to inter George Washington's body underneath the rotunda of the Capitol building. If Republicans had begrudgingly conceded to L'Enfant's original plan to memorialize Washington with an equestrian statue, they recoiled from the idea of moving his remains from Mount Vernon to an elaborate crypt in the house of Congress. The suggestion stirred up associations with monarchy; as far as they were concerned, the move would elevate George Washington to the status of divine king, undermining the principles of democracy for which the Revolution was fought. In the first public debates over the meaning of American memorials, Republicans countered that the most effective and democratically appropriate way to remember George Washington was to immortalize his character through the teaching of American history, a task more suited for books than for monuments.

The controversy ended in a stalemate. The idea for the crypt passed the House but not the Senate and, because of a lack of funds, the equestrian statue was never built. Neither the centripetal notion of symbolic space advocated by the Federalists, nor the diffusionist image advanced by the Republicans, adequately symbolized the paradox of *e pluribus unum*—"one out of many"—that constituted the United States as a political entity. In hindsight, the deadlock reflected a more fundamental obstacle to nation-building than either party could articulate at the time. In fact, it stemmed from a technological rather than a political impasse. It would not be until the completion of America's five transcontinental railroads in 1883 that at least some of America's citizens could experience the new republic *kinesthetically*.[3] Viewing the political territory of America while hurtling at high speeds along the rails was an unprecedented and *lived* experience of the country as a unified and transcendent space, one that encompassed both cultural and geographical diversity. It was also the foundation upon which Americans began to articulate a distinctively modern form of civil religion.

Riding the rails was, first, an opportunity to visit a number of stunning natural locales out West—places like today's Glacier or Yellowstone Parks in Montana and Wyoming—that railroad companies deliberately showcased as both "wonders" of Nature and icons of the nation. The idealization of Nature as the ontological bedrock of the United States already had ample precedents in both eighteenth-century Enlightenment philosophy and mid-nineteenth-century Romantic arts and literature (see Hughes 2004: especially 45–66). It was now left to the railroad corporations to fashion themselves as the escorts into the sublime—though not supernatural— "essence" of America, through both advertising and the scripting of guidebooks to various stops along their lines. Railroad travel thus became the secular analog to religious pilgrimage, with marvelous natural destinations filling in for the traditional *axes mundi* defining older pilgrimage routes (Shaffer 2001: 40–92).

Within a few decades, the federal government had realized the economic and cultural power of these ideas, and began working with the railroads to transform

American tourism into a national rite of passage. In 1916, Woodrow Wilson created the National Park Service "to conserve the scenery and the natural and historic objects and wildlife therein, and to provide for the enjoyment of the same in such manner and by such means as will leave them unimpaired for the enjoyment of future generations" (*National Park Service Organic Act* 1916). The National Park Service subsequently became the custodial agency overseeing most of the nation's monuments, historic as well as natural, and continues to function in this capacity today.

The inclusion of cultural sites to compliment national monuments paralleled further developments in transportation technology. The first mass-produced automobile, the Model T Ford, appeared in 1908, and for the next two decades advocates for a national system of roadways built on the boosterism of railroad companies, advertising the plethora of historic and cultural sites that awaited the patriotic motorist. In the 1930s and '40s, the Federal Writers' Project, one of Franklin Delano Roosevelt's New Deal programs, published the "American Guide" series, a collection of books and pamphlets cataloging the historic attractions along America's roadways—including Indian ruins, technological artifacts, and homes of illustrious Americans—for each state. The series narrated these places as milestones in the nation's history of "progress," conceptualized as the country's ongoing domination of its natural environment. It also celebrated the local folklore and folkways of each state as reflecting America's unique and indigenous culture (Shaffer 2001: 186–202).

The physical act of touring through national space shaped the course of development in Washington, DC, in ways that early planners literally could not have imagined. Most prosaically, the development of a transportation infrastructure facilitated travel to the capital, which in the wake of widespread tourism could no longer claim to be the sole symbolic "center" of America. But more substantively, tourism provided Washington with a new way of conceptualizing and showcasing national memory. Throughout the nineteenth century the city had proceeded in fits and starts to memorialize American history. Some three decades after Federalists and Republicans first battled over the *raison d'être* of national memory, Congress finally commissioned an artist, Horatio Greenbrough, to sculpt a statue of George Washington. In 1841, Greenbrough's piece was installed outside the Capitol, not far from the site where the crypt had been proposed. Featuring Washington as the Roman god Jupiter, seated half-naked on a throne, the statue became a national laughing-stock, and was removed after just two years. Following this débâcle, Congress settled mostly on the planting of memorial trees, and the installation of equestrian-style statues commemorating select military heroes at a number of sites throughout the city, just as L'Enfant had originally envisioned. At least as far as the public was concerned, the results were pleasing enough. With its network of gardens and public art, Washington, DC, became the most popular tourist destination for newlyweds by the 1880s (Savage 2005: 95). And yet, it still lacked a single monumental center reflecting an iconic power comparable to that of its natural landscape.

With the plan to build the National Mall, unveiled in 1901, Washington, DC, came into its own as a memorial hub of the nation. The proposed design of the Mall—as an open, rectangular area of fields lined with elm trees, extending approximately three miles along an east–west axis from the Capitol building to the newly planned Lincoln Memorial—took its architectural inspiration from an earlier monument to George Washington, conceived after the removal of Greenbrough's statue. In 1845, a private association of citizens had successfully proposed to Congress the idea of building a 555-foot-tall obelisk, the Washington Monument, to commemorate America's mythic founder. For its time, the concept was a radical one, not only for the scale of the project—which took over four decades to construct—but also for its design. According to the architectural protocol of the day, great men were commemorated with statues, while obelisks functioned as place markers, most commonly of Revolutionary battlefields. Memorializing George Washington with an obelisk—built, no less, at a site that lacked any historical relevance to the Revolution—succeeded in breaking the old Federalist–Republican deadlock, only to leave observers puzzling over its symbolic significance. Following its completion in 1884, city planners and landscape architects struggled for nearly 20 years to incorporate the Washington Monument into the overall memorial landscape of the capital, failing to agree on a solution.

Then came the idea to build the National Mall *around* the Washington Monument—not simply as an embellishment, but as an iconic space in which the obelisk would stand (Savage 2005: 162–66). Conceptualized during the heyday of patriotic tourism, the Mall was a symbolic compression of the expansive nation as travelers along the transcontinental railroads were then experiencing it. It evoked an experience of Nature's Nation stretching unbroken "from sea to shining sea." The Mall gave meaning, retroactively, to the abstract design of the Washington Monument. From the perspective of the twentieth century, memorializing George Washington as an embodied figure—as either military hero or moral exemplar—would have been to limit the greatness of his legacy. The marvels of technology had made it abundantly clear that modern America quite literally transcended the limitations of physicality by overcoming them. The National Mall, with the Washington Monument near its center, highlighted the immanent splendor of what the nation had become since the days of the Revolution.

The basic structure of today's Mall came to completion in 1922, with the formal dedication of the Lincoln Memorial. Located on the western terminus of the Mall, the monument commemorated Abraham Lincoln not simply as a historical figure, but also symbolically as America's "second founding father." To a certain extent, the Lincoln Memorial was in keeping with the architectural customs of its day: Lincoln as a "great man" was memorialized by a statue of his likeness, enshrined within a Greek-Doric-style temple. Beyond this formality, however, the Memorial reflected its own break with cultural precedent. First, Lincoln's *words* were commemorated as part of the monument: the text of the Gettysburg Address was inscribed on the walls of one interior chamber; that of his Second Inaugural Address in another. The inclusion of these speeches went beyond the mere commemoration of an individual man to underscore the transcendent dimension of the national ideals articulated in his orations. Second, the towering statue of the seated president, with brow furrowed and fingers clenched, evoked the pathos of the Civil War and, by extension, the gravity of the personal sacrifices for which all wars in defense of the nation call. This was a far cry from the triumphal celebration of military heroism reflected in the extant statues of the day.

The Lincoln Memorial does not represent, of course, the first attempt in America to commemorate warfare. On the contrary, war memorials of a more explicit nature have figured as a perennial feature of the national monumental landscape since the early nineteenth century. In commemorating and sanctifying the ultimate sacrifice that citizens undergo for their nation, they come closest to traditional religious monuments—analogous to temples of human sacrifice dedicated to the gods, or shrines built to house the holy remains of martyrs. In his classic discussion of modern nationalism, Benedict Anderson notes that nations, like the religious communities that preceded them, offer their members an ultimate meaning to contingency, suffering, and death. "It is the magic of nationalism to turn chance into destiny," he writes (Anderson 2006: 12), and nowhere more clearly do we see this symbolic transformation enacted than in modern monuments to warfare. A singular difference between religious and national sacrifice relates again, however, to their distinctive notions of time and space. In a traditionally religious context, sacrifice is believed to effect an alchemical transformation of the temporal body into an eternal one; the physical remains of sacrificial victims are charged with sacred power, while their spirits, it is believed, go on to dwell eternally with the gods or God. In the modern context, however, it is the act of sacrifice itself that is venerated; by continually laying down their lives for the country, citizens assure the perpetuation of their nation's existence into the indefinite future.

Throughout the antebellum period monuments to war most commonly took the form of statues to military leaders, as in Horatio Greenbrough's rendition of George Washington as the sword-wielding Jupiter. Thousands of such statues, erected in cities and towns throughout the nation up until the twentieth century, were intended to instill the values of patriotic honor, loyalty, and duty in their onlookers. Also during the antebellum period, citizens memorialized a number of Revolutionary battlefields, erecting obelisks where American blood had been shed. A number of ancient civilizations, including Egypt and Rome, once built obelisks as *axes mundi*, orienting their societies to the timeless realm of the gods. In the modern American context, however, citizens appropriated them to evoke a sense of the timelessness and permanence of democratic ideals. In 1825, Daniel Webster delivered a speech at the laying-of-the-cornerstone ceremony for the Bunker Hill Monument in Boston that captures the secular meaning of national sacrifice in the early decades after the Revolution. Webster began by reminding his contemporaries:

> We are among the sepulchers of our fathers. We are on ground distinguished by their valor, their constancy, and the shedding of their blood. We are here, not to fix an uncertain date in our annals, nor to draw into notice an obscure and unknown spot. If our humble purpose had never been conceived, if we ourselves had never been born, the 17th of June, 1775, would have been a day on which all subsequent history would have poured its light, and the eminence where we stand, a point of attraction to the eyes of successive generations.
>
> (Webster 1825)

Striking here is the absence of any language invoking God or explicitly biblical imagery. The ground is "distinguished" but not holy; it has *become* eminent and worthy of attraction due to the marvelous deeds of America's Revolutionary forebears enacted in ordinary time. For this historic rather than divine reason, a 221-foot obelisk made of granite was raised to mark the Battle of Bunker Hill, becoming the inspiration for the even taller—and equally secular—Washington Monument.

After the Civil War, new military leaders joined the ranks of America's wartime heroes, while hundreds of new battlefields were added to the national landscape, mostly in the South. Just as they had commemorated the Revolutionary War, citizens on both sides of the conflict glorified heroes by commissioning statues, and memorializing the battlegrounds as places of collective sacrifice—in defense of either the Union or the Confederacy. Commemorating the Civil War presented obvious challenges for the Union that former military conflicts had not. The federal government took care to highlight the ideal of national unity even as it acknowledged the gravity of the South's former secession. Even as the War was still raging, Pennsylvania citizens bought up the land where the Battle of Gettysburg had been fought, and began orchestrating the commemoration of the dead, emphasizing Union sacrifices. In the patriotic tours orchestrated by railroad companies after the war, Civil War battlefields were not even included as sites of national pilgrimage, as they detracted from the goal of evoking a sense of the country's singular, mystical essence. At the same time, other battlegrounds—particularly sites of conflict with Native Americans— were showcased as important chapters in an overarching history of America's progress.

While the Lincoln Memorial was not built as a war memorial per se, its associations with the Civil War were inescapable. The anguish etched into the face and hands of Lincoln's statue acknowledged the gravity of the divisions that had led to the conflict, transforming the Mall into what art and architecture historian Kirk Savage has called "a space of engagement with loss and suffering" (2005: 251). Ultimately, however, the inclusion of the Lincoln Memorial reflected the federal government's attempt to consolidate and thus control the politics of memory. In 1933, the National Parks Service took a step further, taking over custodianship of all Civil War battlefields from the War Department, and commemorating them within its master narrative of national unity. During the same period, however, many Southerners took the commemoration of battlefields into their own hands. They remembered them within their own understanding of the South as having fought valiantly to defend "the religion of the lost cause," retaining a sense of collective identity distinct from the rest of the country (see Wilson 1983). Thus the politics of national memory, which had undermined earlier efforts to consecrate the federal capital, were quietly returning again—foreshadowing a new phase of memorializing that would come to characterize the post-Vietnam era.

Decentralized memory

By the 1940s, the infrastructural network of national monuments in America was largely complete. By train, or increasingly by car, citizens could travel to and interact with a constellation of natural and historical sites diffused throughout the nation. The city planners of Washington, DC, had at last succeeded in transforming the city into the memorial capital that L'Enfant had envisioned, by reconceptualizing the very notion of "sacred space." A single governmental agency, the National Parks Service, oversaw, maintained, and commemorated the vast majority of these locales, helping to consolidate and give coherence to national memory. Together they recounted a simple if not simplistic story about the United States, one that emphasized its permanence and glory. America was founded on the ontological bedrock of Nature, enshrined in its many natural parks. Its expansion reflected the unstoppable history of progress, made evident in hydroelectric dams and dynamos, and valorized at historic sites and battlefields. Not even the Civil War had been able to thwart it. On the contrary, the dissolution and reunification of the Union turned out to be a collective experience of redemptive death and rebirth, a message that was writ large in the Lincoln Memorial.

From the hindsight of the twenty-first century, America's heyday of political and symbolic consolidation—lasting roughly from 1880 to 1940—was short-lived. Even at the outset of the Cold War era, the ideal of patriotic tourism was quickly giving way to a decidedly more individualistic notion of enjoying the nation's roadways for recreational or therapeutic purposes. The rising popularity of Las Vegas during the 1950s, or the building of Disneyland at the decade's end, exemplify this trend— which American studies scholar Marguerite Shaffer has characterized as "the ultimate quest for self-indulgent individual pleasure and hedonistic personal freedom in a culture of mass consumption ... revolv[ing] around spectacle, fantasy, and desire" along the American highways (Shaffer 2001: 320). Even in the nation's capital, where John F. Kennedy exhorted citizens to ask what they could do for their country, First Lady Jacqueline Kennedy transformed the White House into Camelot through her own exquisite wielding of pillbox hats and fabulous china. Consumerism, driven by the arousal and satiation of personal appetite, began to vie with America's collectivist ideals of sacrifice for the common good. In light of these individualizing trends, it became increasingly difficult to say what the significance of Mount Rushmore or the White House was for all Americans. The answers were as varied as the citizenry themselves, who continued to flock to national monuments on their own schedules and for their own reasons.

The nation's political culture also underwent a sea change during the 1960s, with the rise of the Civil Rights Movement and the mass protests against the Vietnam War. The National Mall was suddenly transformed from a memorial space of unity into a theater of protest. In different ways, both of these movements exposed and desanctified the violence inextricably linked to the nation's consolidation and expansion. Against their backdrop, the dark underside of earlier monuments glorifying war and conquest became disturbingly clear. To cite just one example, Anglo-Europeans had long memorialized an entire array of locales in the Black Hills of South Dakota—including the iconic, twentieth-century Mount Rushmore National Memorial—as celebrating the myth of American progress. Following the rise of the American Indian Movement (AIM) in the late 1960s, however, Lakota and other Native peoples reclaimed the region as their own, re-inscribing the same locales as memorials to America's orchestrated program of Indian genocide. Two decades earlier, Korczak Ziolkowski, a Polish American sculptor, had begun work on the Crazy Horse Memorial to commemorate one Indian warrior, but now the members of AIM were demanding the return of the Black Hills themselves to the Lakota Nation.

It would be inaccurate, however, to characterize these economic and political trends entirely as postmodern or post-nationalist developments. As we have seen, efforts to memorialize Washington, DC, were undercut during the first half of the nineteenth century by the Republican ethos of political decentralization and individualism. A striking example of this perspective was reflected in the proposal made by John Nicholas, a Virginian congressman and close friend of Thomas Jefferson, during the first debates over how to memorialize George Washington. Rather than building a crypt or erecting a statue, Nicholas suggested leaving a plain tablet in the nation's capital, upon which each citizen could express what the Revolutionary hero meant to him. Further, the ambiguous meanings of Civil War battlefields, as interpreted alternatively by Northerners and Southerners during the heyday of national consolidation, offers a precedent for the political battles over national memory in the late twentieth century.

There are, however, two unprecedented trends discernible in the ways that America memorializes itself today. The first lies in the novel design of many new public memorials built since the 1982 dedication of Maya Lin's Vietnam Veterans Memorial in Washington, DC. Lin's piece, the first major addition to the capital's memorial landscape since the 1930s, came to change the expectations that Americans have about monuments. The Vietnam Veterans Memorial is a stark and minimalist space where individuals can develop their own relationships with the fact of the Vietnam War and/or the American veterans who perished in its wake. It consists of two walls—each approximately 250-feet long and comprised of 140 polished black, marble panels—arranged in a "V" shape and meeting at a 125° angle. On the panels are inscribed the individual names of some 58,000 veterans who were killed or reported missing in action during the War. Constructed below ground level, the Vietnam Veterans Memorial is intended to evoke the experience of descending into a grave. Unlike previous memorials, this one is horizontal rather than vertical. It makes no attempt to depict scenes of the conflict or to create likenesses of combatants. It lacks any iconography such as a flag or an eagle or the Great Seal that might suggest an association with the nation.

At the time of its unveiling, the Vietnam Veterans Memorial awakened a storm of controversy. Secretary of the Interior James Watt initially refused to grant a building permit for the memorial, while some onlookers described Lin's piece as a "black gash of shame" and a "nihilistic slab of stone" (Wills 2007). Despite these initial protests, however, the Vietnam Veterans Memorial has been an immensely popular site since its dedication; over the first decade of the twenty-first century it drew between three and four million visitors each year (National Park Service n.d.). Furthermore, it has become something of a prototype for other architects, who now take pains to distinguish their *memorials* as interactive and emotionally evocative spaces, from *monuments* as static and didactic shrines to nationalism (Doss 2010: 38). Many features of the National September 11 Memorial and Museum, for example, mimic those of the Vietnam Veterans Memorial—including its horizontality, its lack of overt visual references to either the Twin Towers or the attacks upon them, and its inclusion of the individual names of the victims. The Oklahoma City National

Memorial, to cite another example, is also minimalist in its design—organized around a long reflecting pool, remnants of the Murrah Building, and a field filled with 168 empty chairs—inviting visitors into a highly personal and interactive relationship with the memorial space. The new memorials inspired by Lin's have effectively enshrined the iconoclastic and individualistic tendencies of American culture. They simultaneously commemorate the nation, and resist the ideal of proclaiming a singular American memory.

Related to this new architectural trend is the sheer proliferation of memorials in the present-day United States, a veritable "memorial mania" that American studies scholar Erika Doss has studied at length. Among the explanations Doss gives for the phenomenon are an explosion of the historical archives effected by new technologies (Doss 2010: 78), and heightened expectations of individual representation among the citizenry (ibid.: 19). In the first case, the modern idea of "making history," once enacted in the consecration of Revolutionary liberty trees, is now realized through the construction of makeshift or permanent memorials which showcase media representations of highly localized events in the form of photographs, videos, and recordings. In the second case, memorial mania reflects a convergence of the Enlightenment ideal of political individualism with the more Romantic notion of *expressive* individualism, where the voicing of sentiment is a value in and of itself. Given the lack of any single political, social, or religious content unifying this profusion of sites, Doss suggests that we think about memorials primarily in terms of the emotions they embody and evoke, classifying them according to their predominant expressions of grief, fear, gratitude, anger, or shame.

The mania for memorializing reached fever pitch in the immediate aftermath of the September 11 attacks, even spreading for a short time beyond the United States, as sympathizers around the world paid spontaneous tribute to the victims. To cite just one example, on September 12 at London's Buckingham Palace, the Band of the Coldstream Guards played the Star Spangled Banner during the changing of Queen Elizabeth's royal guards. A crowd of mostly American visitors, who had gathered in front of the palace to mourn the recent calamities, tearfully watched on, holding flags and newspaper photographs of the wreckage back home (Graves 2001). Consistent with Doss's analysis, post-September-11 memorials like this one were both decentralized and improvisational. They were driven by a high-tech and internationally coordinated network of media outlets, which repeatedly aired a small set of images portraying America-under-siege, including the now iconic video spectacle of the collapsing Twin Towers. The gatherings were highly affective and—in hindsight—largely ephemeral performances. For just a few months, Americans could imagine themselves as a united people, forgetting all about the contentious "culture wars" that had been raging throughout the nation for at least two decades prior to 2001. In fact, it did not take very long for these divisions to return; within two years, the same footage that had effected a collective national catharsis could be watched again in conspiracy-theory videos, portraying the September 11 attacks as federally orchestrated.

What moral are we to draw from this radical decentralization and destabilization of American memory? On the one hand, Robert Bellah's worst fears seem to have come true. When he penned his first essay on American civil religion in 1967, Bellah spoke of the United States as undergoing a "time of trial," faced with the choice between uniting around common principles, or disintegrating into a multitude of competing political factions (Bellah 1967: 40). Bellah hoped that by directing public attention to the mythic core of national identity—an amalgam of biblical ideals inherited from the Puritans—scholars of American religion could lend a hand to the cause of national reconciliation. But despite the repeated invocation of Puritan-derived, national mythology by American presidents since Ronald Reagan, the nation does not seem to have grown any more unified than it was in 1967—the few months of post-September-11 patriotism notwithstanding. Memorials since the Vietnam Veterans Memorial have enshrined dissent as the unifying ideal of the citizenry. Conversely, the profusion of memorials since the 1960s testifies to the plurality of American identities rather than a single national mythos derived from the New England Puritans.

On the other hand, the present-day decentralization of memory reflects a seamless continuation of post-religious strategies for evoking and perpetuating collective identity. As we have seen, modern notions of horizontal time and space, as well as democratic ideals of individualism, implicitly undermine the ideal of an unchanging and singular tradition. As early as the American Revolution, Puritan cosmology was giving way to new Enlightenment notions of space, time, and community, and the architects of America's memorial network during the late nineteenth and early twentieth centuries unified the country by evoking Nature in a distinctively modern key—as the sublime, though not transcendent, backdrop of national history.

The tensions within the Revolutionary civil religion, which flattened transcendence without obliterating it, have finally given way today to the unqualified celebration of American society as cut loose and free in the boundlessness of horizontal time and space. Despite the loss of a coherent or stable national memory, America continues to replicate itself like never before, in and through countless acts of decentralized and private acts of memorializing, which proliferate endlessly and rhizomatically in a world with no center.

Notes

1 "I consider the work I do memorials, not monuments; in fact, I've often thought of them as anti-monuments. I think I don't make objects; I make places. I think that is very important—the places set a stage for experience and for understanding experience. I don't want to say these places are stages where you act out, but rather places where something happens within the viewer" (Lin 1995: 16).

2 The idea that the nation is based on a new understanding of time as empty and homogenous constitutes the main thesis of Benedict Anderson's now-classic monograph, *Imagined Communities* (rev. edn, 2006). Anderson's analysis underscores the ways in which the rise of print-capitalism—and particularly the dissemination of daily newspapers—enabled readers to imagine themselves existing simultaneously alongside fellow citizens in the same "horizontal" time.

3 "'Annihilation of space and time' was the early-nineteenth-century characterization of the effect of railroad travel. The concept was based on the speed that the new means of transport was able to achieve. A given spatial distance, traditionally covered in a fixed amount

of travel time, could suddenly be dealt with in a fraction of that time; to put it another way, the same amount of time permitted one to cover the old spatial distance many times over" (Schivelbusch 1977: 33).

Works cited

Albanese, C.L. (1976) *Sons of the Fathers: The Civil Religion of the American Revolution*, Philadelphia, PA: Temple University Press.

Anderson, B. (2006) *Imagined Communities: Reflections on the Origin and Spread of Nationalism*, rev. edn, New York: Verso.

Bellah, R. (1967) "Civil religion in America," *Daedalus* 96, 1 (Winter): 1–21.

Bloch, R.H. (1985) *Visionary Republic: Millennial Themes in American Thought, 1756–1800*, Cambridge, UK: Cambridge University Press.

Calvin, J. (1545) "Catechism of the Church of Geneva," in J.K.S. Reid (ed.) (1954) *Calvin: Theological Treatises*, Philadelphia, PA: Westminster Press, 88–139.

Doss, E. (2010) *Memorial Mania: Public Feeling in America*, Chicago, IL: The University of Chicago Press.

Eliade, M. (1954) *The Myth of the Eternal Return, or Cosmos and History*, Princeton, NJ: Princeton University Press.

Fischer, D.H. (1989) *Albion's Seed: Four British Folkways in America*, New York: Oxford University Press.

Graves, D. (2001) "Palace breaks with tradition to honor victims of attacks," *Daily Telegraph* (September 14): A18.

Hughes, R.T. (2004) *Myths America Lives By*, Urbana, IL: University of Illinois Press.

Lane, B.C. (2002) *Landscapes of the Sacred: Geography and Narrative in American Spirituality*, Baltimore, MD: The Johns Hopkins University Press.

Lin, M.Y. (1995) *Grounds for Remembering: Monuments, Memorials, Texts*, Berkeley, CA: Doreen B. Townsend Center. Online. Available: http://repositories.cdlib.org/townsend/occpapers/3 (accessed 7 December 2011).

Lower Manhattan Development Corporation (n.d.) "World Trade Center Site Memorial Competition Guidelines." Online. Available: http://www.wtcsitememorial.org/pdf/LM DC_Guidelines_english.pdf (accessed 11 November 2014).

Mead, S. (1977) *The Old Religion in the Brave New World: Reflections on the Relation between Christendom and the Republic*, Berkeley, CA: University of California Press.

National Park Service Organic Act (1916) 16 U.S.C. 1. Online. Available: www.justice.gov/enrd/ 3195.htm (accessed 17 November 2014).

National Park Service, US Department of the Interior (n.d.) "NPS stats: National Park Service Public Use Statistics Office." Online. Available: www.nature.nps.gov/stats/viewReport.cfm (accessed 17 December 2011).

Ramsay, D. (1811) *The History of the American Revolution*, 2 vols., Trenton, NJ: James J. Wilson.

Richley, R.E. and D.G. Jones (eds) (1974) *American Civil Religion*, New York: Harper & Row.

Savage, K. (2005) *Monument Wars: Washington, D.C., the National Mall, and the Transformation of the Memorial Landscape*, Berkeley, CA: The University of California Press.

Schivelbusch, W. (1977) *The Railway Journey: The Industrialization of Time and Space in the 19th Century*, Berkeley, CA: The University of California Press.

Shaffer, M.S. (2001) *See America First: Tourism and National Identity, 1880–1940*, Washington, DC: Smithsonian Books.

Webster, D. (1825) *An Address Delivered at the Laying of the Corner Stone of the Bunker Hill Monument*, 4th edn, Boston, MA: Cummings, Hilliard, and Company.

Westminster Assembly (1646) "The Westminster Confession," in J.H. Leith (ed.) (1982), *Creeds of the Churches: A Reader in Christian Doctrine from the Bible to the Present*, 3rd edn, Louisville, KY: John Knox Press, 192–229.

Wills, D.K. (2007) "The Vietnam Memorial's history," *The Washingtonian* (November 1). Online. Available: www.washingtonian.com/print/articles/6/174/5595.html (accessed 17 December 2011).

Wilson, C.R. (1983) *Baptized in Blood: The Religion of the Lost Cause, 1865–1920*, Athens, GA: The University of Georgia Press.

Part III
RELIGIOUS TRADITIONS

Introduction to Part III

In the fluid encounter of religion and popular culture—where headlines are made by one resisting (or threatening) the other—it is often easy to overlook their profound symbiotic relationship. But if religious institutions and traditions are embedded in culture, and if culture is one form of meaning-transmission, it stands to reason that there is no way to separate the human experience of religion from the human experience of culture—even "popular" culture. And yet, whether it is Amish "reality" programming, a proliferation of Hindu symbols, Madonna (Madonna!) practicing Jewish mysticism, or entrepreneurs reading up on Zen business practices, much of the critical examination occurs on the popular culture side of the equation. The presumption is too often that religious traditions are immune to change, but that individuals pick and choose elements and aspects of the religious world to construct (and reconstruct) popular culture. The following chapters remind us that—taking a lesson from Heraclitus—the reason one never steps in the same river twice is because both the person and the river are never the same for experience. The encounters between religion and popular culture change both popular culture and the various religious traditions and their institutions.

In his chapter on Buddhism, James Mark Shields explores the popular cultural manifestations in (mostly American) culture. From comics to television, products of commercialism to literary productions, Shields examines various aspects of Buddhism and how they have come to be communicated to, understood by, and reinterpreted by a popular (that is, non-elite) American culture. Yet despite the easy criticism that this form of Buddhism is a bastardized, inauthentic appropriation of an ancient tradition, Shields argues that not only do these various reinterpretations have links in various—and ancient—forms of Buddhism, but that to argue for one "authentic" form of Buddhism is itself a concept foreign to Buddhism. While not abandoning the possibility that some popular manifestations of Buddhism may be worthy of critique (and even reproach), Shields leaves us with an image of Buddhism gone global.

After providing, in his chapter on Roman Catholicism, a foundational account of the history of American anti-Catholicism, Rodger Payne examines the transformed place of Catholics in twentieth-century America. If American dominant (and popular) culture from the colonial period belonged to the Protestant, the mediated culture of the twentieth century belonged to the non-Protestant. And the first such non-Protestant to ascend to that position was the Catholic, whose sights and sounds, rituals and rites, lent themselves to visual culture—perfect for the new medium of film, but then also for an expanding world of mediated culture. And while Catholics continued to represent a religious "other" long into the twentieth century, their integration into both popular and mundane culture not only changed American attitudes toward Catholics, but also changed how American Roman Catholics understood themselves in traditionally non-Catholic cultures.

In her chapter on Hinduism, Sheila Nayar echoes this notion that an aspect of a religious tradition—in this case, the importance of seeing, and being seen—can make that tradition well suited for an encounter with the modern world of popular culture. As she traces the impact of popular culture on Hinduism—on the one hand, examining Western notions (and appropriations) of Hinduism, on the other exploring tradition-based Hindus' use of Western popular cultural forms (such as the Internet) for religious purposes—she is clear that, since there is no such thing as one "authentic" Hinduism, all of the variations are themselves in keeping with the trajectory of the tradition. And while the Hindu identity has historically been tied to India—and remains so for some—the challenges that might be expected as Hinduism (in whatever form) goes global actually have been eased by this adaptability, even if the normal difficulties of inter-religious and intercultural encounter remain.

Those difficulties of encounter are nowhere more apparent than in William Youmans's chapter on Islam. Although this encounter has its roots in the earliest moments of global culture—commercial and cultural interactions between the Muslim and Christian worlds going back centuries—it is also one that has been particularly difficult. Youmans examines in Western popular culture the two-sided coin of Islamophobia/Islamophilia, a coin that, no matter how it is spent, still purchases an essentialization that is a gross distortion of the human reality of actual Muslims; a world of "good" and "bad" Muslims reminiscent of earlier representations of Native Americans or other non-American "others." And yet, even as these tropes are pervasive in contemporary Western popular culture, there is a growing recognition—by both Muslims and non-Muslims—of the international nature of Islam in the non-Muslim majority world, and of the power of popular media to transmit more nuanced images and characterizations.

Taking a slightly different route in his chapter on Judaism, Eric Michael Mazur argues that a coincidence of timing has had a profound effect on the role of Jews in popular culture. In part because of Western liberalization that emancipated the Jew from cultural segregation, and in part because of transformations within Judaism that created new, different, and (in many ways) less visible ways of being Jewish, Jews in Western culture—but (at least initially) primarily in the United States—were not only actually free to participate in larger culture, but felt freer to do so from a religio-cultural point of view. Aspects of Judaism such as religious performativity—a privileging in Judaism of behavior over ideology—provided for Jews an ease of movement into related forms of popular culture, similar to the Hindu emphasis on seeing and being seen, or the Catholic emphasis on sights and sounds. Mazur suggests that, as a result of this transformation within the tradition, a new form of "post-rabbinic" Judaism is becoming visible, particularly through the products of popular culture.

In a similar fashion, in their chapter on Mormonism, Lynita Newswander, Chad Newswander, and Lee Trepanier examine the emergence of this religious tradition into the gentile world. From a history of persecution, Mormons have experienced a series of "Mormon moments," emerging as the quintessential Americans; first with the Osmond Brothers, and most recently with presidential candidate Mitt Romney. Through all of their appearances—including as authors, scriptwriters, fictional characters, and a number of "reality" programs—Mormons have emerged as real people, complex beyond the stereotypes (positive or negative) that have been such a prominent part of their history. In part as a response to it, and in part in conjunction with it, the Mormon community has come to see itself in a more nuanced way as well; to be the quintessential American now means something entirely different from what it meant when the Osmond Brothers first appeared on television. As the American view of Mormons has become more complex, so too has the Mormon view of Mormons.

Self-conceptualization and the challenge of the norm is at the heart of Jodie Vann's chapter on Contemporary Paganism. In her own critique of the processes of "otherness," Vann examines the very processes of meaning making, reminding us that to identify something as "alternative" is to suggest that there is a "central," and that, increasingly in Western culture, the very notion of something being privileged as "central" in the area of religion is problematic. Justifiably, Vann explores not just the history of a religious tradition, but the history of the study of a religious tradition, and finds that the academic study of Contemporary Paganism—as opposed to the theological critique in defense against it—is directly related to the expansion (in the academy) of what was considered a worthwhile pursuit. With the recognition of less institution-tied forms of religious behavior—such elements as identified by the "history of religions" school, including myth, ritual, text, and constructions of sacred space and sacred time—came the recognition that people could be religious in many ways. Vann's analysis explores the ways in which Contemporary Paganism has been expressed through contemporary forms of popular culture, and how it has been represented there. These representations, in turn, have had a powerful impact on how Contemporary Pagans see themselves, and how they have engaged the world around them.

Finally, in his chapter on Protestantism, Clive Marsh acknowledges what most seem to sense, that representations of this broad, diverse, and populous religious tradition are conspicuously absent from Western popular culture. In part, Marsh suggests, this has to do with the pervasiveness of Protestantism in Western (in this case, English-speaking) culture, and in part it has to do with Protestant structures that seem to minimize the appearance of institutional conflict: if you don't like your minister, go find another church. He also suggests that denominationalism contributes to the absence of Protestantism, largely because popular confusion over doctrinal differences obliterates any use in denominational identification. Catholics, it would seem, are all Catholic, and Jews are all Jews; but what is a Protestant? Forces of secularization have complicated the matter, as venues of popular culture turn to the religious fanatic—in this case Protestant—as the representation of the religious adherent.

Marsh's conclusions remind us of the two-way power inherent in the encounter between religion and popular culture. As non-majoritarian religious traditions—everyone except white Protestants—struggle to be fairly represented in popular culture even as they struggle with its influence, does the receding of "mainstream" Protestantism into the background make it a victim of its own successes, or a sign of what awaits the other religious traditions? There is no doubt that the encounter of religion and popular culture has a profound impact on both.

21
BUDDHISM

James Mark Shields

Introduction: commodification, resistance, and the conversion of Captain America

The cover of *Captain America #35* is, from a cultural studies perspective, truly extraordinary. Published in February 1944, at the height of the Second World War, it confronts the reader/viewer with a dynamic tableau of good versus evil. At lower center, his hands clutching a diabolical control wheel, is the bespectacled arch-villain—complete with Asiatic features. Protecting him (and bearing a striking resemblance to the Buddhist guardian deities at the great Nara temple Todaiji) are two muscular green henchmen, facing attack (and certain defeat!) by Captain America and an ally, who fly into the scene with alacrity. And at the center of it all, taking up fully half the vertical space in the image, sits a large Buddha statue, nearly blocking what appears to be a Japanese Imperial flag. Other than the evil scowl and blood-red mouth, the statue is a reasonable facsimile of the great bronze *daibutsu* statue of Kōtoku-in, Kamakura, perhaps the world's most recognizable representation of Amida, the Buddha of compassion.

This 1944 comic projects animosity against Japan as an enemy nation as well as public perceptions (fueled by wartime propaganda) of the Japanese as a "cruel race," as much as (if not more than) it says anything about wartime perceptions of Buddhism in the USA. But that is precisely where it is most interesting: the Buddha comes to "stand for" a whole set of perceptions and assumptions that are deeply dependent on the particular cultural, historical, and political context. The image acts as a synecdoche—or perhaps, more accurately, a cipher. Flash forward 67 years, to 2011, as the Hollywood blockbuster film (or "film-event") *Captain America* is released in theaters worldwide. While the Buddha—evil or otherwise—makes no appearance in the film, the actor who plays Captain America, Chris Evans, is, it turns out, a committed, practicing, "out of the closet" Buddhist. In other words, after nearly seven decades, Captain America has converted—as apparently, have the US media. But what does this mean? And does it make a difference?

By examining a few common narratives and representative tropes of Buddhism in postwar American popular culture, this chapter limns the contours of the tension between ideology and attraction, convention and extension, appropriation and hybridity. I play Devil's (or perhaps, Mara's) advocate, raising questions against those—and they are many—who would too readily dismiss or attack instances of Buddhist "appropriation" or "commodification" by the forces of contemporary popular or consumer culture.[1]

Buddhism and/as popular culture

Since this chapter concerns itself with the specific case of Buddhist traditions, I leave aside here discussion of the more general definition of religion—which allows me to forego discussion of the vexed question of whether Buddhism is or is not a "religion" (as opposed to a "philosophy" or "way of life"). I am more interested in coming to terms with the concept of "popular culture." Rather than turn our neatly boxed magnifying glasses to the fusty pages of the *Oxford English Dictionary*, what better place to begin a discussion of popular culture than the contemporary source that for many typifies popular knowledge: Wikipedia. Here is what we find:

> Popular culture (commonly known as pop culture) is the entirety of ideas, perspectives, attitudes, memes, images and other phenomena that are within the mainstream of a given culture, especially Western culture of the early to mid 20th century and the emerging global mainstream of the late 20th and early 21st century. Heavily influenced by mass media, this collection of ideas permeates the everyday lives of the society.
>
> (Wikipedia.com 2013)[2]

All told, this is a fairly standard and uncontroversial definition of pop culture, understood as a) broadly comprehensive; b) popular or "mainstream"; c) originating in the modern West but increasingly "universalized" due to globalization; d) reinforced by mass media and practices of consumption. We also see here the seeds of discontent—popular culture has been vilified for being vulgar, decadent, superficial, imperialistic, homogenizing, or any combination of these. Though early critics came largely from the intellectual or artistic elite, today opponents of pop culture generally fall into two very different camps: religious conservatives, who see popular culture as a vehicle for liberal, secular, and permissive norms, and secular progressives, for whom the "sin" of pop culture lies not in its permissiveness, but rather in its capitalistic, imperialistic, and homogenizing aspects. The Disney Corporation, perhaps the single most influential shaper of American popular culture since the Second World War, routinely faces criticism from both conservatives and progressives. Interestingly, elements of arguments from both camps align in standard critiques of pop culture's appropriation of Buddhist ideas and imagery, as we will see.

The most exhaustive attempt to theorize popular culture comes from John Storey, whose 2003 work *Cultural Theory and the Study of Popular Culture* notes six competing understandings of the term. Of these, the two most useful for our purposes are the third, which equates pop culture with "mass" or "commercial culture," and the fifth, which, following the work of Antonio Gramsci (1891–1937), locates pop culture at the intersection of a struggle "between the 'resistance' of subordinate groups in society and the forces of 'incorporation' operating in the interests of dominant groups in society" (Storey 2003: 4–5). Although these two definitions seem to underscore the modern aspect of popular culture, I suggest that these can apply, *mutatis mutandis*, to the development, growth, and transmission of many traditional religions, including Buddhism. According to Forbes, popular culture refers to "widespread, common, frequently commercial, and often entertaining aspects" of our cultural context (2000: 4). I suggest that these four criteria equally apply to popular religion.

In the past several decades, Buddhist scholars have turned increasing attention to culture—and particularly material culture—as a way of understanding traditional and contemporary Asian Buddhism. The scholar whose work stands at the forefront of this movement away from the traditional philological and philosophical focus on texts, doctrine, and institutions is Gregory Schopen, who implicitly adopts an understanding of culture (and religion) whereby "cultures are made from the production, circulation and consumption of meanings. To share a culture, therefore, is to interpret the world—make it meaningful—in recognizably similar ways" (Storey 2003: 3; see Schopen 1991). On the level of doctrine, it is worth noting the remarkable similarity between the traditional Buddhist understanding of agency in the midst of complex conditionality and the Gramscian theory of "compromise equilibrium" (Gramsci 1971), which underlies much of contemporary cultural studies. According to both, "culture" is a constant process of "negotiation"—"we make culture and we are made by culture; there is agency and there is structure" (Storey 2003: 4).

Buddhism—still largely Zen, but increasingly Tibetan and Theravadin—is without question a "meme" of great resonance in contemporary United States popular and consumer culture. This fact alone makes the topic of "pop Buddhism" worthy of serious analysis.[3] I suggest, however, that analyses of the relation (and tensions) between Buddhism and US popular culture pay more attention to the Gramscian understanding of culture as the staging ground for negotiation; i.e., the locus where forces of resistance and assimilation (to hegemonic norms) are made manifest. Among other things, this allows us to move beyond the easy dichotomy of outright dismissal of pop Buddhism as being "superficial appropriation" or complete acceptance of such as fully unproblematic expressions of cultural assimilation. To that end, I would like to invoke the spirit of Charles Darwin here, since the Darwinian model of evolution by natural selection provides a useful template for understanding the historical "evolution" of major world religions such as Buddhism. Just as evolution by natural selection relies on the "random" (or non-teleological) appearance of forms that may or may not survive on the basis of (usually) long-term environmental "fit," I suggest that religious evolution works very much in the same way. Specific teachings and practices will over the course of time be interpreted in novel and frequently surprising ways, and these may or may not "fit" with the social, cultural, economic, and political needs and expectations of a given cultural environment. Nowhere in this model is there room for an "essence" or source for "authenticity" other than the capacity to survive and flourish—though religious founders and reformers often do invoke timeless essences and origins as a means to successful innovation.

In what follows, I analyze specific examples of Buddhism in American (largely postwar) popular culture, providing cases gleaned from the six forms of media outlined in Storey's *Cultural Studies and the Study of Popular Culture*: television, fiction, film, magazines, music, and everyday consumption (i.e., advertising and merchandise). Rather than discuss these one by one, however, I have classified the phenomena in the following six common themes or tropes: 1) experience; 2) freedom; 3) *karma*; 4) *nirvana*; 5) humor; and 6) resistance. By way of conclusion, via an analysis of several essays on the status of Buddhism in postwar American culture, I return to my Gramscian-Darwinian counter-critique of the appropriation thesis.

Experience: Siddhartha's quest

One of the most direct and evident influences on the portrayal, perception, and practice of contemporary American Buddhism is the existentialist movement in philosophy and literature. European existentialists picked up and developed the earlier Romantic tradition's quest for freedom via a turn "inwards" toward feelings and senses (rather than reason or tradition), and further highlighted the experience of the "self"—and the self's authenticity—in relation to existence. The Romantic-existentialist quest for authenticity—and privileging of existence over essence— would have enormous impact on postwar Buddhism, particularly as filtered through the literary works of the Beat Generation. The Buddhism of the Beats will be discussed below, but I would like to begin by looking at the work that arguably has had the single greatest "Buddhist" impact on several generations of young American readers: Hermann Hesse's *Siddhartha: An Indian Poem*.

Originally published in German in 1922, this slim novella was first translated into English in 1951[4]—coinciding with the emergence of the postwar youth counter-culture— and became extremely popular in the United States during the 1960s. The story, which takes place in ancient India, tells the tale of a young Brahmin, Siddhartha, who meets the historical Buddha, called here Gotama, and sets off on a path to enlightenment. Though he rejects the Buddha's teaching, Hesse's existentialist hero moves from decadence to asceticism, essentially recapitulating in more detail and with more drama the traditional legend of the Buddha himself, culminating in a final (palpably "Zen") awakening. As in several earlier works (e.g., *Demian*, 1919), Hesse— deeply indebted to German Romanticism—builds upon the traditional *Bildungsroman* by turning the journey inwards (German: *Weg nach Innen*). In *Siddhartha*, this is done via an eclectic pastiche of Indian philosophy (including aspects of Buddhism as well as the philosophy of the *Upanishads*), Zen, existentialism, and Jungian psychoanalysis, which would dovetail perfectly with some of the dominant intellectual and literary trends of postwar America. Particularly noteworthy, however, is the chord Hesse's *Siddhartha* struck with the emerging counter-culture of the late 1950s and '60s; an effect that would not only help to spur interest in Buddhism among the young and disaffected, but would also shape the very image of Buddhism in America. Beyond the fact that Hesse's hero refuses to accept the Buddha's doctrine—not because he believes it false but because it is *doctrine*—another aspect of the novella that aligned with counter-cultural ideals was the insistence that liberation is ultimately a solitary, contemplative affair—a quest for "pure experience"—rather than one rooted in relationships or society.[5] In Timothy Leary's infamous words: "tune in, turn on, drop out."

In terms of popular literature, the "quest/ioning" aspect of Hesse's *Siddhartha* appears as a theme in a number of "Buddhist" works of fiction published since the 1970s. Despite its title, Robert Pirsig's popular philosophical novel *Zen and the Art of Motorcycle Maintenance* (1974) has virtually nothing to do with Buddhism—and thus stands as an early example of what would become a near-ubiquitous usage of the word "Zen" in popular culture to refer to something like "inner peace" or even "spirituality." Yet, as with Hesse's earlier work, it is very much in the tradition of the existential *Bildungsroman*. Since the early 1990s, works of fiction or poetry with the word "Buddha" in the title have proliferated, such that as of October 2012, no fewer than 184 such volumes were listed for sale on Amazon.com—in addition to a further 212 with the word "Zen" in their title.[6] Hanif Kurieshi's *The Buddha of Suburbia* (1990) is typical of this trend: the book tells the tale of a young man living in contemporary London whose father becomes the leader of a group of would-be mystics, propelling the protagonist into a Siddhartha-like exploration of the range of human experience. More recently, Roland Merullo's *Breakfast with Buddha* (2008) explores the gradual transformation of a convinced skeptic via a six-day road trip with an enigmatic guru.

Freedom: *The Dharma Bums*

Like all world religions, Buddhism has long made good use of tales and legends as a vehicle to spread its message among the people, with the early Pali *jātakas* being the best-known example. And yet, it is fair to say that Buddhism in the United States has relied on literature/fiction more than any other cultural avenue, in part because of its incorporation in the work of the most prominent writers of the so-called Beat Generation: Jack Kerouac (1922–69), Allen Ginsberg (1926–97), and Gary Snyder (b. 1930) (see Whalen-Bridge and Storhoff 2009: 2). The Buddhist affinity of several of the leading figures of the Beat Generation is well known, and has been the subject of several published volumes and numerous scholarly articles (for example, see Whalen-Bridge and Storhoff 2009; Tonkinson 1995). Here I will cover only the main points of this affiliation in order to focus attention on the "Americanization" of Buddhism that one sees in the writings of the Beats. To begin, it is important to note the simple fact that Buddhism appealed to the Beats primarily because it was perceived to represent a way of living that contrasted with—and thus could be used as critique of—Western (and particularly postwar American) "bourgeois" society. More specifically, the Beat writers generally understood Buddhism as anti-authoritarian, antinomian, and anti-materialist—and, making a distinction that would solidify into a trope for succeeding generations of youth, "spiritual" without being "religious." Buddhism, and particularly Zen, was perceived as a source for spiritual wisdom that could also support (and, in many cases, justify) the subjective individualism and idealism that the Beats and others had ingested from the Western Romantics, including the American transcendentalists, the European existentialists, and their heirs (many of whom were also attracted to the East in general and Buddhism in particular; see Tonkinson 1995: vii).[7]

In *The Dharma Bums* (1958), Kerouac (via his alter ego, Ray Smith) gives full expression to his eclectic approach to Buddhism, freely mixing it with Christianity and other traditions, as well as offering a critique of the *kōan* tradition as well as the meditation focus of Zen. "All those Zen masters throwing young kids in the mud because they can't answer their silly word questions" (Kerouac 1986: 13). "People have good hearts whether or not they live like Dharma Bums. Compassion is the heart of Buddhism" (ibid.: 132). Here Kerouac appears more inclined toward Larry Darrell of Somerset Maugham's *The Razor's Edge* than Hesse's Siddhartha. As with Maugham's book and Frank Capra's subsequent film, *The Dharma Bums* was read as a blistering critique of bourgeois sensibilities, and particularly the consumerist ethos. The *American Buddhist* proclaimed it "an answer to the literature of disillusion, petulant sensualism and indignation against dry-heart bourgeois hypocrisy ... " (Tonkinson 1995: 27). And yet, along with Hesse's protagonist, Kerouac was reluctant to accept "doctrine" of any sort—even that coming from Buddhism: "But I can't imagine what my rules would be, what rules would conform with pure essence Buddhism, say. That would be, I spose, NO RULES. Pure Essence is what I think I want, and lay aside all the arbitrary rest of it, Hinayana, Shinayana ... Zen, Shmen ... " (Tonkinson 1995: 47). Once again, we see the existential quest for personal authenticity culminating in a freedom that ultimately transcends rules and ideas of any sort.

"Karma chameleon"

Of all classical Indian terms associated with Buddhism, *karma* is without question the one most recognizable to contemporary Americans, as evidenced by its frequent use in popular expressions—often humorous, such as "my karma ran over your dogma"—and in popular music. In early 1983, the British New Wave band Culture Club, led by the flamboyant Boy George (George Alan O'Dowd), released what was to become their signature hit: "Karma Chameleon." The song is a good example of the growing popular awareness of the ancient Sanskrit term *karma* (literally "action"), which in fact predates Buddhism, but provides much of the ethical backbone of traditional Asian Buddhist practice. According to George, "The song is about the terrible fear of alienation that people have, the fear of standing up for one thing. It's about trying to suck up to everybody. Basically, if you aren't true, if you don't act like you feel, then you get Karma-justice, that's nature's way of paying you back" (Bronson 2003: 583). While there are certainly elements here that ring true with traditional Buddhist understandings of *karma*—i.e., that it is primarily about ethical activity and helps to promote individual responsibility—the focus of the song on the negative repercussion of *karma* betrays a slant that is particularly Western, as we see in the common expression "karma's a bitch."

John Lennon may have been the first to employ the term musically in his 1970 hit "Instant Karma (We All Shine On)," which, like "Karma Chameleon," employs *karma* as an admonition for people to take responsibility for their own actions. Lennon, of course, had from the late 1960s been heavily influenced by Indian religious ideas, but here intentionally focuses on the short-term (i.e., "instant") effects that come from one's actions. As he put it in a 1980 interview with David Sheff:

[I]t occurred to me that karma is instant as well as it influences your past life or your future life. There really is a reaction to what you do now. That's what people ought to be concerned about. Also, I'm fascinated by commercials and promotion as an art form. I enjoy them. So the idea of instant karma was like the idea of instant coffee: presenting something in a new form. I just liked it.

(Sheff 2000: 215–16)

As an interesting side note: in 1993, Nike featured "Instant Karma" in a television commercial, which was roundly criticized by fans of Lennon, who felt that Yoko Ono, who owned the rights to her late husband's songs, had "sold out." Her response is worth noting in full, as it picks up an important set of questions related to commercialization of religion, and specifically in relation to the sacred/profane dichotomy and the "goal" of Buddhism:

[L]ook, even if we have something against big business, big business is going to thrive. It's going to be there. The way I see it is: I've got an access there for millions of people to hear "Instant Karma"; and I got $800,000, which went to the United Negro College Fund. That's what I got for that song. You have a problem with that? What's the alternative? … [B]ig business is going to be there no matter what we do. So if it's going to be there, why don't we use it for positive things.

(Kemp 1992: 80)

Whether consciously or not (probably not) Yoko Ono here restates the classical Maháyána Buddhist concept of *upáya*, or skill-in-means, which allows for substantial flexibility in the pursuit of the larger Buddhist goal of easing or releasing suffering—particularly the suffering of other beings. At the same time, her remarks open up the salient question of whether the Durkheimian "sacred" and "profane" distinction, so often invoked, even if implicitly, in discussion of religious "commercialization," can be applied across religious traditions. As Orrù and Wang have argued, this distinction is in fact "marginal to Buddhist thought" (1992: 47; see also Spiro 1966: 95–96). So what does it mean for a company to "profane" Buddhist images or ideas, or for a Buddhist—such as the Dalai Lama, who famously lent his image to Apple for their 1997 "Think Different" campaign—to "sell out"?

More recent songs that allude directly to *karma* include "Karma" (2004) by Alicia Keys: "What goes around, comes around / What goes up, must come down." In a similar vein, glam metal band Ratt's "Round and Round" (1984) and Justin Timberlake's "What Goes Around … Comes Around" (2006), invoke the principle of what we might call "cosmic justice"—framed here in terms of tumultuous romantic relationships. Taking the term in a somewhat different direction, Radiohead's Thom Yorke explains that the group's 1997 song "Karma Police" is about stress and "having people looking at you in that certain [malicious] way, I can't handle it anymore" (Randall 2000: 223). Elsewhere, Yorke and band mate Jonny Greenwood emphasized that the song had a humorous bent—another frequent aspect of references to *karma* in US pop culture.

This humorous treatment of *karma* can be best seen in the popular television sitcom *My Name Is Earl* (NBC, 2005–9), whose entire premise is explicitly based on the reality and power of *karma*. As numerous online critics have pointed out, Earl (and *Earl*) understands *karma* in a fashion that, while not entirely "incorrect," is quite limited compared to the traditional Indian understanding (whether Hindu, Jain, or Buddhist). Namely, as we have already seen with the above examples from popular music, *karma* in the series implies cosmic retribution or punitive judgment for past wrongs (in one's present life), rather than the "effects" of one's actions (for Buddhism, intentions), that works both positively and negatively, and over a series of lifetimes. Also, *karma* is frequently personified as if a divine, conscious being rather than an impersonal force, like gravity. Yet, for all the confusion, *karma* in *Earl* does reflect the way that the term is understood by many Americans—and, as recent studies show, accepted as real by many Americans.

The Dharma Initiative

While *My Name Is Earl* reflects a widespread cultural (mis?-)understanding of *karma*, other fundamental Buddhist terms, such as *dharma* (which in Buddhism generally refers to truth or simply teachings) and *nirvana* (literally, "blowing out"; i.e., the release from suffering that characterizes the condition of enlightenment or awakening) also make sporadic appearances on the American pop culture scene. On television, Dharma, one of the two principal characters of the 1990s light comedy *Dharma and Greg* (ABC, 1997–2002), evokes a stereotypical "hippie Buddhist." While undoubtedly quirky, if not flaky, Dharma nevertheless acts as a moral foundation for her equally stereotypically WASP-y, upper-crust and uptight husband, Greg. More recently, the hugely popular and critically acclaimed drama series *Lost* (ABC, 2004–10) peppered its always complex and oft-convoluted mythology with explicit Buddhist names, terms, and symbols. Most obvious of these is the use of the term *dharma* in the name of the (failed) scientific/utopian experiment that came to the island in the 1970s: the DHARMA (Department of Heuristics And Research on Material Applications) Initiative. The show also references Shambala, a mythical Tibetan Buddhist kingdom, and one character (the leader of the "temple") is named for the well-known Japanese Sōtō Zen sect founder Dōgen Zenji (1200–53). An eight-spoked wheel (*dharmacakra*), representing the Eightfold Path to awakening, appears frequently, as does the number 108, which has significance in Buddhism as the number of *klesha*s or mental defilements; 108 is also the number of beads on a *mala*, used by Buddhists and Hindus in chanting. Textual references include a line from the *Dhammapada*, a classic of basic Buddhist teaching ("Plant a good seed and you will joyfully gather fruit") as well as others that seem to invoke basic Buddhist teachings about suffering, awareness, and the impermanence and mutability of existence (many of these are seen in a video used by the DHARMA Initiative for "brainwashing" purposes).

Here we might reflect upon Dean Sluyter's questions, posed online during the show's second season: "Is mainstream TV really making a meaningful foray into the Buddhist world? Or is it merely rummaging through the thrift shop of Buddhist terminology for the odd hat or trinket in which to play dress-up?" (2006). While this remains a difficult question to answer, it can be argued that while *Lost* exudes a highly generalized vision of "spirituality" that might be connected to various religions, the show promotes an approach to dealing with change and adversity that is palpably Buddhist. Indeed, the central character/hero John Locke is (at least until his sacrificial death and the usurpation of his body by the evil "man in black") a good representative of a lay-Buddhist practitioner who has achieved a type of awakening. For Locke—who as a child is "chosen" as future leader of the island via a test that reflects the procedure of selecting reincarnated spiritual teachers in the Tibetan tradition—the island represents a literal *nirvana*, since it is a place where he is freed from the sufferings (physical and mental) of his pre-crash life in the "real" world. As Sluyter (ibid.) notes, the very opening scene of the pilot—in which Jack Shepherd suddenly comes to consciousness after the crash of Oceanic Flight 815 on a remote tropical island—evokes the theme of awakening.

A beach lover's *nirvana*

While *dharma* is a term that is only rarely found in contemporary pop culture, *nirvana*, like *karma*, has been effectively introduced into the English language as well as the mainstream US cultural lexicon. Also like *karma*, there are definite permutations of the term, some of which stretch the bounds of traditional Buddhist understanding, but, once again, cannot simply be dismissed as "false" and/or "meaningless." The *Oxford English Dictionary* provides two definitions of the term. The first is a solid (though necessarily simplified) rendering of the basic Buddhist understanding: "a state in which there is no suffering or desire, and no sense of self"; while the second nicely captures its more popular usage: "a perfect or very happy state or place: *Toronto is a restaurant-goer's nirvana*." This second sense (called "informal" by the *OED*) creates an inescapable tension with the first, and brings up a larger tension within American Buddhism, especially as filtered through the Beat Generation of the 1950s and 1960s: i.e., between an understanding of Buddhism as being about a relinquishing of desire and selfhood, on the one hand, and as the promise of fulfillment of desire and authentic self-expression, on the other. Let us turn to several examples to flesh out this issue.

In terms of pop culture examples of the use of *nirvana*, first, and most obvious, is the hugely popular early-1990s grunge band Nirvana, led by the charismatic and ill-fated Kurt Cobain. Formed in 1987, the band would become, to some, the flagship band of Generation X, with Cobain (who died of suicide in 1994) as that generation's spokesman. According to Cobain, he chose Nirvana because he "wanted a name that was kind of beautiful or nice and pretty instead of a mean, raunchy punk rock name like the Angry Samoans" (Azerrad 1994: 61–62). Despite the fact, then, that the intentions are not specifically "Buddhist," the connection between *nirvana*, Buddhism, and "peace" are apparent in Cobain's explanation. No doubt the popular meaning alluded to above—*nirvana* as a "paradise" or place of pure freedom—also played a role in the choice. The band's signature album, *Nevermind*, has been credited with transforming popular music in the early 1990s, in ways that could be seen as palpably "Buddhist." According to Brandon Geist, "after 'Nevermind' hit, suddenly it was cool to be in a hard rock band and to sing about your feelings—and to sing about your feelings in a complex way. ... Hard rock became inward-looking ... cathartic as opposed to escapist" (Scalafani 2011).

A much more controversial usage of Buddhist imagery, and one that plays on *nirvana* as a synonym for worldly pleasure, can be found in underwear manufacturer Victoria's Secret's "Buddha bikini" (see Shields 2011). The case of the Buddha bikini makes for a compelling story of the potential backlash faced by any merchandiser who traffics in religious imagery—even, to the evident surprise of Victoria's Secret, Buddhist ones. The swimsuit (called the "Asian Floral Tankini"), first presented in their summer 2004 catalog, was adorned with traditional Tibetan Buddhist iconography, including a prominently displayed Buddha image on the model's left breast. Next to the bikini image was the following *haiku*-like explanation: "A beach lover's nirvana. Halter tankini has side ruching to adjust the length. Ties at neck. Low-rise bottom. Fully lined. Moderate back coverage." Employing the Internet as a source for protest, Buddhists worldwide launched a campaign against Victoria's Secret. Against the growing barrage of criticism, the company discontinued the line, though they did not offer a recall of the sold products, and were initially hesitant to offer an apology to those who were upset by the Buddha bikinis.

Complaints, largely by Asian and Asian-American Buddhists, can be divided into the following three categories: a) against the company's display of ignorance and/or perceived lack of respect for Buddhism as a "foreign religion"; b) the commercialization of images held by Buddhists to be sacred; and last but perhaps most significant c) the *placement* of the sacred images on a *bikini*—symbol of sexual license— and furthermore on parts of a woman's body, such as the breast and crotch, considered by some Buddhists to be "impure." In sum, while the backlash to the Buddha bikini tells us more about the religious, cultural, and gender assumptions of Asian-American and Asian Buddhists than it does about anything specific to Buddhism in US popular culture, the case itself raises significant issues about the meaning and implications of the growing commodification of Buddhism; namely: 1) how does such correlate, if at all, with an increase in Buddhist practice among a subset of Americans; and 2) what are the limits, if any, to public acceptance of "commercialized Buddhism"?

Get your Buddha on the floor

For all that it can teach us about the vagaries of the commodification of religion (and sexuality) in the United States, the "Buddha bikini" was not the first case in which images of the Buddha on designer clothing were the subject of controversy in the United States. In early 2002, trendy retailer Abercrombie & Fitch got into hot water for their new line of Asian-themed T-shirts, one of which was festooned with a stereotypical image of a pudgy Buddha wearing what (inexplicably) appears to be a Hawaiian *lei*, along with the words "Buddha Bash: Get Your Buddha on the Floor." Presumably this is funny because of the similarities of the words Buddha and the contemporary slang term "booty" (i.e., behind), but the Asian-American Students' Association at Stanford University was not laughing: they demanded an apology and called for a boycott of A&F goods. When we examine the "Buddha Bash" T-shirt, we quickly realize that, whatever the reasons for the choice of design, the company is not so much poking fun at Buddhism or the Buddha as assuming that he is already a "figure of fun"—which is why, I believe, the company defended themselves by suggesting that they were laughing *with* Buddhists, not *at* them. Indeed, among the many attributions of the Buddha (and perhaps, though to a lesser extent, Buddhism itself) in postwar US popular culture is that of being "hip," "wacky," and a "party animal." This is fairly explicit on the A&F T-shirt, but one also sees it in the iconography of brands such as True Religion, maker of pricey designer jeans, whose articles display an easily recognizable "fat smiling Buddha" strumming a guitar and giving us the "thumbs up" sign. (One wonders if there is intentional irony in the brand's tagline: "fashion for the senses.")[8]

Of course, the laughing or happy Buddha is not an American invention; such imagery dates back to medieval Chinese devotion to the figure of Budai, a ninth-century Buddhist monk who some claimed was the incarnation of the great Buddha of the future, Maitreya (in Chinese: Mile). When Chinese immigrants first arrived on the western shores of the United States in the mid-nineteenth century, these were the images of "Buddha" that they brought with them; icons that had long embodied the specifically Chinese cultural values of fortune, luck, and this-worldly happiness. It is thus no surprise that contemporary popular images of "the Buddha" in the USA have their iconographic roots in the Chinese Budai. Indeed, students in my class are often shocked to see the early Indian and West Asian Buddha statues, where the Buddha is portrayed as either muscularly Greek or gracefully svelte (and always serious). The image of "happy Buddha" was no doubt furthered by the Beat Generation, who were inclined toward the "crazy wisdom" of the Zen sages and Tibetan gurus; figures who, in their minds (and the minds of their teachers) had passed beyond the realms of conventional morality and conventional tact, such that their every act was at once liberating and—from the perspectives of ordinary society—insane.

A slight variation of the crazy Buddha or Zen/Tibetan adept is the "cool" or "hipster" Buddha, one who, while he may not appear insane, is also not concerned to abide by conventional "bourgeois" practices. A small but indicative example comes from the recent television sci-fi drama *Roswell* (WB, 1999–2002), where the character Kyle Valenti provides the following explanation for his conversion to Buddhism: "This whole aliens-are-among-us thing, it really screwed me up, made me question stuff, life, reality, my place in the universe ... I need a little clarity. I need a little peace of mind." On the show, Valenti's Buddhism is generally fodder for humor, much of it trading on stereotypes of "flaky" Buddhists. In one sequence, another character enters one of Kyle's dreams, where we see him meditating with the Buddha himself, against a dimly lit, mountainous background. Here the Buddha himself, as a bald, muscular, cell-phone-toting hipster, tells him: "You're an alien now, Kyle. Dude, like, accept your destiny." In the recent graphic novel series, *Tales of the Buddha Before He Was Enlightened*, the pre-*nirvana* Buddha is visually represented as the Chinese Budai but acts like an unrestrained seventeen-year-old boy, his life pursuits largely limited to parties, sex, and "weed." It is difficult to trace the genealogy of this particular pop Buddhist sub-genre, but it may well arise out of the association between postwar Buddhism and the counter-culture—particularly that of the beatniks and hippies of the 1960s and early 1970s (with earlier roots in tales of the antinomian antics of Zen and Tibetan masters, embodied most dramatically by Chögyam Trungpa).

A somewhat different set of Buddhist references in animated comedy is in the longest-running series in American television history, *The Simpsons* (FOX, 1989–present). Most famous in this regard is the character Lisa's conversion to Buddhism in episode #275 ("She of Little Faith," September 2001). In typical *Simpsons* fashion, the dialogue is satirical, but also smart: poking fun at American ignorance of foreign ideas while providing evidence that the writers (and at least a few characters) know what they are talking about. Two other popular adult animated sitcoms feature Buddhist characters or references. In *King of the Hill* (FOX, 1997–2010), the Souphanousinphone family, next-door neighbors to the Hills, are Laotian immigrant Buddhists. In Episode #78 ("Won't You Pimai Neighbor," March 2000), the family plays host to a group of (presumably Tibetan) Buddhist monks searching for a reincarnated lama. Though the episode mixes up sectarian traditions, the depiction of Buddhism is realistic, as is the commonly held notion (expressed by Methodist Reverend Stroup) that Americans can practice Buddhist meditation while remaining Christians.[9] Despite their Buddhist affiliation, the series portrays the Souphanousinphones as overbearing, snobbish, and materialistic—in other words, as real people. Finally, episode #68 of the controversial and always irreverent *South Park* series (Comedy Central, 1997–present) introduces the Buddha himself, as part of a team of superhero religious figures known as the "Super Best Friends" (July 2001)—including, besides the Buddha, Jesus, Moses, Muhammad, Krishna, Laozi, and Joseph Smith—who come together to fight evil in the form of magician David Blaine. Actually, as the show notes, the Buddha is an exception among the "friends," since he "doesn't really believe in evil."

American Buddhism: sweet and sour, zen and square

A common critique leveled against pop Buddhism—and, in some cases, against "American Buddhism" more generally—is that it is superficial; i.e., an unthinking adoption (or cynical appropriation) of "Buddhist" terms, concepts, practices, or figures (Zen, *nirvana*, *karma*, meditation, the Buddha, the Dalai Lama) that give an exotic patina to more deeply rooted but unacknowledged Western cultural and religious forms. Victor Sōgen Hori's important essay on "Sweet and Sour Buddhism" (published in the popular Buddhist magazine *Tricycle* in 1994) is a classic instance of this. Hori's argument is based on the premise that there is a fundamental distinction between the way "white Americans" understand Buddhism and the way it is understood by "ethnic Buddhists," and that, in general, the former misunderstand (and misrepresent) Buddhism because of unacknowledged but deeply engrained preconceptions about the self. While there is certainly truth in Hori's basic thesis—i.e., that Western readings of Buddhism tend toward the Romantic/existentialist/New Age focus on self-realization and self-discovery—it seems problematic to suggest, however implicitly, that "ethnic" (i.e., Asian) Buddhists escape any such social, cultural, or linguistic conditioning. How could this be so?

While there does seem to be a Western—once again, Romantic/existentialist—bias in the belief that "Buddhist practice is conceived as freeing the self from incessant social conditioning and releasing its own pure nature [while] meditation is social de-conditioning designed ultimately to affirm and realize the self" (Hori 1994: 49), this may ultimately be more a matter of semantics. After all, the Romantic and existentialist questioning of "conditioned selfhood" and social convention was also ineluctably tied to an ethic of concern for the poor and outcast; i.e., those on the margins of society who "suffer" the most from the alienation imposed by those religious, economic, social, and political structures which over time come to assume a "natural" (and thus unassailable) status. And of course, tracing the genealogy of Romanticism takes us back to Christian conceptions about selfhood, which—at least in theory—also undercut "natural" family and social norms in favor of a radically transformative process in which the "self" is emptied out in a move toward the suffering other (see Abe 1990). By contrast, it is well known that Buddhism in China and other parts of East Asia eventually adopted "Confucian" norms regarding the absolute centrality of the patriarchal family—and by extension the hierarchical state—and that these were often explicitly packaged in Buddhist terms. Thus, while Hori alludes, presumably with approbation, to the "ethnic Buddhist" conception that Buddhist practice is about "breaking habits of selfishness in order to become open, responsible, and compassionate with others," it is highly probable that specific elements of East Asian conditioning will render such "awakening" problematic in Buddhist terms, due to the power of assumption regarding gender, the family, and hierarchical modes of relationship. Might it be, then, that the "ethical-activist" self, a product of specifically Western religious and cultural traditions, aligns with elements of the traditional Buddhist conception in ways that are as "Buddhist" as conceptions that come from Asian cultural traditions, which tend to neglect the threat of conditioning by "external" forces? This takes us back to the Beat Generation, especially the work of Alan Watts and Gary Snyder.

Watts, whose works were instrumental in bringing Buddhism to popular consciousness in the 1950s and '60s, has been maligned, with some justification, for his unabashedly eclectic approach to spirituality. And yet, such criticism fails to bite too deeply, since we are well aware that a promiscuous attitude toward religiosity has been a hallmark of Asian religions for much of their collective history. But rather than his more popular Zen/Daoist manuals, I would like to highlight Watts's 1958 essay "Beat Zen, Square Zen, and Zen," which provides perhaps the first serious attempt to grapple with what we would now call the commercialization of Buddhism in US popular culture. Published in the very same year as Jack Kerouac's *Dharma Bums*, this short piece criticizes "Beat Zen" in ways similar to Hori's argument against "American Buddhism" four decades later.

Watts opens his essay with the line: "It is as difficult for Anglo-Saxons as for the Japanese to absorb anything quite so Chinese as Zen" (Watts 2002: 160). Yet here, already, we see some important differences from Hori. Watts makes clear that Japan is in many ways as culturally distinct from China as the West is from China; he also highlights the specific origins of Zen in (Tang) China—despite the roots of Buddhism in the very different cultural locus of ancient India. In these ways, Watts centralizes the geographic transformations and subsequent cultural adaptations that are

413

inherent to any boundary-crossing religion such as Buddhism, even while suggesting, with Hori, that there may be specifically "Chinese" (seemingly Daoist) elements in Zen that are hard for non-Chinese (including Japanese) to fully understand and/or appreciate. Though his idealization of the archetypal "Chan/Daoist master" as a distinctively "Chinese" cultural form verges on the carefree Buddha stereotype, Watts's attempt to show that there are limits to both "Beat Zen" (identified with "self-defensive bohemianism") and "Square Zen" (defined in terms of a rigid [Japanese?] formalism) does provide a more nuanced appreciation of the problems of searching for a "Buddhism" that escapes cultural assumptions.

A second point raised in "Beat Zen, Square Zen" is the appeal of the "naturalness" of Buddhism in general, but (Chinese) Chan/Zen in particular, in which the Westerner weary (and wary) of the domineering spirit of both institutional Christianity and technology finds "a view of the world imparting a profoundly refreshing sense of wholeness to a culture in which the spiritual and the material, the conscious and the unconscious, have been cataclysmically split" (ibid.: 162). Watts contrasts the "Chinese humanism and naturalism of Zen" with "Indian Buddhism or Vedanta," which attracts only "displaced Christians—people in search of a more plausible philosophy than Christian supernaturalism to carry on the essentially Christian search for the miraculous" (ibid.). Interestingly, then, Watts, like Hori after him, connects part of the appeal of Buddhism to Westerners who have not gotten past their Western (in this case, Christian) assumptions—but he disconnects this particular appeal, along with the type of Buddhism (and Hinduism) associated with such, from the appeal of Chinese Zen "humanism." This too, has its charms, but only to those who, like Watts himself—and, one might argue, Gary Snyder—are attracted to a spiritual ideal/path that is humorous, immanent, immediate, and accessible. Now, the question inevitably raised at this juncture is whether this vision of the Zen "holy fool" is authentic, or whether it, too, is a "projection" based on Western assumptions or desires.

But there, again, is the rub. Can we avoid this collusion between our cultural and psychic preconceptions and elements of a "foreign" tradition? It would seem that, at least in the initial stages—what Buddhists traditionally called "entering the stream"— this is not only unavoidable, but positively helpful, as it provides the primary vehicle for transmission. D.T. Suzuki was well aware of this, as were his fellow twentieth-century transmitters of Asian Buddhism to the United States, from Nyogen Senzaki (1876–1958) and Sokei-an Sasaki (1882–1945) through Shunryū Suzuki (1904–71) and Chōgyam Trungpa.

Finally, I would like to highlight another aspect of Watts's "Beat Zen, Square Zen": his affirmation of the necessity of "truly understanding" Western religious foundations, specifically Christianity. Beyond coming to a deep understanding of Zen on its own terms:

> the Westerner who is attracted to Zen ... must understand his own culture so thoroughly that he is no longer swayed by its premises unconsciously. ... He must be free of the itch to justify himself. Lacking this, his Zen will be either "beat" or "square," either a revolt from the culture and social order or a new form of stuffiness and respectability. For Zen is above all the

Liberation of the mind from conventional thought, and this is something utterly different from rebellion against convention, on the one hand, or adopting foreign conventions, on the other.

(Watts 2002: 165)

In the end, then, the difference between the respective analyses of Watts and Hori comes down to this: whereas Hori is suspicious that Westerners who are attracted to Buddhism—however serious or pure their intentions—may never "get over" their culturally embedded assumptions regarding selfhood, Watts believes that such an "awakening" is indeed possible, so long as that person is willing and able to "deal with" these *a priori* assumptions.

Hybridity: Buddhist resistance?

Neither Watts nor Hori goes so far, however, as Beat poet Gary Snyder, who suggests the potential benefits of a (self-conscious) "fusion" of religio-cultural tendencies. The young Snyder, of course, was the model for Kerouac's character Japhy Snyder—"the number one Dharma Bum of them all" (Kerouac 1986: 9). Indeed, it is fair to say that Snyder's attraction to Buddhism was deeper, longer lasting, and ultimately more influential on his fellow writers than Kerouac's on-again, off-again flirtation (though this is partly due to his much longer life and career). Inspired by translations of Asian Buddhist texts by Ezra Pound, Arthur Waley, and R.H. Blyth, Snyder traveled to Japan in the mid-1950s, where he took the robes in 1955, thereby "officially" becoming a Buddhist. He remained in Japan until 1969, effectively missing the heyday of Beat culture in the United States. While Buddhist—and particularly Zen—themes populate his entire oeuvre, one of the most intriguing expressions of Snyder's Beat Buddhism can be found in the short piece entitled "Buddhist Anarchism" (1961; republished in 1969 as "Buddhism and the Coming Revolution"), in which the author outlines a progressive manifesto for Buddhist social and political activism. In an echo of modernist movements in Japanese Buddhism some seven decades previous, Snyder argues that, since

historically, Buddhist philosophers have failed to analyze out the degree to which ignorance and suffering are caused or encouraged by social factors, considering fear-and-desire to be given facts of the human condition ... [i]nstitutional Buddhism has been conspicuously ready to accept or ignore the inequalities and tyrannies of whatever political system it found itself under.

(Snyder 1995: 177)

While rare in the writings of the early Beats, Snyder's political Buddhism—portrayed as a buttress against the restricting tendencies of the "Judaeo-Capitalist-Christian-Marxist West"—would eventually find its voice in the Socially Engaged Buddhism that would emerge in the 1970s and 1980s.

Now, I by no means intend to suggest that all forms of pop Buddhism are unproblematic. Clearly, some of the phenomena described above, such as the "Buddha bikini" or the "Buddha Bash" T-shirt, as well as other examples such as Visa's "Enlightenment Card," can and should be critiqued in terms of the way they seem unreflectively to appropriate Buddhist terms, images, and iconography for purposes that seem entirely disconnected from any conceivable "Buddhist" aims. Still, the traditional "plasticity" of Buddhism, noted by Hori, prompts us to reflect upon popular Buddhism as part of a growing trend toward what Carl Bielefeldt (2001) calls "secular spirituality." Clearly, the "values" associated with the various forms of the Buddhist cultural meme—freedom, naturalness, peace, harmony, well-being, simplicity, but also resistance, nonconformity, and justice—correlate with "values" already present in US and Western culture. At the same time, these or related values clearly do have undeniable Asian and/or Buddhist roots, and it may be, as it was with the Beats, that the utilization of Buddhist terms helps to clarify or extend these values in new—and "legitimately" Buddhist—ways.

Like Hori before him, Bielefeldt—a prominent Buddhist studies scholar at Stanford University—is dismissive of such hybridization/accommodation/commodification, attributing it to a bourgeois longing for some "psycho-spice" or "inner herb" to allow for "guilt-free self-satisfaction" beyond the bounds of religion: a species of "I-dolatry." Yet this hybridization, whether conscious or not, is not necessarily superficial or selfish. Indeed, such an assumption forestalls us from the critical task of examining more closely the "causes and conditions" that have led to our current state of affairs, one that will take us back through, among others, the Beats, Watts, Hesse, and Suzuki, and from there back to Dharmapala, Shaku Sōen, the 1893 Parliament of Religions, Theosophy, Unitarianism, and the Japanese modernists of the Meiji period. This will require a more thorough, evolutionary or genealogical exploration of the various tropes and images noted above. Moreover, if judgment is indeed warranted, then the question becomes: where do we (whoever "we" may be) draw the line? For nineteenth-century Orientalist scholars, practicing Asian Buddhists—especially those exhibiting Maháyána tendencies—had long since crossed the line into "cultural" degeneration and superstition; for postwar critics, it was the Beats who had "used" Buddhism for their own selfish and hedonistic ends; as mainly middle-class, white Americans began to practice Buddhism in the 1970s and 1980s, they too faced criticism for being "supermarket Buddhists"; finally, now that "convert Buddhism" is largely acceptable, it is "media Buddhism" that comes under attack.

In short, while we do need to be ever on guard against the spectre of Orientalism (in its various forms), there is no small irony to the fact that criticism of pop Buddhism in the United States continues to rely on lingering (Protestant?) assumptions about "authenticity" and "essence"—categories that have long been decried by Asian Buddhists as fundamental stumbling blocks to awakening. Even critiques of the "commercialization" of Buddhism, which might appear to stand on firmer ground, run into the problematic fact that religion in Asia has long been imbricated within commercial culture and economic activity, such that the Eliadean distinction between "sacred" and "profane" falls apart at the seams.

Notes

1 Mara is the Buddhist "lord of death," and thus roughly equivalent to the Devil in the Western tradition. During the night of Shakyamuni Buddha's awakening under the bodhi

tree, it is said that Mara tempted him with various objects of sensual delight (including Mara's own daughters).

2 By their very nature, Wikipedia entries are notoriously fluid. However, the definition presented is the one for "popular culture" found at the time this was written.

3 Despite the recent trend toward studies of various facets of Western or American Buddhism, scholars have been thus far reluctant to tackle the phenomenon of Buddhism in popular culture. What analysis exists tends to be found on Web sites (such as Rod Meade Sperry's "The Worst Horse"), blogs, and popular magazines such as *Tricycle*. One rare exception is Jane Iwamura's *Virtual Orientalism* (Oxford, 2010).

4 That same year, D.T. Suzuki returned to the United States as a lecturer at Columbia, and another generation-defining work, *Catcher in the Rye*, written by that famously reclusive Zen Buddhist, J.D. Salinger (1919–2010), was published.

5 See, e.g., Hesse 2008: 32, 42, 93. As Richard Gombrich has noted, while Buddhism and existentialism do share a number of common features, the traditional (though perhaps less Zen) emphasis on ethics is a significant point of divergence (Gombrich 2006: 64).

6 Of the 184 "Buddha" books, 152 (83 percent) are novels or collections of stories, while 32 (17 percent) are collections of poetry. Of 212 books with the word "Zen" in their title, 92 (43 percent) are novels or collections of stories, while 120 (57 percent) are collections of poetry.

7 The primary Asian teachers of the Beats were D.T. Suzuki (1870–1966), who administered a modernist version of Japanese Zen wisdom, and, somewhat later, Chögyam Trungpa (1939–87), an iconoclastic Tibetan *tulku* (reincarnated teacher or *lama*) whose mission was to bring the "crazy wisdom" of Tibetan Buddhism to the United States.

8 This is a Buddhist "inside joke": if there is one constant within traditional (at least pre-*tantra*) Buddhism in India and South East Asia, it is that it is very wary of the "senses," since they are a (or the) primary cause of addiction, and thus of suffering. Thus to use this tagline as a way to sell clothes festooned with an image of the Buddha is either a self-consciously ironical way of saying "we know this has nothing to do with Buddhism whatsoever or, more likely, another example of the uncritical adoption of Beat interpretations of Buddhism along the lines of "anything goes."

9 The episode was screened (and praised for its "good writing and fearless satire") at the International Buddhist Film Festival, held in San Francisco, February 2006.

Works cited

Abe, M. (1990) "Kenotic God and dynamic Sunyata," in J. Cobb and C. Ives (eds), *The Emptying God: A Buddhist-Jewish-Christian Conversation*, New York: Maryknoll, 3–65.

Azerrad, M. (1994) *Come as You Are: The Story of Nirvana*, Garden City, NY: Doubleday.

Bielefeldt, C., D.K. Swearer, W. Cadge, J. Nattier, and C.S. Prebish (2001) "Tensions in American Buddhism," *Religion & Ethics Newsweekly*. Online. Available: www.pbs.org/wnet/religionandethics/week445/buddhism.html (accessed 20 November 2012).

Bronson, F. (2003) *The Billboard Book of Number One Hits*, New York: Billboard Books.

Forbes, B.D. (2000) "Introduction: Finding Religion in Unexpected Places," in B.D. Forbes and J.H. Mahan (eds), *Religion and Popular Culture in America*, Berkeley, CA: University of California Press, 1–20.

Gombrich, R. (2006) *How Buddhism Began: The Conditioned Genesis of the Early Teachings*, 2nd edn, London: Routledge.

Gramsci, A. (1971) *Selections from Prison Notebooks*, London: Lawrence and Wishart.

Hesse, H. (2008) *Siddhartha*, trans. S. Bernofsky, New York: Modern Library.

Hori, V.S. (1994) "Sweet-and-sour Buddhism," *Tricycle: The Buddhist Review* 4, 1: 48–52.

Kemp, M. (1992) "She who laughs last: Yoko Ono reconsidered," *Option* (July/August): 74–81.

Kerouac, J. (1986) *The Dharma Bums*, New York: Penguin Books.

Orrù, M. and A. Wang (1992) "Durkheim, religion, and Buddhism," *Journal for the Scientific Study of Religion* 31, 1: 47–61.

Randall, M. (2000) *Exit Music: The Radiohead Story*, London: Omnibus Press.

Scalafani, T. (2011) "Why Nirvana's 'Nevermind' spoke to a generation," *MSNBC.com*. Online. Available: http://today.msnbc.msn.com/id/44524115/ns/today-entertainment/t/why-nirvanas-nevermind-spoke-generation/#.UJfl9hjoX2Y (accessed 5 November 2012).

Schopen, G. (1991) "Archaeology and Protestant presuppositions in the study of Indian Buddhism," *History of Religions* 31, 1: 1–23.

Sheff, D. (2000) *All We Are Saying: The Last Major Interview with John Lennon and Yoko Ono*, New York: St. Martin's Griffin.

Shields, J.M. (2011) "Sexuality, blasphemy and iconoclasm in the media age: the strange case of the Buddha bikini," in E.M. Mazur and K. McCarthy (eds), *God in the Details: American Religion in Popular Culture*, revised 2nd edn, New York: Routledge Press, 80–101.

Sluyter, D. (2006) "Let's Get Lost: Television to meditate to," *Tricycle.com*. Online. Available: http://www.tricycle.com/reviews/lets-get-lost-television-meditate (accessed 6 February 2015).

Snyder, G. (1995) "Buddhism and the coming revolution," in C. Tonkinson (ed.), *Big Sky Mind: Buddhism and the Beat Generation*, New York: Riverhead Books, 177–79.

Spiro, M.E. (1966) "Religion: problems of definition and explanation," in M. Banton (ed.), *Anthropological Approaches to the Study of Religion*, New York: Praeger, 85–126.

Storey, J. (2003) *Cultural Studies and the Study of Popular Culture*, 2nd edn, Athens: University of Georgia Press.

Tonkinson, C. (ed.) (1995) *Big Sky Mind: Buddhism and the Beat Generation*, New York: Riverhead Books.

Watts, A. (2002) "Beat Zen, square Zen, and Zen," in D. Lopez, Jr. (ed.), *A Modern Buddhist Bible: Essential Readings from East and West*, Boston: Beacon Press, 160–71.

Whalen-Bridge, J. and G. Storhoff (2009) "Introduction," in J. Whalen-Bridge and G. Storhoff (eds), *The Emergence of Buddhist American Literature*, Albany: State University of New York Press, 1–17.

Wikipedia.com (2013) "Popular culture." Online. Available: http://en.wikipedia.org/wiki/Popular_culture (accessed 10 January 2013).

22
ROMAN CATHOLICISM

Rodger M. Payne

Stung by critics who considered his masterpiece *Birth of a Nation* (1915) overtly racist, American filmmaker D.W. Griffin responded with another epic film, sardonically titled *Intolerance: Love's Struggle Through the Ages* (1916), in which he interwove four separate storylines that attacked injustice and fanaticism in four distinct historical eras. One narrative, titled "The Modern Story," presented working-class Irish Catholics in their struggles against the self-righteous and hypocritical urban reformers known as "The Uplifters"—clearly a swipe at Griffin's own critics—while another plotline, "The French Story," depicted in gruesome detail the atrocities of the 1572 St. Bartholomew's Day Massacre, when Catholics, through the manipulations of the queen regent Catherine de Medici, slaughtered unsuspecting Protestant Huguenots. While the story of the massacre reflected American Protestant opinion at the time regarding the covert evil represented by Roman Catholicism, the Catholic protagonists in the "Modern Story"—identified simply as "Dear One" and the "Boy"—are among the most sympathetic in the film, and the only characters who ultimately triumph over the intrigues of those who seek to do them harm. Through the purity of her Catholic values—a religious morality that is unsullied by any attempt to impose it upon others—the Madonna-like Dear One redeems the Boy from a life of crime and eventually saves him from a wrongful death, even while a third plot narrative, "The Judean Story," intersperses the account of their ordeals with the crucifixion of Christ.

Intolerance was the first American feature film to present explicit images of Catholics and Catholicism and was emblematic of the inconsistent and often contradictory role that such images have had in American popular culture. While remarkable for its sympathetic portrayal of working-class and immigrant Catholics during an era when anti-Catholicism was a still an acceptable prejudice for most Americans, it also perpetuated many of the same anti-Catholic stereotypes that were a part of the legacy of colonial Puritanism. The Catholic was at once the epitome of the promise of America and yet, paradoxically, the sinister "other" whose religion was a threat to the American values of freedom and tolerance. Submission and ruthless authority went hand in hand; for every pious Dear One there was a merciless Catherine de Medici.

The legacy of anti-Catholicism

The representation of Catholics and Catholicism in American popular culture began during the colonial era.[1] Appearing in pamphlets, broadsides, and other published materials designed for mass consumption, anti-Catholicism not only reflected the Puritan conviction that the Church of England had been insufficiently purged of its medieval Catholic elements, but also the collective fears of the British colonists that Catholicism—especially in the form of their Spanish and French military adversaries—presented a grave threat to religious and political liberties. Such deeply seated fears appeared to be justified when, on November 5, 1605, several English Catholics were arrested for plotting to blow up the House of Lords in London on the following day when King James I was expected to be present. Although not the lead conspirator, a Catholic layman by the name of Guy Fawkes became the figure synonymous with this "Gunpowder Plot," and following his arrest and execution, Fawkes lent his name and symbolic presence to a new popular festivity—Guy Fawkes Day—during which an effigy of Fawkes or an equally threatening figure (such as the pope or Satan) was paraded throughout many towns and villages, to be burned at the end of the celebration in a public bonfire. English colonists brought this tradition to the colonies in North America, where it became known as Pope Day, since the effigies employed were invariably of the pope as the key symbol of the "Catholic menace." Although Puritan authorities tried unsuccessfully to ban the celebration—troubled more by the feasting, drinking, and frivolity that accompanied it than by the message it conveyed—Pope Day became one of the more significant public celebrations in the British colonies, especially in New England, where the Puritan hostility to more traditional Christian holy days such as Christmas was enforced by law (Billington 1952: 18–19).

Although observations of Pope Day declined during the period of the American Revolution (when it became an embarrassment to the rebellious colonists seeking alliance with predominantly Catholic Quebec), anti-Catholic sentiments remained just below the surface of American political and religious life. The rise in foreign immigration during the early decades of the nineteenth century—particularly the immigration of Irish Catholics—in addition to other factors, led to a revival of anti-Catholicism that expressed itself in theological discourse, to be sure, but also in populist politics and popular culture. While nativist demagogues might take advantage of such a climate to create the "Know-Nothing" political parties that exercised significant influence in the 1850s, as David Brion Davis (1960: 205) notes, popular forms of anti-Catholicism had "to come from the people, and the themes of counter-subversion would be likely to reflect their fears, prejudices, hopes, and perhaps even unconscious desires." These "themes of counter-subversion," despite almost two centuries of alteration and renegotiation, remain embedded in American popular culture.

Although all Catholics were charged, implicitly at least, with sharing in the designs of Rome to undermine and eventually to overthrow American liberties, even the most virulent of anti-Catholic writers generally viewed the laity as unwitting pawns, held in thrall by the superstitions and ritualized magic of the Catholic hierarchy. Thus, the focus of anti-Catholic hatred came to be centered on the figure of the priest, who appeared in the antebellum literature as a willing agent of religious and societal subversion. In Samuel F.B. Morse's *Foreign Conspiracy Against the Liberties of the United States* (1835), the father of the telegraph and Morse Code accused foreign-born priests, especially Jesuits, of biding their time until, on a given signal from Rome, they would lead the immigrant masses in revolt. While the priest as political threat certainly expressed popular fears of Catholic despotism, it was the darker image of the priest as a social misfit that lodged itself in the collective American unconscious. William Hogan's book *Popery! As It Was and As It Is* (1851) included an "exposé" of the Catholic practice of auricular confession during which, according to Hogan (himself an excommunicated priest), the confessor, in private audience with impressionable young women, groomed such to become his victims for sexual exploitation. The echo of this charge came from the very popular genre of the tales of "escaped nuns," the most infamous of which was *Awful Disclosures of the Hotel Dieu Nunnery of Montreal* (1836), purportedly written by Maria Monk, a young novice who had encountered false imprisonment, forced sexual activity, and even infanticide during her initiation into a religious order. Although Monk's book was undoubtedly a forgery (written most likely by a notorious anti-Catholic), the image of the lecherous priest, whose vow of celibacy was a mere cloak for his illicit activities, became an enduring one in American popular culture. Commenting upon the frankly pornographic intent of such literature, Davis (1960: 217) observes that the "projection of forbidden desires [upon the priest] can be seen in the exaggeration of the stereotyped enemy's powers, which made him appear at times as a virtual superman." Within the Catholic faith, the priest stood apart, removed from natural human desires and the stability of being part of a family. Such an ambiguous figure, who moved between this world and another (whether that other world was divine or satanic), could easily be molded to fit various agendas.

The image of the Catholic priest as sexual aggressor and the attendant imagery of the innocent female victim, whether naïve novice or adolescent penitent, was a reflection of larger Protestant fears regarding the "sensuality" of Catholic practice. In a tradition steeped in the primacy of the written and spoken word, many Protestants were apprehensive about the lure of images, incense, and other forms of Catholic material culture that were designed to engage the senses. According to Ryan K. Smith (2006: 54), even the simple Latin cross for many Protestants "served as a Catholic trademark, a piece of visual shorthand representing the sensual tools of Catholicism and the oppressive authority of the Church." Similar to the way in which a priest might use the sacrament of penance to lure a credulous victim into sexual activity, so might the ritualism of the Catholic Church lure unsuspecting Protestants into spiritual domination and exploitation. Yet, as Smith observes, not only crosses but other visual decorations would soon become part of the fabric of many places of Protestant worship, along with a neo-Gothic style of architecture that had long been dismissed as gloomy and medieval. By the late nineteenth century, despite a resurgence of anti-Catholicism that accompanied postbellum immigration, the sensual style of the Catholic Gothic had begun to replace the rectilinear Federalist style as the preferred mode of Protestant church architecture and thus contribute to a visual landscape in which the sacred could be better distinguished from the secular.

The anti-Catholicism of the nineteenth-century United States produced an enduring image of Catholics and Catholicism as the "other" in American life, not only in terms of religion, but also politically and socially. Even as the more overt forms of anti-Catholicism began to lose acceptance in a society willing to embrace religious diversity, the image of Catholicism as authoritarian rather than democratic, sensual rather than rational, subversive rather than loyal, and irredeemably foreign rather than indigenous continued to lurk in the shadows of popular culture.

The Catholic as liminal figure

Given the harsh and at times violent legacy of colonial and nineteenth-century anti-Catholicism, it would seem surprising that in the twentieth century Catholicism slowly became an integral component of American popular culture. A number of reasons might explain this. By the end of the Civil War, Catholicism had become the largest single denomination in the United States, although Catholics remained outnumbered by Protestants almost three to one. The end of the era of European immigration brought by the passage of the *Johnson-Reed Act* in 1924 allowed the American Catholic population to stabilize and to produce second and even third generation offspring who were better assimilated into the larger culture than their parents and grandparents. As Jay Dolan (2002: 73) comments, these children and grandchildren of immigrant Catholics "were the ones who had pianos in their parlors, lace curtains on their windows, and steam heat in the winter." For most of the twentieth century—certainly until the election of John F. Kennedy as president in 1960—Catholicism remained a distinct sub-culture within American life, but one that was beginning to develop many intersections with the larger American culture.

Another compelling reason for this embrace of culture, argues priest and sociologist Andrew Greeley, resides within Catholic theology. "Catholicism," he suggests (2001: 77), "has the most richly developed popular tradition [of any religion] because it is the least afraid of the imaginative dimension of religion. ... It is the least likely to be afraid of contaminating God by using creation as a metaphor with which to describe Him." This "Catholic imagination" (Greeley's term) can be discerned not only in the high culture of the fine arts or the architecture of a soaring neo-Gothic cathedral, but in the everyday items of the "enchanted world" of Catholicism. Thus, for the Catholic, nothing in the world can be utterly profane; everything has the potential of being "sacramental," a conduit of grace or a revelation of the divine, from the bread and wine of the Eucharist, to religious trinkets, to popular culture where, according to Greeley (1988: 115), "[g]race is to be found." Not all agree with Greeley (even among Catholics), but there is great value of such a sacramental imagination in analyzing the relationship between Catholicism and popular culture in the twentieth and twenty-first centuries. Whether in overt religious symbolism (a clerical collar, a religious habit, a crucifix) or in more unlikely artifacts (films, songs, or sporting events), Catholicism provides both a rich and varied material culture and an ideology of sacramental connection between the material and the spiritual that informs such imagery with a rich imagination.

It is not surprising that Catholics began to merge into the American mainstream—socially, politically, and economically—as twentieth-century mass culture was beginning to develop. In particular, filmmakers like D.W. Griffith found that the robust visual culture of Catholicism—clerical vestments, religious icons, and sacramental practices—provided a visual shorthand that could be exploited to stand for any religious elements within the plot. In *Intolerance*, for example, Griffith could reify internal despair through the confession of the Boy to a priest in clerical garb; similarly, he could suggest sexual repression and misguided superstition when the father of the Dear One forces her to kneel before an image of the Virgin and Child upon his discovery of her affection for the Boy. If Griffith was the first to utilize such imagery, he was far from the last, and as the century progressed, the imagery offered by Catholicism—particularly the figure of the priest or nun—came to represent a multitude of contrasting, and even paradoxical, ideas.

Although American Catholics took little note of *Intolerance* when it was released, by the 1920s Catholic characters were being represented in ways that provoked a significant response. In 1927, MGM released *The Callahans and the Murphys*, a comedy about two Irish families that not only reiterated base stereotypes regarding Irish immigrants, but used these to mock their Catholicism. In one scene, a character is too inebriated even to make the sign of the cross, and in another a drunken brawl erupts during a St. Patrick's Day celebration. The film drew harsh condemnation from various Catholic groups and led to the formation of the Legion of Decency, a watchdog group that began as separate diocesan chapters but rapidly developed into a national organization. Through the use of an annual pledge by which its lay members promised "to arouse public opinion against" offensive films, and by its threat to boycott such films, the Legion of Decency became a powerful group that helped shape the portrayal of Catholics and Catholicism in American mass culture (Skinner 1993: 37).

The outcry against *The Callahans and the Murphys* and the formation of the Legion of Decency also served as catalysts for the formation of the Production Code Administration (PCA), which imposed a type of self-censorship on the American film industry for three decades. Such a code had been proposed before, most recently as a list of "Don'ts and Be Carefuls" compiled by Will Hays, the president of the Motion Picture Producers and Distributors of America. Although a devout Presbyterian, Hays appointed a lay Catholic, Joseph Ignatius Breen, to head the PCA, and together they adopted a revised and more extensive code based on one that had been written by Fr. Daniel Lord, a Jesuit and professor of drama at St. Louis University, and Martin Quigley, a Catholic layman and the publisher of an industry journal. The so-called "Hays Code"—produced and enforced largely by Catholics—regulated the content of American cinema until the 1960s.

Although the Hays Code prohibited the negative depiction of any member of the clergy, Catholics benefited the most by this restriction. Since filmmakers often preferred to employ the figure of the Catholic priest as a representative of morality and organized religion, the Code ensured that they would be presented in a positive light. The first major test of the Code regulations—and thus the first test of the power of Catholic censorship—came in the 1930s with the emergence of the "gangster" genre in films such as *Little Caesar* (1930) and *Public Enemy* (1931). Not only were the protagonists invariably Irish or Italian (and thus implicitly Catholic), but Catholics shared with other Americans the fear that such films glorified criminal behavior. This prompted Breen to demand that such films must present "compensating moral values" (Black 1994: 173–74). The 1938 film *Angels With Dirty Faces* provided the earliest demonstration of how Catholicism—specifically members of the clergy—might provide these compensatory values. The film begins with boyhood friends and fellow altar boys Rocky Sullivan (James Cagney) and Jerry Connolly (Pat O'Brien) being chased by the police, and while Jerry escapes, Rocky is caught and begins a descent into a life of crime. Returning to his old neighborhood after prison, Rocky discovers that Jerry has become the parish priest, and both begin a battle for the hearts and souls of a gang of delinquents. For most of the film, Rocky seems easily to be winning this battle until he begs not to die while being escorted to the death chamber, his display of cowardice having been suggested by Jerry as an object lesson for the boys. Although many complained that the film still glamorized Rocky's life of violent crime and thus made a mockery of the intent of the Code, Pat O'Brien's portrayal of Fr. Jerry Connolly established the figure of the Catholic priest as the moral conscience of the era. Under the Code, Catholic priests became exemplary and heroic figures, ranging from Spencer Tracy's portrayal of Fr. Flanagan in *Boys Town* (1938) to Karl Malden's Fr. Barry in *On the Waterfront* (1954). Unlike the conflicted and overwrought Fr. Farley in *Intolerance*, the celluloid priests of the Code era were "muscular Catholics" who could face down both opponents and corrupt systems with equal composure. Fr. Connelly was a collegiate football star and a former boxer; Fr. Flanagan could take down an opponent with a single punch (but not before removing his collar); and Fr. Barry was based on an actual priest, Fr. John M. Corridan, who worked on the docks in New York City. During the war years of the 1940s, films such as *The Fighting 69th* (1940), *The Fighting Sullivans* (1944), and *God Is My Co-Pilot* (1945) featured priests and other Catholics as exemplary American patriots, transforming, in the process, the stereotypical image of Irish belligerency into a core American value. Thus, while the moral symbolism invoked by the image of the priest had shifted significantly from that of the lecherous figure featured in previous anti-Catholic literature, the priest still remained an ambiguous and liminal figure who could transgress social boundaries.

Such transgression continued in the films of the 1940s, during a period when the larger American culture was beginning to open itself more to the inclusion of non-Protestants. Thus the "muscular" priests of the earlier Code era gave way to the image of the priest as a more approachable figure, but one who still moved when necessary between various social roles. One character in particular came to symbolize the priest as one well assimilated into American culture, Bing Crosby's Fr. Charles Francis Patrick O'Malley, who solved problems with his charm and musical talents rather than his fists. Fr. O'Malley appeared in two films, *Going My Way*, which won numerous Academy Awards including best picture for 1944, and its sequel, *The Bells of St. Mary's*, which appeared in 1945. In both films, Crosby's character presented an understanding of life outside the Catholic sub-culture—he was a former singer who had once been involved in a romantic (but undoubtedly chaste) relationship—and an effective foil to an older and more insulated form of Catholicism represented in *Going My Way* by Barry Fitzgerald's Fr. Fitzgibbon. In

The Bells of St. Mary's, Fr. O'Malley is paired with an equally clever nun, Sr. Mary Benedict, played by Ingrid Bergman, and although the plot to save a Catholic school from foreclosure was less satisfying than the more subtle infighting between the progressive O'Malley and the old-fashioned Fitzgibbon, the film became a quintessential symbol of the assimilation of Catholicism into the mid-twentieth-century "American Way of Life," with its title appearing on movie marquees in films such as *It's a Wonderful Life* (1946) and *The Godfather* (1972). The practical and even-tempered Fr. O'Malley represented for most Americans the image of Catholicism in popular culture, and indeed, one might argue, popular culture had itself been re-imagined within a Catholic context. "Thanks to Hollywood," claims Anthony Burke Smith (2010: 64), Catholicism "had become the popular religion of modern America."

For many Americans, however, deep suspicions remained regarding the ability of Catholics to assimilate fully into American life, much less to represent it. The image of Fr. O'Malley notwithstanding, many non-Catholic Americans continued to view the Catholic as the "other", not only in terms of religious difference, but in other ways as well. The fact that so many of the immigrants in the nineteenth and early twentieth centuries had been Catholic—whether Irish along the east coast, Germans in the Midwest, or Italians in virtually every urban area—meant that Catholicism was usually associated with "foreignness." Further, despite the positive cinematic representations of priests under the Code, for many they still remained symbols of distrust and disloyalty. With the gradual decline of the ability of the Code to preserve Joseph Breen's "compensating moral values," the image of the priest in films after the 1960s became more conflicted, although it was not until the 1980s—in films such as *The Monsignor* (1982), starring Christopher Reeve in the title role—that some of the harsher characterizations of the antebellum anti-Catholic traditions began to reappear. Even in *The Exorcist* (1973), in which a younger priest, Fr. Damien Karras (Jason Miller), is taught the value of the old and mysterious Tridentine rituals as a way to combat satanic evil by Fr. Lankester Merrin (Max von Sydow), the character of Fr. Karras is deeply flawed and teetering on the loss of faith when summoned to help the aging and ailing Fr. Merrin drive out a demon that has taken possession of a young girl. The final result of the battle between good and evil in the film requires the death of Fr. Karras, not only as a way to save the girl but as a way to redeem his own sinfulness.

If the liminality represented by priests such as Fr. Karras caused his character to remain too dangerously transgressive, the emergence of other Catholic characters in American film continued to push Catholicism toward greater acceptance by other Americans. Nuns were similarly ambiguous figures, but were, for the most part, presented in a generally favorable light. Ingrid Bergman's Sr. Mary Benedict was the female equivalent of Fr. O'Malley; it was her prayers, coupled with his charm, which saved her school. Similarly, the sisters of the fictional Order of the Holy Endeavor in *Come to the Stable* (1949) and the sisters in *Lilies of the Field* (1963) relied upon their prayers and their persistence to bring about their desired ends. Following both the rise of feminism and the Second Vatican Council in the mid-1960s, the cinematic image of the nun became more complex, as characters struggled with fulfilling their vows or challenging the restrictions they imposed; but in general, religious sisters in

American films fared much better than did priests in representing a thoughtful and devout Catholic life. On the whole, nuns are much more likely to be featured in comedies than as morally conflicted characters. The musical comedy *Nunsense*, which premiered off-Broadway in 1985, has spawned a number of sequels and imitators including *Late Nite Catechism* (1993), an audience-participation comedy in which a teaching "Sister" in full habit expresses her nostalgia for the pre-Vatican II culture marked by Holy Days of Obligation and fish on Fridays. A much darker presentation is Christopher Durang's one-act play *Sister Mary Ignatius Explains It All for You* (1979)—later made into a Showtime movie version entitled *Sister Mary Explains It All* (2001)—which regards this former Catholic culture as one marked by oppression and mindless authoritarianism. The lead character is a dogmatic nun whose conviction of the simplicity of religious truth is exceeded only by her inability to grasp the psychological damage that her unquestioning faith had on her parochial school students. The play generated significant opposition from many Catholics and remains one of the very few to present a nun as leading character in such a harsh light, although the 1985 film *Agnes of God*, starring Meg Tilley as an apparently psychologically disturbed novice, echoed Maria Monk's famous book in its evocation of a mysterious pregnancy and possible infanticide. More recently, in the 2008 film *Doubt* (based upon the 2004 play *Doubt, A Parable*, by John Patrick Shanley) the conservative Sister Aloysius (played by Meryl Streep) tries to destroy the career of Father Flynn (Philip Seymour Hoffman), despite the lack of substantial evidence for her suspicions that he has behaved inappropriately with a young male student. While offering a more sinister version of the clash between traditionalist and progressivist protagonists, the story draws upon the contemporary sexual abuse crisis within the Catholic Church to suggest that Sister Aloysius's irrational malice reflects her own repressed sexuality.

Holy wars

Catholic males found other ways to enter the popular consciousness as exemplary figures of faith and patriotism. While the World War II films had presented Irish Catholics as solid patriots, it was largely through another route that lay Catholic males could allay suspicion of their religion—through the "muscular Catholicism" expressed through collegiate football, especially the Fighting Irish of the University of Notre Dame, which became perhaps the most popular symbol of Catholicism in the mid-twentieth-century United States. By combining religion, ethnicity, masculinity, and athletics into a potent mixture of an aggressive and uniquely Catholic gospel of athletics, Notre Dame football became the emblematic program that represented American Catholic self-identity, even for those who never attended a college or sent their sons to South Bend, Indiana (the university did not become coeducational until 1972).

Notre Dame football rose to national prominence in the 1920s, the "golden age of American sport," according to historian William J. Baker (2007: 129), under the leadership of the legendary coach Knute Rockne, a Midwestern Norwegian Lutheran who converted to Catholicism only in 1925, eight years after becoming head coach.

Rockne was certainly an innovator on the field, famous for introducing the backfield shift, but he was far more important for his contributions to the Notre Dame "mystique," in which Catholic sensuality and muscular athleticism blended into a seamless whole. The pregame ritual of the entire team attending Mass together in the campus grotto of Our Lady of Lourdes—including, by special episcopal dispensation, even the few Protestant players—balanced perfectly with the powerful backfield of the 1924 team who became known as the "Four Horsemen of Notre Dame"—an intentional reference to the symbolic figures of Conquest, War, Famine, and Death in the biblical book of Revelation. In concert with the team's chaplain, Fr. John O'Hara—who distributed blessed religious medals before games and promoted the masculine piety of the entire student body—Rockne could access, in the words of Baker (2007: 138), "a religious heritage of vast mythic and ritualistic resources" that he "wisely and regularly tapped." In a way unmatched by any competing collegiate team, the Fighting Irish during the administration of Rockne and O'Hara helped establish the controlled violence of the gridiron as a "clean" and healthy game by incorporating it into the ethos of the American immigrant Catholic experience.

No single event exemplifies this more than the story of Rockne's famous halftime speech in 1928 when Notre Dame was behind Army, 0–6. The speech itself was undoubtedly Rockne's own creation, but by citing the death eight years before of George Gipp and Gipp's deathbed admonition to tell the team "when things are wrong and the breaks are beating the boys" to "win just one for the Gipper," Rockne fabricated one of the most powerful myths of American popular culture. Despite the fact that Gipp himself was the antithesis of the saintly piety promoted by O'Hara, Rockne's speech and Notre Dame's eventual 12–16 victory secularized the religious idea of the "good death" and came to symbolize the ultimate triumph of the faithful despite apparent defeat. The full incorporation of the story into popular culture came with the 1940 film *Knute Rockne, All American*, in which the young Ronald Reagan in the role of Gipp made his request to Pat O'Brien's Rockne. With Reagan's subsequent entry into politics, winning one for the Gipper—a nickname Reagan adopted—became the central axiom of the "Reagan Revolution" in the late twentieth century. As numerous scholars have noted, however, this was not empty sloganeering. According to David Chidester's analysis of such civil religious rhetoric, "George Gipp stood as the central cinematic *figura* of redemptive sacrifice in the worldview of Ronald Reagan"; and thus through his "mystical" invocation of the redemptive death of Gipp in connection with the Cold War and "atheistic" threats posed by Soviet Communism—for example, during a commencement speech delivered at Notre Dame University in 1981—Reagan was able "to unify Americans in common cause against a common enemy, just as the sacrificial death of George Gipp enabled a team torn by dissention and factionalism to join together in a common cause and attain the unattainable" (Chidester 2005: 95, 109). Michael Paul Rogin (1987) extended the symbolism of Gipp even further, asserting that Reagan came to identify himself so closely with his own celluloid version of Gipp, especially in the aftermath of John Hinckley's failed assassination attempt, that Gipp became a type of "real presence" in the mind of Reagan, allowing him to interpret his own near death and recovery with that of the nation. "By shifting the source of personal identity from the living body of George Gipp to his [Reagan's] spirit," Rogin argued,

"Gipp's sacrifice turned the body mortal into the *corpus mysticum*." Therefore Reagan "could claim to embody the nation, exploiting the boundary confusion between the president's body and the body politic, because he had risen from the confusion between life and film" (Rogin 1987: 16). Rockne's own image became inseparably enmeshed with the "redemptive sacrifice" of the Gipper's hagiography, especially during the season that followed Gipp's death when Rockne was forced to coach games while confined to a wheelchair due to phlebitis, and then again in 1931 when he died at the age of forty-three in an airplane crash—still clutching, so the legend says, his rosary in his hands.

Ultimately, it was Rockne who became "a symbol of Catholicism to countless Americans" (Chowder 1993), and, as with the figure of the priest, the power of this symbolism was in the way in which Rockne (and by extension Gipp) transgressed boundaries; in this case, boundaries of athletics, nationalism, and religion. The rise to prominence of football at Notre Dame occurred at the same time that a renewed anti-Catholic fervor was beginning to develop, exemplified most ominously by the organization of the "second" Ku Klux Klan at Stone Mountain in Georgia in 1915. Founded by William J. Simmons, a former Methodist minister who had been influenced by D.W. Griffith's depiction of the original Klan in *Birth of a Nation*, this new Klan added immigrants, Jews, and Catholics to its list of un-American groups while maintaining the white supremacy of the Reconstruction-era Klan. Although still strong in the South, the second Klan was in many ways more prominent and more powerful in the Midwest, especially in Indiana, where a population that contained few African Americans and even fewer Jews meant that the Klan's vitriol could be focused on Catholics. In 1924, a Klan convention in South Bend was disrupted by Notre Dame students, but street brawls could not counter Klan ideology as effectively as could sustained prowess on the gridiron. With "[t]heir patriotism called into question by Hoosier rednecks and white-collar politicians alike," observed William Baker (2007: 33), Catholics "excelled at the All-American game of football. Knute Rockne was Notre Dame's answer to the Ku Klux Klan." Athletic success of the type embodied by Rockne and Gipp provided a way for Catholics to cross symbolically into an otherwise still hostile national culture that valued both a defiant masculinity and individual sacrifice for the good of the many. In much the same way that other "minority" groups have engaged in athletics as a type of parallel patriotism, sports such as football and boxing—the latter promoted especially by the Catholic Youth Organization (CYO) that was organized in Chicago in the 1930s—provided a way for Catholic males to physically and visually perform their Americanness for public consumption. Athletic performance or even the willingness to engage physically one's opponent was a symbol of belonging—even in films such as *Going My Way* when Fr. O'Malley first presents himself to Fr. Fitzgibbon wearing the training uniform of baseball's St. Louis Browns, or *The Bells of St. Mary's*, in which Sr. Benedict in full habit can still play baseball or teach a male student how to box. Such pugilistic patriotism was solidified in the 1950s when the Red Scare finally replaced the Catholic Menace as the greatest perceived threat to the American Way of Life, and Senator Joseph McCarthy, for all of his methodological flaws, demonstrated to all Americans that Catholics could take the lead in fighting "godless Communism."

No professional team has come to represent this "muscular Catholicism" to a national audience to the same degree that Notre Dame football was able to do, but a number of professional teams have adopted Catholic symbols for historic or cultural reasons. Major League Baseball's San Diego Padres signify the region's Catholic past and the "chain" of missions that began with the founding of San Diego de Alcala by the Franciscan Junípero Serra in 1769; the team's tonsured mascot is known as the Swinging Friar and wears a Franciscan habit. The most overtly and intentional Catholic identification, however, belongs to the New Orleans Saints of the National Football League. Playing their home games in an area with a substantial Catholic population, "the Saints" is an appropriate nickname for a team that was officially established on November 1, 1966—All Saints' Day in the Catholic liturgical calendar. The team's founder, David F. Dixon, was a devout Catholic and sought the approval of New Orleans Archbishop Philip M. Hannan for the name, fearing that some might think it sacrilegious; Hannan not only approved of the name but also wrote a prayer for the team as well (Catholic News Agency 2010). The team logo, the fleur-de-lis, not only reflects the French heritage of New Orleans and the Gulf Coast region, but has long been a Catholic symbol used to represent the Holy Trinity as well as the Blessed Virgin Mary in paintings and other artistic representations. Fans of the team often adopt Catholic clerical and religious vestments to wear during the games including cassocks, stoles, religious habits, and episcopal miters (often displaying the phrase "Bless You Boys"). It cannot be denied that for many fans, such overtly religious symbols have little to do with any intended public representation of Catholicism, but the fact that Catholics are willing to countenance such activity lends support to Greeley's assertion that in the Catholic imagination, few distinct lines can be maintained between what is sacred and what is mundane.

Festivity and the Catholic imagination

Indeed, the revelry on display by mitered fans in the New Orleans Superdome during football season illustrates one form of evidence that Greeley offers for his thesis: the element of "festivity" that has been a part of Catholic life since at least the Middle Ages. Certainly with the coming of Protestantism and its attitude of "worldly asceticism" as famously defined by the great sociologist Max Weber, festivity—in the form of feasting or public spectacles such as parades and processions—has become a very visible marker of the Catholic presence in popular culture. Both Christmas and Easter were initially outlawed as "popish celebrations" by colonial Puritans, and the contemporary way in which both are observed by Christians and non-Christians alike is largely the result of practices brought into the United States by Catholic immigrants during the antebellum period. "While Episcopalians and Lutherans had always observed a cyclical year of regular festivals and sacraments," notes Ryan K. Smith (2006: 138), "evangelicals began their experiments in the 1820s and 1830s" as "the rich productions surrounding Catholic festivals like Easter and Ash Wednesday enchanted their Protestant audiences." By the last decades of the nineteenth century, the sensual appeal of decorating even Protestant churches with Easter flowers, engaging in the drama of the liturgical calendar, and displaying Christmas trees had flowed outward into popular culture.

If "enchanted" Protestants could at least accept the trappings of festivity that came with liturgical holidays such as Christmas and Easter, they remained, nevertheless, resistant to the broader sacramental imagination of Catholics. Clearly "extra-biblical" observances—saints' days or devotions to the Blessed Sacrament, for example—remained beyond the bounds of liturgical acceptance. Surprisingly, however, the most widely celebrated public festival associated with a saint, St. Patrick's Day, began among Protestant Irish immigrants during the colonial era, and became an expression of Irish Catholicism in the United States only in the mid-nineteenth century. But while the Protestant version was observed by "dinners, speeches, and formal gatherings," the Catholic adaptation was much more "public and unpretentious" (Cronin and Adair 2001: 9). Although Protestant celebrations had also often included military marches, the key Catholic innovation was the street parade and festival, which transformed the holiday into a phenomenon of popular mass culture. As the physical movement of people through a landscape, the street parade is a very public and expressive event that has its foundation in the processions of medieval Europe, when holy relics or images were paraded around the city walls as a symbolic designation of community boundaries or as a protective shield against invasion or disease. Robert Orsi's classic study of Italian immigrant devotion to Our Lady of Mt. Carmel in early twentieth-century New York explores the way in which the procession of a statue of the Madonna "mapped out and gave a divine sanction to the borders of Italian Harlem, [and] ... together with the street life of the festa, sacralized the streets" (2010: 183). Public festivity is not, therefore, a clerical indulgence designed to appeal to baser human instincts, but a creative, expressive, and often quite literal embodiment of the self-creation and self-identity of a group.

Perhaps the best illustration of the intersection between festival and the theological imagination in the United States occurs, again, in south Louisiana and the Gulf Coast region. The annual festivities of the Carnival season that begin on Twelfth Night (the evening of January 5) and continue through midnight on Mardi Gras (Fat Tuesday or Shrove Tuesday) may be best known for their drunken debauchery, but this rather recent decline into decadence fueled by tourist dollars obscures the very Catholic religious structures that lie deeply buried beneath the colorful parades, bare breasts, and mountains of cheap plastic beads. Devout Catholics know that sometime on Ash Wednesday they will need to repent of their overindulgence and get ready for a season of fasting for which the Carnival was merely a preparation.

The roots of Carnival stretch deep into the Middle Ages, when the 40-day Lenten fast was not only prescribed by the Church but dictated by the dwindling supply of foodstuffs that had been stored from the previous year's harvest. The feasting of Mardi Gras, therefore, became a way of indulging human appetites—literally and figuratively—beneath the veneer of the liturgical calendar. While the parading culture of New Orleans, Baton Rouge, and Lafayette, Louisiana, or even Mobile, Alabama, displays elements that are more connected to the medieval "feast of fools"—such as the reversals of social status represented by ersatz royalty who dispense worthless baubles of beads and coins to the adoring masses—the aspect of communal feasting has been retained in the Mardi Gras celebrations of heavily Catholic southwest Louisiana. In "Cajun" communities such as Mamou, Eunice, Crowley, and Church Point, masked riders, in wagons or on horseback, still seek donations for a community meal. Indeed, while even these traditional celebrations have become tourist attractions complete, in some cases, with street festivals and small parades where spectators catch the ubiquitous beads, the symbolic creation of a specifically local and decidedly Catholic community remains strong. Folklorist Carl Lindahl (1996: 133) notes that among the excluded in the Basile, Louisiana Mardi Gras are "Protestants and African Americans [who] do not desire and are not invited to participate." Such exclusion is not meant to be discriminatory, but rather reflects the original boundary-making of the festival community, which expresses its identity as ethnically Cajun and religiously Catholic. According to Cajun folklorist Barry Ancelet (1989: 2), the "ritual chaos" of masked and mounted riders begging, dancing, and indulging in other sorts of normally forbidden activities—all lubricated by copious amounts of alcohol—retains its own "processional nature which has roots in African as well as European tradition … the Mardi Gras moves about through the landscape, taking its celebration to the people, sometimes whether they like it or not." Thus, although a primary concern of the Cajun Mardi Gras is to preserve and reify intersecting boundaries of ethnicity, culture, and religion, it is also, at its best, transgressive of these same boundaries and necessarily performed within the larger public landscape.

Catholics and contemporary popular culture

By the middle of the twentieth century, the "American Way of Life" had expanded to incorporate non-Protestant religions such as Judaism and Catholicism. This was due in part to the positive images of the priesthood and Catholic life promoted in a cinematic industry still under the authority of the Code, but also by the advent of new popular media such as radio and television. By the mid-1950s, the fictional Fr. O'Malley had been replaced as the face of the Catholic priesthood by a real priest, Bishop (later Archbishop) Fulton J. Sheen. Sheen had begun his broadcasting career in the 1930s on radio, but it was his television program *Life Is Worth Living*, which ran from 1952 to 1957, that made him a media star. Always appearing in his full episcopal attire (minus the miter), Sheen was an unlikely choice to represent Catholicism to a national audience. Mark S. Massa (1999: 86) notes the irony of Sheen's popularity, arguing that the television career of this Thomist philosopher turned prime-time star symbolized "the paradoxical nature of the Catholic 'arrival' in the American cultural mainstream." That Sheen's overt Catholicism—his Thomism, his vestments, and a stage prop image of the Virgin Mary that became known as "Our Lady of Television"— was accepted by a largely non-Catholic audience was indeed a sign of Catholicism's cultural acceptance; but as Massa observes, such acceptance actually contributed to the loss of the distinctiveness of the Catholic sub-culture. Within the decade after *Life Is Worth Living* left the air, the Second Vatican Council and the election of John F. Kennedy to the presidency removed the last vestiges of anti-Catholic suspicions from all but the most incalcitrant cultural corners of the American public square, although such ideas would remain embedded within the larger popular culture.

At the opposite end of the spectrum from the very public figure of Bishop Fulton Sheen, the Trappist Monk Thomas Merton came to symbolize the Catholic contemplative tradition, especially through the publication of his popular spiritual autobiography *The Seven Storey Mountain* (1948). Merton's spirituality reflected a very different and much more personal form of Catholicism than that represented by Sheen, but like Sheen he became the face of Catholicism to many of those outside the faith, some of whom adopted his contemplative lifestyle despite—or perhaps because of—its rejection of the values of the larger consumerist culture. Merton's book marked the beginning of a mid-century flowering of a new American Catholic literary tradition that was aided by the embrace of novels by English Catholics such as Graham Greene and Evelyn Waugh. Foremost among American authors was the figure of Flannery O'Connor, a writer in the Southern Gothic tradition of William Faulkner. O'Connor's two novels and her numerous short stories became known for their strong use of Catholic imagery, despite the fact that her characters were usually depicted as southern Protestants. While Hazel Motes, the protagonist of her first novel *Wise Blood* (1952), assures one inquirer that his newly established and ironically named "Church Without Christ" is indeed Protestant, by the end of the narrative Motes has engaged in forms of asceticism—including blinding himself—that suggest a more sinister version of the Catholic imagination than Merton's self-effacing life of prayer and silence. According to O'Connor, such severe physical penance—even violence—always lay at the heart of the sacraments, and was "strangely capable of returning my characters to reality and preparing them to accept their moment of grace" (O'Connor 1970: 112). The literary use of violence for redemptive purposes, however, seems to have been lost upon subsequent writers, who have instead used it to return to earlier themes of corruption.

The novels of Dan Brown, for example, including bestsellers such as *Angels and Demons* (2000) and *The Da Vinci Code* (2003), revive anti-Catholic themes of secretive cabals, self-serving clergy, and mass deception as tools used by the Church for dominance and power. A similar claim can be made of the film *Stigmata* (1999), in which a young woman (Patricia Arquette) is possessed by the spirit of a dead priest and receives the stigmata, although her very physical wounds seem to be more demonic than divine. Ultimately, *Stigmata* and the novels of Brown use the institution of the Catholic Church only instrumentally, as less of an attack on Catholicism itself than an indictment against contemporary Christianity, which is presented as being far removed from the simple religion of Jesus. Yet Catholicism, with its medieval vestments, authoritarian tone, and supernaturalism, supplies the most obvious example of such excess, especially when coupled with the assumed power of its hierarchy over the hearts and minds of its devotees. At the end of *Stigmata*, viewers discover that the supernatural possession and agonies of the heroine are due to the Church's suppression of the Gnostic Gospel of Thomas, which the Vatican "refuses to recognize ... and has described ... as heresy" – an ominous-sounding statement (provided in a postscript) of a simple and well-known fact.

Perhaps no recent work of popular literature or film has associated violence with Catholicism in quite the same way as has the *Godfather* trilogy of Francis Ford Coppola. Coppola's cinematic narrative, based on a book by Mario Puzo (*The Godfather*, 1969), details the rise of the Corleone family from immigrant poverty to leadership of a crime syndicate, with Catholic symbolism appearing along the way as a background for the family's use of violence to achieve its ends. Many of the most violent scenes are interspersed with Catholic rituals—the wedding of Don Vito

Corleone's daughter Connie opens the first film (*The Godfather*, 1972), while the execution of rival dons, ordered by her brother Michael, concludes the film as the camera cuts between the murders and the baptism of Connie's child (during which Michael, as the baby's godfather, pledges to renounce the works of Satan). In 1974, *The Godfather, Part II* offered both a sequel and a prologue to the original film, as it charted the rise of both Vito Corleone, who carries out his first murder during a street festival in honor of San Rocco, and Michael, who assumes his role as Vito's heir in the "family business" at a party celebrating his son's confirmation. This film climaxes again with a murder ordered by Michael, in this case that of his own brother Fredo, who is shot for disloyalty to the family while reciting the "Hail Mary." *The Godfather, Part III* (1990) departs significantly from the Puzo text (the script was primarily written by Coppola); it opens with Michael receiving a papal honor for his donation of "blood money" to a Vatican foundation, although this attempt to purchase redemption fails, since Vatican officials prove to be just as ruthless as any crime family. The criminal corruption within the Church eventually leads to the assassination of Pope John Paul I, a fictionalized version of the very real rumors that accompanied the sudden death of the real pontiff in 1978. Coppola's combination of Italian crime syndicates and a duplicitous clergy bent on world domination clearly reflects themes from both antebellum forms of anti-Catholicism and the ethnic gangster movie genre of the 1930s. Similarly, the HBO series *The Sopranos* (1999–2007) offered television viewers a comparable mixture of Italian ethnicity, organized crime, and Catholicism, although in this case the relationships between these things were much more ambiguous. In the series, protagonist Tony Soprano's Catholic faith certainly does not encourage his criminal career, but neither does it present him with any significant moral issues; outwardly, his family was one of the most religious on television, although their Catholicism is largely disconnected from their anxieties and personal conflicts. At best, their faith is innocuous; at worst it is hypocritical.

The degree to which popular media present the Catholic Church as just another failed religious institution is, ironically, a reflection of the successful emergence of Catholicism into the mainstream of American life in the late twentieth century. Pockets of the extreme religious anti-Catholicism of the antebellum period still remain, but these have been pushed to the social fringe. One such remnant is Chick Publications in California, best known for its cartoon tracts that attack evolution, Halloween, homosexuality, and virtually any and all religions outside of founder Jack Chick's own very fundamentalist variety of Protestantism. In the early 1980s, Chick gained national notoriety with a series of comic books supposedly written by a former Jesuit priest that "exposed" various Catholic conspiratorial activities including the Holocaust, the mass suicides at Jonestown, and the "accidental" creation of Islam as a "counterfeit" religion, but such ridiculous claims find little support in contemporary culture. Rather, historian Philip Jenkins (2003) argues that a "new anti-Catholicism" that has arisen in American popular culture since the 1980s reflects a politically liberal bias against an institution that seems hopelessly mired in proposing traditionalist solutions to contemporary social issues.

Such a "new anti-Catholicism," therefore, may have less in common with earlier claims that Catholics represent a religious "other" in American society and more to do with the reasoning that saw filmmakers adopt Catholic imagery in the early twentieth century: the (presumed) coherence of a Catholic worldview that can be expressed easily in the popular media through verbal and visual symbols. Don Novello's character of Father Guido Sarducci (seen mostly on *Saturday Night Live* [NBC, 1975–present]), the faux gossip columnist for a Vatican newspaper, may be read as a parody of any religious figure trying to appeal to contemporary society, for which his vestments offer an immediate visual representation. Similarly, *SNL* comedian Molly Shannon's Catholic schoolgirl Mary Katherine Gallagher could be any naïve and socially inept preteen, since Catholicism itself provides only a visual setting in which her antics take place (although each skit ended with a sexually suggestive flash of Mary Katherine's panties beneath her school uniform). Another *SNL* alumna, Julia Sweeney, has made her journey from a Catholic childhood to atheism the subject of a lengthy comedic monologue (*Letting Go of God*, 2008), but despite her rejection of religious belief, she still views her former faith with nostalgia and even affection. "I was raised Catholic and for me, it was, all in all, a good experience," she comments; "for me, it was mostly wonderful. I always felt lucky to be a Catholic." While certainly darker comedies—such as the previously discussed *Sister Mary Ignatius Explains It All for You*—have been more visceral in attacking the beliefs and practices of Catholicism, on the whole the presence of Catholic imagery and symbols in popular culture has tended to be informed by the Catholic imagination rather than used as a tool against it, particularly since such usage often comes from former Catholics themselves.

In his book on the Catholic imagination, Greeley (2001: 147) observes that "[o]nce a Catholic, always a Catholic," meaning (at least in part) that the formation of a Catholic imagination in childhood leaves such an indelible imprint on one's perception of the world, that even those who have renounced their faith and left the Church—the clichéd "lapsed" Catholics—are often still deeply influenced by a Catholic sensibility. In American literature, even as authors such as Jack Kerouac and Anne Rice have struggled with or even renounced their Catholic faith, they seem to have retained their Catholic creativity. Kerouac's novels, especially *On the Road* (1957) and *The Dharma Bums* (1958), were among the founding documents of the counter-culture of the late 1950s and 1960s and are known for their improvisation style and popularization of Buddhist ideas. But Kerouac remained an "unsuccessful Catholic" whose own literary influences included Thomas Merton and the Irish Catholic writer James Joyce. Rice has been very public about her own uneven relationship to the Catholic Church, but her novels, which helped to launch a popular culture fascination with liminal figures such as vampires and zombies, can be read as inverted presentations of a Catholic sensibility. Like the priest, the vampire transgresses the boundaries of the human experience and other worlds—one who also offers a communion of blood and flesh that brings a type of resurrection and eternal life. Such a connection was made even more explicit in the HBO series *True Blood* (premiered 2008), in which the medieval priesthood provided a surreptitious cover for vampirism, especially during the period of the Spanish Inquisition. While subsequent episodes have presented a ruling "Authority" with its own scriptures and bloody sacraments, the parallels to Catholicism again appear to be a critique of conservative political and religious ideology rather than a direct attack on the Church itself (McDevitt 2012).

In American popular music, entertainers such as Madonna, Bruce Springsteen, and Jimmy Buffett similarly qualify as lapsed Catholics, with Madonna having famously adopted a version of Jewish mysticism in the place of her former faith. Yet, as Mark D. Hulsether (2000: 82) argues, Madonna's music videos from the late 1980s, such as "Oh Father" and "Papa Don't Preach," served to "reconceptualize Catholic teachings about families and bodies, making them usable in the life of an Italian Catholic taught by nuns." Such utility comes in the form of joining Catholic sensuality with expressive eroticism, thus using Catholic sensibilities to challenge the institutionalized teachings of the Catholic Church. This blending of sexuality and salvation clearly reflects the use of sexual metaphors adopted by many Catholic saints, most of them female, to express the human longing for the divine during the late medieval and early modern periods. One need only think of Bernini's statue of the Ecstasy of St. Teresa for the most aesthetic example; but Bernini's (and Teresa's) insight presents itself as too problematic for many contemporary Catholics. Thus, Madonna's song and music video "Like a Prayer" (1989) generated both a condemnation by the Vatican and a threatened boycott by American Catholics against the Pepsi Cola Company, which had used the song and scenes from the video in a commercial for its soft drink product (Hulsether 2000: 85). The lyrics of the song echo the longing of the soul for the divine in a way similar to the canonical Song of Songs, originally a collection of erotic Hebrew poetry that the Church chose to interpret as a metaphor for the relationship between the devotee and God. But the video extends this imagery into a complex mixture of Southern racism, urban violence, and religious devotion, the last of which appears in the form of a gospel choir, burning crosses, and the suggestion of self-inflicted stigmata. The central figure of this "reconceptualized" passion play, however, is an unidentified Black saint (St. Martin of Porres?), who is simultaneously a devotional statue in a Catholic church, Madonna's lover, and an African-American male who saves her from sexual violence but then is unjustly arrested for the assault. The video was, according to Greeley (1989), "a morality story filled with Catholic imagery" and a "sense of sacramentality" that Madonna "has ... carried with her from her Catholic childhood," although Madonna seemed less sanguine about the lessons from her childhood. Following the release of the video, Madonna told an interviewer for Andy Warhol's *Interview* magazine,

> I have a great sense of guilt and sin from Catholicism that has definitely permeated my everyday life, whether I want it to or not. And when I do something wrong or that I think is wrong, if I don't let someone know that I have wronged, I'm always afraid that I'm going to be punished. ... And that's something you're raised to believe as a Catholic. Everyone's a sinner in Catholicism, and you must constantly be asking God to cleanse your soul and begging him for forgiveness.
>
> (Johnston 1999: 65)

Yet, as many commentators have noted, the video assuages such guilt by utilizing such traditional Catholic symbols as votive candles, holy images, and crucifixes (the last of which Madonna had famously made a fashion accessory) as symbols of racial and sexual liberation rather than religious oppression. "By frequently employing graced everyday artifacts from common experience," Tom Beaudoin (1998: 77) observes, "Madonna participates in the symbolic and sacramental life of her Catholic Church while unhinging sacramentals from their exclusive relationship to Catholicism." This subversive sacramentalism is expressed most powerfully in the imagery of incarnation, since both the Black saint and the female Madonna are identified with Christ: the former by his undeserved subjection to institutionalized injustice, and the latter when she decides to redeem him, her resolution to act visually represented by her slicing open her palms in imitation of the stigmata. The implication that the two might also be lovers joins the sensuality of Catholicism with the theme of liberation, thus reversing older anti-Catholic fears. "Seeking racial reconciliation," Beaudoin argues, "is a spiritual task, and 'Like a Prayer' reminds us again that spirituality and sensuality need each other" (ibid.: 91).

Bruce Springsteen was certainly less controversial than Madonna, but numerous scholars have remarked upon the religious themes that also permeate his music. According to Kate McCarthy (2001: 25–26), the most prominent of these religious ideas is that of the "promised land," which evokes ideas and attitudes ranging from the biblical account of the exodus, to the American dream of creating a "city on a hill," to personal sexual fulfillment. The promised land is both this-worldly and other-worldly; or, perhaps more accurately, the other-worldly aspect can be experienced sacramentally through this world, at least for those willing to search for it in typical American fashion by taking to the road. Thus, while McCarthy emphasizes the Americanness of Springsteen's promised land, Greeley finds it to be an expression of Springsteen's Catholic imagination. In his review of Springsteen's 1988 album *Tunnel of Love*, Greeley remarked that

> Springsteen sings of religious realities—sin, temptation, forgiveness, life, death, hope—in images that come (implicitly perhaps) from his Catholic childhood, images that appeal to the whole person, not just the head, and that will be absorbed by far more Americans than those who listened to the Pope … . Troubadours always have more impact than theologians or bishops, storytellers more influence than homilists.
>
> (Greeley 1988)

Indeed, as cultural historian Robin Sylvan (2002: 4) argues, not only can popular musicians have significant impact beyond the pronouncements of any officially "ordained" (in the generic sense) cultural elite, but popular music can itself serve a specifically religious function within a society by providing "a cultural identity, a social structure, and a sense of belonging to a community." The ability both to form a "religious" community and to express the "lapsed" Catholic form of the imagination may be traced in the music of Jimmy Buffett and in the devotion of his followers, known as Parrotheads.

At first glance, Buffett's music might appear to be the exact opposite of anything that can be construed as a form of the Catholic imagination. "By all accounts," notes Julie J. Ingersoll (2001: 255), "Jimmy Buffett has led a life that flouts traditional religious sensibilities. He glorifies sex and drugs, he seemingly advocates irresponsibility in the name of freedom, and he openly derides traditional religion." In his autobiography *A Pirate Looks at Fifty*, Buffett (1998: 3) writes that as a young man, he "broke out of the grip of Catholicism and made it through adolescence without killing myself in a car," and, like Madonna, he recalls his Catholic childhood only in terms of inculcating a sense of guilt and a need for confession (ibid.: 228). Yet, in a study of the "philosophy" of Buffett, Matthew Caleb Flamm and Jennifer A. Rea (2009: 127, 130) argue that his lyrics remain "quintessentially Catholic," calling him a "singing Catholic rebel." Indeed, Buffett's body of work—both his song lyrics and his books and short stories—contain numerous references to Catholic ideas and practices, which might ridicule his childhood memories of sin and guilt as spurious while simultaneously constructing an alternative "promised land"—Margaritaville—that is itself authentically Catholic.

Margaritaville, the title of a 1977 song that has become synonymous with an empire of restaurants, foods, alcoholic beverages, clothing, and a variety of additional consumer goods, is also, as Buffett has stated many times, a state of mind that can be indulged anywhere. Thus, like Springsteen's promised land, it is always sacramentally present, because "it's always five o'clock somewhere" (title and chorus of a 2003 duet with country singer Alan Jackson). Despite his professed break with Catholicism, Buffett's own Margaritaville is still populated by "saints and guardian angels" (particularly St. Christopher), who beneficently intervene when occasion might arise (see Buffett 1998: 98). And while it may be a place where one is encouraged to "Commit a little mortal sin / It's good for the soul" (Buffett 1973), it is also a place where confession of one's sins is likewise required.[2] In the song "Margaritaville," the singer must ultimately admit that his failed relationship is his "own damn fault," while in the song "Coastal Confessions" Buffett sings "So bless me father yes I have sinned / Given the chance I'll prob'ly do it again / I don't need absolution just a simple solution will do ... I've got coastal confessions to make / How 'bout you?" (Buffett 2004). For Parrotheads, Catholic and non-Catholic alike, Margaritaville is a true mystical paradise where confession may be required but from which guilt is banished—a perfect version of heaven for a postmodern world.

Conclusion

From the lecherous priests of antebellum literature to the breezy shade of a palm tree in mythical Margaritaville, the image of the Catholic as at once both alien and quintessentially American has been a significant expression within American popular culture. The visual imagery of the Church, coupled with its own sacramental theology, has endowed popular culture with an array of powerful images that celebrate the transcendental through the mundane and material. Even in its guise as American "other," as expressed in various forms of anti-Catholic literature and art, Catholicism has long been a way in which Americans have imagined themselves and, on occasion, reframed that meaning in celebration of, or in contradistinction to, the Catholic imagination.

Notes

1 As the most widespread form of Christianity in the world, Catholicism has influenced—and been influenced by—numerous cultures. This chapter will focus only upon the

American context, where a historically strong Protestant hegemony, coupled with governmental neutrality in religious affairs, has created an environment in which Catholics are perceived as both "insiders" and "outsiders" in popular culture.

2 Lyrics for all of Jimmy Buffett's songs can be found in the "Discography" section of *Jimmy Buffett's Margaritaville*: www.margaritaville.com/jimmybuffett_discography.html.

Works cited

Ancelet, B.J. (1989) *"Capitaine, voyage ton flag": The Traditional Cajun Country Mardi Gras*, Lafayette, LA: Center for Louisiana Studies.

Baker, W.J. (2007) *Playing with God: Religion and Modern Sport*, Cambridge, MA: Harvard University Press.

Beaudoin, T. (1998) *Virtual Faith: The Irreverent Spiritual Quest of Generation X*, San Francisco, CA: Jossey-Bass.

Billington, R.A. (1952) *The Protestant Crusade, 1800–1860: A Study of the Origins of American Nativism*, New York: Rinehart.

Black, G.D. (1994) *Hollywood Censored: Morality Codes, Catholics, and the Movies*, New York: Cambridge University Press.

Buffett, J. (1973) "Grapefruit, Juicy Fruit," *A White Sports Coat and a Pink Crustacean*, ABC/Dunhill.

——(1998) *A Pirate Looks at Fifty*, New York: Random House.

——(2004) "Coastal Confessions," *License to Chill*, RCA.

Catholic News Agency (2010) "Catholic history of New Orleans Saints runs deep." Online. Available: www.catholicnewsagency.com/news/catholic_history_of_new_orleans_saints_runs _deep/ (accessed 14 June 2013).

Chidester, D. (2005) *Authentic Fakes: Religion and American Popular Culture*, Berkeley, CA: University of California Press.

Chowder, K. (1993) "When Notre Dame needed inspiration, Rockne provided it," *Smithsonian* 24, 8 (November): 164–77.

Cronin, M. and D. Adair (2001) *The Wearing of the Green: A History of St Patrick's Day*, New York: Routledge.

Davis, D.B. (1960) "Some themes of counter-subversion: an analysis of anti-Masonic, anti-Catholic, and anti-Mormon literature," *Mississippi Valley Historical Review* 47 (1960): 205–24.

Dolan, J.P. (2002) *In Search of an American Catholicism*, New York: Oxford University Press.

Flamm, M.C. and J.A. Rea (2009) "An altar boy covers his ass," in E. McKenna and S.L. Pratt (eds), *Jimmy Buffett and Philosophy: The Porpoise Driven Life*, Chicago, IL: Open Court, 125–38.

Greeley, A.M. (1988) "The Catholic imagination of Bruce Springsteen," *America* 158, 5 (February 6): 110–15.

——(1989) "Madonna's challenge to her church," *America* 160, 18 (May 13): 447–49.

——(2001) *The Catholic Imagination*, Berkeley, CA: University of California Press.

Hulsether, M.D. (2000) "Like a sermon: popular religion in Madonna videos," in B.D. Forbes and J.H. Mahan (eds), *Religion and Popular Culture in America*, Berkeley, CA: University of California Press, 77–100.

Ingersoll, J.J. (2001) "The thin line between Saturday night and Sunday morning: meaning and community among Jimmy Buffett's Parrotheads," in E.M. Mazur and K. McCarthy (eds), *God in the Details: American Religion in Popular Culture*, New York: Routledge, 253–66.

Jenkins, P. (2003) *The New Anti-Catholicism: The Last Acceptable Prejudice*, New York: Oxford University Press.

Johnston, B. (1999) "Confession of a Catholic girl: *Interview* Magazine, 1989," in A. Metz and C. Benson (eds), *The Madonna Companion: Two Decades of Commentary*, New York: Schirmer Books, 52–74.

Lindahl, C. (1996) "The presence of the past in the Cajun Country Mardi Gras," *Journal of Folklore Research* 33: 125–53.

McCarthy, K. (2001) "Deliver me from nowhere: Bruce Springsteen and the myth of the American promised land," in E.M. Mazur and K. McCarthy (eds), *God in the Details: American Religion in Popular Culture*, New York: Routledge, 23–46.

McDevitt, C. (2012) "Rick Santorum inspires 'True Blood' vampire," Politico.com (June 19). Online. Available: www.politico.com/blogs/click/2012/06/rick-santorum-inspires-true-blood-vampire-126569.html (accessed 20 April 2013).

Massa, M.S. (1999) *Catholics and American Culture: Fulton Sheen, Dorothy Day, and the Notre Dame Football Team*, New York: Crossroad.

O'Connor, F. (1970) *Mystery and Manners: Occasional Prose*, ed. S. Fitzgerald and R. Fitzgerald, New York: Farrar, Straus and Giroux.

Orsi, R.A. (2010) *The Madonna of 115th Street: Faith and Community in Italian Harlem, 1880–1950*, 3rd edn, New Haven, CT: Yale University Press.

Rogin, M.P. (1987) *Ronald Reagan, The Movie: And Other Episodes in Political Demonology*, Berkeley, CA: University of California Press.

Skinner, J.M. (1993) *The Cross and the Cinema: The Legion of Decency and the Catholic Office for Motion Pictures, 1933–1970*, Westport, CT: Praeger.

Smith, A.B. (2010) *The Look of Catholics: Portrayals in Popular Culture from the Great Depression to the Cold War*, Lawrence, KS: University Press of Kansas.

Smith, R.K. (2006) *Gothic Arches, Latin Crosses: Anti-Catholicism and American Church Designs in the Nineteenth Century*, Chapel Hill, NC: University of North Carolina Press.

Sylvan, R. (2002) *Traces of the Spirit: The Religious Dimensions of Popular Music*, New York: New York University Press.

23

HINDUISM

Sheila J. Nayar

"Truth is One; the wise call it by many names."

Rig Veda

"You've got The Elephant Man, Johnny Six-Arms, Papa Smurf ... . Hey, these guys are pretty cool!"

Homer describing Apu's gods, *The Simpsons*

There is no (one) Hinduism

Hinduism, the world's oldest living religion, did not name itself. Invading Persians in the first millennium of the Common Era applied the term "Hindu" to peoples living along the Sindhu (now Indus) River (Fuller 2004: 10).[1] As a result, many of the rituals and practices that now constitute an artificially unitary Hinduism derive from fairly localized traditions—often practiced in different languages, and centering on the worship of different gods (Vertovec 2000: 8). Hinduism has, in some sense, always been cognizant of itself as *Hinduisms*; and because there has never been a single Hinduism, there has rarely been inclination or need to undergo any sort of "house cleaning" (Viswanathan 1992: xii). Evolution in Hinduism does not imply that the old must be discarded in order to make way for the new. Indeed, at least one of the Puranas (literally, texts that are "ancient") makes space for multiple versions of a single story, fully recognizing and accepting that different eras generate narrative discrepancies (Doniger 2009: 668). Thus, in the words of the fifteenth-century poet Tulsidas, the god Ram "incarnates in countless ways and there are tens of millions of Rámáyanas [epic tales of his life]" (Lutgendorf 1995: 217).

This accounts not only for Hinduism's malleability, but also its accretive complexity, which can sometimes be read as chaos. But this "chaos" is what gives Hinduism an air of liberation and freedom. It is also what has likely permitted Hinduism to survive. Uncommonly incorporative when it comes to what to believe, Hinduism allows for Hindus who are more animist sharing space with those more polytheistic; pantheists besides panentheists; monotheists among monists (Vertovec 2000: 8). Although the majority of Hindus believe their multiple gods to be forms of the one

440

Supreme God, Brahman, ultimately religious practice (orthopraxy) matters more than religious dogma (orthodoxy). Indeed, the Hindu emphasis placed on *dharma* (duty) underscores the significance of action, of obligation—of performing religion. Further, Hinduism makes epistemic space for different manifestations of God. For example, the Vishnu-oriented school of Hinduism, Śrīvaiṣnavism, acknowledges five equally divine manifestations—from the transcendent God to icons in shrines—that are distinguishable by their increasing accessibility (N. Nayar 1991: 105–38). Or, as the father-figure proclaims in *Am I a Hindu?*, a self-proclaimed primer for "non-resident Indian" (NRI) parents struggling to teach their American-born child about Hinduism, "Son, even Adi Sankarachharya, the great apostle of Advaita philosophy, did not look down upon the practice of worshipping many gods. ... [P]eople are at different stages of understanding the truth" (Viswanathan 1992: 219).

Seeing—and being seen by—popular culture

So crucial is the relationship between divinity and devotee that the focus of the encounter is situated in *darshan*, in the auspicious act of seeing and of being seen by the god (Eck 1981: 3). *Darshan* entails "a two-way look" (Dwyer and Patel 2002: 33), which indubitably makes the looking profoundly active. Perhaps that is why "one of the most ubiquitous manifestations of modern religion in South Asia" has been in the form of lithographs (see Figure 23.1): colorful, mechanically reproduced pictures of deities and other sacred figures (Babb 1995: 6). These pictures often can be found beside the cash register of Indian restaurants, whether in Tulsa or Toronto or Taipei: Laxshmi, goddess of material and spiritual prosperity, adrift on her lotus; Ganesh, remover of obstacles, with his potbelly, elephant head, and one broken tusk.

Saraswati, goddess of knowledge, music, and the creative arts, may bedeck Indian school corridors or hang over a library's circulation desk, just as Nataraja (Shiva as Lord of the Dance) may be found in a theater, or Rama and Sita in a marriage hall (Smith 1995: 36). These lithographs certainly demonstrate how inexpensive imagery can contribute to the growth of a new and distinctly popular omnipraxy, one that is "inconspicuous, casual, informal, and unmediated by specialists" (Babb 1995: 7). What they also reflect is a particularly Hindu cultivation of "an awareness of the power of images and symbols" (Hawley 2004: 117)—not to mention the easy, sometimes arbitrary blurring of sacred and secular in Hindu culture, and in Indian culture more generally.

The more recent Hindu embrace of film and television is no doubt because such visual media lend themselves well to that "ritual exchange of glances," as well as to "religious edification through mythological storytelling" (McLain 2009: 16). A 1980s television serial that recounted the Rámáyana in 78 episodes (*Ramayan*, directed by Ramanand Sagar, 1986–88) proved to be "a feast of darsan," with each character's intense emotional state conveyed through "repeated zoom shots—a convention favored in Hindi films"—and a narrative flow periodically halted "to focus on stylized, poster-like tableaux, accompanied by devotional singing" (Lutgendorf 1995: 230–31). For the majority of its Hindu viewers, the serial "was not simply a program to 'see,' it was something to *do*—an event to participate in" (ibid.: 243). It was followed

Figure 23.1 Seeing—and *being seen by*—the gods (color lithograph), Godong/Getty Images.

soon after by a 98-episode *Mahabharat* (directed by Baldev Raj Chopra and Ravi Chopra, 1988–90).

A similar sort of embrace-cum-transplant of devotional practice is found in the films of "Bollywood"—the Hollywood of Bombay (now known as Mumbai). Bollywood song-and-dance numbers (which, until very recently, were mandatory in every Hindi film) often draw on regional forms of folk theater and re-enactments of mythological tales (Derné 1995: 197). Even the exaggeration inherent in such films, as

Derné notes—as well as the films' reliance on lengthy performances, predictability, elaborate speeches, and digressions—derives from readings and performances of the Rámáyana and Mahábhárata (ibid.). Pleasure derives from a familiarity of form (ibid.): of plots that revisit well-known stories and ceremonial prayers evocatively woven into musical scores (Nimbark 2004: 104; see also S. Nayar 2004). Some argue that second-generation Indians in the United States have developed "Hindi cinema Hinduism"; that is, their traditional rituals and activities are based no longer on actual life-practice, rather on retrogressively mythical (as opposed to mythological) movie versions of Hinduism (Desai 2005: 63; see also Dwyer 2009).

Today the new medium for the Hindu message is cyberspace, and it, too, "is being increasingly mobilized for traditional as well as alternative expressions of faith, spirituality and religion" (Mallapragada 2010: 110). Hindu-temple culture has made its way to the Web, in the form of temple homepages and commercial sites where one can pay for rituals to be performed at prominent temples in India. There are also virtual *mandirs* (temples) at which one can meditate and offer *puja* to a deity (Mallapragada 2010: 110). At Eprarthana.com, for example, digital temple doors open to reveal a deity in his or her inner sanctum and, as virtual incense burns, one is given the option of cracking a virtual coconut or tendering virtual flowers. Earlier mediated forms of seeing and being seen by the divine have, in this way, been repurposed for a digital age.[2] One may also find more philosophical, text-based forms of Hinduism online (e.g., vmandir.com), enabling the centuries-long provision in Hinduism of multiple modes by which the divine may manifest and be understood to be replicated and carried on.

And yet, mainstream popular culture of the United States isn't much interested in *darshan*, or even *dharma*. It is *karma* onto which the North American public has latched—though often in ways that challenge the term's traditional meaning. The root meaning of the Sanskrit term ("to do or to act") implies that "people reap what they sow" (Shouler and Anthony 2009: 58)—and not, as Alicia Keys erroneously croons in her song "Karma," that "[w]hat goes around, comes around" (Brothers, Keys, and Smith 2003). Then again, popular culture is neither social analysis (Fuller 2004: 8), nor necessarily concerned with getting right a people's understanding of their own tradition—especially a tradition that, in the American context, makes up less than one percent of the population (The Pew Forum on Religion and Public Life 2010). The farther audiences tend to be from the direct, lived experience of (in this case) Hinduism, "the more likely they are to construct imagined worlds that are chimerical, aesthetic, even fantastic objects" (Appadurai 2000: 326). When Hinduism is all around you—as is the case in India, where 80 percent of the population is Hindu—how the religion gets represented in, and how it circulates as, fantasy follows a very different trajectory.

Early pop-culture Hinduism in the USA

Hinduism's influence could be felt in America as early as 1836, with the Transcendentalists' romantic imagination of the East as a source to counteract or compensate for industrialization (Iwamura 2011: 9). However, it wasn't until 1893, when the magnetic Swami Vivekananda appeared at the Parliament of World Religions in Chicago, that Hinduism really entered American popular consciousness and culture. Vivekananda spoke about the divinity of the soul and, during an ensuing tour of the United States, attracted admirers who later founded the first of America's Vedanta Societies (Hawley 2004: 112–13). These societies, like Vivekananda himself, focused on a few attractively simplified teachings and on an ethos of "work and worship" (Bardach 2011).

More important to popular culture than Vivekananda's speech, however, is the practice of yoga that he exported from India. Few who sustain today's $6 billion annual American yoga industry are aware "that they owe their yoga mats to Vive-kananda" (Bardach 2011). Perhaps that is because the ascetic seams between the Old and New Ages were frayed as early as 1927, with the release of Katherine Mayo's non-fiction bestseller *Mother India*, in which Indian religious life is depicted in a "devastatingly negative" way (Melton and Jones 2011: 4). The book's opening pages alone reflect an unsubtle rhetorical pattern that carries through the entire work: an initial (fleeting) admiration for the "big, western, modern" city of Calcutta that swiftly gives way to the lamented "Indian town" behind it, one of mosques, bazaars, and temples like the Kali Ghat shrine, in which, dimly lit, resides the figure of the goddess Kali. "Black of face she is," as Mayo describes, "with a monstrous lolling tongue, dripping blood. Of her four hands, one grasps a bleeding human head, one a knife, the third, outstretched, cradles blood" (ibid.: 5). It is worth pointing out that Mayo's project had been facilitated by British Central Intelligence, which sought to discredit Mahatma Gandhi and reinforce the need for British control of India (A. Singh 2006). Alas, due to the book's popularity, it was reprinted 30 times within just a few years of its initial release.

Thirty years later—post-Partition, post-Indian Independence—another pendulum swing in the West paved the way for a mystically inclined "visibilization" of Hinduism (Jacobs 2010: 121), one partly contingent on the disillusionment of European and American youth with the mores of their parents' generation and the empty materialism of the day (ibid.: 143). Thus, despite the fact that Hermann Hesse's 1922 novel *Siddhartha* was translated into English in 1951, it wasn't until the 1960s that it "created a literary lure for the mystical East" (Williamson 2010: 44). At approximately the same time, Asian teachers arrived on Western shores perpetuating Eastern religion as something existing "outside of cultural and sociological realities" (ibid.). These spiritual gurus often presented under the veil of science or empiricism "only the mystical practices of their traditions" (ibid.).[3]

The establishment in the 1960s of the *bhakti*-oriented International Society for Krishna Consciousness (ISKCON)—or the "Hare Krishnas," as they are more popularly known—arguably mitigated to a degree the West's ignorance of Hinduism as a tradition. Before that, however, some decidedly tawdry depictions of the religion appeared on the Hollywood screen. There was, for instance, the puckishly problematic Beatles film *Help!* (1965), which opens with a satirical worship of Kali—one that blends faux Buddhism, European medieval tropes, Roman armor, and masks straight out of ancient Greek tragedy—and includes a beautiful maiden being sacrificed to that "Drinker of Blood," that "Mother of Darkness." The focus here is not on aspects of Hinduism that are customary or that are popularly illustrated—life- and love-loving

Krishna, for instance, or time-devouring Kali for whom devotees feel affection. Rather, the focus is on a random assortment of ghastly practices (human sacrifice, blood-imbibing) that appear lurid and orgiastically "other."

And yet, this indictment seems unfair, given that the subsequent influence of the Beatles on the growing public consciousness of Hinduism was paramount—and positive. Consider, for instance, the Beatles' association with Maharishi Mahesh Yogi, who not only became their guru but was also the first to popularize one of those empirical, scientific (and accessible) strains of Hindu practice, transcendental meditation (TM).[4]

More specifically, Hindu devotee George Harrison's 1969 recording of the "Hare Krishna Mantra" made the British singles charts, and his 1970 song "My Sweet Lord" includes a chanting of the "Hare Krishna" mantra along with that of the Christian "Allelulia." That song spent time at number one on both sides of the Atlantic (Jacobs 2010: 121) and a video recording of its performance has received more than seven million hits on YouTube.[5] Because of his association with the Beatles, the Maharishi was well enough known by the mid-1970s to appear as guest of honor on the *Merv Griffin Show*. During the show, Hollywood star Clint Eastwood "strode onstage … opened his suit jacket and reached in as if he were going to pull out Dirty Harry's .44 Magnum. Instead, he produced a flower and handed it to the Maharishi." After that program, "TM initiations soared" (Shouler and Anthony 2009: 213).

Hinduism became increasingly aligned with counter-cultural practices and experientially intense (and purportedly liberating) forms of self-expression—rock music, psychedelic art, hallucinogenic drugs—precisely because of its having been extricated from its original and often more conservative intentions. Somewhat ironically, A.C.B. Swami Prabhupada, who founded the Hare Krishnas, envisioned ISKCON's consciousness-raising mantra as a healthy alternative to "psychedelics and antiwar protests" (Prabhupada 1983: xi). These misappropriations were precisely what motivated hit Bollywood film *Hare Krishna Hare Rama* (1971), directed by Dev Anand, in which a brother seeks out his estranged pot-smoking, guitar-loving, love-loving hippie-sister. Sings the sister from within her largely foreign enclave of long-haired hippies, "Puff away and let your sorrows melt away / Chant morning and evening / Hare Krishna, Hare Ram … " The ensuing provocative dancing so repels her dharmic brother that musically he entreats them not to defame the Hindu gods: "Wake up, you careless people / Win over your mind by reading the Gita / … / Don't let your life be a slave to intoxication / Ram abandoned all pleasures with a smile / … / Krishna taught us the theory of karma / You have turned away from your duties / Save us, O Lord Ram … ." (Paradoxically, it's the drug-induced portion of the song that still gets broadcast today—a tribute, perhaps, to the general trump of musical intemperance over reprimand.)

Post-Nri pop-cultural Hinduism

It wasn't until the late 1960s that Indians settled in significant numbers in the United States, thanks in large part to the *Immigration and Naturalization Act of 1965*. The brief wave of Indians who had come before this act had been prior to the passage of federal laws in 1917 and 1924 that intentionally prohibited Asian immigration (McLain 2009: 201). Participants in the post-1965 wave were particularly eager (and numerically better able) to retain their religious identity and to "establish visible and permanent places for Hinduism" in their new homeland, which they did by building temples and community centers, and by importing religious authorities (ibid.: 202). Many of them were unlikely architects of their religion, professionals who suddenly needed to construct a "new and practical form" of Hinduism (ibid.).[6] As a result, in addition to hosting weddings, celebrations of the Festival of Lights (Diwali), and birthdays of major deities, the more than 200 temples that now exist in the USA also frequently function in non-religious, culturally inflected capacities—such as settings for Bollywood-inspired bridal showers and birthday parties (Nimbark 2004: 109).[7]

Although 98 percent of all Hindus still reside in India, the more than one and a half million currently in the United States have crafted a Hinduism that responds to—and also sometimes necessarily insulates itself from—pop-cultural depictions of Hinduism that are externally produced by mainstream media culture. This was especially the case in the 1970s–1990s, before the digital communications explosion. Thus *Am I a Hindu?* was published in 1992 to help religiously isolated parents who found themselves "unable to explain a range of Hindu customs, practices, and doctrines" (Kurien 2007: 10). Ample use was also made of India's easily transportable comic-book series *Amar Chitra Katha* (Immortal Picture-Stories), in which tales of gods, goddesses, and important mythological and historical figures are vividly recounted. These comics, originally intended to teach overly Westernized, English-medium schoolchildren in India about their own history and mythology, experienced a second life abroad (McLain 2008: 298). If the comics remain beloved today, it may be because they helped NRIs define their own self-understanding of Hinduism and India. Perhaps that legacy also explains their current availability as an iPhone application (see Figure 23.2).

These comics can be ideologically problematic, however; all of the heroines are portrayed as submissive, long-suffering, husband-worshiping wives—projecting an orthodox Hindu ideal of the feminine—while, at the same time, they are depicted visually as "voluptuous, fair-skinned … and draped in revealing silken clothes" (McLain 2009: 61). Nevertheless, for diasporic parents without formal religious instruction, this inexpensive, colorful series has served to articulate "what Hindus believe and why" (ibid.: 201).[8] Still, as Vasudha Narayan cautions, "unlike a person in India, where newspapers and regular television programming carry glimpses of *varied* rituals and synopses of religious discourses," young Hindus in the USA who have been fed a unitary diet of *Amar Chitra Katha* may not envisage "alternative versions of a story" (ibid.: 205–6).

Of course diasporic Hindu youth today could be said to have more in common with contemporaneous middle-class Hindus in India than ever before, given that both of these communities are better able to afford the same technologies and are therefore privy to the same religious television shows, Bollywood-film channels, and temple Web sites. They heed the same jet-peripatetic gurus and partake in the same pilgrimage tours—quite distinct from the more ascetic nature of pilgrimages of old. The exchange has become more complicated, though not necessarily disagreeably so,

Figure 23.2 App for the ACK comic on Mirabai, devotee of Krishna. Excerpt from iRemedi-
ETHER*MEDIA Amar Chitra Katha iPad App Comic book from www.ether
media.net.

because of the multidirectional flow in which Hinduism travels, back and forth
between India and the West. No longer must the medium be physically transported—by way of cassette tapes of devotional songs (*bhajans*), familiar prayers
(*artis*), *filmi artis* (prayers made popular because of their presence in a Bollywood
film), or even Bollywood disco scores, with their lyrics now praising (for example)
the Mother Goddess (Manuel 1993: 115).[9] Diasporic Hindus no longer rely on isolated weekly television or radio programs that contained "a peculiar blend of
religious-spiritual discourse and legal-commercial advice," and offered "their NRI
listeners heavy doses of religious chants and hymns" (Nimbark 2004: 103). This sort
of miscibility of the financial with the faithful is nothing new (see Sinha 2011: 201).
What is new is a "sense of simultaneity that [is] not firmly anchored in national or
even international space" (Hawley 2004: 118).[10] In addition to the expressly Hindu
television channels, Web pages, and radio stations generated by "cyber-savvy"
Hindus on behalf of their respective sects (Nimbark 2004: 103), there are satellite-
imported TV "soaps" from India, in which characters regularly perform *pujas* or

offer *aarti* to Krishna and Radha; and gurus like Sri Sri Ravi Shankar and Swami Guru Ram Dev who have parlayed YouTube.com into mobile meditation zones. Facebook pages, like the one for *Hinduism Today* magazine, stream daily inspirations and articles to one's smartphone. Of course, NRI communities partaking of these variously mediated forms of Hinduism may be differently motivated than their counterparts in India. Nevertheless, these forms are (for the most part) intended for Hindus.

But what about Hinduism in mainstream popular culture dominated (and consumed) by non-Hindus?

Pop-American Hinduism

In the last few decades, a number of mainstream representations of Hinduism have instigated protest campaigns, often because of the perilously decontextualized nature of those representations. As journalist Mark Pinsky argues—specifically in the context of the animated television series *The Simpsons*, with its recurrent Hindu character Apu Nahasapeemapetilon—most Americans who see images of Hindus or Hinduism on television or in the movies "don't have a clue about the ancient and profound Hindu beliefs and customs. ... When it comes to the Hindu references, the uninformed audience sees only the denigration, the inflated tale, the twisted view" (Pinsky 2001: 154–55). Anti-defamation groups have protested against the caricature of Hinduism on programs like *The Simpsons*, but also against the sassy (and sometimes sacrilegious) representations of Hindu deities in commercial manufacturing and advertising. These appropriations run the gamut, from toilet seats pasted with images of the gods (Kurien 2007: 186) to depictions of Rama on shoes and designer bikinis (Sinha 2011: 199). True, some of the more chic items "are also readily available in India, as Hindu imagery and symbolism have been made exotic, glamorous," such that the gods have been "embraced by popular culture in the fashion houses of Mumbai and Delhi" (ibid.). One may find—purchased by Hindus and non-Hindus alike—"Hindu icons and emblems ... on tote bags, t-shirts, lunchboxes and as tattoos on human bodies" (ibid.). Mouse pads are stippled with images of Krishna, drink coasters with Hanuman, and funky throw pillows playfully display "a psychedelic-looking Saraswati" (Wax 2010). Pronounces one product emblazoned with an image of Ganesh, the elephant-headed god: "Ganesh is a foodie, and is crazy about ladoos [Indian sweets]" (ibid.).

A problem emerges, however, when cultures that don't worship these deities—conceiving of them instead as mere exotica—go so far as to decorate underwear with a celestial being or with the words "Shiva in Training." Kohler Company published in the *New York Times* an ad for shower fixtures using a woman in the Nataraja pose of the lord Shiva (*The Hindu Universe* n.d.); *Newsweek* also appropriated the same pose for its cover image of US President Barack Obama on November 22, 2010. (One finds it hard to imagine, in the Christian context, a scantily clad woman taking a shower in the pose of the Virgin Mary, complete with baby Jesus in her arms; or India's prime minister positioned as a crucified Christ on the cover of *Newsweek*.) American-born Hindus, "cut off as they are from the full range of Hindus and Hinduisms that they would experience in India" (Doniger 2009: 651), may be more susceptible to the narrow presentations of Hinduism offered by the American media. But this is nowhere near as concerning—or as brash—as the degradation of the Hindu swastika. The swastika (Sanskrit: "luck," "wellbeing"), a symbol no less auspicious to Buddhists and Jains as to Hindus (Viswanathan 1992: 299),[11] still has not recuperated from its forced association with Nazism.

Although some NRI Hindus may shrug noncommittally at many of these wryer depictions, insufficient work has been done regarding "what it means for white American youth to consume these symbols of 'otherness'" (Maira 2005: 13). To complicate matters, Acharya Palaniswami, the editor of *Hinduism Today*—who is Euro-American—reminds us that humor is often an indicator of cultural receptivity:

> Hindus in America don't yet understand that ridicule is actually part of the process of acceptance of minorities here. … It does seem strange, even cruel, but the creation of "stock jokes" about a minority is part of letting them in, so to speak, welcoming them into the great melting pot.
>
> (Pinsky 2001: 154)

Then again, some analysts argue that Hindus abroad actually defy the "traditional image of America as a great melting pot," since they rely instead on their own sources of news and advertising. According to a recent survey, 84 percent of respondents indicated that they got their information from ethnic sources (Nimbark 2004: 100). These include publications like *India Abroad* and *News India*, whose pages on religious worship and spiritual activities have more than doubled since the 1980s (ibid.: 101), and cable channels out of India, such as *Aastha*, whose Web site proudly promotes itself as "India's No. 1 socio-spiritual-cultural television channel" and boasts two hundred million viewers in thirty million households worldwide (www.aasthatv.co.in). According to Nimbark, this reflects a patent preference among NRIs for an "unabashed Hindu identity" over one that is "racialized"—because of their being a visible minority—or that capitulates to "the 'pseudo-secularism' of [those] NRIs who are neither traditional nor truly modern in their beliefs" (ibid.). In other words, disputations about pop-cultural representations of Hinduism in the West exist as much among Hindus *in* the West as they do between Hindus *and* the West. As religion is collapsed with ethnic identity—as has been the case for many other diasporas (e.g., Irish Catholics, North African Muslims)—the accuracies of those parameters are themselves often quite distorted, religiously speaking.

And yet, parallel popular-cultural trends may work to undercut Hinduism's integration into mainstream popular culture. To be sure, there have been welcoming public representations, such as in the United Kingdom, where for a brief time *The Kumars at No. 42*—part interview show, part Hindu-family comedy—was broadcast; and in Canada, where, in 2011, the national postal service launched two Diwali stamps in advance of that religious celebration (see Canada Post Website [www.canadapost.ca/diwali]). There are also feature films, such as the Sanskrit *sloka*-importing *Matrix Revolutions* (2003) and Nina Paley's animated *Sita Sings the Blues* (2008), a film that endearingly and complexly retells the Rámáyana from Sita's point of view.[12] Add to these a handful of television shows like the American version of

The Office (NBC), whose "Diwali" episode (first aired 2 November 2006) offers a send-up of that Hindu festival of lights.

But it is perhaps the religiously excised practice of *hatha yoga* and spiritual vegetarianism that have been "Hinduism's biggest contributions to American pop-culture" (Chander 2009). Ironically, *hatha yoga*—which is only one form of yoga (*bhakti* being another)—was traditionally only practiced by certain ascetics who could handle its "psycho-physical techniques for purifying the body and mind" (Williamson 2010: 15). Today, *hatha yoga*, not unlike meditation, has come to symbolize "[r]etreats for urban people who want to relax and procure its health benefits" (ibid.), a sort of "Spandex yoga."

Others agree—at least concerning yoga's increasing disassociation from its ascetic roots. Only 31 percent of Americans who tried yoga in 2006 said they were pursuing "spiritual development," with far more "focused on six-pack abs or non-denominational inner serenity" (quoted in Grossman 2006). In fact, one entrepreneur blended recent fads by borrowing from the Jewish mystical tradition to produce the training DVD *Kabbalah Yoga* (Grossman 2006). Perhaps there is, in the popular imagination, a relative ease in seeing ancient forms of worship combined; maybe antiquity encourages appropriation. In all of these situations, religious iconography becomes a style rather than part of a tradition composed of rituals, prayers, and ethics (Williamson 2010: 4). Even yoga, which in formal terms is supposed to be a link to God (literally, a yoke), becomes evermore wrested from the divine.

Importantly, the same thing also is taking place in India—at least among the cosmopolitan classes. Middle-class urban India, too, has begun to use yoga to pursue inner peace. Sri Sri Ravi Shankar's movement (the "Art of Living," with hundreds of outlets across India) has "made deep inroads into the newly affluent society," in part because the movement provides "a yogic alternative to going to a shrink, stigmatized even today in India as an evidence of mental imbalance" (Joseph 2011). Instead, the modern affluent of India pay for advice on how to breathe, meditate, and manage stress; they participate in "a brand of Hindu philosophy that is secular in nature," and frequently proffered in the form of "stock phrases ('Do not fall in love, rise in love')" (ibid.). Shankar—no relation to the famous sitar player—has also succeeded in taking his Art of Living westward, and onto YouTube. He has "emphasized the branding of India as the spiritual home of the world," a claim some consider "one of the most enduring and absurd of myths" (ibid.). Nevertheless, Indian gurus certainly appear to have a better chance of succeeding globally than do gurus from, say, Hungary or Guinea Bissau, and "because Hinduism is not a structured faith with a central authority or chain of command" (ibid.), new gods and exotic gurus easily appear on the horizon.

Deepak Chopra, an endocrinologist originally from India and part of the TM movement, is probably one of the most popular and international of these charismatic, if slightly enigmatic, self-help leaders.[13] In the West, he has single-handedly parlayed the purveying of "alternative spirituality in the new millennium" (Iwamura 2011: 109) into a multimillion dollar industry. Although the clean-cut Chopra makes an appearance in the scatological comedy *The Love Guru* (2008)—in which Mike Myers plays a Deepak Chopra-wannabe—he altogether eschews the "guru-speak," guru apparel, and eccentric, Bollywood-ish guru enclave of the sort common in

450

Hollywood representations of Hinduism. Fusing New Age oriental monk-dom with "classy" corporate capitalism, Chopra proffers a philosophy based on a simplified Hinduism (ibid.), pulling especially from its "vast corpus of ancient wisdom on healing," and offering "a melange of treatments ... many of which draw from the types of indulgences made common during the me-decade of the 1970s: aromatherapy, music therapy, bliss technique, diets, pulse diagnosis, primordial sound ... ," yoga, TM, and so forth (Prashad 2000: 66–67).[14]

Orientalism or orientation?

It is perhaps in mainstream popular culture that the "Orient" as a construction that Ashis Nandy argues long served as an inversion of the "West"—set up to perform as its shadowy, mystical, non-rational underbelly (Malhotra n.d.)—continues, especially today. Even in the multicultural educational system of the West, Hindu religious beliefs and traditions are routinely ridiculed: "from mocking the Hindu vegetarian diet, to demonizing the Goddess in school textbooks, to implying that Hindu beliefs are laughable superstitions" (Banerjee 2007a: 263). Madhu Kishwar claims that dominant forms of global mass media tend

> to see the cultures and faiths of non-European peoples as ... mainly of anthropological interest, existing as a curious hangover of a lower stage in the evolution of human kind. Therefore, instead of leading to greater understanding, fleeting mass media images of alien practices ... have so far tended to increase divisions, strengthen prejudices and negative stereotypes.
> (Banerjee 2007b: 315)

In 2006, for example, the Oxford University Press published an American social studies textbook intended for sixth graders. "[The monkey-god] Hanuman loved Rama so much," recounts the text when discussing the Indian epics, "that it is said that he is present every time the Ramayana is told." Regrettably, the textbook then proceeds to ask its readers to "look around—see any monkeys?" seeming to invite the 11-year-olds "to tease or ridicule their mostly brown-skinned Hindu classmates: 'See any monkeys?'" (Banerjee 2007a: 263). In another example, an exhibit at the Walters Gallery in Baltimore, Maryland, used a Freudian reading to interpret an eleventh-century carving of Ganesh, describing "his limp trunk" as forever serving as "a poor match for [his father] Siva's erect phallus" (see Rampersad 2007b: 24).

Frequently the only Hindu text that an American will know by name is the Kama Sutra. It is peddled to many visitors to India in the form of ancient text, sex guide, or DVD (Indians are not unwilling to commercialize their own culture for a profit). Still, the Kama Sutra draws comparatively little attention in India, a fact that perhaps reveals more about the "West" than about the "Orient."[15] Indeed, the title is used for a wide array of products in the West. There are Kama Sutra wristwatches that display "a different position every hour," and a "Kama Sutra Pleasure Box" and a "Kama Sutra Weekender Kit," whose creams and oils are "packaged in containers decorated with quasi-Hindu paintings of embracing couples" (Doniger 2009: 646).

SHEILA J. NAYAR

Books of erotic paintings or sculptures, with titles like *Illustrated Kama-Sutra*, abound, as do cartoon Kama-sutras and Kama-sutra "apps" (admittedly amid many other Hindu applications that offer everything from mantras and meditations to rituals and a history of the Bhagavad Gita); and there is of course the 1996 film by Mira Nair, *Kama Sutra: A Love Story*, which explores the political ramifications of love and sexuality. As for the actual Kama Sutra text, its treatment of sex is highly secular and highly technical and so "has earned India a reputation for sensuality that is rather misleading" (Shouler and Anthony 2009: 6). As Wendy Doniger avers, the Kama Sutra has fallen prey to "a great deal of lustful marketing and misrepresentation," and is being misread (by both Americans and Hindus) as little more than a "dirty" book (2009: 646).

But Western culture—or, perhaps more accurately, Christian culture—too often conceives erroneously of that text as representative of Hinduism, and of Hinduism as an embodiment of a wholly mystical and sensuous "otherness" (quite distinct from the sensuous materiality of actual Hindu practice). This incongruity of representation is something that *The Everything Hinduism Book*—arguably as much a piece of American popular culture as a pedagogical entré into Hinduism—tries hard to stifle. The book opens with an outline of the four aims of Hindu life—*artha* (material wellbeing); *dharma* (duty); *kama* (love); *moksha* (liberation)—swiftly asserting thereafter that "Hinduism is not an otherworldly philosophy that demands its adherents subscribe to exotic doctrines. On the contrary, it is a most practical religion" (Shouler and Anthony 2009: 1). All of this points to one of the great hermeneutical tensions; after all, the relative prominence that the Kama Sutra is given becomes illusory proof of its central place in Hinduism, both alluring to the outsider, and also objectionable. Perhaps this reflects a "U-turn" syndrome that enables appropriations of source traditions "while simultaneously denigrating" them (Rampersad 2007a: 81).[16]

Is it possible that mainstream media sometimes accidentally promote the "U-turn" syndrome? Consider Homer from *The Simpsons*, who with comical flippancy refers to Ganesh as "The Elephant Man"; or his son Bart, who dresses up as a cardboard Ganesh in order to reunite Apu, the Hindu proprietor of the Kwik-E-Mart, with Apu's estranged bride by exhorting, "I order you to get back together—or I'll suck your blood—blah, blah!" True, his world-weary sister Lisa responds, "Bart, stick to the script. Don't be a jerk"; but many viewers, unaware of Ganesh's obstacle-removing gentleness, may still erroneously assume a vampire-like aspect to the god. In this case, it may be less an issue of mainstream media representing Hinduism stereotypically than of their perpetrating—at least in the United States—an egoistic (though not necessarily conscious or even malicious) selectivity in terms of what gets represented. Then again, maybe the focus on Ganesh in this episode is because non-Indian Americans, by virtue of their NRI neighbors and friends, more often have come into contact with this god, who as "a transsectarian figure worshiped by Hindus of many inclinations," is ideal for worship in NRI temples comprising regionally diverse Hindus (Hawley 2004: 115). The issue is not whether to represent but how to temper the oft subconscious human inclination to jockey for cultural-religious supremacy; how to "balance our freedom of expression" with a respect for that "other" culture which produced those rituals and rites, and which may revere those gods (Pitzl-Waters 2010).

Is Britney Spears sporting "Om" and "Hare Rama Hare Krishna" symbols (Chaitanya 2006) raising cultural awareness? Is Madonna donning a sari and singing "a self-composed Sanskrit song at the MTV awards before a backdrop of Hindu god images" (Estulin 2004) rendering Hinduism accessible or exotica? When in *Michael Clayton* (2007), Tom Wilkinson, playing attorney Arthur Edens, intensely declares "I'm Shiva, the god of death!" (Doniger 2009: 647), does this enfold Shiva into the American pantheon of familiar deities, or does it—because Shiva is being associated exclusively with death—estrange him? Wilkinson's declaration may well be an even more specific allusion to physicist Robert J. Oppenheimer, who acknowledged how, after witnessing the first detonation of the atomic bomb—a bomb he himself had helped to design—the following words from the *Bhagavad Gita* sprang to mind: "Now, I am become Death, the destroyer of worlds" (Hijiya 2000). But is this yet another instance, even if unwittingly, of Hinduism being positioned as something strange, something to fear?

Kali: a case study

And then there is Kali. Indeed, it could be said that Kali provides the "most ambiguous and misrepresented notion" of Hinduism in visual media (Chaitanya 2006). Shorn of any piousness, this goddess typically becomes transmuted exclusively into a picture of demonic devouring, as in *Indiana Jones and the Temple of Doom* (1984) and the aforementioned *Help!* One finds her represented in TV series like *Xena: Warrior Princess* (1995–2001) and *Highlander* (1992–98), and even in an advertising script for a brand of mints.[17]

As self-proclaimed Pagan blogger Jason Pitzl-Waters (2010) sagaciously notes, Kali has become "part of America's cultural (and sub-cultural) short-hand in invoking an 'exotic' Indian other (along with Ganesha and the dancing Shiva)." But why just these particular deities, given the breadth of the pantheon? Where, for instance, is the goddess Saraswati, who has "come to symbolize the independent woman as thinker and a gifted creator," as Sanjay Patel writes in his darling *Little Book of Hindu Deities*? After all, "Sarasvati enjoys playing her instrument, the veena, as loud as she wants and can sit glued to her favorite books, the Vedas, guilt-free for hours. … Gods, eat your heart out, because this goddess is not available or interested—that is, unless you have a library card or can play back-up sitar" (Patel 2006: 39). So, why is she not prominent—as is neither Rama nor Laxshmi?

The image of Kali is further complicated by the Indian comic series *Amar Chitra Katha*, which expurgated the fierce bloodthirstiness of Kali (as depicted in the ancient Devī Māhātmya) from its comics. The comics' originator, Anant Pai, considered her blood drinking "a degradation of Hinduism" that would alienate modern, middle-class, Hindu readers' sensibilities (McLain 2008: 319, 317). Indeed, even in calendar art and god-poster imagery today, Kali is only rarely depicted in her gruesome form, her tongue verging instead on something close to "soft-focus eroticism" (ibid.: 319). But then, every culture "has its own category of the exotic," as Rachel Fell McDermott and Jeffrey Kripal aptly point out; and "for those in the Hindu mainstream, this includes Kali's various provenances—Tantra, tribal culture, historical links to social revolution, and a bloody cult—all of them both alluring and dangerous'" (McDermott and Kripal 2003: 9). Is there a class or socio-cultural bias to this sort of visual excision, a desire on the part of educated Hindus to soften, or even censor, the religion's more extreme aspects? Very possibly—just as has historically been the case for certain Catholic imagery prevalent in earlier times, such as that of St. Bernard of Clairvaux imbibing from the lactating breast of the Virgin Mary. Paradoxically enough, then, the very representations that middle-class Hindus have been trying to excise from (or subdue in) Hinduism are the ones that non-Hindu popular culture, with its different motivations, often actively foregrounds.

Kali's depiction in *Xena: Warrior Princess* offers a particularly fruitful case in terms of the tensions that play out—and sometimes that don't play out—vis-à-vis depictions of Hinduism in American commercial media. A 1999 episode ("The Way") raised the hackles of the World Vaishnava Association because of the way that episode treated Vedic culture: as a veritable "treasure chest" from which plotlines could be pulled and characters fictionalized—including the highly revered god Krishna (Luthra 2001: 132–33).[18] In the episode, after discussing with her companion the ethically and existentially thorny duties of being a warrior ("Is this my right spiritual quest?"), Xena is aided by the Hindu monkey god Hanuman in her pursuit. Hanuman assists her in combating demons who are trying to thwart her attempts to reach the "Avatar" (and also compliments her on her monkey fighting skills, which she tells him she learned from the Amazons). Hanuman then leads her to Krishna— or "the ultimate manifestation of the supreme deity," as Hanuman describes him—with whom Xena further pursues her philosophical questioning and to whom she ultimately prays. "[T]he fact that Xena prays to Krishna for help is of utmost significance," as Fillingim (2009) points out. "Xena has rarely if ever sought the help of any god, and in the rare instances where she does … it [is] almost always in the form of tit-for-tat bargaining that exploits the gods' petty desires. … The fact that Xena explicitly seeks the help of Krishna gives the Hindu god a very special status in the Xenaverse."

Producers explicitly acknowledged at the episode's end that they had taken liberties with "Hindu deities and historical timelines." However, they insisted they had done so "to illustrate the beauty and power of the Hindu religion." Still, anti-defamation groups found the sanctity of Krishna, as well as the very real place he holds in religious mythology and history, thoughtlessly scrambled and recast into a temporally amorphous Xena-land. But how can one sufficiently and satisfactorily represent a Hindu god (or a Hindu scripture or symbol), considering the polysemic nature of Hinduism? Dr. Ravi Arvind Palat, an expert in Hinduism who served as consultant on "The Way," suggested that "the self appointed guardians of the Hindu faith" were, through their protests, "subverting the very meaning of being Hindu" (Green n.d.). Meanwhile, in an editorial for the Vaishnava News Network (vnn.org), Jagannatha Tirtha Das wrote that "Krishna's holy name and Krishna personally [getting] nationwide airtime [was] a miracle" and that Krishna's intervention in the episode was "not offensive in any way, just a little inaccurate"; if anything, Das said, the producers ought to be "complimented for transmitting Krishna's holy name to millions" (Green n.d.).

Even more interesting is the fact that American Hindus Against Defamation (AHAD), which went to such lengths to expose and excoriate the episode's trivialization of Krishna, never once mentioned Kali in their official protest (see American Hindus Against Defamation n.d.), particularly given what occurs at the climax of the episode: Krishna informs Xena that "her way for this lifetime is the way of the warrior" and that "it is by fighting for just causes that she will attain good karma" (Fillingim

2009)—a clear allusion to when, in the Bhagavad Gita, Krishna informs Arjuna about his karma. Further, Xena must perform without attachment, Krishna says— again, just as Krishna directs Arjuna in the Gita. As a result, Xena cuts off the evil Indra- jeet's hand; and, in the same way that Indrajeet's father, Ravan, could sprout heads, Indrajeet grows six limbs in his missing hand's place. When Indrajeet cuts off Xena's arms, Krishna envelops her in a magical blue light, and she is reborn as Kali: the warrior goddess, multi-armed, with savage teeth, her face black-colored though its bottom half is red. One could argue that this depiction of Kali actually makes sense— as a force, both creative and destructive, that must temporarily manifest darkly in order to combat utterly dark forces (just as a mother might in order to protect her brood).

Certainly in this scenario Kali is neither evil nor demon, for how else to explain our heroine Xena taking her form? Nevertheless, AHAD was utterly indifferent, almost blind, to Kali's presence. Yes, this disregard might have had to do with the prominence of Krishna as Supreme Lord in some contemporary Vashnavite sects; but it might also speak to the privileging of male deities over female ones, and to the often patriarchal making of hierarchies that, sadly, can be fundamental to Hindu religion (Fuller 2004: 4). Difficulties arise when one's historically figured deities are also well embedded in lore and mythology; and yet, by being both historical and mythological, they also have the power to be incorporated into today's popular-cultural myths and, in this way, commandingly to persist.

Perhaps, then, we might draw some wisdom from Homer Simpson's outsider proclamation about Apu's gods: "Hey, these guys are pretty cool!" For although both insiders and outsiders may see truths, as Arvind Sharma solemnly puts it, genuine understanding arises "at the point of their intersection" (Braverman 2004). If both insiders and outsiders remain insulated from each other, false notions of intel- lectual sovereignty develop. And so it is that, in this world, each is needed—for "[e]ach is required to call the other's bluff" (Rosser 2007: 387–88).

Notes

1 For the British, "Hindu" more broadly denoted individuals who had not converted to Islam, were not Sikh, etc. (Shouler and Anthony 2009: 34).

2 For the north Indian ritual of Karva Chauth, women fast from sunrise to sunset so that their "husbands will be blessed with longevity. While some local traditions differ, most women look at the moon through a sieve or a cloth before eating or drinking." Now there is a mobile application "that turns the screen of your phone into a sieve through which women can see the moon" (Hiranandani 2011).

3 Such excision of some elements of Hinduism from Hinduism-at-large continues. Much like the book from which it was adapted, the "Pray" segment of the film *Eat, Pray, Love* (2010) extricates Hinduism from India—in spite of its taking place there.

4 Instructors in transcendental meditation, including the Maharishi, did not consider TM "to be specifically Hindu, since it does not require either belief in or devotion to a deity" (Shouler and Anthony 2009: 214). However, a federal district court in Newark, New Jersey, ruled that it was, pointing "to several religious factors": the use of mantras, the inclusion of traditional religious acts, and the fact that the movement "was accepted in India as a form of Shaivite Hinduism" (ibid.: 216).

5 Harrison was sued by Bright Tunes Music Corporation for copyright infringement, speci- fically for copying the 1963 hit "He's So Fine," written by Ronnie Mack and made famous

by the Chiffons. Harrison was found guilty of "subconscious plagiarism" (Caldwell 2005: 143–44).

6 Prashad claims that today's "U.S. desis may desire a 'culture,' but not one that openly challenges the cultural hegemony of white supremacy"; as a result the particularly chauvinistic expression of Hinduism that is growing in the United States—"Yankee Hindutva," as he calls it—"operates in a 'private' domain, such as temples and homes, but notably through the Internet" (Prashad 2000: 143).

7 Religious activity in groups is "not generally a part of Hinduism in India except during temple and village festivals"; but because of desire for community, American Hindu temples "frequently adopt a congregational format, offering special Saturday or Sunday puja and bhajan 'worship services'" (Kurien 2007: 9–10).

8 The comics also have proven to be a valuable way for Hindus abroad—"from Australia to Brazil to Kuwait to London to Singapore to Tanzania"—"to explain facets of Indian culture to others in their community who are not familiar with it and who may even have absorbed negative stereotypes about India and Indians" (McLain 2009: 201).

9 Devotional music in India is not limited to Hinduism, but also includes Muslim *qawwali*, Jain *bhajans*, and Sikh *shabd kirtan* (Manuel 1993: 119).

10 John Hawley made this statement more than 15 years ago, before the explosion in digital and social media.

11 The symbol is not exclusive to India, and can be found in the artwork of Chinese, Egyptian, and Native American communities as well (see Schmidt 2005).

12 The *sloka* "Asatoma Sat Gamaya, Tamasoma Jyotir Gamaya, Mrityorma Anritam Gamaya"—about moving from "the unreal to the Truth, from darkness to Light, from the ephemeral to the Eternal"—is used in *The Matrix* during a fight sequence between Neo and the evil agent Smith. Chaitanya (2006) champions the *sloka*'s inclusion as a "studied integration" rather than a thoughtless gloss—very unlike Stanley Kubrick's *Eyes Wide Shut* (1999), where recitations from the Bhagavad Gita provided the soundtrack for an orgy scene.

13 According to Iwamura, "the most confounding aspect of Chopra's fame seems to be the dissimulation between reality and image that the popular press senses yet is not able to dispel or contain. As *Time* anxiously quotes: 'It's my destiny to play an infinite number of roles, but I'm not the role I'm playing,' says Chopra with characteristic inscrutability" (2011: 110).

14 The capitalism reference here is no mere hyperbole: Chopra was one of three Indian scientist-authors who penned "Letter from New Delhi," which appeared in the October 1991 volume of *JAMA* (*Journal of the American Medical Assocation*). His article, which "purported to be a scientific evaluation of a traditional form of Indian medicine called Ayurveda," was in fact "a thinly disguised advertisement" for TM's Ayurvedic product line (Barnett and Sears 1991: 188)—for which Chopra was "chairman and sole stockholder" (Iwamura 2011: 109).

15 There is, admittedly, a brand of condoms named after it.

16 At the same time, "U-turn reversals" may lead, for example, to the notion that the reincarnation that one seeks to escape in Hinduism becomes popularly transmuted by many a Westerner into a good thing.

17 The text reads: "Kali is a Hindu goddess that represents death, destruction, time and change. And what food comes to mind when you think of death, destruction, time and change? Curry! These exotic spice mints are great on their own or as an accompaniment to basmati rice and garlic naan" (Pitzl-Waters 2010).

18 Although the episode was pulled in Canada because of the burgeoning anti-defamation campaigns at the time, it did air in the United States (Luthra 2001: 133)—and is now available for instant viewing on Netflix.

Works cited

American Hindus Against Defamation (n.d.) "Urgent clarification sought from producers of 'Xena.'" Online. Available: www.hindunet.org/anti_defamation/xena/ (accessed 19 September 2012).

Appadurai, A. (2000) "Disjuncture and difference in the global cultural economy," in F.J. Lechner and J. Boli (eds), *The Globalization Reader*, Malden, MA: Blackwell, 323–30.

Babb, L.A. (1995) "Introduction," in L.A. Babb and S.S. Wadley (eds), *Media and the Transformation of Religion in South Asia*, Philadelphia, PA: University of Pennsylvania Press, 1–20.

Banerjee, A. (2007a) "An American community gets awakened," in K. Ramaswamy, A. de Nicolas, and A. Banerjee (eds), *Invading the Sacred: An Analysis of Hinduism Studies in America*, New Delhi: Rupa and Co., 262–79.

——(2007b) "Character assassination," in K. Ramaswamy, A. de Nicolas, and A. Banerjee (eds), *Invading the Sacred: An Analysis of Hinduism Studies in America*, New Delhi: Rupa and Co., 303–23.

Bardach, A.L. (2011) "How yoga won the west," *New York Times* (October 2): Sunday Review 4.

Barnett, R. and C. Sears (1991) "JAMA gets into an Indian herbal jam," *Science* 254 (October 11): 188–89.

Braverman, A.M. (2004) "The interpretation of gods," *University of Chicago Magazine* 97, 2 (December). Online. Available: http://magazine.uchicago.edu/0412/features/index.shtml (accessed 28 October 2012).

Brothers, K., Jr., A. Keys, and T. Smith (2003) "Karma," *The Diary of Alicia Keys*. J Records.

Caldwell, J. (2005) "Expert testimony, scenes a faire, and tonal music: a (not so) new test for infringement," *Santa Clara Law Review* 46, 1: 137–70.

Chaitanya, M. (2006) "Britney's bindi," *Hindustantimes.com* (January 24). Online. Available: www.hindustantimes.com/News-Feed/AtlantaDiary/Britney-s-bindi/Article1–42129.aspx (accessed 23 August 2012).

Chander, V. (2009) "Princeton to hold 'Hinduism in the 21st century' week," *ISKCON News* (April 4). Online. Available: http://news.iskcon.com/node/1880 (accessed 12 September 2012).

Derné, S. (1995) "Market forces at work: religious themes in commercial Hindi films," in L.A. Babb and S.S. Wadley (eds), *Media and the Transformation of Religion in South Asia*, Philadelphia, PA: University of Pennsylvania Press, 191–216.

Desai, J. (2005) "Planet Bollywood: Indian Cinema abroad," in S. Davé, L. Nichime, and T.G. Oren (eds), *East Main Street: Asian American Popular Culture*, New York: New York University Press, 55–71.

Doniger, W. (2009) *The Hindus: An Alternative History*, New York: Penguin Press.

Dwyer, R. (2009) "Hinduism," in J. Lyden (ed.), *The Routledge Companion to Religion and Film*, New York: Routledge, 141–61.

Dwyer, R. and D. Patel (2002) *Cinema India: The Visual Culture of Hindi Film*, New Brunswick, NJ: Rutgers University Press.

Eck, D.L. (1981) *Darśan: Seeing the Divine Image in India*, Chambersburg, PA: Anima Books.

Estulin, C. (2004) "Hands off my gods," *Time.com* (August 30). Online. Available: www.time.com/time/magazine/article/0,9171,689493,00.html (accessed 22 August 2011).

Fillingim, D. (2009) "By the gods—or not: religious plurality in Xena: Warrior Princess," *Journal of Religion and Popular Culture* 21, 3 (Fall). Online. Available: www.usask.ca/relst/jrpc/art21(3)-PluralityInXena.html (accessed 5 September 2012).

Fuller, C.J. (2004) *The Camphor Flame: Popular Hinduism and Society in India*, Princeton, NJ: Princeton University Press.

Green, M.E. (n.d.) "Xena: the way of the censor," *The Little River Review*. Online. Available: www.littlereview.com/getcritical/xena/waycensr.htm (accessed 27 September 2011).

Grossman, C.L. (2006) "Hindu lite: pop culture plays fast and loose with an ancient faith," *USA Today* (February 16): 9B.

Hawley, J.S. (2004) "Global Hinduism in Gotham," in T. Carnes and F. Yang (eds), *Asian American Religions: The Making and Remaking of Borders and Boundaries*, New York: New York University Press, 112–40.

Hijiya, J. (2000) "The Gita of J. Robert Oppenheimer," *Proceedings of the American Philosophical Society* 144, 2 (June): 123–67.

The Hindu Universe (n.d.) "Nataraja: Lord Shiva as a scantily clad woman hawks shower fixtures." Online. Available: www.hindunet.org/anti_defamation/kohler/ (accessed 12 September 2012).

Hiranandani, K. (2011) "Digital devotion: mobile app updates Hindu ritual Karva Chauth," Asiasociety.org (October 17). Online. Available: http://asiasociety.org/blog/asia/digital-devotion-mobile-app-updates-hindu-ritual-karva-chauth (accessed 18 October 2012).

Iwamura, J.N. (2005) "The oriental monk in American popular culture," in B.D. Forbes and J. Mahan (eds), *Religion and Popular Culture in America*, rev. edn, Berkeley, CA: University of California Press, 25–43.

——(2011) *Virtual Orientalism: Asian Religions and American Popular Culture*, New York: Oxford University Press.

Jacobs, S. (2010) *Hinduism Today*, London: Continuum.

Joseph, M. (2011) "Spiritualism made for the modern age: letter from India," *New York Times* (July 7): 2.

Kurien, P.A. (2007) *A Place at the Multicultural Table: The Development of an American Hinduism*, New Brunswick, NJ: Rutgers University Press.

Lutgendorf, P. (1995) "All in the (Raghu) family: a video epic in cultural context," in L.A. Babb and S.S. Wadley (eds), *Media and the Transformation of Religion in South Asia*, Philadelphia, PA: University of Pennsylvania Press, 217–53.

Luthra, R. (2001) "The formation of interpretive communities in the Hindu diaspora," in D.A. Stout and J.M. Buddenbaum (eds), *Religion and Popular Culture: Studies on the Interaction of Worldviews*, Ames, IA: Iowa State University Press, 125–42.

McDermott, R.F. and J. Kripal (eds) (2003) *Encountering Kali: In the Margins, at the Center, in the West*, Berkeley, CA: University of California.

McLain, K. (2008) "Holy superheroine: a comic book interpretation of the Hindu *Devī Māhātmya* scripture," *Bulletin of the School of Oriental and African Studies* 71, 2 (June): 297–322.

——(2009) *India's Immortal Comic Books: Gods, Kings, and Other Heroes*, Bloomington, IN: Indiana University Press.

Maira, S. (2005) "Trance-formations: orientalism and cosmopolitanism in youth culture," in S. Davé, L. Nishime, and T.G. Oren (eds), *East Main Street: Asian American Popular Culture*, New York: New York University Press, 13–31.

Malhotra, R. (n.d.) "Stereotyping Hinduism in American education," infinityfoundation.com. Online. Available: www.infinityfoundation.com/mandala/s_es/s_es_malho_stereo.htm (accessed 23 August 2012).

Mallapragada, M. (2010) "Desktop deities: Hindu temples, online cultures and the politics of remediation," *South Asian Popular Culture* 8, 2: 109–21.

Manuel, P. (1993) *Cassette Culture: Popular Music and Technology in North India*, Chicago, IL: University of Chicago Press.

Melton, J.G. and C.A. Jones (2011) "Reflections on Hindu demographics in America: an initial report on the first American Hindu census." Unpublished paper delivered at the Association for the Study of Religion, Economics, and Culture, Washington, DC (April). Online. Available: www.thearda.com/asrec/archive/papers/Melton_Hindu_ Demographics.pdf (accessed 19 September 2012).

Nayar, N.A. (1991) *Poetry as Theology: The Srivaisnava Stotra in the Age of Ramanuja*, Wiesbaden: Otto Harrassowitz.

Nayar, S.J. (2004) "Invisible representation: the oral contours of a national popular cinema," *Film Quarterly* 57, 3: 13–23.

Nimbark, A. (2004) "Paradoxes of media-reflected religiosity among Hindu Indians," in T. Carnes and F. Yang (eds), *Asian American Religions: The Making and Remaking of Borders and Boundaries*, New York: New York University Press, 98–111.

Patel, S. (2006) *The Little Book of Hindu Deities: From the Goddess of Wealth to the Sacred Cow*, London: Plume.

The Pew Forum on Religion and Public Life (2010) "U.S. religious landscape: affiliations." Online. Available: http://religions.pewforum.org/affiliations (accessed 22 January 2012).

Pinsky, M.I. (2001) *The Gospel According to The Simpsons: The Spiritual Life of the World's Most Animated Family*, Louisville, KY: Westminster John Knox Press.

Pitzl-Waters, J. (2010) "The pop-culture Kali of America," *The Wild Hunt: A Modern Pagan Perspective* (June). Online. Available: www.patheos.com/blogs/wildhunt/2010/06/the-pop-culture-kali-of-america.html (accessed 23 August 2012).

Prabhupada, A.C.B. Swami (1983) *Chant and Be Happy: The Power of Mantra Meditation*, Los Angeles, CA: The Bhaktivedanta Book Trust.

Prashad, V. (2000) *The Karma of Brown Folk*, Minneapolis, MN: University of Minnesota Press.

Rampersad, P.I. (2007a) "De-spiritualizing tantra," in K. Ramaswamy, A. de Nicolas, and A. Banerjee (eds), *Invading the Sacred: An Analysis of Hinduism Studies in America*, New Delhi: Rupa and Co., 73–95.

——(2007b) "Religious studies: projecting one's shadow on the 'other,'" in K. Ramaswamy, A. de Nicolas, and A. Banerjee (eds), *Invading the Sacred: An Analysis of Hinduism Studies in America*, New Delhi: Rupa and Co., 17–26.

Rosser, Y.C. (2007) "*University of Chicago Magazine*: obscuring the issues," in K. Ramaswamy, A. de Nicolas, and A. Banerjee (eds), *Invading the Sacred: An Analysis of Hinduism Studies in America*, New Delhi: Rupa and Co., 378–96.

Schmidt, N. (2005) "Reclaiming the Symbol," *Index on Censorship* 34, 2: 52–53.

Shouler, K. and S. Anthony (2009) *The Everything Hinduism Book*, Avon, MA: Adams Media.

Singh, A. (2006) "Teaching journal: Katherine Mayo's *Mother India* (1927)," Amardeep Singh (blog) (February 7). Online. Available: www.lehigh.edu/~amsp/2006/02/teaching-journal-katherine-mayos.html (accessed 24 October 2011).

Sinha, V. (2011) *Religion and Commodification: "Merchandizing" Diasporic Hinduism*, New York: Routledge.

Smith, H.D. (1995) "Impact of 'god posters' on Hindus and their devotional traditions," in L.A. Babb and S.S. Wadley (eds), *Media and the Transformation of Religion in South Asia*, Philadelphia, PA: University of Pennsylvania Press, 24–50.

Vertovec, S. (2000) *The Hindu Diaspora: Comparative Patterns*, London: Routledge.

Viswanathan, E. (1992) *Am I a Hindu?: The Hindu Primer*, San Francisco, CA: Halo Books.

Wax, E. (2010) "Traditional Indian piety makes way for pop culture images of Hindu gods," *Washington Post*, (June 13): A11.

Williamson, L. (2010) *Transcendent in America: Hindu-Inspired Meditation Movements as New Religion*, New York: New York University Press.

24
ISLAM
William Lafi Youmans[1]

Introduction: between Islamophobia/-philia and "good"/"bad" Muslims

Without a doubt the most influential theoretical architecture for understanding the Western representation of Islam and Muslims is Edward Said's landmark study, *Orientalism* (1978). Since its publication, it has helped launch the field of post-colonial theory and inspired numerous studies that advance the basic arguments, further articulate them, caricaturize them, resist them, or reject them. The book chronicles the long history of European thinkers, writers, leaders, and artists who construct "the Orient," and represent it as a timeless, regressive, mystical wonderment. The study historicizes a problematic scholarly, artistic, and popular Western engagement with the Orient generally that positions it as a subject place and set of peoples to be understood, feared, and conquered. Said traces a particular, dominant mode of communicating "the East" to intellectual and artistic formations within the context of Western imperialism, as Great Britain, France, and then the United States sought the physical, material conquest of that part of the world.

As testament to the work's influence, the accusation of being an Orientalist—aimed at either a work or a scholar—is deeply damaging, and suggests that the target analysis is a flat, condescending, simplistic, ill- or uninformed treatment of an implied "other," a "them." It is a disposition imbued with the presumptions of power, positionality, and bias. Such works make grand claims about Islam, and may also treat Muslims as engineered differently, as easily characterized *en masse* as if they are of one mind—or two or three minds—and incapable of independent thought and action outside of group doctrines and perceived historical tendencies. One of the most common Orientalist maneuvers is to reduce what Muslims do or think to the singular force of Islam, as opposed to the other explanatory variables, such as psychological, sociological, economic, or political factors.

Said later extends the analysis to US news media coverage in his 1981 work *Covering Islam: How the Media and the Experts Determine How We See the Rest of the World* (revised in 1997).[2] Said argues that Islam has been framed negatively; for Americans and Europeans, "Islam is 'news' of a particularly unpleasant sort" (1997: 144). The book illustrates how American news media have presented Islam as a monolithic religion, absent understanding or nuance, and entirely explanatory of conflict in the

Middle East and other parts of "the Muslim world." Worse, this depiction justifies treating Muslims as an enemy class. He takes note of entertainment programming, such as movies and TV shows "in which Muslims are uniformly represented as evil, violent, and above all eminently killable" (ibid.: xxvii).

While Said writes of historical discursive formations, he very much has his eye on the contemporary scene. He works backwards, understanding contemporary knowledge of the East through its lineage of knowledge production in the context of imperial domination. His arguments have resulted in a greater sensitivity to the misrepresentation of Arabs and Muslims, especially. Nonetheless, other visions of Islam in the West have painted it in more menacing terms.

One of the most influential geopolitical analyses to gain prominence after the September 11, 2001, attacks is Samuel Huntington's *The Clash of Civilizations* (1996). Taking this title from a sentence in an essay on "Muslim rage" by Bernard Lewis (1990), Huntington reasons that world conflict will increasingly fall along civilizational lines. He is writing about the future after the end of the Cold War, and his emphasis is on cultural clash. For Huntington, the world is constituted of civilizations as cultural blocs. The primary flashpoint therefore is between Western civilization based on "Judeo-Christian" values and Islamic civilization. "Islam," for Huntington, is "a different civilization whose people are convinced of the superiority of their culture and are obsessed with the inferiority of their power" (1996: 217–18).

Huntington's argument became popularized after the 2001 attacks when it was taken up by some in the Bush administration and his 1996 book advancing this argument was a bestseller. While the argument mutated the more influential it became—like many academic notions that gain currency in the public realm—its popular usage retained its basic attribute of accentuating religious-cultural differences between civilizations as the essential fault-lines in future conflict. One difference between his work and how it was presented in its popular rendering was that Huntington was a realist who believed countries should pursue their interests rather than advance their particular value systems (McAlister 2005: 286).

With regard to popular culture, the greater clash is the tension between mutated versions of Said's views and Huntington's views. On the one hand, *Islamophilia*, as Said himself noted in later writings, transforms into a sort of misplaced sentimentality for, even a romanticization of, "good" Muslim traits. On the other hand, *Islamophobia* is a literalist caricature of Huntington's prediction, a popular panic about the expanding presence and role of Muslims in society. This manifests in anxiety about mosque construction as well as in the religious views of American non-Muslim leaders. Said's and Huntington's works do not create either of these sensibilities, to be sure. Rather, they both have long-standing currency in American politics. This is to say that 9/11 was not the starting point for thinking about how representation of Islam matters, but it is the defining event for the reframing of Islam along these dichotomous lines.

Islamophobia/Islamophilia

Islamophobia refers most literally to the state of a "generalized fear of Islam and Muslims" (Shryock 2010: 1). A 1997 Runnymede Trust (UK) report defined it as "unfounded hostility toward Islam, and therefore fear or dislike of all or most Muslims" (Commission on British Muslims and Islamophobia 1997). This term and its derivatives—"Islamophobe" and "Islamophobic"—are often used as descriptors of negative representations of Islam and Muslims and their perpetrators. When a statement or work is called Islamophobic, it suggests that rather than expressing a fair and informed understanding of the religion, it betrays a deeply skewed, anxious, or charged depiction meant to further resentment toward Islam or Muslims.

Some contend that, as an analytical concept, it suffers from a lack of clarity (Allen 2010: 63). The idea that fear of Islam is the basis for unjustifiable antagonism is controversial, broad, and difficult to define. Some state that it is often used as a charge to silence criticism and marginalize those who express views that contradict the religion. Nevertheless, the term is commonly used, and features in the titles of numerous reports. The number of books and articles on the subject is growing. There is a nascent academic journal, *Islamophobia Studies Journal*, dedicated to publishing research and theorizing the topic. National civil rights groups have adopted combating it into their advocacy agendas. As a mode of discourse and critique, it exists, though hostility toward Islam and Muslims in general predates the use of this term.

Islamophilia is also problematic, as an overly simple, essentialist disposition that glorifies the religion and its followers, or is "selectively positive" (Shryock 2010: 9). It made its appearance in English texts well before Islamophobia. Intended to critique the adulation of Islam and Muslims, it has been deployed since in several ways.

As a critique, it is the inversion of Islamophobia as an unfounded hatred of Islam: Islamophilia refers to an unfounded warmth or exuberance (Shryock 2010). This use of "Islamophilia" is intended to tarnish those betraying an overly positive bias. It suggests that they are apologetic and defensive to the point of delusion. For those who wish to criticize Islam as a whole, in general terms, seeing positive or even neutral commentary on the religion strikes them as overly partial and dishonest. It can also be a polemic weapon invoked by public figures and commentators in response to being accused of Islamophobia. One suspected of phobia would naturally accuse the accuser of suffering from the corresponding "-philia".

In a different strain, Islamophilia is used by critical scholars, following Said's notion of Orientalism, to signify a romantic veneration of the religion or the culture(s) of its followers. In this critical sense the -philia is a blind reverence, a fetishization, or exoticization, that equally lacks nuance. On the face of it, it is harmless, but this treatment reduces the religion—or rather, constructs it—as something to fit with the desires and wants of the -philic. It is not an honest engagement, nor is it directed at achieving real understanding of the ethnographic or lived Islam of Muslims. A variation of this stance is the attempt to force Muslims into "friendship" (Shryock 2010: 9), pitting them as opposition to the "bad" Muslims while ignoring legitimate gripes they may have. This denies their agency by undercutting their desire to avoid a binary friend/enemy categorization. It also risks vilifying those who do not fit neatly into the friend role while being far from enemies. Notes Shryock (2010: 11), "In our rush to identify Muslim friends who think and act like 'us,' we turn those who think and act differently into potential enemies." It cannot be surprising that many Muslims acquiesce to this "friendship" role or celebrate unfounded apologetics out of concern for the negative consequences of being mistaken as villains, or out of sheer desire just to be accepted in this new society. The decades after the 9/11 attacks clearly have been polarized times, with the notion of the "clash of civilizations" circulating as a popular lens on world affairs. The desire by Muslims to belong is certainly understandable.

Just as Islamophobes can use the label Islamophilia as a shield against their critics, Islamophilic tendencies may be a defensive overreaction to the charges leveled against the religion. These are apparent in equally ahistorical, over-generalized statements that, like the -phobe's accusations, have some basis in truth. Thus, when some denigrate Islam as an intolerant religion, the -phile responds that Islam is the most tolerant religion because of how followers of other religions flourished under Muslim rule and how the Quran calls for protection of "people of the book" (followers of other Abrahamic religions named in the Quran). If it's called a sexist religion, the -philic retort is to hail Islam as a progressive religion that has advanced women's rights considerably, pointing to particular provisions in divorce and inheritance. While both of these defenses reasonably could describe particular epochs of Muslim rule and sources of religious authority, they tend also to conflate what Muslims do with the religion, and are equally essentialist moves. They gloss over extant problems in both theology and practice. This results in an unfortunate level of generality—both in scrutiny and in adulation—that no religion or people should have to fit so neatly.

"Good" Muslims and "bad" Muslims

In the years after the September 11, 2001, attacks, Americans displayed a greater curiosity about Islam. College enrollment in related courses, sales of Qurans, and newspaper primers on the religion increased. For Muslim Americans, this was a double-edged trend. While interest in, and inquiries about, the religion were welcome as opportunities for dialogue, the insinuation that intrinsic qualities of the religion offered guidance into the attacks was troublesome. The notion that the rationale for the attacks could be located in a holy text well over a millennium old was clearly a stretch, yet this is what motivated the increase in Quran sales.

Presuming that there was a link between the violent attack on citizens and the underpinning theology suggests that religiosity could predispose Islam's adherents toward violence. This was not such an absurd presumption. Al Qaeda and its members themselves cloaked their actions and views in religious terms. This linkage alarmed Muslims who disavowed such violence and were anxious about potential backlash, but it also unnerved Western governments that feared religion would be used to recruit more militants. The Bush administration confronted this by asserting that the West was not at war with Islam and that there was a fundamental difference between "good" Muslims and "bad" Muslims. During his address to a joint session of Congress after the 9/11 attacks, he said: "The enemy of America is not our many Muslim friends; it is not our many Arab friends. Our enemy is a radical network of terrorists, and every government that supports them" (Bush 2001). "Bad" Muslims were an aberration who distorted religious teachings to suit their anti-American agendas, while "good" Muslims held religiously and (more importantly) politically moderate views. "Bad" Muslims, the marginal minority according to official rhetoric, threatened an otherwise peaceful inter-civilizational coexistence and provoked Western countries into reluctant wars only necessitated by national security.

This "good"/"bad" distinction is not actually new. It was integrally linked to a geopolitics rooted in colonialism and the Cold War, and given expression through the logic of the "war on terror" (Mamdani 2004). Said (1980) noted that the "good" Muslims in the early days of the Reagan Administration were the Afghans who fought the Soviet Union. They were good because they were aligned with American foreign policy aims in the Cold War. Re-watching *Rambo III* (1988) is illustrative. In it, Rambo (Sylvester Stallone) goes to Pakistan/Afghanistan to rescue his friend, a captured military colonel, and is aided by "good" Muslim fighters as he takes on the Soviets. Many of those same forces went on to form the Taliban and Al Qaeda, holding roughly the same ideological views. They became "bad" Muslims when they were no longer needed in the Cold War. The Taliban, which formed out of the remnants of the Afghan mujahedeen, fell out of favor as its human rights record grew increasingly grotesque in the 1990s. The Taliban, "born of a brutalized society, was to brutalize it further" (Mamdani 2004: 161). It was when Al Qaeda began attacking the United States that this transformation of previously heroic mujahedeen into "bad" Muslims occurred.

Extremity of religiosity matters in the "good"/"bad" calculus, but can also be overridden by political convenience. Take the most prominent and stereotypical markers of extreme religious practice from American eyes: the use of capital punishment, the forced covering of women, beards on men, the wearing of non-Western clothing, and intolerance for other religions. Many see Iran as a brutal example of a theocracy, and condemn and lampoon it in the strongest terms. Yet American ally Saudi Arabia enforces even stricter codes based on a very particular interpretation of Islam mixed with Gulf-specific cultural practices. It most clearly enforces officially the practices and aesthetics of religious extremism, yet it is "good," while Iran is "bad."

Rather than being informative about what took place that dreadful day in September 2001, President Bush's Manichean distinction between "good" and "bad" Muslims obfuscated the independent political causes of the attacks. This allowed most of the public to avoid considering the underlying reasons outlined and articulated by Osama bin Laden. Though widely published and well known among Muslims, the rationales bin Laden gave for attacking the United States were expressly political, explicit qualms with American foreign policy—from the presence of American soldiers in Saudi Arabia, to the war and sanctions on Iraq, support for Israel, and backing unpopular regimes in the region. But by framing Al Qaeda's marginal place as "bad" Muslims, it never became important to consider these reasons publicly, within the United States. To do so, many reason, would be to give the terrorists what they want. But couldn't considering the motives of terrorists be just as useful in crafting a counter-terrorism program? The problem with labels of "good" and "bad" is that designating someone or some idea as "bad" puts them beyond the scope of reasonable discussions. They simply must be eliminated, punished, or rehabilitated, but not engaged or considered on any sort of equal footing.

Delineation of good and bad Muslims is problematic for other reasons as well. As Shryock (2010: 10) notes, the "traits that define the good Muslim are just as likely to be based on wishful thinking and a politics of fear." This sets up an impossible standard for Muslims, as they are made to fit an ideal-type, the image of a safe Muslim. A common name for the good or safe Muslim is the "moderate Muslim," whose moderation is always defined against what comes to be seen as typifying bad Muslims, often by those who are largely ignorant and hold skewed understandings of Islam or Muslims. To fit within the category of "good," Muslims must contort themselves and their views, offer themselves as sanitized, de-politicized, overly friendly to other denominations, and seem non-controversial. Like members of other marginalized groups throughout history—but possibly to a greater extreme—they do not have the luxury of being who they are.

-Phobia/-philia, "good"/"bad": toward "simplified complex representation"

What is the relationship between Islamophobia/-philia and the "good" Muslim/ "bad" Muslim binary? Is it as simple as adoration for "good" Muslims being equated with Islamophilia and hatred for "bad" Muslims with Islamophobia? Not necessarily. Both produce their own differentiated "good" and "bad" Muslims.

Latent Islamophobia may obsess over "bad" Muslims, see them as representative of the whole, but generate the creation of a class of "good" Muslims to deny the analysis is motivated by phobia. It is the equivalent of a racist invoking defensively a friend of the racial background he or she is accused of deriding. Of course, many Islamophobes are not so soft-bellied. A co-chair of Rudy Giuliani's 2008 Presidential campaign in New Hampshire told the press, "I don't subscribe to the principle that there are good Muslims and bad Muslims. They're all Muslims" (quoted in Cole 2008: 136). That he was released from the campaign afterward, while Giuliani campaigned against religious extremism, shows how the "good"/"bad" device can be crucial for moderating and making palatable a discourse of phobia. A patriotic Muslim American who supports the "war on terror" and is not too religious would likely please the -phobe. Another "good" Muslim is the Muslim who adopts phobic views to become an outward critic of the religion as a whole. He puts forward an equally essentialist view of the religion as a cause of violence and pre-modern culture, and pushes the religion to reform, and assimilate the more palatable ways of Western culture and politics.

By the same token, for any form of Islamophilia to be credible, it relies on modeling a particular "bad" Muslim who stands in contrast to what is seen as the more dominant and representative "good" Muslim. Full-blown -philics who think all Muslims are "good" are rare and easily cast as suspect in this context of the polarizing "war on terror" discourse.

Islamophobia/-philia signify the two polar orientations toward the religion, its doctrines, and its cultural underpinnings. The "good"/"bad" binary is a device that interacts with these, allowing a tactical communicative shift toward moderation and digestibility. It is a sort of faux-complexity that can be made to appear as knowledge, familiarity, sophisticated thought, and so forth. "Good"/"bad" can also serve strategically in the contest between -phobia and -philia. The -philes use the "good" to challenge the -phobes, just as -phobes use the "bad" to challenge the -philes. For instance, Islamophobes point to instances of honor killings or stonings to undercut -philic claims that "Islam means peace." Islamophiles bring up the contribution to science and learning that Muslims made historically, or the hospitality culture of "good" Muslims, to show that -phobes tell an incomplete and skewed story.

The tension is at work in popular culture, but they both hold Islam out as object of description with the feel that a Muslim audience is not being addressed. Most mass, popular culture about Muslims is clearly crafted as if it were not to be read by Muslims. Latent to both -phobia and -philia is an "othering," reflecting a "culture talk" mode that sees religion as essential to who people are, when other factors may be more important. The -phobic and -philic views are overly deterministic regarding religiosity, seeing the religious identity as core and explanatory.

This dualism emerged in popular culture as outright vilification of the "bad" in tension with celebration of the "Good." It is especially difficult to locate reasonable representations of Arabs and Muslims in American TV and movies between the 1970s and 2001 (Shaheen 2009). However, after the September 11, 2001, attacks, the motivation for asserting there are good Muslims becomes greater. Alsultany (2013: 161) writes, "a strange thing happened": the representation of Arabs and Muslims on US television became more sympathetic. It was as if the creative forces behind American TV took a collective cue from President Bush's distinction. She finds that TV entertainment programming depictions of Arabs or Muslims as terrorists increasingly are matched by Arab or Muslim protagonists, often as allies or aids in efforts to defeat the antagonists. Furthermore, the associations are blurred by the presentation of non-Muslims as the enemy terrorists in police dramas and national security shows (a novel post-9/11 genre) and movies. This representation strategy reflects a post-racial sensibility, she argues, as the TV creators seek to avoid the typical race-baiting and negative stereotyping of past eras. She terms this almost mechanical construction of proto-complexity a "simplified complex representation" (Alsultany 2012: 21). It was a limited strategy in that it still often led to affirmation of anti-terror policies—such as torture—and legitimized the prosecution of terrorism, even as its representation was less racialized. In Alsultany's analysis, we see both "good" and "bad" Muslims in most popular culture representations.

Old and new movements in popular culture

There is a great deal of scholarship on problematic media depictions. Wilkins (2009: 23) explores action-adventure films' use of villains who represent "simplistic, limited stereotypes with harmful repercussions." Few have shown as completely persistent bias in the depiction of Arabs and Muslims in cinema as Jack Shaheen, who has chronicled through intensive cataloging a history of Hollywood movies' character-izations of Arabs and Muslims (Shaheen 2009), with a special emphasis on post-9/11 (Shaheen 2008).

This section focuses on areas of greater complexity, showing some openings in media representation whereby old assumptions are challenged and provoked. Layers of meaning make the simple application of "good"/"bad" and "-phobia"/"-philia" binaries more difficult. This section will focus on just two areas of change: television and Internet memes.

Television

Analyzing specific post-9/11 television shows—*Law & Order* (NBC, 1990–2010), *NYPD Blue* (ABC, 1993–2005), *CSI* (CBS, 2000–present), *24* (FOX, 2001–10), *The Grid* (TNT, 2004), and *The Wanted* (NBC, 2009)—Alsultany writes at length, identifying a clear trajectory in which shows go from overt and simple to a bit more complex (though still binary and incomplete, and therefore problematic). Considering this trajectory, it is worth evaluating more recent shows in light of the above analysis of Islamophobia/-philia and "bad"/"good" Muslims. More recent shows are more complex in their representations; the question is whether this makes for necessarily more fair depictions.

The Emmy-winning series *Homeland* (Showtime, 2011–present) is the subscription channel's most popular scripted drama. It centers on a returning war prisoner, US Marine sniper Sergeant Nicholas Brody (Damian Lewis), who, in the early days of the US invasion, was captured in Iraq, sold to an Al Qaeda leader, Abu Nazir (Navid Negahban), and imprisoned in Damascus. His captors isolate and torture him, but Abu Nazir shows him acts of kindness and then adopts him. Under Abu Nazir's influence, Brody converts to Islam and goes to Abu Nazir's home to teach his son, Issa, English. Brody grows to love the boy. When Issa is later killed in a drone attack, Brody swears to kill Vice-President William Walden, who ordered the strike and then lied about it on television. After being moved to Afghanistan, Brody is freed in a military raid on an Al Qaeda compound. Brody returns to the United States as a war hero.

The audience is captivated at the start by whether Brody is or is not a terrorist. This becomes the primary obsession of the CIA agent-protagonist, Carrie Mathison (Claire Danes), who was previously tipped off to the possibility of an imminent attack by a returning war prisoner. Brody wins a seat in Congress while continuing to work as an agent of Abu Nazir. The show exploits the intrigue between forces of terrorism and counter-terrorism to heighten its dramatic appeal. Dealing with current events, it makes an attractive claim to realism, despite the inevitable turn to the "often fanciful and ridiculous" (Beaumont 2012) that television drama requires.

For several critics (Al-Arian 2012; Beaumont 2012), the show's first two seasons are markedly anti-Muslim. Al-Arian focuses on some of the most troubling elements of the story that make it, in her words, "insidiously Islamophobic." In explaining Brody's motivations, she writes, the show hints at his witnessing of US military strikes abroad and the lies of politicians. It also suggests possible brainwashing, of "Stockholm" syndrome. The only consistent fact through these different explanations is his new religiosity, Al-Arian explains.

Like Brody, Al-Arian argues, the most menacing "bad" Muslim characters have infiltrated acceptable American society: a mainstream, Oxford-educated journalist who wears skirts, a Saudi diplomat, an academic married to a white woman. As intelligent, assimilated, and patriotic as these characters appear, they are in the service of the character's prime villain, an Al Qaeda head. This is "insidious" because it suggests even peaceful, neighborly Muslims could be hiding a terrorist agenda. The perfect symbol of this is the fact that the professor and his wife use their display of an American flag to communicate secret codes to other terrorists. The message: even "good" Muslims should be suspected. Brody is the ultimate example.

In a telling deployment of the "good" Muslim prototype to offset claims of Islamophobia, Yair Rosenberg (2012) argues against the accusation that the show is anti-Muslim by naming the good characters: a Lebanese-American CIA analyst who gets shot and is accused, and then exonerated, of working for the terrorist mastermind Abu Nazir; a "longtime Muslim informant" for the CIA in Beirut; a Muslim military chaplain; and a local imam's wife. Most of these are posited as "good" because of their role in prosecuting the "war on terror." For example, Brody's decision to aid the US government's assassination of Abu Nazir was an act of rehabilitation, making him a "good" Muslim in the end. It's not anti-Muslim, Rosenberg argues, because it suggests Muslims are capable of being "good."

Representations of Muslims, while ubiquitous in national-security-themed shows, also make their way into other genres. In *The Killing* (AMC, 2011–present), a murder mystery police drama, two Seattle police investigators try to solve the gruesome murder of a local high school student. One of their early suspects is her teacher, Bennett Ahmed (Brandon Jay McLaren), a Somali-American involved with the local mosque. His religious background is invoked as a natural explanatory factor in the likelihood of his culpability. While the show stoked audience prejudices to insinuate Ahmed's guilt, it shows Ahmed as a victim himself. He suffers a brutal attack by the dead woman's father. Even his non-Muslim wife suspects him, the school administration suspends him, and students walk out of his class. The local mosque is vandalized with Islamophobic graffiti, a clear reference to the anti-Muslim backlash after 9/11.

The case against the teacher dissipates, and he's left as a tragic but admirable secondary character. Ahmed's suspicious behavior, which his wife had noticed and reported to the police, had been caused by his efforts to help a young Somali-American girl avoid genital mutilation by her family. He was in fact not a "bad" Muslim, even though he acted surreptitiously to avoid detection by the community and defy her family. He is nearly a "good" Muslim, as a moderate, practicing Muslim and devoted schoolteacher, but we do not quite see him serve the purpose of fighting terror.

This show's representation of Islam and Muslims is quite complex. It raises the issue of a physically painful and dangerous cultural tradition while avoiding the vilification of the community as a whole. By linking it to an ethnic community, it suggests this is more of a cultural practice than a religious one; a local councilman and mayoral candidate frequently refers to the Somali community as integral to Seattle. By showing how non-Muslims on the program enact prejudice and then victimize Somali-Americans, *The Killing* reflects a more nuanced representation than do earlier shows.

The most refreshing treatments in popular culture of Islam and Muslims are those in which religious persuasion is an afterthought, part of a character's background but not blatantly relevant to his persona. This is de-essentialization, a removal of "culture talk." Faith becomes a matter of no greater significance than for other characters—an inessential fact that bears little on storyline or plot. In other words, like the many presumed Christian or Jewish characters, Muslims are not merely reduced to their faith; they are something more. This is the "new normal" for which to strive.[3]

One such character whose Muslim background is incidental is Abed Nadir (Danny Pudi) on *Community* (NBC, 2009–present), a show depicting a group of friends at a community college. Abed is an eccentric film student who is revealed early on to be of Palestinian (specifically Gazan) and Polish descent. In two separate episodes, he says he is a Muslim but not devout. Abed is an avid pop culture junkie, which he uses to seek solace from his strict father—who wants him eventually to run the family falafel restaurant—and his estranged mother. Initially, his father is depicted stereotypically, trying to crush Abed's dreams of filmmaking and attempting to grab him and take him from school. In a later episode, Abed makes a film that wins his father over, revealing him to be more flexible than originally depicted. In another episode, Abed's cousin Abra visits from Gaza adorned in a *niqab* (a full body cover). Abed's father is highly controlling of her, presenting him as enacting stereotypical gender relations through the desire to control a woman's body, a behavior that is found in some places (increasingly, according to reports, in Gaza). For safety reasons, he restricts her from playing on an amusement park ride. She fights with him, and then sneaks in by having someone else wear the *niqab* and pretend to be her. We see in Abed's father a stereotypical patriarch, but we also see him bend, and we see a young woman's resistance. The show is neither clearly phobic nor -philic, and relies on no clear construction of a "bad" Muslim/"good" Muslim dichotomy, even if it hints at occasional stereotypes. *Community* is not a show that takes itself too seriously, however. It is too hip, playful, and ironic to rely on unimaginative stereotypes around a group so often treated simplistically in media representations.

Compared with the more popular shows Alsultany reviews, these more recent serials are more intricate and layered—ranging from depictions of the insidious (*Homeland*) to playful nuance with stereotypes (*Community*) and fitting outside of the "good"/"bad" paradigm (*The Killing*)—and seem to suggest that television is getting smarter about Islam. These three programs may not be representative, however; there are other areas of popular culture that merit greater concern, and may better typify Islamophobia/-philia in action.

Memes and Internet politics

The Internet hosts vibrant digital cultures and sub-cultures. Highly active sharing engenders the rapid circulation of Internet content, from jokes, to videos, to Tweets. While this can result in information overload, a deluge of images and information, occasionally a particular meme—a popular term, item, image, or other unit of content that is widely disseminated ("goes viral")—stands out from the crowd and becomes the object of widespread attention. It becomes a reference that many people know, reaching audiences that may be significantly larger than that for most movies and television programs. Some memes, however, travel within relatively closed networks, groups of connected people who share similar interests or identities. Memes that are shared widely speak to a certain zeitgeist, even if only to a segment of the population. While such memes are famously fleeting, some are recycled, and certain patterns show continuity among the types of audiences in which they proliferate. In this case, lower-level memes expressing Islamophobia are worth examining.

Islam-related themes can depict a certain degree of phobia. In 2007, "Islamic Rage Boy" spread rapidly. It portrays Shakeel Ahmad Bhat, a Kashmiri political activist who was frequently photographed and recorded shouting vigorously at protests. His face has been used in innumerable "Photoshopped" images and YouTube videos, mostly as attempts at humor, but they also have elicited violent reactions and hatred from some observers. A blogger at *Jihad Watch* quips, "I just want to put my fist down his throat," while the late journalist Christopher Hitchens refers to him as a "religious nut bag" (French 2007). He is quite clearly cast as the "bad" Muslim: hateful, fanatical, and violent.

Not all memes are phobic. A 2011 meme from Reddit, "Ordinary Muslim Man," takes an image of a traditionally dressed and bearded Pashtun. At the top of the image is the phrase "I am da bomb," which then continues at the bottom: "at making falafel." This meme became enormously popular as a subversion of anti-Muslim stereotypes. One version said at the top, "72 virgins"—a reference to the myth that Muslim suicide bombers are motivated by the promise of receiving such a reward in heaven—but then continues, "went to a Star Trek convention." Another has him say, "I will blow up your family … portrait to 20" x 30" so you can display it on your living room wall." This meme lampoons the "bad" Muslim construct directly, and there is evidence that it has had more currency and greater reach than "Islamic Rage Boy."[4]

That said, the strong reception online for Islamophobic material often ends up in an exchange with other views. The intentionally provocative film *The Innocence of Muslims* was created for the purpose of exposing the violence and immorality of Islam. While initially ignored in the United States—exposing the limits in the contagion of Islamophobia—its Arabic-dubbed trailer on YouTube inspired anti-American protests in Egypt and elsewhere (Flock 2012). The subsequent attention generated nearly ten million "views," creating a small-scale diplomatic issue for the United States when Egyptian protestors scaled the walls of the American embassy in Cairo (Flock 2012). Many of those viewing it were critical of the film; even mass media outlets responded. On September 24, 2012, *Newsweek* published a cover image of Muslims protesting under the phrase "Muslim Rage," hoping to generate a Twitter discussion of the cover with use of a hashtag (a keyword that allows Twitter users to comment on the same subject). Unfortunately, they chose the questionable cover phrase "#MuslimRage." Such hashtags, like memes, can just as easily be mobilized ironically, or used in a manner that is completely opposite of their original, intended meaning. This hashtag was soon populated with satirical "Tweets" making fun of Muslim problems; noted one, "I'm having such a good hair day. No one even knows" (Chappell 2012).

It would be difficult to argue that such responses are necessarily Islamophilic. They do not glorify the religion. Instead, like the "Ordinary Muslim Man," they seek to demystify the religion. Muslim comedians and other performers speak of their work as humanizing Muslims (Tugend 2013). This is only because common misperceptions exist about Islam, some of which are hostile and others just ignorant. A sense of ordinariness in representation online and in television programming approximates the "new normal" for which Muslims strive. It is easy for them to feel ill at ease and alienated given the dynamic and vocal politics of Islamophobia expressed by a small network of organizations and actors who hold events to burn the Quran, oppose mosque construction in New York City or small cities in Tennessee, and who see everywhere a Muslim conspiracy bent on American domination (Lean 2012). Hate crime levels are still significant (Potok 2012).

Self-representation

Muslims and Islam are most profoundly ordinary in their own media products, where self-representation is an option. In the past decade, Muslim American media have proliferated, from literature, theatrical productions, and music to comedy, cinema, and television programs. However, few have reached the audience and achieved the acclaim of the Canadian situation comedy TV series, *Little Mosque on the Prairie* (CBC, 2007–12).

Set in Mercy, a fictional small town in Saskatchewan, the show's subject is the local Muslim community. It is close-knit and in many ways a microcosm of larger Muslim diaspora populations, with its diversity of outlooks, nationalities, and religious devotion (and presentation). The program revolves around a mosque located in a space rented from a church, and begins with the arrival of a new imam, Aamar Rashid (Zaib Shaikh), who has moved from Toronto, leaving behind a career as a corporate lawyer. The town's previous imam, Baber (Manoj Sood), is a traditionalist who tends to express the most conservative positions on various issues that arise, from gender separation to interreligious relations. The new imam develops a budding interest in a local doctor, Rayyan Hamoudi (Sitara Hewitt), who wears a hijab and lives with her parents, the oddly matched Yasir Hamoudi (Carlo Rota) and his Muslim convert wife, Sarah Hamoudi (Sheila McCarthy). Yasir is a contractor and the typical businessman, who is always looking to make deals. Sarah works in public relations for the shady mayor, and always seems a bit confused about her commitment to her religion. A right-wing "hate" radio DJ (Neil Crone) lobs accusations at the Muslim community, yet spends most of his time in a restaurant that is a favorite gathering spot for the Muslim community, in part because he has a romantic interest in the owner, Fatima Dinssa (Arlene Duncan), a Nigerian Muslim immigrant.

The show approaches the Muslim community with depth and nuance. This is not surprising, given that the show's creator and head writer, Zarqa Nawaz, is a British-Canadian Muslim who lives in a small town. As a journalist, filmmaker, and freelance writer, much of her work has been about Muslim communities in the West and their relations with other religious groups and society at large. The show seems to suggest that Islam is, and should be, indigenized to the new countries where Muslims now live. In this program, they are simultaneously Muslim and small-town Canadian. The show seems to essentialize the community, in that Islam is one of the main underlying factors that makes its members who they are. One might ask whether this is overly positive in a way that approaches Islamophilia. Yet *Little Mosque* does not shy away from facing tough issues head-on, and allows the characters to represent varying perspectives reflective of actual positions. It is clear Nawaz is concerned with the role of women in the community, and gender relations are a marked theme of the more tense episodes.

Why representation matters

For Americans, television is the primary medium. Americans spend on average nearly three hours per day watching television, making up the majority of their leisure time (Shah 2013), making its programming elemental to what Americans learn about the world. It is a source of public education and miseducation. When it comes to a religion to which many have had little exposure, the frames, purported facts, and notions of the religion communicated through television can be quite potent. Even in an avowedly multicultural society like the United States, Muslims make up less than five percent of the national population, and are concentrated in larger cities and in a small number of states. Many Americans have no interpersonal relations on which to draw to better understand the religion. While people rarely fully subscribe to, learn from, or remember what they watch, the less pre-existing knowledge about Islam and familiarity with Muslims they have, the more vital television programs, from news to entertainment, may be in shaping their views.

For Muslims—particularly those living in Western countries—how media and institutions represent them and their religion is quite consequential. They may feel themselves to be in a tenuous state of citizenship, as not quite belonging in countries that either celebrate their Christian or Jewish and Christian heritage in public discourse (e.g., the United States), or subscribe to notions of secularism that penalize public displays of religiosity (e.g., France). Where there are "wars on terror" being waged, Muslim populations tend to be treated as suspicious classes, increasing their marginality in society and the polity. Media can therefore serve as a mirror for positioning Muslim populations. They take it as a barometer of their inclusion. If popular culture takes Islam as foreign or threatening, Muslims are more likely to feel alienated, and may seek greater insularity. In some ways, the enclave provides shelter.

Institutionalized Islamophobia: domestic foreign policy

Islamophobia is most dangerous when it becomes institutionalized in government policy, law, and practice. While local, state, and federal governments in the United States often take great care to avoid blanket profiling and discrimination, civil rights groups still learn of many instances of mistreatment. On the face of it, some laws may have a disparate impact. When these laws have a high profile, they tend to harm relations between Muslim communities and governments. Some of the more egregious examples of institutionalized Islamophobia include secret surveillance programs by local police and federal law enforcement that targeted mosques and their members.

New York City was a central location for this form of institutionalized racism. In the summer of 2013, a report that the New York Police Department secretly designated specific mosques as terrorist organizations alarmed many in New York (Bruinius 2013). These designations were connected to "terrorism enterprise investigations" that lasted years, and also involved the infiltration of secular civic and social services groups, such as the Arab American Association of New York. Its director, Linda Sarsour, describing the impact of this program, noted that it "chills free speech in our communities" (ibid.). The report about this internal designation emerged just as a coalition of rights groups launched a federal lawsuit against the city for what it called an "unconstitutional religious profiling and suspicionless surveillance program" (American Civil Liberties Union 2013). City officials denied that the report was accurate; Police Commissioner Ray Kelly called it "fiction" (Bruinius 2013).

It is difficult to say whether the NYPD takes its cue from popular representation of Muslims or whether its orientation helps shape those cultural representations. In certain cases, it is quite clear that media have an impact on how the police understand Islam. In 2010, the NYPD showed nearly 1,500 police trainees *The Third Jihad*, a film that Muslim groups have roundly criticized as promoting suspicion of all Muslims (Gross and Hays 2012). Commissioner Kelly appeared briefly in the film, and later apologized when news about showing it to trainees emerged in 2012. Mayor Michael Bloomberg acknowledged that "anything like this doesn't help credibility, so Ray's got to work at establishing, re-establishing or reinforcing the credibility that he does have" (Sacirbey 2012).

Institutionalized Islamophobia is at its worst when programs carried out to promote positive government–community relations are revealed to be fronts for surveillance. This brings about a crisis of trust, suggesting prejudicial treatment of the community. The Federal Bureau of Investigation (FBI) was at the center of such a controversy, in which "mosque outreach" programs designed to improve communication with the Muslim community were actually an information-gathering operation. Government documents show that agents tracked the names of congregants and the subjects of sermons, sought information about financial contributions, and later "secretly sought background information of congregants, including those whom they met with separately in the name of improving community relations." Government documents pertaining to the program reveal what the American Civil Liberties Union characterized as a "secret and systematic intelligence gathering program" not based on any reasonable, individualized suspicion (Huus 2012).

These sorts of wide-ranging programs erode trust with the community, making it less likely that they will cooperate with law enforcement. Taking community relations seriously requires trust-building, which would encourage members of Muslim communities to cooperate with law enforcement and make law enforcement officials less likely to presume that anyone who was critical of American foreign policy or was religiously devout was a terrorist. This reflects the same distinction in popular culture between external representations of Muslims and Islam, and those by Muslims. The former are most likely to present flat, superficial, and naïve views of the religion, while self-representation captures a richness, diversity, and vibrancy that is much closer to reality. In both American political institutions and popular culture, however, Muslim empowerment is still marginal. Entertainment and news, like the institutions of national security and law enforcement, can still represent Muslims as "good" or "bad."

Said suggests the circulation of Islamophobia/-philia in American discourse is wedded to US foreign policy as a power in Muslim-majority regions. As American political engagement with the Middle East accelerated after World War II, so did American popular culture's grappling with Islam. Melanie McAlister stressed the role of representation—specifically, "the intersection between cultural texts, foreign policy, and constructs of identity" (2005: 307)—in shaping events. Cultural matters, such as the way the Middle East was understood popularly, do not reflect larger politics, but make them, are intrinsic to them. Popular conceptions of Islam are rooted in media coverage, religious views, entertainment, and the series of tropes emanating in the framework of American racial politics—from threat and paranoia to fetish and envy—that get projected onto an understanding of "othered" peoples. Islamophobia/-philia in the United States are the "byproducts of its imperial policies" (Tamdgidi 2012: 78), as they both assert a simple, instrumentalized Islam that fits well with the state's regional objectives.

Even in the long view of the historic, conflictual encounter between Christian and Muslim civilization, during the Crusades, Mastnak (2002) argues that Europe's hostility to Islam was more a function of intra-European politics and peace-making than it was the direct result of the Muslim conquest of Spain. He writes that Islamophobia has been the dominant Western disposition toward Islam since the first Crusades, and he is unconvinced that its -philic counter is anything but "marginal and full of contradictions" (Mastnak 2010: 42). Even supposed affection for "good" Muslims can be framed in a way that asserts what have come to be seen as the deep flaws of the religion. He cites the example of a United Nations initiative, "The Alliance of Civilizations," which was meant as a critique of Huntington's "clash," yet not of his construction of "civilizations." It took for granted that the Muslim world was in dire need of rehabilitation and modernization, and that Islam's "special relationship to violence" was the central problem (ibid.: 46), and it refused to confront Islamophobia in the West as a possible challenge to alliance. For Europe, the panic over the influx of Muslim immigrants as well as the deep opposition to the inclusion of Turkey in the European Union speaks to the relationship between the fraught cohesiveness of Europe as a place on the one hand, and the Muslim question, the age-old challenge Europeans grappled with to define the appropriate fit for Muslims within and next to Europe on the other.

This domestic/foreign distinction in both Europe and the United States is a bit of an artifice. Islam is by nature transnational, and Muslims have been part of both places for centuries. It is common knowledge that many of the African slaves taken to the new world were Muslim (Diouf 1998). Muslims have been a part of Europe for more than a millennium, despite various efforts to "cleanse" them. European empires in countries like Algeria (France) and India (Great Britain) also bestowed on Muslims subject status, an imperial pathway to citizenship. It is, of course, a multi-layered history, yet Islam is seen as a foreign, non-Western religion. The more popular culture embraces the presence of Islam, and Muslims as Americans, the more effectively Muslims will gain the status of the ordinary and the everyday.

Notes

1 Thanks to Evelyn Alsultany, Yousra Fazili, E.J. Baker, Raed Jarrar, Niki Akhavan, and Andrew Shryock for their inspiration, advice, and feedback.

2 The word "covering" in the title of the book, he notes, has a double meaning; it refers both to "coverage" in the sense of reportage, but also to the synonym of obscuring or removing from sight.
3 I am appropriating this concept from the title of a short-lived television program (*The New Normal* [NBC, 2012–13]) to mean something previously taboo that has become accepted, and even taken for granted.
4 A November 2014 search on the search engine Google for each of the phrases in quotation marks shows that the phobic meme "Islamic Rage Boy" generates 240,000 results, whereas "Ordinary Muslim Man" gets three times as many: 750,000.

Works cited

Al-Arian, L. (2012) "TV's most Islamophobic show," *Salon* (December 15). Online. Available: www.salon.com/2012/12/15/tvs_most_islamophobic_show/ (accessed 10 November 2013).
Allen, C. (2010) *Islamophobia*, Burlington, VT: Ashgate Publishing Company.
Alsultany, E. (2012) *Arabs and Muslims in the Media: Race and Representation after 9/11*, New York: New York University Press.
——(2013) "Arabs and Muslims in the media after 9/11: representation strategies for a 'postrace' era," *American Quarterly* 65, 1: 161–70.
American Civil Liberties Union (2013) "Rights groups file lawsuit challenging NYPD's Muslim surveillance program as unconstitutional" (June 18). Online. Available: www.aclu.org/national-security/rights-groups-file-lawsuit-challenging-nypds-muslim-surveillance-program (accessed 3 November 2013).
Beaumont, P. (2012) "Homeland is brilliant drama. But does it present a crude image of Muslims?" *Guardian* (UK) (October 13). Online. Available: www.theguardian.com/tv-and-radio/2012/oct/13/homeland-drama-offensive-portrayal-islam-arabs (accessed 14 November 2013).
Bruinius, H. (2013) "NYPD labeled mosques as terrorist organizations, report says," *Christian Science Monitor* (August 28). Online. Available: www.csmonitor.com/USA/Justice/2013/0828/NYPD-labeled-mosques-as-terrorist-organizations-report-says-video (accessed 14 November 2013).
Bush, G.W. (2001) "Transcript of President Bush's address," *Washington Post* (September 21): A24.
Chappell, B. (2012) "'Muslim Rage' explodes on Twitter, but in a funny way (yes, really)," *NPR* (September 17). Online. Available: www.npr.org/blogs/thetwo-way/2012/09/17/161315765/muslim-rage-explodes-on-twitter-but-in-a-funny-way-yes-really (accessed 10 December 2013).
Cole, J. (2008) "Blowback from the GOP's holy war," *Salon* (February 1). Online. Available: www.salon.com/2008/02/01/islamophobia (accessed 14 November 2013).
Commission on British Muslims and Islamophobia (1997) *Islamophobia: A Challenge for Us All*, London: Runnymede Trust.
Diouf, S. (1998) *Servants of Allah: African Muslims Enslaved in the Americas*, New York: New York University Press.
Flock, E. (2012) "How 'Innocence of Muslims' spread around the globe and killed a US diplomat," *U.S. News & World Report* (September 12). Online. Available: www.usnews.com/news/articles/2012/09/12/how-innocence-of-muslims-spread-around-the-globe-and-killed-a-us-diplomat (accessed 10 December 2013).
French, P. (2007) "The surprising truth about Rage Boy, America's hated poster-boy of Islamic radicalism," *Daily Mail* (UK) (November 11). Online. Available: www.dailymail.co.uk/news/article-492864/The-surprising-truth-Rage-Boy-Americas-hated-poster-boy-Islamic-radicalism.html#ixzz2ePZXAKXa (accessed 14 November 2013).

Gross, S. and T. Hays (2012) "Muslims call for NYPD chief to resign over movie," *Wall Street Journal* (January 26). Online. Available: http://online.wsj.com/article/APbe6d40631fdb4cc89bc868e32ba0aace.html (accessed 14 November 2013).

Huntington, S.P. (1996) *The Clash of Civilizations and the Remaking of World Order*, New York: Simon & Schuster.

Huus, K. (2012) "ACLU: FBI 'mosque outreach' program used to spy on Muslims," MSNBC.com (March 29). Online. Available: http://usnews.nbcnews.com/_news/2012/03/29/10907668-aclu-fbi-mosque-outreach-program-used-to-spy-on-muslims (accessed 14 November 2013).

Lean, N. (2012) *The Islamophobia Industry: How the Right Manufactures Fear of Muslims*, London: Pluto Press.

Lewis, B. (1990) "The roots of Muslim rage," *Atlantic Monthly* (September): 47–60.

McAlister, M. (2005) *Epic Encounters: Culture, Media, & U.S. Interests in the Middle East Since 1945*, Los Angeles, CA: University of California Press.

Mamdani, M. (2004) *Good Muslim, Bad Muslim: America, the Cold War, and the Roots of Terror*, New York: Pantheon.

Mastnak, T. (2002) *Crusading Peace: Christendom, the Muslim World, and Western Political Order*, Berkeley, CA: University of California Press.

——(2010) "Western hostility toward Muslims: a history of the present," in A. Shryock (ed.), *Islamophobia/Islamophilia: Beyond the Politics of Enemy and Friend*, Bloomington, IN: Indiana University Press, 29–52.

Potok, M. (2012) "FBI: anti-Muslim hate crimes still up," *Salon* (December 10). Online. Available: www.salon.com/2012/12/10/fbi_anti_muslim_hate_crimes_still_up (accessed 10 December 2013).

Rosenberg, Y. (2012) "'Homeland' is anything but Islamophobic," *Atlantic* (December 18). Online. Available: www.theatlantic.com/entertainment/archive/2012/12/homeland-is-anything-but-islamophobic/266418/ (accessed 14 November 2013).

Sacirbey, O. (2012) "Muslims call for NYPD chief to resign over video," *Washington Post* (January 26). Online. Available: http://articles.washingtonpost.com/2012-01-26/national/35440103_1_muslim-community-nypd-muslim-american-groups (accessed 10 December 2013).

Said, E. (1979[1978]) *Orientalism*, New York: Vintage Books.

——(1980) "Islam through Western eyes," *Nation* 230, 16: 488–92.

——(1997) *Covering Islam: How the Media and the Experts Determine How We See the Rest of the World*, rev. edn, New York: Vintage Books.

Shah, N. (2013) "Americans worked less, watched more TV in 2012," *Wall Street Journal* (June 20). Online. Available: http://online.wsj.com/news/articles/SB10001424127887323300004578557703281646888 (accessed 10 December 2013).

Shaheen, J.G. (2008) *Guilty: Hollywood's Verdict on Arabs after 9/11*, Northampton, MA: Olive Branch Press.

——(2009) *Reel Bad Arabs: How Hollywood Vilifies a People*, Northampton, MA: Olive Branch Press.

Shryock, A. (2010) "Introduction: Islam as an object of fear and affection," in A. Shryock (ed.), *Islamophobia/Islamophilia: Beyond the Politics of Enemy and Friend*, Bloomington, IN: Indiana University Press, 1–25.

Tamdgidi, M.H. (2012) "Beyond Islamophobia and Islamophilia as Western epistemic racisms: revisiting Runnymede Trust's definition in a world-history context," *Islamophobia Studies Journal* 1, 1: 54–81.

Tugend, T. (2013) "Oy! 'The Muslims Are Coming' to your town," *Jewish Journal* (September 12). Online. Available: www.jewishjournal.com/tomstopics/item/oy_the_muslims_are_coming_to_your_town (accessed 10 December 2013).

Wilkins, K.G. (2009) *Home/land/security: What We Learn about Arab Communities from Action-Adventure Films*, Lanham, MD: Lexington Books.

25
JUDAISM

Eric Michael Mazur[1]

At its core, Judaism is a religion of performance. This is to suggest neither that there is no performative element to other religions nor that there is no interior spiritual aspect to Judaism. But there is a certain irony in the fact that this tradition, perceived as the foundation of Western monotheism—the belief in one God—has since before the destruction of the second Holy Temple in Jerusalem (70 CE) been predicated upon the willingness of its adherents to perform some, most, or all of 613 *mitzvot* (positive and negative behavioral commandments).[2] Performance has shaped the Jewish experience; periods of persecution have been punctuated by prohibitions on Jewish behaviors, while Jewish survival has often depended on the performance of ritualized or commanded acts.

Some might presume that Jews are therefore perfectly suited for participation in the mediated world of popular culture (with its emphasis on performance) and might point to the presence of Jews in the various popular culture venues as evidence. However, the role Jews have played in popular culture, particularly in the West, has had more to do with a comparatively recent, continuous negotiation that many Jews have performed between their own religio-cultural identity, the predominantly (if increasingly vague) Christian identity of Western public culture, and the demands of modernity that have had such a powerful impact on both.

This chapter is not intended as a traditional history of Jewish involvement in popular culture, nor is it designed to recount specifically where Jews have been involved in the construction, distribution, or consumption of popular culture. Rather, it is an interpretive analysis of the context of that participation, and Judaism's transformation—experienced by most Jews, primarily in the West—from a segregated religio-ethnic community to an acculturated, increasingly fluid identity integrated at all levels of contemporary popular culture. The scholarship on Judaism in modernity is legion, and on Judaism in popular culture increasingly so. The following is intended as a synthesis of the trends presented by that material.

Periodization of Jewish history

In the broadest terms, Jewish history can be divided into distinct periods, each with its own presentation of Judaism. The first ("biblical") period—from the moment of creation to the establishment of the Davidic Kingdom—at the very least established for Jews a sense of being in the world and a relationship to the Divine that, because of its emphasis on kinship, has played a significant role in the conception of Jewish community across time and space. The second ("Temple") period—from the establishment of the Davidic Kingdom to the second destruction of the Holy Temple in Jerusalem by the Romans—among other things established in Judaism a sense of place (Israel, and Jerusalem specifically) as well as a sense of discipline (enacted in the processes of exile and return) in the relationship between its adherents and God.

But it is the most recent ("rabbinic") period that is of greatest import for our purposes. This period—beginning just before the second destruction of the Holy Temple and the near-complete destruction of the Jews by the Roman Empire shortly thereafter—emerged from the teachings of those who reinterpreted Judaism from a location-specific religion to one that could be performed anywhere. The rabbis for whom this period is named emerged from the Pharisees, a religio-social party that functioned as teachers, scribes, and interpreters of the not-yet-complete Tanakh outside of the Temple. Their ability to re-imagine the nature and central identity of Judaism as separate from—but related to—the Holy Temple was crucial to Jewish survival into the Roman period and beyond. It is during this period that post-scriptural Judaism takes shape, with its emphasis on various behaviors, some of which are familiar to those outside of the Jewish world: *kippot* (skullcaps), *kashrut* (the system of dietary restrictions), liturgical use of Hebrew, and various life-cycle rituals.

To many Christians, a particular version of rabbinic Judaism—a broadly European ethnic variation known as *Ashkenazi* Judaism (pl.: *Ashkenazim*)—became synonymous with all of Judaism, and many depictions (stereotypes) of Jews from the medieval period to the present have been based on this form. It is not the only ethnic form, but because of a strong cultural barrier imagined between Christian Europe and Muslim North Africa and the Middle East, Ashkenazim have played a greater role in "Western" culture than the other Jewish ethnic forms, and therefore a greater role in "Western" popular culture.

Over the course of centuries, Ashkenazim in Western and Eastern Europe lived increasingly different lives. Starting in the thirteenth century, Western Ashkenazim faced ghettoization and a series of expulsions, from England (1290) to Spain (1492) and Portugal (1497). Eastern Ashkenazim also experienced ghettoization, as well as segregation in rural *shtetlakhim* (small villages), at times accompanied by severe persecutions and expulsions. This has meant that, while many Ashkenazim retain fond memories of this portion of their inherited past, particularly those from Central and Eastern Europe often recall it as a period of suspicion, segregation, and persecution.

By law and by practice, Ashkenazim kept to themselves. Individuals might leave their enclosed world—and risk the consequences of being persecuted by non-Jewish authorities, or mourned (as if dead) or placed under a *herem* (rabbinic censure) by Jewish authorities—but those who lived in it engaged in a form of Judaism that by definition reinforced mechanisms of separation. Christian governments segregated the Jews, but so too did Jewish observance of the *mitzvot*, which necessitated walking to synagogue, having access to Jewish services (like kosher butchers), and observing social restrictions related to interactions with non-Jews. Even language maintained a separation; Yiddish—an amalgam of languages drawn primarily from an older form of German—was the vernacular of Eastern European Jews. Hebrew was the language of the Divine (and therefore used only in prayer), and the dominant cultures' languages—Polish, Russian, German, etc.—were considered profane.

Across the Jewish world, rabbis placed great emphasis on studying Torah and performing the *mitzvot* in order to bring an end to the exile experience. This is not to suggest, however, that life was puritanical. Wine, for example, was not only a central element of liturgical practice, but its consumption at times was encouraged, sometimes in great amounts; four glasses were to be consumed by each adult participant at the *Pesah seder* (Passover liturgical meal) and participants were expected to get so drunk on the holiday of Purim that they could not tell the difference between the hero in the Book of Esther and the villain. Purim in particular was a jocular holiday; in addition to the alcohol (or maybe because of it), a tradition developed of dressing as the hero and heroine, and putting on skits portraying (or related to) the central themes and events of the holiday. It also was common among Ashkenazi wedding guests to tell jokes or perform skits or dances to entertain the bride and groom as part of the usual wedding celebrations. But these events—and others like them—were kept within the community, and performed within the context of religious observance (see Most 2013). Popularly consumed literature or public performances accessible to non-Jews were significantly less common.

Modernity and the end of rabbinic Judaism

In many ways, the European Enlightenment marks the beginning of the end of Western rabbinic Judaism (see Mendes-Flohr and Reinharz 1980). France granted Jews full civil rights by the end of the eighteenth century, as did other European countries over the remainder of the nineteenth century. Western Ashkenazim acculturated, gaining positions in non-Jewish society unknown to Jews for centuries. At the same time, Jewish writers and public intellectuals known as *maskilim* ("enlighteners") were re-imagining Judaism to maintain its Jewishness while bringing it into the mainstream of "modern" culture. However, this transition often came at a cost, and imagined or real, Western European Jews felt pressure to abandon outward expressions of Judaism to fit in. By the 1820s, Reform Judaism was making these (and other) transitions central to its conceptualization of Jewish identity and practice, seeking to integrate Judaism into the modern world by abandoning seemingly anachronistic and particularistic behaviors in favor of a more modern ethics-based approach.

In more traditional Jewish communities, all adult men were expected to be sufficiently knowledgeable to participate in—and lead, if necessary—any and all religious services. Few Jewish rites required a rabbi, who was seen as a member of the broader Jewish community and functioned primarily as a judge, teacher, scholar, and interpreter of the sacred texts and the *mitzvot*. In the "modern" era, however,—particularly in places most directly influenced by the European Enlightenment—the rabbi became the presumed leader of a congregation, its spokesperson, its representative in official or ecumenical matters, and most significantly, its employee (see Sarna 1995). North America provides a good example of this transformation; Jews fleeing

Iberian expulsion settled on the edges of New Spain as early as the 1520s, and in New Amsterdam in the 1650s, but there was no ordained rabbi on the continent until the arrival in the 1830s of Reform rabbis who fit this newer model (see Faber 1992).

The challenges of modernity and the commodification of the rabbi led to a flowering of Jewish denominational diversity as more traditional Jews responded to the changes endorsed by the Reform movement. The greatest extent of this flowering took place in the United States and not in Europe, in part because of long-established historic institutional patterns of both Jewish life and non-Jewish anti-Semitism, in part because of the ethnic diversification of American Judaism, and in part because of the evolving nature of authentic religious freedom experienced by that increasingly diverse American Jewish population. North America was a relatively clean slate, and waves of immigrants brought Jews from Catholic and Orthodox Christian as well as Protestant and Muslim dominant cultures. The first "wave"—from the beginning of North American exploration through the 1820s—primarily was made up of *Sephardim* (Jews from Southern Europe, North Africa, and the Middle East), who were acculturated but attuned to the Atlantic trading world (see Faber 1992). The second "wave"—during the middle of the nineteenth century—was heavily populated by Jews from what today is Germany who were heavily influenced by ideas from the European Enlightenment, and who brought with them the continent's first rabbis. This wave swept Jews who felt less tied to communal forms of Jewish practice across the expanding American frontier (see Diner 1992).

It is the third "wave"—from the 1880s until the 1920s—that most dramatically elevated both the demographic and the cultural presence of Jews in the United States.[3] These Jews from Central and Eastern Europe were more traditionally observant and less directly influenced by the Enlightenment than their Western European co-religionists, and initially scornful of their efforts to rid rabbinic Judaism of its historic traditions. In response to Reform modernizations, its leaders helped found the American Orthodox movement.[4] Eventually, a third, more centrist (Conservative) movement was established, as was a fourth, more self-consciously inclusive (Reconstructionist) movement (see Raphael 1984).[5]

The creation of denominations and the commodification of rabbis also facilitated a transition of Jews into the broader non-Jewish mainstream.[6] Diverse ways of being Jewish—of performing (or not performing) the *mitzvot*—provided greater flexibility for members of the community to take on more central (if symbolic) roles. The *shokhet* (kosher butcher) had always played an important role; but in the New World, leadership (and role models) came from those performing non-religious communal functions. In the United States (and Western Europe), the Jewish politician, financier, magnate, and lawyer replaced the rabbi as the model spokesperson for (and often, defender of) the Jewish community (see Alexander 2001; Auerbach 1990), offering non-religious yet seemingly Jewish ways of participating in the mainstream.

As incongruous as it may seem, one example of this transition is reflected in the rise of the Jewish American gangster. The result of difficult economic conditions related to immigration and a desire to forge an alternative route to "success" in American society, Jewish gangsters achieved elevated status among some Jews who saw them as wealthy, powerful, and above all, beyond the reach of authorities who had traditionally oppressed Jews and Judaism (see Fried 1980). Not surprisingly, many of the Jewish gangsters also saw themselves in this way, and maintained their Jewish identity (and even Jewish practice) as they engaged in nefarious adventures (see Rockaway 2000; Cohen 1999).[7]

The Jewish emergence of pop culture Jews

Jews have been depicted in forms of popular culture for centuries, though rarely positively, and often as biblical or medieval stereotypes.[8] The Oberammergau Passion Play, performed since the seventeenth century in Bavaria, is but one example (see A.J. Goldman 2010), but negative images of Jews in pre-modern forms of popular culture are common (see Felsenstein 1999).[9] By the end of the nineteenth century, however, newly emancipated Jews of Europe and the United States attained a level of positive celebrity among non-Jewish audiences; negative stereotypes continued (see Lindemann 1991), but increasingly, Jewish artists and performers gained acceptance.

The emergence of Jews into Christian culture, the concomitant sense of pressure to shed visible elements of Jewish practice, and the lessening of religious authority in the Jewish community, combined with the coincidence of the largest wave of Jewish immigrants, technological advances in consumer and mediated culture, and debates over the place of the newly liberated African American and the "Americanness" of the (primarily non-Protestant) immigrant, all had a significant impact on Jewish popular artists, many of whom struggled with issues of acceptance, particularly in a culture where class, race, and religion were largely connected (see Mazur 2012). Many of the Jewish products of popular culture from the end of the nineteenth and beginning of the twentieth century examine issues of assimilation into the American "melting pot" (a term first used by a Jewish playwright; see Zangwill 1917) and differentiation (from other immigrants, and from the more culturally marginal African Americans). Performance in "blackface" was common, but for American Jews it seems to have served as a lived metaphor for the anxiety over marginalization and fitting in to white Christian American culture (see Brodkin 1998; Erdman 1997; Rogin 1996).

Not all Jews were willing (or able) to make the transition into Anglo-Protestant "Americanness." Well into the first half of the twentieth century, staples of Jewish Europe and the urban Jewish immigrants—Yiddish-language music and theater (which evolved into Yiddish-language film; see E.A. Goldman 2010)—enabled non-English speakers to maintain a connection to their country of origin. As this generation passed and English became their children's primary language, Yiddish-language entertainment production diminished considerably.

But it was the emergence of the English-language film industry that provided Jews with the most powerful springboard into American popular culture. Considered by some to be a poor man's alternative to proper theater, early films often carried messages designed to "improve" the viewer; not only a Christian message but also a typically Progressive Era message of social reform and Americanization. Representative of those struggling with generational difference, economic disenfranchisement, the trials of immigration, and the challenges of inter-group relations (or even intermarriage), a number of early plots were resolved by the near total acculturation of the (often younger) characters into the "American way of life." More because of their status as "ethnic" immigrants than as non-Christians, Jews were often among those portrayed in this struggle (see Lindvall 2011). When faced with monopolistic exclusions in New York, a handful of Jewish entrepreneurs relocated to California, and established film studio empires (see Gabler 1988).[10] Once there, they (and their writers) were able to transform stories central to immigrant Jews into stories that were of interest to a nation of immigrants.

Up to this point, Jews had been visible not just in film but also on the stage (see Lane 2011; Merwin 2006) and, in the 1930s and 1940s, on radio (see Siegel and Siegel 2007). But with increased visibility came increased anti-Semitism, and in the years before and after World War II, the "Jewish" character diminished noticeably. Programs with obviously Jewish characters that had flourished during the "golden age" of radio—like *The Goldbergs* (NBC [radio], 1929–36; CBS [radio], 1936–46; CBS [television] 1949–51; NBC [television] 1951–52; Dumont 1954–56)—lost their appeal as they and other programs transitioned to television (see Brook 2003). Characters like the one played by Al Jolson (born Asa Yoelson) in *The Jazz Singer* (1927), who felt required to choose between obeying his father's wishes for him to become a *hazzan* (ritual chanter of Jewish liturgy) or becoming a popular singer, faded behind characters portraying broader "American" values (see Friedman 1987; Erens 1984).[11] As comfort with Jewish characters diminished and Jewish actors moved on to play other parts, non-Jews filled the few Jewish roles. An award-winning film of the period—*Gentleman's Agreement* (1947)—portrays a journalist seeking to "break the story" on anti-Semitism by pretending to be Jewish, something that Jews themselves seemed unable to do.

Changes in the American religious landscape in the late 1950s had a significant impact on American Judaism. Post-World War II economic and educational growth enabled more Americans to move into the middle class, creating a suburban culture that often eased tensions between religious groups as it leveled cultural difference. Many American Jews reflected what sociologist (and rabbi) Will Herberg (1955) described; that Protestantism, Catholicism, and Judaism were all versions of one American identity. Others—many of them members of the "baby boom" generation (born between World War II and 1963)—rejected this level of assimilation and became involved in various forms of cultural protest: the "Beat Generation," Christian or messianic Jewish groups that blended Judaism with Protestantism, or the various Asian religions newly present in American society because of changes in immigration law (see Melton 1993).

In the era of the "hyphenated" American, the rejection of Judaism as "establishment" also created a re-awakening among Jews in their ethnic self-consciousness as "Jewish Americans" who again found their place as an ethnicity. Elements of popular culture of this period reflect a growing curiosity about (and pride in) (primarily Ashkenazi) Judaism, with current events seeming to raise Judaism's profile, from Brooklyn/Los Angeles Dodgers pitcher Sandy Koufax's refusal to pitch in the first game of the 1965 World Series (because it conflicted with Yom Kippur) to the decisive Israeli victory in the June, 1967, Six-Day War. Some aspects were subtle— Leonard Nimoy's slight modification of a familiar Jewish hand gesture as the Vulcan greeting on *Star Trek* (NBC, 1966–69)—while others were rather blunt—for instance the song "They Ain't Makin' Jews Like Jesus" by "country & western" group Kinky Friedman and the Texas Jewboys (led by Richard Samet "Kinky" Friedman). Mark Spitz's seven gold medals in the 1972 Olympics—the same Olympics at which eleven Israeli athletes were murdered by Palestinian terrorists—broadly televised Jewish identity, and by 1973, *The Jewish Catalog* (Siegel *et al.* 1973)—a self-described "do-it-yourself kit"—was circulating widely in the American Jewish community. The 1978 broadcast of the mini-series *Holocaust* (NBC) rivaled the viewership of *Roots* (ABC) broadcast one year earlier (Diamond 1978).

Social discomfort remained, particularly in depictions of Jews on television—often the product of Jewish writers and actors. The first network program to feature an openly Jewish character since the cancellation of *The Goldbergs* in 1956, *Bridget Loves Bernie* (CBS, 1972–73) explored the issue of interfaith marriage—until significant protest from the Jewish community over the issue's positive portrayal led to the program's cancellation (Zurawik 2003). Nonetheless, the die was cast, and for the remainder of the century the appearance of Jews on television—on programs like *Rhoda* (CBS, 1974–78), *Mad About You* (NBC, 1992–99), *The Nanny* (CBS, 1993–99), *Friends* (NBC, 1994–2004), and *Dharma and Greg* (ABC, 1997–2002)—was often dependent on their relationship to non-Jewish partners (see Brook 2003).

A version of this discomfort—the so-called "self-hating Jew"—had been a popular element of Jewish humor since the end of World War II, and in-group Jewish rhetoric at least since the beginning of the modern period (Glenn 2006). By the 1980s, this phenomenon began to fade, in part because cultural differences among Jews diminished with the waning of Jewish in-migration, and in part because those generations who had struggled so hard to acculturate gave way to a younger generation that was almost entirely acculturated. A measure of this change can be seen in the public reception of Woody Allen (born Allen Stewart Konigsberg) as a Jewish comedian and filmmaker; while many older Jews felt great disdain for his work and his characters' love-hate relationship with Judaism, the younger generation felt comfortable with his presentation of these issues to the non-Jewish world where—according to a 1979 issue of *Playgirl* magazine—he was considered one of the sexiest men in the country (Hirsch 1990: 3).

Post-rabbinic Judaism and the "New Jew"

Despite more recent controversies that surround him, Woody Allen is a good example of a transitional figure in American Judaism precisely because of how he is received differently across the generational dividing line in the American Jewish community. Those Jews who sociologist Robert Wuthnow (1998) might identify as the "dweller" generations of twentieth century American society—immigrants from the beginning of the century and their children who grew up in the middle of the century—preferred keeping to their own cultural cohort: Jewish neighborhoods, clubs, philanthropies, and the like for the former; civic organizations, synagogues, the Parent–Teacher Association, and the like for the latter. These generations transplanted their roots from somewhere else, or planted new roots in their new suburban communities. But those Jews who were the product of the post-World War II experi-ence—religious "seekers" of the "baby boom" generation—came of age in the late 1960s and early 1970s, and fueled an initiative to explore new ways of being Jewish, likewise increasing the way Jews and Judaism were represented in popular culture. While many retained their more institution-based patterns, those who were more sig-nificantly affected by the era's cultural changes (see Roof 1993) were more comfortable identifying themselves as "spiritual" but not religious, and pursued innovative, non-institutional, non-rabbinic expressions of Judaism, including feminist reinterpretations and various manifestations of the Jewish Renewal movement (see Magid 2006).

As a result, since the 1980s, a new form of Judaism has emerged in American popular culture: the "New Jew," identified by his or her comfort with being a post-ethnic, post-denominational, non-*halakhic* (that is, non-practicing), almost entirely unaffiliated Jew (as a character or a celebrity), but also by how little impact that Jewishness actually has in his/her presentation (in film, television program, song, or celebrity "news"). While name changing continues (e.g., Winona Ryder, born Winona Horowitz), it is countered by confusion created with a growth of non-Jews with "Jewish sounding" last names (e.g., Leonard Albert "Lenny" Kravitz), mostly as a result of intermarriage,[12] and non-Jews who, in a more Protestant way, have "come to" (or felt "drawn" to) Judaism but do not undergo any of the rabbinic traditions for formal conversion (e.g., Madonna).

With the emergence of the "New Jew" has come greater visibility for things Jewish—cultural as well as religious—in the public sphere, most noticeably the popular use of Yiddish. In advance of the presidential election in 2008, the pro-Obama political action committee Jewish Council for Education and Research used "New Jew" comedienne Sarah Silverman in an online video to encourage young Jewish voters to visit their "*bubbes* and *zaydes*" ("grandmothers and grandfathers") in Florida to convince them to vote for their candidate ("The Great Shlep", 2008). The video went viral, attracting over seven million "hits" in its first two weeks on line (Itzkoff 2008). In the video, Silverman makes light of Jewish anxieties over Amer-icanization when, in pointing out the fear older American Jews might harbor because of Obama's middle name (Hussein), she responds "you'd think that somebody named Manischewitz Guberman might understand."

No longer coded as a "Jewish thing," Yiddish is used broadly in popular culture in song lyrics ("*mazel tov*" ["good luck"] in "I Gotta Feeling" by the Black Eyed Peas), political campaign buttons (see Figure 25.1), and film titles (*Shrek* [2001], which is Yiddish for "terror") and scripts. Lampooning the American appropriation of Yiddish, a very not-Jewish Ed Begley, Jr. (playing a very not-Jewish "Lars Olfen" in the 2003 mockumentary *A Mighty Wind*) recalls his experience with the fictional folk group the Folksmen:

> The *nakhes* ["pride"] that I'm feeling right now ... 'cause your dad was like *mish-poche* ["family"] to me. When I heard I got these ticket to the Folksmen, I let out a *geshreeyeh* ["yell"], and I'm running with my friend ... running around like a *vilde chaye* ["wild beast"], right into the theater, in the front row! So we've got the *schpilkes* ["nervousness"], 'cause we're sittin' right there ... and it's a *mitzvah* [in this context, "good deed"], what your dad did, and I want to try to give that back to you. *Oy keinehora* ["Oh, no evil eye"], I say, and God bless him."

Figure 25.1 Gore–Lieberman presidential campaign button, 2000. (From the author's personal collection; photograph by the author.)

On 13 March 2014, "New Jew" Jon Stewart had to admit on *The Daily Show* (Comedy Central, 1996–present) that his guest (Jason Bateman) and not he had correctly translated the Yiddish word *hazerei* ("garbage") in an on-air interview.

While the "New Jew" has caused some anxiety in the institutional Jewish world (see Pew Research Religion and Public Life Project 2013), these self-identified Jews— mostly young, mostly progressive—have been the foundation of a new style of Jewish public presence. Non-rabbinic, non-traditional, non-institutional, and almost Protestant in the freedom to choose Judaism as an identity (rather than be "chosen" by God to receive the "gift" of the *mitzvot*), the "New Jew" has become the model for a growing subset of American Jews, the Jewish version of Wuthnow's and Roof's spiritual seeker in late twentieth- and early twenty-first-century America.

And it is this Jew who is appearing more frequently in American popular culture. In 2000, the film *Keeping the Faith* responded to a century of intermarriage narratives by presenting the story of three friends (two boys and a girl) who remain friends into adulthood, when one of the boys becomes a Catholic priest and the other a rabbi. The film's conflict revolves around the boys' love interests for the (non-Jewish) girl, reaching the moment when (as adult men) they must choose between their religious commitments and their feelings for the woman. The priest reconfirms his religious vows—a plotline that could have gone either way. But the surprise ending comes not when the rabbi forfeits his pulpit (which might have been in keeping with the trajectory of representations of Jews on film), but when the woman (stereotypically blonde) converts to Judaism so that she can marry him without him having to do so, a decidedly less traditional twist. While not specifically a depiction of the "New Jew," this film does illustrate one important aspect of the representation of Jews and Judaism in contemporary popular culture. Not only has Judaism become "aspirational" (see Shukert 2012), it has become normal; more characters happen to be Jews and, more to the point, are as comfortable being Jews—no more, no less—as any other character is about being some other religion, or as any other character is with them.

Hanukkah: taking back the (silent) night

One of the best ways to track Jewish acculturation into American culture, Dianne Ashton (2010: 197) reminds us, is to trace the way Jews have celebrated the holiday of Hanukkah in the United States; for our purposes, one need only shift the focus to how Jews, Judaism, and Hanukkah have been presented in popular culture.[13] This is because the holiday—religiously marginal and neither commanded in the Torah nor described in the Tanakh—has become an important aspect of Americanization because of its temporal coincidence with Christmas.[14]

Despite its lesser scriptural location, its observance has long been part of the Jewish calendar, complete with making (and eating) *latkes* (potato pancakes) or *sufganiot* (fried jelly donuts), lighting candles (one for each night of the holiday, plus the *shammes*, or "servant" candle), and playing with a *dreidl* (a squared spinning top). Until the twentieth century, gift giving was minimal but the sharing of *gelt* (originally coins; today, aluminum-covered chocolates) was common.

Jews also have been "celebrating" Christmas for centuries. In Eastern Europe, rabbinic scholars chose this one night *not* to study Torah or Talmud, for fear that it would seem that they were honoring the Christian God and not their own. Some spent the evening playing cards, others spent it tearing toilet paper—a necessary (yet fittingly profane) practice given the prohibition against tearing paper (even toilet paper) on Shabbat. They even renamed the Christian holiday: *Moydredike Nahkht* ("fearful night"), *Goyim Nahkht* ("gentiles' night"), and most popularly, *Nitl Nahkht* (see Plaut 2012: 31–32; Wex 2005: 21–22).[15]

By the nineteenth century, Hanukkah was a practice primarily of the more observant; those inclined to assimilate were not inclined to display their Judaism so obviously, and many of the more acculturated German-American Jews were just as likely to celebrate Christmas (Joselit 1999). The third "wave"—who were both more traditional and more numerous—revived the popular celebration of Hanukkah, in reaction to assimilation and as an expression of people-hood that could be woven into the American narrative without violating traditional Jewish practice (Ashton

2010). This revival coincided with the dramatic increase in the public celebration of Christmas, making comparisons inevitable (Stein 2012). Notes American Jewish historian Jenna Weissman Joselit (1999: 312–13), by the 1920s, Hanukkah "showed clear signs of having been thoroughly Americanized, modernized, and commercialized," and by the late 1930s it had taken on most of the social and commercial trappings now common for both Hanukkah and Christmas.

By the mid-twentieth century, America's expanding pluralism made it necessary to recast broad expressions of Protestantism into inclusive expressions of civic virtue, including an Americanized version of Christmas. This is nowhere better reflected than in the popularity of the song "White Christmas" by Irving Berlin (born Israel Isidore Beilin), which almost single-handedly recast Christmas from a theologically significant Christian event to a familial and nostalgic American event (see Mazur 2007; Rosen 2002). Berlin and other Jewish songwriters created an American (as opposed to a Christian) Christmas songbook based on broadly "American" values (such as God blessing America, another sentiment put to song by Berlin) and "American" sentiments (such as snow in winter), contributing such popular tunes as "The Christmas Song" (also known as "Chestnuts Roasting on an Open Fire"), "I'll Be Home for Christmas," "Let It Snow, Let It Snow, Let It Snow," "Silver Bells," "Winter Wonderland," "Sleigh Ride," "Rudolph the Red-Nosed Reindeer," "Holly Jolly Christmas," and even the music in the 1966 television cartoon *How the Grinch Stole Christmas* (see Tracy 2009; Foer 2005; Martin 2001). Many Jews also observed their own moderately "Jewish" Christmas, complete with greenery (often called a "Hanukkah bush") and ritual meal (Chinese food; see Nathan 2012).[16]

Post-World War II events gave new currency to the nationalistic aspect of Hanukkah (particularly the narrative of the righteous few defeating the oppressive many). Early Jewish settlers in Israel had incorporated this into their own "civil religion" before World War II (see Liebman and Don-Yehiya 1983). But in the United States, this reinterpretation was conflated with lessons of the Holocaust (see Eichler-Levine 2010) and emerging narratives of American pluralism—the Herbergian example of what Americans who are Jews do when Americans who are Christians do something else—elevating it culturally if not theologically. Celebrating Hanukkah as equal to Christmas enabled this lesser Jewish holiday to become the way Jews could seem American without becoming Christian, or sacrificing too much as Jews.

The rise of American Evangelicalism in the late 1970s elevated the place of religion in public rhetoric, and whether Hanukkah was used as a "culture war" counterweight to the saturation of Christmas or as a symbol of unity with conservative religio-social politics, it became a much more public (that is, not exclusively Jewish) phenomenon. In 1979, President Jimmy Carter helped light a Hanukkah menorah installed by the haredi group Chabad in Lafayette Park (see Katz 2009: 244), and later acknowledged—for the first time by an American president—that the annual Christmas message need not presume the Christianity of all citizens. In 1989, the United States Supreme Court ruled that the presence of a *hanukkiah* (a traditional Hanukkah candelabra)—along with a variety of other "seasonal" items—effectively neutralized any inappropriate appearance of governmental endorsement of Christianity.[17] That same year, President George H.W. Bush put on public display a hanukkiah he had been given by the Synagogue Council of America. In 1993 the residents of Billings, Montana, admirably posted menorahs (or pictures of them) in their windows after hate-groups increased their level of violent activity in town (*New York Times* 1994; see also Eichler-Levine 2010).[18] That same year, President Clinton invited local Jewish children into the Oval Office for a Hanukkah candle-lighting ceremony. In 1996, the United States postal service issued a stamp to honor Hanukkah, the first non-Christmas stamp in the 34 years of Christmas stamp issuing (Broadway 1996). In 2001, President G.W. Bush hosted the first Hanukkah party, complete with a candle-lighting ceremony in the White House residence (see Sarna 2009). And in 2009, Utah Senator and Mormon Orrin Hatch composed, sang, and recorded his own Hanukkah song (Leibovich 2009), taking mathematician and comedian Tom Lehrer at his word when he said that the reason he had taken it upon himself to write "(I'm Spending) Hanukkah in Santa Monica" for Garrison Keillor's radio program *American Radio Company* (syndicated, 1989–93) in the early 1990s was because all of the other Jewish song writers were too busy writing Christmas songs (Tugend 2000).

Much like the place of American Judaism itself, even as Hanukkah became more of a "public" event, there was some sense of unease about how it fit into the predominantly (if increasingly vague) Protestant dominant culture. This is evident in the way that it was presented in American popular culture. On December 16, 1972, *Bridget Loves Bernie* aired "'Tis the Season," likely the first American prime-time television examination of Hanukkah. On December 15, 1987, ABC likewise aired an episode of *thirtysomething* ("I'll Be Home for Christmas"),with a Hanukkah-themed secondary plot line, and on December 16, 1991, CBS aired "Seoul Mates," an episode of the comedy *Northern Exposure* (1990–95), with a Hanukkah-themed secondary plot line; other programs—like *The Nanny* (CBS, 1993–99) and *Friends* (NBC, 1994–2004)—followed (see Rockler 2006).[19] In all of these programs, the celebration of Hanukkah was either a secondary plot line, an element of conflict between Jewish and non-Jewish characters (that often ended in the cooptation of the Jewish holiday for the Christian one), or both. Many of these episodes were written by Jews, but the situation was not made better by non-Jewish writers who, particularly in children's television programming, "outed" Jewish characters for the Christmas holiday season, when—presumably in the spirit of ecumenical pluralism—the religion of some secondary character could offset either the desire of the protagonist to celebrate Christmas or the ignorance that not everyone else did so (see Rockler 2006: 456).

But even as this unease was being expressed, the cultural self-confidence of the "New Jew" was emerging elsewhere. Beginning in the mid-1980s, Jewish organizations seeking to preserve endogamous marriage began hosting Christmas eve Jewish "singles" events (often called "Matzo Balls"; see Lee 2008); around the same time, companies began selling Hanukkah cards with decidedly "insider" humor (Silberman-Federman 1995). On December 16, 1989, "Hanukkah Harry"—making his first appearance in "The Night Hanukkah Harry Saved Christmas" on the NBC late-night sketch comedy program *Saturday Night Live* (1975–present)—helped a sick Santa complete his toy deliveries, quite possibly the first time since the death of Jesus that a Jew was portrayed (in popular culture, at least) as "saving" a Christian holiday! On December 17, 2005, another *SNL* skit revisited the historic Jewish fear of Christmas with the song "Christmastime for the Jews," humorously describing a sense of

Jewish liberation to do things in public which they are never ordinarily able to do—listen to Barbra Streisand music playing loudly outdoors, play for the Los Angeles Lakers basketball team, see *Fiddler on the Roof* with real Jewish actors, and so on—because all of the Christians are indoors celebrating Christmas.

Evidence that the world of Hanukkah had transformed entirely appeared on December 3, 1994, when, according to journalist Michael Norman (2008), the holiday went from "getting token attention in American culture to receiving its own prominent spot on the nation's holiday mantel." That night, on the popular "Weekend Update" segment of *SNL*, writer and comedian Adam Sandler introduced "The Chanukah Song." In the twenty years since, this anthem has found regular radio play between Thanksgiving and New Year's Day, can be found in various official and "bootlegged" versions on YouTube, was "spoofed" by Steve Carell for *The Office* (NBC, 2005–13), and "covered" by Jewish singer-songwriter Neil Diamond—albeit on a 2009 Christmas album. Less a holiday song than a declaration of identity, it reassures those listening—particularly Jewish kids who "feel like the only kid in town without a Christmas tree"—that they are not alone by listing "people who are Jewish, just like you and me."[20] Sandler's song had such an immediate impact that in 1996, children attending a Manhattan Jewish day school identified Sandler as their second favorite Jewish hero, behind Jerry Seinfeld (whose program *Seinfeld* had been on NBC for nearly seven years by then), but ahead of New York "shock jock" Howard Stern (who placed third) and the Almighty (who placed an embarrassing fourth) (Shandler 2009: 8). The song later appeared on the soundtrack for the 2002 animated film *Eight Crazy Nights* (dir. Seth Kearsley), co-written by Sandler and named from a line in the song. Though otherwise forgettable, this film is significant because—starring a Jewish figure who struggles with issues of loss, estrangement, and alcoholism—it was the first feature film of the "Christmas season" (the season that celebrates the birth of a Jew who grows up to be the Christian messiah) to focus on the life of a Jew.

A slight backlash toward Christmas and the winter holidays followed Sandler's breakout moment. Probably the most critical is the episode of *South Park* (Comedy Central, 1997–present)—"Mr. Hankey, the Christmas Poo" (aired 17 December 1997)—in which the lone Jewish character Kyle Broflovski not only sings a song lamenting the difficulties of being Jewish during Christmas ("It's Hard to Be a Jew at Christmas"), but also invents a scatological alternative to Santa Claus. The next day (December 18), NBC unleashed "The Strike"—"the most potent rebellion against Christmas" (Feller 2008: 160)—an episode of the popular comedy program *Seinfeld* (NBC, 1989–98) in which the Costanzas celebrate "Festivus" ("for the rest of us"), whose observance includes an aluminum pole, "feats of strength," and most uncomfortably, the "airing of grievances."[21] The film *Bad Santa* was released in 2003—directed and produced by Jews, disparaging Santa and Christmas, and becoming a seasonal cult classic (Chandler 2013)—the same year that the popular youth drama series *The O.C.* (FOX, 2003–7) aired "The Best Chrismukkah Ever" (on December 3), inventing a new term (a Christmas literally without "Christ-") and industry (see Chandler 2012; Bernstein 2008; Shandler and Weintraub 2007).

But as the Catholic League and the New York Board of Rabbis noted in a joint statement denouncing Chrismukkah, "those who seek to synthesize our spiritual traditions may be well intended, but they are insulting both of us simultaneously" (see Neuhaus 2005: 68). While many Jews continue to observe Hanukkah (and Christmas; recent polls indicate as many as one third of all Jews had a Christmas tree the previous year; see Goodstein 2013) according to older patterns, the transition of what we might call a "new" Hanukkah has been profound; for many American Jews, Hanukkah has moved from entirely within the Jewish world, through the shadow of Christmas, into independent existence. On December 6, 1996, Nickelodeon aired a Hanukkah-themed episode of the popular children's program *Rugrats* (1991–2003), and in 2003 the Disney Channel aired the made-for-TV movie *Full Court Miracle*, based on a true story about a team of basketball players at a Jewish high school in need of a coach. That same year saw the release of *The Hebrew Hammer* (dir. Jonathan Kesselman), "the baddest Heeb this side of Tel Aviv," a Jewish superhero in the pattern of John Shaft (*Shaft*, 1971) who, in stopping an evil Santa, saves Hanukkah (see Clanton 2006). In English, *maccabee* means "hammer."

As Michael Norman (2008) concludes, Hanukkah has become "almost hip"—culturally, if not theologically. Internet sales of Hanukkah materials make it easy to festoon one's house like neighborhood Christians, and references to the holiday appear in Christmas specials; not as counterweights to make the specials more inclusive, but in an almost ironic way, as if to acknowledge the differences between Christian and Jewish culture. Dan Clanton (2006) reminds us that the struggle that gave rise to Hanukkah was not only between the Jews and the Greek Empire, but also between the "pious ones" and those Jews who had chosen to assimilate into Greek culture. In many ways, it still is, but the emergence of the "New Jew" and "hip" Hanukkah suggest that, in a way, they have made a separate peace. On November 23, 2008, the song line-up on Stephen Colbert's *Colbert Christmas* (Comedy Central) included a duet with Jon Stewart titled "Can I Interest You in Hanukkah," a humorous nod to the differences between the two holidays. Two years later, in 2010, an all-male a cappella group from Yeshiva University uploaded to YouTube a video of "Candlelight" (Westrich 2010)—a cover version of Taio Cruz's hit "Dynamite"—where it was viewed nearly one million times in fewer than eight days, and replayed on *Today* (NBC, 1952–present). Their newfound fame earned them an invitation to CBS's *Early Show* (1999–2012) and an opportunity to open for Orthodox Jewish reggae-rapper Matisyahu (Hesse 2010).[22] Although produced by young men at one of the more traditional institutions of Jewish higher learning, the video has more in common with something produced by contemporary (secular) boy bands than with the 1950s *hazzanim* (pl.) who studied at their school before them.

Today, in some ways, Jews now "own" their own version of Christmas. The "Hanukkah bush" is now a "Menorah Tree" (Markoe 2013) and the traditional Jewish Christmas dinner of Chinese food can be had "kosher-style" (Tracy 2012), or even kosher (Fine 2012)—as can an edible version of the gingerbread house, complete with *mezuzah* (Alpern 2012) (see Figure 25.2). And that Santa in the Mall? He's just as likely to be Jewish as not (Zeveloff 2012).

But the complete "liberation" of Hanukkah was most evident in 2013 when, because of a rare coincidence, the first full day of the holiday fell on Thanksgiving. The last time this had occurred was in 1888 (see Elliott 2013; Petrecca 2013);

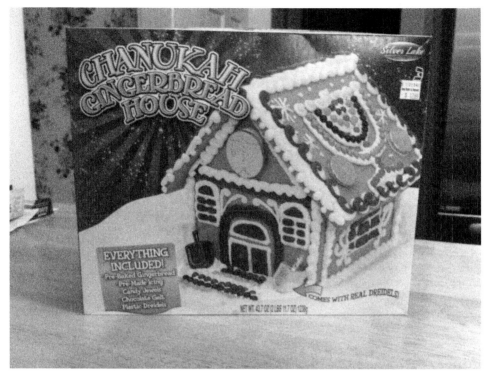

Figure 25.2 Kosher Hanukkah gingerbread house. (Courtesy of Dr. Claudia Pitts; photograph by the author.)

according to some, the next time it will occur will be in 79,811 CE (Zelizer 2013). No matter; much was made of this coincidence, and a new, entirely American Jewish holiday was born. A Massachusetts marketer is credited with coming up with the name "Thanksgivukkah" (having had the foresight to register it as a trademark)— Manischewitz and other vendors avoided trademark infringement in true Hanukkah fashion, by using a host of spelling variations (Elliott 2013)—and a nine-year-old New Yorker invented the "Menurkey"—a menorah made in the shape of a turkey, with the requisite number of tail feathers to accommodate the Hanukkah candles (see Figure 25.3). No longer in need of Christmas—or Christian culture—for the development of their own identity, American Jews joyously celebrated two holidays whose themes actually compliment each other (see Zelizer 2013).

In some ways, the American Jewish celebration of Hanukkah had come full circle. Blair Stein (2012) notes that late nineteenth-century American Jewish leaders—in an attempt to make Hanukkah (and Judaism) seem more American—had made a concerted effort to connect it not just with the non-Christian, cultural aspects of Christmas, but also with the patriotic aspects of the Fourth of July. The connection of Hanukkah to Thanksgiving illustrates how this holiday has paved the way for Jews to find their own place in American society, without Hanukkah being mistaken as the "Jewish Christmas."

Figure 25.3 Thanksgivukkah "Menurkey." (Courtesy of Leslie Needham; photograph by Dana Needham.)

Conclusion: *hosti gezeyn in dayne lebn?*

In a film flashback, a sheriff recalls his youth, and the time during his family's journey to the American West when, "from out of the West," came "the entire Sioux Nation." The "chief," noticing that they're African American (*"schvartes"* ["blacks," meaning African Americans]), restrains his second-in-command, chastising him ("no, no, *zayt nisht meshuge"* ["No, no, don't be crazy"]). To ensure that the family will be protected, the leader yells out to the rest of the group *"Loz im geyn!"* ["Let 'em go"— actually "Let him go," but why quibble?]. Once the family has thanked him for safeguarding their passage and moved on (with the appropriate *"abi gezint"* ["In good health ... " as in "You're welcome"]), the chief ponders the moment: *"Hosti gezeyn in dayne lebn?"* ["Have you ever seen such a thing in your life?"]. "And the rest," the now-adult sheriff concludes, "is history."

The question posed at the end of this scene—from Mel Brooks's 1974 comedy *Blazing Saddles*—could just as easily be asked of Judaism in contemporary popular

492

culture. To go from a culture segregated and persecuted to one so nearly completely acculturated is, from the vantage of global Jewish history, a remarkable (if at times frightening) thing. Stories (possibly apocryphal) circulated after the film's release that Yiddish-speaking Jews were impressing non-Jews with their knowledge of Native American languages. Today, Yiddish—like Jews and Judaism generally—is much more common. Bagels are served in fast food restaurants—granted, often with ham and cheese, bacon and cheese, or sausage and cheese; but like pizza and egg rolls, they have become an American food in the process. And with dramatic transformations in American Judaism—from rabbinic to post-baby boom, "seeker"-driven Judaism—so has Judaism been transformed in American popular culture.

The 2013 film *This Is the End* epitomizes this transformation, and the rise of the post-rabbinic "New Jew" in popular culture. Written by long-time friends Seth Rogen and Evan Goldberg—who met on the "bar mitzvah circuit" and started the script for the film *Superbad* (2006) at the age of 13 (National Public Radio *Fresh Air* 2013)—the film examines a Christian version of the end of the world, with Jewish tongue firmly in cheek. The cast is littered with celebrities—in large, small, and cameo roles—but focuses on several members of what has come to be known as the "Jew Tang Clan" (Abrams 2012: 32): Rogen, James Franco, Jonah Hill, Michael Cera, Paul Rudd, Jason Segel, and Jay Baruchel (whose paternal grandfather was Jewish). The film, whose script at one point bore the subtitle "based on the book by God," is drawn from the two Jewish writers' reading of the Christian New Testament—whose imagery they thought was "crazy" and "unbelievable"—and plays with their interpretation of Christian theology: "that if you're good you go to heaven, that if you're bad you go to hell." Reflecting (even if subconsciously) a long history of difficult interfaith relations, they understood this to mean, for some Christians, the equation of being Jewish with being "bad" (National Public Radio *Fresh Air* 2013).

The actors in the film purport to be playing themselves—that is, friends Rogen and Baruchel decide to attend a party held at Franco's home, at which Hill and others (also supposedly playing themselves) are in attendance. The film is not a documentary, nor even intended to represent actual events or relationships; but it does blur the line between Jewish actors playing parts (whether of Jews or not) and Jewish actors revealing something about themselves as Jews, and suggests a great deal about how Jews feel they are free to represent themselves in contemporary American popular culture.

Biblical epics have been a staple of the film industry from the beginning, but even then they were usually imbued with Christian rather than Jewish interpretive value (Gross 2011). Even the film retelling one of the most central narratives to Jewish identity—*The Ten Commandments* (1956), about the exodus of the Hebrews from Egyptian bondage to the Promised Land—regularly is shown around Easter, which comes close enough to Pesah to provide some solace for American Jews (Surrency 2011). Another Exodus narrative, *The Prince of Egypt* (1998), made after consultations with hundreds of Jewish, Christian, and Muslim scholars to minimize offense, was (according to studio executive Jeffrey Katzenberg) not intended to be religious, and rarely mentions God, Hebrew, Israelite, or a Promised Land (Tooze 2003). But in the early years of the twenty-first century, not only can Jews participate in the production and consumption of popular culture; they can more comfortably locate themselves there, and non-Jews can locate them there, too.

It is therefore hard to know which film—in the words of Jon Stewart—is "Jewier": *This Is the End*, which appropriates Christian theology through a Jewish lens (an uncommon switch in moviedom) or *Noah* (2014), which re-appropriates a Jewish narrative for a broader, largely non-Jewish audience. But there is no question that, as Jews (for the most part) have become more comfortable in contemporary, predominantly Christian culture—and Christians have (for the most part) become more comfortable with Jews (and other non-Christians), Jews and Judaism have found a greater place in contemporary popular culture.

Notes

1 Thanks to my wife, Claudia, who suggested *This Is the End* for its interesting use of Jewish identity and Christian theology. This chapter is written in honor of my friend Richard D. Hecht, who taught me how to juggle notions of modern Jewish history, the history of religions, and the lived experience of religion. Thanks, Richard!

2 According to traditional Judaism, God gave the entire *Chumash* (Pentateuch) at Mt. Sinai, making every direction therein (613 of them) a *mitzvah* ("commandment"); in Hebrew, the "Ten Commandments" are identified as *devarim* ("words," "things spoken") and not *mitzvot*, and are understood as general categories of behavior.

3 By the American Revolution, there were about three thousand Jews in the colonies. Between the 1880s and 1920s, the American Jewish population increased from roughly three hundred thousand to three and a half million (Sorin 1992).

4 Although often used interchangeably, "traditional" Judaism and Orthodox Judaism are not synonymous. The former refers to pre-modern rabbinic Judaism; the latter describes a movement in, and then a denomination of, modern Judaism.

5 Raphael (1984) notes that all but the last of these movements began in Europe. Because of the tragic events of World War II, this point is, for most Jews, largely moot.

6 These transitions also coincided roughly with the emergence of African-American forms of Judaism (see Gold 2003).

7 Many gangsters were strong Zionists, and raised money, transported weapons, or even relocated to the young Jewish nation; others moved to evade prosecution (see Rockaway 1994).

8 For example, William Shakespeare's play *The Merchant of Venice* presents a negative image of Judaism despite the fact that Jews were prohibited in England during the playwright's lifetime, having been expelled in 1290 and not legally readmitted until 1655.

9 Positive portrayals are extant; see George Eliot's *Daniel Deronda* (1876).

10 These "empires" then enabled other Jews to find work in the industry. Some joked that MGM stood for "Mayer's *ganse mishpochah*" (Yiddish for "entire family").

11 A familiar literary representation of this phenomenon was the comic book character Superman—created by Jerome "Jerry" Siegel and Joseph Shuster, both children of Jewish immigrants—who masks his difference from society until he's needed; the dream of any immigrant, to be sure, but one common enough in the twentieth-century American Jewish experience. This trope continued, to an extent, in the work of the second-generation comic book artist Stanley Martin Lieber, better known as Stan Lee—also the child of Jewish immigrants.

12 While the history of Jewish matrilineality has been the subject of debate—does it date to rabbinic literature from the beginning of the Common Era or the Tanakh (Book of Ezra, fifth century BCE)?—there is little debate that it was the Jewish foundation of community identity throughout the rabbinic period (see Cohen 1985; Schiffman 1985); until 1983, a

child was not considered Jewish unless the mother was Jewish (or converted to Judaism before the child's birth) or the child converted. In 1983, the Reform movement expanded the definition of Jewish identity to include those born of a Jewish father (and non-Jewish mother) so long as the children were raised in a Jewish environment. Lenny Kravitz, born of a Jewish father and non-Jewish mother, does not consider himself to be Jewish (Heath 2009).

13 For a complete cultural history of Hanukkah in America, see Ashton (2013). Because it is only properly spelled in Hebrew, and because Hebrew contains sounds not easily replicated with English letters, there are more than twice as many spellings of the holiday as there are days in the holiday (see Stein 2012).

14 The holiday—described in the Books of the Maccabees, texts retained in the Catholic translation of Hebrew Scripture that were excised from the Jewish canon—celebrates the victory of a small band of religious Jews (*hasidim*, "pious ones," a term often used for today's haredim) led by the Maccabees over the eastern Greek Empire in the second century BCE. Greek priests had desecrated the Holy Temple in Jerusalem; the holiday takes its name from the Hebrew word for the Temple's rededication after the Maccabees reclaimed it. The holiday's length comes from the "miracle of the oil," when a small amount of consecrated oil used for the Temple's *ner tamid* ("constant light," representing the constant presence of the Divine) lasted long enough (eight days) to be replenished (see Stern 1979).

15 Some suggest that "Nitl" is an acronym for "*Nit iden Toreh lerner*" ("Jews do no Torah learning/study"); see Plaut (2012: 35).

16 While it is possible to make kosher Chinese food (see Grossman and Grossman 1963), the bond between American Jews and Chinese food is largely based on shared immigrant experiences and the fact that many American Jews consider Chinese food to be "safe treyf" (Tuchman and Levine 1993).

17 *County of Allegheny v. American Civil Liberties Union*, 492 U.S. 573 (1989).

18 The town's response came as Hanukkah/Christmas approached, after Jewish homes were vandalized, and not by Thanksgiving when African Americans, Latinos, Native Americans, gays, lesbians, and "welfare recipients" had been targeted.

19 "The Hanukkah Story" (aired 16 December 1998); "The One with the Holiday Armadillo" (aired 14 December 2000).

20 Different versions identify different Jews, some not Jewish according to rabbinic law.

21 "Festivus celebrants", conclude Eric Shouse and Bernard Timberg (2012: 143), "participate in ceremonies that mock the most basic elements of contemporary Christmas and Hanukkah celebrations—family and togetherness." While the purported creator of Festivus is not Jewish, all four of the principal actors are, and George Costanza—although ostensibly Italian—is "coded" as Jewish (see Brook 2003: 106).

22 By March of 2014, the video had been viewed over nine million times, or enough for every single Jew—man, woman, child—in the United States to have seen it once, and half of them to have seen it a second time (see Goodstein 2013).

Works cited

Abrams, N. (2012) *The New Jew in Film: Exploring Jewishness and Judaism in Contemporary Cinema*, New Brunswick, NJ: Rutgers University Press.

Alexander, M. (2001) *Jazz Age Jews*, Princeton, NJ: Princeton University Press.

Alpern, L. (2012) "How-to guide to Hanukkah gingerbread house: there's blue M&M's, Sno-Caps and a vanilla taffy mezuzah," *Forward* (December 4). Online. Available: http://forward.com/articles/167136/how-to-guide-to-hanukkah-gingerbread-house (accessed 4 December 2012).

Ashton, D. (2010) "Modern Maccabees: remaking Hanukkah in nineteenth century America," in P. Nadell, J.D. Sarna, and L. Sussman (eds), *New Essays in American Jewish History:*

Commemorating the Sixtieth Anniversary of the Founding of the American Jewish Archives, Cincinnati, OH: American Jewish Archives, 197–228.

——(2013) *Hanukkah in America: A History*, New York: New York University Press.

Auerbach, J.S. (1990) *Rabbis and Lawyers: The Journey from Torah to Constitution*, Bloomington, IN: Indiana University Press.

Bernstein, E. (2008) "The santafication of Hanukkah: escaping the 'December dilemma' on Chrismukkah.com," in D. Janes (ed.), *Shopping for Jesus: Faith in Marketing in the U.S.A.*, Washington, DC: New Academia Publishing, 275–85.

Broadway, B. (1996) "A sticky church–state issue: Postal Service's Hanukah stamp rekindles debate over holiday commemoratives," *Washington Post* (October 19): D8.

Brodkin, K. (1998) *How Jews Became White Folks and What That Says About Race in America*, New Brunswick, NJ: Rutgers University Press.

Brook, V. (2003) *Something Ain't Kosher Here: The Rise of the "Jewish" Sitcom*, New Brunswick, NJ: Rutgers University Press.

Chandler, A. (2012) "Intermarriage scores vital SkyMall endorsement: Hanukkah tree topper seems weak in body, strong in meaning," *Tablet* (December 3). Online. Available: www.tabletmag.com/scroll/118185/intermarriage-scores-vital-skymall-endorsement (accessed 4 December 2012).

——(2013) "All-star team of Jews defiles Christmas in Billy Bob Thornton's *Bad Santa*: how the Coen brothers and Terry Zwigoff helped create a holiday classic that angers gentiles," *Tablet* (December 17). Online. Available: www.tabletmag.com/jewish-arts-and-culture/156296/bad-santa (accessed 17 December 2013).

Clanton, D.W., Jr. (2006) "From Mr. Hankey to *The Hebrew Hammer*: Hanukkah in pop culture," in L.J. Greenspoon and R.A. Simkins (eds), *Studies in Jewish Civilization: American Judaism in Popular Culture*, Omaha, NE: Creighton University Press, 201–16.

Cohen, R. (1999) *Tough Jews: Fathers, Sons, and Gangster Dreams*, New York: Vintage Books.

Cohen, S.D. (1985) "The matrilineal principle in historical perspective," *Judaism* 34, 1 (Winter): 5–13.

Diamond, S.A. (1978) "'Holocaust' film's impact on Americans," *Patterns of Prejudice* 12, 4: 1–19.

Diner, H.R. (1992) *A Time for Gathering: The Second Migration, 1820–1880*, Baltimore, MD: The Johns Hopkins University Press.

Eichler-Levine, J. (2010) "The curious conflation of Hanukkah and the Holocaust in Jewish children's literature," *Shofar* 28, 2: 92–115.

Eliot, G. ([1876] 1909) *The Writings of George Eliot: Daniel Deronda*, 3 vols, New York: Houghton Mifflin Company.

Elliott, S. (2013) "Manischewitz urges consumers to celebrate a hybrid holiday," *New York Times* (October 28): B6.

Erdman, H. (1997) *Staging the Jew: The Performance of an American Ethnicity, 1860–1920*, New Brunswick, NJ: Rutgers University Press.

Erens, P. (1984) *The Jew in American Cinema*, Bloomington, IN: Indiana University Press.

Faber, E. (1992) *A Time for Planting: The First Migration, 1654–1820*, Baltimore, MD: The Johns Hopkins University Press.

Feller, W.V. (2008) "Holidays and leisure," in B.F. Shearer (ed.), *Culture and Customs of the United States*, Westport, CT: Greenwood Press, i: 153–92.

Felsenstein, F. (1999) *Anti-Semitic Stereotypes: A Paradigm of Otherness in English Popular Culture, 1660–1830*, Baltimore, MD: The Johns Hopkins University Press.

Fine, D. (2012) "A very kosher Christmas in SoHo: how a trendy eatery is battling the laws of physics to redefine kosher cuisine," *Tablet* (December 26). Online. Available: www.tabletmag.com/scroll/120213/a-very-kosher-christmas-in-soho (accessed 31 December 2012).

Foer, J.S. (2005) "A Beginner's Guide to Hanukkah," *New York Times* (December 22): A27.

Fried, A. (1980) *The Rise and Fall of the Jewish Gangster in America*, New York: Holt, Rinehart, and Winston.

Friedman, L.D. (1987) *The Jewish Image in American Film: 70 Years of Hollywood's Vision of Jewish Characters and Themes*, Secaucus, NJ: Citadel Press.

Gabler, N. (1988) *An Empire of Their Own: How the Jews Invented Hollywood*, New York: Crown Publishers.

Glenn, S.A. (2006) "The vogue of Jewish self-hatred in post-World War II America," *Jewish Social Studies* n.s. 12, 3 (Spring): 95–136.

Gold, R.S. (2003) "The Black Jews of Harlem: representation, identity, and race, 1920–39," *American Quarterly* 55, 2 (June): 179–225.

Goldman, A.J. (2010) "New kind of passion in an 'alpine Jerusalem,'" *Forward* (May 26). Online. Available: http://forward.com/articles/128345/new-kind-of-passion-in-an-alpine-jerusalem (accessed 20 February 2014).

Goldman, E.A. (2010) *Visions, Images, and Dreams: Yiddish Film, Past and Present*, rev. edn, Teaneck, NJ: Holmes and Meier Publishers.

Goodstein, L. (2013) "Poll shows major shift in identity of U.S. Jews," *New York Times* (October 1): A11.

Gross, A. (2011) "Bible Films," in E.M. Mazur (ed.), *The Encyclopedia of Religion and Film*, Santa Barbara, CA: ABC-CLIO, 65–70.

Grossman, R. and B. Grossman (1963) *The Chinese-Kosher Cookbook*, New York: Eriksson.

Heath, C. (2009) "Lenny Kravitz interview," *Telegraph* (June 16). Online. Available: www.telegraph.co.uk/culture/music/rockandpopfeatures/5549844/Lenny-Kravitz-interview.html (accessed 6 May 2014).

Herberg, W. (1955) *Protestant, Catholic, Jew: An Essay in American Religious Sociology*, Garden City, NY: Doubleday.

Hesse, M. (2010) "Harmony group's Hanukkah anthem lights a fire on Web," *Washington Post* (December 4): C1.

Hirsch, F. (1990) *Love, Sex, Death, and the Meaning of Life: The Films of Woody Allen*, rev. and updated, New York: Limelight Editions.

Itzkoff, D. (2008) "Message to your grandma: vote Obama," *New York Times* (October 7): C1.

Joselit, J.W. (1999) "'Merry Chanuka': the changing holiday practices of American Jews, 1880–1950," in J. Wertheimer (ed.), *The Uses of Tradition: Jewish Continuity in the Modern Era*, New York, NY: Jewish Theological Seminary, 303–25.

Katz, M.B. (2009) "Trademarks of faith: 'Chabad and Chanukah in America,'" *Modern Judaism* 29, 2 (May): 239–67.

Lane, S.F (2011) *Jews on Broadway: An Historical Survey of Performers, Playwrights, Composers, Lyricists and Producers*, Jefferson, NC: McFarland and Company.

Lee, J.B. (2008) "A season of more than Christmas," *New York Times* (December 24): 19.

Leibovich, M. (2009) "Mormon senator's (nonreturnable) gift to the Jews," *New York Times* (December 9): A20.

Liebman, C.S. and E. Don-Yehiya (1983) *Civil Religion in Israel: Traditional Judaism and Political Culture in the Jewish State*, Berkeley, CA: University of California Press.

Lindemann, A.S. (1991) *The Jew Accused: Three Anti-Semitic Affairs (Dreyfus, Beilis, Frank) 1894–1915*, New York: Cambridge University Press.

Lindvall, T. (2011) "Silent film," in E.M. Mazur (ed.), *The Encyclopedia of Religion and Film*, Santa Barbara, CA: ABC-CLIO, 393–400.

Magid, S. (2006) "Jewish Renewal: toward a 'new' American Judaism," *Tikkun* 21, 1 (January/February): 57–60.

Markoe, L. (2013) "Move over Hanukkah bush, here comes the menorah tree," Religion News Service (November 21). Online. Available: www.religionnews.com/2013/11/21/move-hanukkah-bush-comes-menorah-tree/ (accessed 25 November 2013).

Martin, D. (2001) "Albert Hague, 81, a composer and actor," *New York Times* (November 15): D10.

Mazur, E.M. (2007) "Going My Way? Crosby and Catholicism on the Road to America," in W. Raubicheck and R. Prigozy (eds), *Going My Way: Bing Crosby and American Culture*, Rochester, NY: University of Rochester Press, 17–33.

——(2012) "Religion, race, and the American constitutional order," in R.D. Jacobson and N.D. Wadsworth (eds), *Faith and Race in American Political Life*, Charlottesville, VA: University of Virginia Press, 33–55.

Melton, G. (1993) "Another look at new religions," *Annals of the American Academy of Political and Social Science* 527 (May): 97–112.

Mendes-Flohr, P.R. and J. Reinharz (eds) (1980) *The Jew in the Modern World: A Documentary History*, New York: Oxford University Press.

Merwin, T. (2006) *In Their Own Image: New York Jews in Jazz Age Popular Culture*, New Brunswick, NJ: Rutgers University Press.

Most, A. (2013) *Theatrical Liberalism: Jews and Popular Entertainment in America*, New York: New York University Press.

Nathan, J. (2012) "Our Jewish Christmas traditions: my family never observed Christmas, but we did mark the holiday every year, with our own recipes," *Tablet* (December 17). Online. Available: www.tabletmag.com/jewish-life-and-religion/118426/our-jewish-christmas-traditions (accessed 17 December 2012).

National Public Radio *Fresh Air* (2013) "Seth Rogen, Evan Goldberg: friends till 'The End'" (June 11). Online. Available: www.npr.org/2013/06/11/187350045/seth-rogen-evan-goldberg-friends-til-the-end (accessed 6 January 2014).

Neuhaus, R.J. (2005) "The Public Square: While we're at it," *First Things* (December): 68.

New York Times (1994) "Montana outrage stalls skinheads" (February 20): 38.

Norman, M. (2008) "Hanukkah is becoming almost hip," Cleveland.com (December 20). Online. Available: www.cleveland.com/religion/index.ssf/2008/12/hanukkah_is_becoming_almost_hi.html (accessed 14 December 2010).

Petrecca, L. (2013) "Retailers eat up 'Thanksgivukkah': rare holiday mash-up lights imaginations," *USA Today* (November 15): 1A.

Pew Research Religion and Public Life Project (2013) "A portrait of Jewish Americans" (October 1). Online. Available: www.pewforum.org/2013/10/01/jewish-american-beliefs-attitudes-culture-survey/ (accessed 2 October 2013).

Plaut, J.E. (2012) *A Kosher Christmas: 'Tis the Season to be Jewish*, New Brunswick, NJ: Rutgers University Press.

Raphael, M.L. (1984) *Profiles in American Judaism: The Reform, Conservative, Orthodox, and Reconstructionist Traditions in Historical Perspective*, San Francisco, CA: Harper and Row.

Rockaway, R.A. (1994) "Hoodlum hero: the Jewish gangster as defender of his people, 1919–49," *American Jewish History* 82, 1–4: 215–35.

——(2000) *But He Was Good to His Mother: The Lives and Crimes of Jewish Gangsters*, New York: Gefen Publishers.

Rockler, N.R. (2006) "*Friends*, Judaism, and the Holiday Armadillo: mapping a rhetoric of postidentity politics," *Communication Theory* 16: 453–73.

Rogin, M. (1996) *Blackface, White Noise: Jewish Immigrants in the Hollywood Melting Pot*, Berkeley, CA: University of California Press.

Roof, W.C. (1993) *A Generation of Seekers: The Spiritual Journeys of the Baby Boom Generation*, San Francisco, CA: Harper San Francisco.

Rosen, J. (2002) *White Christmas: The Story of an American Song*, New York: Scribner.

Sarna, J.D. (1995) "The evolution of the American synagogue," in R.M. Seltzer and N.J. Cohen (eds), *The Americanization of the Jews*, New York: New York University Press, 215–29.

——(2009) "How Hanukkah came to the White House," *Forward* (December 11). Online. Available: http://forward.com/articles/120124/how-hanukkah-came-to-the-white-house (accessed 6 January 2014).

Schiffman, L.H. (1985) "Jewish identity and Jewish descent," *Judaism* 34, 1 (Winter): 78–84.

Shandler, J. (2009) *Jews, God, and Videotape: Religion and Media in America*, New York: New York University Press.

Shandler, J. and A. Weintraub (2007) "'Santa, shmanta': greeting cards for the December dilemma," *Material Religion* 3, 3 (November): 380–403.

Shouse, E. and B. Timberg (2012) "A festivus for the restivus: Jewish-American comedians respond to Christmas," *Humor* 25, 2: 133–53.

Shukert, R. (2012) "Intermarried a-listers and us," *Tablet* (October 4). Online. Available: www.tabletmag.com/jewish-arts-and-culture/113208/intermarried-a-listers-and-us (accessed 7 October 2012).

Siegel, D.S. and S. Siegel (2007) *Radio and the Jews: The Untold Story of How Radio Influenced America's Image of Jews, 1920s–1950s*, Yorktown Heights, NY: Book Hunter Press.

Siegel, R., M. Strassfeld, and S. Strassfeld (eds) (1973) *The Jewish Catalog: A Do-It-Yourself Kit*, Philadelphia, PA: Jewish Publication Society of America.

Silberman-Federman, N.J. (1995) "Jewish humor, self-hatred, or anti-Semitism: the sociology of Hanukkah cards in America," *Journal of Popular Culture* 28, 4 (Spring): 211–29.

Sorin, G. (1992) *A Time for Building: The Third Migration, 1880–1920*, Baltimore, MD: The Johns Hopkins University Press.

Stein, B. (2012) "'The Charnukah being observed now': understanding Hanukkah through American newspapers, 1880–1915," *Journal of Religion and Culture* 23: 39–61.

Stern, M. (1979) "The period of the Second Temple," in H.H. Ben-Sasson (ed.), *A History of the Jewish People*, Cambridge, MA: Harvard University Press, 185–303.

Surrency, D. (2011) "Holidays," in E.M. Mazur (ed.), *The Encyclopedia of Religion and Film*, Santa Barbara, CA: ABC-CLIO, 220–25.

Tooze, G.A. (2003) "Moses and the reel exodus," *Journal of Religion and Film* 7, 1 (April). Online. Available: www.unomaha.edu/jrf/Vol7No1/MosesExodus.htm (accessed 28 April 2014).

Tracy, M. (2009) "Have yourself a Jewish little Christmas: the top 10 Christmas songs written by Jews," *Tablet* (December 24). Online. Available: www.tabletmag.com/jewish-arts-and-culture/music/22910/have-yourself-a-jewish-little-christmas (accessed 11 December 2012).

——(2012) "Why Jews eat Chinese on December 25, and how a hip Brooklyn deli is modernizing that tradition," *Tablet* (December 25). Online. Available: www.tabletmag.com/jewish-life-and-religion/53569/jewish-christmas (accessed 29 January 2013).

Tuchman, G. and H.G. Levine (1993) "New York Jews and Chinese food: the social construction of an ethnic pattern," *Journal of Contemporary Ethnography* 22, 3 (October): 382–407.

Tugend, T. (2000) "Tom Lehrer: an equal opportunity offender," Jewish Telegraphic Agency (May 31). Online. Available: www.jta.org/2000/05/31/life-religion/features/tom-lehrer-an-equal-opportunity-offender (accessed 19 December 2013).

Westrich, U. (2010) "The Maccabeats—Candlelight—Hanukkah," YouTube.com (November 26). Online. Available: www.youtube.com/watch?v=qSJCSR4MuhU (accessed 14 March 2014).

Wex, M. (2005) *Born to Kvetch: Yiddish Language and Culture in All Its Moods*, New York: St. Martin's Press.

Wuthnow, R. (1998) *After Heaven: Spirituality in America Since the 1950s*, Berkeley, CA: University of California Press.

Zangwill, I. (1917) *The Melting-Pot: Drama in Four Acts*, New York: The Macmillan Company.

Zelizer, G.L. (2013) "Let's celebrate the convergence of Thanksgiving and Hanukkah: latkes with cranberry sauce make for a perfect holiday," *Forward* (November 15). Online. Available: http://forward.com/articles/187288/lets-celebrate-the-convergence-of-thanksgiving-and (accessed 16 January 2014).

Zeveloff, N. (2012) "When Santa at the mall is Jewish: red suit, white beard, no yarmulke for Father Christmas," *Forward* (December 13). Online. Available: http://forward.com/articles/167577/when-santa-at-the-mall-is-jewish (accessed 14 December 2012).

Zurawik, D. (2003) *The Jews of Prime-Time*, Hanover, NH: Brandeis University Press.

26
MORMONISM

Lynita K. Newswander, Chad B. Newswander, and Lee Trepanier

Though it has resided for over a century at the fringes of America's geography and society, the Church of Jesus Christ of Latter-day Saints (commonly known as the LDS Church or "Mormons," because of their belief in the Book of Mormon as a sacred work of scripture) has a rich history closely tied to its land, people, and culture.[1] Founded in 1830 by young farm-boy Joseph Smith, who claimed to have seen heavenly messengers in vision, the religion grew steadily in small numbers until it built up a devout membership (Remini 2002). They gathered together first in New York, later in Ohio, Missouri, and Illinois, before making the final trek to the Salt Lake Valley. Each time, they were met with challenges from neighbors who were offended by the teachings of the new faith or threatened by the political power of the rapidly growing group (Wicks and Foister 2005). Skirmishes led to official government action against the Mormons: first an extermination order from Governor Lilburn Boggs of Missouri, later military action ("the Mormon War"), and court rulings that ultimately disincorporated the Church and froze its assets (see Arrington and Bitton 1979).

Though the last century has seen many positive changes for the faith, it has remained largely isolated from the American mainstream. This may be credited partially to the fear or distrust of outsiders who do not understand or appreciate what Mormons hold sacred (see Givens 2007). These misgivings and misinterpretations have contributed to a muddled public identity: one which is, on the one hand, staunchly traditional, squeaky clean and lily white, and on the other, secretive and untrustworthy. Such depictions persisted through much of the twentieth century, and characterized the Mormon as from another time and place, an "other" and an outsider.

Recently, Mormonism has been the focus of unprecedented media interest. What some have called "The Mormon Moment" (see Kirn 2011, and accompanying cover photo)—spurred by Mitt Romney's 2012 presidential campaign and an increased public relations effort by the Church of Jesus Christ of Latter-day Saints—has resulted in a significant increase in screen time for the religion. This attention comes both from inside and outside of the LDS Church, and spans the gamut of today's media outlets: reality shows and scripted television series, radio, movies, books, and even

Broadway—not to mention blogs, news articles, and network newsmagazines. The coverage is certainly widespread, and as a result, Americans are reshaping a collective image of what Mormonism is and what its influence on their lives should be.

A generation ago, Donny and Marie Osmond were the poster children of traditional values. Complete with matching bellbottoms and "big" hair, they were part of a real-life *Brady Bunch* family and exhibited much of what was synonymous with Mormonism at the time: clean living, big families, the Mountain West, and the white upper-middle class. Today, by contrast, popular attention for the faith comes from a variety of often conflicting images; as more Mormons are represented on "reality" television programs and in other media, the public is introduced to a multidimensional view of the faith that includes members from various backgrounds, cultures, and ethnicities, with a wide range of interests. While many of these images go beyond the strict standard of traditional LDS values, the Church has embraced the new aggregate image of itself as a worldwide faith whose people and message are suddenly new and relevant. In an effort to regain control of the image of "Mormons," the Church has launched a vast public relations campaign that capitalizes on current trends in popular culture to reintroduce the public to the once misunderstood religion.

It isn't that Mormons have not received media attention before. Although their traditional families and conservative culture reflect mainstream values, they have been portrayed as outsiders, anomalies in the American melting pot. For much of the twentieth century, Mormonism was a boutique religion isolated in the Rocky Mountains and largely unfamiliar to the broader population. With official LDS headquarters in Salt Lake City, the culture seemed miles away from the rest of society. This is evident in early depictions of Mormons in the media as strange or peculiar, often innocent and naïve of the cultural values of the "real" world. However, the vision of Mormons in popular culture today has started to distance itself from the stagnant, homogenous image of a very particular and peculiar people to one that is more diverse, ready to accept a variety of styles and systems of belief, and decidedly contemporary. Over the last several decades, the portrayal of Mormons in popular media has mirrored the broader shifting tides of American culture: as widespread values have become more pluralistic, more accepting of breaks from tradition, and more rewarding of well-crafted public personas, the image of Mormons has also changed.

Traditional depictions of an American faith

There was a time during the Cold War period when the simple, one-dimensional depiction of Mormons as honest, family-oriented, white, and wholesome was happily embraced by consumers of American media. Even though this depiction of LDS culture overlooked the nuances and deep traditions of this particular faith (Givens 2007; Bloom 2006), the image sold records and produced successful business careers. For some, the vision of Mormons as innocent is still able to capture the American imagination and media attention. For others, however, that same image seems stagnant, staid, and is associated with classism, sexism, and racism. As popular culture evolves, the image of Mormons projected by popular media—and promoted by

Mormons themselves—has transformed into something new, and no longer beyond the mainstream.

In the beginning, there were the Osmonds …

The popular personification of these twentieth-century Mormon values began with four brothers, between the ages of nine and three, who started singing as a barbershop quartet in their hometown of Ogden, Utah, in order to raise funds for their deaf older brothers to serve missions for the LDS Church. This was the humble beginning of the Osmond Brothers (later simply the Osmonds)—Alan, Wayne, Merrill, and Jay, with Donny joining later—a group of clean-cut Mormon boys who made a name for themselves in pop music in the early 1970s with hits like "One Bad Apple" (Billboard's #1 for 1971; Whitburn 2004: 445). The musical Osmond family found longevity in their success in part by tapping into the public's collective yearning to maintain traditional family values. As the children grew, their sound changed, as did their ambition. In 1976, the family put most of its efforts into two of the younger family members, who launched their own variety show, *Donny and Marie* (ABC, 1976–79). The siblings were teenagers (18 and 16, respectively), but already had over a decade of experience in the family business of music and entertainment. Together, they were quite a pair; she was "a little bit country," he was "a little bit rock and roll," and the combination seemed to be precisely what America was looking for: youth, beauty, and success, with strong family values and a sense of civility. In fact, their public image was so impeccable that after the show was cancelled, Donny felt that he was disadvantaged in his attempts at a solo adult career by the public perception of him as "unhip" and a "boy scout" (Burgess 1999). One professional publicist even suggested that he should intentionally get arrested for drug possession (BBC News 2004).[2]

What was it about the Osmonds that made them a particular "moment" in American popular culture? First, although entertainment generally and music specifically were pushing new limits of tradition and public decency, the Osmond family—with other big, happy families, like *The Brady Bunch* (ABC, 1969–74) and *The Waltons* (CBS, 1971–81)—fit into a definite, persistent niche of simple American values onto which many wanted to hold. The difference was that, in the Osmonds, America had a real-life manifestation of the (perhaps already fading) dream that a family could find success on a large scale while maintaining their love for one another and dedication to their personal values.

Their position was always a precarious one, however, because while the values they upheld remained the same—as Mormons, they did not smoke or drink, they respected their parents and saved themselves for marriage—those of the crowds upon which they relied to sell their records were changing. This period also saw the rise of another side of music notoriety, populated by groups like Led Zeppelin, KISS, the Rolling Stones, and Pink Floyd, which popularized adult themes, lewd behavior, and an altogether new standard for the musical genre. Perhaps, however, this very tension was the key to the period of the Osmonds' success: in times of swiftly changing societal standards, their image was a happy reminder of a simpler time when a teenager's worst troubles concerned their hair and bellbottoms.

As the tides of time continue to push culture away from these so-called outmoded values, it only reinforces the unique characteristics that many members of the LDS Church tend to reflect. For example, David Archuletta, Brooke White, and Carmen Rasmusen developed a large fan base from their time on *American Idol* (FOX, 2002–present), thanks in part to their straight-laced sensibility coupled with an image of innocence. Archuletta was said to have a "guileless grin" with the "eyes of Bambi" (Slezak 2008a). Although White was cast as a "wide-eyed nanny" (Slezak 2008b), she was more optimistically characterized by her sense of "vulnerability" (Silvesan 2008). Rasmusen was said to be naïve and have a squeaky-clean image.[3] Even though these characteristics were occasionally cast in a negative light, they were also sources of the singers' popularity. Each of these would-be idols was able to tap into the public's fascination with a value system that was considered out of step with the times, but was nonetheless appealing.

Another member of the LDS community who captured the national spotlight in recent years is Brigham Young University basketball player, Jimmer Fredette. Professional basketball superstar Kevin Durant called him the "best scorer in the world" (Durant 2011). The phenomenon known as "Jimmermania" hit its zenith in 2011 as his team reached the "Sweet 16" in the NCAA Tournament, and he was named the National Player of the Year. Although his talent pushed him onto the national stage, as it had with Archuletta and others, it was his humility that seemed to separate Jimmer from his peers in the sports world. Instead of focusing on how to highlight his own achievements through high-profile antics, he praised his teammates and allowed his performance to speak for itself. His soft-spokenness and kind demeanor informed by a strong family narrative, including stories of his time spent with his brother, seemed to some to reflect a particular LDS identity.

Business, politics, and the white-collar image

The stereotype of good old-fashioned Mormon values has been popular in American business, as well. Because the LDS Church (like other Protestant communities) is run and administered by lay members rather than specially trained and paid clergy, each member shares a load of the responsibility, meaning that the rigors of church membership can help prepare Mormons for working in a bureaucracy and adapting to business life. Additionally, the rational-legal ideals of hierarchy, rules, specialization, and division of labor have been part of the structure and practice of the faith from the early twentieth century (Bowman 2012; Quinn 1984). This fit is reinforced by Mormon religious values, particularly the standards of clean living, integrity, and hard work. Howard Hughes, notorious billionaire and embodiment of so much of the excess Las Vegas came to exemplify, preferred to surround himself with Mormons (*Time* 1976); he liked that they didn't drink or smoke, and he felt the need to be surrounded by an inner circle whose advice he could trust. And Hughes was not the only one to capitalize on the benefits that clean living and a strong work ethic bring to the boardroom. Political scientist James Q. Wilson (1993: 102) notes that "there are business executives who prefer Mormons as employees because they believe that Mormons are more honest." The representation of Mormons as leaders in business and on Wall Street led *Businessweek* magazine to refer to the Mormon mission (the two years Mormon men are required to serve proselytizing, often in a foreign country) as "God's MBA" (Winter 2011).

Perhaps the figure who best represented traditional LDS beliefs in business was Stephen R. Covey. He was able to connect LDS and American values by translating his religious ethic into a system of tools for effective leadership. His *Seven Habits of Highly Effective People* has sold over fifteen million copies worldwide since it was first published in 1989, and Covey readily admits that Mormonism is central to his seemingly secular work. Seven years before *Seven Habits* hit the shelves, he wrote *The Divine Center*, a religious book for an LDS audience, in which he encouraged others of his faith to "testify of gospel principles" using vocabularies that would resonate with the "experience and frame of mind" of non-Mormons (Covey 2005: 240). In this manner, Covey's Mormonism was translated into business terms and was readily accepted by an eager public.

He was able to do this by presenting a softer version of capitalism that rested on balance, not excess. Rejecting the strains of casino and predatory capitalism that were the rage of the 1980s economic boom, Covey called for business leaders to be less competitive and more harmonious. According to him, competitive and aggressive business cultures not only eroded character, but created climates that estranged employees from each other and their beliefs. His call for synergy and balance created an indelible mark in the business community. Purpose informed by habits provided the means to achieve a meaningful life. Profits were partially a by-product of achieving a balanced life. Covey was able to mix together church and business in a way that was seamless and attractive.

This is the formula that helped launch Mitt Romney's business success. He was well educated, successful in his business pursuits, an accomplished public servant, and a devoted spouse and family man. Like Donny and Marie—champions of American popular culture for an earlier generation—Romney was a clean-living, tradition-saving, Book of Mormon-toting representation of his faith. Unfortunately for him, the circumstance surrounding his media attention was different, and voting Americans indicated that while certain attributes may be entertaining in one arena, they are not necessarily desirable in others. Also working against Romney were the changing tides of popular culture, which portrayed twentieth-century Mormon values as backward and regressive in an increasingly progressive society (see Grossman 2012).

In 2012, Romney's attempt to define himself primarily as a business leader was successful; he became the first Mormon to win the presidential nomination from one of the major American political parties. Building Bain Capital and saving the 2002 Salt Lake Winter Olympics apparently had given him credibility. In particular, the financial rescue of the Winter Olympics gave him the reputation of being willing and able to use his managerial expertise for the common good (Johnson 2007). In a way, Romney represented the ideals of Covey's multifaceted business leader operating on the principles of character. As a result, these managerial skills informed by a service orientation made him an attractive candidate to help correct the country's economic downturn.

Yet, Romney had a hard time disclosing his identity completely, especially as it related to his Mormonism. Republican leaders, who worried that anti-Mormon views were prevalent among the public—and especially among Evangelical Christians, who form a sizable part of the party's base—worked to dispel the religious stigma. In an address before the Republican National Convention in Tampa, for example, former Arkansas Governor and Baptist minister Mike Huckabee declared that he cared "far less" about where Romney went to church than about where he would take the country; and Paul Ryan, the Republican vice-president nominee and Catholic, noted that he and Romney went to "different churches" yet shared the "same moral creed" (Davis 2012).

On the night Romney accepted his party's nomination, there were several heartfelt testimonials from his friends, who spoke directly about the candidate's religious faith and how it formed his moral views. Fellow Mormons Ted and Pat Oparowski and Pam Finlayson spoke of Romney's help and kindness to their families as they dealt with tragedy. Serving time as a bishop and later as a stake president of the LDS Church, Romney oversaw several congregations in a district similar to a Catholic diocese, counseling LDS members on their most personal concerns (such as marriage, parenting, and faith), and working with immigrant converts from other countries. Grant Bennett, a congregational assistant to Romney, told Republican delegates that Romney had "a listening ear and a helping hand," devoting as many as 20 hours a week as stake president (Zoll 2012).

In his acceptance speech, Romney, however, was more cautious about his faith. He recalled growing up as one of the few Mormons in his Michigan town but portrayed it as any other type of mainstream Christian faith: "We were Mormons and growing up in Michigan; that might seem unusual or out of place but I don't remember it that way. My friends cared more about what sports team we followed than what church we went to." Romney also referred to his faith when his family moved to Massachusetts: "We had remarkably vibrant and diverse congregants from all walks of life and many who were new to America. We prayed together, our kids played together and we always stood ready to help each other out in different ways" (Romney 2012).

Although Romney never distanced himself from his faith, he also never fully utilized it in a way that could add to his campaign. Instead, he focused on how his business expertise and experience qualified him to be the next president, reinforcing the stereotype of a staunch, white-collar fiscal conservative, leading to a series of problems beginning during the Republican primaries and hitting full stride during the general presidential campaign. Specifically, Romney's opponents were able to characterize him not only as aloof and distant from the people, but also as a representative of the Wall Street breed of vulture capitalists. The accusation of taking advantage of people by destroying small towns through firing people or outsourcing their jobs was an image that was tough to shake. Though many of these qualities are the result of Romney's own fiscally conservative Republicanism and personality quirks, his position as a public Mormon figure resulted in negative associations with the faith as tired, white, and aging (Prince 2012).

Romney did not help his own presentation with a series of gaffes. Most notably, he was caught on video explaining his belief that there were "47% of the people ... who believe that they are victims, who believe the government has a responsibility to care for them, who believe that they are entitled to health care, to food, to housing, to you-name-it" (Korte 2012). This message confirmed the predatory capitalist image, one that Romney was unable adequately to counter. He struggled to keep his public image from being considered one-dimensional, old-fashioned, and un-hip. In this instance, however, the clean-cut Donny and Marie image was a negative rather than a positive marker in a culture that was already open to accepting a new, more dynamic vision of Mormonism.

An evolving image

Thanks to the unprecedented contribution and recognition of members of the LDS faith to the core of contemporary popular culture, the definition of Mormonism has expanded into what appears to be a much more inclusive culture (see also Mauss 1994). The traditional representation is not necessarily out of sync, but is now informed and complemented by a newly popularized, broader image of the faith. Ironically, however, this culture appears to be increasingly at odds with the values of Donny and Marie. While Mormons in the media today continue to hold on to some aspect of the clean-cut visage molded over the last several decades, they embody a reality that includes the hip, the unkempt, the controversial, and the contemporary, as well as the traditional. These new images have emerged from "reality" TV, books, movies, TV shows, and a Broadway play.

"Reality" TV and real Mormons

Because Mormons have had the reputation of being innocents who are unversed in the ways of the world, they make for an appealing foil in "reality" TV. All the more appealing is the chance to see individuals break out from the mold and demonstrate a spark of personality—especially when that spark comes into conflict with values traditionally associated with Mormonism. "Reality" shows like *American Idol*, *The Real World* (MTV, 1992–present), *Survivor* (CBS, 2000–present), *America's Next Top Model* (CW, 2003–present), *The Bachelorette* (ABC, 2003–present), *America's Biggest Loser* (NBC, 2004–present), *The Rebel Billionaire* (FOX, 2004–5), *Dancing with the Stars* (ABC, 2005–present), *So You Think You Can Dance* (FOX, 2005–present), and others, permit members of the LDS Church not only to represent themselves, but also to shape new, contemporary, and nuanced visions of their faith, enabling the American public to see Mormons as they really are: some good, some bad, some indifferent, and perhaps, in the end, not quite so different from everyone else.

One of the first Mormons to make a name for herself in "reality" television was Julie Stoffer, who appeared on MTV's *The Real World* in 2000. At the time, Stoffer was a student at BYU, a private school owned by the LDS Church that requires its students to abide by a strict honor code. Growing up, Stoffer had not been allowed to watch MTV at home, but she caught episodes of *The Real World* at a friend's house, and she saw her audition as an opportunity to experience something new and different. The show's producers were interested in her strict religious background and the drama it might create on screen were she to represent the traditional wholesome image associated with those of her faith (Larsen 2000). Although Stoffer did not engage in specifically immoral behavior on the show, the fact that she was rooming with men (participants on *The Real World* live together under one roof) was a breach of her BYU honor code contract. After the show aired, she was suspended from the school; she never appealed the decision.

Like Stoffer, other members of the LDS Church appearing on "reality" TV have capitalized on the appeal of their clean-cut images, even (perhaps especially) when the show encourages them to reach beyond the morality in which they were raised. Aimee, a contestant on *America's Next Top Model*, made a point of telling the judges early on that she was an "ex-Mormon"; she believed that modeling went against her previous faith (and her mother's wishes) because she would have to wear "risqué clothing." Jef Holm, winner of the eighth season of *The Bachelorette*, was "raised Mormon" in a family whose members were still devout in the faith (Carbone 2012). During the show, he displayed a unique appeal—he upheld a wholesome image while also appearing modern and up to date. Although the LDS Church encourages Mormons to marry within the faith, Holm became engaged to *Bachelorette* Emily Maynard (the engagement ended in 2011). Todd Herzog, winner of the fifteenth season of *Survivor*, was an openly gay Mormon who also appeared up to date and able to relate to his surroundings. Although he played the game in a manipulative and cunning fashion, he was able nonetheless to make key connections that earned him the title of sole survivor. By contrast, Dawn Meehan, who was in the twenty-third season, struggled to make connections with younger contestants. Despite this (and a resulting emotional breakdown), the BYU English professor became a maternal figure to the group, adapting and adjusting to her context. Her game was more subtle but less strategic than Herzog's, and eventually she was voted out.[4]

A broad range of personalities emerges from the Mormon "reality" star contestants, and there is no singular depiction that can capture the nuance that exists within the Mormon community. Some Mormons have been traditional while others have been less so. It is the same with other Mormon public figures, who today more than ever are speaking freely and esoterically about their faith. Joanna Brooks, for example, presents a liberal progressive strain in Mormon thought by picking up on the themes of yearning and change in her book *The Book of Mormon Girl* (2012). As she describes her LDS life experiences, Brooks embraces the heritage of Mormonism reflected in the values of community and charity. While being positive about the service culture of Mormonism, she challenges the beliefs of her church, namely its position on women and homosexual issues. By taking this route, her work is one of clear "unorthodoxy." In recognizing this, Brooks declares that she is "not an enemy" (2012: 160). She just opposes the doctrine, but supports the traditions and people that flow from it. She does not shy away from this depiction, but celebrates it.

In contrast, Glenn Beck fuses together entertainment and enlightenment to present his particular conservative outlook. Although Beck is a political personality and does not attempt to be a spokesperson for a strain of Mormon thought like Brooks, he does embody aspects of traditional Mormon beliefs and culture with a contemporary twist. His presentation style is irreverent, emotional, and engaging. Like a good Mormon, he is not timid to express his feelings or weep openly in front of an audience when he is passionate about something. He also pushes "outlier" topics such as emergency preparedness in case of societal breakdown—a topic that also carries a strong influence from one strain of LDS teachings. Beck is not afraid to gin up controversy; his bombastic style, tone, and willingness to push issues partially led to his ouster at *Fox News* (Beck 2009). Despite these antics and personal causes, he advocates a libertarian message that not only resonates with a broad swath of the American public, but has its roots in one current of Mormon thought.[5]

Vampires, polygamy, and a musical: Oh, my!

Perhaps the most popular contemporary representations of Mormons in the media are those with which the LDS Church would rather not be associated.[6] Edgy movies about teen lust and angst, the modern-day practice of polygamy (which the LDS Church gave up over 120 years ago), and a lewd and crude Broadway musical have done much to keep the faith in the public eye. For her own part, Stephenie Meyer, the author of the *Twilight* series, has projected a mixture of the conventional and the new with her characters. She has not discarded the wholesome image of Donny and Marie, but has revamped and packaged it in a way that is alluring and modern. The ability to encapsulate this tension between traditional values and of-the-moment culture is partially a reason why the *Twilight* series has become a global phenomenon in print and on screen. In crafting her universe, which is filled with vampires and werewolves, Meyer draws on her beliefs to add depth to her story. According to one writer, this is the "key to understanding her singular talent" (Grossman 2008). She does this by capturing particular Mormon sentiments that are grounded in its historical and religious ethos. The Cullens, the immortal vampire family that serve as the primary characters in the series, exist on the fringe of civilization, always looking from the outside with an understanding that they will never be a part of normal society. Even with their marginal status, they are not traditional vampires marked by debauchery; rather, they are immortal creatures who chiefly celebrate and strive to live a life of self-control. They have renounced their natural proclivities, or in LDS terminology they have rejected the "natural man." This requires them to live in a paradoxical state; they must be in the world, but not of it.

Meyer explores the characters' ability to adhere to this standard when the vampire Edward Cullen falls in love with a human. Instead of being repulsed, Bella Swan, the chief protagonist of the story, desires to be a vampire so she can be immortal to experience eternal love. In capturing this young love, Meyer is able to draw on the "erotics of abstinence." The yearning of sex, love, and sacrifice become driving themes that pull the characters apart and together. Young love must be constrained and channeled in the proper way. The arc of this narrative fits into the broader theology of LDS beliefs of eternal marriage and its conception of the good life. Love grounded in self-discipline, sacrifice, and service represents the embodiment of what it means to live up to a human and heavenly potential. These underlying themes coupled with a feeling of alienation have drawn millions of readers and viewers.

Similarly, Glen A. Larson, the creator of *Battlestar Galactica* (ABC, 1978–79), embedded LDS beliefs in his series, drawing on different theological aspects to develop the main narrative. Most notably, the threat of extermination after a devastating attack pushed survivors to let go of their homeland and to search for a lost land/tribe/planet. Themes of search and discovery amid the backdrop of forced estrangement allowed the creator to explore issues of what it means to belong while fighting for survival. In addition, Larson also used details of Mormon practices and beliefs—such as the governing structure of the church and eternal marriage—to fill in minor details of his universe, providing the show with greater depth, nuance, and character (Trepanier and Newswander 2012).

The updated version (Syfy, 2003–10) continued to draw on these same themes. However, it overlaid them with a darker reality reflected by a post-9/11 world. Subjects related to searching for a new identity after a devastating attack—what it means to live where war appears to have no end, the difference between terrorism and resistance, the tension between military and civilian relations, and whether one has to become like the enemy in order to ensure victory—posed questions similar to those being raised by the very real "war on terror." In addressing these contemporary topics, Larson's overall vision remained intact, even though the issues surrounding how to find a new home became more complex and difficult to answer. Like Meyer, Larson's theme of alienation, hope, and discovery were partly rooted in an LDS worldview.

It is not only Mormons who have shaped this evolving image of their faith—significant contributions have come from those on the outside, as well. On the one hand, HBO's fictional Henrickson family might not have appeared too different from the Osmonds: a slew of children, a peaceful Utah setting, and happy parents. But *Big Love* (2006–11) was no *Brady Bunch*. Its central family was polygamist, members of an offshoot of the LDS Church who held on to certain doctrines and beliefs that the mainstream LDS Church no longer practices. Still, the family is described as Mormon, and the LDS Church received much critical attention during the height of the show's popularity. Reacting to some of the themes depicted in the show, and the outcry of many of its own membership, the LDS Church released an official statement:

> The Church has long been concerned about the continued illegal practice of polygamy in some communities, and, in particular about persistent reports of emotional and physical child and wife abuse emanating from them. It will be regrettable if this program, by making polygamy the subject of entertainment, minimizes the seriousness of the problem ... placing the series in Salt Lake City, the international headquarters of The Church of Jesus Christ of Latter-day Saints, is enough to blur the line between the modern Church and the program's subject matter, and to reinforce old and long-outdated stereotypes. ... *Big Love*, like so much other television programming, is essentially lazy and indulgent entertainment that does nothing for our society and will never nourish great minds.
>
> (The Church of Jesus Christ of Latter-day Saints 2006)

Responding to this statement, HBO Entertainment president Carolyn Strauss said, "It is interesting how many people are ignorant about the Mormon Church and think that it [the LDS Church] actually does condone polygamy. So in an odd way, the show is sort of beneficial in drawing that distinction" (Wilson 2006). It is a distinction the Church desired to have clearly made—it wanted no association with or publicity related to the project.

Although HBO emphasized the distinction between the Mormons portrayed on the show and members of the LDS Church, it appropriated the theme of the struggles of whether an outside group or belief can be accepted by the in-group. During its last season, the show pushed two similar themes: the redefinition of marriage and the redefinition of who can hold the priesthood. Both of these themes center on Bill Henrickson, husband to three wives. On one front, he champions the cause to normalize polygamous relations by using his elected office as a state senator to introduce a bill that would make polygamy legal. Although fellow polygamists are wary of his attempts to shed light on this practice, his belief—which would be verified by a personal revelation—mobilizes his followers to embrace the challenge of redefinition. On the other front, he actively resists one of his wives' attempts at receiving the priesthood, which traditionally in the LDS Church (and fundamentalist Mormon sects) has been given only to males. Because Bill sees this as a violation of God's law, he is willing to lose his wife in order to uphold his belief. Yet, in his dying moments after being shot by an enraged neighbor, Bill asks one of his wives to exercise her priesthood and give him a blessing. The show concludes suggesting that the source of change and progress is not found in the mainstream, but on the fringe. The final moments of the show also raise questions about the future trajectory of Mormonism—if the group is willing to make certain changes (discontinuing the practice of polygamy, or allowing black men to hold the priesthood), what is to stop it from embracing gay marriage or female clergy?

Similar to *Big Love*, The Learning Channel's *Sister Wives* (2010–present) also promotes the theme of acceptance and normalization of unconventional practices. The family life of Kody Brown, his four wives, and 17 children shows that they not only live in the midst of the broader population, but that they are also like them to a very large extent. Brown and his family are members of a fundamentalist sect, the Apostolic United Brethren, which separated itself from mainstream Mormonism in the late nineteenth century. Still, the correlation in the public mind between mainstream Mormonism and polygamy remains near the surface. The Brown family has received a warm reception from its television audience, but not from state officials in Utah, who investigated the family on charges of bigamy, causing the family to leave the state and relocate to Nevada. Kody and his wives were interviewed by Oprah Winfrey just after the show premiered in 2010, where they described themselves as an average American family with common values (Oprah.com 2010).

Like *Big Love* and *Sister Wives*, another recent media portrayal of Mormons is not "Mormon" at all: *The Book of Mormon* musical (2012), which has enjoyed critical and popular success on Broadway, is actually the creation of *South Park* writers Trey Parker and Matt Stone, with Robert Lopez (who co-wrote *Avenue Q*), none of whom are members of the LDS Church. The play's main characters are two LDS missionaries in Uganda—Elders Price and Cunningham—who are youthful and naïve in their own separate ways. The task of preaching the word of God in a war-torn, poverty-filled, AIDS-stricken village governed by a ruthless warlord saps them of any faith or hope. Price momentarily quits after having his aspirations dashed, while Cunningham stays and adapts his message to make it more palatable to the villagers. This message, one based on fantasy, science fiction, and Mormon theology, is what captures and converts the villagers. Realizing that doctrinal religious commitments are of limited use, the two missionaries embrace the notion that religious stories and metaphors are what truly serve people. In the play, zealous commitments to a set of codified doctrines that are claimed to be manifestly true are what not only marginalize people of faith like Mormons, but also prevent them from fulfilling their mission of service. Soft commitments to a set of stories that are claimed to be helpful are a way to be accepted and achieve a transcendent purpose.

The new face of Mormonism

Interestingly, *The Book of Mormon* musical—separate as it is from the official faith and doctrine of the LDS—elicited a much different reaction from the Church than *Big Love* did only a few years prior. While the latter inspired a strong media statement refuting the show and emphasizing the Church's stance, the former has been met with a very different attitude. *The Book of Mormon* musical was popular from its early press, and speaking against it would reinforce the twentieth-century image of the LDS Church as stodgy, old-fashioned, and distanced from the times. And so the Public Affairs bureau of the LDS Church went about things in an unprecedented and unexpected way: they capitalized on the fame and launched a large campaign in New York City's Times Square. Billboards, subway ads, and ads on top of taxi cabs all shared images of a new Mormonism—one represented by regular people doing regular things. For example, one ad showed an Asian woman riding a surfboard with the tagline "I am a Mormon" (Kaleem 2011). The result has been an increase in missionary contacts and traffic to the Church's official Web site. As Peggy Fletcher Stack (2011) of the *Salt Lake Tribune* put it: "there's no business like show business—to boost a religion."

Branding Mormonism

This effort is part of a larger campaign to "brand" Mormonism. As Church spokesman Michael Purdy explains: "There's a national conversation going on about Mormonism and we want to be a part of it" (Kaleem 2011). Part of this conversation is getting the message out that the Church is not the stiff, immovable bureaucracy it once was. In so doing, it does not actively distance itself from uncharacteristic portrayals of its faith as it had previously. *The Book of Mormon* musical is not the only example of this shift in behavior, which has also been manifest in other areas. For example, although *Real World* participant Julie Stoffer was kicked out of BYU for sharing living quarters with men, more recent *Survivor* favorite Dawn Meehan was not. In fact, she returned for another season, all while maintaining her status at the university. BYU's more forgiving attitude toward honor code violations by students and faculty in the public eye is indicative of a broader trend of rebranding the faith as one welcoming to members from a variety of backgrounds and perspectives, none of whom are perfect.

The LDS Church itself understands the implications of outside forces defining what it means to be Mormon. It has also grappled with internal issues that raise similar questions regarding the shifting Mormon identity. As the LDS Church continues to grow, it is no longer confined to the Mountain West, but has become a global presence (see Bushman 2008; Ostling and Ostling 2007; Bushman and Bushman 2001). Today, more Mormons live outside the United States than in it. The growing religion can no longer simply be identified by a pioneer stock that was expelled from the borders of the United States in the nineteenth century. As a result of these external and internal forces of change, the Church hired two large advertising agencies to find out what Americans thought of Mormons. Through focus groups, the answers were clear and not very flattering: "secretive," "cultish," "sexist," "controlling," "pushy," and "anti-gay" were among the common perceptions (Goodstein 2011).[7]

Brandon Burton, president and general manager of Bonneville Communications (an advertising agency owned by the Church), explains that this revelation required a quick and decisive change of pace in the Church's public relations campaign (Goodstein 2011). In late 2011, it unveiled its plan to affirmatively present its visions of what it means to be Mormon, and also to counter negative images and stereotypes. Previous advertisements had explained LDS doctrine with the intent to persuade viewers that Mormons are, in fact, Christian, and ended with an invitation to call a toll-free number and order a copy of the Book of Mormon or the Bible. Though there was some success through these efforts, they still had not dispelled some of the negative imagery of the Mormon people as a whole.

Consequently, Burton and his team took a very different approach. Rather than highlighting the Church's central focus on the traditional family and middle-class American values, the new "I am a Mormon" campaign portrays a vibrant faith with a varied, multicultural membership. To alleviate some of the more negative consequences associated with perceived differences, the campaign highlighted real members of the faith—from world champion surfers to stay-at-home moms—with the message that stereotypical perceptions of Mormons as insular, fundamentalist, or otherwise outside of the norm were far from the truth. The driving theme of the campaign was that members of the Church are diverse and different, but are united by a common belief in certain articles of faith. The practice of the faith as outlined by LDS Church standards provides a common backdrop that defines the faith and allows members to express their individuality and celebrate their own cultural heritage.

The campaign has been touted as "very savvy branding" by others in the advertising business (Riparbelli 2011). "Previous campaigns focused on what we believe, and we also want people to know who we are because of what we believe," said Purdy. "This is one way to get to know us" (Riparbelli 2011). The message that comes across, according to Kathleen Flake, a religion scholar from Vanderbilt Divinity School, is "We're like you" (Marrapodi 2011). In other words, Mormons are the people next door—black, white, Hispanic, single parents, large families, loud and quiet. Over a century after Brigham Young gloried in the peculiarity of his people, the message being sent from the LDS Church today is that they aren't so different, after all.

It may seem an odd approach for a church to have a public relations department as active and expensive as the Mormons' (estimates are that the "I am a Mormon" campaign alone has cost over $6 million; see Goodstein 2011). In addition to handling its own image on a corporate level, Church members serve as public affairs representatives on a local level in communities around the world. The mission of public affairs is just as important to the community as any other duty expected of Mormon members. Specifically, they are expected to "establish key relationships" with opinion leaders, or "those who can affect the public reputation of the Church or who can help or hinder the Church in the achievement of its mission" (The Church of Jesus Christ of Latter-day Saints n.d.). The goal is not proselytizing or converting, but building relationships; in other words, creating and maintaining control over an image that will foster better understanding between the LDS Church and the communities wherein its adherents reside.

Experience has proven that the public image of the LDS Church is inextricably tied to its continued growth and success with would-be converts (see Arrington and Bitton 1979). Instructions given to those involved in local public affairs remind individuals of the importance of perception:

> Above all, you will be helping influential people who are not of our faith to recognize The Church of Jesus Christ of Latter-day Saints as a positive influence in the world and its members as sincere and diligent disciples of the Lord Jesus Christ.
>
> (The Church of Jesus Christ of Latter-day Saints n.d.)

The LDS Church as an organization, with the help of millions of members around the world who are happy to declare "I am a Mormon," continues to work to build a reputation through media, personal relationships, and whatever means available.

Conclusion

The change in the public perception of Mormons, driven by both Mormons and non-Mormons alike, is reflective of the change in American society over the past 50 years: from traditional, staid, and white to pluralistic, dynamic, and multi-ethnic (see Mauss 2003). Whether in entertainment, politics, business, or even in the LDS Church's promotion of itself, the perception of Mormons has evolved along the same pattern as Americans' perception of themselves as a more culturally diverse society. This transformation in the public's perception of Mormons therefore should not be surprising, as Mormons have become more integrated and accepted into mainstream American society and culture.

As American society first started to recognize in popular culture its cultural diversity in the late 1960s, Mormons were portrayed as representing traditional, wholesome, and all-American white values, such as shown by the Osmonds. Likewise in business with Stephen Covey and in politics with Mitt Romney, the public perception of Mormons recalls a time of American prosperity, decency, and dominance of the world. However, this portrayal of Mormons as representative of these values is ironic for two reasons. First, the public perception of Mormons as representing these traditional values came at a time when these very values were being displaced by new ones of diversity, pluralism, and secularism. As American society became more conscious of its ethnic and religious diversity, the Osmonds stepped onto center stage in American music and TV; as American businesses began to lose their global dominance, Stephen Covey's *Effective Habits* shot to the top of the best-selling business book list; and as the Republican Party currently is faced with the challenge of changing electoral demographics, Mitt Romney became their nominee. In each of these cases, Mormons entered and were accepted by mainstream American society as they represented a set of values that were fading in influence and power.

But perhaps even more ironic is that Mormons have, from time to time, served as the public persona for traditional America—a group that previously has been marginalized, persecuted, and perceived as representing quintessentially anti-American values. With a history of exile from upstate New York to the Midwest and eventually to Salt Lake City, Mormons have faced discrimination, oppression, and even the murder of their founder, Joseph Smith, in Carthage, Illinois, at the hands of the American public. From their military confrontation with the US federal government in 1857 to the many rejected applications for statehood (first as Deseret, then as Utah), Mormons traditionally have been viewed with suspicion, if not downright hostility, by Americans. The irony of American culture and society in the past 50 years is that Mormons have often been used to represent these traditional values, a set of values that initially marginalized and persecuted them (see Trepanier and Newswander 2012).

But more recently Mormons also have contributed to the more culturally diverse conversation about American culture. Whether in "reality" TV shows like *Survivor* or musicals such as *The Book of Mormon*, Mormons are depicted as having a diverse set of values reflective of American society itself: some are conservative like Glenn Beck; some are progressive like Joanna Brooks; and others are a combination of both. Perhaps the most telling of this changing perception of Mormons in popular culture is the LDS Church's "I am a Mormon" campaign to show to the American public that its religion is varied, multicultural, and inclusive. Mormons are not a homogenous set of strangers living in the Intermountain West, but one's neighbor, co-worker, and friend.

As American society recognizes and respects more its cultural diversity, Mormons are no longer stigmatized and are allowed to participate in the public conversation about the nature and direction of mainstream American culture. But as Mormons began to participate in this conversation, the American public discovered that Mormons themselves are as diverse as American society, with its own cultural diversity and individuality celebrated before a backdrop of common religious beliefs. No longer just seen as a proxy for traditional American values, Mormons are starting to be viewed as being as diverse as America itself. As American society continues to change, Mormons likewise will, too, being both reflective and contributing to this new understanding of what it means to be an American—and a Mormon—today and in the future.

Notes

1 Mormons are those who subscribe to the Book of Mormon, while LDS refers more specifically to those Mormons who subscribe to the authority of the Church of the Latter-day Saints in Salt Lake City.

2 In the interview, Michael Jackson suggests that Osmond change his name because it is considered too wholesome.

3 Rasmusen later appeared on *Fear Factor* (NBC, 2001–12) and wrote a book, *Staying in Tune* (2007), which details the choices she's made to keep her time in the media spotlight consistent with her religious and personal values.

4 Other Mormon "reality" TV stars embody more traditional values. For example, *Survivor* participant Neleh Dennis brought the Bible and Book of Mormon as her luxury items, and Ashlee Ashby talked about waking up at five a.m. every weekday morning as a teenager to study doctrine as part of the LDS church-wide seminary program. For more about these participants, see the *Survivor* Web site (www.cbs.com/primetime/survivor/).

5 As some see it, Beck's unique style—and consequently his success—come from his affiliation with the LDS Church. For example, many of Beck's core political values, such as an almost worshipful admiration of the American Founders and the Constitution, are deeply seated in LDS theology and did not appear in Beck's public persona until after his conversion in 1999. Furthermore, some argue that Beck's politics are inspired by the prominent Mormon (and staunchly conservative anticommunist) Cleon Skousen, who Beck cites in *The Real America* (2003) and whose work he has promoted on his radio program.

6 For example, despite all of its success, Mormon Stephenie Meyer's *Twilight* books are not available through Church-owned Deseret Book. In 2009, the bookseller cited "mixed review[s]" as a reason for discontinuing sales of the series. Though the books are still available by special order, the message is startlingly clear: even though Meyer is a Mormon and a BYU graduate, and the novels are bestsellers, the appropriateness of their content is not unquestionable (see Thomas 2010).

7 Church public relations efforts began in the 1970s when the two terms most commonly associated with Mormonism were "polygamy" and "racist." The result was the famous "Family: It's all about time" catchphrase (see Boorstein 2011).

Works cited

Arrington, L.J. and D. Bitton (1979) *The Mormon Experience: A History of the Latter-day Saints*, New York: Knopf.

BBC News (2004) "Donny Osmond" (December 6). Online. Available: http://news.bbc.co.uk/2/hi/programmes/hardtalk/4054629.stm (accessed 8 April 2013).

Beck, G. (2003) *The Real America: Messages from the Heart and Heartland*, New York: Simon and Schuster, Inc.

——(2009) "Glenn Beck story pulled because of his Mormon faith," *Glenn Beck* (January 4). Online. Available: www.glennbeck.com/content/articles/article/200/19594/ (accessed 23 September 2012).

Bloom, H. (2006) *The American Religion*, New York: Chu Hartley Press.

Boorstein, M. (2011) "Mormons, winning the Web," *Washington Post* (August 18): C01.

Bowman, M. (2012) *The Mormon People: The Making of an American Faith*, New York: Random House.

Brooks, J. (2012) *The Book of Mormon Girl: A Memoir of an American Faith*, New York: Free Press.

Burgess, S. (1999) "Donny Osmond: we suffer for his art," Salon.com (September 21). Online. Available: www.salon.com/people/feature/1999/09/21/osmond/index.html (accessed 5 April 2013).

Bushman, C.L. (2008) *Contemporary Mormonism: Latter-day Saints in Modern America*, Westport, CT: Praeger.

Bushman, C.L. and R.L. Bushman (2001) *Building the Kingdom: A History of Mormons in America*, New York: Oxford University Press.

Carbone, G. (2012) "The Bachelorette's Jef Holm on whether or not he's Mormon and how faith fits into his life," WetPaint.com (July 23). Online. Available: www.wetpaint.com/the-bachelorette/articles/the-bachelorettes-jef-holm-on-whether-or-not-hes-mormon-and-how-faith-fits-into-his-life (accessed 8 April 2013).

The Church of Jesus Christ of Latter-day Saints (2006) "Church responds to questions on TV series," The Church of Jesus Christ of Latter-day Saints: Newsroom (March 6). Online. Available: http://newsroom.lds.org/ldsnewsroom/eng/commentary/church-responds-to-questions-on-hbo-s-big-love (accessed 23 September 2012).

——(n.d.) "Getting started," The Church of Jesus Christ of Latter-day Saints: Public Affairs Training. Online. Available: http://publicaffairs.lds.org/eng/getting-started (accessed 4 March 2013).

Covey, S.R. (2005) The Divine Center, Salt Lake City, UT: Deseret Book.

Davis, J.H. (2012) "Romney speaks of Mormon faith to try to dispel prejudice," Bloomberg News (August 30). Online. Available: www.businessweek.com/news/2012-08-30/romney-speaks-of-mormon-faith-to-try-to-dispel-prejudice (accessed 23 September 2012).

Durant, K. (2011) "Jimmer Fredette is the best scorer in the world!!" Twitter.com (January 26). Online. Available: https://twitter.com/KDTrey5/status/30490973544910850 (accessed 2 May 2013).

Givens, T.L. (2007) People of Paradox: A History of Mormon Culture, New York: Oxford University Press.

Goodstein, L. (2011) "Mormons' ad campaign may play out on the '12 campaign trail," New York Times (November 18): A01.

Grossman, C.L. (2012) "Few informed, many wary of Mormon beliefs," USA Today (January 25): 1A.

Grossman, L. (2008) "Stephenie Meyer: a new J.K. Rowling?" Time (April 24). Online. Available: www.time.com/time/magazine/article/0,9171,1734838,00.html#ixzz0gT11bdmP (accessed 23 April 2013).

Johnson, K. (2007) "In Olympics success, Romney found new edge," New York Times (September 19): A1.

Kaleem, J. (2011) "Hundreds of Mormon ads launched in New York City," Huffington Post (June 22). Online. Available: www.huffingtonpost.com/2011/06/22/mormon-ads-new-york_n_881834.html (accessed 5 April 2013).

Kirn, W. (2011) "Mormons Rock!" Newsweek (June 13/20): 38–45.

Korte, G. (2012) "Romney: Obama voters 'believe they are victims,'" USA Today (September 17). Online. Available: http://usatoday30.usatoday.com/news/politics/story/2012/09/17/romneys-47-remark/57797246/1 (accessed 8 April 2013).

Larsen, K. (2000) "Stoffer, parents criticize BYU following suspension," MormonsToday.com (July 31). Online. Available: www.mormonstoday.com/000730/P2Stoffer01.shtml (accessed 24 April 2013).

Marrapodi, E. (2011) "With 'I'm a Mormon' campaign, Church counters lily-white image," CNN Belief Blog (November 2). Online. Available: http://religion.blogs.cnn.com/2011/11/02/with-im-a-mormon-campaign-church-counters-lily-white-image/ (accessed 8 April 2013).

Mauss, A. (1994) The Angel and the Beehive: The Mormon Struggle with Assimilation, Urbana, IL: University of Illinois Press.

——(2003) All Abraham's Children: Changing Mormon Conceptions of Race and Lineage, Urbana, IL: University of Illinois Press.

Oprah.com (2010) "Inside the lives of a polygamist family" (October 14). Online. Available: www.oprah.com/oprahshow/Inside-the-Lives-of-a-Polygamist-Family/1 (accessed 8 April 2013).

Ostling, R. and J.K. Ostling (2007) Mormon America: The Power and the Promise, New York: Harper Collins.

Prince, G.A. (2012) "Mitt Romney is *not* the face of Mormonism," *Huffington Post* (September 19). Online. Available: www.huffingtonpost.com/gregory-a-prince-phd/mitt-romney-is-not-the-face-of-mormonism_b_1897404.html (accessed 2 May 2013).

Quinn, D.M. (1984) *The Mormon Hierarchy: Origins of Power*, Salt Lake City, UT: Signature Books.

Rasmusen, C. (2007) *Staying in Tune: From American Idol to Nashville, How the Young Women Values Have Helped Me Remain True to the Gospel*, Provo, UT: Spring Creek Book Co.

Remini, R. (2002) *Joseph Smith*, New York: Penguin Press.

Riparbelli, L. (2011) "Mormon NYC campaign 'savvy branding'," ABCNews.com (June 21). Online. Available: http://abcnews.go.com/Business/mormon-nyc-ad-campaign-savvy-branding/story?id=13888304 (accessed 8 April 2013).

Romney, M. (2012) "Transcript: Mitt Romney's acceptance speech," National Public Radio (August 30): Online. Available: www.npr.org/2012/08/30/160357612/transcript-mitt-romneys-acceptance-speech (accessed 23 September 2012).

Silvesan, C. (2008) "Brook White's performance on American Idol," *Yahoo Voices* (May 1). Online. Available: http://voices.yahoo.com/brooke-whites-performance-american-idol-4-29-2008-1424881.html?cat=33 (accessed 24 April 2013).

Slezak, M. (2008a) "Nine guys finish last," *Entertainment Weekly* (February 27). Online. Available: www.ew.com/ew/article/0,20180597,00.html (accessed 8 April 2013).

——(2008b) "American Idol: never mind the bollix," *Entertainment Weekly* (May 1). Online. Available: www.ew.com/ew/article/0,20196803,00.html (accessed 8 April 2013).

Stack, P.F. (2011) "Also playing on Broadway: new Mormon ad," *The Salt Lake Tribune* (June 20). Online. Available: www.sltrib.com/sltrib/news/52005719–78/church-mormon-lds-musical.html.csp (accessed 8 April 2013).

Thomas, E. (2010) "'Twilight' loses luster with Deseret Book," *Deseret News* (April 23). Online. Available: www.deseretnews.com/article/705299108/Twilight-loses-luster-with-Deseret-Book.html (accessed 1 April 2010).

Time (1976) "The keepers of the king," 108, 24 (December 13): 33.

Trepanier, L. and L.K. Newswander (2012) *LDS in USA: Mormonism and the Making of American Culture*, Waco, TX: Baylor University Press.

Whitburn, J. (2004) *Top R&B/Hip-Hop Singles: 1942–2004*, Menomonee Falls, WI: Record Research.

Wicks, R.S., and F.R. Foister (2005) *Junius and Joseph: Presidential Politics and the Assassination of the First Mormon Prophet*, Logan, UT: Utah State University Press.

Wilson, B. (2006) "LDS Church rejects polygamous accusations," *Deseret News* (February 28). Online. Available: www.deseretnews.com/article/1,5143,635188091,00.html (accessed 24 April 2013).

Wilson, J.Q. (1993) *The Moral Sense*, New York: Free Press.

Winter, C. (2011) "God's MBAs: Why Mormon Missions Produce Leaders," *Businessweek* (June 9). Online. Available: www.businessweek.com/magazine/content/11_25/b4233058977933.htm (accessed 8 April 2013).

Zoll, R. (2012) "Romney makes Mormonism part of his big night," *US News and World Report* (August 31). Online. Available: www.usnews.com/news/politics/articles/2012/08/31/romney-makes-mormonism-part-of-his-big-night (accessed 23 September 2012).

27
CONTEMPORARY PAGANISM

Jodie Ann Vann

Introduction: reconciling the popular and the alternative through the religious imagination

Any thorough understanding of the relationship between religion and popular culture must consider those varieties of expression that have traditionally been understood as "alternative." Contemporary Paganism and alternative religions offer a rich source of data that is simultaneously beneficial and problematic. They help us understand how religion functions in the context of the now, and yet they challenge almost every notion upon which popular definitions of religion rely. One of the biggest challenges is determining who can accurately be considered "Pagan" or "alternative." Some Pagans practice in communities with a designated leader; others are solitary. Some groups claim a particular creed; others are essentially eclectic. Many Pagans include a variety of gods and goddesses in their practice, while some may have only a few, and others, none at all. The definitions of these groups are highly flexible and their boundaries are highly permeable, making a strict categorical description not only impossible, but in direct conflict with the foundational elements of most of these groups. For the sake of clarity, we will include in Paganism those varieties of religion—including, but not limited to, Asatru, Druidism, Heathenism, New Age, Wicca, and other forms of "nature religions" or "spiritualities"—that view nature as inherently meaningful, and draw from ancient, usually indigenous forms of practice aimed at a comprehensive understanding of the cosmos.

We can examine the relationship between Contemporary Paganism (and related forms of alternative spiritualities) and popular culture using the concept of the religious imagination. Contemporary Paganism and other alternative religions rely upon a particular type of religious imagination that is grounded in postmodern thought.[1] This same imagination is present in the popular cultural universe (see du Gay et al. 1997) in the form of products of the fantasy genre. As we will see, alternative religion and fantasy are two related, somewhat parallel streams that rely upon a particular formulation of the religious imagination.

The religious imagination is the activity through which experience is filtered and made meaningful (Cady 2011). It provides the framework for interpreting reality, and for understanding the symbols, actions, myths, and signs in which and through which we live. It balances somewhere between reality and fantasy, between objective and subjective—it is the realm in which the "what should or could be" influences the conception and expression of "what is."

According to Mark C. Taylor (2009: 20) "the activity of the imagination ... has two sides: figuring, which is emergent (i.e., productive and creative), and refiguring, which is recombinant (i.e., reproductive and re-creative)." Using the very popular fantasy series *The Lord of the Rings* (1954–55) and *Harry Potter* (1989–2007) as examples of *refiguring* we can explore the ways in which Pagans have looked to these series as literary models, and have borrowed various elements from them in the creation of dynamic and inventive worldviews. By examining the television series *Charmed* (WB 1998–2006) and *Merlin* (BBC/Syfy, 2008–present) as products of a certain type of *figuring* of the imagination, we can begin to identify a particular understanding of religion in general, and of Paganism and alternative spiritualities more particularly. Lastly, we will investigate the role of the computer (and most especially the Internet) as a new mode of both production and consumption of meaningful elements. All of these products are vital in the formulation of alternative religious identities. Examining ways in which these fantasy elements are produced and consumed—and how they deal with the representation of Pagans and other groups—will help us flesh out the relationship between the popular and the alternative. Through all of these examples, we will see that the religious imagination is central.

The idea of the religious imagination is vital to our exploration of Paganism and alternative spiritualities. On the whole, Contemporary Paganisms and alternative spiritualities present categorical problems because they are not part of the scholarly "world religions" model (Masazawa 2005).[2] For the larger portion of the history of the academic study of religion (as a field separate from theological studies), a majority of scholarship has been centered around Buddhism, Christianity, Hinduism, Islam, Judaism, and other identifiable traditions. Any groups outside of this model, such as indigenous religions, have fallen under the purview of anthropology or cultural studies. In recent years, there have been serious efforts to transgress such distinctions between fields so that scholars have access to an entire arsenal of tools, the better with which to explore the dynamic and complex world of humans acting out their lives in cultural context.

Challenging these categorical distinctions is absolutely essential if we are to bring Paganism and alternative forms of religious expression into the broader conversation on what it means to be religious (that is, meaningfully human) in a postmodern world. Foundational to this relationship is the historical fact that Paganism and associated traditions have been found on the fringes of the mainstream. Alternativity relies on centrality; historically in the academic study of religion, the center has been made up of those traditions included in the "world religions" paradigm. We will examine how the relationship between the fantasy genre and so-called alternative religions challenges many of these assumptions about categories and boundaries. Contemporary Paganism and many products in the fantasy genre share traits, including the use of central archetypes and a particular type of religious imagination that allows for a dynamic creation and interpretation of reality (or realities).

This is neither a suggestion that reading fantasy literature will somehow lead people to witchcraft or Paganism, nor that Pagans understand created fantasy worlds to be depictions of reality in any wholesale manner. Instead, it is an investigation into how both Paganism and fantasy share in some foundational roots; they are, in some ways, parallel streams of thought that engage a certain type of imagination, rely on central archetypes, and share a dynamic understanding of the relationship between history, myth, and the construction of a meaningful reality. Understanding the ways in which the religious imagination is active in both the production and consumption of these products of the fantasy genre can help us better understand the postmodern religious imagination in general.

Following the example of Paul du Gay and his colleagues (1997: 11) in their seminal study of the Sony Walkman, we can explore Contemporary Paganism and alternative religions "as a clue to the study of modern culture in general ... the distinctive ways of making sense and doing things—which are the basis of our culture." By using visual media to explore how depictions indicate general, often implicit and subtle understandings of alternative groups, we can see that these so-called fringe groups have had an impact on popular culture in a very dynamic and complex way. Many ideas, practices, and beliefs that are born in the periphery are incorporated into the popular, while themes and trends in the general cultural universe occasionally become vehicles of meaning within alternative religious modalities. In order to accomplish this, we must focus on the ways in which the religious imagination plays an active part in the construction of interpretive structures of meaning.

Nonetheless, we must keep in mind that the environment in which Contemporary Pagans and related groups develop their religious identities is one already colored by popular cultural understandings of religion in general, and alternative religions more specifically. The ways in which alternatively spiritual people use, adopt, and borrow from various cultural sources with the express intention of constructing individualized religious identities is evidence of the progressive biography of universal religious pluralism. One of the foundational elements of many alternative religions is the assertion that all religions are valid, all religions have the potential for significance for practitioners, and religion can include meaningful elements from any source. As elements from the religious fringe become part of religion in general, this foundational tenet of Paganism has become the foundational tenet of progressive, postmodern religion as a whole.

This chapter is aimed at examining postmodern expressions of religion in a way that takes seriously the experience of practitioners of New Religious Movements and alternative forms of religious expression. An examination of modern Western religious history demonstrates that the ideas and practices that develop within the "alternative" spiritual sphere have had an impact on mainstream religion, and similarly that popular cultural elements can be explored through applying a certain understanding of the postmodern religious imagination (Bender 2010; McFarland Taylor 2007; Chidester 2005; Braude 1997). Like Courtney Bender (2010: 5), I, too, begin "with the view that spirituality, whatever it is and however it is defined, is *entangled* in social life, in history, and in our academic and nonacademic imaginations."

A brief history of alternative religions

Historically, times of social change are often characterized by expansions of religious freedom (see Bender 2010; Clifton 2006). Sometimes this has been met with an equally fervent backlash, such as was often the case in colonial and early American religious history. Witchcraft accusations, for example, were most often levied against those who were perceived to be a threat to the status quo, particularly those who had different ideas about the ways in which reality (that is, nature) worked.

Changes in cultural norms have historically been most immediately reflected in the religious practice on the fringes, where change and flexibility are accepted elements of practice.[3] By examining religion outside of the framework of the mainstream "world religions," scholars are better able to understand how popular cultural elements influence and are simultaneously influenced by religious expressions.[4] As American religious historian Sarah Pike (2004: 24) noted, in the nineteenth century "American occult religion became popular and blended with European imports like Mesmerism and Swedenborgianism to flourish in movements such as Transcendentalism, Spiritualism, the Theosophical Society, and New Thought, all of which influenced and are reflected in New Age and Neopagan religions." Practitioners of these movements put priority on the development of the self in relation to the world. The emphasis on re-enchanting the world through freedom of personal expression remains influential (see Pels 2010; Pike 2004; Partridge 2004; Morris 2000; Latour 1993). It was also common for religious expression outside of the mainstream (Protestant Christianity) to be quicker to respond to changing social norms. Notes Pike (2004: 51), "spiritualism fit the mood of the time with its democratic inclusiveness, the opportunities it offered women … ." Such is the historical relationship between the popular and the alternative; many of the elements that are born and develop on the fringes of culture foreshadow larger changes in popular conceptions.

The period after the Second World War saw a resurgence of interest in alternative religions, this time alongside the postmodern movement (see Foucault 1994; Latour 1993; Pels and Meyer 2003). World War II had fractured many people's sense of security and challenged modern reliance upon forward-thinking industrialization as the source of all that is good. In many ways the age of the atomic bomb led to the Age of Aquarius; if technology was so devastating, many people believed that a return to nature could heal the wrongs of the modern age. For some, this desire to reconnect with the earth manifested in attempts to reconnect with mythic history— one in which people's individual and collective religious identities were intimately tied to nature (see McFarland Taylor 2007; Clifton 2006). This was also a period of great creativity; technological advances in television, radio, and general industry provided swiftly moving and nearly pervasive vehicles for popular culture. The last 75 years of human history have provided perhaps the quickest shift in the modes of culture; in many parts of the world, televisions can be found in nearly every home, and most people have access to the Internet at almost every moment. This—coupled with a nostalgia for an idealized past—has allowed for a burgeoning of postmodern ideals, and for their quick and efficient dissemination.

Among nearly all forms of Contemporary Paganism, there is an emphasis on the use of archetypes. For many, this is most apparent in the formulation of divine personages. More feminist-leaning Wiccans use Diana as a central figure, calling upon centuries of layered meaning in the construction of this most powerful feminine deity. Druids use the legends and folklore of Britain and Ireland to ground their contemporary practice; Glastonbury, England, central in King Arthur lore, is also a center of Contemporary Druidism. These groups, on the whole, strike a delicate balance between individual and community, between tradition and change, and between affiliation and eclecticism, all while continuing to emphasize the importance of the natural world as a source of ultimate meaning. All of these factors are active elements in the religious imagination that provides the foundation for alternative religious expression; as Mark C. Taylor (2009: 23) notes: "every religious position is also temporally and historically situated—it grows out of a past that shapes it and anticipates a future that can transform it." This possibility for transformation through religious imagination is vital to contemporary expressions of Paganism.

Imagination at play: popular fantasy literature and alternative spirituality

Although Paganism has no central text, no essential bible of alternative religion, text has nonetheless played an important role in the history, development, and propagation of these traditions. In his examination of the history of Paganism in the United States specifically, Chas Clifton (2006: 13) notes that Paganism's "propagation and its ongoing life occurred through textual means." Authors such as Silver Raven Wolf, Starhawk, Scott Cunningham, Raymond Buckland, and Isaac Bonewits have made careers of publishing various historical and how-to books, attending Pagan conferences, and otherwise building communities of Pagans around the world primarily through textual means. Many Pagans look to these written resources, both in print and in digital format, as guides for the development of their religious expression. Because a majority of Pagans' paths—personal spiritual affiliations, usually in relation to particular traditions (such as Wicca, Druidism, or Asatru)—do not have any central authority, the Pagans are adept at research and discovery, both in solitary and community formats. Additionally, notes Clifton (ibid.: 4), "fantasy characters" may serve as "role models of a sort to a community overloaded with 'beginners' and short of 'elders.'" That love of and emphasis on reading extends to books beyond the realm of strictly Pagan literature. Indeed, as Clifton illustrates, in some ways the development of Paganism and the fantasy genre—in which "religious concerns find expression in other cultural forms so that cultural products perceived to be secular can carry authentic and meaningful religious content and deal with sacred concerns" (Ostwalt 2003: 7)—occurred side by side, and often through the same authors.

John Ronald Reuel (J.R.R.) Tolkien's seminal fantasy series, *The Lord of the Rings*, has been a particularly strong influence in many Pagan communities. The story—a follow-up to the successful children's fantasy book, *The Hobbit* (1937)—is a classic hero's journey tale, set in the fantastic Middle-earth. It follows Frodo Baggins, a young hobbit entrusted with the destruction of a powerful magical artifact, the One Ring. The story contains many elements common to fantasy stories, including a variety of magical races (dwarves, elves, and goblins, among others) and fantasy creatures (such as dragons, talking trees called ents, and giant spiders). Magic is presented as a natural force, harnessed most explicitly by the wizard Gandalf. Much work has been done on the religious undertones (or sometimes, overtones; see Wood 2003) of the series, but considerably less has been done on exploring how

JODIE ANN VANN

Pagans have used the series as a source of meaningful elements in the construction of religious identities which exist outside of the fantasy world created by Tolkien.

One of the clearest examples of the influence of this story and the world it presents is a Pagan gathering place called Lothlorian. This nature sanctuary in southern Indiana, named for the elves' realm in Tolkien's Middle-earth, plays a central role in the local eclectic Pagan communities, though it is open to all "earth-respecting" traditions. The Web site of the organization maintaining the sanctuary describes it as "an alternative community of free thinkers and environmentally conscious citizens," themes that are present in the fantasy world which Pagans endeavor to bring to our world (see *Elvin H.O.M.E.* n.d.). One of the founders explains the name choice as a natural progression: the group associated elves with the care of the forest, and identified Lothlorian as the home of these elves.

By drawing upon the well-known formulas found in fantasy literature, Pagans are calling into play many of the archetypes that are common in popular thought, especially in the English-speaking world. The name choice of Lothlorian is intended to call to mind a particular type of scene, replete with elves, magic, and otherworldliness. The power of language to conjure such mental images, emotional responses, and powerful associations was clearly, if not consciously, an element in the founders' decision to draw from Tolkien's masterpiece. The explicit connection between alternative religion (in this case, most influentially, eclectic Paganism) and fantasy literature is expressed through language; the ways in which fantasy comes alive for Pagans are dependent on the highly active engagement of the religious imagination.

Tolkien's work as a whole fits perfectly into the postmodern project; *The Lord of the Rings* was first published in several stages in 1954 and 1955, during perhaps the most prolific period of postmodernist scholarly production. Although this series is a continuation of a larger body of work on Middle-earth, this particular text is central, and demonstrates several experimental elements of the postmodern movement. While we may acknowledge the use of common archetypes and a subtle critique on industrialization, we must still credit Tolkien for his most obvious postmodern theme: the subjectivity of language. Language is one of the simplest elements to carry from one world to the next; it is portable and dynamic. As a symbolic system, it carries more than the simple denoted meanings of various words and phrases; as the example of Lothlorian demonstrates, language can carry an entire world of meaning, spiritual and religious. A philologist and professor of literature as well as a fantasy author, Tolkien understood the structures of language as both subjective and created, creating several languages (including Elvish) for his imaginary world. The use of language in the series fleshes out the fantasy world of Middle-earth; in a unique way, it makes it real.

Pagans also see the presence of archetypes in the book as imaginative use of ancient cultural and religious ideas (see Aloi 2001; Vikernes n.d.). In particular, Gandalf is often interpreted as an archetypical construction of an ancient Druidic figure; wise, capable, and a community leader. He is cleansed by fire (the Balrog) and emerges pure, as Gandalf the White. Pagans point to Tolkien's education and position within the academy, and his knowledge of folklore and myth, as support for their own Pagan reading of the stories. They also point to the author's development of Middle-earth—through dense descriptions of the landscape and the rich

524

characterizations—as evidence that this world is (in some ways) real. Pagan fans of the series (book or film) point to the blending of archetypes, ancient folklore and myth, and contemporary elements as an almost magical, alchemical mix that results in a universal fantasy world to which they may look for inspiration and dynamically meaningful material for the construction of self. Many understand themselves to be recreating or reconstructing the religions of the ancient world; Tolkien provides them a rich and dynamic portrait of that world, allowing them, if only for a brief time, to immerse themselves in the meaningful alternate and ancient reality that inspires their real contemporary practice. Indeed, some fans have pointed out that, while Tolkien was influenced by Christian values, the world he created is one that mirrors pre-Christian Europe (Rosson 2005). Pagans point to this fantasy world as a place where real-world issues are sorted out: struggles of good versus evil, questions of racial relationships, and the power of love, honor, and loyalty are all at play within Tolkien's world, and are interpreted as models for life enacted here in reality.

More than 50 years after *The Lord of the Rings* was published, the *Harry Potter* series emerged and seized the public's attention. *Harry Potter and the Sorcerer's Stone*, the first book in the series, introduces a young boy wizard, an orphan raised by his magic-hating aunt and uncle southwest of London. The full series of seven books follow Harry through his years at Hogwarts, a famous wizarding school, to his final encounter with the evil wizard Voldemort. Blending the "English school story" model with the familiar hero's journey, *Potter* engages many elements found in Contemporary Pagan practice: herbalism, divination, and the foundational connection between nature and magic. Witches and wizards are born, though their powers must be developed through education and practice.

It is unlikely that the author, J.K. Rowling, set out to convert a generation of children to Paganism, and it is equally unlikely that the texts would somehow entice young readers to take up witchcraft in the real world. However, there is some connection between these two streams of thought. Starhawk (2001), a popular Pagan author, noted that "the magic in Harry Potter takes us back into an animate universe," reflecting the sense from within the Pagan community that the essential aspects of Paganism are preserved in fantasy; that both work toward re-enchanting reality and reconnecting with the world as a magical place (Hutton 2007; McFarland Taylor 2007).

Since the first of seven books was published in 1997, the *Harry Potter* series has been at the center of a dynamic, rich, and often contentious conversation. There is a range of opinion among both Christians and Pagans, from celebration to tolerance to vehement and active disapproval. As with *Lord of the Rings*, some Pagans point out that Harry's world is built upon archetypes and myths rooted in a pre-Christian past. They often argue that, while the specific type of magic is not real, the values present (hope, loyalty, love, the power of nature, and the triumph of good) are all vital. Some Pagans have equated the banning of *Harry Potter* to the banning of imagination.

Interestingly, some Christians point to the same element of *Potter* to discount it that Pagans often use in its defense. Caryl Matrisciana, for example, warns parents that the series desensitizes children to the dangers of occultism. In an interview with Terry Meeuwsen on the Christian Broadcasting Network (CBN), she notes that

---

Rowling admitted taking "more than a third of the research and the content of these so-called fantasy books" from occult sources.[5]

Many arguments condemning *Potter* are grounded in the series' earliest volumes, when parts of the story were not yet developed. Rowling was hesitant to outline religion in the series, particularly at first, for fear that she might reveal too much. In response to questions about religion in her books, she later responded that Hogwarts was "a multi-faith school" (Adler 2007). More recently, in an interview with Oprah Winfrey in 2010, Rowling more clearly outlined her position:

> I'm very frustrated with fear of imagination. That's—I don't think that's healthy … . I'm not pushing any belief system here, although there is a lot of Christian imagery in the books … . On the "you must not discuss witchcraft, you must not have witches or magic depicted in a book," I think that's nonsensical … . It will always be with us … it's a belief system that humanity passed through. It still has huge attractions. There's a quotation that I almost used in the *Harry Potter* book … . "In magic, man has to rely on himself" … . I'm not saying I believe magic is real. I don't. But that's the perennial appeal of magic—that we ourselves have power and we can shape our world.[6]

Rowling's statement demonstrates the complexity of the issue, as does the epigraph for the final volume, *Harry Potter and the Deathly Hallows*, which comes from two sources (Aeschylus's "The Libation Bearers" and William Penn's "More Fruits of Solitude") and which she identifies as Pagan and Christian respectively.

Certainly, not all Christians take issue with *Potter*. After the publication of the final book—with its clear references to life after death, and with Harry portrayed as a resurrected Christ-figure—many argued that the entire series was a Christian allegory. Some have identified Dumbledore as God the Father, Harry as Christ, and the complicated Professor Snape as Judas (see Diamant 2007). Beyond the direct correlations, however, pro-*Potter* Christians argue that the broad themes of love, charity, kindness, and the pervasive power of good are evidence that the text is, at base, richly Christian. Many pro-*Potter* Pagans see these virtues as universal morals, and interpret the perhaps Christian elements of the story and characters as examples of ancient archetypes and story formulas, of which both the Christ narrative and *Potter* story are parallel examples (see Littlefield n.d.).

The imagination is at play in both sides of this debate; as Rowling herself stated in an interview with Katie Couric on October 20, 2000, for the *Today Show*, in response to a question about anti-*Potter* backlash: "people tend to find in books what they want to find."[7] For Contemporary Pagans, the importance lies in the way in which *Harry Potter* has been used as a rich source of inspiration for thinking about moral values, and for conceptualizing how natural powers ought to be enacted in the real world. I have found none who think the *Potter* world is directly real. Neither have I found evidence for vast conversions to Paganism by individuals after reading the books or watching the films.

The re-enchantment of the world, the return to an animate universe, is not, of course, the sole purview of either Paganism or fantasy literature. During the past few decades, there has been a marked shift in understanding the earth as a holistic system, reflected in ecological movements, environmental ethics, and a variety of religious traditions. What is unique in the relationship between Paganism and popular fantasy, however, is that both of these look to the mythical past for inspiration and examples for bettering the world. Both require the use of an active imagination, both borrow from various archetypes and meta-narratives, and both engage with reality in a way that allows for different interpretations and understandings of how things are and perhaps how they ought to be. This tendency to look to fantastic structures and archetypes as models for the construction of meaningful identities in the real world further strengthens connections here. It is Pagans' tendency to draw meaningful elements from fantasy worlds to serve them in the real world that allows us to examine this dynamic relationship.

Both *Lord of the Rings* and *Harry Potter* are stories about worlds that are created by particular authors' imaginations; they are fantasies woven out of myth, archetype, common tropes, and particular contexts. Both incorporate magic, a vital part of many contemporary Pagans' practice. And yet, the relationship between these works of fiction and Pagan thought is not a simple one-to-one correspondence. To say that reading either of these, or other fantasy stories, is equal to or results in witchcraft or Paganism is too simplistic. However, if we are to understand how the religious imagination functions in a postmodern world, we cannot ignore the complex, slippery, and often messy relationship between alternative spirituality and popular fantasy literature. Both use archetypes in the construction of a person-driven cosmology; Pagans in the personae of their deities, and fantasy in the construction of the various characters. Both understand nature to be special—somehow sacred—and generally related to magic, if in various ways. Both demand a flexible and active imagination in the construction of complex worlds. And both are dynamic sets of symbols, histories, and other elements that are used in the construction of uniquely meaningful identities.

Of course, as du Gay *et al.* (1997: 5) point out, "meaning making is an on-going process. It does not just end at a pre-ordained point." This makes Paganism a rich source for the study of cultural processes of meaning making. As Partridge (2004: 32) observes, "epistemological individualism leads, in turn, to eclecticism," and Pagans are, at foundation, involved in a very dynamic process of meaning making. According to Pike (2004: 119), they "make use of whatever tools are available to them and borrow from the sources at hand." The common Pagan focus on the development of individual spiritual paths indicates a certain understanding of truth and knowledge; both must be sought.

Fantasy genre elements, whether in literature, television, or film, are dynamic examples of how, as Clark puts it, "religious communities sometimes make use of popular secular ideas, products, and practices to further their own so-called 'sacred' goals" (Clark and Clanton 2012: 15). Religion theorist Talal Asad notes that sacred and profane "do not denote *types* of action but *aspects* of almost any kind of action" (1993: 161; emphasis in original); in Contemporary Paganism, particularly for groups and individuals that encourage eclecticism, the boundaries between the sacred and the profane disappear. This is particularly important in the context of eclectic Paganism, wherein practitioners may draw from almost any source available in the construction of their worldview. The inclusion of elements from outside the realm of religion in the religious expression of these individuals and communities ought not to be interpreted as problematic or as a lessening of their religious authenticity. The distinctions between sacred and profane, while sometimes highlighted in ritual practices, fall away in the quotidian framework of meaning that Pagans create and recreate continuously.

The fantasy of the "other": depictions of Paganism in popular culture

In the postmodern era, notes Conrad Ostwalt (2003: 7), "there is a tendency for religious institutions to employ secular and popular cultural forms like television and the movies to make religious teachings relevant for a modern audience," and representations of Pagans, most particularly witches and other magicians, are abundant in popular culture, particularly in fantasy film and television. While few Pagans are involved in the production of these depictions, the ways in which pop culture portrays Paganism and alternative or nature religions indicates much about these groups vis-à-vis the mainstream religious landscape. While those who practice magic are often portrayed in problematic or negative ways, there is also a romanticization of the types of power with which alternative spiritualities are associated.

As Paganism has become more common in the real world, popular culture has had to account for it as part of the cultural universe. The religious imagination facilitates a holistic worldview that includes the self, "other," and the world at large; as Paganism has moved into popularity, pop culture has worked through how it ought to be included in this holistic paradigm. The resulting depictions have, for the most part, portrayed Pagans as "other": in other times, other places, or other realities. In the 1960s and '70s, a majority of these depictions moved from Hollywood's "B" movies into the mainstream horror and fantasy genres with films like *Rosemary's Baby* (1968) and television shows such as *Bewitched* (ABC, 1964–72) and *Dark Shadows* (ABC 1966–71). While these depictions are incredibly problematic, the contemporary increase in the number of depictions of Pagans and practitioners of alternative religion indicates a shift in the popular cultural universe.

In the late 1990s and early 2000s, the series *Charmed* (WB, 1998–2006) became one of the network's most popular shows.[8] The series follows the lives of three sisters, Prue (later replaced by Paige), Piper, and Phoebe, as they uncover and develop their magical powers as witches. The main characters are described as "Wiccan" or "witches" interchangeably, and some attention seems to have been paid to depicting Wicca accurately. For example, the sisters base their actions on the Wiccan Rede— "An' it harm none, do what ye will"—which they find inscribed in their family's *Book of Shadows*. During the first episode ("Something Wicca this Way Comes," aired 7 October 1998—an obvious play on the nearly identical title of Ray Bradbury's 1962 classic novel), two detectives, Andy and Darryl, set out to solve a string of murders. Andy observes a pattern in the murders: the victims are all witches. While Darryl is skeptical, Andy follows his instinct and visits occult shops, learning about the role of pentagrams and athames (ceremonial knives used as tools for directing energy while working magic) in contemporary Wiccan practice; his knowledge of occult realities eventually allows him to solve the crimes. The underlying elements of Wicca present in the series—in the tools used, the foundational moral code, and the emphasis on familial or path traditions—demonstrate a level of accuracy in the fantasy of the show. What is most important for our purposes is the obvious attempt to include Wicca as a real—that is, not simply a fantastical—system in the real world. The writers and producers of the series seem to have worked diligently to develop a product that, whether they intended it or not, has helped bring Wicca into the popular cultural universe.

The influence of *Charmed* is undeniable. The main characters, the most powerful witches in history, are very "normal," average young women. Witchcraft, at least the type these three employ, is made appealing, non-threatening, and (to some degree) sexy. This occult classic presents an understanding of alternative religion—through a romanticized presentation of Wicca—that normalizes the religion as a valid and authentic spiritual option.

It is clear that the show's creators took creative license with regard to some of the more fanciful elements of the series (orbing, telekinesis, etc.). However, religious imagination is clearly active in both the production and consumption of *Charmed*. The creation of such a show relied upon the inclusion of Wicca as a cultural element; the viewers of the show employed the religious imagination in reframing their schemata to include Wicca as an element of reality. By bringing Wicca into the popular cultural universe, *Charmed* demands the active participation of creators and viewers as both work to incorporate alternative religiosity into their holistic understanding of reality.

Charmed has produced very vocal responses from the Pagan communities, and online forums reveal a vast (and often extreme) spectrum of opinion. The show is referred to, in various ways, as television that appeals to people who are generally into "witchy" things. Many object to the show's incorrect portrayal of Wicca, while some attribute their initial interest in Wicca to seeing its characters' enactment of ritual. Some view the sisters' transformation (through their growth in Wicca) from normal girls to powerful women as a positive understanding of the empowering value of Paganism, while others have gone as far as to adopt into their real life some of the terms and practices depicted, especially "orbing" (teleporting—not necessarily physically, but mentally; something akin to astral projection) and employing a "white lighter" (a positive guiding influence, similar to a guardian angel).

The use of these (and other) elements has not gone unchallenged within the community, and a brief perusal of the various online discussion forums clearly demonstrates the split within the community. Those who borrow from *Charmed* and similar shows are referred to as "fluffy bunnies," and are considered by some to be trendy, uncommitted Pagans. Some discuss (sometimes blatantly argue, or engage in "flame wars") what is the appropriate or authentic use of elements from popular culture, and *Charmed* seems to be at the center of that debate. At the heart of all of this is the understanding that Paganism is diverse, dynamic, and full of contestation. Popular cultural products such as *Charmed* highlight the fault lines within the various communities, and allow a better understanding of the various ways in which popular culture has an effect on and is affected by alternative religion.

In recent years, the British television series *Merlin* has captured the imaginations of many viewers even outside of the UK. The show follows a young version of the familiar wizard as he works to fulfill his destiny alongside the Crowned Prince of Camelot, Arthur Pendragon. Under the monarchy of the detestable King Uther, magic has been criminalized throughout the kingdom. In order to maintain his status as personal servant to Arthur and assistant to the palace physician, Gaius, Merlin must constantly battle his in-born nature and hide his magical abilities. Mentored by both Gaius and the Last Dragon (whom Uther has imprisoned beneath the palace), Merlin learns how to control his magic, while using it surreptitiously for the benefit of others.

As in most fantasy series, magic is shown to have both a positive and a negative side, though of course, the hero of the series uses it only for good. What is intriguing for us is how the source of magic is portrayed. Both the Dragon and Gaius tell Merlin on several occasions that he is "a child of the old religion," which is bound up in the "magic of the earth itself," both of which are explicit references to nature-oriented religions, of which Paganism is the most obvious example. Notably, the Druids follow this ancient tradition, and appear as mysterious and powerful outlaws under Uther's rule. There is, then, an implicit understanding that there is real magic at play in the ancient world; more importantly, this magic is natural, innate, and powerful. That the Druids are associated with the preservation of the old religion suggests a vibrantly positive message about the community, particularly in the face of the vile and self-serving King Uther, who understands nothing of the good in magic.

The various types of magical abilities speak toward a particularly eclectic understanding of Paganism. Merlin's abilities manifest most obviously in the mentally charged power to move objects and influence the elements. While this might not be a power that is very realistic in the context of Contemporary Paganism, it does indicate one central tenet: that is, the connection between individuals and the materiality of the world.[9] Other characters also display powers and abilities that mimic elements that are often found in current Pagan practice. The Lady Morgana (who is, on occasion, referred to as the last Priestess of the Triple Goddess, a clear reference to Contemporary Wicca) experiences prophetic dreams, even before she becomes aware of her magic. In one episode ("The Beginning of the End," aired 8 November 2008), a young Druid boy is caught in the city; he is portrayed as having telepathic powers (by which he communicates with Merlin), perhaps indicating a latent gift in the young wizard as well. And the Great Dragon seems to be clairvoyant.

While there are those who use magic to dark ends, on the whole the magic of the earth (which, in "The Dragon's Call," aired 20 September 2008, is related to "the oldest gods") is portrayed as both good and natural. The heroic, self-sacrificing, and ultimately magical Merlin is contrasted with the terrible, self-centered, and anti-magic Uther—and the implication is quite apparent. Like *Charmed*, *Merlin* presents an understanding of magic as a natural force, bound in the power of the earth itself. Again, while there are some liberties taken for the sake of production, the overall message in *Merlin* is that nature religion is good, powerful, and above all else, real. The show presents magic and earth-religion as foundation elements, allowing them to become a part of the popular cultural universe, and demanding that an active engagement of the religious imagination works to incorporate alternative religion into the schemata of holistic reality.

Pagan reactions to *Merlin* are perhaps more complicated than the other examples we have discussed here. Historically, particularly in Britain, the Arthur legends have been interpreted through both a Pagan and a Christian lens. In this re-imagining of the story, Pagans see, once again, a particular version of the pre-Christian world, one in which the "Old Religion" is alive and well. Pagan and non-Pagan reviewers point to the program's clear attempts at outlining a rich spiritual tradition; as *Guardian* columnist Cole Moreton (2009) observes, "the BBC uses pagan spirituality as a source of inspiration" for this series, among others, and the success of the show, both in Britain and abroad, is attributed to the trend toward mainstreaming Paganism. Some Pagans do respond to the negative portrayal of Morgana as Priestess of the Triple Goddess, and negative critique has focused on the lack of historical and mythical accuracy. But the majority of Pagan responses are positive regarding the religious aspects of the series, and overall, Pagans see *Merlin* as a positive example of popular culture engaging with their traditions through this familiar historical myth.

Although the stories and formats of these series are quite different, both *Merlin* and *Charmed* share one very important characteristic: their main characters are born with magic, which is portrayed as the ancient power of nature itself. The heroes and heroines, the characters who use magic for good, have innate power. While this power must be harnessed, developed, and consciously directed, the fact that the main characters are born with magic mirrors the sentiments of many Contemporary Pagans. While few currently practicing Pagans are raised in Pagan households, they do commonly express the idea that Paganism fulfills their natural and innate spiritual inclinations (Clifton 2006; Pike 2004). According to Sarah Pike (2004: 117), many "describe finding Neopagan and Wiccan communities or particular paths as coming 'home' and discovering 'family.'" Many Pagans state that they first became interested in Contemporary Paganism through books, the Internet, and sometimes in encounters with Paganism in popular media, including the examples included here. In my own field research, I have heard many times that people were already practicing variations of Paganism before they discovered the communities that nourished and helped to develop their identities. While practicing Pagans do not claim to have been born with magical powers, many do claim an innate tendency toward the types of religious experiences and practices that Paganism offers.

Parallel worlds: the Internet and alternative religious identities

The tools Pagans use to develop their personal religious identities have changed much over the last few decades, and any discussion would be incomplete if we were to neglect an examination of the ways in which new technologies have changed the relationship between contemporary alternative religions and popular culture. "[A]s transcendence gives way to immanence," notes Mark Taylor (2009: xvii), "transforming the world into a work of art is realized through new technologies that increasingly obscure the line supposedly separating image and reality." It is therefore no surprise that one of the most influential developments for Pagans in recent years has been the Internet. The personal computer provides a rich new environment through which Pagans find new meaning for their religious expressions. Through the digital (namely imagined) world of the Internet, time and space are compressed in such a way as to allow for the dynamic construction of alternative (though related and connected) realities. The technology of the Internet allows many Pagan conceptions and ideals to take on new dimensions.

For most people who use the Internet, even for the most technologically savvy, this tool mimics the mysterious and powerful force that has, at certain points in history, been called magic (Pels 2010). Individuals must employ religious imagination to conceptualize the virtual realities and the collapse of both time and space that the Internet facilitates. Of course, the Web is not only a tool for religion, but at its most foundational level, it challenges preconceived notions of reality in a way that only the religious imagination can rectify and bring into the holistic paradigm in a meaningful way. As a product of the postmodern postindustrial age, the Internet provides a perfect example for exploring how, as Partridge (2004: 53) argues, "the religious worldview has not collapsed." Rather, it is "still operative at ambient levels and is gradually beginning to surface, permeate, and shape Western society and culture." Indeed, through the prevalence of the Internet—and as individuals rely upon it to greater and greater extent—the religious imagination is called into more common usage.

One of the ways this has had an impact on Pagan and other alternative spiritual groups is in community building. The popular Web site the *Witches' Voice* (n.d.) provides event notices, opportunities to find groups with specific path orientations (whether Asatru, Druid, Wiccan, or others), and to post and read various articles and letters on Pagan topics. As Pike observes (2004: xi), many New Age and Neopagan movements have "successfully promoted themselves through publishing and on the internet. The popularization of their ideas," she concludes, "has been an important development." Indeed, the Internet has encouraged communication not only within Pagan communities, but has allowed interested persons to seek out groups wherein they might develop their religious identities.

After decades, and perhaps centuries, of maintaining their traditions underground and in the dark, Pagans and Paganism have been able to emerge (as they say) "out of the broom closet" via the Internet. Pagans use computers to connect with one another in virtual communities constructed with the explicit use of a dynamic religious imagination, or to connect with others who share their beliefs and practices in ways that encourage face-to-face meetings. Demographics of practitioners indicate that aside from creative and artistic fields, the most common vocations for Pagans are in technological and computer-related industries (see Clifton 2006; Pike 2004; Berger 1999; Harvey and Hardman 1996). Practitioners of alternative religions are drawn to technology for various reasons, but as Mark Taylor (2009: 3) observes: "postmodernism is inseparable from the emergence of postindustrial network culture ... deregulated, decentralized, and distributed networks effectively collapse distance and compress time to create a world in which to be is to be connected." The Internet acts as a tool for both the production and consumption of alternative religious identities.

It also serves as a tool for the regulation of those constructions. A recent Google search of "Wicca" drew more than three million hits, "pagan" returned more than fourteen million, and "alternative religion" nearly two hundred million. In comparison,

"Christianity" drew over one hundred ten million, "Buddhism" over eight million, and "Hinduism" more than five million, making it clear just how active Pagans and practitioners of alternative religions are online. As a tool for the production and consumption of religious information, the Internet has possibly had a greater impact on this collection of spiritual communities than on any other. The presence of online discussion boards, Pagan Web sites, and other vast quantities of data provides one other valuable tool for practitioners: through it, their practices and beliefs are regulated. Alternative religions change and shift rapidly, and the Internet facilitates these dynamic processes. Most Pagans rely on trial and error, personal taste, and inspiration from the many texts, both academic and fantastic, which they use in various ways for the development of individual religious identities. The Internet has made these elements available in number and accessibility in a way that was, before the current era, unimaginable.

Looking toward the future

One of the challenges with a strict application of the circuit of culture model employed by du Gay *et al.* with the Sony Walkman is that Contemporary Paganism is very unlike a piece of technological equipment. Nor is it a television series or a book. At stake in our examination of these groups are the religious, spiritual, social, personal, communal, ideological, moral, and cultural realities of living people. And yet, if we understand religion to be, in some ways, a cultural product, we might be able to use an adapted, more richly nuanced version of the circuit of culture model to help us better understand the relationship between Contemporary Paganism and popular culture. It is absolutely vital to reiterate that what we have examined here is the phenomenological dimension of the relationship between Paganism and the popular cultural product of fantasy; central are the ways in which the structures of Paganism and those of fantasy are parallel. The type of imagination required in the construction of a Contemporary Pagan worldview is similar to that which is demanded in the encounter with fantasy. In some ways, the eclectic individualism of Paganism is mirrored in the creation of alternative realities of fantasy worlds. Elements of the fantasy genre are products of a particular type; they exemplify and in some ways embody a dynamic stream of thought. These products give us access to a particular way of imagining the world that we might otherwise not be able to access. Popular cultural depictions of Paganism and alternative religions have brought these conversations into the broader cultural universe.

As we observed earlier, boundaries between the popular and the alternative are permeable and constantly in flux. Our examination of Contemporary Paganism has allowed us to trace the ways in which cultural elements on the fringes find their way into the mainstream, and vice versa. Pagans are unique in their express and conscious use of various popular cultural elements in the construction of individualized religious identities. The popular and the alternative define one another in some ways; by applying theories of the religious imagination to both, we can see how these boundaries are penetrable and flexible in ways that allow individuals and communities to draw from various sources that they deem meaningful. In this schema, religion is best used as an adjective. As Taylor (2009: xiii) notes, it is "not a separate domain but pervades all culture and has an important impact on every aspect of society." The religious imagination is that active element which allows us to consider all of these examples under a shared rubric of alternative religiosity.

As Pike observes, Paganism is

> rooted deeply in time and history, yet with a contemporary focus on self-knowledge and personal experience ... these religions are eclectic at heart, blending old and new ... to meet the needs of late twentieth- and early twenty-first-century people.
>
> (Pike 2004: 12)

This process of blending, borrowing, and creative construction is essential in understanding how the religious imagination works in this context. When there are no strict boundaries between the religious, the popular, the cultural, and the secular, everything is available for incorporation into a meaningful schemata. What is important, and what allows for the comprehensive inclusion of elements from any and all of these arenas, is the active dimension of the religious imagination, which is vital in the creation of self-identities.

The "secularization thesis"—the argument that, as societies become modernized through advances in science and technology, religion necessarily declines—is never far from any discussion of contemporary religion. While it is true that affiliation with major organized religious groups appears to be in decline in the United States, the number of people who claim some sort of "spirituality" is steadily rising. Indeed, as Partridge (2004: 42) argues, it seems that the processes of secularization and the increase in identification with spirituality are "two aspects of the same process," which he identifies as "a fundamental process of social and cultural change in which identical forces can be seen to be responsible for the decline of the one and the emergence of the other.'" If this is so, it might not be that fewer people are engaging their religious imaginations, but that the arenas in which they do so are less often the organized ecclesiastical institutions of traditional Western religions, and more often the eclectic, alternative forms of religious expression. This being the case, so-called "alternative" forms of being religious are now becoming part of the mainstream, part of the cultural universe in which we all find ourselves and in which we all develop religious and cultural identities.

Luckily (for our purposes), there have been scholars who have examined this historic shift in some detail. Notes Conrad Ostwalt:

> Contemporary American culture witnesses secularization occurring in two directions: 1) the churches and religious organizations are becoming increasingly more attuned to the secular environment, particularly to popu-lar culture, and are in some cases trying to emulate it in an effort to remain relevant; 2) popular culture forms, including literature, film, and music, are becoming increasingly more visible vehicles of religious images, symbols, and categories. *These two directions of secularization demonstrate the blurred or*

malleable boundaries between religion and culture—the sacred and the secular—that define the relationship of religion and culture in the Postmodern era.

(Ostwalt 2003: 28–29; emphasis added)

By looking at the ways in which religious imagination encounters popular culture, and how popular culture engages the religious imagination, we may come to a richer understanding of the relationship between these two overlapping spheres. It is this multidirectional nature of influence and change that is essential to our understanding of the relationship between alternative religiosity and popular culture.

Incorporating Paganism and other alternative religions into a fruitful discussion of contemporary religion requires a shift in the definition and conceptualization of religion. We must begin to rethink "the ways that the religious (or ... the spiritual) is not only *lived* but *produced* within nonreligious sectors" (Bender 2010: 46; emphasis in original). By using ideas and theories of the religious imagination in our examination, we have begun to unravel how, for many practitioners of contemporary Paganism and alternative spiritualities, "the divine is not elsewhere but is the emergent creativity that figures, disfigures, and refigures the infinite fabric of life" (Taylor 2009: xvii–xviii). The process of reconsidering the relationship between the popular and the alternative has only just begun; there is work yet to be done.

Notes

1 I use the term "postmodernism" to describe a particular current of thought that takes up as its main characteristics the ideals of relativism, idealism, pluralism, and constructivism. I draw the theoretical basis for this understanding from Pierre Bourdieu (1977) and Michel Foucault, both of whom are continuously present throughout this chapter.

2 Unless otherwise stated, I use "religion" and "spirituality" interchangeably.

3 I am borrowing here from Ann Braude (1997), who argues that women's history is American religious history. Like Braude, I see that broader shifts in cultural and religious trends are first taken up by groups outside of the mainstream.

4 It is this mutually constitutive relationship that is foundational here; the religious imagination at work in this investigation is one that simultaneously shapes and is shaped by experience and new information.

5 The interview was aired on 5 December 2001, and can be seen on YouTube.com: www.youtube.com/watch?v=GUlNjr9NXrA (accessed 10 January 2014).

6 A transcript of the interview can be found on a Harry Potter fan Web site (see Harry Potter's Page 2010).

7 A transcript of the interview can be found on a Harry Potter fan Web site (see Accio Quote! 2000).

8 In this and the next example, I have specifically opted to focus on more recent depictions that, to some degree, are more positive and/or realistic in at least one aspect of Paganism.

9 Generally, Pagans and other nature-revering practitioners of alternative religions do not separate matter from spirit. Rather, they integrate earth-stewardship into their religious identities. Both animism and monism are common among these practitioners.

Works cited

Accio Quote! (2000) "Katie Couric interview of J.K. Rowling." Online. Available: www.accio-quote.org/articles/2000/1000-nbc-couric.htm (accessed 24 March 2013).

Adler, S. (2007) "'Harry Potter' author J.K. Rowling opens up about books' Christian imagery," MTV.com (October 17). Online. Available: www.mtv.com/news/articles/1572107/jk-rowling-talks-about-christian-imagery.jhtml (accessed 19 March 2013).

Aloi, P. (2001) "The fellowship of the ring—Peg's view," *Witches' Voice* (December 22). Online. Available: www.witchvox.com/va/dt_va.html?a=usma&c=media&id=3769 (accessed 20 March 2013).

Asad, T. (1993) *Genealogies of Religion: Disciplines and Reasons of Power in Christianity and Islam*, Baltimore, MD: The Johns Hopkins University Press.

Bender, C. (2010) *The New Metaphysicals: Spirituality and the Religious Imagination*, Chicago, IL: The University of Chicago Press.

Berger, H.A. (1999) *A Community of Witches: Contemporary Neo-Paganism and Witchcraft in the United States*, Columbia, SC: University of South Carolina Press.

Bourdieu, P. (1977) *Outline of a Theory of Practice*, trans. R. Nice, London: Cambridge University Press.

Braude, A. (1997) "Women's history *is* American religious history," in T. Tweed (ed.), *Retelling U.S. Religious History*, Berkeley, CA: University of California Press, 87–107.

Cady, L. (2011) "Religious imagination in the late secular age: extending liberal traditions in the twenty-first century," *American Journal of Theology and Philosophy* 32, 1: 23–42.

Chidester, D. (2005) *Authentic Fakes: Religion and American Popular Culture*, Berkeley, CA: University of California Press.

Clark, T.R. and D.W. Clanton, Jr. (eds) (2012) *Understanding Religion and Popular Culture*, New York: Routledge.

Clifton, C.S. (2006) *Her Hidden Children: The Rise of Wicca and Paganism in America*, Oxford: AltaMira Press.

Diamant, J. (2007) "'Harry Potter' and the gospel of J.K. Rowling," *Washington Post* (June 30); B09.

du Gay, P., S. Hall, L. Janes, H. Mackay, and K. Negus (1997) *Doing Cultural Studies: The Story of the Sony Walkman*, London: Sage.

Elvin H.O.M.E. (n.d.) Online. Available: www.elvinhome.org (accessed 11 February 2013).

Foucault, M. (1994) *The Order of Things: An Archaeology of Human Science*, New York: Random House.

Harry Potter's Page (2010) "Transcript of Oprah interview with J.K. Rowling." Online. Available: www.harrypotterspage.com/2010/10/03/transcript-of-oprah-interview-with-j-k-rowling/ (accessed 19 March 2013).

Harvey, G. and C. Hardman (eds) (1996) *Paganism Today: Witches, Druids, the Goddess and Ancient Earth Traditions for the Twentieth Century*, London: Thorsons.

Hutton, R. (2007) *The Druids*, London: Hambledon Continuum.

Latour, B. (1993) *We Have Never Been Modern*, Cambridge, MA: Harvard University Press.

Littlefield, C. (n.d.) "Harry Potter as a metaphor for struggling with God," *Harry Potter for Seekers*. Online. Available: www.harrypotterforseekers.com/articles/hpasametaphorforstrugglingwithGod.php (accessed 5 April 2013).

McFarland Taylor, S. (2007) *Green Sisters: A Spiritual Ecology*, Cambridge, MA: Harvard University Press.

Masazawa, T. (2005) *The Invention of World Religions: Or How European Universalism Was Preserved in the Language of Pluralism*, Chicago, IL: The University of Chicago Press.

Moreton, C. (2009) "'Everyone's a pagan now,'" *Guardian* (June 21). Online. Available: www.guardian.co.uk/world/2009/jun/22/paganism-stonehenge-environmentalism-witchcraft (accessed 19 March 2013).

Morris, R. (2000) *In the Place of Origins: Modernity and Its Mediums in Northern Thailand*, Durham, NC: Duke University Press.

Ostwalt, C. (2003) *Secular Steeples: Popular Culture and the Religious Imagination*, Harrisburg, PA: Trinity Press International.

Partridge, C. (2004) *Enchantment of the West, vol. 1*, London: T&T Clark.

Pels, P. (2010) "Magical things: on fetishes, commodities, and computers," in D. Hicks and M.C. Beaudry (eds), *The Oxford Handbook of Material Culture Studies*, Oxford: Oxford University Press, 613–33.

Pels, P. and B. Meyer (2003) *Magic and Modernity: Interfaces of Revelation and Concealment*, Stanford, CA: Stanford University Press.

Pike, S. (2004) *New Age and Neo-Pagan Religions in America*, New York: Columbia University Press.

Rosson, L. (2005) "Pagan but 'consonant with Christianity,'" *The Busybody* (December 11). Online. Available: http://lorenrosson.blogspot.com/2005/12/pagan-but-consonant-with-christianity.html (accessed 20 March 2013).

Rowling, J.K. (1998) *Harry Potter and the Sorcerer's Stone*, New York: Scholastic. (Also published as *Harry Potter and the Philosopher's Stone*.)

——(2007) *Harry Potter and the Deathly Hallows*, New York: Scholastic.

Starhawk [Miriam Simos] (2001) "Why I like Harry Potter" (December). Online. Available: www.starhawk.org/pagan/harrypotter.html (accessed 23 February 2013).

Taylor, M.C. (2009) *After God (Religion and Postmodernism)*, Chicago, IL: The University of Chicago Press.

Tolkien, J.R.R. (2012 [1937]) *The Hobbit*, New York: Random House.

——(2012 [1954–55]) *The Lord of the Rings, 50th Anniversary Edition*, New York: Mariner Books.

Vikernes, V. (n.d.) "Paganism: part iii—the one ring," Burzum.org. Online. Available: www.burzum.org/eng/library/paganism03.shtml (accessed 20 March 2013).

Witches' Voice (n.d.). Online. Available: www.witchvox.com (accessed 28 February 2013).

Wood, R.C. (2003) *The Gospel According to Tolkien: Visions of the Kingdom in Middle-earth*, Louisville, KY: Westminster John Knox Press.

28

PROTESTANTISM

Clive Marsh[1]

Protestants are more notable in popular culture in the modern period for their absence, rather than their prominence. It is the purpose of this chapter to explore what that statement means, why it is so, and what the consequences are. The claim may be a cause of surprise given the evident influence of Protestantism in social, cultural, political, economic, and religious life throughout the English-speaking West (and beyond) across many centuries. But it is an important observation to make, both to press a contemporary cultural interpreter to ask why and when Protestantism does become explicitly present, and what it means that, for much of the time, Protestantism is either simply not present, or its presence is hidden (consciously or unconsciously) or merely implied.

It is, though, necessary first to note that Protestants have always had a lot to say about popular culture deriving from or portraying life outside of churches, whether or not they have been evident within it. This may be why they are so often absent now, for much of what they have said has been negative. Or at least it has been cautious and controlling, expressing concern about the potential corrupting influence of any human creativity exercised without awareness that, as creative, it is derivative from divine creativity. At least since the Puritans there has been ambiguity about the fruits of all human labor issuing in what would now be termed the arts and popular culture. Despite the Protestant Reformation owing much of its early success to its close alliance with a major technological development (printing) and thus new form of media (popular pamphlets, using both words and visual images), this did not lead inevitably to a positive view of human artistry. John Calvin was more positive—at times—than is often recognized about the extent to which human endeavor could reflect the beauty of divine creation. But there still remained quite a split "between the world of God and this world" (David Cooper, cited in Dyrness 2004: 75). Human artistic activity might, at best, be evidence of the displacement of God's presence throughout the created order, of which glimpses might be seen. The legacy of this strand of Protestant thinking and belief, its negativity about human creativity and resulting art and popular culture, is still evident in contemporary cultural life through attempts to categorize what is valuable (or seemly) to consume, or to censor. Christian guides to movies "suitable for families" may not be wholly negative about human creativity but often do wish to demarcate clearly what is acceptable, and to distinguish what is of "this world" as opposed to "God's world."

And popular cultural productions with a clearly Christian Protestant theme (such as the American TV series *7th Heaven* [CW, 1996–2007]) tend to follow a similar line: it is important to delineate that which is Christian, and acceptable to Christians, from that which is not.

That said, the legacy of the Reformation, and of Puritanism in particular, is not totally one-sided. In a stimulating study of "The godly and popular culture" in *The Cambridge Companion to Puritanism*, Alexandra Walsham remarks: "Acquiring much of their substance and meaning from their confrontation with each other 'Puritanism' and 'popular culture' must … be seen as an example of reciprocal and mutually reinforcing processes of cultural and religious self-fashioning" (2008: 279). She shows how even the most devout of Puritans were frequently much more engaged in the cultural life of their times, and participants in popular practices in ways, and to an extent, which might surprise current interpreters looking back into the past. Puritanism and popular culture "interacted in more nuanced and complex ways than has often been allowed" (ibid.: 289). In the present, Protestant interaction with popular culture more directly takes the form of a complex, ambiguous relationship with consumerism. Whether it is popular music, blockbuster films, "feel good" or "reality" TV, Protestant Christianity makes use of secular popular culture (and may even need it) even while being repelled by it.

In many ways, then, what Walsham concludes about Puritanism—too easily assumed to have created an unqualified legacy of negativity toward human culture—applies to Protestantism's interaction more generally: it has been very cautious, often highly critical, deeply suspicious, and wanting to distinguish itself sharply from it, even while being profoundly dependent upon it, and shaping itself in constant interplay with it.

In his recent study of Protestant contributions to the Hollywood film industry, *Reforming Hollywood*, William Romanowski (2012) shows that the assumed negativity is sometimes not quite as it seems. Romanowski's detailed study logs a concern to work for self-regulation for moral ends, rather than simple censorship of what was deemed unacceptable. This approach, Romanowski argues, was widespread across denominational boundaries and theological persuasions. Whether or not Romanowski is right about the specifics of Protestant engagement with film, he is exploring the same ambiguous yet continual interplay noted by Walsham with respect to Puritanism. It is the same ambiguity that is reflected in the appearance and absence of Protestantism within recent Western popular culture, and which this chapter will map and examine.

The case of the absent clergy

Protestantism sounds like a single phenomenon and yet is, by definition, diverse. Its strain of protest has contributed to its own constant tendency to divide so that there are only multiple Protestantisms: Lutheranism, Presbyterianism, Congregationalism, the Baptist movement, Mennonites, the Society of Friends (Quakers), Methodism, Pentecostalism, to name but some of the most obvious. Of these, most have authorized ministers. But it is rare, save for very specific cases where the denomination is specific to a plot (in a book, film, or TV show), for such labels to be used, or to matter, in popular culture, and rarer still for ministers of those traditions to appear. Even where a Protestant minister is a central character, such as Reverend Eric Camden (played by Stephen Collins) in the American family drama *7th Heaven*, the denominational affiliation is (presumably for pragmatic, ratings-related reasons) relatively non-specific. Camden is minister of "Glen Oak Community Church."

This feature of popular cultural life—the relative absence of Protestant clergy—is well documented with respect to TV in Richard Wolff's *The Church on TV* (2010), in which by far the majority of characters considered are Roman Catholic. Scott H. Clarke's helpful 2005 study, undertaken with respect to American TV in September 2002, showed more Protestant characters overall (though still only 2.7 percent, compared to 52.8 percent of the population; see p. 146), and he was not focusing solely on clergy. The specificity of Clarke's study, while instructive, may be limiting. Kozlovic's (2002) survey of "sacred servants" in cinema indicates much larger numbers of Catholic characters. Even allowing for a perhaps substantial difference of approach in the two media of popular culture, Protestantism is sparsely represented.

Wolff's rationale for this state of affairs is persuasive. Protestant diversity, he suggests, means that throughout the 1960s and 1970s, Protestants always had the option of finding like-minded fellow Christians in some church or other. Catholics, by contrast, were committed to each other more directly within the same institutional framework, and so the tensions were more publicly apparent. As a result, this made for more compelling television (Wolff 2010: 45–46). Even now, when it can be argued that we live in "post-denominational" times, the point remains: the sheer diversity of Protestantism is a problem for popular culture and is better suppressed.

The fact that Protestant clergy are not prominent in popular culture is, however, significant in one further important respect. Protestantism has championed the religion of the everyday. It has been a major spur to secularization as a result. Protestantism should therefore not be represented primarily by its appointed leaders. This means, though, that characters labeled or identifiable as Protestants rarely appear at all in standard plots. This is a first clear pointer to the hiddenness of Protestantism in popular culture. Ministers scarcely appear, as it would be too much trouble to identify and clarify what type of minister was appearing. And because Protestantism is best not represented by clergy, it is the lay people—standard characters—whose Protestantism may be assumed. In UK culture (until relatively recently), if a person's religious background was assumed, then in England it was assumed to be Anglican (Episcopalian); in Scotland, Presbyterian (Church of Scotland). It is only in recent years that the "religious nones" have appeared in large numbers in statistical surveys (e.g., an increase from 15 to 25 percent of those stating "no religion" between 2001 and 2011 in England and Wales; from 15 to 20 percent in the USA between 2007 and 2012). Prior to this recent development, in England at least, "C of E" (Church of England) affiliation would have been declared in practice, and could thus have been assumed of fictional characters. Working class characters might have been Roman Catholic.

In the USA, Presbyterianism once might have been assumed of business leaders, for Calvin's influence in shaping the "Protestant work ethic" runs deep. Whether or not the Protestant work ethic is ultimately sustainable as a concept, the alliance between Protestantism, hard work (or at least an entrepreneurial spirit), and prosperity has often been maintained, and has been something of a hallmark of a Europe-linked form of Christianity. Even so, in popular culture, it has not usually been necessary to define other figures as Baptist, Lutheran, or Methodist. Garrison Keillor (1985) could explore the distinctions delightfully, and even play with the nuances between German and Norwegian Lutherans in Lake Wobegon. But in that literary instance, religion is itself the subject matter. Otherwise, labels are unnecessary. Marlee Matlin's portrayal of Joey Lucas, the feisty Quaker pollster in *The West Wing* (NBC, 1999–2006), and Dan Parker (John Corbett), a Lutheran pastor in the not very well-received film *Raising Helen* (2004), are striking exceptions to prove the rule. Lucas's Quakerism may have been opportunistic, providing a needed character to oppose the death penalty; Parker's day job at least dovetailed into the characters' everyday lives. Even so, such identification is unusual.

Meanwhile, white Anglo-Saxon Protestantism in more general terms is the backdrop against which secular society has developed and presented itself in Western popular culture. There is no need for clergy, and scarcely any need for Protestantism to make itself explicit at all. And, in a way that indicates a US echo of the UK scene, US popular culture reflects the extent to which Catholic association with urban life could be portrayed in a way that would not work for Protestants, who are associated much more with suburban life (Wolff 2010: 119).

To illustrate the normativity of Catholicism in the portrayal of clergy one need only think of such a scene as the incidental appearance of a priest in the *Friends* (NBC, 1994–2004) episode "The One After Vegas" (aired 23 September 1999), in which Chandler and Monica seek to avoid drawing the most obvious of conclusions—that they should marry. As they are seeking a "sign" as to how to decide— purporting to hope that they receive a sign that they should not wed—the elevator opens to confront them with the figure of a priest. Wearing a Roman collar, he could admittedly be Episcopalian (Anglican) or Lutheran, though is more likely being identified as Roman Catholic. Western popular culture needs its Christian priests, in other words, to be clearly visible and recognizable. As such, and again confirming the tenor of Wolff's study of American TV, and despite Clarke's evidence indicating how few religious figures there are at all, they are not usually specifically Protestant.

The decline, and confusion, of denominationalism

Popular culture has to wrestle, admittedly, with the sheer confusion of Protestantism. For those outside of the multiplicity of Protestantisms—with not the slightest inkling of what the difference might be between a Methodist, a Baptist, and a Presbyterian, unless explained or functioning as an intrinsic element of a plot—denominational labels are unnecessary. But they remain a feature of Western life. Secularization continues throughout Western societies, though for different reasons and at different rates (Bruce 2009; Davie 2002; Bruce 1996). Contrary to the now largely discredited secularization thesis, religion as a phenomenon has far from disappeared from Western industrialized society. Its resurgence may take some unwelcome forms at times, yet religion of some kind, however minimal, clearly seems to be a necessity for most human beings. But even in the face of that basic insight, the detail of Protestant differences seems somewhat trivial. This, at least, is the verdict of popular culture. However significant denominational difference may have been in the past, and whatever theological freight the distinctions still carry, there is neither time nor space to dwell on them for too long.

A range of examples from the 1970s TV comedy series M*A*S*H (CBS, 1972–83) illustrate this. Father Mulcahy, the chaplain to the mobile hospital, is a Roman Catholic, in itself a confirmation of the point made above: popular culture needs its Christian priests to be clear-cut and visible, and Protestantism does not supply this. His Catholicism provides, however, a foil for other characters around him whose Protestantism need not be explicit, but surfaces occasionally. Colonel Sherman Potter (Harry Morgan), the camp commander in the second phase of the series, is, inconsistently, a Methodist and then a Presbyterian. Scriptwriters acknowledge, in effect, a "general Protestantism" and do not need him to be anything more specific. As to what that Protestantism amounts to, however, it is not clear. Working back from the character of Potter, Protestantism could be assumed to be constituted of firm, no-nonsense, but fair and (largely) clear leadership, with a deep vein of compassionate humanity. It would be comforting to think that Protestantism was always so rich and positive.

A second example from the series is an aside from (Lebanese-American) Corporal Max Klinger (Jamie Farr), referring in the episode "Fade Out, Fade In" (aired 20 September 1977) to Captain B.J. Hunnicutt's (Mike Farrell's) "Presbyterian features." A contrast is being drawn between the variety of cultures that make up contemporary America (then and now) and the tall, white, blond European. In popular culture, then, Protestantism has, or at least had in the late 1970s and early 1980s, still to develop an identity independent of its European roots.

A third M*A*S*H example merely confirms this, adding a distinct class dimension, and accentuating the fact that Protestantism is influential but remains hidden. Its embeddedness in Western (especially North American) culture, indeed, causes a blurring of the boundaries between religious and secular. Major Charles Emerson Winchester III (David Ogden Stiers) joined in the sixth season. A patrician from a wealthy Boston family, Winchester is a combination of condescension and compassion. Brilliant at his job—having made the best use of a privileged education—yet struggling to adjust to his new, demanding context where his enjoyment of high culture has few outlets, his aloofness is more overtly apparent than his altruism. The latter does, however, surface on many occasions, often evoked when combined with appreciation for the arts.

Winchester's religious background is never made explicit. The cultural context created for him, however, suggests Protestant roots through the New England connections. Winchester expects to lead, and assumes close alliance between high culture, educational privilege, and social standing. Though such "highbrow" Protestantism stands in marked contrast to the social context and background of so many branches of the Protestant movement past and present, it is important to note how these aspects of the portrayal of Protestantism have taken effect via implicit means in North American popular culture. It is a form of the bourgeois "cultured" Culture

Protestantism (*Kulturprotestantismus*) identified in Europe in the later ninteenth and early twentieth centuries, where political, economic, and social leadership were closely linked to religious background and high cultural interests.

The dominant value system of the M*A*S*H TV series, however, is not explicitly religious at all. Its therapeutic theme is called forth by its context—the Korean War as a substitute for contemporary comment on US involvement in Vietnam. Beyond physical healing, however, is a more overarching therapeutic thread, fashioned by the humor itself, but also by the theme of mental and emotional healing which runs through the whole series. It interweaves with themes which could be claimed as religious (e.g., redemption and salvation, and above all forgiveness). In a memorable episode ("Dear Sis," aired 18 December 1978), written by Alan Alda, Father Mulcahy himself needs to be released from his own sense of lack of self-worth. His forgiveness is brokered by Hawkeye (Alda) in a clear act of secular absolution. Though it could be argued that the forgiveness and self-acceptance that Father Mulcahy receives need not be understood within a framework of salvation or redemption at all, this would clearly be how Mulcahy himself understood it (i.e., theologically). As a popular cultural example of redemption interwoven with a secular narrative of forgiveness, however, it is a striking case of the collaboration that is possible between secular and religious narratives. In 1970s US culture, secular narratives were clearly gaining the upper hand and displacing religious (and especially Christian) narratives in wider culture. Three decades later, Protestant theologian David Kelsey (2005) could remark just how prominent redemption would be in the arts and cultural life. Forgiveness remains far from the prerogative of religious (let alone Protestant) traditions to interpret. But I suggest that here in M*A*S*H we see the workings of what would, and will, continue to be the case across (secular) Western culture: that religious motifs and language will continue to be drawn upon when ethical and philosophical reflection on everyday experience is undertaken.

When this example of "secular absolution" from M*A*S*H is linked with the role played by the army psychiatrist, Major Sidney Freedman, it is clear that the dominant set of values espoused in the series may be called secular liberalism, but that it would be misleading to imply that such values are disconnected from religion. Though not specifically Christian, and claimable by no individual tradition alone, the interplay between M*A*S*H's therapeutic theme and the religious roots and overtones of the self-help, personal development culture of the decades in which M*A*S*H appeared should therefore be noted. The liberal Protestantism that would lie behind Winchester's family tradition would undoubtedly have fed into that mix, just as it fed "talking cures" such as American psychologist Carl Rogers's person-centered therapy. Hawkeye's secularized voice was perhaps more influenced, and significantly so, by liberal Protestantism than he might have cared to admit. Therapy of the best kind, in other words, needs ecumenical backing and attention.

A quite different, more recent, and more explicit example of the appearance and role of multiple Protestantisms in popular culture can be found in *The Simpsons* (FOX, 1989–present). In many ways *The Simpsons* represents one of the most developed and thoughtful engagements with the theme of contemporary religion in Western popular culture. Though it is far from even-handed in its treatment of religious diversity (Buddhism, Hinduism, Islam, and Judaism are given quite cursory attention, and

Roman Catholicism is somewhat caricatured as opposed to being simply satirized), the series does important work in teasing out some of the nuances and complexities of at least some aspects of Western society. With respect to the diversity of Protestantism, *The Simpsons* gets under the skin of a variety of types of Christianity and probes in particular the interplay between this variety of Protestantisms and the (largely) secular framework within which they, and all religious traditions, need to operate.

Mark I. Pinsky (2007) has done an excellent job of mapping all of this terrain in *The Gospel According to The Simpsons*. In leaning heavily on his entertaining survey of religious themes evident in the series, I wish simply to draw out insights germane to my point about the confusion created by Protestant denominationalism, and the decreasing significance of the diversity in ecclesiastical cultures beyond the churches themselves. Whether this apparent indifference to Protestant diversity signifies the end of denominations, or at least pinpoints a major question for denominations (as to whether their origins and *raison d'être* have much to say to society today), we shall assess in due course.

Springfield, the town where the action in *The Simpsons* takes place, has a number of Christian congregations, including Roman Catholic, Episcopalian, and African Methodist Episcopal churches. However, the majority of people in the town—and the series implies that the majority of people still do attend church—go to the First Church of Springfield, a congregation within the fictitious "Western Branch of American Reform Presbylutheranism." This fictional label indicates awareness of the complexities created by Protestantism's fissiparous tendencies. In merging denominations into their fictional church, the creators of the series show that serious fun can be had, for the issues are still real, at the expense of Protestant infighting. They have connected (and reconnected) some traditions while showing full awareness of, for example, the class and cultural differences which are frequently held to exist between Episcopalians/Anglicans and other Protestants, and the fact that all so-called "mainstream denominations," for all their own known diversity in practice, too often perceive themselves as largely white, or are under-represented in their leadership structures by members from a range of ethnic backgrounds.

In comparison with M*A*S*H, *The Simpsons* marks a new phase in popular culture's handling of Protestant diversity. Two and three decades later, references to denominations are more overt, if playfully garbled. In being a portrayal of suburban life, as opposed to offering an examination of contemporary American life through a distant army hospital, its sphere of observation is more everyday. These denominations (or churches like them) really do exist. People really do go to them, in the USA at least (even if not in Europe to the same extent) in large numbers (though see Pinsky 2007: 76). Committed religious characters interact with the less- and non-religious. A somewhat tired minister, Reverend Timothy Lovejoy, serves the First Church of Springfield. His existence as a clearly defined Protestant minister, even if of a fictional denomination, is a further example of a mild climate change in popular culture: he is at least present. Yet his tiredness (and dullness) reflects a waning confidence in the church's impact on social and political life. He does his job, but would rather be spending time on his hobby (model trains). His now lost youthful optimism—which had coincided with an upsurge of hopefulness in Christianity's potential in the 1960s and 1970s to work in a more united way, and to contribute to social and political betterment—has given way to a rather functional contribution to civic life.

More impressive in many ways is the religious commitment of a lay church-member, Ned Flanders, who, while in significant respects being the antithesis of the secular liberalism that M*A*S*H espoused, has become something of a sympathetic character for viewers. In Pinsky's view, he has become "the fairest and most sympathetic portrayal of an evangelical Christian in American popular culture" (2007: 46). While irritating in his nitpicking and over-scrupulousness, and in those respects reflecting Protestantism's ever-present tendency to legalism, his sheer desire and attempt to be and do good is a profound challenge to Homer Simpson. That such a character is Christian, and Evangelical, is itself of major note.

With Ned Flanders, however, we have moved beyond denominational categories. In this respect popular culture again reflects concerns and developments within Protestantism in recent decades. With Reverend Timothy Lovejoy, a hopeful, outward-looking form of Christianity, linked to Protestant denominationalism yet rising above it through ecumenical cooperation, has lost its inner drive. This does not present the full picture of where Protestantism has gone, for charismatic and Pentecostal forms have taken root even in mainstream traditions. It does, though, say something about Protestantism in its denominational forms. Protestantism has turned in on itself, or, more accurately, in both this particular popular cultural portrayal of Protestantism and across the West, mainstream denominations in their traditional forms have lost their cultural dominance. Other voices and forms of Protestantism are challenging the mainstream. The First AME Church of Springfield offers an alternative style of worship that pays more attention than the First Church of Springfield to emotional fervor and contemporary music. Ned Flanders—though a member of the First Church of Springfield—is taking note of where more passionate, expressive forms of faith are to be found.

Protestants and/as Evangelicals

The First AME Church of Springfield remains, as the Episcopal and Catholic churches that also function as alternatives to the First Church of Springfield, denominationally identified. Striking though this denominationalism is, the greatest attention in Springfield is paid to the church of the fictional denomination. Just as in *7th Heaven*, then, the focal point of the Protestant church portrayed is not denomination-specific. What is to be learned from this?

Aside from the persistent point about ratings (no single denomination must be singled out, as one would not want to lose Baptist/Episcopalian/Lutheran/Methodist viewers), the ethical (even pedagogical) point of this is so that all Protestants—or at least, as many as possible—can identify in some way with the characters being portrayed. That is often how the popular arts work. Viewers need to be able to "connect." The more specific a character or set of characters might be, the less likelihood there might be of a viewer, Protestant or not, finding a point of connection.

There is, though, a further insight to be explored. Increasingly in the final decades of the twentieth century, denominations became less significant than theological, and especially moral, convictions (and thus than political groupings, too). One might even assume that among Christian voices, especially in North America, Protestantism and Evangelicalism could be easily equated. Protestant denominations could continue to thrive, but more as mainstream historical traditions than as living, contemporary communities with active voices which would need representation in popular cultural life. Hence, such an influential and informative series as *The West Wing* would lay out key features of this move to post-denominationalism in Protestantism in ways which confirm the observations already made above, and add a new dimension to the mix: the suggestion that although Evangelicalism is far from a single entity, it is the leading set of voices, in practice, in public life from within the contemporary Protestant movement. In some respects, from the perspective of popular culture, Evangelicalism is Protestantism.

Again a Roman Catholic figure is a foil against which this new post-denominational Protestantism becomes apparent. Unlike in *M*A*S*H*, the main Roman Catholic character in *The West Wing* is a lay Catholic, the President himself: Josiah ("Jed") Bartlet (Martin Sheen). The shift from a clerical to a lay figure is itself not insignificant, reflecting the public stage on which religious and political debate would in future occur with respect to moral questions. Priests would no longer command authority. Ministers/pastors perhaps never did (at least in popular culture). But in *The West Wing*, with the exception of one or two walk-on characters, some of whom will be noted below, where theological debate does occur it is conducted by lay participants.

Two issues arising in episodes of *The West Wing* illustrate this, though in very different ways: how the Bible is to be understood today, and the question of whether or not to welcome into the USA asylum-seeking Chinese Evangelical Christians. The first of these, biblical interpretation, appears in "The Midterms" (aired 18 October 2000), an episode in the second season. In an exchange allegedly inspired by public discussion of the talk-show performances of Dr. Laura Schlessinger, President Bartlet challenges the approach to the use of the Bible displayed in the radio chat show fronted by Dr. Jenna Jacobs. Bartlet uses biting satire to point out the inconsistency in using the Bible to condemn one practice (homosexuality) while not confronting others (slavery, touching a dead pig, sowing two different crops alongside each other, wearing clothes made of two different types of cloth) that are treated with equal seriousness in the Hebrew Bible/Old Testament.

Public discussion of the appropriate use of the Bible in contemporary Western culture is not, of course, an issue important to Protestants alone. Its long-standing particular significance for Protestants, however, and the fact that biblical interpretation is so central in much intra-Protestant discussion, makes this an important scene in popular culture's treatment of the Bible's use. In this short three-minute clip, the application of reason and the appeal for respect for historical distance and context (past and present) in the task of biblical interpretation are both brought starkly to the fore. Striking too is the fact that a lay Catholic is found offering in public an appeal for the exercise of now standard critical approaches to the understanding of biblical texts. It stands in sharp contrast to the more clichéd example in the film *The Shawshank Redemption* (Frank Darabont, 1994) of the Bible's use by the hypocritical (probably Protestant) prison warden (played by Bob Gunton).

Despite criticism of the Bible's use, however, the Bible is not itself being belittled or disregarded, and there are other occasions throughout *The West Wing* where the Bible is used positively. It might, though, be argued that Protestants (and Evangelicals in particular) are portrayed as figures of fun, easy to lampoon, and all of one mind (as "the Religious Right"), were there not other features of the series pointing to a more complex reality. Reverend Al Caldwell, Mary Marsh, and John Van Dyke appear in the very first episode as representatives of Evangelical Christianity whose knowledge of the Bible is less impressive than expected. By the second season, however, a more sympathetic presentation of Caldwell is evident. In "Shibboleth" (aired 22 November 2000), Caldwell offers financial support from his Church for the Chinese Christians who have found their way to the USA. He represents the (fictional) "Christian League," and his church is left undefined—a further illustration both of the decline of denominationalism and of the switch to politico-theological groupings—although this is an acknowledgement of a concern for human wellbeing which transcends, or is evident in and through, any religious group.

Protestantism is not, then, collapsed into Evangelicalism in popular culture. But there is a clear reflection of the shift from denominations and mainstream traditions to different kinds of cross-denominational affiliations as carrying cultural influence.

Protestants as fanatics and sectarians

In the two-edged way just described, *The West Wing* acknowledges the contemporary power of the Evangelical voice in American life. While Evangelicalism does not speak for, or represent, the whole of Protestantism in Western culture, its prominence is appropriately reflected in the series. It is important to link the positive, moral intent of Evangelicalism with the many denominations of Protestantism as they surface in popular culture. Even when poking fun at many of Protestantism's characteristics, popular culture may just about maintain a view that the Protestant voice is a good thing in society, though admittedly a substantial research project would be needed to establish this. And there are plenty of portrayals suggesting otherwise.

Mary Marsh, who accompanies Reverend Al Caldwell on his White House visits in *The West Wing*, is somewhat humorless in her fervor. While her commitment might be deemed admirable, her lack of charity is less so. In this respect she embodies a negative side to Protestantism as popular culture understands it. This is a Protestantism long portrayed in the arts: the Protestantism of the fanatic and of the sect. If the latter is not necessarily dangerous (merely a little odd, at times) then the former is more so.

Robert Duvall's *The Apostle* (1997) and Paul Thomas Anderson's *There Will Be Blood* (2007) are but two filmic examples of this strain of Protestant practice. (Kozlovic [2002] adds others under his "Fundamentalist, Rigid, Ascetic, Puritanical, Fascist and Nasty" and "Scheming, Corrupt, Frauds & Tricksters: Real & Implied" headings.) Duvall both directs and acts in the 1997 film, in which he plays Sonny Dewey, the "apostle" of the film's title, an individual wracked by guilt, though unable to face the consequences of his past actions, and fervent in his commitment to the rightness of his convictions. The story of his life reflects Protestantism's own themes, in many ways: how to handle internal torments (as a movement) when the easiest solution is to split and start something new.

Anderson's film also compresses many stock features of Protestantism, though it does so in a rich, rewarding, if somewhat demanding film. There is stubbornness on the part of the preacher, Eli Sunday (Paul Dano), who is a key figure in the film. There is, again, the desire to set up a new Church (here, the Church of the Third Revelation). The frontier, and the entrepreneurial risk-taking which went with it, suggest the constant interweaving of Protestant spirituality with commercial expansion.

If Protestants are often portrayed as driven individuals, popular culture also sees them presented as aloof. In one strand of this sectarian tendency, the effect is quaint, quirky, but harmless. A very well-known example, the portrayal of an Amish community in *Witness* (Peter Weir, 1985), is sympathetic, linking a clearly defined historical tradition—and presenting it to a contemporary audience in an informed and informative way—with a question about what kind of communities are needed to create a safe society. A more art-based filmic tradition has trodden similar territory. The now over-used *Babette's Feast* (Gabriel Axel, 1987) is also ultimately sympathetic to Protestant sectarianism, though its gentle humor leaves behind a basic question about Protestantism's propensity to promote a colorless life. More disturbing are Lars Von Trier's *Breaking the Waves* (1996) and Michael Haneke's *The White Ribbon* (2009), both studies of closed communities. Though admittedly located more in the art-film genre than in popular culture, they display graphically how abuse can all too easily develop within a sectarian lifestyle. Even if the ending of Von Trier's film is puzzling, the abusive element lingers in the viewer's memory.

Sectarianism is, in other words, a trope of Protestantism. The fact that it is necessary to turn to film, and art-film in particular, to illustrate this point, however, suggests that while it is present in artistic cultural portrayals, it is perhaps not widely evident in popular culture, at least not in explicit form. The question arises whether it might nevertheless feature implicitly as "odd" or "anti-social" behavior. Explicitly religious characters in detective dramas or thrillers, to cite a further example, are often the ones who turn out to be twisted, although one must admit that it is rarely any particular background (other than "generally Christian") that is being targeted.

One perhaps surprising point at which the sectarianism of Protestantism might be deemed identifiable in Western popular culture is in the idealization, even idolizing, of the family. It is telling, for example, that *7th Heaven* presents itself first of all as a family drama, focusing on a family who happen to be that of a pastor. Again this is understandable, so that identification may be possible, even in the case of non-religious viewers who might be interested. There has, however, been concern for some time that Protestantism has allowed its concern for the primary focus of everyday life to take on too much of a domestic focus. When allied with the effects of social mobility upon family patterns, and the resulting emphasis on the nuclear family, domestic life has arguably come to dominate lives even ostensibly shaped by a religious faith. This tension lies at the heart of the "culture wars" in the USA, and is logged in the work of such an influential thinker as Stanley Hauerwas. Hauerwas (2001: 506–12) argues for the primacy of the church as a social grouping, both to challenge the idolization of the (privatized) domestic space and to press for the importance of theological voices in public discussions about ethics. The way in which he presents his case bears a particularly North American stamp, the church–state distinction being so marked, though his voice has carried influence much further afield. In terms of the impact upon popular culture as the barometer of contemporary Western life, it might be said that friends (or even *Friends*) has replaced "family" as the focus of where fundamental thinking about the practice of human relationships occurs, and that the former is avowedly urban and secular, and the latter, in its Protestant form, begins to look suburban but dated.

There are questions to be raised about this partially true picture of Protestantism in popular culture, and of the sectarianism implied by a focus on the family. But that it is in part true indicates there is work to be done in identifying and exploring the picture mapped above, and in suggesting what is to be done in response.

The surprising persistence (and reappearance) of Protestantism: the resurgent rev

Before turning to some reflective observations about the overall picture of Protestantism in popular culture there is one, final, recent development in Protestantism's portrayal to be noted. Alongside the relative absence, or "general Protestant" portrayal, of post-Reformation Christian figures in popular culture, there is one new feature of TV culture that merits attention: the new form of denomination-specific clergyman. In contrast to where we began, the clergyman is now portrayed (and in each of the two cases, we are talking of a male cleric) as a vulnerable, sometimes weak figure, very much caught up in the messy, demanding complexities of urban living. In the case of both *The Book of Daniel* (2006) in the USA and *Rev* (2010–present) in the UK, clergy are presented as struggling with life and ministry. In the former, Episcopalian priest Reverend Daniel Webster wrestles with his own inner self, while caught up in a range of family and church situations that read like a catalog of contemporary social and ethical issues. The series was short-lived and controversial, but at least it tried to reflect the church's (any church's) current realities. The UK series, also centered on the life of an Anglican (Episcopalian) priest/vicar, follows a similar line, though as a situation comedy rather than as a serious drama. At the time of writing, a US version—replacing the London-based vicar with a Chicago-based Episcopalian priest—is being considered. While it also runs the risk of parading a standard range of contemporary social, ethical, or ecclesiastical issues and, apart from a handful of leading figures, depends on a set of mostly stock characters, it has begun to do a wonderful job of requiring cultural critics who do not normally attend, or attend to, church life to reconsider what is actually happening in the UK today. Well-informed in its construction, it becomes an example of Protestantism as vulnerable and fragile, and yet "still there," undertaking work of profound value among people often neglected. Such Christian practice is not the preserve of Protestants, though in the UK scene, as well as offering a reminder of Christianity's persistence in secular culture, it is a reminder too of a lingering church–state association. In this most recent popular cultural form, then, Protestantism is seen as eccentric and yet fiercely resilient.

Has the absence of Protestants, the fun at their expense, or the satire about them (*South Park* [Comedy Central, 1997–present] comes to mind in addition to *The Simpsons*) bottomed out? Is something new happening here? It is too early to say. *Rev* (BBC 2010–present) may in some ways simply be continuing the tradition of the well-trodden trope of "bumbling Anglican vicar" played out in continuity with a tradition in English literature, reflected in popular culture on UK TV in *All Gas and Gaiters* (BBC, 1967–71) and *Dad's Army* (BBC, 1968–77), and in film, on a number of occasions, by clerical characters played by Rowan Atkinson (*Four Weddings and a Funeral* [1994] and the darker comedy of *Keeping Mum* [2005], for example). To some extent, *The Vicar of Dibley* (BBC, 1994–2007, intermittent) continues that tradition, though it offers a character of a woman vicar who, while often lacking confidence, is also shrewd and likeable. And one message is clear: rural life still needs churches. On the other hand, then, there may be a new preparedness, in the midst of an evidently more secular age, to signal the different ways in which quite specific religious traditions—different kinds of Christianity, with diverse emphases, as well as a range of other religions—continue to contribute to social and political life. It is perhaps being seen as vital that popular culture too (and not just academics or religious leaders) emphasizes the extent to which religions are not just belief systems but institutions, which foster social practices and which shape people's everyday lives. The complex but profound ways in which they do this may need portraying in more detail than has often been the case, and than can be undertaken satisfactorily in popular culture. But perhaps the days of "absent" or "unspecific" Protestantism are over.

Protestantism and popular culture: the consequences of a Protestant form of secularity

The contention of this chapter has been that Protestantism has been present in Western popular culture over the past 50 years or so, though perhaps not as much as might have been expected. Christianity's past dominance in the West is reflected in popular culture. Ironically, however, it is Roman Catholic figures that have been more apparent, due to a more overt priestly presence being more distinctive when a generalized Christianity was required. Behind the scenes, Protestantism could assume its cultural hegemony, complacently perhaps, even while secularization continued at a rapid pace. Protestant-specific portrayals may have come to the fore more recently due to a decline in Protestantism's cultural influence. It has become more important to articulate (including visually) what religious groups exist, and what they might now be for. Past influence or cultural prominence, or knowledge of what specific religious groups did or do, can no longer be assumed. The chapter has also suggested that while Protestantism might have been dominant in the background, as secularization (and the stark separation of church and state in the USA, even if more ambiguous than sometimes assumed) was taking its effect, it was not appropriate to pinpoint where Protestantism might actually be having an impact on so-called "secular liberalism." Perhaps times have changed and a postmodern culture is more open to having the precise identities and sources of influences on culture and thought pointed out, in all their variety, including religious.

In conclusion I offer two contrasting "takes" on what has been mapped all too sketchily in this chapter. First, I ask what we might have expected in "looking for Protestantism" in popular culture, given how Protestantism is usually defined. Second, I ask what we have actually found, so that we can see how these two pairs of lenses square up.

First, then, what might we have expected? It is not easy to sum up what constitutes "Protestantism." As often noted, Protestantism has such regional variants that "simple generalizations" concerning the development of Protestant thought, let alone variety of practice, will not do (McGrath 1993). That said, independence of spirit, refusal to rely on external authority, willingness to question, openness to critical thought, individualism and individual salvation, attention to everyday life (and to the sacred in the secular), and support for the entrepreneurial (and commercial) spirit have long been features of Protestant piety and practice, and thus of Protestantism's influence on public life. Such observations actually fit in well with what we have found portrayed in popular culture, both in the way in which secular mores (partly influenced by hidden Protestantism) have developed, and in the way that Protestantism has been explicitly portrayed. For good and ill, we might say, Western secular culture has a Protestant shape, and this is evident in popular culture. From the secular liberalism of M*A*S*H to the independent spirit of Homer Simpson, the individual's wellbeing, though shaped by communal settings of public life (workplace), home life, and church, remains paramount.

Protestantism has, however, through its emphasis on the everyday, in many ways produced more secular results than it would have expected. This is one of the insights of Brad S. Gregory's recent *The Unintended Reformation* (2012). Applying Gregory's line of thinking to this brief and impressionistic survey of popular culture, it is possible to say that in the same way that atheisms take the forms of the theisms they oppose, similarly Western secularization has followed the flow of (and inevitably been influenced by) the hegemonic Protestantism which it has often wanted to play down or replace. Is it now time, though, to recover the theological sense of that secular life not simply in the academy (Gregory 2012: 381–87) but more broadly in cultural life (Taylor 2007: 726–27)? The popular culture and theology/religion dialogue is vitally important not to reassert Protestant hegemony, but to ensure that the quest for a good theology can be fashioned from the many conversation partners (religious and not) who need to be around the table as meaningful debate occurs about the values by which people choose to live. Without keeping theological debate alive at the heart of secular culture, then the impact of the "central, most powerful symbol in terms of which human life in the West has been ordered and oriented" (Fiorenza and Kaufman 1998: 153) will be respected neither in the impact it has had on secular living, nor with regard to the different institutional contexts (Protestantism included) out of which such insights have come. The damage done (socially, ethically, politically) when the theological reflection operating implicitly and explicitly in society is insufficiently examined will be vast.

One of *South Park*'s creators, Matt Stone, is quoted as expressing surprise, when they set out to produce their often controversial series, at how little religion there was on TV (cited in Pinsky 2007: 268). This has changed. Despite the frequently satirical tone when religion does appear, there is serious intent too. Perhaps the resurgent interest in Protestant specifics might be part of a questioning of some aspects of secularity that, while welcome in its openness to people of all faith and none, sometimes hides aspects of its value system that, in the West at least, were sown on Christian soil. On TV at least, despite the numerical decline of support for Protestantism, a substantial gap remains between characters portrayed and *de facto* support for Protestant traditions. Here, popular culture does not reflect the society of which it is a part. But whether the tide is turning, only time will tell.

Note

1 I am grateful to John Lyden, Vaughan S. Roberts, Nicky Sorsby, and Isobel Woodliffe for contributions to this chapter.

Works cited

Bruce, S. (1996) *Religion in the Modern World: From Cathedrals to Cults*, Oxford: Oxford University Press.

——(2009) "Secularization," in R.A. Segal (ed.), *The Blackwell Companion to the Study of Religion*, Oxford: Wiley-Blackwell: 413–29.

Clarke, S.H. (2005) "Created in whose image? Religious characters on network television," *Journal of Media and Religion* 4, 3: 137–53.

Davie, G. (2002) *Europe: The Exceptional Case. Parameters of Faith in the Modern World*, London: Darton, Longman and Todd.

Dyrness, W. (2004) *Reformed Theology and Visual Culture: The Protestant Imagination from Calvin to Edwards*, Cambridge: Cambridge University Press.

Fiorenza, F.S. and G.D. Kaufman (1998) "God," in M.C. Taylor (ed.), *Critical Terms for Religious Studies*, Chicago, IL: University of Chicago Press: 136–59.

Gregory, B.S. (2012) *The Unintended Reformation: How a Religious Revolution Secularized Society*, Cambridge, MA, and London, England: The Belknap Press.

Hauerwas, S. (2001) "The radical hope in the Annunciation: why both single and married Christians welcome children," in J. Berkman and M. Cartwright (eds), *The Hauerwas Reader*, Durham, NC and London: Duke University Press: 505–18.

Keillor, G. (1985) *Lake Wobegon Days*, New York: Viking Penguin.

Kelsey, D. (2005) *Imagining Redemption*, Louisville, KY: Westminster John Knox Press.

Kozlovic, A.K. (2002) "Sacred servants in the popular cinema: research notes towards a taxonomic survey of the mundane holy," *Journal of Mundane Behavior* 3, 2 (June). Online. Available: www.mundanebehavior.org/issues/v3n2/kozlovic.htm (accessed 4 February 2013).

McGrath, A.E. (1993) "Protestant theology," in A.E. McGrath (ed.), *The Blackwell Encyclopedia of Modern Christian Thought*, Oxford: Blackwell: 476.

Pinsky, M.I. (2007) *The Gospel According to the Simpsons: Bigger (and Possibly Even Better!) Edition*, Louisville, KY: Westminster John Knox Press.

Romanowski, W.D. (2012) *Reforming Hollywood: How American Protestants Fought for Freedom at the Movies*, New York: Oxford University Press.

Taylor, C. (2007) *A Secular Age*, Cambridge, MA: The Belknap Press.

Walsham, A. (2008) "The godly and popular culture," in J. Coffey and P.C.H. Lim (eds), *The Cambridge Companion to Puritanism*, Cambridge: Cambridge University Press.

Wolff, R. (2010) *The Church on TV: Portrayals of Priests, Pastors and Nuns in American Television Series*, New York: Continuum.

INDEX